Thinking about Religion

To my teachers:

John Barone, Robert Bolger, Donald Evans, Frank Cochran, Peter Frank, Herbert Hingert, Stanley Insler, Elmer Kremer, Sam Mackintosh, Sister Sarah Marie CSC, Ed Murawski SJ, Ninian Smart, Edward Synan.

Thinking about Religion

An Historical Introduction to Theories of Religion

Ivan Strenski

Blackwell
Publishing

BLACKWELL PUBLISHING
350 Main Street, Malden, MA 02148-5020, USA
9600 Garsington Road, Oxford OX4 2DQ, UK
550 Swanston Street, Carlton, Victoria 3053, Australia

First published 2006 by Blackwell Publishing Ltd

1 2006

Library of Congress Cataloging-in-Publication Data

Strenski, Ivan.
Thinking about religion : an historical introduction to theories of religion /Ivan Strenski.
    p. cm.
Includes bibliographical references and index.
ISBN-13: 978-1-4051-2011-1 (hardcover : alk. paper)
ISBN-10: 1-4051-2011-8 (hardcover : alk. paper)
ISBN-13: 978-1-4051-2012-8 (pbk. : alk. paper)
ISBN-10: 1-4051-2012-6 (pbk. : alk. paper) 1. Religion—Methodology. I. Title.

BL41.S72 2006
200′.7—dc22

2005015485

A catalogue record for this title is available from the British Library.

Set in 10pt/12pt Goudy-Roman
by Spi publisher services
Printed and bound in the United Kingdom
by TJ International Ltd, Padstow, Cornwall

The publisher's policy is to use permanent paper from mills that operate a sustainable forestry policy, and which has been manufactured from pulp processed using acid-free and elementary chlorine-free practices. Furthermore, the publisher ensures that the text paper and cover board used have met acceptable environmental accreditation standards.

For further information on
Blackwell Publishing, visit our website:
www.blackwellpublishing.com

Contents

Acknowledgments

I should like to thank the following for their assistance, encouragement and constructive criticism along the way: Greg Alles, Scott Bartchy, Philippe Besnard, Paola Castro, Winston Davis, Joseph L. Esposito, Dan Hardy, Sian Hawthorne, Andrew Jacobs, Robert Alun Jones, Lionel Joseph, Henrika Kuklick, Joan Leopold, Arie Molendijk, Scott Morris, Diana Marroquin, Donald Nielsen, Laurie Patton, Bill Pickering, June O'Connor, David Rapoport, Jean Rosenfeld, Tom Ryba, Robert A. Segal, Ninian Smart, Jon Stone, Ellen Marie Strenski, Megan Maureen Strenski, Edward Tiryakian, and the students of Religious Studies 100. I have also been blessed to work with the superb editorial staff at Blackwell Publishing, Sophie Gibson, Rebecca Harkin, Andy Humphries, Cameron Laux, and Karen Wilson.

Admiration and thanks go out as well to the persons and institutions facilitating my research: Judith Ann Schiff, Chief Research Archivist, Manuscripts and Archives, Yale University Library, for assistance regarding quotations from the Malinowski Archives; the staff and collections of the Rivera Library, University of California, Riverside and the Young Research Library, University of California, Los Angeles. This book could not have been written as efficiently as it was without that great gift to scholars everywhere – the internet. I would finally like to express my gratitude for the supportive research environment of the University of California, Riverside, and especially for funding from the Holstein Family and Community Endowment.

Introduction: Thinking about Religion, Instead of Just Believing

From Religion to the 'Problems of Religion'

In George Eliot's *Middlemarch*, the ardent Dorothea Brooke confronts Will Ladislaw with a question embracing an essential option reflected in *Thinking about Religion*: "What is *your* religion?," Dorothea asks. But, then adding immediately lest her pious query be misunderstood – "I mean not what you *know about religion*, but the belief that helps you most?" (Eliot 1872, p. 381). However, as the title *Thinking about Religion* indicates, unlike Miss Brooke, I would have much preferred to ask Will the other question and a follow-up – what did he *know about religion* and *how did he come to think about religion* as he did? Still, in that simple yet forceful question Eliot's fervent heroine captures a perennial distinction in the life of religion itself. Unlike the purpose of *Thinking about Religion*, Dorothea wants to know about how Will has tended to *be* 'religious' or to have *practiced* a 'religion.' She cares not at all for the central concerns of *Thinking about Religion* – how religion itself has become a *problem* as well as the focus of 'theorizing' about religion. Much as all readers of *Middlemarch* come, thus, to admire Dorothea Brooke, I, for one, wish she had asked *my* question!

For better or for ill, *Thinking about Religion* takes its stand squarely on the importance of understanding how and why people have come to *think about religion* – how people have sought to "know about religion," how they have made of religion an area of human curiosity by submitting religion to endless interrogation, understanding, and explanation. *Thinking about Religion* then rests on the view that *knowing about religion* is, therefore, inseparable from having questions about religion, from interrogating religion, from seeing religion as an arena of problems. What, for example, was the first religion? How many religions are there? Are all religions equally true, or is there only one, and so on? Even more recently, certain thinkers responded to these problems by proposing '*theories*' that aim to solve these problems.

It is true that from place to place, in rare outbursts of creative curiosity, people have asked such basic questions about the nature, value, and justification of religion. But these were fleeting episodes in the spotty history of human curiosity, that left behind no major books or treatises, no sustaining institutions or 'schools,' no lasting cultural influences in the forms of lines of inquiry or major questions about religion. On the contrary, religion did not become a real arena of problems, rigorously interrogated and systematically researched, until fairly late in the history of the West. There would never have been the study of religion as we know it, unless religion itself had first become a problem in some sustained way. This book tells the 'story' of important attempts to raise and solve many of the chief problems of religion by inventing what we can call 'theories' of religion.

As the British cultural critic Terry Eagleton explains, the appearance of 'theories' indicates the existence of perceived *problems* – the sense that "something is amiss." Theories aim to fix these problems by explaining how and why they occur. Problems of religion pop up like dreaded "small bumps on the neck," warning us that "all is not well" in the religious world (Eagleton 1990, p. 26). In the modern West, we have experienced a rash of such 'problems' – what Eagleton calls "a really virulent outbreak of theory," something indeed "on an epidemic scale" (Eagleton 1990, p. 25). This 'epidemic' of problems of religion has ignited intense theorizing about religion that has conspicuously engaged practically every major Western thinker of any note since the 1500s – Spinoza, Locke, Hume, Kant, Hegel, Marx, Durkheim, Max Müller, Freud, and many others. *Thinking about Religion* proceeds from the main premise that both this 'epidemic' and the attempts of 'theories' to address it cry out for understanding. *Thinking about Religion* seeks to provide an understanding of both some main problems of religion and the theories constructed to deal with those problems. The present study is committed to understanding both the intellectual and cultural causes of our theorizing about religion and the theories themselves. This book is, then, about how our 'theories' about religion – theories about its nature, truth, utility, value, and such – emerged in the history of the modern West. This book is about the ways some remarkable thinkers tried to understand and explain religion as a result of its becoming a *problem*, and about *why they thought they were right* in coming to their theoretical answers to these problems.

Religion is not unique in having emerged from what we take for granted in ordinary life, only then to become the subject of theories. Ordinary people have engaged in everyday artistic or economic behaviors for a long time and in many places. Artistic and economic life was just *lived*, without becoming the subject of academic study, such as esthetic or economic theories. Something special must happen to raise these commonplace features of everyday life to the level of academic, intellectual, or theoretical discourse. Something special must happen in order to link these everyday activities with academic programs or government departments and ministries. It is a very long way from the more or less unexamined economic *life* of that vendor of "parsley, sage, rosemary and thyme" at Scarborough (market) fair in the folk song, to the *theory* of supply-side *economics*, or to economic 'problems' under the consideration of the US Council of *Economic* Advisors. Certain faint continuities are recognizable, but the science of economics was a product of modern thinkers in the modern world, not a persistent feature of human history. So too have departments of religious studies created their own buzz with the 'theories' of religion they both teach and create.

So, like art and economic life, religion became the object of a disciplined academic or systematic program of self-reflection – what can be called 'science.' Only in the past century and a half has there been anything called a "science of religion." Although we tend not to use the term 'science of religion' these days, it is still the normal way the study of religion is identified, for example, in France, where the "*sciences religieuses*" can claim a solid history of over a century and a half. Likewise, in the German-speaking world, under its formidable-sounding title, *Religionswissenschaft* holds sway, as it does in the Netherlands, as we will see, in the title of the Dutch scholar Cornelis P. Tiele's major work, *Elements of the Science of Religion*, itself inspired by Max Müller's project for a "Science of Religion" at Oxford. All these represent major and deliberate efforts to go beyond belief, and even to go beyond everyday curiosity about religion. If this situation were otherwise, we would have to explain why the documentary evidence for a 'natural' or much earlier disciplined and systematic study of religion is simply non-existent.

Up to the time when thinkers started studying religion in terms of scientific ideals, critical or radical self-reflection about religion was the main business of the religions themselves, and served the special needs of religious communities. Shakers, for example, worried about how they might expand their membership. Muslims meditated about whether their chief leadership should be confined to blood relatives of Muhammad. Roman Catholics disputed among themselves about how to deal with the role of women and the like.

While the problems that the individual religions wrestled with were real problems, they were 'in-house' problems. They were not the kind of problems that mattered to any and all religions, or for religion *as religion*. Shakers, Muslims, Catholics may well have had their problems, but they were those only afflicting Shakers, Muslims, and Catholics respectively. As such, the answers offered for their problems were not like scientific theories, since they did not need to appeal to the broad range of human belief and experience. Shakers did not have to satisfy Catholics about the answer they gave to their own 'in-house' Shaker problems, and vice versa. But the theories provoked by the general problems of religion did need to speak across sectarian and religious lines. These theories needed to speak in the manner of 'science' and try to appeal to the broadest consensus about the nature of facts, evidence, and such that they could. The new scientific studies of religion had therefore to be *comparative*, and never allow one individual religious perspective to hold a privileged place.

Therefore, in the West, beginning no more than 300 years or so ago, religion in this general and comparative sense became *theorized*. As a consequence, religion thus became the object of many sorts of concerted inquiry or disciplined study. In this critical and inquiring mode, people typically ask of religion a series of questions, mentioned at the beginning of the introduction: What is religion? What was the first religion? Does it make sense to inquire about the chronological origins of religion at all? How many religions or *kinds* of religion are there? Do religions change? If so, do they change according to any regular principles we might discover, such as evolution or degeneration? Is religion essentially private or instead essentially social? Do all religions require a belief in god? Afterlife? The supernatural? What makes a religion simple? What makes it complex, and so on? (Strenski 2003). These are only some of the myriad questions that stimulated the curiosity of some of the bravest and most adventurous thinkers of our history. They took a fateful step and dared to imagine that they could offer *explanations* of what is commonly thought to be the epitome of the unexplainable in human life – religion. *Thinking about Religion* seeks to help students of religion understand what these thinkers said about the nature of religion, and how and why they had the courage to *think they were right* in doing so.

But, Why *Did* They Think That They Were Right?

By focusing on the question of why the great theorists in the study of religion *thought they were right* about the ultimate meaning of religion, *Thinking about Religion* differs funda-mentally from most of the ways we have tended to approach the theories in the study of religion. This book does not seek exclusively or even primarily to assemble a series of devastating criticisms of the major *methods and theories* in religious studies. This book is not about targeting a theory or theorist for 'execution.' This is not a book that primarily shows how one can do a neat 'butchering' job on theories of religion by 'cutting them up.' To be sure, readers will find criticism and analysis enough in the pages to follow. And, thus, readers will find ample discussion of why a given theory may be said to be *wrong*.

Thinking about Religion concentrates on why thinkers thought they were right, rather than on why they may have been wrong, because I think we can learn much more by approaching theories this way. I should add that I am not some kind of relativist who believes that all theories and methods are equally true. I believe that we should not delude ourselves about the shortcomings of any theory of religion. All are flawed in some way, and it would be foolish to think otherwise. No perfect Prince Charming of theories waits to carry us off to some intellectual paradise. It is not likely that some single theory of religion just waits to be discovered or created to solve all the problems encountered with religion. *Thinking about Religion* does not operate from assuming the likelihood of the arrival of Prince Charming.

But just because Prince Charming is not on his way, it is another thing entirely to make the flaws in theories our main preoccupation in the study of theories of religion. For that reason, while this book notes the weaknesses of theories, I believe that it is not productive simply to *dwell* upon the shortcomings of theories. Such a self-satisfied and negative position surely cannot be the end of critical inquiry into our theories of religion! It is just too easy making a career out of showing how any theory falls short by leaving things out, or does not match up well with the 'facts,' and thus cannot meet the standards of being 'true.' Once we have exposed the weaknesses or fatal flaws of a theory, what have we finally accomplished? Do we draw the conclusion that theorizing is a relatively worthless activity, since any theory can have holes shot in it? Do we scorn theorizing in the same way biblical Creationists disparage Darwinian evolution, because it is, after all, 'only theory'? Or, if we still think theorizing may be a worthy activity, what have we learned about how theories actually come to be – and thus perhaps how we ourselves might construct them – merely by shooting holes in them, or by cutting them up? Every course in methods and theories that I know seems to conclude by leaving a trail of wreckage – a littered scene of disabled or terminated theories breathing their last. Is this what we really want as the end result of our critical inquiry into theories of religion? *Thinking about Religion* was written and conceived in the belief that those who value theorizing in the study of religion want *more*.

Leading Questions: On Seeing Both the Forest and the Trees

This 'more' is to deepen our understanding of past theorizing so that we get the point of what the great theorists were trying to achieve – even when they failed to achieve it. This process involves a delving into the contexts of the creation and formation of theories, so that we can begin to see what the theorists were really trying to achieve, and how the theories they created measure up to what they hoped to produce.

As such, this effort at understanding theories of religion essentially entails something of an *historical* approach to theories and theorizing about religion. Understanding the development of the study of religion reminds me of what it was like finding my way around my present home city of Los Angeles. There is no 'pole star' against which to set a straight and single course across an otherwise simple expanse of land. Like such a great and often random-seeming city, the development of the study of religion presents us rather with a sprawl of historical details, frustrating encounters with grid-locked arguments, broad boulevards of ignorance across which no easy crossing is obvious. Learning how to navigate such a city requires getting one's bearings with respect to different and shifting landmarks and, as our position in the cityscape changes, against new points of reference again.

Thinking about Religion offers us at least two such major orienting points of reference that the great theorists seemed to use to focus their efforts. The first is their repeated search for Natural Religion, whether conceived as the 'first' religion, the common denominator of all religions, or some fundamental human capacity for religiousness, analogous to a moral sensibility or the esthetic sense. The answers given for the quest for Natural Religion by the first wave of great theorists dominate the polemic of Parts I and II of *Thinking about Religion*. The second way this book finds its way through the landscape of theoretical thinking about religion is by noting how the a second wave of more modern thinkers in Part II tend to address the central problem of the ultimate nature and status of religious *experience*. Long gone is the historical quest for an absolute beginning point, now replaced by attempts to explain how and why the proclaimed experiences of religious folk have come to be. Is the feeling of absolute dependence upon a great power, often constituting the essence of the reports of encounters with the sacred by believers, to be taken at face value? Or, as Freud would suggest, are we not rather in the presence of mythologized versions of our childhood memories of parental power? Or, again, to follow Durkheim, are we better advised to trace these indubitable feelings to the even more indubitable fact of our absolute dependence upon society? Part III of the present volume seeks to lay out some of the more influential accounts of the real nature of so-called religious experiences.

One final suggestion for students as they read through the book. Be alert to three steps I tried to follow as I wrote each chapter. First, each chapter tends to be organized around a basic *problem* of religion emergent at a particular time because of various changes that occur in a society. Such a change might be the discovery of heretofore unknown prehistoric societies of Europe, and the way they put into question the Bible's version of the human past. This, in turn, put into question the account of the world and humanity given in the sacred scripture of the West, and thus of the religious life led in accord with its guidance. Or, such a change might be the 'discovery' of the Freudian unconscious, and the revision this has caused in many quarters, of our sense of our own ability to know ourselves – and especially to know if we can trust our religious experiences. Second, once these 'shocks' to the religious self-consciousness are felt, what reactions by way of new *theories* of religion emerged? What, for example, did Robertson Smith have to say about modern Christianity, with it strong emphasis on *belief* in God, once what he took to be the earliest levels of biblical religion seemed totally devoid of beliefs as such? What was Freud to make of the prevalence of modern Christian religious experience of absolute dependence upon God the father, when to him it seemed as if this might be based on childhood memories of the power of our own human fathers? Third, and finally, no matter whether we find that thinkers like Robertson Smith or Freud were wrong or not about their conclusions about religion, the job of understanding these (and all the other) theories is only complete when we have satisfied ourselves that we understand *why the theorists thought that they were right*! How and why, for example, could anyone, like Robertson Smith to take a case in point, think that there could even be people, much less religious people, who lacked beliefs!? How could he have thought such things? Whatever else students take from this book, I at least hope they will feel that they understand how and why some remarkable folk *thought about religion*. And, that, incidentally, is why I titled this book *Thinking about Religion*.

References

Eagleton, T. 1990. *The Significance of Theory*. Oxford: Blackwell.
Eliot, G. 1872. *Middlemarch*. New York: New American Library.
Strenski, I. 2003. Why It Is Better to Have Some of the Questions than All of the Answers. *Method and Theory in the Study of Religion* 15, 169–86.

The Prehistory of the
Study of Religion:
Responses to an
Expanding World

PART I

Naturalism, God-Given Reason, and the Quest for Natural Religion

1

'Big' Problems, 'Big' Questions

People began studying religion because people began having *'big' problems* concerning religion – fundamental problems about the very nature of religion itself. What was the first religion? How many religions are there really? Is religion a good thing? Have people always been religious? Of course, religious people have always puzzled about questions that are not quite as 'big' – mostly because they are only questions *interior* to one religion and not others, or that are only of local or personal interest, or that do not challenge the basic nature of religion as a whole – like the question of whether, for example, religion is a good thing at all. Religious folk have thus wondered about the nature of their God, their chances at attaining Nirvana or Moksha, whether they live forever in eternity, or pass away without remainder, whether they are doomed to eternal reincarnation or damned to eternal hellfire, and so on. But, as compelling as such questions are, they are not the 'big' kinds of problems that spurred the study of religion as we have come to know it. The questions that gave the study of religion its start were 'bigger' in the sense that they were far more sweeping in their implications about the nature of religion itself, and thus far deeper, since they struck at the very heart of religion as such.

One such often-asked 'big' question about religion that figures in this chapter was what the true religion was. Sometimes this question took the variant form of asking which religion, if any among the many, could claim to have been the first or oldest religion. Are all the many different religions perhaps derived from some primal religion that no longer exists in the world but, like the supposed religion of Adam and Eve, has been lost in the fog of past history? At other times, this fundamental question was posed in terms of questioning what the essential nature of all the many religions was – what they all had in common that made them religions (Byrne 1989, p. 183). I shall speak of these questions as belonging to the quest for "Natural Religion" – a form of religion that is alternately thought to be the oldest and primal, or that forms the common content of the many religions, or that constitutes what we could call the true and essential nature of religion.

This kind of fundamental questioning about the nature of Natural Religion began in the sixteenth century in Europe with a small and scattered number of individuals, typically unknown to one another and operating for the most part as lonely scholars. Their questioning proceeded basically like any other rational philosophical or intellectual inquiry of the day. They went about their fundamental studies of the nature of religion much as scientists of the same era, such as Galileo or Copernicus, carried on their pioneering investigations into the natural world – by observation, logical reasoning, and scientific hypothesizing. What they sought to avoid was proceeding in terms of the *revealed* truths of religion, such as were contained in the Bible, for example, or in the orthodox teachings of a church. For this reason, we can describe these first studies of religion as *naturalistic* or *rational*. I shall also use the name *deist* – written in lower case – to label them, even though this term belongs to a later period of inquiries about religion, practiced by the *Deists* proper (written in the upper case), than those at the very beginning of such efforts. Thus, in the deist quest for Natural Religion, one sees the beginnings of nothing less than a 'scientific' approach to religion – what we can call a naturalistic or 'academic' approach to religion because it proceeded according to rules similar to those governing the secular study of nature. In this nascent scientific and philosophical context, those we have called 'deists' tried to understand and justify their belief in Natural Religion. The British-born American revolutionary, Tom Paine, neatly sums up the main points of this ideal of Natural Religion upheld by the Deists in his powerful tract on religion, *Age of Reason* (1794). For Paine, Natural Religion was the "only religion that has not been invented, and that has in it every evidence of divine originality, is pure and simple Deism. It must have been the first, and will probably be the last, that man believes" (Paine 1794, p. 233).

Natural Religion

Natural Religion is, however, even a far subtler notion than Paine reports. Despite its name, although *Natural* Religion suggests a religion of nature worship – "naturism" – Natural Religion is not always to be identified with the religion of nature worship. Natural Religion embodies the belief that religion is an innate, built-in feature of being human. It is therefore "natural" in the sense that it is a "normal" part of being human. Natural Religion reflects the belief that all people are born with a capacity or talent for being attracted to the ultimate reality. People are, on this view, religiously 'musical' by birth, so to speak. The desire to attain nirvana, ultimate reality, or the godhead is born into every human being just by virtue of their being born a human being. We do not have to be indoctrinated in any way to have elemental religious feelings and orientations.

Those that adhered to the idea of Natural Religion typically felt that human beings therefore can *know* about ultimate truth by their own human abilities. Divine intervention is not required for people to know God, for example. In this sense, the belief in the natural capacity of human beings for religiousness parallels belief in the natural human capacity for moral sensibility or esthetic judgment. We would tend to think that person deficient in terms of their humanity were they to lack moral sense or esthetic perception, such as in the cases of sociopaths, psychopaths, or cultural philistines, respectively. The thinkers that brought forth the ideas of Natural Religion felt the same way about the essentially human quality of the religious sense, and presumed as much in their attempts to come to terms with the diversity of religions. One could not truly be human if one lacked the natural religious sensibility represented by the idea of Natural Religion.

Others, however, among the more religiously orthodox, felt that this natural knowledge of the divine could – and in most cases, *should* – be supplemented, from time to time, by divine or "supernatural" intervention into the natural world. Such intrusions of the divine into the natural or human are what we call 'revelation.' In these cases, Natural

Religion is generally opposed to 'revelation' or the stuff of 'revealed' religion. Here, religious knowledge is said to require the direct revelation of religious truth from the supernatural realm. The Koran, the Bible, the Vedas and so on would be examples of *revealed* religion, because these documents all claim divine sources. They claim supernatural origins, and are not believed simply to have come to be as normal features of human nature. Revealed religion is 'special'; Natural Religion is 'normal.'

The distinction between natural and supernatural religion, between the religion of human nature and the religion of revelation in turn raised the question about the relationship between natural and revealed religions. Here are some important ways the two have been thought to be related.

From the side of revealed religion, the view was fairly clear. Since it is merely human, Natural Religion is considered lacking in some way. Divine providence therefore needed to provide 'revelation' to supplement what humans could not apprehend by their own rational powers, even though these powers of reason were understood as God-given. By virtue of this, revealed religion was *superior* to Natural Religion, and rendered Natural Religion obsolete. Natural Religion may have been needed in order to *start* down the path to eternal salvation, but it was insufficient for reaching ultimate religious goals. Humans alone cannot effect their own salvation. Only the divine could bring humans home to their eternal resting place. Revelation embodied the divine guidance that made ultimate salvation possible.

From the side of Natural Religion tradition, the relation of revealed to natural religion was considerably more complex. Since it is from the Natural Religion tradition that the study of religion ultimately derived, I shall elaborate its viewpoint along several lines. Thus, one reaction to the opposition of revealed and natural religion had to do with evaluating their relative importance to one another. All thinkers in the Natural Religion tradition agreed, for example, that Natural Religion provided the *necessary* basis or foundation upon which revealed religions rested. Without a natural religious sensibility, there could be no hope for the acceptance of revealed religion. Indeed, why would revelation be accepted had there not been a predisposition for religion that was natural to human nature in the first place? For this reason, these thinkers judged Natural Religion superior to revealed religion.

Another reaction to the opposition of natural to revealed religion took a radical turn. Building on the notion that Natural Religion served as a *necessary* prerequisite for revealed religion, these thinkers pressed the case for the superiority of Natural Religion further. These partisans of Natural Religion tended typically to defend this idea by pointing out that if Natural Religion was the basis for revealed religion, it therefore must embody the essentials of religion – and therefore the best of the religions. This led these thinkers to conclude that revelation was then not really needed at all, and that Natural Religion could replace revealed religion! What need had we of revealed religion when we already had its essence – Natural Religion? Tom Paine makes such a stance plain in his *The Age of Reason* (1794):

> there is no occasion for such a thing as revealed religion. What is it we want to know? Does not the creation, the universe we behold, preach to us the existence of an Almighty power, that governs and regulates the whole? And is not the evidence that this creation holds out to our senses infinitely stronger than any thing we can read in a book, that any imposter might make and call the word of God? As for morality, the knowledge of it exists in every man's conscience. (Walters 1992, p. 223)

To the 'deists,' Natural Religion was a kind of purified religion, and in that sense a higher religion than even revealed religion. The deists preferred such a 'purified' religion, free as it was of elaborate social organization, hierarchy, ritual, extravagant mythology, and most of the other features we associate with the particularist cultural dimensions of revealed religions. They preferred a rather intellectual religion, one that did not conflict with reason and the rising status of science, so powerful in Europe from the sixteenth century. The deists sought a religion that emphasized morality and a simple belief in a supreme being.

Contemporary Unitarians and Unitarian Universalists reflect much of the sensibility and basic tenets of Natural Religion as articulated by the thinkers under discussion in this chapter, as do most of the founding fathers of the United States. In addition to Tom Paine, whom I have already cited, one can get a specific sense of what those who adhered to Natural Religion felt that it was. Benjamin Franklin, for example, described his religion in ways that would conform to many an expression of what I have called Natural Religion. In reply to a letter of March 9, 1790, from Ezra Stiles, then president of Yale College, querying Franklin on his religious beliefs, the great man said:

> Reverend and Dear Sir , . . . you desire to know something of my Religion. . . . Here is my Creed. I believe in one God, Creator of the Universe. That he governs it by his Providence. That he ought to be worshipped. That the most acceptable Service we render to him is doing good to his other Children. That the soul of Man is immortal, and will be treated with Justice in another Life respecting its Conduct in this.

Sounding the universal human note characteristic of Natural Religion, free of all adherence to a particular revealed religion, Franklin adds: "These I take to be the fundamental Principles of all sound Religion, and I regard them as you do in whatever Sect I meet with them." When it comes to revealed religion, Franklin is equally clear about his disdain for sectarian differences and most of all for any claims about the truth of the *supernatural* character of religion. Here, the subject is what Franklin may think of Jesus. To begin, he applauds Jesus's *humanistic* ethical teachings: "As to Jesus of Nazareth, my Opinion of whom you particularly desire, I think the System of Morals and his Religion, as he left them to us, the best the World ever saw or is likely to see." But when it comes to *supernaturalist* claims about Jesus, Franklin withdraws into his preference for a Natural Religion: "but I apprehend it has received various corrupting Changes, and I have, with most of the present Dissenters in England, some Doubts as to his Divinity" (Walters 1992, p. 105).

Not Out of Thin Air: Objectification and the Birth of 'Religion'

Convictions about the content of Natural Religions such as Franklin's did not emerge out of 'thin air,' but rather represented solutions to problems of religion that pressed in upon people of the time. I claimed in the opening lines of this chapter that people began "studying religion" because people began having *'big' problems* about religion. Those people who began studying these fundamental problems of religion turn out to be the very same people who articulated the main ideas of Natural Religion that we have just been discussing. What then was the set of *'big'* problems for which Natural Religion was the answer? Who were some of the first thinkers to formulate these answers, and why did they do so?

I believe one can best understand the rise of an idea as momentous as Natural Religion by reference to the ferment of the times that in effect gave this idea birth. As in the case of human childbirth, the emergence of the infant from the womb is often a violent and shocking event. So as well were the events that gave birth to the idea of Natural Religion as a solution to the first problem of religion – the nature of the true, first, or most essential religion. Of these shocks, two stand out for particular attention – the Protestant Reformation and the European discovery of the New World.

The shock of the Protestant Reformation initially, of course, hit Catholics first and hardest, since it stood for a claim that two groups of Christian peoples really differed. This in turn meant that each 'objectified' the other – saw the other as other, as different. Martin Luther declared this difference in a sharp, practical way by explicitly listing his grievances against Rome. He thus set the Protestant Reformation in motion by posting 99 theses on the main door of the cathedral at Wittenberg in 1517. John Calvin declared a kind of independence of Rome as well in beginning his attack on Catholic hegemony over religious matters in Europe by 1532. No more powerful statement of objectively perceived difference can be made, of course, than warfare. And, in this sense we can understand the French Wars of Religion (1562–98) as living and dying expressions of objective difference. Likewise, the St. Bartholomew's Day massacre of Protestant nobles by agents of the French Catholic crown in 1572, with all it involved in the dehumanizing violation of one's opponents and the abrogation of confidences and trust, gave added emphasis to the break within Christendom. The Spanish Armada of 1588, aimed at a Protestant England in rebellion against Rome, witnessed the seriousness with which European powers took religious differences. In England, in the century following, King Charles I was beheaded at the behest of Protestant rebels. The Protestant general, Oliver Cromwell, then succeeded in establishing a Calvinist Commonwealth to replace the monarchy. Republican rule in England, however, only lasted from 1642 to 1659, ending with the restoration of the Stuart monarchy under Charles II, who ruled from 1660 to 1685.

While it is true that before the Reformation there had been many disagreements among Christians leading to divisions – and even schism – within Christianity, nothing was as radical and severe as the break between Catholics and Protestants during the Reformation. The conflict between Protestants and Catholics was not restricted to theological debate. The series of protracted religious actions – in the form of religious wars that ensued – not only exacerbated their theological differences, but created the objective social conditions and relations of difference. As there seemed to be no end to the back and forth violence provoked by the religious revolutions of the time, there thus seemed no end to the depth of the severing of relations between Protestants and Catholics.

Out of this social and political objectification of the other, the very idea of there being 'religions,' in the plural, and thus the first 'problem' of religion, resulted. Historian John Bossy argues that the battles ignited by the Reformation that divided Christianity not only pitted military forces objectively against each other, but changed the way we thought about 'religion': Religious wars thus brought home the reality of

the simple existence of a plurality of embodied, and embattled, faiths . . . Objectification arose, then, out of that the need to describe one's own or other people's way of belief and life, as if from outside, in circumstances where a plurality of such ways had come into existence. It was, at first, forced upon people who wished to maintain the historic sense.

Marking this emergence of the concept of many 'religions,' Bossy goes on to note:

> We can take, in English, writing simultaneously in the 1590s from the Anglican and the Catholic side: Richard Hooker and Robert Parsons. In important works, both started off with the traditional sense of religion as worship or worshipfulness: "Christian religion" or "Catholic religion." Both ended up by talking about "religions": a plurality of objective entities erected around a set of doctrines or principles and therefore true or not true, but above all different. (Bossy 1982, pp. 5–6)

Going a step further, Bossy then argues, however, that Westerners found such radical difference a disagreeable notion to swallow. Like our proponents of Natural Religion, these thinkers generated an idea of an objectified and general notion of ' religion.'

> From this unwillingly conceded notion of a plurality of "religions," one passed, principally during the first third of the seventeenth century and especially in the minds of people who felt this plurality as problem which urgently required solution, to an abstractable essence of them, "religion" in general, or rather "the Christian religion" in general . . .

Next, Bossy notes a further development. "From this abstracted generality it was possible to pass to the larger generality, an essence of all those entities visible in the world of which the Christian religion could be thought an example." We arrive at a notion close to our idea of religion as such, and to the notion of universal religion espoused by the theoreticians of Natural Religion, even if not perfectly so aligned (Bossy 1982, p. 6). Jean Bodin, whom we will consider shortly, comes close enough to such a modern, objectified idea of religion to link with the shifts of meaning that Bossy outlines, even if Bodin is not a perfect representative of this usage.

The second shock came with the discovery of the new world of the Americas by European explorers and their encounter there with totally new religions and new peoples. Hernan Cortez had conquered Mexico by 1521 after a two-year campaign that took him through parts of Central America as well. By 1608, the Jesuit order had established a presence in Paraguay. In 1620, Massachusetts Bay colony was established by the Pilgrims. As early as 1584, Sir Walter Raleigh had established a colony in Virginia, and in 1608 the Jamestown settlement was founded there as well. The efforts of the British and the Spanish were followed rapidly in the seventeenth-century by Dutch exploits in Asia and the French entry into India.

In terms of European expansion into the New World, it too had its own religious dimensions. The fifteenth- and sixteenth-century Spanish and Portuguese enterprises of discovery and navigation were in part driven by the need to get round a virtual blockade between Europe and India produced by Islamic dominance of the overland trade routes in the near East. Likewise, the colonial efforts of Protestant powers, such as England and the Netherlands, were very often motivated by desire to compete with the Portuguese and Spanish on religious and economic grounds as well. Portuguese and Spanish commercial, colonial, and missionary activity in the New World can be seen as competing with British and Dutch Protestant efforts in the same areas.

This shock of the New World struck both Catholics and Protestants in relatively equal measure. What was particularly stunning, however, about these encounters was the novelty the European explorers found in the Americas. The indigenous cultures differed radically from anything known in Europe, Africa, or the near East, or from historical relations found in the Bible. The peoples of the New World were literally unprecedented, and thus presented unprecedented problems for anyone concerned about religion – whether Catholic or Protestant.

Taken together, then, both the Reformation and the New World discoveries shook the self-confidence of Western civilization in its own sufficiency, by challenging an endless list of longstanding assumptions about the nature of religion in human history. How could it be that Christianity could be so deeply divided between Protestants and Catholics as to present seemingly insuperable disagreements that no one could mediate? How could it be that the Christian unity seemed beyond the grasp of people of good faith? As for the Americas, how could it be that in the New World one discovered entire peoples and civilizations that could not be accounted for within the mental framework of knowledge of the world at that time? How could God's revelation in the Bible have failed Christians so thoroughly in preparing them for these strange encounters?

On the other hand, these shocks generated immense intellectual curiosity and energy. Thoughtful people entered a period of healthy skepticism about what could be known about the world, and thus began construction of a new edifice of knowledge that would encompass both the realities of Christian division and the unprecedented novelty of the New World. Foremost among the skeptical questions thoughtful people asked were precisely those radical questions about the very nature of religion itself that I mentioned from the outset. Thoughtful individuals began raising questions about the nature of religion in general because their assumptions about the religious life had now been radically questioned.

Some of these questions were motivated by the desire to dampen the fires of warfare caused by disputes between Catholics and Protestants over the Reformation, by the desire to mediate the differences between Christians in some "fair" and peaceful way – a way which did not prejudice the case of one against the other, or provoke any side to violence. Was there any objective middle ground available for settling differences between the claims of Catholics and Protestants? Or was the only alternative endless bloodshed and violence? The recent history of the West in those days had not been promising.

In the case of the encounter with the religions of the New World, Christians were simply stumped about what to make of them. This puzzlement gave rise to whole series of questions. Here were religions which seemed, at any rate, to owe nothing to Jewish or Christian origins. As different as Islam was from Christianity, at least Christians realized that it was part of the Abrahamic tradition. Both Islam and Christianity, not to mention Judaism, understood each other as members of one, if somewhat dysfunctional, family each vying for the favor of the Father. Where, however, did these New World religions come from? How had they come to be? Were they newly evolved from a form of humanity close to that of Adam and Eve, and close therefore to a 'primal' form of religion? Or did their apparent 'primitive' condition represent religions that had suffered a long historical decline or degeneration from more 'advanced' forms of faith? How, then, were these strange religions to be evaluated? Were they, in some sense, valid religions, or part of some true religion? Had they perhaps broken off from the line of development that had seen its fulfillment in the Abrahamic religions? Or was it possible that they were not even *religions* but only appeared so to be – like some sort of mocking imitation of the true thing? Some thinkers even wondered whether these newly discovered 'religions' were actually 'superstitions,' or worse yet, Satanic cults – much as the Spanish conquistadors thought about the Aztec religions that required human sacrifice in ancient Mexico? Perhaps, despite their apparent differences, the New World religions might be, for example, distant echoes of our own past, corrupted survivals of the religion of Paradise. European explorers were often struck by the gentleness and lack of a sense of guilt and sin among some of the folk met in the New World. Some wore little or no clothing, some showed no signs of aggressiveness, thus suggesting the primal innocence that was believed to have prevailed in the Garden of Paradise before the Fall. Were these folk blessed remnants of some pure "first" religion, or even perhaps distant, far-flung, marooned relatives of Christianity or Judaism? Had they known Christ? Had some apostle brought the gospel to them in the early years after the death of Christ, as tradition claims that St. Thomas had evangelized India? Likewise, the European belief in the noble savage – a kind of innocent and unsullied humanity – reflected this belief in the survival of human beings relatively untouched by the sin of Adam, or uncorrupted by modern civilization.

Figure 1.1. Early depiction of Native American religious figure, suggesting that religion was 'natural'

Source: A Soothsayer (The Flyer). Watercolor by John White. Engraved by G. Veen in De Bry's *Virginia,* Plate 11 (about 1585–90). Reproduced by permission of the British Museum.

(See figure 1.1.) In our own day, for example, many members of the Church of the Latter-Day Saints (Mormons) believe that the native Americans are themselves historical survivors of one of the lost tribes of Israel. There was really no end to the speculation about the real identity of these 'Others,' just as today we would imagine all sorts of scenarios were we to make contact with intelligent creatures from another planet.

A Time of Problems, and Creative Ferment Too

Along with this incessant questioning about the nature of religion sparked by the dual shocks of Reformation and New World discoveries, we would do well to appreciate that beyond the destructive conflicts rocking European consciousness, the centuries marked by the Reformation and the discovery of the New World were also times of extraordinary cultural vitality. In England, the late sixteenth to the late seventeenth centuries saw the glorious reigns of the Tudors, Henry VIII (1491–1547), his daughter, Elizabeth I (1533–1603), and James I (Stuart) (1566–1625), and the cultural ferment their reigns produced in the figures of Shakespeare (1564–1616), Francis Bacon (1561–1676), Thomas Hobbes (1588–1679). This period also saw the publication of the celebrated English translation of the Bible, the King James version. On the continent, an illustrious list of names can be counted, such as Leonardo Da Vinci (1452–1519), Niccolo Machiavelli (1469–1527), Erasmus of Rotterdam (1466–1536); the critical theologians and biblical scholars, Laelius (1525–62) and his nephew, Faustus (Sozzino) Socinus (1539–1604), the political philosopher and jurist, Hugo Grotius (1583–1645), the Spanish humanists, Francisco de Vitoria (c. 1485–1546) and Bartolomé de las Casas (1484–1576). The beginnings of the study of religion are to be found precisely in this same world of creative intellectual ferment, born though it was of war and conquest.

It is one of the ironies of human history, then, that both the negative and positive developments of the late fifteenth and early sixteenth centuries spurred many thinkers to give some account of the religious differences of their newly complex world, and in some cases some account of how these differences could be overcome. The first and most prominent solution to these early problems of religious diversity, conflict, and novelty was what I have called the thesis of existence of 'Natural Religion' – the belief in the existence of a universal and fundamental human religion that was built into the very make-up of human being. To these thinkers of the early-modern period – to those I have somewhat anachronistically applied the name 'deists' – we owe the beginnings of serious and open critical inquiry into the nature of religion.

One point about this deist quest for Natural Religion should be noted before moving on, since I shall reiterate this theme throughout the book. The deist quest for Natural Religion was not only a rational and scientific quest, it was at the same time and equally well a religiously motivated quest (Byrne 1989; Preus 1987). Thinkers in these early years of the rise of science did not necessarily oppose religion and science, belief and knowledge, in part because, as we have noted, they took reason to be itself a God-given endowment to humanity. Instead a more common view was that science and religion complemented one another. The deists, for instance, were quite comfortable embarking on the scientific quest to discover what for them was a religious goal – the identity of Natural Religion – by rational, God-given means. Furthermore, this entire rational quest was itself *motivated* by religious zeal. The deists felt that such *religious* goals as the discovery of the identity of Natural Religion could be achieved – in many cases but not all, as we will see – by human, God-given reason, unaided by divine intervention in the form of revelation or personal illumination from above.

Asking the First 'Big' Questions about Religion: Jean Bodin and Universal Law

Perhaps the earliest figure articulating such a naturalistic or 'academic' approach to questions of religious difference was the French Renaissance humanist and Sorbonne professor, Jean Bodin (1530–96). As we will see as well, despite his being among the first to take a secular or naturalistic approach to religion, he was nonetheless motivated by a deep religious and ethical purpose of his own – the quest for Natural Religion much like that articulated centuries later by Benjamin Franklin and Tom Paine, for example.

Bodin was both a jurist and diplomat, besides being an early form of academic historian and philosopher. The model of a 'Renaissance man,' Bodin was concerned with a wide series of issues such as the methodology of history writing, especially as it applied to understanding the nature of Roman law and to the reforms of medieval interpretations of Roman law that he sought to introduce, the nature of modern jurisprudence, and the rules by which affairs of state ought to be conducted among nations. Bodin's involvement in everyday life also suggests that religion and the study of religion can – and should – be seen as well as a part of everyday life, despite religion's being distinct 'enough' for separate study.

As a jurist, Bodin realized along with others that in a modern, postmedieval nation-state such as the France of his day, "a systematic jurisprudence could not be erected on a purely Roman basis" (Franklin 1963, p. 36). One of the reasons Roman law could no longer serve as the basis of French law was that, thanks to the discoveries of humanist philologists and historians of ancient Rome, Bodin and others discovered that Roman law was conceived for very particular purposes of the Roman society of its time. It was not therefore necessarily applicable to modern-day Renaissance France. Bodin thus sought a new, more universal, foundation for the laws of France, independent of the particular historical and cultural conditions of Roman society. A man of the greatest intellectual ambition, Bodin believed he could appeal to a "universal history" encompassing all the known world's legal systems to derive such local French law (Franklin 1963, pp. 37, 58)! Bodin's contribution to this effort at legal reform are contained in his 1556 *Methodus ad facilem historiarum cognitionem* (*Method for the Easy Comprehension of History*) in 1566.

Bodin was not alone in such efforts at reforming French law by comparing ideas about law from different nations. In fact, we might see the beginning of comparative study of religions in this period, where the practice of an elemental cross-cultural comparison was employed for the first time in a systematic way in the West. As a Renaissance humanist, Bodin was particularly predisposed to eschew parochialism, and took an accordingly wide and *comparative* view of human affairs. The humanists felt, for example, that by *comparing* French laws with those from other times and places – by placing French law within a larger *human* context – they could arrive at solutions to specifically French problems otherwise harder to obtain. Bodin's contemporary, the jurist Charles Du Moulin (1500–66), for example, argued that the local customary laws from all over the realm might be brought together into a common code, and then critically *compared* and synthesized into a unified system of French law. The spirit of comparison in law was carried so far indeed that some of these progressive jurists felt that despite the fact that Frenchman had the right to their own laws, they could not ignore the laws and history of the barbarians who had peopled modern Europe, such as the Franks, Angles, Saxons, Goths, and so on. Nor, in the opinion of certain reformist jurists, could French reformers even remain ignorant of the laws and history that lay beyond the boundaries of European Christendom, notably Saracen or Turkish history (Franklin 1963, p. 45)! Bodin, too, operated very much in the progressive spirit of a time that sought to overcome the limits of parochialism by looking beyond his immediate surroundings to the larger, more encompassing comparative context provided by the history of humanity.

Bodin's solution to the restructuring of jurisprudence and his establishment of law upon a universalist basis was not only based on *comparison*, but also employed an early rudimentary form of *historical scholarship*. "The best of jurists," says Bodin, are those

> who have diligently traced the sources and root of law to its ultimate beginning; who have accurately rendered the entire history of legislators and jurisconsults together with the knowledge of antiquity . . . who have shown perfect knowledge of the Greek and Latin languages in which the laws have been commanded and described. (quoted in Franklin 1963, p. 62)

His method of the comparative study of religion, as well, reflects this early form of *historical* and comparative approaches to law. Says Bodin in *Methodus* (107B–8A)

> I have appended the laws, universally collected, of all the peoples who have been famous for military and civil training. For this purpose I have used historians as well as jurisconsults so that to the laws of the Persians, Greeks, and Egyptians no less consideration should be given than to the Roman. I have resolved moreover to take all the best things from the pandects of the Hebrews also, and especially from the books of the Sanhedrin and, in which enterprise J. Cinquarbes and Mercier, royal teachers of the Hebrew language, have promised to assist me. Nor do I doubt that I can arrange to have the laws of the Spanish and the British made available as well as those of all the most famous cities of Italy and Germany . . . in order to conjoin with our own. And this too I hope, that we may soon have access to the civil law of Turkey, or that the public law at least, on which this flourishing and formidable power is established, should in one way or another, come into our possession. (quoted in Franklin 1963, pp. 71–2)

This commitment to an historical perspective, however rudimentary in its techniques, was doubtless one of the reasons, as we will see, that Bodin would argue that the true religion – Natural Religion – would necessarily have to be the *oldest* or *first* religion.

Being Diplomatic about Religion

In his 'other life' as a diplomat, Bodin tried to work out the practical details of helping warring factions in the French Wars of Religion 'get along' with one another. Bodin was thus a person professionally trained and deeply committed to finding ways in which people of vastly different religious persuasions could manage together to make a civil social life, free of violence and strife (Preus 1987, p. 6). In doing so, he tried to maintain an impartial even-handedness. Although a Catholic, Bodin risked speaking up for the Protestants (Huguenots) in an assembly dominated by the Catholic League, where the King himself, Henry III, was aspiring to become head. Even though he was a Catholic, Bodin tried to thwart the popular Catholic attempt to reopen the war against the Protestants by facilitating negotiations between both sides. Despite his efforts, he failed, and the nation was once more plunged into fratricidal bloodshed (Bodin 1955). The Catholic League resumed its violent attacks on the Protestants, and undertook a murderous reign of terror against them. Out of a prudent desire to survive in the face of religious fanaticism, Bodin himself joined the hated Catholic League, and retired into a state of political quietude. This retreat did not mean, however, that Bodin gave up on the problems of religious violence. Bad as the sheer intensity of the French religious wars was, it did not even seem theoretically *conceivable* or *imaginable* to mediate the differences between Catholics and Protestants. It was to these theoretical tasks then that Bodin put his mind. Part of the answer that he would conceive was to propose a quest for a fundamental religion of humanity that underlay *both* Catholic and Protestant faiths. In this way, Bodin felt that some underlying unity between the warring factions could be found, and perhaps their deadly differences overcome. This became Bodin's idea of Natural Religion.

The problem for Bodin was both to know how to *conceive* this common root religion of both Protestants and Catholics, and then to seek a way to *discover* how and where it existed. As M. J. Tooley has argued, nothing expressed Bodin's generous humanist thinking more than the application of his fine mind to so hotly contested a matter as religion in the public domain. Says Tooley,

> What French humanists of the first half of the sixteenth century were interested in was the integration of concrete facts into comprehensive and comprehensible systems. Religion being the urgent topic of the day, it was the search for the universal and comprehensive religion which most engaged their attention, and encouraged the hope that some sort of agreed formula could be reached which would unite Catholic and Huguenot. (Bodin 1955)

Withdrawing within himself as he was robbed of his place in the world of real-life diplomacy, he turned his mind toward these 'consolations of philosophy' – that is to say, to his work on Natural Religion.

It is these last works that matter most to us. Bodin worked out a carefully thought-out process, much like constructing a legal brief or courtroom argument. He sought, first of all, to shift the grounds of discourse about religion from one where entrenched, dogmatic beliefs ruled the interchange between religions to one where dialogue, rational argument, and shared polemic assumptions would dominate. His major work on religious difference, *Colloquium heptaplomeres* (*Colloquium of the Seven about Secrets of the Sublime*, 1587), illustrated this method. Suitably enough, it was written in the form of a dialog and debate, many-sided, but fought out civilly among adherents of various religions all focused ultimately on the question of the nature of the best and truest religion. In the France of Bodin's day, such formal rational procedures were becoming routine in the courtroom and at negotiating sessions between warring governments. The *Colloquium* then worked like the processes in a court of law, with all sides making their arguments according to agreed-upon codes of evidence and procedures. Protestant and Catholic, as well as Jews and Muslims, would make their arguments and contend in civil fashion, striving to resolve the questions at hand. In Bodin's case, the main issue under dispute was the identity of the best or truest religion.

As the *Colloquium* proceeded, the interlocutors attempted to find common ground between their feuding religious positions. In the guise of a representative of one of the religions, Bodin took the position that the *best* religion was one that could be shown to be the *oldest*. By the standards of knowledge of Bodin's time, this would needs be the religion of Adam. Indeed, this religion must have been one with which Adam's human nature had been endowed. In that sense, it must also have been a virtually natural, inborn faculty of Adam's humanity – a minimal definition of Natural Religion. Furthermore, Bodin argued that as the first human, Adam would carry within himself elemental features of being human. And, as such, Adam's religion must also have been somehow passed on to all human beings in his line. All humans, therefore, must carry within us the same *innate* aspects of Adam's religion – aspects that we would have to discover at a later date, however, since so much time had passed and so much confusion had accumulated around the nature of true religion in the interim (Preus 1987, pp. 12–13). One thing was certain, however, about the content of this innate religion of Adam: it would surely need to be monotheistic in the fashion proclaimed by Moses (Preus 1987, pp. 11–13).

What more there was remained unclear, except for one interesting thing. While the religion of Adam was not known in all its detail, the religion of Moses was better known. This, of course, was Judaism. But in Bodin's view, Moses did not just create a *new* religion in his day, he also restored Natural Religion – the religion of Adam – or at least goodly portions of it. As such, for Bodin, Judaism enjoyed a high status, insofar as it recalls the religion of Adam, and must be sufficient for human salvation as well. The implications of this view tended further to suggest that Judaism was the oldest religion then known to people. And thus in the course of thinking about the oldest religion, Judaism rapidly advanced to the position of being a strong candidate for being the best among religions alive at that time. Quite understandably for the time, this provisional conclusion led Bodin's enemies to charge him with being a "Judaizer" – a person either secretly a Jew or one who sought to advance the cause of Judaism among Christians. While it is not known whether the charge of Judaizier had merit, it is true that Bodin was one of the first students of religion to place Christianity on the same level as its religious rivals, such as Islam or Judaism. Indeed, one of the characters in Bodin's *Colloquium* even explicitly challenges the universal truth of Christianity (Preus 1987, pp. 12–13)!

Aside from the Judaizer issue, it is critical to observe the procedures Bodin proposed for resolving the question of the nature of the best or true religion. These procedures, significantly, were rather modern, and relied on rational bases. Thus, the *age* of a religion was something that could be determined in the same way the age of any other feature of the human world was established, and thus one could establish common, rational ground for discussion and debate between and among religions. Appeals to additional supernatural or extrasensory 'revelation' or divine authority were unnecessary. Reason was by its nature God-given from the start. Nor, of course, could revelation or sacred authority settle these questions of the antiquity of a religion anyway, since those very approaches themselves were part of the dispute. They relied on sources of knowledge that were peculiar to the different religions, such as papal authority, for example, and therefore could not in principle form the bases of a common human consensus about what was acceptable evidence (Preus 1987, ch. 1). Bodin shows himself in this the consummate and eternal jurist.

Although the term 'natural religion' came into currency some two centuries later than Bodin's time, I shall continue to refer to supposedly oldest and innate religions by the term Natural Religion. Bodin's quest for the original religion is particularly significant because it introduces a concept guiding many subsequent academic or naturalistic approaches to religion, later going by the name of the quest for (or rejection of the existence of) such a Natural Religion. Bodin argued that once one had discovered the oldest of all religions one would have *ipso facto* discovered evidence of a fundamental and innate natural religious sensibility or faculty, if not the original religion itself. Bodin also asserted that this oldest religion, this "Natural Religion," would be sufficient for human salvation. This meant that "revealed religion" as found, for example, in the Jewish and Christian Bibles was superfluous for the purpose of humanity attaining ultimate happiness. Like other partisans of Natural Religion, he then believed as well that the idea of the divine, the idea of God, was the basis of the religious sensibility that was implanted in human nature.

Natural Religion is What All Religions Share: Edward, Lord Herbert of Cherbury

A generation or so later in England, the quest for Natural Religion took a different turn that was epitomized by the seventeenth-century thinker, also often identified as the first deist (in the general sense), Edward, Lord Herbert of Cherbury (1583–1648). Edward was the brother of the famous English metaphysical poet, George Herbert, and himself a notable poet and composer of songs as well. Many of his verses show an attractive love of life and humane, irreverent wit. In a short three-line poem called "Epitaph for a Stinking Poet," his barbed wit was aimed at one of his recently interred poet enemies. The poem reads simply "Here stinks a poet I confess, yet wanting breath stinks so much less." When it came to love, Herbert could be equally impious and even a bit raucous. A poem called "Kissing" contains the following lines of gentle good humor:

> Come hither, Womankind, and all their worth,
> Give me thy kisses as I call them forth;
> Give me thy billing kisses; that of the Dove, the Kiss of Love;
> The Melting Kiss, a Kiss that doth consume to a Perfume;
> The extract Kiss, of every sweet apart;
> A Kiss of Art;
> The Kiss whichever stirs some new delight, the Kiss of Might;
> The twacking smacking Kiss, and when you cease,
> A Kiss of Peace . . .

Like Bodin, Herbert also pursued the career of a professional diplomat, serving the English crown in France. While in royal service on the Continent, Herbert came to know many of the great philosophical skeptics and free-thinking intellectuals of the day, such as Marin Mersenne, Pierre Gassendi, and Hugo Grotius. As a thoughtful individual caught in the midst of religious strife during the English Civil War, Herbert was concerned with the attainment of both religious and political peace. Although sympathetic to the Protestant theological cause, Herbert of Cherbury remained neutral between contending parties throughout the vicissitudes and disorder of the English Civil War. Early on, as a member of the landed gentry, Herbert was a royalist, but then later did not resist occupation of his estate by parliamentary forces in 1644 (Hill 1987, p. 16). Above all, he argued for moderation among all parties to the conflict and avoided taking sides as long as he could. For this, he earned the dubious epithet of being an "ambidexter" (Hill 1987, p. 15). At his death, Herbert was ready to receive the last rites. But, he so irritated the officiating clergyman by his obvious indifference to the whole affair that the ceremony was summarily cancelled (Hill 1987, p. 16).

Herbert's views on religious tolerance are recorded principally in his 1633 treatise, *De Veritate*. So 'catholic' in scope and ambition was it in its openness to religious pluralism, that the Vatican promptly entered it onto the Catholic Index of forbidden books. Despite the rationalist implications of Herbert's thought, Herbert conceived his investigations into the origin of religion out of a deep, if progressive and experience-based, piety. In this sense he departed from the practice of many of his skeptic contemporaries in his belief in the ability of the human mind to attain certainty – albeit a certainty that was itself God-given.

Herbert and Francis Bacon: Ordinary Experience and Its Divine Illumination

But Herbert was also one of those thinkers who believed that God-given reason and religion could collaborate in finding the truth. On the one hand, along with Bacon, Herbert possessed a confidence in human knowledge that approached the spirit of the Renaissance philosopher of science, Sir Francis Bacon (1561–1626), known for pioneering inductive and experimental method. Bacon, for example, stood for the practice of rigorous *empirical* methods of experimentation, a key to naturalistic approaches to knowledge. For example, he urged people seeking scientific knowledge to discipline their *experience* of the world through cautious experimental method. Thus Bacon says

> In a selection of our reports and experiments, we consider that we have been more cautious for mankind than any of our predecessors. For we admit nothing but as an eyewitness, or at least upon approved and rigorous examined testimony; said that nothing is magnified into the miraculous, but our reports are pure and unadulterated by fables and absurdity.

Such scrutiny of information in turn meant that erroneous data could be purged from the human record:

> May, the commonly received and repeated falsehoods, which by some wonderful neglect have held their ground for many ages and become inveterate, are by us distinctly proscribed and branded, that they may no longer molest learning . . .

Hence, for the first time in the West, Bacon proposes a thorough and rigorous method of interrogating nature in terms of the criteria provided by ordinary human experience:

In every new and rather delicate experiment, although to us it may seem sure and satisfactory, we yet publish the method we employed, that, by the discovery of every attendant circumstance, men may perceive the possibly latent and inherent errors, and be roused to proofs of more certain and exact nature, if such there be. (Bacon 1620, p. 341)

But while Bacon did so very much to advance empirical and naturalistic methods in the natural sciences, he was also skeptical that the loftiest of truths could be known in this way. Herbert felt much the same. Thus while Bacon always felt that humanity's great discoveries were ultimately due to the power of God working inside the thinker, he waxes eloquent as he describes God acting in behalf of the advances of science. To Bacon, God "gavest the light of vision as the first fruits of creation and hast inspired the countenance of man with the light of the understanding as the completion of thy works" (Bacon 1620, p. 342). No matter how much Bacon contributed to the naturalistic search for causality and the propagation of the experimental method, for him, God was to be acknowledged to be the very power behind reason itself. In concluding his autobiography, Herbert shows a similar mixture of naturalism and supernaturalism concerning the quest for knowledge. He tells us how he overcame his indecision about publication of *De Veritate*, thanks to a kind of controlled experiment – in this case what we might call an omen – mediated by a divine sign.

as I knew it would meet with much opposition, I did consider whether it was not better for me awhile to suppress it. Being thus doubtful in my chamber, one fair day in the summer, my casement being opened toward the south, the sun shining clear, and no wind stirring, I took my book, De Veritate, in my hand, and kneeling on my knees, devoutly said these words: "*O Thou eternal God, Author of the light which now shines upon me, and Giver of all inward eliminations, I do beseech Thee, of thy infinite goodness, to pardon a greater request than a creature ought to make; I am not satisfied enough whether I shall publish this book De Veritate; if it be for thy glory, I beseech thee give me some sign from heaven; if not, I shall suppress it.*"

I had no sooner spoken these words but a loud though gentle noise came from the heavens (for it was like nothing on earth), which did so comfort and cheer me, that my petition is granted, and that I had the sign I demanded, whereupon also I resolved to print my book. This, however strange so ever it may seem, I protest before the Eternal God is true, neither am I in anyway superstitiously deceived herein, since I did not only clearly hear the noise, but in the serenest sky that ever I saw, being without all cloud, did to my thinking see the place from whence he came. (Cherbury 1888, pp. 176–7)

Herbert, like Bacon, then, was a person for whom religion and science were not at odds with one another, even as both men advanced the cause of a rational or naturalistic understanding of the world – and in Herbert's case, knowledge of the nature of religion.

Not only did he see reason as a divine gift, but he also saw religion as a natural quality of being human. After all, neither God nor animals had 'religion'! Only humans had religion. Furthermore, like men of his time, Herbert also accepted the additional support to the God-given provided by special revelation. Ironically, Herbert believed in order to discover the universal religion of humanity, not even God-given reason was enough. Divine revelation was necessary for this task, as indeed it was to attain intellectual firm certainty about the world (Byrne 1989, pp. 23–33). Herbert especially abhorred the way some believers appealed to unique revelation to assert the superiority of their own religious position. He felt that claims to a specially revealed religious truth encouraged the fierce and intractable religious conflicts of his day (Preus 1987, p. 25). If such conflict was to be avoided, one then had to find a rational and neutral way to overcome the differences dividing contestants in the religious battles of the time.

Herbert's 'Ambidextrous' Theory of Natural Religion

In response then to the previous hundred years of religious warfare in England and on the Continent – including his own firsthand experiences of combat for the Protestant forces in the Netherlands – Herbert undertook a double – some might say, 'ambidextrous' – project regarding Natural Religion. First, although we have noted his departure from the radical skepticism of his era, together with the 'skeptics' he tried to undermine claims to *absolute* knowledge – even by Christians (Hill 1987, p. 20). For this, he was widely regarded either as an atheist or certainly an enemy of Christianity in that he, like Bodin, saw Christianity as "one particular religion among many particular religions, none of which can appeal to the reasonable observer" (Hill 1987, p. 32). Second, Herbert seems to have been so repelled by religious conflicts that he was motivated to seek a "universal" religious common ground independent of any particular religious tradition – what I have chosen to call Natural Religion (Preus 1987, p. 23). Ironically, Herbert's belief in the existence of this common universal religion followed necessarily from his own Christian humanist religious convictions: to wit, the goodness of God required that no part of the human family, past, present, or to come, could in theory be cut off from the necessities of salvation. Like Bodin, Herbert believed that each human being had implanted in them a special, divinely originated faculty that whetted the human appetite for true religion.

Herbert's answer to religious conflict was then, like Bodin's, to posit a universal essential religion that all the particular historical religions shared. But unlike Bodin, Herbert believed that this common religion would be something of a 'lowest common denominator' of the key shared beliefs of the religions. In Herbert's view, the basic tenets of Natural Religion were – much like Franklin's – first, the belief in God; second, that God should be worshiped; third, that virtue and piety are mutually related; fourth, that our crimes must be repented; and finally, that judgment about good and evil would be made in the afterlife. The universal religion was, in a sense, the true essence of all the religions because all religions shared these beliefs. If people were only able to grasp this!

Thus, Herbert was not the complete naturalist his outlook on universal religion might suggest. He was, however, a 'step on the way' to the more thoroughgoing naturalism that would follow (Byrne 1989, p. 22). Because he accepted revelation as a source of knowledge about the world, and especially about the religions, Herbert did not take the final step into naturalism. Thus, for him, in order to arrive at a sense of a common human religious foundation, one needed not only to assemble data on the world's religions and inductively reason back to the elements they held in common, but in doing so hope that one's mind would be guided by divine light (Byrne 1989, pp. 32–3). Nevertheless, in Herbert's work we can see how the quest for Natural Religion generated one of the first attempts to make sense of the nature of religion in itself. We also see how, together with Bodin, the affairs of the world, such as religious warfare, produced shocks to the thinking of Western people that compelled them to think hard about the nature of religion. The quest for the first religion, for original religion – for Natural Religion – was thus a spur to thinking about religion as such.

Herbert's Critics: John Locke and David Hume

Herbert was not without critics in his own time, although his critics hardly set an example for consistency themselves. One such critic, the philosopher John Locke (1632–1704) argued against Herbert for clinging to the divine inscription and innateness of human religious ideas, like Natural Religion, rather than being fully open to the discipline of experience. If, as Locke affirms, all knowledge is a function of human experience, how can Herbert permit revelation to find a way back into our inquiries – even about religion?

Yet, despite Locke's protest against the role of revelation in what is supposedly a naturalistic matter, he falls into the same kind of thinking for which he attacks Herbert. While Locke thought that his sturdy empiricism would bring the study of religion down to earth, and do away with the need for revelation, he wound up leaning on revelation himself. Thus, Locke's approach to religion shows how tenacious appeals to revelation could be. How otherwise to explain how and why Locke rejected Herbert's view of the innate nature of the key elements of religion, yet accepted the universality of Natural Religion? The "Precepts of Natural Religion are plain, and very intelligible to all Mankind, and seldom come to be controverted," says Locke. Moreover, this is so much so that the pious Locke added that "it would become us to be more careful and diligent in observing" it (Locke 1975, p. 490). But Locke never answers the obvious objection: how could such universality across the human species be possible if people did not possess, as Herbert implies, some kind *pre-experiential*, natural, built-in capacity for Natural Religion – like a predisposition for language or morality?

Locke also took issue – quite fairly – with Herbert's view that human reason required a supplementing divine guidance to comprehend religion. Herbert has no real answer to this. But the problem with Locke leveling this criticism against Herbert was that Locke *himself* could not make up his mind about this crucial matter: he granted revelation extraordinary privileges too! Locke was utterly unable to reconcile his view that experience and reason should be our final guides with his equally sincere view that human knowledge had been corrupted in the Fall and required revelation to 'complete' it (Byrne 1989, pp. 45, 48, 49, 51). Deeply religious men that they were, neither Bacon, Herbert, nor Locke could then quite let go of the need to understand ordinary human empirical knowledge as sufficient unto itself in matters of knowing about religion. They always left open the door to assistance from supernatural sources in their attempts to understand religion – even Natural Religion!

That they should have wanted *both* naturalism and supernaturalism to be in play in their approaches to understanding the nature of religion and Natural Religion in particular, should not, however, diminish our appreciation for the progress that they in fact made over straightforwardly pious and wholly supernaturalistic approaches to understanding religion. While Bodin, Herbert, and Locke differed among themselves about Natural Religion, and with the degree of naturalism they would permit in the study of religion, they nonetheless at least made a beginning in producing a naturalistic study of religion. They made more plausible than had been so before that, despite claims about the supernatural origins of biblical religion, at least some part of human religiousness was the result of features of our general human nature. They succeeded in putting before us the proposition that – as Natural Religion – religion was a normal part of being human, just as were our senses of morality or beauty. Thinkers like Bodin, Herbert, and Locke – at least in part – believed one might discover the existence and features of this Natural Religion in the same ways one unlocked various secrets of nature more or less as described by Francis Bacon – without aid of special divine revelation, but primarily, for them, by means of the powers of human, albeit God-given, disciplined experiment and deductive or inductive reason. Normal powers of human perception and argument were for the first time granted at least a level of sufficiency – however conflicted or partial – to know all there was to know about the nature of religion. In this sense, then, of adhering to naturalistic conceptions of knowledge in their studies of religion, Bodin, Herbert, and Locke might well be designated incipient naturalistic scholars of religion.

The Deists Proper

The final breakthrough for naturalism in the study of religion came with other proponents of the thesis of Natural Religion in the generation or so following Herbert and Locke. Here, I refer to the advent of the Deists proper: Charles Blount (1654–93), Matthew Tindal (1657–1733), John Toland (1670–1733), and William Wollaston (1660–1724). Revelation was finally put aside, and reason – understood as itself a divine endowment – became the only accepted basis needed for arriving at the identity of Natural Religion.

This by no means meant that the Deists were in any way enemies of religion. These Deists (in the full sense of the word) were intensely and confidently religious. We can perhaps better grasp the power of their spirituality in the exuberant religious architecture of the Renaissance and Enlightenment, such as that of Sir Christopher Wren. In his splendidly open and elegant churches, for example, divinity is suggested by the intense flow of natural light into the sacred precinct. Or, one may see traces of such a bold and worldly spirituality, at peace with humanity, in other great church architecture, such as the Church of the Madeleine in Paris, where Jesus is depicted in the friezework as a healthy and muscular man, unconflicted about his humanity. (See figure 2.1.)

The Deists showed once more, therefore, how spiritual and religious motivation could be similarly at peace with one another as driving forces in the sciences. To them, this meant that the tenets of Natural Religion were considered both eminently reasonable and majestically sacred. After declaring that the "only religious Title therefore that I shall ever own, for my part, is that most glorious one of being a Christian," Deist John Toland proceeds to declare "that there is nothing in the Gospel contrary to Reason, nor above it; and that no Christian Doctrine can be properly called a Mystery" (McGinnis et al. 1997, pp. 13, 17). The Deist William Wollaston likewise declared in his *The Religion of Nature Delineated* (1724) that Natural Religion "has always seemed to me not only evidently true, but withal so obvious and plain, that perhaps for this very reason it has not merited the notice of authors..." Furthermore, Natural Religion requires no compulsion or wrenching of the human spirit, such as in forms of ascetic denial. Wollaston thus goes on to add that regarding Natural Religion, the use and application of it is so easy, that if things are but fairly permitted to speak for themselves their own natural language, they will, with moderate attention, be found *themselves* to proclaim their own rectitude or obliquity; *that is*, whether they are disagreeable to it, or not. (Wollaston 1724, p. 7)

Like Herbert, the Deists had an abiding humanist belief in the goodness of God and a refusal to accept the divine as punitive or domineering. In effect, the Deists can be seen to have married the humanism of Herbert to the empiricism of Locke in advancing their own articulation of Natural Religion. In the bargain, and perhaps without realizing it, they thereby also provided some of the intellectual bases for the future development of a 'science of religion' – a project that would be self-consciously pursued, as we will see in chapter 3, under this very name by Friedrich Max Müller, a latter-day deist of his own kind. The humanism of the Enlightenment Deists led them to reject the idea of a special, historically restricted revelation only open to the lucky few. The words of Matthew Tindal's *Christianity As Old As the Creation: or, the Gospel, a Republication of the Nature of the Religion of Nature* (1730) assert that all peoples have an equal opportunity to attain eternal happiness: "God, at all Times, has given Mankind sufficient Means, of knowing whatever he requires of them; and what those Means are." Going further, the summary of chapter 2 of the same volume states that Natural Religion is all the religion one needs, and therefore that revelation is superfluous: "That the Religion of Nature is an absolutely perfect Religion; and that external Revelation can neither add to, nor take from its Perfection; and that True Religion, whether internally, or externally revealed, must be the same" (Tindal 1995, p. vi). In this sense, like Herbert and Bodin, Tindal affirmed a full humanism in asserting that Natural Religion was a religion of reason – *human* and God-given at the same time: "the Religion of Nature consists in observing those Things, which our Reason, by considering the Nature of God and Man, and that Relation we stand in to him, and one another, demonstrates to be our Duty; and that those Things are plain; and likewise what they are" (Tindal 1995, p. v).

Taken together, this cluster of beliefs constituted the core of the naturalistically based humanism of the Deists. To wit, this meant that if there be any justice in the world, religion must therefore be natural to the human species and universal in the sense of salvation being open to all people at all times and in all places. If religion is thus natural and universal, inquiry into religion should be an open affair. All the religions of the world, therefore, are comparable to one another, and can be studied in comparison with one another without supervening dogmatic restrictions. As a natural part of universal human nature, all religions, in principle, therefore, are to be included in a program of rational scrutiny and universal comparison (Byrne 1989, pp. 52, 53).

Taking leave of Herbert's belief in innate ideas, the eighteenth-century Deists, Blount, Toland, and others, embraced Locke's empiricism as the epistemological basis of inquiry into religion – arguably even more so than Locke himself. The Deists were also more consistent and thoroughgoing than Locke in that they did not stray from the view that all knowledge is a function of experience – as Francis Bacon argued centuries before (Bacon 1620, pp. 339, 340, 342) – of "sensation, reflection and reason." Thus, unlike Bodin, Herbert, Locke, and even Bacon himself, claims to 'revelation' were not exempt from the rule of naturalistic knowledge (Byrne 1989, p. 40). Unlike Locke, the Deist Charles Blount rejected the insistence on the necessity of special revelation to repair our 'corrupted' postlapsarian human cognitive capacities (Byrne 1989, pp. 56 ff.). Human reason was the final court of appeal in the realm of knowledge, and no appeal to 'revelation' could save religion or anything else for that matter. Deist John Toland thus embraced Locke's empiricism and at the same time rejected Locke's view of reason needing completion from revelation. Toland also agreed with the spirit and much of the letter of Locke's *The Reasonableness of Christianity* in that he thought that there was nothing irrational in "true Christianity" (Byrne 1989, p. 71). But this concurrence with Locke did not mean that Toland accepted Locke's view that revelation was needed to supplement human reason or that it was a justification for or "ground of proper belief." So-called 'revelation' might be a "source" of novel religious ideas – notions not commonplace in human thinking – and in this sense, 'revelation' may be said to be "above reason." But Toland maintained a more consistent empiricism even than Locke in stating that even such 'revelation' would have to pass before the bar of rational scrutiny as well (Byrne 1989, p. 72). Cutting the last ties with revelation, the Deists of the eighteenth century can, therefore, be seen to be to streamlining the quest for Natural Religion begun over a century earlier by Jean Bodin. Whatever else they achieved, I take it to be a major victory for modern religious studies that the Deists established the intellectual bases of a comparative, naturalistic, academic study of religions.

In addition to their intellectual creativity, the Deists showed great political and moral courage which in effect gave intellectual legitimacy to the naturalistic study of religion that would follow in the generations after them – such as in the work of the aforementioned Friedrich Max Müller. Given the political and institutional realities of official and unofficial ecclesiastical establishment in the West, institutional pressures worked to afford Christianity a place of privilege among the other religions of the world. Against this presumption of Christian privilege, the Deists were pioneers in breaking the Christian monopoly over religion and the study of religion. They furthered a naturalistic study of religion by setting "Christianity in a larger context of the history of religion," and as a result they, in effect, showed "how an anthropocentric, naturalistic history of it might be possible" (Byrne 1989, p. 80). This was no small achievement, since in order to do so, the Deists had to 'decenter' Christianity, and thus fly in the face of many orthodox Christian powers of the day. Such decentering of Christianity was an essential step in advancing the future of the study of religion, since it made possible the very practice of comparative study that would be the mainstay of the naturalistic study of religion.

David Hume: Radical Skeptic, Radical Empiricist

Ironically, the first consequential comparative study of religions in English came from the same pen as one of the most radical critiques of deism. Here I refer to Locke's great successor empiricist, David Hume (1711–76). Hume is particularly interesting to us because he is heir as well to two aspects of the broad skeptical tradition. On the one hand, he shared the skeptical tradition's suspicion of revealed religious sources of knowledge, such as biblical or ecclesiastical authority. On the other hand, Hume shared the spirit of Francis Bacon's attempts to assure the reliability of sense experience through the method of controlled experiment, but was not naive about the fallibility of sense impressions. He knew full well the pitfalls of an uncritical attitude to sense experience, against which Bacon, of course, warns. Yet, despite Hume's wariness about the bases of knowledge and certainty, he wrote what is probably the first history of religions, based upon naturalistic, and thus empiricist, principles – *The Natural History of Religion* (1757).

As both suspicious of sense data as a perfect basis for knowledge, but yet also forced to rely upon them for his histories, Hume presents an interesting figure. Let us first consider how he challenged the bases of deist arguments concerning Natural Religion from the point of view of his skepticism.

First, good skeptic that he was, Hume not only challenged the 'deist' belief in the God-given nature of reason, he also confronted deist belief in the adequacy of rational argument alone to discover natural religion. Since religion was a matter of human fact, whatever else it might be, it could not be known outside the normal ways in which matters of fact are known. There was for Hume no evidence for God-givenness in an activity to rife with error and misperception. The best we could hope was to appeal to sense experience – no mater how fallible this was as well. Good empiricist that he was, Hume challenged deists to provide concrete evidence of Natural Religion in the form of empirical or historical examples, ultimately derived from sense experience as they must be. If such a thing as Natural Religion exists now or in the past, Hume in effect asked, one should be able to produce a concrete example of it, or find sense-based historical records of it – even as one will need to maintain an historian's skepticism all the while.

In his *The Natural History of Religion* (1757), Hume accordingly claimed to find no evidence for the existence of a real, historical Natural Religion. Indeed, the only example of a religion that might qualify to be Natural Religion in the sense of being the oldest or simplest religion was not the lofty monotheism assumed by Herbert, for example, but a rude and unruly polytheism! According to his empiricist criteria, only polytheism could claim to be called any sort of "primary religion." From all available reliable evidence from America, Africa, Asia and other places, polytheism seems to be "the first and most ancient religion of mankind . . . [with] not a single exception to this rule," says Hume (Hume 1963, p. 33).

Hume also had theoretical reasons to feel that he was right in identifying polytheism as the Natural Religion. He was an early pre-Darwinian evolutionist, but nonetheless a progressivist believer in a developmental view of the course of human history. Hume believed in the evolution of the human mind such that "the mind arises gradually from inferior to superior" (Hume 1963, p. 34). For Hume, polytheism thus *must* be the first religion because it fit his evolutionist beliefs. According to Hume's developmentalist theories of human growth, primal humanity was ignorant of the true nature of the causes active in the world, and thus ignorantly projected human experience of multiple human agency onto the heavens in the form of 'gods.' Early human populations were an "ignorant multitude" and worshiped familiar objects, rather than stretching their imaginations in the direction of a "perfect Being." To Hume, it was unthinkable that this polytheism might represent degeneration from a monotheism, such as Herbert and the deists conceived the primal or Natural Religion. Hume believed that once people had tasted of the glories of monotheism, they would never have reverted to polytheism. Having done so would conflict with Hume's sense reason's workings (Hume 1963, p. 35).

The problem for Hume was, then, thus how to account for the *origins* of polytheism. The contemplation of nature could not direct the human mind toward polytheism because "all things in the universe are evidently of a piece" (Hume 1963, p. 37). On the other hand, the vicissitudes of human affairs are many. Thus, people who do not understand the causes of things resort to projecting human models onto the unknown, thus giving us polytheism. Or, people who are in awe of human authorities project their leaders and heroes into a heavenly realm, and see them as deities (Hume 1963, p. 58). Hume, it must be added, held no brief for monotheism. He saw all religions as rife with "absurdities" (Hume 1963, p. 75). "Examine the religious principles which have, in fact, prevailed in the world. You will scarcely be persuaded that they are anything but sick men's dreams" (Hume 1963, p. 97). Ordinary sense experience – the only source of knowledge that human beings have – only takes us so far. On a somewhat mystical note, Hume sums up his view on the limited nature of the human ability to know about the world: "The whole is a riddle, an enigma, an inexplicable mystery" (Hume 1963, p. 98).

Secondly, along with the deists, Hume rejected any possibility of a special revelation – such as the Bible, Koran, Vedas, and such. But, he went further down the skeptical road and also rejected the concept of nature as a source of religious truth. Hume therefore dismissed the deist belief in the idea of an essentially benevolent divine architect of the universe, the contemplation of whose works would lead one straightaway to the divine throne. In Hume's view, nature is far too unpredictable to exhibit design – much less benevolent design, given the occurrence of natural catastrophes such as earthquakes, floods, and famines (Preus 1987, p. 90–2). Later, as we will see in our treatment of Biblical criticism, Hume rejected the occurrence of miracles as well. God was supposed to have created a unified world, and thus any break in natural regularity, such as a miracle, seemed to contradict the ideal of divine omniscient foresight (Preus 1987, pp. 88–9). If God was perfect, then he must have created a perfect world. If so, why would it be necessary for him to intervene in it by way of miracles?

Thirdly, and explicitly against the claims of Herbert of Cherbury, Hume also opposed the idea of there being any inborn religious capacity or faculty – any idea or feeling for the divine that was built into human nature. The religious instinct is not "original" or a "primary impression of nature," such as pleasure and pain, hunger and thirst, sex, gratitude, self-love, and so forth. Further, even if one could identify such a primary religious "impression," there would not be general or universal agreement about it or the "origin of religion in human nature." Some nations even reject religion altogether, or are without it entirely (Hume 1963, p. 31). Without unanimity about the nature of religious ideas found around the world, how could one conclude that such an inborn religious faculty, sensibility, or capacity exists? And while it is even true that belief in an invisible, intelligent power is widespread, there is little agreement on the nature of the details of its nature (Hume 1963, p. 44). Most people are theists by force of dull habit and tradition (Hume 1963, p. 55–6).

In this way, Hume employed an even more severe empiricism than Locke, and a far more skeptical attitude towards the possibilities of knowledge than did Herbert. Since it is not God-given, reason cannot lead us to discover Natural Religion. Nor, therefore, can religion be based upon reason. Religion arises instead from sense experience and emotions, and it is to this kind of experience that we must turn if we wish to know about religion. By advancing this critical empiricism, Hume thus proves to be the single most notable precursor to nineteenth-century classical anthropology of religion, embodied especially in the writings of Edward Burnett Tylor, who is effusive, as we will see, in his praise of the methods and results of Hume (Preus 1987, pp. 84–6). In fact, I shall argue that Hume represents the most perfect model of a figure in what I have called the "prehistory" of the study of religion. Despite the limits of his thinking, he shows us a serious and relatively open engagement in a study of religion that conforms with modern standards of knowledge.

References

Bacon, F. 1620. *Great Instauration and the Novum Organum*. London: Kessinger Publishing, 1997.

Bodin, Jean. 1955. *Six Books of the Commonwealth*, trans. with an intro. by M. J. Tooley. Oxford: Blackwell.

Bossy, J. 1982. Some Elementary Forms of Durkheim. *Past and Present* 95, 3–18.

Byrne, P. 1989. *Natural Religion and the Nature of Religion*. London: Routledge.

Cherbury, E., Lord Herbert. 1888. *The Autobiography of Edward, Lord Herbert of Cherbury*. London: Walter Scott.

Franklin, J. H. 1963. *Jean Bodin and the Sixteenth-Century Revolution and the Methodology of Law and History*. New York City: Columbia University Press.

Hill, E. D. 1987. *Edward, Lord Herbert of Cherbury*. Boston: Twayne.

Hume, D. 1963. The Natural History of Religion. In *Hume on Religion*, ed. R. Wollheim. London: Collins.

Locke, J. 1975. *An Essay Concerning Human Understanding*, ed. P. H. Nidditch. Oxford: Oxford University Press.

McGinnis, P., A. Harrison, & R. Kearney, eds. 1997. *John Toland's "Christianity not Mysterious."* Dublin: Lilliput Press.

Paine, T. 1794. *Age of Reason: Being an Investigation of True and Fabulous Theology*. New York: Citadel Press, 1974.

Preus, J. S. 1987. *Explaining Religion*. New Haven: Yale University Press.

Tindal, M. 1995. *Christianity As Old As the Creation, The Gospel, A Republication of the Religion of Nature*. Chippenham, UK: Thoemmes Press.

Walters, K. S. 1992. *The American Deists: Voices of Reason and Dissent in the Early Republic*. Lawrence, KS: University of Kansas Press.

Wollaston, William. 1724. *The Religion of Nature Delineated*, intro. by S. Tweyman. Delmar, NY: Scholars' Facsimiles and Reprints, 1974.

The Critique of Religion Also Begins with the Critique of the Bible

2

Since Reverend Doctors now declare
That clerks and people must prepare

To doubt if Adam ever were;
To hold the flood a local scare . . . ,
That David was no giant-slayer . . . ,
And Joshua's triumphs, Job's despair . . . ,
And Daniel and the den affair,
And other stories rich and rare,
Were writ to make old doctrine wear
Something of a romantic air. . . .

Since thus they hint, nor turn a hair,
All churchgoing will I forswear,
And sit on Sundays in my chair,
And read that moderate man Voltaire.

–Thomas Hardy, "The Respectable Burgher,
On 'The Higher Criticism' "

The Bible's New Readers: Skeptics and Seekers

What the search for natural religion should, in part, teach us is how religion became a problem because of the imagination, curiosity, and courage of both believing as well as skeptical individuals, like the "deists" Jean Bodin, Herbert of Cherbury, John Locke, and their chief skeptical critic, David Hume. In attempting to respond to the tumultuous political and religious crises of their times, Bodin and Herbert sought to devise a view of the nature of religion that would offer an alternative to the proud assertion of religious particularity that they thought instigated the interreligious strife in their day. For a certain class of unimaginative believer, it was typically considered impious and even blasphemous to employ everyday reasoning to treat the sacred subject of religious truth. While it was becoming acceptable in the seventeenth century to apply God-given reason to politics, jurisprudence, diplomacy, science, and common human affairs, such reason was thought somehow inappropriate for application to the equally God-given domain of religion! But, in full confidence that reason itself was a divine endowment, the deists went boldly ahead and brought God-given reason to bear on questions concerning religion. In doing so, in principle, they brought religion into the arena of shared human knowledge for the first time in the West.

In forging ahead into this unknown territory, bolstered in part by their confidence in the divine origins of reason itself, the early naturalists not only opened up a veritable Pandora's Box of questions, but also took steps to answer at least some of them in the form of the idea of Natural Religion. For them, human experience, rational argument, and historical data became the bases for evidence as to the nature of Natural Religion. Natural facts, then, became the bases for agreement about what we can say and what we can know about religious claims, at least in a minimal sense. At a certain point in the intellectual history of the West, giving an account of religious life in terms of facts, common to human experience, became a basis for talking about religion – at least by certain critical thinkers. Of course, many religious believers continued as they always had, relying from case to case upon strictly religious forms of discourse. They thus continued to justify their views about religion based upon their personal religious experiences, dreams, visions, and such, or grounded in both scriptural and ecclesiastical authority. But the emergence of thinkers like Bodin and Herbert as well as empiricists and skeptics like John Locke and David Hume, meant that a new – naturalistic – approach to fundamental religious issues could be said to have first seen the light of day by the end of the eighteenth century. The 'deists,' and of course their critics, such as David Hume, can be said then to have been the first to put 'religion' into play as a subject of rational, naturalistic inquiry.

The 'deist' breakthrough into the naturalistic study of religion, tempered as it was by Hume's hostile skeptical critique, brings us to the subject of the present chapter – the significance for the study of religion of the rise of the critical study of the Bible. (I shall adopt the convention of calling the new methods of criticism of biblical texts 'Higher Criticism,' a term that properly came into prominence during the last third of the nineteenth century.) The 'deists' and skeptics contributed to the rise of the historical-critical study of the Bible primarily by means of encouraging an entire range of natural-istic studies in the humanities – of sciences of philology, history, and the study of ancient literatures. In addition to their support of scientific approaches to religion, the 'deists' also gave impetus to the *art of interpreting* these documents: "hermeneutics" (Byrne 1989, p. 94). In theory, therefore, the 'deists,' skeptics, and Higher Critics of the Bible all shared the conviction that the Bible *could and should* be scrutinized like any other piece of literature – in a rational, empirical, that is to say, naturalistic way, all the while recalling the 'deist' sense of human reason as a divine endowment. It was left to people trained to do this kind of critical work to fulfill the implications of the deist critique of religion.

If opposition or suspicion dogged deist attempts to apply critical tools to the religions, biblical criticism itself has known controversy from the start – and for good reason. While historical inquiry may have grown out of a pious desire to deepen knowledge of the scriptures, for some religious folk the application of historical analysis to sacred texts seemed impious. Even when it was not immediately considered to upset ordinary expect-ations about the nature and content of the Bible, critical study of the Bible promised reorientation of entrenched views among Western religious folk. Of this impact of historical critical methods of Bible study, the historian Van Harvey notes that the great modern theologian Ernst Troeltsch (1865–1923) "discerned that the development of this method constituted one of the great advances in human thought; indeed, that it presupposed a revolution in the consciousness of Western man" (Harvey 1966, pp. 3–4). Some defenders of unexamined understandings of the sacrosanct character of the Bible would even describe the results of historical criticism of the Bible as "traumatic" (ibid.). Still others felt that the "method itself...was based on assumptions quite irreconcilable with traditional belief." Supernaturalism, miracles, Christian uniqueness, reliance on faith as a fundamental basis for life – all these came into question with the advent of the kind of methods the leaders of this revolution brought forward (Harvey 1966, p. 5). Such prophecies would, naturally enough, often come true. One of the most radical of biblical critics, David Friedrich Strauss, fell by the wayside. His adoption of historical critical methods eventuated in his own slide into heresy. Although Strauss began by promising only strict historical criticism, he ended being a proponent of a religion of humanity (Harvey 1966, p. 7).

But, as in the quest for Natural Religion, critics like Strauss did not monopolize the field and drive out the believers, nor do they today. Higher Criticism of the Bible had as many, if not more, of its Herberts and Bodins as it had of its Humes. More typical of the spirit of biblical criticism than Strauss were liberal Protestants who saw critical historical study of the Bible as an aid to more mature religious conviction. Thus, William Robertson Smith, himself a student of Julius Wellhausen, one of the Higher Critics of the Bible to be discussed later, affirmed the Christian virtues implicit in taking the critical scientific and historical path:

> The higher criticism does not mean negative criticism. It means the fair and honest looking at the Bible as a historical record, and the effort everywhere to reach the real meaning and historical setting, not of individual passages of the Scripture, but of the Scripture Records as a whole; and to do this we must apply the same principle that the Reformation applied to detail Exegesis. We must let the Bible speak for itself. Our notions of the origin, the purpose, the character of the Scripture books must be drawn, not from vain traditions, but from a historical study of the books themselves. (Smith 1912, p. 233)

Despite his religious optimism, Robertson Smith was hardly blind to the potentially upsetting impact of the critical work of a Strauss: "The science of Biblical Criticism has not escaped the fate of every science which takes topics of general human interest for its subject matter, and advances theories destructive of current views on things with which everyone is familiar and in which everyone has some practical concern" (Smith 1881, p. 1). "In this process the occasional destruction of some traditional opinion is a mere incident....the historical critic must destroy the received view, in order to establish a true one" (Smith 1881, pp. 24, 25). But this shaking of the received religious foundations is no reason for a daring religious soul to draw back from the challenges science presents:

> We must not be afraid of the human side of Scripture. It is from that side alone that scholarship can get at any Biblical question....In this department of intellectual life science and faith have joined bands. There is no discordance between the religious and the scholarly method of study. They lead to the same goal; and the more closely our study fulfils the demands of historical scholarship, the more fully will it correspond with our religious needs. (Smith 1881, p. 27)

Such, at any rate, was an outline of Robertson Smith's progressive Christian resolution of the problem of the relation between criticism and biblical piety. It is one that continues to inform the spirit of contemporary Higher Criticism of the Bible today as well. Of course this is not to claim that all biblical critics shared Robertson Smith's progressive Christian vision. Skeptics like Renan felt little desire to celebrate the supernaturalistic elements in biblical narratives, nor did those like Strauss resist the opportunity critical study of the Bible provided to launch their own post-Christian theological agenda. Each critic will have to be taken on their own terms.

Representing the Sacred: Why Biblical Words Matter More than Sacred Images

Before engaging the major protagonists of Higher Criticism of the Bible, it is worth dwelling on the deeper reasons why critical examination of biblical *texts* made a dispro-portionately greater impact upon Christian self-consciousness at all! Why, for example, did not critical examination of other religious media, such as visual and graphic repre-sentations, stir as much controversy, create as many problems of religion? Why should disputes among the faithful about the reading the biblical narrative differ so much from those regarding the 'reading' of iconographic representations of Jesus? Why has criticism of the Bible caused such an extraordinary amount of acrimony and ill-will, while Christians – the iconoclastic controversy of the eighth and ninth centuries for the moment excluded – at any rate, seem rather free and easy about how Jesus, for instance, is represented in visual or plastic form (Pelikan 1974, ch. 3)? (See figure 2.1.)

The reason for this asymmetry between feelings about these religious media needs to be traced back to a radical shift in the way the Bible was read in the course of the history of Christianity. Reading the Bible exclusively in a literal way – as being a document that was assumed to correspond to a state of affairs *in the world* as well as in eternity – came rather relatively late. For over a thousand years, the Bible had been read in numerous ways. In fact, the most prominent way of reading the Bible before the Protestant Reformation was as *allegory* or *symbol* – and not only literally. For Christians for over a thousand years before the Reformation, God had graciously provided humanity with two 'books,' as it were. God had given people knowledge of himself *both* through the book known as 'the Bible,' but also through the 'book of nature.' Seeing God's creation – nature – as revealing the creator meant that the entire 'natural' (really on this view a world suffused with the *super*natural as well) world spoke to pious Christians in various and sundry ways. Everything, no matter how humble and useless to human purposes, *revealed* the divine purpose. Everything bore the mark of its divine origins. Everything was a symbol of some, often quite small, part of the divine plan. "Animals," for example, as historian Peter Harrison tells us, "had a 'story.' They were allocated meanings, they were emblems of important moral and theological truths, and like the hieroglyphics of ancient Egypt they were to be thought of as the characters of an intelligible language" (Harrison 1998, p. 2). Similarly, alongside the handiwork of the divine author of nature – the 'book of nature' – the biblical book was as well a source of powerful sacred meanings, evidence of hidden divine codes and symbols of divinity. To wit, the Bible was not *always*, nor perhaps even principally, taken *literally*. Christians of the first thousand years of the history of the church did not, therefore, see the Bible as some kind of protoscientific or historical text.

Figure 2.1. Jesus depicted as Greco-Roman god on the tympanum over the main entry to the Church of the Madeleine, Paris (1807–45)
Source: Church of the Madeleine, Paris.

The Book of Genesis was revelation of God's power, majesty, and love, not an early version of today's high-school biology textbooks! It was instead a *religious* document – a powerful source of revelation of the wisdom and beneficence of God's sustaining power and love for humanity.

Not to be disrespectful in any way to believers, I would hazard a comparison of the way the Bible was read in those early centuries of the Christian movement with media that today might be said to *reveal* truths about life to people today. One might liken this pre-Reformation way of reading the Bible to the way, say, J. R. R. Tolkien's *Lord of the Rings* is read – or 'watched' in our modern cinemas. Without doubt the world of Middle Earth, Mordor, the Marches, and such are depicted, in Tolkien's books and in the film versions of them, as highly realistic and concrete. We are shown maps of that world, plans of how difficult it will be for our heroes to penetrate the redoubt of Mordor and destroy the ring. Not only that, but Tolkien provides an elaborate history explaining the evolution of the world's many humanoid peoples – Elves, Fairies, Hobbits, Orcs, Nazgul, Wizards, Men – into the world we inhabit, sadly depleted of wondrous beings such as Elves, Hobbits, and such, but happily free of Orcs and their ilk. Part of the joy of reading/watching the *Lord of the Rings* comes precisely from the credible details of a lost world that Tolkien provides.

But I would suggest that the putative *historicity*, so to speak, of the Tolkien books is only part of the reason for their hold on the good-hearted spiritual imaginations of modern readers. No modern reader – or at least very, very few – believe that these books are to be read, indeed *ought to* be read, literally. But, what matters here for our comparison with reading the Bible literally is that the lack of real *historicity* of the Tolkien books in no way depletes their value – indeed, their *religious* or spiritual value. What is paramount for readers of the Tolkien books is their symbolic or allegorical meaning, and not whether, say, Orcs, Gandalf, or Frodo really lived in *historical* time or whether Middle Earth, the Shire, or Mordor can be found on any automobile club map, or unearthed by some enterprising archeologist. Thus, whether the *Ring* trilogy recounts actual occurrences in actual places in history – whether it is *literally* true or not – means nothing for the *spiritual* or *religious* impact of the Tolkien books. It makes no difference that Frodo does *not* 'live.' What matters to readers is what the *Ring* trilogy, its key characters, struggles – both internal and external – and such, *mean*. To any attentive reader or viewer, it seems clear that the many struggles depicted in the Tolkien books present edifying spiritual virtues at work or under threat – values like courage, faithfulness, honesty, love, honor, kindness, affection, steadfastness in the face of evil, and so on. What is the point of the common graffito like "Frodo lives!"? Ironically, although posed as a claim about someone's really being alive, it is itself a clearly meant to be read as a *symbolic* statement – just like pre-Reformation allegorical or symbolic readings of the Bible. A graffiti artist who thought they were declaring a fact that *could* even qualify as historical would surely have misfired. And viewers would have missed the point entirely of such a graffito, if they as well thought that Frodo *could have had* an actual historical existence that could be asserted! Furthermore, they would have missed the whole point of the way Tolkien wanted his books to be read if the *historicity* of Frodo mattered to the real meaning of his books. One might just as well pack the detailed maps of Middle Earth packaged in the *Lord of the Rings* on one's next road trip across the United States, or along the borders of England and Wales!

It is revealing, therefore, that iconic representations of Jesus, for example, have been commonly accepted by Christians as not needing to conform to the actual (historical) way that Jesus looked. Indeed, we do not know with any degree of certainty how Jesus looked – just what some skeptics of the New Testament's recording Jesus' exact utterance would say as well. Rather, without loss of their sacred character, graphic representations of Jesus have typically been seen as symbols of various Christian truths. Jesus' solidarity with humanity is exemplified in biographical scenes, such as the nativity, not the precise historical details of a stable and manger of the first century! The range of graphic representation of Jesus has, as well, been fairly broad across the centuries of Christian history, indicating a spirit far from the literalism that can attach to the biblical narrative. When the earliest Christians rendered their understanding of Jesus pictorially, they often did so to represent their savior to the world and to themselves in sometimes abstract symbols of new life and resurrection – in emblems declaring Jesus' conquest of death. Jesus as cosmic divinity is also evident in the powerful Pantokrator and world-ruler images from the great western European cathedrals or Eastern orthodox icons of Christ in glory.

Evidently, there is much theology and straightforward religious instruction, and of a good broad range of it as well, occurring in the way Jesus has been represented in *visual* terms. What I want to underline is how *relatively* little controversy this wide range of representation has provoked. I do not say no controversy, since Christians have disagreed on a number of ways in which Jesus has been represented visually, such as with the Iconoclast Controversy in the eighth century. In this light, it is hard to evaluate why the catacomb art of the early Christians represented Jesus in abstract cryptic symbols and codes, rather than in more graphic representations of the image of Jesus and the saints.

The abstract representations of early Christianity included such symbols as, for example, the Greek letters, χρ (chi rho), usually laid one over another indicating the first two letter of the Greek word, "Christos." Or the earliest Christians would indicate Jesus by the sign of the fish – the "Ichthos" – a coded form of the pious declaration, "Jesus Christ, Son of God," where the "I" stood for the Greek form of Jesus (Iesu), the "ch" for "Christos," and the "thos" for the Greek word for God, "theos." Beyond these examples, the earliest Christians freely shared and declared other dimensions of their young faith in Jesus, such as that found in the baptistery of Dura Europos, where Jesus is depicted as the Good Shepherd or Man of Wisdom, and so on. Thus was abstraction rooted in some sort of theological position, much as it is in Islam's interdiction against depicting living animal forms. Did the Iconoclast movement of the eighth century somehow pick up this strand of early Christian piety by trying to outlaw *any* visual representation of religious subjects at all? We do not know. There are also controversies surrounding presentation of what today may be the most prominent image of Jesus – the crucified, suffering, dying lord. There are, for example, no Christian representations of the crucifixion of Jesus for the first 400 years of Christian history! Reacting to Roman Catholic emphasis upon depicting suffering Christ, the Protestant Reformers stood against its depiction, preferring instead the symbol of the empty cross to signify the centrality of the resurrection over the passion.

What one wants to take from this brief treatment of representations of Jesus is that in our times – at least ever since the Reformations, both Protestant and Catholic – the status of the *literal* biblical narrative has become a heated issue, in a way that *visual* depiction has not. Instead, a swarm of problems has settled round the nature of the biblical narrative. To what extent is the Bible like or unlike competing genres of narrative form, such as 'history' on the one hand, and 'myth' on the other? Here is where our controversies about representing Jesus cluster. By the early nineteenth century, the level of controversy rose so high as to provoke another one of those 'problems of religion' around which the study of religion has been constructed. When it came to *literary* or *putatively historical* representations of Jesus, it became controversial indeed how Jesus would be rendered in narrative, how his presence there would be interpreted in texts and documents such as the Bible.

"Frodo Lives!": Myth, History, and Mystery

The Jesus of the gospel narrative then became controversial because of the post-Reformation dominance of literal readings of the Bible. Literal readings were powerful for all sorts of reasons, not least of which was the superficial similarity of some of them to literary modes, like 'history,' which was at the same time enjoying an increasing prestige. But unlike allegorical or symbolic readings of the Bible, reading it literally also put it at risk of conflict with other kinds of narratives purporting to give a different or contrary account of the same events narrated in the Bible. These accounts are what we may call 'history.' On the one hand, if one read the Bible literally, one also ran the risk of too close a resemblance to other narratives, like 'myth.' These were but two of the most prominent genres for classifying ancient documents such as the Bible that occurred to those trying to understand the nature of the biblical narrative.

Concomitant with the rise of the historical sciences were, as well, their ancillary 'sciences' – the comparative philological and literary sciences directed at writing ancient history. (The same kind of conflict arises, incidentally, for alternative accounts of the 'book of nature' – what we may call 'science' or, in its original terminology, 'natural philosophy.') As for the alternatives of 'history' and 'myth,' the status of the Bible was thrown into controversy as the literatures of the ancient world came to be uncovered and published. Just to take one small example, it might be thought that the classic deities, Attis or Cybele, as depicted in the mythologies of the ancient world, were not actual historical persons. We might call them 'fictional' or 'mythical' creations, but ones that were nonetheless religious and redolent with powerful meanings – like say the Gandalf or Frodo characters of Tolkien's *Lord of the Rings*. That is why we frequently refer to the narratives in which all such characters appear as 'myths,' and why we speak of them as 'mythical' personages – even though we also sometimes *seem to wish* they were historical figures, as seems to be the case for those who proclaim that "Frodo lives!"

When, however, scholars reflected on the reasons for such classifications, they found good reasons to suppose that the character of Jesus, as represented in the Bible, was equally 'mythical' as, say, the figure of Attis was, and that the gospel narratives could plausibly be called 'myths' in the same sense as the stories relating the life and death of Attis, to take but one example. These scholars reasoned that the Jesus of the gospels – depicted as a kind of magician or wonder-worker, multiplying loaves and fishes, raising the dead, transforming water into wine, as well as having been born miraculously of a virgin, then finally killed as part of some cosmic sacrificial or expiational drama, only to rise to life again from the dead – seemed about as "mythical" a figure as any from the "mythology" of the ancient world. How could such a representation be "*historical*," then – not least of all because the events and patterns of behavior of Jesus conformed so well with those of the accepted "mythical" figures from the "myths" of the ancient world?

Reasoning further, some of these Higher Critics of the Bible posed the question of whether, despite the "mythical" qualities of the gospel narrative, parts of the gospel might contain *historical* elements nonetheless. Once this move to sift out the historical features concerning Jesus from the mythical ones began, the *quest* for an "historical Jesus" was launched! Here we seek information about Jesus, the flesh and blood man, who lived during the time of Caesar Augustus in Palestine. We seek to know about Jesus in the same sense as we would seek to know about any other historical personage, such as Socrates, Plato, Caesar, and so on.

Another way of talking about the historical Jesus was also by contrasting him with the "mythical" one. The term for this 'Jesus,' friendlier to Christian believers and more current in today's religious discourse, is to refer to the opposition between the "Jesus of history" versus the "Jesus of faith." Here, the Jesus whose acts and words can be affirmed by the historical sciences is the "historical Jesus," the Jesus, for example, whose existence was attested to by the Jewish historian of the first century, Flavius Josephus (37–100 CE). The Jesus of faith would then be that understanding of Jesus affirmed in Christian creedal statements, but either of a dubious historical nature or none at all. Here would be aspects of Jesus' career such as his "sitting at the right hand of the Father" – not the kind of claim even put forward as a candidate for "history," since it would be a state of affairs occurring in eternity. But, although it is believed by Christians to have occurred in time and space, the resurrection of Jesus would qualify as a state of affairs encompassed by the rubric, the "Jesus of faith," because of its miraculous nature. Indeed, *believing* that the resurrection was an historical fact is for many Christians a defining feature of Christian orthodoxy.

In recent days, two major activities of scholarship taking part in the quest for the historical Jesus are the work of the Jesus Seminar and the investigation of the so-called

Gnostic gospels. In both cases, the results of the scholarship, if accepted, would tend to change Christianity in the way Christians understood themselves. The Jesus Seminar consists of a large team of scholars, each of whom was asked to read through the New Testament and to rank sayings and passages there in terms of the likelihood of their being actual sayings of Jesus. The consensus reached by these scholars is that the majority of sayings attributed to Jesus in the gospels are fabrications. Nor, did Jesus perform miracles or physically rise from the dead, according to the scholarly consensus among the members of the Jesus Seminar. The implication of their work is that much of what we understand as Christianity is in fact the creation of the church and Jesus' followers, rather than of Jesus himself. As one might imagine, these conclusions created a scandal among Christians and created immense theological *problems* for them. Ramon E. Morales of San Gabriel, California, wrote in a letter (March 18, 1995) to the *Los Angeles Times*:

> It is ludicrous for the Jesus seminar to state that their "findings" do not act to tear down any people's faith. They claim the Jesus didn't speak the words attributed him, he didn't perform any miracles and that he didn't physically resurrect after his death. Since most of the New Testament theology is depended on at least one of those three things, that leaves us following some wimpy do-gooder who got in trouble with the law and was crucified. Not much point to that.

If the past experience of resistance to attempts to lay before believers an image of Jesus at variance with what is commonly held in the hearts of believers be a guide, this and similar reactions may be expected to future efforts at Higher Criticism of the Bible.

The point to be made here is that such conflict – the raising of questions or problems – has been one of the leading ways that religion has been put into question in the West. It has as well been a constant prod to new thinking about the nature of religion, starting by way of critical inquiry into the source documents of Judaism and Christianity. For that reason alone, we need to appreciate the vital role in the making of modern-day religious studies of Higher Criticism of the Bible. At this point, to do this with the right degree of depth and polish, we need to press on and learn something of the ways that Higher Criticism first challenged received understandings of the Bible. First, we will need to know further about the *methods* employed to force a new look at the status of the Bible. Second, we will need to know something about how the first *major players* in the Higher Criticism of the Bible brought about a fresh way of looking at the Bible.

Biblical Criticism's New Methods

We began understanding the rise of Higher Criticism of the Bible by noting that, like the 'deists,' some were motivated by skepticism (Renan and Strauss, for example) while others were tribunes of progressivism (Robertson Smith). The rise of the Higher Criticism of the Bible differs from the circumstances of 'deist' approaches to religion in that it announced the appearance of at least the four new disciplines for studying religion – history, philology, text criticism, and hermeneutics. Now more than ever, anyone wishing to study the Bible critically needed to be more than just masters of polemics like the jurist Bodin and philosopher Herbert were. One needed to be a good *historian* as well as someone adept in the ancient and exotic *languages* of the Bible, knowledgeable about how texts were *put together*, and adept at *interpreting* them.

First, *history*. In their commonly-held belief in the value of the naturalistic treatment of religious *texts* – especially those of Christianity – 'deists,' skeptical empiricists, and Higher Critics of the Bible each advanced the naturalistic study of religion in their own ways. Like the 'deists' in their quest for what might lie behind or precede 'revelation,' we will see that the Higher Critics of the Bible sought to uncover the 'historicity' of, the actual historical substrata underlying, biblical narratives. As skeptical, empirical historians, Higher Critics of the Bible wondered, for instance, whether there really had been a great historical flood as related by Genesis? Did the walls of Jericho, also, *in fact* 'come tumbling down'? Or, at least, is there empirical evidence that they did so when and if an historical Moses was in fact on hand to expedite their collapse? In this connection, historical approaches to religion raised questions of religious documents, such as which events narrated actually occurred in the past in contrast to events which were only imagined, such as stories and myths.

We will recall that Hume set something of an example of the way in which *history* could be applied to the study of religion. His *Natural History of Religion* set out an object lesson in how one could submit religion to the rigors of historical inquiry and criticism. Hume showed, in effect, that it was not enough just to be clever at dialectic, as he supremely was. Nor was it enough to excel in legal polemics or in working the nuances of concocting diplomatic compromises, as both Bodin and Herbert of Cherbury were. A firmer grasp was needed of 'doing history.' We will recall as well that by training and inclination, the 'deists' and skeptical empiricists tended on the whole to be philosophers. Thus, when Bodin did historical work, as he had in his legal histories, he pursued this discipline in relative isolation rather than in a growing movement with others engaged in a definite kind of special inquiry. The rise of Higher Criticism of the Bible represents something altogether different – namely the growth of an historical mentality or consciousness, as Van Harvey has argued.

> To be sure, Western culture, in contrast to many others, has always been characterized by a sense of history. But only in the nineteenth century did this manifest itself in a sustained and critical attempt to recover the past by means of the patient analysis of evidence and the insistence on the impartiality and truthfulness of the historian. . . . This revolution in consciousness found its formal expression in he creation of a new science, history. (Harvey 1966, p. 4)

The 'deists,' then, had been concerned with comparing religious doctrines and beliefs, or religions as institutions. The Higher Critics of the Bible, on the other hand, were devoted to the historical study of the religious scriptures common to both Judaism and Christianity, and to the historical contexts in which these documents arose. We will look more closely into the work of critical historians in exploring the contributions of representatives of the influential 'Tübingen School' based at the progressive Eberhard Karls University (Tübingen) in the Germany of the early to mid nineteenth century, F. C. Baur and D. F. Strauss

Next, *philology*. Once the historicity of religious texts was established, the texts had to be either read in their own languages and/or translated into modern European languages – quite often by the same persons we have identified as 'critical historians.' Addressing such historical questions demanded many new skills of students of religion. Most of all, the biblical critics needed to be trained in *philology* – the serious study of language in all its dimensions. As such, a new syllabus of questions presented themselves. The new biblical scholars had often to determine, for example, the identity of the very languages in which the Bible had been originally and subsequently written. How correct were the translations made along the way? Typically, philologists needed to construct afresh the grammars of the ancient tongues, some of which had never been formalized in this way. Dictionaries of exotic languages had to be assembled as well, often without the help of native speakers to assist the process. As students of ancient texts and obscure literary forms, these scholars were in effect involved in elaborate projects of the reconstruction of lost cultures and civilizations through the media of studying ancient languages.

Taken together, history added to philology became indispensable for another discipline – *text-critical* approaches to scripture. From the time of the late middle ages to the Renaissance, two cultural developments set in motion the need to develop text-critical methods of biblical study. The first was the discovery of apparently ancient biblical and other religious manuscripts purporting to be of great, yet undetermined, antiquity. The second was the development of printing. Both produced a great increase in the number of actual physical texts – copies – in circulation throughout Europe. Some of these 'copies' were authentic, others forgeries (Popkin 2003, p. 219). This inevitably gave rise to questions about how to distinguish the real versions of old texts from false ones. How do we determine authenticity, and find the 'best' physical text? What concrete version of something purporting to be an ancient text actually was truest to the original? Once the historical location of a text was secured and its linguistic pedigree established, how was a given text in fact *constructed* over the course of its life?

What applied to any ancient text applied in this respect to the Bible itself. Since different versions of the biblical texts circulated at a particular time, it made sense to ask whether a particular text was authentic or a clever counterfeit, whether one text contained fewer errors than another, whether one was a 'better' one than another? Historians might also want to know, for example, which particular version of the text, or part of a text, was the oldest? Or, they might want to know which particular text may have been based or derived from another text? How indeed could we assign dates of composition or of creation to the texts in hand, since most of the texts did not come with such explicit identifying markers; or if they did, how could one be sure these were accurate? Students of the ancient literatures want to know, for instance, whether there might be textual errors in the Bible, mistakes that perhaps had crept in during the course of copying and recopying by medieval and ancient scribes? Were there even deliberate distortions made to the texts by unscrupulous scribes or scheming clerics? How do we know that we possess the most authentic rendition of the words and thoughts of the four evangelists, Paul, Jesus, Moses, the prophets of Israel, or King David? And how do we know what the words of these texts meant for the people of the time of their creation? Was the text at hand the product of a single author, and who was that author, if it be only one? Or is the text the edited sum of the works of several authors or voices? Who indeed are they? And what have they to do with each other? Are they allies, opponents, or something yet different again?

The Jewish philosopher Baruch Spinoza (1634–77) provides a fine, very early example of how sacred texts were studied in order to unpack the mysteries of their authorship. But, as we will see, it fell to the Tübingen School, especially F. C. Baur, D. F. Strauss, and others, to produce a rigorous practice of biblical criticism. Nonetheless, Spinoza can be seen as precursor of Tübingen School scholars in his querying of Mosaic authorship of the

Torah, or in further unpacking the order and make-up of the composition of an ancient text in order to understand the evolution of the present form of a text from possible earlier versions of it. The critical study of texts as a science thus entailed the systematic and rigorous study of documents for the purpose of determining their actual authenticity, their factual authorship, their true date of creation, the cultural and social circumstances of their origins – what the German Higher Critics of the Bible called *Sitz im Leben*, their situation in a particular living context. This new textual criticism of the Bible thus worked more concretely on religion than the 'deists,' in ways such as seeking to evaluate something as seemingly mundane as the origins of the physical texts that they held in their hands. Again, were they originally composed in the form in which they now existed? Or were they perhaps compilations and/or redacted versions of more primitive texts? Like the gospels, had they issued from a single author as the Bible itself claimed? Or were names like 'Matthew' and 'Mark' codenames for entire schools of biblical authors? If they were compilations, then the critics sought to disentangle the chronology and contents of ancient religious texts as they had developed in order to write a history of the physical text, so to speak.

In their close attention to the empirical details of religious data, then, the Higher Critics of the Bible fostered a naturalistic study of religion. Revelation was not denied because the Bible was now to be studied naturalistically – historically and empirically; it was just something that had to be squared with the naturalistic investigations of religious texts. Together with 'history,' the close study of texts thus produced distinctions that we now take for granted, such as that between the early and later versions of a text, the 'source' document and its derivatives, the 'canon' and the noncanonical, and so on. In turn, this enabled scholars to conjecture about the degree to which a document was historical or legendary or mythical. Indeed, the very category of scripture itself, especially as implied in distinctions between 'history' and 'scripture,' or other literary forms, became an issue. Nowhere did these distinctions come to bear with more consequence than in Higher Criticism of the Bible. One great contribution to the naturalistic study of religion, made by the Higher Criticism of the Bible, then, was to approach a sacred text such as the Bible as a *human* document that could be pulled apart and held up to the light of critical scrutiny (Harvey 1966, ch. 1).

Finally, *hermeneutics*. Once these languages had been identified, their grammars mastered, and some notion of the composition of the biblical text achieved, the students of the Bible were faced with the most interesting and intellectually challenging problems of all: interpreting what the biblical texts meant in their original and present form, and how they should be construed in the future. This eventually called forth a general theory of interpretation, *hermeneutics*, to begin to deal with a host of problems afflicting the intelligent reading or interpretation of sacred texts such as the Bible. How, for example, does the whole of a text shape the way we interpret any given part? Paradoxically, can we even understand any part of a text until we grasp the meaning of the whole? As the philosopher Friedrich Schleiermacher (1768–1834), generally acknowledged as founder of philosophical hermeneutics, put it: "The sense of every word in a given location must be determined according to its being-together with those that surround it" (Bowie 1998, p. 44). This is not even to begin querying the many other questions of interpretation that arise in the context of understanding the Bible, such as how recent interpretations of the biblical text can be squared with earlier ones. Or how past readings of the meaning of sacred texts conform to those that were traditionally taught – since it is often held that religious truth is one and unchanging. At one time, as we know, biblical texts were chiefly interpreted *allegorically*, only later to become interpreted *literally* – some would say like 'history' or 'science.' Indeed, some folk still interpret the words of the Bible in this way today, even down to believing that creation, for example, happened in seven days. But others see the biblical narrative in more *spiritual* ways, reading the same creation narratives as signs of divine love and concern for humanity (Evans 1963).

The major figure in the development of a formal theory of hermeneutics, Schleierma-cher, devoted himself to constructing a system for interpreting texts correctly. For him, it became the subject of a formalized, complex, high-level intellectual inquiry. Schleier-macher set out this serious intellectual inquiry in his formidable *Hermeneutics and Criticism* (1838), a document that modern readers will find more reminiscent of a technical manual in engineering than a treatise on how to read the Holy Book. There, Schleiermacher argued on the one hand, along with our 'philologists,' that proper interpretation required mastery of the *objective* rules of correct language use (Bowie 1998, p. 6). For Schleiermacher, then, hermeneutics was first of all a demanding form of rule-governed activity – "requiring the talent for language" (Bowie 1998, p. 11). Aside from normal attention to grammar, Schleiermacher asserted, for example, that proper understanding of particulars required an understanding of how they were situated within the whole of a text. He thus advanced appropriate methodological maxims, arranged in numbered paragraphs, such as the following:

20. The vocabulary and the history of the era of an author relate as the whole from which his writings must be understood as the part, and the whole must, in turn, be understood from the part.
   1. Complete knowledge is always in this apparent circle, that each particular can only be understood via the general, of which it is a part, and vice versa. And every piece of knowledge is only scientific if it is formed in this way . . . (Bowie 1998, p. 24)

23. Even within a single text the particular can only be understood from out of the whole, and a cursory reading to get an overview of the whole must therefore precede the more precise explication. (Bowie 1998, p. 27)

Second Canon: The sense of every word in a given location must be determined according its being-together with those that surround it. (Bowie 1998, p. 44)

But Schleiermacher went further than a concern with the relative placement of objective materials in pursuit of adequate interpretation. He argued that hermeneutics also involved understanding the *subjective* or "psychological" presuppositions that readers brought to the texts. Schleiermacher also tells us that hermeneutics is a high art calling for a "talent for knowledge of individual people" (Bowie 1998, p. 11). This attention to the knowing subject eventuated in Schleiermacher's assertion that hermeneutics con-tained a "subjective element . . . a talent," as well as the rigorous objective knowledge and skills that he outlined (Bowie 1998, p. 12). In the subjective vein, and more controver-sially, Schleiermacher advanced an approach to interpretation known as "divination" – "the ability to arrive at interpretations without definitive rules . . . hermeneutics [as] an 'art,' because it cannot be fully carried out in terms of rules" (Bowie 1998, p. xi). Among others, Schleiermacher has been read in this way by the philosopher Wilhelm Dilthey (1833–1911) as principally meaning that the interpreter must *empathize* with the text: "Before the application of the art one must put oneself in the place of the author on the objective and the subjective side," says Schleiermacher (Bowie 1998, p. 24). It is a point of some controversy whether this language actually implied that Schleiermacher advocated what later came to be attributed to him as a Romantic theory of "empathetic understanding." We will see that something quite close to the Romantic theory of empathetic understanding featured prominently in the methodology of the phenomenologists of religion, although mostly attributed to Dilthey. But, doubtless because of Dilthey's intellectual admiration for Schleiermacher, the method of empathetic understanding as identified with Dilthey came to be attributed as well to Schleiermacher (Bowie 1998, pp. vii, xx, xxix). Not coincidentally, Dilthey's biography of Schleiermacher, *Leben Schleiermachers* (1922), is regarded as Dilthey's finest realization of the method of empathetic understanding (Ermarth 1978, pp. 267–71). Following the lead of Schleiermacher in more recent times, the existential theologian Rudolf Bultmann, a sophisticated proponent of a "demythologizing" interpretation of biblical narratives, echoes this subjective aspect of Schleiermacher's rich hermeneutical theories:

> Schleiermacher (1768–1834) already recognised that such [grammatical and philological] hermeneutic rules are not sufficient for the real understanding of a text. He demands the completing of the philological interpretation by a psychological one, and he calls it an interpretation by divination. A literary work has to be understood as a moment in the author's life. The interpreter must reproduce in himself the incident out of which the work which he has to interpret grew. He must, so to speak, produce the work again. (Bultmann 1957, p. 111)

Together with history, philology, and textual criticism, hermeneutics lives on, along with more recent innovations of its own, in present-day Higher Criticism of the Bible.

Higher Criticism: Internal Discrepancies

It is easy to understand resistance to the application of scientific procedures to religious scriptures such as the Bible. Such critical studies meant that the status of the Bible (or any other allegedly divinely inspired text) as God's inspired word, along with its lofty position as eternal revealed truth, was put into a very different context than it had had for the believer who had not interrogated the text. In the light of the textual-critical sciences, the Bible was a human document like any other, and thus was subject to the same scrutiny as any other text. The critical study of the biblical text, therefore, launched a whole raft of questions quite often challenging innocent faith. It is possible to divide these questions into two broad categories. On one hand were queries spurred by an "internal" critique of the biblical narrative; on the other were problems generated by what one may call an "external" critique of sacred scripture. Let us consider the matter of "internal" critique first. All such questions arose once the proposition was entertained that the biblical texts seem to have a human side with an equally human history, a history that might include honest errors or deliberate distortions, dictated by political or religious interests.

As one investigated the *internal* character of the biblical narrative, for example, puzzles were thrown up about certain oddities and discrepancies found there. Right from the very beginning of the Bible in the Book of Genesis, ch. 1, a version of creation is given that differs from that in the very next chapter! In ch. 1, for example, God creates things in a certain order, heaven and earth, light, day and night, etc. But in ch. 2, God creates in another order – the earth already exists, and then is followed by the creation of man. Pointedly, in ch. 1, verse 26, man is created in God's image, while in ch. 2, verse 7 and following, Adam is formed from dust and moisture. Another early discrepancy occurs in ch. 4, where Genesis recounts the story of Cain and Abel, Adam and Eve's only children. As we know, Cain kills his brother, Abel. Shortly thereafter, God asks Cain where his brother is, only to receive the now classic retort, "Am I my brother's keeper?" Unhappy with this answer, God curses Cain and dooms him to bear the mark of his murder – the infamous "sign of Cain" – and to be forbidden henceforth to settle and practice agriculture. What, however, struck the new critics of the local narratives was the fact that in the first 17 verses of ch. 4, the Bible tells us that Cain subsequently went on to marry, produce a son, Enoch, and continue his life as a city dweller – despite the fact that the Bible gives no account of the origin of the wife that Cain took in the process. How, indeed, could Cain have found a wife to marry, if he and Abel were the only offspring, as the Bible relates, of the first parents of the human race? The Bible is silent on this matter, but critics of the biblical narrative fell upon this as a sign of the human character of the biblical text. Equally noteworthy was the discrepancy in the Genesis account of Noah and the flood in ch. 7. There, in verses 1 through 6, the narrative relates how God commanded Noah to take *seven pairs* of each kind of ritually clean animal into the Ark, but with only one pair of each kind of unclean animal. Yet verses 6 through 10 relate a flood story beginning with the statement that Noah was 600 years old when the flood came upon the earth and concluding with the onset of the flood after the entry of *only single pairs* of animals of the earth into the Ark. Critical students naturally question why two flood stories occurred in the passages relating to Noah. Historians considering such an oddity might be tempted to suggest that the different texts reflect different historical dates of origin, later fused together into a single narrative. In the New Testament we find similar internal discrepancies in the genealogies attached to Jesus. Matthew, ch. 1, traces Jesus' origins to Abraham. Yet, in Luke, ch. 3, Jesus' genealogy is traced as far back as Adam. Another example: at the Last Supper, Luke records that Jesus used two cups, 22:17 and 22:20, while Matthew 26:26 and Mark 14:23 mention only one.

In the viewpoint of the historical, philological, and hermeneutic sciences, these discrepancies did not necessarily invalidate the claims of Christianity or ancient Judaism. At the very least, they opened up a vast range of problems and questions about the composition and character of biblical texts, with possible implications to our present-day understanding of the nature of Christianity and Judaism. We know, for example, that early Christians assembled the Bible, and that in this sense the Bible is the daughter of the church. Thus, the church decided which books and which teachings were to be included in the Bible – placed in the "canon" – and which were not to be included. Recent scholarship on these so-called Gnostic gospels, not to mention their popularization in Dan Brown's runaway bestseller *The Da Vinci Code*, conveys some of the excitement and scandal that new readings of the Christian canon can produce (Brown 2003).

Elaine Pagels is one of the leaders in the new scholarship of these excluded texts. Pagels believes that the study of such noncanonical texts, such as the notorious Gnostic "gospels," may help us understand the development of Christianity. Her inquiries raise a whole set of historical, textual-critical, and hermeneutic problems with the status and content of the biblical narrative. What were the bases of the decisions that the early church made about the content of the New Testament? Why were some 'gospels' included and others (the so-called Gospel of Thomas, for example) excluded from the New Testament canon? Do passages in the New Testament retain older, conflicted versions of Christian religious thought? Should these be challenged or at least revisited? For example, these days it is often asked why women have traditionally had an inferior role within Christianity. But in the Gnostic gospels, on the other hand, the role of women there is often quite prominent. Raising the hermeneutic question, one wonders how this discrepancy with the New Testament canon should be interpreted. Could the casting of women in inferior roles in the canonical gospels have been more a matter or early Christian misogyny than, say, straightforward loyalty to the words and wishes of Jesus? What, therefore, is the *meaning* these differences? What *meaning* should we attach to the way women are portrayed in the New Testament? This juxtaposition of canonical and noncanonical "gospels" thus has the power to make us think anew about commonly accepted assumptions about religious orthodoxy. It creates one of those "problems of religion" that I mentioned in my introduction, and that are so important in the development of critical studies of religion.

Higher Criticism: The Question of the "External" Fit of Biblical Narrative with "Facts"

On the other hand, proponents of the "external" criticism of the Bible were more concerned with the *factual truth* of the biblical narrative – its 'historicity' as explained above – rather than with issues of "internal" consistency. "External" critics challenged various doctrines, such as the trinity, the virgin birth, the resurrection of Jesus, and the occurrence or performance of miracles and other supernatural events, such as the multiplication of the loaves and fishes or ascension of Jesus into heaven.

One strategy for checking the factual nature of events narrated in the Bible brings us back to the matter of historical methodology discussed earlier. How do biblical accounts of events square with those of contemporaneous documents of indubitable historical value? Is the Bible good 'history'? Do Roman or Jewish records of the time confirm biblical accounts of the same period? Is the Bible 'historical,' and to what extent, and in what sense? Was there really a Roman procurator in Judea named Pontius Pilate, and was he involved in the condemnation of Jesus to death – if indeed such a person as Jesus of Nazareth existed? Did Jesus exist, and to what extent did his existence conform to the picture given of him in the Bible? If Pilate existed, the usually factual, and thus historically reliable, Roman records should confirm Pilate's existence to be a 'fact.' If they do not, one would tend to be skeptical of the biblical account, since Roman records for these matters tend to have a high degree of historical accuracy, and would not be motivated to overlook such a routine matter.

A second strategy for checking the *factual* accuracy of the Bible – especially regarding miracles – is by comparing claims made there to our knowledge of the natural world. Is it possible, for example, that Moses could have caused the Red Sea to divide? Is the virgin birth of Jesus or any other human being a biological possibility? When the Bible says that God made the sun stand still at the battle of Jericho, could this really have been the case – especially since we know that relative to the sun it is the earth that moves? There are additional, conceptual, problems with claims about miracles. If we understand a miracle to be a God-caused intervention into nature, how can we tell if it was God who caused the event? We may note an irregularity in nature and observe an apparent suspension of a law of nature. Human beings only *see* the event. But we do not *see* God causing it. How do we know that an apparent suspension of or an anomaly in a natural process was God-caused? The answer is faith. I would suggest that we might conceptualize the notion of a miracle as a believer's seeing an event *as an intervention* of God in natural processes.

Major Jewish Players: Spinoza and the "Scientific Study of Judaism"

I have already mentioned in passing some of the early figures in the development of Higher Criticism of the Bible, such as F. C. Baur, D. F. Strauss, and others, but how and where did the critical study of the Bible begin? While it is generally true that Protestant Christian scholars in German-speaking countries of the late eighteenth and early nineteenth centuries, such as members of the Tübingen School, were the most prominent practitioners of critical methods of studying the Bible, full credit should be given to the independent developments in Jewish critical biblical scholarship of the same vintage – the Wissenschaft des Judentums (Science of Judaism) movement and earlier (Neusner 2000, p. 102). In Germany, as early as 1822, the Jewish scholar Immanuel Wolf, one of the founders of the Wissenschaft des Judentums movement, put forth a view of the desirability of a historical, scientific study of scripture identical with that of the Christian Higher Critics of the Bible. Says Wolf of the Wissenschaft des Judentums,

> the aim will be to depict Judaism, first from a historical standpoint, as it has gradually developed in taking shape; and then philosophically according to his inner essence and idea. The textual knowledge of the literature of Judaism must precede both methods of study. Thus we have, first, the textual study of Judaism. (Wolf 1980, p. 194)

In 1819, the Jewish historian Leopold Zunz founded an independent and private organization for the scientific study of Judaism, the Verein für Cultur und Wissenschaft der Juden (Albert 1977, p. 251). Together with Abraham Geiger, Zunz launched the official organ of the movement, the *Monatschrift für Geschichte und Wissenschaft des Judentums*. Its express aim was to publish original work on all aspects of the history of Jewish life the world over, including critical studies of the Bible.

In the same period, the Jewish historian Heinrich Graetz aspired to a critical historical study of rabbinic literature. This marked the beginnings of the study of the Talmud as history. For Graetz, the Talmud should be regarded as a human document, and whatever its spiritual values, should be studied using the same methods of historical, philological, and critical resources applied to profane literature (Neusner 2000, pp. 100 ff.). Taken cumulatively, the movements of critical scholarship with which Graetz can be associated had lasting effects for the Jewish community. In the words of Jacob Neusner,

> Alongside the historicistic frame of mind shaped in the aftermath of the Romantic movement, there was an enduring critical spirit, formed in the Enlightenment and not to be eradicated later on. This critical spirit approached the historical allegations of ancient texts with a measure of skepticism. So for biblical studies, in particular, the

history of ancient Israel no longer followed the paths of the biblical narrative, from Abraham onward. (Neusner 2000, p. 102)

Although it would take us too far afield to explore all these effects, Neusner also notes additional, perhaps unintended consequences of the work of supposedly critical historians like Graetz. He and his ilk were far less mere critics than they make out. They sought, ironically, to achieve positive "theological results" for reinvigorating and shaping the future of Judaism (Neusner 2000, p. 103).

As early as the 1830s, French Jews too became interested in developments within the German university system, and sought actively to lure German scholars to France. Among those attracted by emigration to France were a number of German Jewish scholars connected to the group Geiger and Zunz had assembled in 1819. Having refused to convert to Christianity in pursuit of higher careers in the German professional world, their careers were effectively stymied. In pursuit of the benefits of emancipation, some therefore emigrated to France. Thus within a short time of the establishment of the Wissenschaft des Judentums itself, the originally German movement was carried to France, subsequently to become part of the intellectual scene of the study of religion in France flourishing within the milieu in which Durkheim and his collaborators worked on the social-scientific study of religion. In this regard, perhaps doing most to set the pace for avant-garde French Jewish scholars was Salomon Munk. For Munk, Judaism stood alongside other religious traditions like Islam and Christianity as an equal – and equally appropriate – object of scientific study, not as a separate, autonomous entity. Like the Durkheimians, Munk was a comparativist and an original proponent of interdisciplinary work. He sought to orient the study of Judaism toward the disciplines of archeology, history of antiquity, and philology (Simon-Nahum 1991, pp. 90–5).

In some respects, these critical attitudes to Jewish scriptures and religion, as well as their modern successors, can be linked all the way back to an earlier thoroughgoing naturalistic critic of the Bible, such as the Jewish religious thinker Baruch Spinoza (1634–77) (Simon-Nahum 1991, p. 12). In his most dedicated critical work on the Bible, A *Theologico-Political Treatise*, Spinoza tells us of his desire to study the sacred text according to the light of reason – scientifically or naturalistically – like the 'deists' Bodin and Herbert. Spinoza's determination to steer clear of 'religious' approaches to religious documents like the Bible, also echoed the 'deists' in pursuing Natural Religion. Spinoza undertook his efforts to construct a religiously *neutral* approach to biblical interpretation for the same purposes of overcoming religious conflict followed by the 'deists.' In his case, Spinoza was driven to undermine conflicts and fanaticism that religious disagreements over interpretations of meaning in the Bible had caused in his time (Spinoza 1670/1951):

> As I pondered over the facts that the light of reason is not only despised, but by many even execrated as a source of impiety, that human commentaries are accepted as divine records, and that credulity is extolled as faith; as I marked the fierce controversies of philosophers raging in Church and State, the source of bitter hatred and dissension, the ready instruments of sedition and other ills innumerable, I determined to examine the Bible afresh in a careful, impartial, and unfettered spirit, making no assumptions concerning it, and attributing to it no doctrines, which I do not find clearly therein set down.

Beyond such sincere scientific resolutions, made in the interests of seeking social peace, Spinoza laid out a series of procedures and questions that might inform a naturalistic or scientific approach to biblical study. He may then be said to have assembled perhaps the first program of problems or questions that could be used to guide critical or naturalistic inquiry into biblical narrative, and by way of this point of entry the first syllabus of problems of a critical or naturalistic study of religion.

> With these precautions I constructed a method of Scriptural interpretation, and thus equipped proceeded to inquire – What is prophecy? In what sense did God reveal Himself to the prophets, and why were these particular men chosen by Him? Was it on account of the sublimity of their thoughts about the Deity and nature, or was it solely on account of their piety? These questions being answered, I was easily able to conclude, that the authority of the prophets has weight only in matters of morality, and that their speculative doctrines affect us little. (Spinoza 1670/1951, p. 8)

The implications of Spinoza's methods for Bible study conform as well to the naturalistic approach of the 'deists' and skeptical empiricists to religion in general, and anticipate the critical historical approach of the Wissenschaft des Judentums. For him, the scriptures should be studied like any other bit of nature, in particular by means of the systematic method of investigation that Spinoza borrowed from Descartes – even though the more pious Descartes refused to submit holy writ to his own scientific method! For Spinoza, the Bible's "speculative doctrines affect us little." That is to say, that it was not a true *source* of knowledge in his view, although the Bible had valuable moral guidance to offer. Instead, it was chiefly as an *object* of inquiry that the Bible held interest for the scientific student of religion. We should then go forth and apply the methods of scientific scrutiny to what had heretofore been considered exempt from it (Popkin 2003, pp. 242–3).

Similarly, in our own day of religious turmoil and change, scholars from religious traditions outside the ambit of Western culture are applying the same kinds of critical tools to the analysis of their sacred texts as Christian and Jews had from the early nineteenth century. The critical approach is even penetrating the Islamic tradition, despite continued resistance to historical critical study of the Koran. A Muslim scholar in Germany writing under the pseudonym Christophe Luxenberg has argued that the Koran has been misread and badly translated for centuries. Luxenberg's scholarship concerns itself with the earliest extant copies of the Koran, and argues that parts of Islam's sacred scripture are derived from preexisting Christian literature, later misinterpreted by Islamic scholars preparing editions of the Koran that are still read today (Stille 2002: p. A1).

Major Protestant Players: Ferdinand Christian Baur and the Tübingen School

Despite the brilliant beginnings made by Spinoza, it took nearly 150 years before his theoretical insights began to appear in the concerted work of other scholars in the West, both among Jews and now Christians. It took at least that long before Higher Criticism of the Bible in the style in which it has come to be known provoked "problems of religion" that challenged the way the bulk of Europe's religious population conceived and studied religion, especially religious documents, scriptures, or texts.

The first seminal figure fully to articulate and extensively practice the historically skeptical approach adumbrated by Spinoza was the German Protestant historian and philosopher Ferdinand Christian Baur (1792–1860). Inspired by G. W. F. Hegel's historicizing philosophical thought, Baur took the view that the Bible should be submitted to rigorous historical interpretation and criticism in the same way as profane literature. One should not grant privileges to traditional readings of scripture or the feelings of pious believers about the nature of the Bible. Instead, one had to apply critical methods of interpretation to attain a proper understanding of the teachings of the Bible. Therefore, while the Bible may remain divinely inspired, close attention to the nature of religious texts did not support the view, for example, that the entirety of scripture had fallen whole and supernaturally formed from the hands of God. Rather, the Bible itself reflects human authorship, as Spinoza and the Wissenschaft des Judentums thinkers argued as well. And if human authorship had to be taken into consideration, we had to apply our understanding of human processes to the interpretation of the Bible.

For Baur, a principle source for understanding human processes was Hegel's philosophy of history. It was in terms of Hegel's conception of the logic of historical change as a dynamic interaction between 'thesis' and its opposite, 'antithesis,' subsequently resolved into a 'synthesis,' that Baur's reading of the Bible took shape. In particular, Hegel made Baur sensitive to this pattern of opposed tensions and struggles, resolved into resolutions that shaped the profane human history of nations and peoples. In this logic of dialectical struggle and synthesis, the forces represented in the Bible were no different. After all, in the Bible one could discern how different theological parties contended for dominance in shaping religious history just as literal military forces contended for political supremacy in profane human history. As one might expect, Baur's approach greatly upset many of the faithful, since it challenged the entire conception of the Bible as a simple revelation of a preformed divine plan. Instead of serene supernatural origins and reassuring ideas of divine inspiration in holy scripture, Baur claimed that the Bible was a record of human – albeit religious or theological – struggles.

Baur thought that an excellent example of such a tension within early Christianity conforming to this pattern of Hegelian dialectic tension was what he detected in the Pauline letters. When read through Hegelian eyes, the letters of Paul reveal a theological battle between two opposed factions of early Christians. On one side was the party of Jewish Christians associated with the apostle Peter (Petrine); on the other were those new Gentile Christians recently evangelized by Paul (Pauline). Their fight was nothing less than one to define the nature of early Christianity and, in effect, how the church would evolve from that point forward – in part at least, whether to become a Christian one had first to become a Jew, and among other things, whether male converts and newborns had to undergo circumcision.

> It was my study of the two Corinthian letters that first caused me to concentrate my attention more directly on the relation of the apostle Paul to see that this relationship was one quite other than is ordinarily assumed; that where it is taken for granted that there existed a complete harmony between all the apostles, there was actually an opposition, one which even went so far that the very authority of the apostle Paul was brought into question by Jewish Christians. (Baur 1851)

Engaging this struggle required that Baur do some of the first extended work in *historical* criticism and *textual criticism*. For one, in order to retrieve the historical position held by Paul – and not just ones piously attributed to the Apostle by the Gentiles – Baur had to sort out the authentic Pauline letters from those *claiming* his authorship, but which were not *authentic* products of Paul himself. To Baur, historical criticism thus entailed skepticism about traditional assignment of Pauline authorship to scriptural books such as the Letters of Paul. Baur, in fact, concluded that Paul had only authored four of the ten letters traditionally ascribed to him.

Having sorted out the authentic texts from the inauthentic, Baur then argued that one party was aligned with those still clinging to their Jewish identities – the party of Peter – while the other fell in with the more radical universalizing line taken by the 'new apostle to the Gentiles' – Paul of Tarsus. Baur here tried to capture the dynamic logic of opposition embodied in the Hegel's logic of dialectic confrontation of thesis with antithesis, with the Petrine and Pauline forces playing their respective contending roles. In Baur's view, the Gospel of Matthew resolved these oppositions into a harmonious synthesis. Despite such a seemingly innocent resolution to the struggles that Baur saw in the New Testament, his entire approach was so profoundly disturbing to the received wisdom of traditional believers that Baur was severely attacked over the years, and finally isolated from his colleagues. In their religious cowardice and stiff-necked resistance to changing their old habits, Baur's opponents thought it better to reject the fruits of the God-given endowments of human reason that led Baur better to understand the real message of Paul. For them, ironically clinging to their human-originated habits of reading the Bible, it made no difference that, thanks to Baur, they now were in a better position to understand the depths of God's word by better understanding Paul, for example!

Major Players in the Quest for the Historical Jesus: Renan and Strauss

Beyond the critical studies of the Bible by Baur and others in the early nineteenth century, one major question has dominated the fortunes of historical criticism right up to our day. This is the so-called 'quest for the historical Jesus.' Although more than just a single 'quest,' it was an attempt to sort through the traditional narrative representations of Jesus in order to provide a historically reliable biography (Harvey 1966, p. 9). It was this quest that attracted some of the most prominent figures of nineteenth-century biblical criticism, such as a one-time student of Baur's, David Friedrich Strauss (1808–74), as well as the French rationalist historian and former Catholic, Ernest Renan (1823–92).

Born in the traditionally conservative Catholic milieu of Brittany, Ernest Renan trained for the academic clergy, specializing in philology and history with a special attention to Jewish studies. An avowed devotee of the ideals of Higher Criticism of the Bible as a "positive, creative faculty," Renan exhibited a love of science that led him both to appreciate religion as an object of scientific study and to make science itself a kind of religion in his life (Chadbourne 1968, pp. 39, 46). And, although dedicated to science and the autonomy of scientific endeavor, Renan did not deliberately set out to antagonize the Catholic faithful, who might well have found his critical ideas threatening to their faith. Renan thereby set the tempo for the relatively tolerant, undogmatic, though critical and skeptical style of modern religious studies in France, much in the spirit of one of France's first critical students of religion, Jean Bodin.

Reflecting the great strides that scholarly study of sacred texts had taken in the nineteenth century, Renan studied Hebrew at the seminary of Saint Sulpice, and maintained his love of the language throughout his life. Along with certain other Gentile savants, Renan was even recognized for contributions to Jewish studies with election into the Société des Études Juives – the official professional society of French Jewish learning, the 'French' cousin of the German Jewish Verein für Cultur und Wissenschaft der Juden, which in turn launched the movement known as Wissenschaft des Judentums, which we have discussed above. As a model nineteenth-century philologist and critical historian of religion, Renan published major works on the history of Semitic languages, his *Histoire générale des langues sémitiques* (1855), a seven-volume study of the origins of Christianity (1863–81), his *Les Origines du Christianisme*, and the five-volume history of the Jews (1887–93), *L'Histoire du peuple d'Israël*. Renan was named professor at the prestigious Collège de France in 1862, only to be suspended for having, in effect, denied the divinity of Jesus (Houtin & Sartiaux 1960, p. 396).

Although one can see that Renan's record of weighty publications ranks him as a major scholarly figure in his own right, he owed tremendous intellectual debts to the pioneering work of people like F. C. Baur, D. F. Strauss, and the entire Tübingen School (Carbonell 1979, p. 61). In 'Catholic' France, however, this association doomed Renan to incessant conflict with the Roman Catholic church's teaching on the inerrancy and immutability of the Christian scriptures. In 1845, Renan finally and reluctantly broke with the church over the very 'Protestant' issues of the freedom of intellectual inquiry and the liberty of the individual conscience. James Frazer felt that Renan always retained a profound sympathy for Roman Catholicism and remained emotionally attached to it throughout his days (Frazer 1923, p. 38). While being constitutionally incapable of converting to Protestantism, Renan so admired the liberating ideals of his colleagues in the Tübingen School, that he is supposed to have voiced the desire to have been "born a German Protestant!" (Chadbourne 1968, p. 94).

Renan's *Vie de Jésus*

Giving voice to his critical attitude to the biblical narrative, Renan declared what we can call a classically *rationalist skepticism* toward such elements of the Bible as miracle and myth. In his *Life of Jesus* (1861), Renan thus declares:

> If the miracle has any reality, this book is but a tissue of errors. If the Gospels are inspired books, and true, consequently, to the letter, from beginning to end, I have been guilty of a great wrong in not contenting myself with piecing together the broken fragments of four texts, like as the Harmonists have done, only to construct thus an *ensemble* at once most redundant and most contradictory. If, on the contrary, the miracle is an inadmissible thing, then I am right in regarding the books which contain miraculous recitals as history mixed with fiction, as legends full of inaccuracies, errors, and a systematic expedients. (Renan 1861, pp. x–xi)

His reference to Jesus in his inaugural lecture as an "incomparable man" won him an immediate suspension of his teaching privileges! (Houtin & Sartiaux 1960, p. 396). But this and more severe censures did not stop Renan. He continued in this vein with the publication of his rationalist biography of Jesus, *Vie de Jésus*, and won dismissal from his chair at the Collège de France. The story of the inspiration of Renan's great popular work in part, at least, may help us understand the thrust of his intentions. A trained and expert archeologist, Renan had been supervising a scientific expedition to 'Syria' in 1860–1, when he was struck by the pious realization that he was "treading the same ground" and "breathing the same air" as Jesus and his disciples had centuries earlier. Renan's desire to convey this sense of the reality of the milieu in which Jesus lived led him to undertake the project that later became *Vie de Jésus*. Contrary to standard expectations, although Renan's work here is often characterized for the rationalist impieties it deploys in debunking sacred Christian traditions surrounding Jesus, it is abundantly evident that *Vie de Jésus* nonetheless sprang from Renan's genuine, heart-felt religious motivations. Renan is reported, for example, to have "knelt briefly" at a local shrine in pious memory of Jesus, revealing an attitude of sweet reverence that suffuses Renan's "least scientific and most personal" work (Chadbourne 1968, p. 115).

There has hardly been a more popular attempt to produce a biography of Jesus than Renan's. As late as the 1970s, distinguished historians of Christianity, such as Owen Chadwick, still judged Renan's work in extraordinary terms:

> The *Life of Jesus* was a landmark; no landmark in theology, where its influence was negligible or neglected, but in the attitude of the middle class to religion. It was the first time that a biography of the man was written, which excluded the supernatural and at the same time was aimed at the general reader and written by a master of the evidence. It was also the last time that such a biography of the man was written by a scholar, for the progress of inquiry made men see that the historic materials were not sufficient to enable the writing a biography which excluded the supernatural. (Chadwick 1975, p. 219)

Much the same verdict about the book's popular appeal was reached on the opposite shore of the Atlantic a century earlier by Renan's American contemporary, the Harvard philosopher John Fiske. His review of *Vie de Jésus* begins with these words of dubious praise. "It is by far the most readable book which has ever been written concerning the life of Jesus. And no doubt some of its popularity is due to its very faults" (Fiske 1876, p. 77). The problems Chadwick, Fiske, and subsequent scholarly critics find with what is, in effect, a kind of historical novel is precisely with its fidelity to history:

> Renan is certainly very faulty, as a historical critic, when he practically ignores the extreme meagreness of our positive knowledge of the career of Jesus, and describes scene after scene in his life as minutely and with as much confidence as if he had himself been present to witness it all. Again and again the critical reader feels prompted to ask, How do you know all this? or why, out of two or three conflicting accounts, do you quietly adopt some particular one, as if its superior authority were self-evident? (Fiske 1876, p. 77)

But, again, at the time there was a public demand for accounts of the life of Jesus, and the then rapidly growing reading public wanted something that at least *looked* historical. (One thinks of parallels from our own time, such as the runaway popularity of books written in a similar vein, like Dan Brown's *The Da Vinci Code*.) To the mass-market reader, the complaints of Fiske and his ilk must have seemed pedantic academic quibbles – as the chagrined Fiske himself admits in the same review:

But in the eye of the uncritical reader, these defects are excellences; for it is unpleasant to be kept in ignorance when we are seeking after definite knowledge, and it is disheartening to read page after page of an elaborate discussion which ends in convincing us that definite knowledge cannot be gained. (Fiske 1876, p. 77)

D. F. Strauss: Mythologist and Religious Humanist

As great as Renan was, he owed immense intellectual debts to the German Protestant pioneers of Higher Criticism of the Bible in the Tübingen School, F. C. Baur, and especially D. F. Strauss. Indeed, Strauss might be called his generation's chief protagonist in pressing the critical historical examination of the life of Jesus. His *Life of Jesus* (*Leben Jesu*) (1834) – marked a major event in the progress of critical study of the Bible. Although it was not the rationalist skeptical and demythologizing biography of Jesus that Renan achieved, its theological assaults on received conceptions about the character of Christianity created scandal enough in its time. Like Renan, Strauss challenged a host of traditional beliefs about Jesus in his great work – the historical accuracy of the birth stories, the narratives of Jesus' temptation by Satan, his baptism by John, the many reported occasions of miraculous healing performed by him, and, of course, Jesus' transfiguration, resurrection, and ascension (Harvey 1966, p. 11). But, unlike Renan, Strauss went beyond mere naturalist skepticism of the French rationalist, and sought to build on the ruins of the biblical narrative a new religious vision entirely – religious humanism (Harvey 1966, p. 7). As Van Harvey sarcastically puts it:

> The issue [of the motivations behind Higher Criticism of the Bible] was frequently clouded by the fact that the earliest biblical critics sallied forth into speculative theology in the name of a factual science. D. F. Strauss, for example, after a thousand or so pages of reasoned historical argument in his *Life of Jesus*, took pen in hand and charted a theological program for the future in which the doctrine of the Incarnation was to be supplanted by the idea of the deification of humanity. (Harvey 1966, pp. 6–7)

Strauss's constructive theological ambitions aside, even though he worked a generation before Renan, in many ways his style of interpretation of the biblical narratives might be seen to supersede Renan's. One's evaluation of Strauss's *Leben Jesu* will depend in part on one's evaluation of the value of the Hegelian notions that Strauss imbedded in his work. For the French positivist, the Bible was rife with plainly dissembling or erroneous materials. Renan's aim was simply to get down to a historical bedrock beneath the 'mythical' overlay obscuring the core of the biblical message. Although with Strauss, we find at first the same skeptical attitude to miracles so well worked out in the writing of David Hume, Baur, and others, we also, however, are introduced to a technical concept of 'myth' that greatly enriches critical approaches to sacred texts. Thus, while Strauss, like Renan, argued that any biblical passage containing reference to the occurrence of miracles could not, *ipso facto*, be considered 'historical,' he would perhaps say more about the religious consciousness, and say it, perhaps, more subtly than his French follower.

It was true for Strauss that Christians, for example, proclaimed Jesus' resurrection, and equally true that Jesus really did not reanimate – in an *historical* sense. Yet Strauss did not believe that the evangelists or early Christians were *lying*, mistaken, or holding back what they knew to be true, as Renan in a sense implied. True, the critic needed to separate the miraculous and mythical from the real and historical, as Strauss eagerly did. Instead, Strauss felt that in calling attention to the miraculous and 'mythical' character of parts of the biblical narrative, he was saying that the people of biblical times thought about the world differently than modern folk, who thought 'historically.' They thought about the world 'mythically' because their minds had not yet developed an historical consciousness. The 'Spirit' – in the Hegelian sense – that shaped the mentalities of people at various stages in the mental development of the human race simply had not evolved to the same level that it would later in modern times. Wrong as they might be, people of biblical times did not deliberately *fabricate* "myths" about Jesus, but rather naively and sincerely saw the world in an unpremeditated 'mythical' way. They were only expressing themselves in a way appropriate to their level of mental development. People of today, informed as they were by an historical and scientific consciousness, could no longer see the world in this 'primitive' way. 'We' had to ask historical questions of the biblical narrative, and inform our religious belief and practice according to the results of historical inquiry. There was no other way for modern folk to continue being religious, because failing to do so would fly in the face of knowledge. Critical study of the Christian sacred scriptural writings thus was fated to have a huge impact on the future of religious faith among Christians in the West.

Taken together, then, the combined influence of the representatives of Higher Criticism of the Bible – from Spinoza, through Baur, Strauss, and Renan – would then be to put into question a whole range of issues about the status of the biblical narrative. In bringing to bear questions about the historicity of the Bible, in querying the character of the versions of the Bible in circulation, in raising the matter of the authenticity of the authorship of various sacred books, in interrogating sacred scripture about its internal discrepancies, the Higher Criticism of the Bible opened a new and extensive chapter in the study of religion.

Looking Forward to the Perils of Comparison

One final source of external criticism of the biblical narrative, and one that would become another indirect source of questions about the nature of religion, emerged in comparing Jewish and Christian religious documents with those originating outside Judaism and Christianity. While the founders of Higher Criticism of the Bible did not themselves press the implications of interreligious comparison, a loyal student of theirs would. As we will see in the work of Friedrich Max Müller in the next chapter, cross-cultural comparison would be employed to raise questions about one of the core beliefs of so-called 'orthodox' Christians – the uniqueness of Christianity, and especially of the Bible itself. Significantly, as we will see, Max Müller was deeply influenced by the founders of Higher Criticism of the Bible and conversant with their methods. I should like to make a transition to the next chapter and conclude this chapter on the Higher Criticism of the Bible by anticipating Max Müller's impact on the study of religion from just the sort of cross-cultural comparisons of religious narratives that called into question the Bible's uniqueness.

Consider unidentified narratives, for example, such as the following. Here, one immediately thinks of Jesus accepting his impending suffering and death for the sake of human salvation: "The Lord resolved to take upon itself the burden of all human suffering. 'I am determined to take his own, not to turn or run away, not to tremble or to be terrified.' " Yet, this text is Buddhist in origin, and articulates the career of the *bodhisattva* – the person in the process of becoming the Buddha. What does this parallel mean? What sort of problems of religion does it raise? Does it signify that the older text – in this case the Buddhist one – was borrowed by the younger – Christian – one? Or does it suggest – if looked at in the manner of the 'deists' – that both Buddhism and Christianity are rooted in a common religious source, however unknown it may be to them? Likewise, what would seem more Christian than these phrases celebrating the love of God for humanity, articulating a religion of grace and devotion to God?

> In Him alone seek refuge with all your heart, all your love, and by His grace, you will attain eternity and everlasting peace.
>   Keep Me in mind, love Me and worship Me, bow down before Me, and if you do, I promise that you will be with Me. You are dear to Me, so put aside matters of the Law, and turn to Me your true refuge. I will deliver you from all evils. Have no cares.

This is drawn from the Hindu scripture, the *Bhagavad Gītā*. As such, does it indicate that the oft-heard claim that Christianity is a unique religion of grace and love for the savior might not be so unique after all? And if that is so, are not the same problems of religion, related to borrowing and such, raised? And what would it mean to Christian belief if it were discovered that Christianity had borrowed from a 'pagan' and even *polytheist* religion, such as much of Hinduism is? Or who, when presented with the following quote, would not identify it – at least at first glance, and certainly in terms of its spirit – as the story of the Prodigal Son in Luke 15:11–32?

> A man left his father's house and went to live in another city. He lived there for many years. But while the father continued to grow rich, the son became miserably poor. In the course of time, the son wished to see his father and went on a journey back home. When he arrived, however, he found that the father had moved to a distant land. All the while, the father too thought of the son he had lost many years ago, and grieved inwardly: "I am old, well advanced in years, and though I am rich, have lost my son. It would be bliss indeed if my son could someday enjoy all the wealth that I have acquired."

The real source of this excerpt is the Buddhist scripture, the *Lotus Sutra*. Could it be that the gospels hide within themselves elements planted there from other religions? And again, if that is so, what does this mean not only to claims of the uniqueness of Christian revelation, but what does it mean to the relations of religions to one another as a whole? The close critical study of the Bible is for a good reason an excellent source of some of the great problems of religion.

From Deism to "Mr. Tylor's Science" to Müller's Comparative Study of Religions

As we will see with regard to Friedrich Max Müller in the next chapter, the method of the Higher Criticism of the Bible was combined with *comparative* method, and extended in principle to *all* religious texts from *all* traditions. Applying these methods to the study of ancient Indian texts, Max Müller too sought to identify and to reconstruct the character of the different historical strata of Indian religion in a naturalistic way from evidence provided by the systematic study of language. Are the Vedas as primitive as the Hindus of today claim? If so, does linguistic evidence indicate this? Or are such claims theological and political? Does the study of the Vedic language point to the existence of a religion that historically preceded and materially contributed to the character of the Vedas? From linguistic evidence, such as comparative phonology, can we deduce that the Vedas have precedents, near relatives, and such among other religious traditions outside India, such as other scriptures composed in Indo-European languages, such as the Avestan of Iran? Why are so many of the features of Vedic religion like those found in *comparison* with ancient Iranian, Greek, and Roman religion, and so on? These kinds of questions asked by Max Müller of ancient India were typical of the same kinds of questions critical textual scholars and historians had been asking about the Bible for well over a generation.

Now, while Max Müller was no anthropologist, since he limited himself to the study of written texts, the advent of the historical linguistic study that he practiced bore on the work of future anthropologists of religion such as Tylor and Frazer. I argue that we cannot really understand the context of E. B. Tylor's work, the man called the 'father of anthropology,' without taking into consideration his relations with the theories of Max Müller, his great Oxford colleague, rival, and critic, as well as the leading critical philologist and historian of (Indian) religions of his time. Both thought they had been able, in their related but different ways, to uncover the nature of the origins of religion – and certainly the methods by which one could do so. Yet they disagreed about both their methods and results. Second, the historical critical method of the study of the biblical texts, as developed in Germany under Paul Lagarde and Julius Wellhausen, made direct methodological contributions to the development of the anthropology of religion associated with William Robertson Smith, Durkheim, and the Durkheimian school.

References

Albert, P. C. 1977. *The Modernization of French Jewry: Consistory and Community in the Nineteenth Century*. Hanover, NH: Brandeis University Press.

Baur, F. C. 1851. Autobiographical Reflection on His Studies in Paul (1851): Die Einleitung in das Neue Testament als theologische Wissenschaft.

Bowie, A., ed. 1998. *Schleiermacher: Hermeneutics and Criticism and Other Writings*. Cambridge: Cambridge University Press.

Brown, D. 2003. *The Da Vinci Code*. New York City: Doubleday.

Bultmann, R. 1957. *History and Eschatology: The Presence of Eternity*. New York: Harper and Row.

Byrne, P. 1989. *Natural Religion and the Nature of Religion*. London: Routledge.

Carbonell, C.-O. 1979. Les historiens protestants dans le renouveau de l'historiographie française. In *Les Protestants dans les débuts de la Troisième République (1871–1885): Actes du colloque de Paris, 3–6 Octobre 1978*, eds. A. Encrevé & M. Richard. Paris: Société de l'histoire du protestantisme français.

Chadbourne, R. M. 1968. *Ernest Renan*. New York: Twayne.

Chadwick, O. 1975. *The Secularization of the European Mind in the Nineteenth Century*. Cambridge: Cambridge University Press.

Ermarth, M. 1978. *Wilhelm Dilthey: The Critique of Historical Reason*. Chicago: University of Chicago Press.

Evans, D. 1963. *The Logic of Self-Involvement*. London: SCM Press.

Fiske, J. 1876. The Jesus of History. In *The Unseen World and Other Essays*, ed. J. Fiske. Boston: Houghton and Mifflin.

Frazer, J. G. 1923. Ernest Renan et la méthode de l'histoire des religions (1920). In *Sur Ernest Renan*. Paris: Claude Aveline.

Harrison, P. 1998. *The Bible, Protestantism and the Rise of Natural Science*. Cambridge: Cambridge University Press.

Harvey, V. A. 1966. *The Historian and the Believer*. New York: Macmillan.

Houtin, A. & F. Sartiaux. 1960. *Alfred Loisy: sa vie, son oeuvre*. Paris: Editions du CNRS.

Neusner, J. 2000. Conservative Judaism. In *The Encyclopaedia of Judaism*, vol. 1, eds. J. Neusner, A. J. Avery-Peck, & W. S. Green. Leiden: E. J. Brill.

Pelikan, J. 1974. *The Spirit of Eastern Christendom (600–1700)*. Chicago: University of Chicago Press.

Popkin, R. 2003. *The History of Skepticism*. New York: Oxford University Press.

Renan, E. 1861. *The History of the Origins of Christianity. Book 1. Life of Jesus*. London: Mathieson & Co.

Simon-Nahum, P. 1991. *La Cité investie: La "Science du Judaïsme" français et la République*. Paris: Cerf.

Smith, W. R. 1881. *The Old Testament in the Jewish Church*. New York: D. Appleton.

——. 1912. What History Teaches Us to Seek in the Bible. In *Lectures and Essays of William Robertson Smith*, eds. J. S. Black & G. Chrystal. London: Adam and Charles Black.

Spinoza, B. 1670/1951. *A Theologico-Political Treatise and a Political Theatise*, trans. R. H. M. Elwes. New York: Dover.

Wolf, I. 1980. On the Concept of a Science of Judaism. In *The Jew in the Modern World*, eds. P. R. Mendes-Flohr & J. Reinharz. New York City: Oxford University Press.

Classic Nineteenth-Century Theorists of the Study of Religion: The Quest for the Origins of Religion in History

PART II

The Shock of the Old: Max Müller's Search for the Soul of Europe

3

From Science of Religion to Natural Religion and Back Again

One lasting achievement of Higher Criticism of the Bible for the study of religion was to complicate the reading of religious texts – to cause an entire series of problems to come forth from a source that heretofore had been relatively unproblematic. Although the original critics of the Jewish and Christian Bibles may not have realized it, in opening the religious scriptures of their own respective traditions to naturalistic critical scholarship, they suggested that the same techniques could be applied to any and all religious texts. In looking at religious texts for the first time as shaped by historical and human processes – rather than being some timeless visitation from beyond upon the human realm – a substantial portion of the scholarly community had set into motion a great revolution in our approaches to religion. In religious texts, one read not only inspired words that moved the spirit in traditionally accepted ways, but also words often driven by different theological or religious agendas.

Texts, therefore, can be said to have 'come to life'– both in reflecting the conditions of the human religious *life* of their inception, and also in revealing *lively* dramas lying behind the decisions made in their inception, inclusion in a canon, selective editing, and so on. Granted, therefore, that the 'gospels' may be 'good news' and speak to broad spiritual concerns. But why are there four and not five, or only one? Why do Matthew, Mark, Luke, and John differ from each other about the 'good news'? Why indeed do the orthodox only call these four documents "Gospels" as well? What do we make of those other extracanonical texts, also called "Gospels," such as the Gnostic Gospels, that were left out of the New Testament canon altogether? Why do they reflect different human theological concerns? Why do they branch off from the original source documents of the Gospels from which they seem to derive? Careful reading of the biblical texts reveals different political agendas at work in these otherwise sacred narratives. For example, feminist biblical scholars have observed that patriarchy rules out the significant role of women in the New Testament scriptures. The same, however, cannot be said for the Gnostic gospels, which include women in prominent roles in the divine economy. What does this say about the formation of early Christianity, indeed about the legitimacy of such traditional gender relations?

The significance of these innovations in scholarship about religious texts cannot, therefore, be underestimated for its implications for the study of the religions. As we know from the cultural crises provoked by so-called religious 'fundamentalists' – more properly biblical 'literalists' – over issues like the historical Jesus, Darwinian evolution, or homosexuality, the pronouncements of the critical study of the Bible stir controversies still. The 'shocks' to Western religious consciousness first felt in the early nineteenth century continue to ripple forth. The same religious 'shocks' are also beginning to threaten to unsettle religious traditions in other parts of the world today as well. Time will tell how much and how far these will progress.

But for our immediate purposes, we will consider only two of the most germane issues for this study of the development of academic ways of studying religion. First, if the Bible can be read as scriptural "revelation," as sacred, why cannot *other* sacred texts from *other* religions of the world be read as "revelation" or its sacred equivalent as well? We have already seen how selected texts from non-Christian religious traditions so closely resemble in spirit those of Christianity, for example, that the uniqueness of the biblical text can be brought into question. If that is so, perhaps religions share some common territory of what the sacred is, of what a revealed truth might be? If these common features are observed as well, it becomes more reasonable – even to a partisan of a given faith – that other religions convey sacred truths too. Second, if the Bible can be looked upon as an *historical* document, fit to be judged by normal historical and empirical standards of scholarship and knowledge – and not faith or supernormal cognition – then why cannot any and all religious scriptures be seen in terms of the human historical and empirical character that they possess? Why, therefore, should not all the texts of all the religious traditions of the world be subject to critical textual and historical examination for the purpose of understanding the ways that they have changed over the eons? Despite their claims to supernatural, divine, or transhistorical origins, are not all religious scriptures *at least at some level*, documents owned by human beings and transmitted by human beings to their descendants?

This brings us to one of the first scholars who was convinced of these new perspectives on religious texts, and who put them to work on a wide range of the religious scriptures of the world – Friedrich Max Müller (1823–1900) (van den Bosch 2002, p. 517). From the outset, however, we should note that while Müller expanded the application of the same critical approaches originally brought to bear on the Jewish and Christian Bibles, respectively, to the study of religious texts of the world's religions, he did so in the name of a "science of religion" – in much the same spirit as had the Higher Criticism of the Bible we discussed in the previous chapter. Müller looked on all the world's religious texts as equally sacred, as 'revelations.' But, at the same time, however, he approached all of them as well in a spirit of *scientific* historical curiosity and discovery. "I had been at a German university, and the historical study of Christianity was to me as familiar as the study of Roman history.... [It] left me with the firm conviction that the Old and New Testament were historical books, and to be treated according to the same critical principles as any ancient book" (Müller 2002a, pp. 191–2). This stance left Müller open to the charge of 'agnosticism' – a label he cheerfully accepted. "In one sense I hope I am, and always have been, an Agnostic," because for Müller an agnostic was someone

> relying on nothing but historical facts and in following reason as far as it will take us in matters of the intellect, and in never pretending that conclusions are certain which are not demonstrated or demonstrable. This attitude of the mind has always been recognized as the *conditio sine qua non* of all philosophy. (Müller 1901, pp. 355–6)

True to his commitment to the science of history, Müller then set aside the claims of the faithful that the Bible embodied special divine revelation and a record of miracles.

"A belief that these books had been verbally communicated by the Deity, that what seemed miraculous in them was to be accepted as historically real, simply because it was recorded in these sacred books, was to me a standpoint long left behind" (Müller 2002a, p. 192). In place of strict adherence to the literal sense of the words of the biblical text, Müller undertook historical and philological studies of all the sacred texts of the world, the Bible included. He carried on the equivalent of the Higher Criticism of the Bible that in the previous chapter we traced back to Spinoza – not coincidentally the subject of Müller's doctoral thesis. As for the Bible, Müller tells us: "To me, the questions that occupied my thoughts were to what date these books, such as we have them, could be assigned, what portion of them were of importance to us, what were simple truths they contained, and what had been added to them by later collectors" (Müller 2002a, p. 192).

An historical note can perhaps illuminate Müller's unique approach to the sacredness of religious texts. The new Higher Criticism of the Bible was beginning to put in an appearance in the Oxford of Müller's day, and while Müller was altogether sympathetic to its efforts, he was anything but antireligious. Even though he was part of the movement of criticism of myth-laden religions, he did not engage in destructive 'debunking' or demythologizing of sacred texts. Quite the contrary; as we will see, Müller did not wholly disparage myths, even though he felt that religion at its deepest transcended them. Religion – even religion that was believed to be true – was not therefore at 'war to the death' with mythology, as some of the Deists, David Hume and D. F. Strauss, for example, believed. Instead, religion transcended and fulfilled myth, and thus myth had some measure of relative religious value. For him, historical studies and the other sciences assisted religion in purifying itself. Müller shared the view of the liberal Christians of his day in believing that the Higher Criticism of the Bible would bring out the "original Christian message by undoing it from the accretions of supernatural and superstitious beliefs" (van den Bosch 2002, p. 78). Müller's own words on the higher, more mature, religious value of the Higher Criticism of the Bible tell the whole story:

> I gladly acknowledge that some of the happiest, and not only some of the happiest, but also some of the best men and women I have known in this life, were those who would have shrunk with horror from questioning a single letter in the Bible, or doubting that the serpent spoke to Eve, and an ass to Balaam.
>
> But can we prevent the light of the sun and the noises of the street from waking the happy child from his heavenly dreams? Nay, is it not our duty to wake the child, when the time has come that he should be up and doing, and take his share in the toils of the day? (Müller 1986a, p. 12)

Thus, Müller was an unashamedly, if progressive, pious man, motivated by a rich and subtle combination of heart-felt religious and scientific motives. For his ability to merge in one person both these human tendencies, Müller presents us with a remarkable and challenging story about how his style of the study of religion took shape.

Despite these progressive values, Müller did little publicly to promote them, and even less to confront his theological enemies. He found the Anglican ecclesiastical establishment that dominated the academic and religious scene in Oxford in the latter half of the nineteenth century truly stifling. Yet he avoided confrontation with the established church and "stood aloof from the conflict of parties, whether academical, theological, political. I had my own work to do, and it did not seem to me good taste to obtrude my opinions, which naturally were different from those prevalent at Oxford" (Müller 2002a,

p. 156). Thus Müller disturbed the certainties of the religious system of his day not by a radical undermining of religion altogether in favor of a rationalist empiricism, but by gently compelling the orthodox Christian establishment of his time to take seriously the religious alternatives to Christianity found round the world, especially in India. That is where he both found the problems of religion of his day, and where he exacerbated them!

It was a measure, however, of the complacency and conventional thinking of the Oxford of Müller's time that even his gentle and pious unsettling of the received views of the Christian ecclesiastical establishment should be met with ferocious hostility. Various high-placed forces sought unsuccessfully to prevent the publication of Müller's *Sacred Books of the East* – what he called the "Bibles of humanity" (Chauduri 1974, pp. 355–6). On the occasion of the great honor of his offering the Gifford Lectures, Müller was treated to vicious attacks by the Catholic Monsignor Munro of St. Andrew's, who cast Müller as a kind of "Judas" to traditional Christianity, blasphemer, pantheist, or atheist in disguise.

> The Gifford Lectures delivered by Professor Max Müller were nothing less than a crusade against Divine revelation, against Jesus Christ, and against Christianity. The guilt of those who permitted that anti-Christian doctrine in a university founded to defend Christianity, was simply horrible; It was a strange thing that in a Christian university, public feeling should have tolerated the ostentatious publication of infidelity.
>
> As to Max Müller: "Professor Max Müller was incapable of a philosophical idea, and ignorant of Christianity he sought to overthrow. His theory uprooted our idea of God, for it repudiated the idea of personal God." (Quoted in Chauduri 1974, p. 362)

This attack is not entirely unfair, even if its tone reveals a panicky recognition of the radical impact Müller's research would have for creating problems for religion. Müller's theosophical monistic tendencies did, after all, remain with him from his German romantic heritage, even if Müller always believed that his *avant-garde* beliefs could be reconciled with Christianity. Accordingly, Müller did not intend to paint a uniformly bright and uncritical picture of the other religions at the expense of Christianity. While it is true that he suppressed many explicitly sexual passages in the scriptures collected in his *Sacred Books of the East* series, Müller was just exercising the Victorian prudery proper to his social class. Unlike the British anthropologists E. B. Tylor and J. G. Frazer, as we will see, he never intended to use comparative materials to undermine the religion of the realm. In his introduction to the *Sacred Books of the East*, Müller remarked, "The time has come when the study of the ancient religions of mankind must be approached in a different, less enthusiastic, more discriminating, in fact, in a more scholar-like spirit" (Chauduri 1974, p. 352).

Despite his attempts to avoid antagonizing his theological enemies, Müller's application of philological and textual-critical techniques to scripture met a good deal of hostility from the churches. When he tried to broaden the study of religion and religious texts with his publication the 49-volume series, *Sacred Books of the East*, he naturally wanted to include the Hebrew Bible and the New Testament. The series had been planned by him to make all the major religious texts of the world available in English translation. However generous Müller's intentions, fierce objections from powerful figures at Oxford thus forced Müller to drop plans for including the Western Bible. Commenting on the parochial enmity faced by Müller for his open and 'catholic' views, the anthropologist E. B. Tylor contrasted Müller with his enemies in sharp terms:

Nowhere, perhaps, are broad views of historical development more needed than in the study of religion. Notwithstanding all that has been written to make the world acquainted with the lower theologies, the popular ideas of their place in history and their relation to the faiths of higher nations are still of the medieval type. It is wonderful to contrast some missionary journals with Max Müller Essays, and to set the unappreciating hatred and ridicule that is lavished by narrow hostile zeal on Brahmanism, Buddhism, Zoroastrianism, beside the catholic sympathy with which deep and wide knowledge can survey those ancient and noble phases of man's religious consciousness ... (Tylor 1958, p. 22)

Notwithstanding this setback to the inclusion of the Bible in the *Sacred Books of the East*, Müller carried on this great work for over two decades – from 1879 until his death in 1900. The series was completed posthumously in 1910. This monumental task would alone suffice to put us in Müller's debt forever.

But Müller's importance in the theoretical development of the study of religion – his stimulation by and engagement in what I have called 'problems of religion' – was perhaps just as significant. Deeply impressed, like many of his contemporaries, by the discovery of vast and long-lived religious traditions heretofore unknown in the West, Müller responded with energy, curiosity, and intellectual daring. Müller was, for example, one of the first systematic and persuasive agents of cross-cultural comparative methods in the study of the religions of the world. He also sought to articulate a nonconfessional, scientific, global, and systematic account of the undeniable diversity of religious history that presented itself to the Western mind. His name should always be connected with a new and unprecedented academic discipline that he sought to establish – the "science of religion." In this sense, unlike the Deists of the early-modern and renaissance periods, Müller devised a professionalized academic and putatively scientific plan for the study of religion.

In another sense, however , despite these scientific ambitions, Müller was remarkably like some of the early naturalists, but also unlike others. He was himself embarked on a profound progressive religious quest through the pursuit of his own scientific work. Like the very first figures who made 'religion' a problem – the Deists – and who also made the academic, comparative, naturalistic, or scientific study of religion possible, Müller too was on a quest for Natural Religion – a quest which was at the same time as deeply religious as aspects of the same quests undertaken by Herbert and Bodin. Thus, intimately connected with his scientific philological and textual activities was also an abiding and powerful existential interest in discovering the characteristics of the natural religion of humanity.

In this respect, Müller's application of rational critical techniques to sacred scriptures was clearly not motivated by the desire to discredit them and their religious value. Indeed, just the opposite can be said to be true when one considers his progressive yet profound piety. Unlike that nineteenth-century pioneer of debunking critical approaches to the Bible, David Friedrich Strauss, who we met in the previous chapter, Müller saw his critical studies of sacred texts as leading to a deeper and truer religiosity (Stone 2002, pp. 167–8). Müller's work can therefore be seen as an answer to Hume's challenge to those Deists discredited by Hume for making claims about the existence of natural religion without adequate historical or empirical evidence for it. In the most ancient of the religions of India – or at least not very far behind them – Müller would argue that, in effect, he had found *empirical philological evidence* of the Natural Religion to which the inquiries of Herbert and Jean Bodin pointed, but that Hume had dismissed for their lack of historical evidence. Müller will argue that the best historical and scientific evidence we have for the first religion – for Natural Religion – was of a kind of mystical religion of transcendent and infinite oneness, hinted at by the nature worship of Vedic India that pre-dated Hume's polytheism.

Both this naturism and its more abstract consummation in the form of Natural Religion were religious sensibilities that attracted Müller personally, and to which he seems to have been piously devoted. Thus, if one only looked more deeply, beyond Hume's polytheism, there were layers of more ancient and more sublime religious sensibilities to be found. Hume had only scratched the rough surface below which lay what for Müller was a depth of purest religious sensibility. Likewise, beyond Strauss's debunking of the gospels and the exposure of their mythological elements, Müller felt that mythological critique had not pressed far enough. While much of the gospel narratives, like those of his own area of special research – the Vedic scriptures of ancient India – may indeed be 'mythological' and for that reason religiously corrupted (at least in the eyes of Müller's generation), this was no reason to conclude that their value began and ended there. What lies beneath and behind what appears to us as corrupt or childish on the surface? Müller believed a profound religiosity, something like devotion to the Natural Religion of the Deists, lay beneath what looked corrupt and shabby. One only needed a discerning eye to see through the dust of the ages to the profound levels of pure religion that lay beneath. What if the mythological gospel or Vedic texts, for example, represented residues of something grand that had fallen into decline – like the dusty images found in archeological sites, which when once restored, reveal their original radiance? Why should we assume a fashionable, but facile, story of evolutionary progress in all things, and thus judge the old as inferior to the new? Why should we likewise freeze our perceptions of things in the superficial present and judge things as they appear at the moment? If historical change be a reality, then things – religion included – may change in many directions. Religion may develop and grow as easily as it may decline and degenerate. The intellectual challenge to a science of religion is to determine where a given institution is on the historical line of march.

Müller tended on the whole to see things in decline and as permeated by a sense of loss. Müller was thus determined to answer the challenges of rationalists and skeptics, and plunge into what he took to be the deepest levels of human religiosity, employing in aid of this religious quest the new techniques and scholarship only recently available to him and his generation. Once more, Müller shows how traditions of sound scientific schol- arship have, at least in part, been driven by deep religious motivations. These, in some sense, are the same kinds of drives that moved the scholarship of Herbert and Jean Bodin in their pursuit of natural religion, but here in the middle of the nineteenth century, they were backed up by Müller's critical and historical research into ancient religions and their texts.

A Word about Natural Religion, Naturism, and the Religion of Nature

Since I have spoken rather generally about natural religion and nature, it would be well at this point to make some distinctions among the different types of use of the word "natural" or "nature." For the 'deists' Herbert and Jean Bodin, although they had varying degrees of regard for the natural world, they were on the whole not unduly enamored of nature. The romantics, and especially the English and German romantics, loved nature both as a source of recreation, but most importantly as a revelation of divinity. For this reason, we should distinguish four terms: the *naturalistic* study of religion, *natural* religion, *naturism*, and the *religion of nature*. By a naturalistic study of religion, as we have seen from the very beginning of the present study, we mean a study of religion that proceeds within the limits of ordinary reason and experience. Claims made within a naturalistic study of religion then cannot be based on religious faith. The latter two terms, 'naturism' and 'religion of nature,' are synonyms. They indicate an actual religion consisting in the worship of 'nature.' Here 'nature' might be understood as referring to violent shows of power, such as thunderstorms, volcanic eruptions, and earthquakes, or to gentler happenings, like the sunrise, sunset, or eclipses. Then again, the 'nature' that is worshiped might take the form of great natural phenomena such as vast oceans, tall mountains, or high heavens, or as well prominent heavenly bodies – the distant sun and moon. Natural religion, on the other hand, while it may be described as including the importance of natural phenomena and objects, differs in that the worship of nature is usually not entailed. What is asserted instead is the fact that religion or the religious sensibility is a given of human nature, rather then being God-given outside the normal course of human events. Natural religion historically has also often been rather abstract. The ultimate reality, divinity, is often not represented in imaginary form at all, but regarded as a kind of divine geometer or cosmic principle, or a kind of distant architect of the universe. We will recall, for example, how the deists regarded the universe as designed by some type of cosmic architect, the knowledge of which is simply part of the make-up of human beings. Natural religion is therefore in contrast with revealed religion, whereas naturism would contrast with other sorts of religion such as animism, the worship of souls, or polytheism, the worship of many gods. What makes Müller particularly interesting is his qualified fusion into one of both streams of religion involving nature. He is therefore both a naturist, in the modern sophisticated sense typical of the Romantics – and not therefore in the naive sense of nature worshippers described in ethnographic literature, or even perhaps of the Veda; but he is also, without qualification, a devotee of Natural Religion. Part of the puzzle in understanding his thinking about the study of religion is to understand how his religious pursuits – both in regard to nature and in regard to natural religion – contributed to the development of a study of religion that he took to be naturalistic at the same time. Müller's belief in the ability to reconcile religion and science was thus so strong that he called his approach to study of religion a "science of religion."

Romanticism and the Making of Germans

The conditions motivating Müller's quest for natural religion were, however, quite different than those active in the sixteenth, seventeenth, and eighteenth centuries. Although he was a man of generally ecumenical spirit, Müller was less motivated in his quest for a common Natural Religion by revulsion against the religious warfare that ravaged the seventeenth century, than by the pain he felt in the face of the advance of the soulless, secular, modern industrial age. Müller's reaction set him on a nostalgic quest for a lost world of simplicity and piety associated with his own bucolic past. In an autobiographical reflection upon his youth, he refers to the small town of Dessau in

Figure 3.1. Friedrich Max Müller at 30

Source: Müller, *An Autobiography: A Fragment* (London: Longmans, Green, 1901).

which he grew up as "a little oasis in the large desert of Central Germany" (Müller 2002a, p. 1). A certifiable romantic, Müller celebrates the virtues of Dessau's intimate face-to-face life, altogether lacking the alienated complexity of the urban and industrial life then reaching a high-water mark all across Western Europe.

> I was born and brought up in Dessau, a small German town, an oasis of oak trees where the Elbe and the Mulde meet, a town then overflowing with music. Such towns no longer exist.
>
> When I went to school at Dessau, this small capital of the small Duchy of Anhalt-Dessau counted, I believe, not more than 10 or 12,000 inhabitants. Everyone knew everybody. As a boy I knew not only the notables of Dessau, I knew the shops and the shopmen, the servants, the day laborers who sawed and split wood in the street, every old woman that sold apples, every beggar that asked me for a pfennig – mark, not a penny, but a tenth part of penny. It was a curious town, with one long street running through it, the *Cavalierstrasse*, very broad, with pavements on each side of the street that had to be weeded from time to time, there being too little traffic to prevent the grass from growing between chinks of the stones. (Müller 1898, pp. 4–5)

But some years later, reflecting on the harshness and depersonalization brought by the modern age, he observed with sadness:

> All this is changed now; few people remember the old streets, with distant lamps swinging across to make darkness more visible at night, and with long water spouts frowning down on the pavements like real gargoyles, and not frowning only, but during

a thunderstorm pouring down buckets of water on a large red and white umbrellas of the passers-by.

Dessau was then the very poor town, but a *laeta paupertas* reigned in it; everyone knew how much everybody else possessed or earned, and no one was expected to spend more than was justified by his position. We can hardly understand now with how little people then managed, not only to live, but thoroughly to enjoy the highest pleasures of life.... there was a curious mixture of simplicity of life and enjoyment of the highest kind. I remember in my grandfather's house delightful social gatherings, musical and literary performances. I remember Mozart's "Don Juan," Beethoven's "Fidelio" being performed there, the latest works of Goethe and Jean Paul being read and appreciated with a cup of tea or glass of wine. (Müller 1898, pp. 5–6)

When it came to nature itself, Müller imbued it with a religious significance, typical as well of the romantics. In 1858, Müller penned a biographical sketch of his father, Wilhelm Müller, the Romantic poet and one of Franz Schubert's greatest librettists. There he comments on the then increasing popularity of nature as a source of recreation and esthetic appreciation. His reference to "cockneys" – London's East End working-class inhabitants – also hints at the sources of this new sensibility in the revulsion against the increasingly unpleasant condition of the smoke-choked, grimy, and teeming Dickensian industrial cities of Western Europe. Something of the religious also informs this paean to the natural world. For although Müller speaks only in lyric and poetic terms here, his oblique references to gods of Greek mythology – the "Titans" – hints at a deeper theological significance for him in the romantic love of unsullied nature:

It is well known how many of the most beautiful spots in Scotland, and Wales, in Cornwall, were not many years ago described as wastes in wildernesses. Richmond and Hampton Court were admired, people traveled also to Versailles, and admired the often admired blue sky of Italy. But poets such as Walter Scott and Wordsworth discovered the beauties of their native land. Where others had only seen bare and wearisome hills, they saw the battle-fields and burial places of the primeval Titan struggles of nature. Where others saw nothing but barren moors full of heather and broom, the land in their eyes was covered as with a carpet softer and more variegated then the most precious loom of Turkey. Where others lost their temper at the gray cold fog, they marveled at the silver veil of the bride in the morning, and the gold illumination of the departing sun. Now every cockney can admire the smallest lake in Westmoreland or the barest moor in the Highlands. Why is this? Because few eyes are so dull that they cannot see what is beautiful after it has been pointed out to them, and when they know that they need not feel ashamed of admiring it. (Müller 1858, pp. 114–15)

With feelings like this, reinforced by his own father's significance, Müller places himself comfortably in the tradition of the German Romantics.

In large part, Müller's personal spiritual quest was also enriched and complicated at the same time by being bound up with an emergent search for a German national soul. But to reach this point, we will have to detour through India, much as the early German romantics themselves did. Although the sources of the romantic movement are in dispute, it seems clear that romanticism was in part a reaction against the coming urbanization and industrialization of Western societies, as well as the advance of strange and often frightening new forms of politics and government inspired by the French

Revolution and promoted beyond the borders of France by its militant herald, Napoleon Bonaparte. The romantic reactions to these two great historic trends – on the one hand, assertion of the value of the spirit and nature, and on the other, resistance to the universalizing tendencies of France in favor of a sense of rooted local German nationalism – produced a potent mix of cultural creativity. German romantic nationalists began to find a broad field of inspiration for their own struggles in the image of the classic India that started by the end of the eighteenth century gradually to become known in Europe. In the India that they fashioned for themselves, the German romantic nationalists first saw a model of a culture of spiritual profundity, sharply opposed to the reputation for rationalist, materialist superficiality of the French Enlightenment. They perceived likewise a religious tradition that seemed to them to celebrate the very natural world that they felt was being violated daily by the forces of secularism, urbanism, and industrialism, rooted as well in the Enlightenment. India virtually 'magnetized' the imagination of German romantic nationalists in much the same way that they had also been fascinated by the image of the glories of ancient Greece.

The European Discovery and Invention of India

Given the broad popularity of the religions of India today in the West, it is hard for us to imagine just how dramatic the discovery of the literatures of ancient India in the late eighteenth and early nineteenth centuries was for thoughtful Europeans, and especially for an emergent sense of German national identity. India was taken to heart by German Romantics and nationalists like Müller in an imaginative way. An entirely new and heretofore unknown ancient civilization, rivaling in sophistication those of ancient Rome, Israel, Greece, or Egypt, suddenly thrust itself into the consciousness of Europe. The discovery of this ancient India, apparently so profoundly spiritual and full of mystery, whet the curiosity of some of the most imaginative and adventurous thinkers of the early nineteenth century. It spurred them on to creative efforts of cross-cultural comparison and borrowing – one of which was the comparative study of religion that Müller was to undertake throughout his long life.

Significantly, some of the most active thinkers exploiting this new knowledge of the literatures of India were the first romantics, particularly the Germans, such as the von Schlegel brothers, August Wilhelm (1767–1845) and Friedrich (1772–1829), and the philosopher Friedrich von Schelling (1775–1854). They were intrigued by the example of India – everything from its metaphysics of monistic absolutism to its extravagant mythology. These key figures came to the knowledge of Sanskrit in Paris from Alexander Hamilton, the first Sanskrit professor in England and an army officer retired from service in India. In the long run, however, thanks in no small part to romanticism and the German desire to root their new national identity in a noble ancient civilization, it was Germany that would become the home of European "Indomania." With figures such as the poet-philosophers the Schlegels and the philosopher Schelling as its chief proponents, German "Indomania" became a prominent cultural force from the early nineteenth century into the twentieth. Müller was part of this great cultural vogue, and one of its most productive agents in the world of the human sciences (Trautmann 1997, pp. 138–40).

Germany was not alone in its fascination with what it learned about India. In some sense this movement swept through Western Europe and North America. No less than the American poet-philosopher Ralph Waldo Emerson (1803–82) responded to the presumed monistic mysticism of the religion of ancient India in a manner instructive for what it tells us about early attempts to assimilate the culture of the subcontinent. It incidentally tells us a good deal about Müller, since Müller dedicated his *Lectures on the Science of Religion* to Emerson on the occasion of the American transcendentalist's visit with him in Oxford in 1873, and in celebration of what he termed the "constant refreshment of head and heart derived from his writings during the last twenty-five years." We ought not to forget that Emerson was also the author of at least two works that fit the general spirituality of the German romantic idealists. These are the lecture entitled "Natural Religion" (1869) and his famous "Divinity School Address" of 1838.

In his short lyric poem "Brahma," Emerson meditates, for instance, on the mystery of the Hindu absolute.

Brahma (1857)

If the red slayer think he slays,
Or if the slain think he is slain,
They know not well the subtle ways
I keep, and pass, and turn again.

Far or forgot to me is near,
Shadow and sunlight are the same,
The vanished gods to me appear,
And one to me are shame and fame.
They reckon ill who leave me out;
When me they fly, I am the wings;
I am the doubter and the doubt,
And I the hymn the Brahmin sings.

The strong gods pine for my abode,
And pine in vain the sacred Seven;
But thou, meek lover of the good!
Find me, and turn thy back on heaven.

The poet is moved by the ability of this Brahma to transcend time and space, to overcome death, to show that what appears to be different is not really different – mainly all those mysterious beliefs characteristic of Indian religious beliefs in nonduality, in the oneness of all things so much at odds with both the materialism and even individualist spirituality of the West. Thus the poet shows us how the individual is stymied by a series of apparent contradictions typical of Western thought. Although they make no rational sense for Western materialists, they are the essence of the higher spiritual truths imputed to Indian religion by the Romantics. For instance, the line, "I am the doubter" is followed by one in which the same speaker/doubter is identified with the object of doubt itself – "the doubt." Duality, so essential in the materialist worldview, is simply cast aside. Even those who would flee Brahma, as in the line "when me they fly," actually flee Brahma by the power of Brahma itself, since Brahma is the essence of us all. Western self-sufficiency is also then dealt a fatal blow, as the Romantics saw it. All the materialism and hard-nosed empiricism of a Hume, Locke, or Bacon was seen, then, as a shallow and simplistic approach to a magical world that far exceeded their puny attempts to grasp it. "They know not well" and "They reckon ill" are phrases that tell us how disdainfully Emerson and Romantics like him regard the world of everyday knowing.

Müller's Discovery of India in Language

The growing European consciousness about ancient India was part of an overall European effort to learn about the civilizations of the ancient world by recovering and translating their ancient scriptures and uncovering their often long-forgotten historical sites. The new knowledge of India came at first primarily through the recovery of ancient manuscripts collected by Sir William Jones, a British jurist posted in India in the late eighteenth century. Jones was also the first person to argue systematically that the ancient sacred language of India, Sanskrit, was a close relative to Latin, Greek, and even English. Sanskrit words such as *pitar, matar*, and *bhartr* were simply too close to their Latin counterparts, *pater, mater*, and *frater*, and to the English *father, mother, brother*, Jones argued, to be mere accidents. There had to be some kind of – as yet unknown – historical links between 'East' and 'West.'

The texts collected by Jones were soon made available to scholars in France and Germany, where they also spawned great enterprises of textual study and scholarly research of all kinds. The spread of Sanskrit studies in Germany was especially great since the country was divided into a large number of small states, each with its own university, and each therefore requiring its own chair of Sanskrit. Nevertheless, because of Napoleon's sponsorship of oriental studies, apart from London, Paris was the reigning center of Sanskrit studies in the first half of the nineteenth century. It was there that the leading German Sanskrit scholars of the future did their original training, and from there that they carried their expertise back to their many provincial home universities.

Picking up the thread laid down by Jones and sustained by Alexander Hamilton's teaching and scholarship in Paris, was the German scholar Franz Bopp. In 1816 he published the first systematic comparative grammar of Indo-European languages, linking Sanskrit, Greek, Latin, Persian, and the Germanic languages (Sharpe 1986, p. 22). It was thus not just the British who made original discoveries such as Jones's. French and German scholars were also active in the translation and acquisition of ancient manuscripts from India and elsewhere in the ancient world. A Latin translation of the Hindu scriptures, the Upanishads, was completed in 1802 by the freelance scholar Anquetil du Perron. The hieroglyphics of ancient Egypt were first deciphered by the French in the early nineteenth century, thanks to Napoleon's invasion and his sponsorship of Egyptological research. Cuneiform script from ancient Babylon also finally yielded to painstaking deciphering efforts at about the same time. Müller was an eager and industrious heir to this remarkable period of intellectual initiatives and the successive rounds of scientific successes they produced.

By 1841, the University of Leipzig had established a chair in Sanskrit, first occupied by Hermann Brockhaus. There under Brockhaus, Müller first came to study that ancient tongue but, true to his broad and catholic intellectual appetites, he wrote his doctoral thesis instead on an aspect of the philosophy of Spinoza (Stone 2002, p. 10). This pursuit of philological and philosophical interests at the same time seems in a way to typify the way Müller's mind worked. Although Müller wrote his thesis on part of Spinoza's *Ethics*, he also continued to work on Sanskrit. Likewise, Müller never stopped delving into the implications of the works of the great masters of German philosophy, such as Kant, Hegel, and, most importantly, Schelling. While Kant and Hegel were known to Müller only through their books, Müller attended the lectures of Schelling in Berlin. As an admirer of Friedrich von Schlegel, for instance, he came under the influence of such pieces of early theoretical glorification of India as *Über die Sprache und Weisheit der Indier* (On the Language and Wisdom of India, 1808) – the first work persuasively to argue for substantial "intellectual" links between Europe and India (Sharpe 1986, p. 22). In fact, one can say that Müller's philosophical pursuits did not deter him from concentrating increasingly on his Sanskrit studies. Like some of his masters in the German philosophical world, such as Schlegel, the two interests reinforced one another. Thus, while to some commentators this span of interests may mark Müller as an 'eclectic,' it may easily be a measure of his voracious intellect. Besides that, Müller believed that moving on these two tracks was necessary since the deep general philosophical and religious questions that intrigued him could only be finally resolved by pursuing philological studies. He, like just as many other Romantics, believed that the answers to his philosophical and spiritual questions lay in India, and India could not be understood apart from understanding its ancient tongues.

To open a brief parenthesis here, we might take the opportunity to observe that since Müller was working in both philosophy and in the study of ancient religious literatures, he could hardly have overlooked Spinoza's 1670 *A Theologico-Political Treatise*. Yet overlook it he apparently did. Spinoza's work, as we noted in the previous chapter, first articulated a critical philological approach to the Bible, even while he was considering Schelling's newly conceived philosophy of mythology. We know that Müller was aware of the great cultural trends in modern scholarship, such as the critical study of the Bible pioneered by D. F. Strauss as well as others working in the same area, such as the Semiticist and author of a highly popular critical life of Jesus, Ernest Renan in France (Stone 2002, pp. 167–8, 25–9). Yet Müller is silent about the Higher Critics of the Bible, and published nothing at all on them or their approach to sacred texts, so close in so many ways to his own historical and philological studies of the ancient Indian scriptures. We will return to this point indirectly in a while, because it bears on Müller's general attitude toward religion and the application of critical reason to it.

To return to Müller's progress toward a career in Indic studies, then, we find in him yet another example of a young German migrating to Paris for the higher studies that would fuel his "Indomania." After his studies with Brockhaus, Müller perfected his Sanskrit scholarship in Paris under Eugène Burnouf in 1845–6. There, Müller began the major intellectual project of his life – the critical edition and translation of the *Rig Veda* – the single most important scriptural text of the earliest level of the religions of India. A monumental effort, the task required not only over 20 years of Müller's life, but also a total reorientation of his living conditions as well. Unable to complete this work in the French capital because the British kept the only complete set of Sanskrit manuscripts of the *Rig Veda* in Oxford, Müller abandoned the Continent for England, where he would live the rest of his life.

Müller therefore departed the Continent for an entirely new life in Oxford. Along the way, he needed to master not only a new language, along with the manners and customs of an England far more insular in all respects than can be imagined today, but also finally to win himself a sinecure in the university. Müller succeeded famously in making a new life for himself, largely through his own courage and effort, but also though the timely aid and assistance of the sponsorship of his extraordinary patron, the Prussian emissary to the

Court of St. James, Baron Christian von Bunsen. It was the Prussian official who agreed to sponsor the publication of Müller's edition of the *Rig Veda*, and thus to secure Müller's career.

The Discovery of Indo-European Languages

Among the stunning facts thrown up by the Vedic texts was the fact that the language in which they were written – an early form of Sanskrit – was soon recognized as remarkably similar to the ancient tongues of Rome and Greece, not to mention the modern languages of western Europe. So remarkable and unprecedented was this that it set scholars on a series of speculative ventures that fed the curiosity of some of the best minds of the West. What could such affinities mean? Could this mean that the civilization of ancient India, although a vast distance from Europe, conceivably shared in some substantial fashion aspects of the ancient civilizations at the basis of modern Europe? Was this some sort of 'forgotten ancestor' of Western civilization, some sort of 'lost kin'? How is this similarity, made all the more puzzling by European ignorance of ancient Indian civilization all these years, and made altogether implausible by the vast distances between India and Europe, to be explained? Let me reconstruct, very briefly and rather liberally, how the facts of similarity of language were welded into a major scholarly discipline – Indo-European studies – and how this new science of the Indo-European languages formed the basis of the comparative study of religion that Müller pioneered.

It is, of course, commonplace to recognize family resemblances among the languages of peoples living close to one another and sharing a common history. The Romance languages of French, Portuguese, Spanish, Italian, Catalan, and Provençal have all been recognized as descendants of Latin for some time. But it is less well-known that at least one language of a nation separated geographically from the Mediterranean home of the Romance languages is also derived from Latin – namely Romanian, for instance. Similarly, although many languages of the Indian subcontinent are all derived in part from Sanskrit – languages such as Hindi, Urdu, Bengali, Marathi, and so forth, it is rather surprising that the far-flung language of the Gypsies – Romany – is itself a sister language of those modern Indic languages derived from Sanskrit. How much more implausible, and thus upsetting, when philologists of the nineteenth century, beginning of course informally with Sir William Jones in 1796, argued that the main languages of Europe and India were part of the same language family!

A small demonstration of related words between branches as widespread as English and Sanskrit would be examples such as the English word "yoke" and "yoga " in Sanskrit. The link in meaning between these two very different words is that in the Sanskrit "yogi" is one literally who "yokes" themselves to a discipline of physical practice. Or, our English word "suture" reflects a Sanskrit word "sutra" in that a "sutra" is literally a series of strands of text or argument woven together into a single discourse, much as a suture is sewn together with thread. Consider also our words having to do with fire – ignition, ignite, igneous, and so on. Is it surprising, given the links we have already seen, that the Hindu god of fire should be named Agni? Upon the first discovery of Sanskrit, it was thought to be the mother tongue of all Indic and European languages. Some scholars even argued that all the major languages of Europe were derived from a mother tongue native to India. Thus Latin and Greek, for instance, ancient as they were, were thought to be daughter languages of Sanskrit, even though they are actually approximate contemporaries of Sanskrit. This later was proven to be false, since the oldest levels of both European and Indian languages derive as equals from a third source, common to both branches of a language family. Some of the more nationalist German linguists argued accordingly that German language and culture were privileged to be directly rooted in the noble language and culture of ancient India. And since the ancient Indians identified themselves as 'Aryans,' the German nationalist linguists adopted the same name for their root identity. For these Aryan nationalists, Indo-Aryan Sanskrit stood alongside Latin, Greek, or Hebrew as an ancient tongue with a vast literature rich in spiritual significance. Ancient Indian civilization thus filled the role for the German Aryanists that the civilizations of ancient Rome, Greece, or Israel played for nineteenth-century Italians, Greeks, and Jews, respectively. Having outlined the discoveries being made in Indo-European comparative linguistics, we need to consider the larger political and cultural developments in Germany that would then merge with what was coming to be known about the Indo-European origins of the German – indeed all European – languages.

The Search for Germany's National Soul in India . . . of All Places

Max Müller's scholarly activity cannot be well understood apart from the motivations given it by the particular social and political conditions of his native Germany in the early to mid nineteenth century. Müller's scholarly activity, like that of all the German romantics, was directly or indirectly bound up with the quest for German national identity. Despite what one may think, Germany is actually a relatively young nation, officially not coming into existence until 1871. England, France, Spain, Poland, and even much smaller Portugal or the Netherlands all could claim centuries of national unity of one degree or another. Even in comparison with the newer nations of the world, such as the United States, Germany only became a nation-state in 1871, during the youth of Max Müller, while the United States, of course, dates from the late eighteenth century. Before the late nineteenth century, what we today understand as 'Germany' was no single nation at all, but rather a loose array of scores of independent city states, duchies principalities and kingdoms of various sizes, sometimes bound together in confederation, but at other times not. Müller, in fact, lived and grew up in one of these small, independent German regions, in the town of Dessau, the capital of a minor state called Anhalt-Dessau in eastern Germany, near Weimar. As a result of a political atomization of the country, German political identities were both numerous and localized. Therefore, although it was possible for a "German" to identify themselves as a Rhinelander, Prussian, Bavarian, Berliner, or Hessian, this name meant nothing in terms of reference to a nation-state. There was no such political reality as Germany, and therefore no "Germans" in the political sense of the term. In the same way, it would have meant relatively little had the various colonies making up British North America never unified into the "United States of America," but had remained autonomous 'states' located as they were in English-speaking North America. Even after official constitutional unification, the new Germany had much to do in order to realize its unity.

People like Müller were among those who took this task to heart. To them, what Germans needed was a noble national story or 'myth' – something to make them less proud of who they 'were' than proud of what they had become in 1871. But what has this quest for German national identity to do with India? In the process of nation-building in Europe, even into the late nineteenth century, a national myth was thought to be an important part of the construction of a national identity. Tiny a land as she was, the Netherlands could point proudly to there being a nation created from the North Sea by the ingenuity of its native inhabitants and their system of dikes. 'Fortress England' stood in magnificent insularity, free from menacing continental Catholic powers such as Spain, whose mighty Armada miraculously fell victim to the vicissitudes of English weather. Poland could point to a thousand-year history of Christian nationhood and militant defense of Christendom at the borders of Western civilization against Muslim invaders from the East. While a region of "Germany" such as Prussia could call upon its mythic origins in the exploits of the Teutonic knights, as a whole, modern Germans lacked such rich mythological accounts of themselves as a people. They had no national 'story' or myth to tell, no way to give an account of themselves to rival what several other European nation-states could offer.

German nationalists like Müller sought precisely the elements of such a national myth to provide the basis of an ideology that would unify the distinct constituents of this new nation-state. In Europe, this not only meant tracing a nation-state's linguistic and cultural roots to various historical predecessors, such as to the motley assortment of ancient 'Germanic' tribes that had invaded the Roman Empire from before the beginnings of the first millennium; it also required that national identity be rooted in a story of noble origins – typically in the form of a link to an ancient high civilization, often articulated in terms of a myth. Even though the Italians, Spanish, and French were as much descended from barbarian invaders as the Germans, they could also trace their historical origins to the glories of ancient Rome – although the Italians came late to nationhood like the Germans. This gave those countries sufficient warrant to identify themselves as the natural heirs of the Roman Empire. After all, they also spoke Romance languages derived from Latin, and had been part of the Roman empire for many centuries. Not so the peoples north of the Rhine, Rome's natural northern border for many years. Even the modern Greeks, compromised as they were by centuries of Turkish occupation, could trace their identity to the noble ancient civilizations of Athens, Sparta, or Macedonia, conveniently leaving aside their cultural debts to the Turks. Even the Jews, scattered as they were across all of Europe and the Middle East in the diaspora since 70 CE, could at least refer to their origins in ancient Israel and therefore could place themselves at the foundations of the religious traditions of the West.

But the Germans lacked an equivalent classical high-cultural ancestor – at least in the ancient Mediterranean world. Were they then only the descendants of barbarians who sacked Rome and pillaged much of civilized Europe? Germany traced its origins to the barbarian tribes that conquered much of the Roman empire, and this conferred a certain vigor upon the Germans. But even Europe's Jews, stateless as they were, could claim the noble heritage of ancient Israel extending into history many thousands of years. The nineteenth-century German nationalists wished to remedy this shortcoming in the make-up of their national identity, and thus sought to establish a noble past uniquely their own. This is where ancient Indian civilization became useful to the German romantic nationalists as a mythical basis for German national identity. For them, the link would be direct. By leap-frogging both the Greco-Roman and Jewish sources of Western cultural identity, the German Aryanists hoped to find in ancient India and its Aryan past the primal soul of their own nation. For this effort, the linguistic scholarship of the Indo-Europeanists provided a scientific basis for the much sought-after connection of German speakers to

Aryan India. It was only left to someone like Müller to forge these links in terms of cultural – in particular, religious – relationships between his own past in a small town like Dessau, and the Indo-European cultural past that was there to see in the newly available documents that he was busy editing and translating, the *Rig Veda*.

The Vedas, the Aryan Bible

I trust that this quick tour through the political and cultural thought-world of Müller's formative years will give readers some idea of how significant the study of the Vedas were for him. We know Müller was prepared to see many things in the Vedas that his location at the heart of the German romantic and nationalist movements favored – love of nature and the native land, the prestige of mystical religion and spirituality, and so on. What must have startled and pleased Müller, however, is how well the Vedas spoke in their own words to the depths of his own heart. The Vedas, for example, lend themselves to being read as exemplifying a religion of nature that we saw suggested in Müller's remarks on the English Lake District. In *Rig Veda* I:113, the Vedic goddess, Ushas (Dawn) is celebrated in rich metaphors worthy of Müller's romantic contemporaries:

> This light has come, of all the lights the fairest:
> The brilliant brightness has been born effulgent.
> [...]
>
> Night now has yielded up her place to morning.
> [...]
> Morning and Night clash not, nor do they tarry.
> [...]
>
> Dawn has awakened every living creature.
> Men lying on the ground she wakes to action,
> Another is aroused for winning greatness;
> Another seeks the goal of varied nurture:
> Dawn has awakened every living creature.
>
> Daughter of Heaven, she has appeared before us,
> A maiden shining in resplendent raiment.
> Thou sovereign lady of all earthly treasure,
> Auspicious Dawn, shine here to-day upon us.

Beyond their being readily open to a naturist reading, so dear to the hearts of German romantics like Müller, aspects of the Vedas lent themselves to what one might call 'deeper' expressions of the religious spirit. Of Ushas and her myths, Müller says

> Ushas the bright now becomes Ushas, the immortal, and after that step has been taken, what is more natural than that she should become an attractive centre for other religious sentiments and thoughts? Even with us a bright morning raises our spirits, and rouses a sense of happiness and gratitude in our heart, though the object of our gratitude may remain nameless. Think what it must have been in early times, when life

and everything was felt to depend on the kindly light of the morning! A bright sunrise was a new life, a sunless, cold, stormy morning meant suffering, often starvation or even death. Need we wonder then that some words should have been stammered forth at the rise of a bright day, words of joy and gratitude, addressed not to a nameless being, but to the kind and brilliant Ushas. (Müller 1892, p. 433)

For Müller, therefore the love of nature and our dependence upon it made eminent sense of the desire to worship it. But there is more. At least some of the natural world so transcends human abilities to encompass it, that it generated in early people the very idea of a realm radically beyond our own, where the gods dwelt. For instance, Müller suggests how early ideas of the transcendent arose in the contemplation of objects like the sun, ocean, great mountains, and the like.

However strange it may seem to us, if we simply follow the evidence placed before us, there can be little doubt that the perception of the Unknown or the Infinite was with many races as ancient as the perception of the Known or the Finite, that the two were, in fact, inseparable. To men who lived on an island, the ocean was the Unknown, the Infinite, and became in the end their God. To men who lived in valleys, the rivers that fed them and whose sources were unapproachable, the mountains that protected them, and whose crests were inaccessible, the sky that overshadowed them, and whose power and beauty were incomprehensible, these were their unknown beings, their infinite beings, their bright and kind beings, what some of them called their *Devas*, the Bright, the same word which, after passing through many changes, still breathes in our own word, *Divinity*. (Müller 1892, p. 218)

In the end, more and more of Müller's mystical and monistic religious ground, so much a part of his German idealist philosophical nurture, came to light. Besides monist idealist philosophers like Hegel, the Schlegel and Schelling known to Müller in his time and through his education, we should recall that Müller was well versed in the thought of Spinoza, also a proponent of a philosophy arguing for the oneness of all things in God. These ideas of cosmic oneness seemed to gain support from the Vedas as much as did the more straightforward naturism that they seemed to confirm. Thus, in *Rig Veda* I:1, a hymn to the Vedic god of fire, Agni, the sacrificial fire, may seem like just another example of nature worship – of fire, in this case. But it is more, and thinkers like Müller recognized this. The fire here is addressed first of all as a person, then addressed directly *as* the person of the god Agni himself, along with the priest offering the sacrifice too.

May that Agni, who is to be extolled by ancient and modern seers, conduct
the gods here.
Through Agni may one gain day by day wealth and welfare which is glorious
and replete with heroic sons.

Readers should note that in the original Indic script in which the hymn is written, there is no capitalization of "agni," such as the English translation above offers. This divinizing capitalization no doubt reflects the theologically loaded conventions prevalent in the West, practices that tend to distort the unifying tendency that the Vedic religious mind seems to intend here. This is to say that, from what we can gather, the Vedas make no distinction between fire and a god of fire. An ordinary fire represents the actualization in our world – the presence, so to speak, of the god of fire *as* fire. Indeed, for the Vedas, any example of warmth or heat, wherever located, is an instance of the presence of the god of fire – Agni. Thus, the sun is Agni in the sky; the family hearth or sacrificial flame is Agni in ritual or everyday cooking fire; body heat is Agni in an animal body – all are real presences of the 'god' of fire, who in some way is not limited by his manifestations, but made real and present in them. Note how the following lines identify fire with the priest who manipulates fire in a ritual, and also see Agni as a priest offering sacrifice – because the fiery consumption of the sacrificial victim is indeed what a sacrifice effects.

> I extol Agni, the household priest, the divine minister of sacrifice, the
>   chief priest, the bestower of blessings....
> O Agni, the sacrifice and ritual which you encompass on every side, that indeed
>   goes to the gods.
> May Agni, the chief priest, who possesses the insight of a sage, who is truthful,
>   widely renowned, and divine, come here with the gods.

Typical of the idealism and romanticism of his generation of young German intellectuals, Müller's own religion tended toward pantheism. He, like others of his class, much admired the later Vedanta philosophy of India, where the unity of all things was not merely suggested in poetic metaphor, as in the Vedas, but asserted outright. Müller's religious sensibilities were accordingly cast in terms of a romantic nature mysticism to which the Vedas might be said to point, married all the while to the constant philosophical bent of his mind. In one of his last essays, he rejects with vigor the notion that he is an 'agnostic' in the vulgar sense of the term. Müller feels he knows, indeed feels, too much of what the truth of things may be ever to accept that epithet:

> If Agnosticism excludes a recognition of an eternal reason pervading the natural and
> the moral world, if to postulate a rational cause for a rational universe is called
> Gnosticism, then I am a Gnostic, and a humble follower of the greatest thinkers of
> our race, from Plato and the author of the Fourth Gospel to Kant and Hegel. (Müller
> 1901, p. 356)

Now when these interpretations of the religious sensibility of the Vedas were linked with the results of comparative Indo-European linguistics, certain German nationalist thinkers, like Müller, felt that Germans had finally found for themselves the ancient forebears they sought. For not only was German language derived from original Indo-European root stock, where Sanskrit occupied a privileged position, but the very spirituality of the earliest strata of Sanskrit religion and literature – the Vedas – conformed with the romantic, monistic sensibility of advanced German thought! For this reason, Müller could declare the Vedas the equivalent of the (Hebrew) Bible. Indeed, Müller called it the "Aryan Bible." Müller was the person who applied the term "Aryan" to designate that group of peoples who spoke original Indo-European, feeling it was more appropriate than the cumbersome, then-current, alternative, Indo-Germanic. In Müller's view, ancient Aryan myths such as the Vedas were a repository of the ancient wisdom of the Aryans. In some real sense, then, the deepest content of the Vedas lay at the root of Western culture, and thus German national identity. "We are by nature Aryan, not Semitic," Müller said in 1865.

Because they seemed to be truly archaic, and thus closer to the natural religion of the dawn of humanity, the Vedas held pride of place for Müller. As such, he believed that they should be recognized as co-equal in cultural stature with the biblical traditions and literature of the ancient Hebrews – but now, most importantly, as the source of properly European (read "Aryan") cultural heritage. In the Vedas, Müller saw a record of the religion of a pre-European golden age. They provided a direct route into a profound philosophy, the primordial wisdom of the human race, and in particular into what he believed to be the mother race of the West – the Aryans.

While all this remains true of Müller's own spirituality, this affection for the ideals of the Aryans as revealed in the Vedas never pushed Müller over into an embrace with the radicalism of some German philosophers. They wished either to jettison Christianity in favor of Indian religion, or to reform Christianity by replacing the Old (Hebrew) Testament with the Vedas, therefore dispensing entirely with Christianity's Semitic heritage. This is not to say that Müller was not tempted by such a radical program, and even by a certain level of anti-Semitism (Strenski 1996, pp. 62–9). Citing the philosopher Friedrich Schopenhauer with apparent approval, Müller records the philosopher's delight in reading the Upanishads: "oh how thoroughly is the mind washed clean of all early engrafted Jewish superstitions, and of all philosophy that cringes before those superstitions!" (Müller 1891, p. 6). Instead of the purging of Semitic elements from Christianity, Müller denied any religion a privileged place before the truth: "we share in the same truth, and we are exposed to the same errors, whether we are Aryan or Semitic or Egyptian in language and thought" (Müller 1891, p. 274). This meant then that Müller relativized all scriptures to one another. As "revelations," the Bible stood alongside the Vedas, not beneath it. Further distancing himself from racist interpretations of Aryanist discourse, Müller argued against German nationalist Aryanists that Indo-European philology had anything to do with biology or race. There are, for instance, no Aryan skulls! But with the genie out of the bottle, not even Müller could control "MaxMüllerism," which took on a life of its own. Those earlier Aryanist ideas influenced the racism of such disciples of Müller's as the American, John Fiske (Poliakov 1974, p. 214).

Comparative Mythology and the Aryan Soul

Alongside the cultural strategies involved in Müller's attraction to the Vedas, he taught us some very practical lessons in how to study myths and religion. Indeed, we need not accept any of Müller's Aryanist or German nationalist ideological baggage at all to learn the lessons his work has to teach the study of religion. The good news, therefore, is that the methods Müller applied to the study of myth and religion have outlived his political and cultural schemes, and can readily be detached from them. I would list the number of these methodological achievements as three.

First, one way that religions can be studied is by tracing their diffusion and distribution across the globe. In the twentieth century, Georges Dumézil, the great French Indo-Europeanist, established an illustrious scholarly reputation on the basis of his arguments that there was an original Indo-European ideology, and that it entailed a tripartite organization of society – the king, the warrior, and the priest. Wherever the Indo-Europeans settled, they left behind this particular tripartite organization of social order that can be detected with the proper kind of historical and philological research (Littleton 1982).

Second, we owe to Müller the development of the notion that there are *families*, *types*, or *styles of religions* – for example, Abrahamic, Indic, Semitic, Greco-Roman, Sino-tibetan, and such – just as there are *families* of languages – Indo-European, Altaic, Semitic, and such. This makes Müller something of a proto-phenomenologist of religion. Significantly, the scholar that we can call the first phenomenologist of religion, the Dutchman Cornelis P. Tiele, makes clear that he owes his impetus in this area to Müller. Indeed, Müller's daughter was the translator of Tiele's manual of religious phenomenology. In our day, Ninian Smart, for one, has used this sort of scheme to bring out comparisons and contrasts between Christianity and Buddhism with great skill. We will see more of the way Smart employs this principle in his modern phenomenological studies of religion. Müller, rather simplistically, thought there were basically three such families of languages – Indo-European, Semitic, and 'Turanian' – and that the major families of religions corresponded, on the whole, one-for-one. We know today that language families are far more complex and numerous. But, Müller gave the effort to classify languages – and religions – a start, and for that he should be credited. As we will see, his engagement in the study of language and religion was also freighted with unsavory ideological projects. These too can be jettisoned without loss to the methodological points he first made about the simple classification of religions. The ideological project to which I refer engaged him and German nationalist thinkers of the nineteenth century in what was for them the distressing fact that European Christianity crossed family lines and incorporated Semitic – Jewish – qualities. Part of Müller's attraction to the Vedas was the possibility of replacing the Semitic elements of European Christianity with the Indo-European Vedas.

Third, we owe Müller a great debt for his practice and promotion of *comparative studies of religion*. Based again on his experience of the comparative study of languages, Müller was the first scholar prominently to show how useful it would be to study religions in relation to one another. He argued that one cannot know one religion unless one knows several, because being acquainted with religions in general would help us understand the particulars of given case. By analogy, would not one trust an automobile mechanic with a new sort of car more, if that mechanic had had previous experience of many sorts of cars? Müller was fond of putting the matter paradoxically by stating that a person who knows only one religion, knows none (Müller 2002b, p. 113). That is to say, that a person who knows only about one religion can never be sure that they know more than just what may be peculiar to that particular religion, rather than something fundamental about religions. By analogy, this would be like a physician who specialized only in diseases of the liver being unable to counsel patients on their general health. If the goal of treatment is general health, the liver specialist would have little to say if they had never strayed beyond their specialty. They could not comprehend the general system of the human body, and thus can say 'nothing' about how the other organs interact – even to influence the workings of the liver!

Ever the scientist and, as it turns out, a respectably modern philosopher of science, Müller insisted that comparison was absolutely necessary if the study of religion was to be scientific. "There is no science of single things, and all progress in human knowledge is achieved through comparison, leading on to the discovery of what different objects share in common, till we reach the widest generalisations and the highest ideas that are within the ken of human knowledge" (Müller 1892, pp. 417–18). In part, Müller was urging the use of comparison because it served the quintessentially scientific activity of generating curiosity. Whatever else a science of religion is or should be, it should be a context in which questions are raised, problems are put, in short, in which the human faculty of curiosity is given full and unbridled expression, and where our work is always subject to revision and improvement. Thus, at the end of his last series of the famous Gifford Lectures in 1892, Müller delivers a view of science worthy of the twentieth-century philosopher of science Karl Popper.

> I do not believe in human infallibility, least of all in Papal infallibility. I do not believe in professorial infallibility, least of all in that of your Gifford lecturer; We are all fallible, and we are fallible either in our facts, or in the deductions which we draw from them. If therefore any of my learned critics will tell me which of my facts are wrong, or which of my conclusions faulty, let me assure them, that though I am a very old Professor, I shall always count those among my best friends . . . those who will correct any arguments that may seem to them to offend against the sacred laws of logic. (Müller 1986b, p. 543)

Here again Müller's experience in comparative historical phonology of the Indo-European languages served him well, since such studies were well practiced in comparison. The following examples should give some sense as to why Müller's approach was so powerful – and in a sense remains so still. Comparison makes us *think*, by suggesting analogies, similarities, and differences we might not have entertained before that.

Comparison occurs at least in two dimensions that can work with great effect together – the historical and the synchronic. Let us look at the synchronic first – the kind of comparison that holds time constant and looks across a field of possibilities, such as the forms of words in present-day English and German. We will see shortly how comparison occurs along the historical axis, as between (say) words in present-day English and their historic Latin roots. One trivial example of such a fruitful use of comparison would be that concerning an explanation of some words in English ending in the silent or soft "-gh" or "-ght" – thus, enough, rough, tough, through, though, although; and right, might, fight, height, night, weight, and so on, respectively. Two questions immediately occur. First, why do we have these endings at all, when they are not sounded, or at least not sounded as they are written? Second, although we speakers of modern English do not sound these endings as they are written, do we have any warrant for believing that any of our linguistic forebears did? And, short of audio recordings, how can we tell how these words may have been pronounced in ages past?

Part of the solution to these puzzles is supplied by *historical* information. To wit, we know from the history of the English-speaking world that English was in part derived from peoples who spoke what today are the modern Germanic tongues – German, Dutch, and the Scandinavian languages. Thus, *synchronic* comparison should tell us that we would find parallel words with the same or similar meanings that look at least a bit in those languages like the soft "-gh" and "-ght" suffixed English words above. And, upon examination, indeed we do. Corresponding to "enough" and "through," the German "genug" and "durch"; the English "right" and "might" likewise find their mates in the German "Recht" and "Macht."

To answer the questions surrounding those oddly spelled English words, we can appeal to comparative data. Thus, to begin, the reason these words are so oddly spelt is that they are rooted in Germanic sources. They are, as it were, old Germanic words left over in English. And thus, the reason they are spelled as they are, with their unsounded "-gh" or soft "-ght" endings, is that at one time they were pronounced to sound those endings much as their German comparisons do today. This can, of course, be checked by attending to poetry of known dates of composition or transcription where words are set to rhyme with the "-gh" and "-ght" suffixed words. If the rhymes are to be made with hard "cht" sounds, then the comparisons will have been borne out.

More impressive still, once we have established these historical connections and parallels, we can make better sense of aspects of language that might have remained closed to us. Comparison might help us understand the meanings of words that have dropped out of modern English, but which still might remain in a parallel or 'sister' language like German, for example. In Shakespeare's England, for instance, one spoke of "barm" as in "make the drink bear no *barm* . . ." (*Midsummer Night's Dream* II.i) – a word form the meaning of which has vanished from modern English. Müller's comparative techniques suggested that we can fill in this empty space left in modern English by resorting to the sister language of modern German. In this case, we can construct the meaning of "barm" by resorting to the modern German word for "yeast" – "Bärm." It takes little imagination to conclude that in "barm" Shakespeare was referring to the foam that beer yeast typically produces. So, synchronic comparison lets us fill in gaps by moving from the known to the unknown.

The First Serious Effort in the Comparative Study of Religions

In terms of religion, say in religious mythology, the same comparative techniques are employed by Müller as he used in comparative historical philology. Indeed, both the comparative study of religion and myth built upon information and analyses derived from the comparative study of language. Thus, consider how Müller *as philologist* did comparison in the historical dimension of language, using the example of the English noun 'divinity' and its verbal relative, 'to divine.' We all know what divinity means in common parlance; a general designation such as one from a dictionary states: "the state or quality of being divine; especially, the state of being a deity." When we begin with a simple *comparison* with a sister language such as French, a near perfect cognate occurs – 'divinité' – meaning deity or god. Likewise, Spanish yields the abstract noun 'divinidad,' with the same meaning as English or Spanish. How do we account for these similarities, at least from the point of view of English? Either 'divinity' originated in one of these tongues, and then passed to the others, or they are all derived as equals from a third source. The kind of historical linguistics that Müller practiced answers this question.

In terms of historical debts owed to our cultural ancestors, what further do these relationships suggest about our own ideas of God, the divine, and such – even apart from biblical or other scriptural sources? Added to that is the fact that even sources of ideas about God deemed to come from 'revelation' would still need to be sifted through the language of the hearer, still need to be translated into a local vernacular. If one of our words for God is derived from the Latin, is it not possible that our conception of God, our fundamental assumptions about the nature of God, are likewise derived to some degree from Roman culture? When we *compare* 'divinity' to the verb 'to divine,' some intriguing possibilities are raised.

The kind of comparative linguistics that Müller practiced answers first with a complex analysis based upon the fact that the nominal form 'divinity' appears to have come along with the verbal form 'to divine.' There we find that before modern English the word occurs in an earlier form of our language, Middle English 'divinen.' This, in turn, can be traced to Old French 'deviner,' which in turn comes from Latin 'divinare.' More interestingly, however, when we trace these to their Latin origins, we find that the noun 'divinity' derives from 'divinus,' a soothsayer, and 'divus,' a god! At least one question Müller's style of linguistic comparison suggests is whether and to what extent our ideas of religious ideas – ideas of divinity – carry some of this original Latin meaning having to do with foretelling the future, such as that retained in our word 'diviner.' Or, how much of the original Latin meaning of the idea of a soothsayer as someone being inspired by a god (divus) carries over into our conceptions of the workings, say, of a 'divining rod' and the 'diviners' who manipulate them?

But, as we know, Müller and his fellow Indo-Europeanists were not satisfied to compare Romance languages to one another, and with their Latin roots. They wanted to push back the origins of modern Indo-European languages to their ultimate roots in the language of the Indo-Europeans themselves, by way of Sanskrit, but even further back still. What are the root meanings of, say, 'divinity' and its semantic relatives, 'divine,' 'diviner,' and so on? Indo-Europeanists answered with a remarkable series of replies. For starters, the Sanskrit word for 'god' was 'deva'– virtually the same word for 'god' as the Latin 'divus.' At the very least, comparison implied that classic European and Indian language about deities may well be a *common* language, shared across the 6,000-mile distance and 5,000-year-long history of the Indo-European crescent, extending from Sri Lanka to Ireland, or even across the Americas to Australasia, if one likes. We are still digesting the implications of such facts today. Imagine how this 'shock of the old' might have struck the minds of provincial folk in a small, bucolic German town like Müller's Dessau, not to mention the salons of London or Paris!

Max Müller therefore cherished the radical belief that the lessons learned in seeking the Indo-European roots of our language could be applied to religions as well. Müller wanted to know how far back – even well beyond the boundaries of the Jewish heritage – we can trace the main religious ideas we take for granted in modern-day Christianity, for instance. While Müller honored the Bible and revelation, he believed, somewhat in the manner of Locke, that the human mind had to be prepared with a natural aptitude for religion in order to receive revelation at all. Müller believed in Natural Religion, and he exploited the comparative method then employed in the study of languages to discover what it was.

Thus, pressing his historical comparisons further, when Indo-Europeanists like Müller delved into the root meaning of words like 'divinity,' 'divus,' and 'deva,' they concluded that even before Latin and Sanskrit, another language, 'Indo-European,' must be designated the mother tongue of this great 'Aryan' language family. In Indo-Europeanist, these experts concluded, there was the root word 'div' from which 'divinity,' 'diva,' and such derived. Now, 'div' meant 'to shine,' and thus all these related cognates of 'divinity' had something to do with what 'shines' or is 'radiant,' and so on. In this heyday of the celebration of German folklore, language, and literature, myth was naturally enough a favored category of cultural expression. This was true for Friedrich Müller, even if myth, in turn, was for him both a derived feature of language ("only a dialect, an ancient form of language"), and moreover something which was symptomatic of a "linguistic breakdown" – his theory of myth, see as a "disease of language" (Müller 1881a, p. 451). Thus Müller says, mythology is inevitable, it is an inherent necessity of language, if we recognize in language the outward form and manifestation of thought; it is in fact the dark shadow which language throws on thought, and which can never disappear till language becomes altogether commensurate with thought, and which it never will. (Müller 1881b, p. 590)

The Myth–Religion Relation

Müller's belief in the importance of myth is thus dependent upon his even deeper conviction about the overriding importance of language in culture. If a people's language should change, said Müller, soon too would its social arrangements follow suit. For Müller, although they were not religion in the strictest sense themselves, myths were like "precious stones...hidden" in the "rubbish" of the highly mythological "physical religion." Thus when it came to the Greeks, Müller could say on the one hand that he did not believe that the *Iliad* was their "Bible." This, however, did not stop him from turning around and declaring in the same lecture that as "the religion of the ancient world," "although mythology was not religion in our sense of the word... yet I would not deny altogether that in a certain sense the mythology of the Greeks belonged to their religion" (Müller 1881b, p. 586). Going even further to assert the link between religion and myth, Müller said that in the case of ancient India, the "Veda... [is] the real theogony of the Aryan races" (Müller 1881a, p. 381). Further affirming the perennial religious value of that great trove of myth and the love of his scholarly life, the Vedas, Müller said that in the Vedas, "we get one step nearer to that distant source of religious thought and language which has fed the different national streams of Persia, Greece, Rome and Germany, and we begin to see clearly that there is no religion without God, or as St. Augustine expressed it, that 'there is no false religion which does not contain some elements of truth' " (Müller 1882, p. 135).

Müller's belief in the priority of myth in Vedic religion was thus in effect part of a deeper theological and sociological idealism, linked with Aryanist cultural ideology. Thus when he encountered the Vedas, Müller felt as if he had fulfilled his own German romantic longings and the promise of his deistic liberal Protestant religious rearing at the same time. In the Vedic myths, he felt as if he had made contact with a pure, primordial, contemplative nature religion, which, as the "Bible of the Aryans," was at the same time the primordial religious lore of his beloved Germany. Mrs. Max Müller said of her husband that his "highest object was to discover reason in all the unreason of mythology, and thus to vindicate the character of our ancestors, however distant." Thus for Müller, despite the failings of myth in capturing the high-flown abstract truth of philosophical religion-as-such which he preferred, the many ancient religions were often constituted by myth, and that proper piety presupposed a special reverence for myth.

Where then does this take students of comparative religions? Does it suggest, for example, that because numerous myths of the Vedas are addressed to the sun, the original Indo-Europeans worshiped through a religion of the sun – that most radiant of all shining objects? Some scholars, like Müller, thought so. As it turns out, this example is well chosen, since worship of the sun is the highest form of the nature religionism that Müller believed characterized the older levels of human religion. Although there was more to Vedic religion than sun worship, Müller argued that a close reading of the Vedas showed that the preeminent *explicit* object of Vedic mythology was the sun, as even the hymns to Agni attest. After all, according to Vedic religious logic, the sun is both the fire (Agni) in the sky as well as a manifestation of the sun as fire on earth. As *Rig Veda* X:1 says:

> High has the Mighty risen before the dawning,
>   and come to us with light from out the darkness.

> Fair-shaped Agni with white-shining splendor
>   has filled at birth all human habitations.
> You, being born, art Child of Earth and Heaven,
>   parted among the plants in beauty, Agni!

> The glooms of night you, Brilliant Babe, subduest, and art come forth,
>   loud roaring, from your Mothers.

Müller much admired the Vedanta philosophy which became a rage among religious liberals as well as Aryanists of his time (Voigt 1967, p. 32). From his adolescence, Müller's religious sensibilities were accordingly cast in terms of a romantic natural mysticism linked with Aryanist cultural theories, where the sun was the leading emblem of an original transcendental, yet natural, unity of the Absolute (Mosse 1964, pp. 70–2, 89). Yet things do not stop there with a single object of nature worship in Müller's view.

As all romantics affirm, the pristine unity of beginnings, like the radiance of the solar Absolute, fade or become clouded, leaving us only to strain for return. After describing the nature worship of the Vedas, Müller rhetorically asks: "And are we so different from them?" In contemplating nature "do we not feel the overwhelming pressure of the Infinite . . . from which no one can escape who has eyes to see and ears to hear?" (Voigt 1967, p. 32). Does it also explain why we naturally think of the gods as heavenly – as resident high above the earth in a celestial realm, such as the sun? Our imaginations do, after all, presume as much. Does the rootedness of our modern languages explain then, in part, why we think so? Müller and those like him thought as much.

Beyond Vedic Mythology to Natural Religion

One reservation put a damper on Müller's unreserved enthusiasm for Vedic religion. Despite his respect and affection for mythology and naturism, and for the personifying of sacred powers these entailed, Müller thought that mythologically informed religions, such as that of the Vedas, could not be considered the epitome of religion. Something serious was lacking in them. Given that Müller assumed that religion must be 'spiritual,' he inevitably came to consider mythologically informed, and thus personified, religions rather base forms of religion. He called such religions, the original natural religions of the ancients, "Physical Religions." As such, in Müller's scheme of evaluating religions, they were lower than the lofty, abstract, and *impersonal* "Philosophical Religions" of his own day. Thus to Müller the Vedas displayed certain "childish" features, such as personified struggles and jealousies among the gods. At the same time, however, this immature form of religion could still represent an approximation of the *impersonal* absolute. The Vedas were natural "revelation" in their own way. Despite their "childish" sacrificial or ritual conceptions of being able to buy off the anger of personal gods, they did show progress on the way to an abstract monotheism or impersonal monism, since they at least admitted that the universal powers were governed by a kind of law.

The unification of divine powers achieved by being brought under law-like regulation, causing us to see the devas acting often in concert with one another, and taking turns in different contexts to represent for their devotees the high god, was not the irrational and unruly polytheism of Hume's view of the earliest level of religious life. Vedic polytheism was, rather, what has come to be called a "henotheism" – a system in which many gods congregate and cooperate under law-like principles, and most of all, an impersonal system in which each takes its turn at the head of the pantheon. The henotheism of the Veda was thus a way-station on the road to an abstract monotheism or impersonal monism, meaning that the "physical religion" of the Vedas exemplified a vital progressive stage in the history of religions.

For the ecumenical but pious Müller, this evidence of ancient wisdom reaffirmed his belief in a divine plan by which all human beings would be led to the truth, despite appearances to the contrary. Thus, the "real history of man is the history of religions: the wonderful ways by which the different families of the human race advanced toward a truer knowledge and a deeper love of God" (Müller 1882, p. 129). In a letter dated December 7, 1878, to A. P. Stanley, the Dean of Westminster, Müller expressed his understanding that a certain narrow orthodox element of the British public would object to his religious liberality:

> Of course I know that many people will be angry with my Lectures. If it were not so, I would not have written them. The more I see of the so-called heathen religions, the more I feel convinced that they contain germs of the highest truth. There is no distinction in kind between them and our own religion. The artificial distinction which we have made has not only degraded the old revelation, but has given to our own almost a spectral character. (Quoted in Chauduri 1974, p. 358)

For Müller, "religion" meant, as we have seen, both the many different historical religions studied by anthropologists, historians, philologists, and others, but also "religion" in a normative sense that can go by many descriptions – real religion, religion in its true essence, "religion-as such" – what we have called Natural Religion. This changeless, fundamental religion is for the many constantly changing historical religions their "deepest" constant essence and nature. It is what they really are at bottom (Müller 1892, p. 104). Thus he can say, for instance, that it is from eternal religion-as-such that the many and varied religions of the world arise, and this is why "religion" – religion as such – cannot be equated with myth. To explain this paradox, we need to see that for him the religions were mélanges of cult, myth, and practice; but religion-as-such was the perfectly spiritual and highly abstract activity of the "perception of the Infinite" (Müller 1891, pp. 294 ff.). This notion of religion-as-such refers to something which existed "before" sacrifice, ritual, and myth, and thus was something which could not be equated with myth. Behind the 'mythical' representations of the oldest religious texts, then, we find important traces of the 'pure' and universal abstractions of primal natural religion to which Müller's scholarship wished to lead his readers. "We also examined the different epithets that were assigned to the Devas," says Müller, then adding telling reference to the Christian God, "and to Him who was recognized in the end as above all Devas, and we found that they closely corresponded to the attributes of God in our own religion" (Müller 1891, p. 337).

References

Chauduri, N. 1974. *Scholar Extraordinary*. London: Chatto and Windus.

Littleton, C. S. 1982. *The New Comparative Mythology: An Anthropological Assessment of the Theories of Georges Dumézil*. Berkeley: University of California Press.

Mosse, G. 1964. *The Crisis of German Ideology*. New York: Grosset and Dunlap.

Müller, F. M. 1858. *Chips from a German Workshop* (3). New York: Charles Scribner's Sons, 1881.

——. 1881a. Comparative Mythology [1856]. In *Selected Essays on Language, Mythology and Religion* (1). London: Longmans, Green.

——. 1881b. On the Philosophy of Mythology. In *Chips from a German Woodshop* (5), ed. F. M. Müller. London: Longmans, Green.

——. 1882. On the Vedas or the Sacred Books of the Brahmans [1865]. In *In Selected Essays on Language, Mythology and Religion* (2). London: Longmans, Green.

——. 1891. *Physical Religion*. New York City: Longmans, Green.

——. 1892. *Natural Religion*. London: Longmans, Green.

——. 1898. Musical Recollections. In *Auld Lang Syne*, ed. F. M. Müller. New York: Charles Scribner's Sons.

——. 1901. Why I Am Not an Agnostic. In *Last Essays: Second Series*, ed. F. M. Müller. New York: Longmans, Green.

——. 1986a. *Anthropological Religion*. New Delhi: Asian Educational Services.

——. 1986b. *Theosophy or Psychological Religion*. New Delhi: Asian Educational Services.

——. 2002a. *My Autobiography*. New Delhi: Rupa and Company.

——. 2002b. On the Science of Religion, Lecture One (1870). In *The Essential Max Müller: On Language, Mythology and Religion*, ed. J. R. Stone. New York: Palgrave Macmillan.

Poliakov, L. 1974. *The Aryan Myth*. New York: New American Library.

Sharpe, E. J. 1986. *Comparative Religion: A History*. La Salle, IL: Open Court.

Stone, J. R., ed. 2002. *The Essential Max Müller: On Language, Mythology, and Religion*. New York: Palgrave Macmillan.

Strenski, I. 1996. The Rise of Ritual and the Hegemony of Myth: Sylvain Lévi, the Durkheimians and Max Müller. In *Myth and Method*, eds. W. Doniger & L. Patton. Charlottesville, VA: University of Virginia Press.

Trautmann, T. R. 1997. *Aryans and British India*. Berkeley: University of California Press.

Tylor, E. B. 1958. *Primitive Culture*. New York City: Harper and Row.

van den Bosch, L. P. 2002. *Friedrich Max Müller: A Life Devoted to the Humanities*. Leiden: E. J. Brill.

Voigt, J. 1967. *Max Müller: The Man and His Ideas*. Calcutta: Firma K. L. Mukhopadhyay.

The Shock of the 'Savage':
Edward Burnett Tylor,
Evolution, and Spirits

4

Mr. Tylor and His Science

It was Max Müller who dubbed the science of culture "Mr. Tylor's science," and since then it has been common, in the English-speaking world at least, to think of Edward Burnett Tylor (1832–1917) as the first 'anthropologist.' Although Müller is thought to have uttered these words ironically, there are nonetheless ample reasons for going along with his description of Tylor and his career (Stocking 1987, p. 195). While, like Muller, Tylor held academic posts at Oxford, unlike Müller, he spent some significant time in the field visiting, and to some degree actively studying, actual traditional societies. Tylor's first venture abroad for what might be called 'fieldwork' was his expedition to Mexico in 1856. This trip to Mexico was inspired by Tylor's meeting of a fellow Englishman, Henry Christy (1810–65), in Havana. Christy, a member of the science-minded Ethnological Society of London, as well as a collector of "ethnographic and archeological artifacts," pressed Tylor to undertake closer study and first-hand contact with the "primitive" religions that were at that time coming into vogue for study. The two men thereupon set off together on an extensive tour of Mexico on horseback, the results of which are recorded in his first book, *Anahuac* (Stocking 1987, p. 195; Stocking 2001b, p. 107; Tylor 1861).

Unlike Max Müller, Tylor undertook what we might call a more direct study of religion – especially its expressed beliefs and customs – rather than the close study of texts. While he was mostly a popularizer of ethnography and not an ethnographer himself, his approach encouraged others to do so. This meant that he also encouraged understanding living traditional or "primitive" peoples rather than investigating them through literature. In a real sense, one can look at Tylor's work as another answer to Hume's challenge to show us empirical support for the existence of Natural Religion. Tylor's pursuit of these questions led to the publication of *Primitive Culture*, his greatest book. Seventy percent of this book dealt with religious themes, and much of that with "animism" – Tylor's answer to the problem of the nature of the first and most funda-mental religion set by the proponents of Natural Religion. Tylor took particular pleasure in the historical precedent for his animism provided by his empiricist forebear, David Hume. This slashing critic of eighteenth-century theories of primal natural religion, such as Herbert of Cherbury's, saw the first religion – polytheism – as a kind of rational, although emotionally charged, extrapolation of the ordinary human experience of powerful persons onto the divine realm. Tylor tells us with pride that Hume's *Natural History of Religion* is "perhaps more than any other work the source of modern opinions as to the development of religion." In Tylor's view Hume still had much to teach the people of the mid-nineteenth century. He asserted the overriding "influence of this personifying stage of thought" in the origins of religion, and thus how people had from the very first most likely been animists. Tylor cites Hume's claims that there

> is a universal tendency among mankind to conceive all beings like themselves, and to transfer to every object those qualities with which they are familiarly acquainted, and of which they are intimately conscious.... Nor is it long before we ascribe to them thought and reason, and passion, and sometimes even the limbs and figures of men, in order to bring them nearer to a resemblance with ourselves. (Tylor 1873, p. 61)

We ought therefore to read Tylor's empiricist approach to the study of religion and his theory of "animism" as being in contrast to Müller's theological ambitions, his mysticism, and his view of Natural Religion as the perception of the Infinite. As Tylor himself put it in *Religion in Primitive Culture* as early as 1873:

> I propose ... to study the animism of the world so far as it constitutes, as unquestionably as it does constitute, an ancient and world-wide philosophy, of which belief is the theory and worship is the practice ... Here let me state once for all two principal conditions under which the present research is carried on. First, as to the religious doctrines and practices examined, these are treated as belonging to theological systems devised by human reason, without supernatural aid or revelation ... (Tylor 1873, p. 11)

By extension, because of his claim to be in Hume's tradition, Tylor also stood opposed to the Deists Herbert of Cherbury and Jean Bodin. The first and most fundamental religion was not what these 'theologians' of Natural Religion claimed it to be (Stocking 2001a, p. 334). It was not monotheistic, nor did it hold that this one god should be worshiped; it neither promised a final judgment that would reward the good for their virtue, or punish for evil their transgressions in a life hereafter. For Tylor, at best, the original religion of animism held out the possibility of immortality, since everything was in its essence spirit. Simple animism was, as it were, the 'real' natural religion. Let us look at how Tylor understood this concept.

Animism as the Real Natural Religion and Real First Science

For Tylor animism was the historically oldest and structurally most fundamental of all religions, the essence of religion itself. Thus, Tylor packaged a *chronological* thesis – which religion was *first* – along with a *logical* one – which religion was most *basic*, fundamental, and essential. For Tylor, animism combined to answer both inquiries, since he felt it to be not only the *first* religion but the *essence* of religion as well. This was his way of replacing all other proposals pretending to discover either the first or most fundamental religion. This is what is meant by saying that animism was, in a way, Tylor's radically revised idea of Natural Religion. Animism was, as Tylor recorded in his unpublished draft of his Gifford Lectures, nothing less than "the common religion of mankind" (quoted in Stocking 2001a, p. 334).

One distinctive feature of Tylor's theory of animism is his assumption that religion was really about giving an account of or explaining the world. This is why Tylor's animistic theory of religion is called rationalist or intellectualist. He took at face value the assertions of the religions, and held them to account as explanations which, like scientific hypotheses, could fail or succeed. It was Tylor's view that when measured against the evidence and claims of the sciences of his day, religion would show itself to be promoting falsehoods. God did not create the world; natural forces did. Adam and Eve were not the first humans; 'Lucy' (a fossil hominid discovered in Ethiopia and thought to be about 3.2 million years old) or someone like her, was. The universe was eons old in age, and not a few thousand years old, as Bishop Ussher (1581–1656) famously calculated from his biblical reckonings. God was not the ultimate, and even less the immediate, cause behind events in the world; natural causes were. It is not hard to see why Tylor came to presume that religions tried to explain things, since religious beliefs such as those we have just listed seem to attempt to do precisely this. Does not one of the Christian creeds, for example, begin with the statement, "I believe in God, the Father almighty, creator of heaven and earth ..." The existence of God as expressed by this creedal statement pretty clearly then tells us that it is a high priority for religion to explain the existence of the world, or so at any rate it seems.

Tylor presented religion in its most fundamental form, animism, as giving special kinds of explanations of the world. Things – impersonal beings – are really not 'things' at all, but personal beings. Animists presumed that the personal model explains things in the world far better than other options, for example impersonal mechanisms such as the play of forces, variations in atomic structures, and such. Religious people talk instead about history as being an example of the action of a divine person, of a provident being, and not as the action of impersonal forces such as fate or sheer chance. For him, animists believe that there is a reality behind events that is personal, that is human-like, that can be addressed by prayer and supplicated to, and which judges and rewards our actions and punishes our misdeeds. Animism *is* thus the real primal natural religion, not the lofty and abstract Natural Religion of a Max Müller. By contrast, the simplest, most primitive religions, says Müller, show us the kernel around which the complex of Natural Religion has developed.

> natural religion, or the natural faculties of man under the dominion of the natural impressions of the world around us, can lead, nay, has led man step by step to the highest conception of deity, a conception that can hardly be surpassed by any of those well-known definitions of deity which so-called supernatural religions have hitherto claimed as their exclusive property. (Müller 1891, p. 197)

The problem was, therefore, that great thinkers like Tylor and Müller disagreed about what that *original* condition of religion might be.

Tylor and Max Müller: From Irenics to Polemics

First, to the Tylor–Max Müller polemic (Stocking 1987, p. 305). In their own ways both Müller and Tylor were heirs of the German tradition of the systematic and scientific study of cultures, *Kulturgeschichte*, connected with such figures as Adolf Bastian and

Gustav Klemm (Müller 1886, p. 267; Tylor 1880, p. 448). Müller worked from the science of languages, Tylor through 'customs.' But despite a shared debt to the Germans, gradually Tylor and Müller came to differ more and more on the question of the character of the *study* of religion (Müller 1886, p. 264). Tylor embraced the study of culture as primary, and thus took up with religion because of its marked location within culture. This difference was in part expressed by Tylor's interests being focused on "customs." That they had apparently always differed regarding their personal attitudes toward religion itself would, in the end, prove decisive in shaping how they felt a 'science' of religion should be constituted.

Tylor, perhaps bristling with Non-Conformist resentments against the Anglican establishment, and certainly broadly antagonistic toward religion, found it agreeable to cast religion in the poorest light possible. In this sense, we can characterize Tylor at least at first glance as a 'critic' of religion, rather than a 'caretaker.' Tylor did not see himself as advancing any sort of positive religious agenda, but rather saw himself, at the very least, as someone who critically examined and evaluated the claims made by religious people against the standards of knowledge current in his day. If I may go a step further, for Tylor and others of his ilk, such as Sir James Frazer (as we will see below), we need to more accurately describe the intended thrust of their work on religion with a term of my own invention. Tylor is the inverse of the believing theologian or 'caretaker' of religion; he is an 'undertaker of religion' (McCutcheon 2001). With as much theological zeal as a traditional theologian, Tylor advances a deliberately antireligious agenda. He is in truth a kind of antitheologian. By contrast, the 'critic' will adopt a position of neutrality regarding *both* the truth claims of religion and its 'undertakers.' But the 'undertaker of religion' adopts as negative a position about religious claims as the 'caretaker' does a positive one. They are the mirror image of one another, and as such depart from the professional ethic of the academic student of religion. As we have noted earlier, the aim of Tylor's studies is not neutral in the way a critic's is, since Tylor tells us that his desire was "Theologians all to expose" (Stocking 1987, pp. 190–1). Müller, on the other hand, was nurtured by the liberal religious, often theosophical, piety of German Romanticism, in the end making him a certifiable Deist at heart and in mind. He was ultimately very much the 'caretaker of religion,' even though he contributed a good deal of what a good 'critic' would add to our understanding of religion, especially by his championing of a comparative study of religions that privileged no religious tradition. Müller at least offered us a way of studying religion that made for a neutral approach to the different religions of the world – even though he nurtured in his heart the faith of a progressive Christian. The position developed by Tylor in these exchanges in some degree helped define our contemporary usage of the phrase "anthropological study of religion," while in some sense Müller would set some of the guidelines for what has become known as Religious Studies – especially the *critical* dimensions of his methodological orientation (Strenski 1985; Strenski 1996a; Strenski 1996b).[1]

The public exchanges between Müller and Tylor always seemed cordial, and frequently laced with compliments. This was due partly to the prestige of historical philology, of which Müller was at the time the chief representative in England. R. R. Marett observed that the entire intellectual climate of Tylor's time was well disposed toward the radical critical research into the Bible and other classical literatures exemplified in part by Müller, but more so for Tylor, as we will see, by German skeptical rationalists like David Friedrich Strauss. "The concept of a veritable science of language, founded on the use of the Comparative Method, became firmly established in mens' minds," Marett observed of the intellectual scene in the mid to late nineteenth century (Marett 1936, p. 44). Early in his career, Tylor therefore saluted Müller's scientific work, especially his exposure of onomatopoeia or "imitation" in theories of the origins of language – even though later Tylor would adopt much the same viewpoint himself (Stocking 1987, p. 163; Tylor 1866a, pp. 545, 552, 555–6). Further, Tylor often lavished praise on the value of the "theory of mythology which Max Müller has put forth with such skill and marked success" (Tylor 1866b, p. 81). For his part, Müller early on was pleased to recognize Tylor as an intellectual ally. In a review of Tylor's *Researches into the Early History of Mankind* (1865), Müller noted with pleasure that his own comparative philology, "the sciences of language," had given Tylor's anthropology its "first impulse" and trademark interest in the 'primitives.' Accordingly, Müller specifically applauded Tylor's work in the "early history of the human race" as exemplary of the "good earnest men who care for facts" (Müller 1886, p. 253). More than that, Müller felt that Tylor's work showed signs of overcoming endemic British positivism, which otherwise would be satisfied with a mere concern for facts. Instead, Tylor improved upon fact-gathering "by giving life and purpose to facts" (Müller 1886, p. 267). It was partly then in this context of the leadership and prestige of the kind of work Max Müller represented so ably and popularly in England that we need to see the beginnings, at least, of Tylor's 'anthropology.'

Yet, despite their common interest in 'scientific' studies of religion, "Mr. Tylor's science" (Müller's epithet [Stocking 1987, p. 195]) finally represented a rejection of the core of Müller's "Science of Religion." However well rooted in historical linguistics and critical history of sacred texts it might be, Müller's idea of 'science' went well beyond what Tylor could accept. Müller's "Science of Religion" was modeled on the practice of historical phonology in constructing hypothetical forms of the Indo-European *Ursprache*. In its embrace of hypothetical thinking, it fell short of being scientific in Tylor's perhaps cramped empiricist sense, even though Max Müller never ceased insisting that his "Science of Religion has to deal with facts, not with theories" (Müller 1891, p. 366).

With all but explicit reference to Müller's interpretation of Vedic and other materials as pointing to a primal natural religion, Tylor exposed what he saw as a major weakness in Müller's claims about the scientific character of "Science of Religion" – reliance on a hypothetical state of primal natural religion. In a veiled reference to Müller, Tylor comments: "In supporting and exemplifying the opinion that we may see in Animism an elementary religious phase … it has not been necessary for me to assume imaginary or hypothetical states of human culture" (Tylor 1866b, p. 85). In characterizing Tylor's evolutionist and empiricist reasons to favor 'anthropology' over against Müller's philo-logical and theologizing of human origins,[2] Marett felt that Tylor's approach rested on the belief that "the best way to understand human nature in its diversity was through ethnology understood as the study of ethnic groups and people in all their *concrete* activity" (my emphasis) (Marett 1936, p. 47).

Müller was not without answers to Tylor, even though the future of 'anthropology' would belong to Tylor and not to the likes of Müller. Against the rising tide of the prestige of Darwin, Müller ridiculed Tylor for the implications of his evolutionism, but without much effect in the hostile intellectual climate of his day. How could Tylor justify regarding children as the logical equivalents of "savages" (Müller 1892, p. 212)? Was not the assumption of an evolutionary process underlying this equivalence as metaphysical and hypothetical as Müller's own assumption of the nature of primal natural religion as worship of the infinite? Müller also remained a skeptic about the value of the testimony of native informants. Why are the 'savages' assumed to be privileged informants about the dawn of humankind? Would we trust Christians of today to tell us about first-century Palestine (Müller 1892, p. 217)? Since it is not then obvious that 'the native knows best,' was Tylor's reliance on native information 'superficial' data at best? What causal models, hidden determinants, or 'structures' lay beneath 'what the native said' (Müller 1892, p. 216)? Finally, if empirical evidence – even from 'savages' – be our guide, Müller claimed, like Andrew Lang and Pater Wilhelm Schmidt would years later, that his ideal of a single high God, an "Unknown" and "Infinite" being, was to be found today in the ethnographic field – even alongside the kind of animistic beliefs cited so often by Tylor (Müller 1892, p. 218).

As a good, hard-headed empiricist, Tylor argued that primal natural religion need no longer be a hypothetical construct or a mere deduction from 'facts.' He believed that he had done nothing less than discover, by unerring empirical means, what everyone from Jean Bodin to Herbert of Cherbury to the English Deists had sought to discover – the true identity of primal natural religion. The only (*sic*) difference was that he identified Natural Religion not in lofty terms, but rather as a meager belief in the existence of spirits animating things – his "animism." The 'earliest' or most 'primitive' of religions does not then indicate or suggest the straining for unity with the infinite and abstract that Müller thinks Vedic (or any other religion) does, but rather the desire to explain the world, a kind of proto-science that posited the existence of immaterial beings or spirits within things. Animism as the primal natural religion is nothing very special, lofty, or even, despite its name, spiritual. It is just an instance of humanity's first efforts to explain natural phenomena. As Tylor put it so well:

> through all these gradations of opinion, we may thus see fought out in one stage after another, the long-waged contest between a theory of animation which accounts for each phenomenon of nature by giving it everywhere a life like our own, and a slowly-growing natural science which in one department after another substitutes for independent voluntary action the working out of systematic law. (Tylor 1866b, p. 82–3)

In this sense, the standard characterization of the opposition between Müller and Tylor, rendered as the opposition of naturism to animism, is somewhat off the mark (Durkheim 1995, pp. 45–69). The real opposition between Müller and Tylor was the problem of the nature of the origins of spirituality or religion – the problem of the nature of that putative primal natural religion that had driven naturalistic studies of religion since the sixteenth century. Müller's primal natural religion was a highly spiritualized meditative religion like the natural religion of the Deists, while Tylor's animism was a product of everyday human reasoning and imagining that could be apprehended empirically (Stocking 1987, p. 160). As Pierre Laplace replied, when asked by Napoléon why he had made no mention of the "author of the universe" in his *Mécanique céleste*, Tylor too was in effect saying of the origins and nature of religion, "Sire, I have no need of that hypothesis." Thus Tylor proposes a level of religion that he believed was more fundamental than Müller's Natural Religion, or even Müller's religion of the worship of nature. Before any other type of religion, there was animism. The main question to which I want to address this chapter is why Tylor thought he was right to believe that animism made sense as a thesis about the nature of religion. To do this, we will have to penetrate Tylor's thought world and the context provided by his life and times. What problems of religion was he seeking to solve? What problems was he seeking as well to make *for* religion?

Why Tylor Thinks Like He Does

From our review of some key – mostly Christian – religious beliefs, it is not surprising that Tylor should come up with a theory of religion based upon the belief in spirits. Even some prominent students of religion of our own day, like Hans Penner, still adhere to a broadly Tylorian theory of religion (Frankenberry 2002). Yet, right or wrong, one still wants to know what considerations might inform how and why Tylor thought he was right about his theory. There were, after all, contrary theories in play. What constraints and encouragements did he have for pressing ahead with the view that animism was the nature of religion?

Taking the most obvious, there is ample evidence in the data for animism explicitly to be found in what we might call primitive religions. The belief both in spirits inhabiting and animating beings, or the existence of souls in things, was widespread in the classic and ethnographic literature. In his article, "The Religion of the Savages," Tylor observes that

> The act of breathing, so characteristic of the higher animals during life, and coinciding so closely with life in its departure, has naturally been often identified with the life itself, and the etymology of words which have that since assumed very abstract or theoretical meanings, still shows their starting point in this primitive thought. Thus in the first chapter of Genesis ... "breath of life" has already come to designate the living creatures which the Earth brings forth, and indeed the Hebrew Bible shows us breath passing into all meanings of life, soul, mind and animal in general. So with Latin, *anima*, *animus*, Greek *psyche*, German *Geist*, English *ghost*, in all which the original sense is that of breath. (Tylor 1866b, pp. 72–3)

We should also note the fact that in the England of Tylor's time, the Spiritualist movement was quite popular, and that Tylor found corroboration for his theory of animism in it (Stocking 1994, p. xvii). Spiritualists believed in the existence of disembodied souls of the deceased, and that contact could be made between them and the living by means of a spirit medium. Such religious practice implied that those who died continued nonetheless to exist in independent spiritual or ghostly forms into another world. We should also not forget that Tylor himself had been born into the Christian sect called the Society of Friends, more commonly called the Quakers. A central practice of Quaker worship meetings was 'waiting for the spirit to move one to speak.' In this spiritual practice, the assembled worshipers, remaining in a state of silence, wait until one of their number feels that the spirit urges them to speak. At that point, someone will rise and address the meeting because they feel the 'spirit has moved them to speak.' Thus Tylor had considerable reason for thinking that the belief in the existence of spirits was important to religion.

Secondly, Tylor suspected that Christianity actually boiled down to this belief in the existence of spirits, or rather the existence of one great spirit or soul, namely God. Here, comparing the ancient religions of Mexico with the Catholicism of the same country, Tylor dryly observes,

> There is not much difference between the old heathenism and the new Christianity ... the real essence of both religions is the same to them. They had gods, to whom they

built temples, and in whose honour they gave offerings, maintained priests, danced and walked in processions – much as they do now, that their divinities might be favourable to them, and give them good crops and success in their enterprises. This is pretty much what their present Christianity consists of. (Tylor 1861, p. 289)

When all was said and done, like primitive animism, Christianity has always preached the existence of a great soul who cares for, acts in, and governs the world.

Upwards from the simplest theory which contributes life and personality to animal, vegetable, and mineral alike – through that which gives to stone and plant and river guardians spirits which live among them and attend to their preservation, growth, and change – up to that which sees in each department of the world the protecting and fostering care of an appropriate divinity, and at last of one Supreme Being ordering and controlling the lower hierarchy – through all these gradations of opinion we may thus see fought out, and one stage after another, a long contest waged between a theory of animation which accounts for each phenomenon of nature by giving it everywhere a life like our own, and a slowly growing natural science which in one department after another substitutes for independent voluntary action the working out of systematic law. (Tylor 1866b, pp. 82–3)

But, one might ask nonetheless, why did anyone believe this? In particular, why did the so-called primitives think that animism was in fact true? Tylor's answer comes in a number of forms. First, ignorance. The primitives are frequently mistaken about the true causes of things because they project everyday familiar experience drawn from social life onto nature and indeed onto everything in their worlds. But this projection of the personal onto the impersonal is a mistake. It suggests a low level of mental development and knowledge. The myths indeed may speak of the fabulous doings of talking serpents, or of the exploits of gods and goddesses contending with each other. But they are simply not true.

A second reason for the belief in spirits comes actually from the more ordinary experiences of human beings everywhere. Consider first the experience of our dream lives. In dreams, we imagine ourselves moving about in space without the resistance that our material bodies cause us. Many cultures have interpreted dreams as being real experiences of our true spiritual nature liberated from the shackles of the body. Thus when we dream, our spiritual selves actually move about in an ether, in a spiritual space where bodies are not needed. There is also the experience that human beings may have of differences between life and death, between a living body and a dead one. If one reflects upon the difference between an animal recently deceased and the living animal, one of the first things that one may notice is the absence of breath. This is significant because the soul has often been either identified with the breath or as a source of the breath. Thus when a person or animal dies, the breath, and along with it the soul, are said to depart, leaving behind the in-animate body. Early medical experiments in Europe were sometimes aimed at trying to detect the absence of this life principle in a dead body. The experiment consisted of placing a body about to die upon the scale and waiting for death. Once the animal or person had died, their weight was registered once again in an effort to detect the difference in weight between the living and dead body. That difference the investigators thought would be accounted for by the absence of the soul or spirit in the body.

While such explanations may account for why traditional or primitive societies might imagine that souls inhabit everything, they do not explain why contemporary religious folk should think the same. Modern religious folk know about science, for example, and therefore should have beliefs that conform with the discoveries of science. That modern religious folk continued, however, to believe in spirits meant for Tylor that they were in fact no better than the primitives. Modern religious believers do not really understand the ways of the universe and the way that life really works because they have not absorbed science into their lives. They simply value their own religious experiences of spirit, of inspiration, of the feeling that God actually acts in their lives, more than what they know from science. Thus modern religious belief in God is a "survival" of primitive ignorance – a key term of Tylor's that we now need to investigate.

"Survivals"

Although, as we will see, Tylor believed in evolution of the human species and human culture, he also believed that various aspects or characteristics of early stages of evolution somehow managed to survive evolution and development. These he called "survivals" because they resisted change over time, and continued some of the features of stages of human developmental growth that had long since been surpassed. Thus a "survival" is a primitive thing, an ancient thing that persists in our culture, even though it is outmoded and unnecessary. Consider, for example, the necktie as a "survival." Originally, the necktie was a kind of scarf worn around the collar of a man's shirt in order both to keep his neck warm and to keep the top of the shirt tightly closed. Thus the necktie was practical for its time and place. However, as time went on, and buttons and zippers and other such fasteners were invented, the necktie scarf became outmoded. It served no useful practical function. Yet, as we all know, the necktie is still worn – but not for its original functional purpose, but rather as an ornament. Thus the fact that we continue to wear this necktie scarf is an example of how an older cultural custom *survives* despite its lack of utility.

For Tylor, animism or the belief in spirits to explain natural phenomena is also, on the whole, just such a "survival." If the belief in spirits to explain things can be said to *evolve or progress*, it does so in essentially insignificant ways – at least from Tylor's anticlerical point of view. Originally spirits were thought to account for the way things happened in the natural world. But modern-day Christians, Jews, or Muslims, for example, still persist in thinking just as animistically, in effect, as their 'savage' forebears. God lies behind and controls the universe and human fate, even when degrees of human freedom are factored in. Modern-day monotheism is just 'primitive' animism 'writ large,' so to speak. While to believers the differences between the two may seem great, and seem as well to evidence *progressive growth and development*, as indeed we will see William Robertson Smith argue in a while, for Tylor such developments were marginal at best. At bottom, modern-day religious folk saw the world as a place *animated* and fundamentally *explained* by the agency of a *personal spirit* – God.

Only with the rise of science – itself, at least since Newton, Galileo and the others, wedded to *impersonal* models of explaining the world – can we speak of a radical move up the steps of progressive evolution from animism. Modern science *replaces* animism, in Tylor's view. Science mounts the 'ladder' of progress and leaves behind the 'lower rungs' of primitive thought, such as animism, once it has got its use out of them – just as modern human beings have moved well beyond their primate animal forebears, even though humanity could not have come into being without those early prehuman stages of biological development. Thus, as Tylor sees science, we learn that spirits – no matter how 'large' – do not account for the way things occur in the natural world. Trees do not thrive because of the existence of life spirits inside them or because of divine providence, but because of the inanimate chemical nutrients that feed their roots. Animals do not die because of the departure of the soul from their bodies or because 'God has taken them to Himself,' but because of the breakdown of their organs.

Yet, as Tylor well knew, this belief in the activity of spirits or God continues to "survive" into our own day – primarily in religion. His contribution to continued human progress was, as he thought, to expose the 'survived' and primitive nature of beliefs in personal spiritual agency in the world. Tylor provides us with a very colorful example of how the survival of ancient sacrificial practices is a part of the unrecognized cultural practice of the modern day. Here, Tylor chooses oddities surrounding funeral rites to make his point about the phenomenon of the "survival." In his "Religion of the Savages," he notes how the possible historical origins of certain religious practices remain unknown to believers:

> From the mind of the Catholic or Protestant, who hangs a wreath of everlastings on the grave cross or flings flowers upon the coffin, the idea of sacrifice, of conferring a practical benefit on the departed spirit, has now mostly passed away. Pressed for an explanation, such a one would hardly maintain that the reason for the funeral offering was anything but a mere sentiment.

For believers, the practice 'explains itself' as an appropriate *traditional* expression of feelings for the dead. Not satisfied with what religious folk say about the nature and meaning of their practices, the scientist reveals the *real reasons and causes* for what people do. Going on, Tylor adds:

> But it is just such mere sentiment that the student of the lower phases of human nature is so often able to trace to their source, when he sees in them the relics, inherited through long and changing ages, of what were once cogent and practical views of life ... [T]he ethnographer ... discerns in such things long lingering remnants of a younger time. From the stage where the soul of the offering is thought to be fed upon by the soul of the departed friend, through the stage where the act of sacrifice is thought to convey to that soul a direct feeling of pleasure, down to the stage where the intention of the funeral garland has dwindled to the satisfaction of the mere imagination, – through all this utter change of signification the ceremony of the offering to the dead has held on its unbroken course, and will hold it till old men forget that they were once children, and a hard middle-age world that it, too, was once younger. (Tylor 1866b, p. 80)

What is radical about Tylor's theory of animism is then that he thought that religion itself is a "survival." Religion, defined as a belief in the existence of spirits, or a great spirit-god, is simply a leftover bit of the most primitive beliefs of the most primitive level of human history. But in the meantime, we have to endure survivals of primitive beliefs, much as we endure all sorts of obsolete oddities of culture like neckties! In time, scientific explanations of the world would gradually be seen to have replaced religious (animistic) ones. But religious people just would not *learn*, and as such would not fully be able to participate in the upward, progressive movement of the human spirit. Part of their minds may be modern and 'progressive,' but the religious parts are still mired in prehistoric ways of thinking such as animism.

1859 and All That: The Discovery of the European 'Primitive'

When we inquire more deeply into why Tylor should think he was right in assigning religion to the dustbin of history, we inevitably come up against his commitment to a theory of progressive evolution. Both the ideas of a 'survival' and animism belong to just such an original theoretical framework of developmentalism. How then does evolutionary thinking bear on the way Tylor thought about the nature of religion, and in particular about animism? To do this, we need to take a step or two back and consider the historical events out of which Tylor's thought in part sprang.

If Max Müller's problems of religion were stimulated by his discovery of the splendid ancient civilization of faraway India, the dramatic eruptions of Europe's own local prehistoric and 'primitive' forebears challenged Tylor to come up with solutions to a series of new problems of religion. What in particular created *problems of religion* for Tylor and those like him were the discoveries of the prehistoric human past, and as we will see later, the puzzle of the existence of 'primitive' peoples in the modern day. From the early nineteenth century a series of spectacular archeological discoveries totally revolutionized the European sense of history and the place of religion in it. Various discoveries on the European continent attested to the existence of peoples utterly forgotten by then contemporary European folk, and in the process greatly extended the sense of the length of the human past far beyond anything imaginable – and certainly far beyond anything suggested by the Bible. This realization only multiplied the effect of the blows to a biblical authority already reeling under the successive impact of Higher Criticism, and to a lesser extent knowledge of the other religions of the world as made known by the likes of scholars like Max Müller. The implications for religious understanding in the latter third of the nineteenth century in Europe thus seemed far-reaching and profound. These events demanded new theories to encompass the new knowledge only lately appearing on the European intellectual scene.

As if religious consciousness had not been shocked enough by these new developments in the European understanding of the world, these intellectual crises only deepened thanks to the publication of Charles Darwin's *On the Origin of Species* (1859). His naturalistic account of the growth and development of all living forms, moving slowly but inexorably at the glacial pace of geological time, left out any sort of divine creative initiative. For many, this explosion in the sense of the scope of the recoverable past presented yet another challenge to the intellectual foundations of religious belief, especially as it cast doubt on the literal truth of the Bible. By any account of our own present-day conflicts between religion and science, Darwin's challenge continues to excite controversy.

The Caves and Their Religion

Now, although Darwin and the revolution he incited in biology bear on the story to be told in this chapter, even more pertinent to our understanding of Tylor and religion was his reaction to the discoveries of European human prehistory. Consider first the shock inflicted upon European self-consciousness by what the archeologists found right beneath the unsuspecting feet of their modern-day contemporaries. In 1859, excavations at Brixham Cave (also known as Philp's or Windmill Hill Cave) near Torbay, Devonshire, on the south coast of England shocked scientific and popular opinion. By sheer accident, in 1858, a builder, Mr. Philp (no first name can be traced), was digging the foundation for the construction of a terraced house, when his pick axe broke through to a subterranean cavern (Gruber 1965). There, the bones of exotic animals such as reindeer, rhinoceri, lions, and elephants were found, setting off a program of archeological excavations that began the following year. Adding fuel to the imagination of the late nineteenth century, some of these rude bone pieces evidenced signs of human fashioning. The early peoples living in the Brixham cave vicinity had apparently been hunters skilled not only at hunting the exotic animals slain by them, but also at manufacturing the weaponry necessary for the task (Oldham 1989).

Darwin happened to be among the scientists particularly impressed by these discoveries. To him, the discoveries at Brixham cave not only "established the great antiquity of man," they also gave to other independently influenced developmental thinkers, like Tylor, the warrant they needed to link "man to some antecedent primate form," and to translate "this interest … into a systematic investigation of human sociocultural origins" (Stocking 1987, p. 172). Giving us some sense of the shock value of the particular import of the archeological discoveries at Brixham Cave, Charles Lyell, the great geologist and one of the first to sustain systematic arguments about the great age of the human species, triumphantly observed in the sixth chapter of his *The Geological Evidence of the Antiquity of Man* (1863): "I may conclude this chapter by quoting a saying of Professor Agassiz, 'that whenever a new and startling fact is brought to light in science, people first say, 'it is not true,' then that 'it is contrary to religion,' and lastly, 'that everybody knew it before'" (Lyell 1863, p. 112). For Europeans, it slowly became clear that literally beneath their feet lay buried an entire prehistoric European ancestor civilization the existence of which they had neither recollections nor records. Who then were these people, and what did they have to do with nineteenth-century Britons?

Tylor was well prepared to accept the redefinition of the human past that these remarkable discoveries entailed. His longstanding adherence to the pre-Darwinian developmentalist thinkers of his time made it easy for him to imagine humanity to have grown up through many long stages of development (Stocking 1987, p. 178). Along with other admirers of Darwin, Tylor especially welcomed the way that these discoveries lengthened the human past far beyond what the Bible proposed (Marett 1936, pp. 198–202). In this sense, we might say that Tylor welcomed the *problems* created for religion – especially for biblical literalists and the rigid theologians who frequented the Oxford of his day. It makes sense then that Tylor would like to provoke problems for religion, since he saw the aim of his studies as being "Theologians all to expose …" (Stocking 1987, pp. 190–1).

In terms of the larger picture, however, the discoveries of the prehistoric world taught mixed lessons about religion. We will see more of the complexities as we develop the discussions in this chapter about the idea of the 'primitive.' But for the moment, consider the difficulties encountered in using the term 'primitive' – even about something like the artifacts and representations of the prehistoric caves that we have just discussed. On the one hand, one might argue that there is something decidedly 'primitive' about these societies marked by undeveloped levels of technology. These are societies that apparently lived by hunting and gathering, and thus had not developed agriculture and settled life in cities. Archeological evidence also indicates that these folk hunted and worked with stone tools rather than with technologies involving metal working. Data such as these led thinkers of Tylor's ilk to regard our ancient prehistoric ancestors as 'primitive.' He had next to nothing to say about what we might call 'fine arts.' Of the four chapters of his *Anthropology* entitled "The Arts of Life," he writes nothing about 'art' as one commonly understands it. Instead, these chapters dwell upon utilitarian material culture – technologies, tools, and implements (Tylor 1881).

Yet, on the other hand, as one can see from cave paintings in southern France and Spain, ranging from 15,000 years to about 35,000 years old, one finds an impressive combination of exquisite esthetic refinement and plausibly a rather sophisticated air of mystery. Animals, typically being hunted, frequently occur. Extinct animals such as wooly mammoths are depicted along with surviving species such wolves, reindeer, horses, or bison. Human figures are rarely depicted, but when they are, they are depicted indirectly, as with the negative of the human hand, made by blowing pigment over the hand placed flat against the cave wall. (See figure 4.1.) On the rare occasions when humans do appear, they do so mostly in the guise of ritual actors or hunters, or some combination of the two. Corroborating the theme of hunting, some of the most

Figure 4.1.   Painting of spotted horses and imprints of human hands on the walls of the Pech-Merle cave, dating from approximately 25,000 BCE. (Cabrerets, Lot, France.)

Source: www.quercy.net/pechmerle/english/visite.html#11.

frequently occurring remains found in caves, such as Brixham, for example, were hunting implements or weaponry such as spear and arrow heads, either made of stone or fashioned from animal bone.

On the other hand, in these paintings there may be something suggesting rather sophisticated conceptions of human agency and cosmic powers. Thus, while the images are often drawn well, even from the perspective of our modern and often quirky esthetics, many of the cave illustrations are sophisticated in capturing the esthetic moment, often in a telling gesture, such as the so-called horned dancer or 'shaman' of the Les Trois Frères cave in southern France.

In the same vein, R. R. Marett, Tylor's biographer and a student of anthropology in his own right, saw the cave paintings he visited in the south of France and in Spain as unmistakably indicating esthetic refinement and even intellectual command. Marett did not deny evolution, only that the folk one called 'primitive' were not deprived of lofty notions and sensibilities recognizable in our own thought and action. Philosopher Georges Bataille suggests, as well, that with the appearance of cave art such as that found in Lascaux, for example, humans moved out of the grim world of the workaday into a richer, and in a sense more human, domain of creative freedom (Bataille 1955).

Yet it is hard to know just what such exquisite representation was about, since the prehistoric folk left us no interpretive tools. We just do not know for sure why they chose to depict what they did, and as they did. The famous horned dancer of Les Trois Frères in France may evoke this sense of the magical and uncanny, for clearly whatever else may be present, what we see is a human dressed up to look like an antelope or deer in an upright position. Marett, for example, felt that the images and human traces he found in the caves of France and Spain suggested a religious sensibility, in particular the concept of *mana*, an notion similar to that of the holy or sacred that we will see developed by the phenomenologists of religion, such as Gerardus van der Leeuw, Rudolf Otto, Ninian Smart, and Mircea Eliade. Religion, thus, can be conceived to have a long history because the Paleolithic cave paintings reveal a deep religious and magical sensibility:

> A visit to certain prehistoric sites of France will suffice to persuade us that there was rudimentary religion amongst ancient no less than there is amongst modern savages, and that its spirit was essentially the same. At Niaux, for instance, there are pictographs and paintings which, so far as can be made out, are connected with rites intended to secure good hunting. The fact, too, that they occur deep within the dark recesses of a mountain, where a certain awe is felt even by a modern mind, afford an additional proof that solemnities were being celebrated; that fine art in this case was but the secondary product of religion . . .

Therefore, the aura surrounding these ritual sites wreaks of sublime power and mystery. The caves are not art galleries, but sacred places, domains where our human ancestors communed with supernatural forces that transcended the ordinary world – mysterious forces such as *mana*:

> Hence we may justly speak of prehistoric sanctuaries. In entering one of these caves to encompass his hope by means of its solemn prefiguration the ancient savage was crossing the threshold that divides the world of workaday from the world of the sacred; and these rites in them, whether the mechanism of spell or of prayer predominated in them, were genuinely religious in so far as they involved a mood and attitude consisting

in a drawing near in awe, to approved traditional usage, to an unseen source of *mana*. (Marett 1914, pp. 203–4)

Tylor had only examined material items such as tools and bones gathered from such sites, and never seemed to have evinced interest in seeing the cave paintings that so impressed Marett. Still, from what we know of them, we might imagine how Tylor could have come to think about religion as he did. The idea of animism, the idea of the existence of spirits that are independent of a given body, might lie behind the graphic art of the cave paintings and thus suggest something of the religious attitude informing them. Might not the representation of the horned dancer, for example, seeming to embody the spirit of the hunter's quarry, suggest that he was part of a ritual to assure success in the hunting of the animal depicted? One might conjecture further that the dancer thinks of himself as somehow possessing the 'spirit' of the reindeer, and in doing so believes that he can control the availability of the reindeer for the coming hunt. Perhaps then Tylor was not far off in thinking that the belief in souls or spirits is some fundamental part of the religious attitude, since we seem to find indications of such beliefs in the human record dating back tens of thousands of years? Of course, given Tylor's general antipathy to religion, we would not expect from him the glowing expressions of religious awe to which his own biographer and disciple, R. R. Marett, was given.

But how did Tylor justify thinking about the belief in spirits as 'primitive'? And indeed, in what sense might such a description be justified? Before we attempt to understand how and why Tylor thought it was right to think that evolution applied to the mental side of human culture, such as religion, art, philosophy, science, etc. – and not just to technologies and physical artifacts – a word or two needs to be said about the discourse of 'the primitive.' Tylor's use of the word 'primitive' and its synonyms, such as 'savage,' was quietly and completely followed by virtually all the major thinkers of his generation. Yet it is a word that can be terribly offensive and even morally objectionable to use in scientific contexts. For this reason, we should pause for a moment to consider it and its uses.

A Word about the Words 'Primitive' and 'Savage'

A revealing instance of Tylor's morally odious use of 'primitive' or 'savage' can be found in his justly famous essay about animism, "The Religion of Savages" (1866). At the core of the moral problems afflicting Tylor's way of talking is the analogy he assumes between 'primitive' peoples and children. The 'savages' or 'primitives' are quite simply and literally humanity's 'children,' and ought to be treated in the same patronizing way children of the late nineteenth century were treated. Europeans, especially those of northern, secular, or Protestant stock, like Tylor, on the other hand, are humanity's right-thinking 'grown-ups' and natural superiors, with all the rights and privileges accorded to adults in Victorian England.

Thus, "The Religion of Savages" conveys an argument for the Tylor's animistic theory of religion with a straightforward appeal to an analogy between those he called 'primitives' and children. Tylor does this by relating the telling of a Christmas Eve story before an audience of small children. In the story, a group of children with families are gathered together for a cozy evening meal. While inside everyone was busy eating and making merry, outside in the cold and dark, an old broomstick lay forgotten by the door. The evening of merriment concluded, the children and adults went on their way back to their individual houses, as the snow gathered on the ground all around them. The broomstick, however, would remain day after day out in the cold, covered with snow, and all alone. At this point, the children in the audience broke in lamenting the plight of the broomstick. Tears flowed copiously and the feelings of the young audience poured out for the misery of the lonely old broomstick. The adult storyteller, however, would have none of this. Instead of sympathizing with the kindly feelings of the children for the broomstick, he sternly rebuked them, saying how 'childish' they were for having any feelings at all for a lifeless object. Better that they should feel sympathy for something of their own kind, for something alive that had real feelings and could respond to them, rather than to lavish their 'childish' emotions on a mere thing. The story breaks off here (Tylor 1866b, p. 71).

Tylor tries to make several points with this little example. The most germane point bearing on our understanding of his theory of religion is observing that children act like children(!) – or at least like what a middle-class man of the late nineteenth century thinks about children. He does not reproach or scold them for this, because as children he believes they evince the behavior fitting to their evolutionary stage of mental maturity. They could hardly do better as long as they remained at such an immature level of mental development. Thus, as children, they do not *know* the real causes of events in the world, nor the true nature of things. As we will see, Tylor believes that the same may be said of those cultures called 'primitive' or 'savage.'

For Tylor and many other thinkers of his time, 'primitives' or 'savages' would include not only the prehistoric European folk, but also people such as Native Americans, Fijians, Khonds of Orissa, Beduoins, Maoris, and even Vedic Indians, among others (Tylor 1866b, *passim*). In terms of the idea of a spirit or soul, Tylor claims that these peoples evince the same *ignorance* about the relation of animate and inanimate things as the children of his illustrative tale. Both groups project life, feelings, and intelligence on everything – whether ultimately deserving or not. The children see spirits and souls everywhere, and not only in animate beings; but so also do the 'primitives.' If children see the broomstick as having a kind of soul, so also do the Hindus of Vedic times (as Müller in fact tells us) see inanimate things, such as fire, as a manifestation of the spirit or god they call Agni. Tylor feels that this sort of talk indicates that neither the Hindus of Vedic times nor the children of our story know any better. Both are ignorant of the real causes of events and nature of things in the world. Humanity would have to wait until the human mind matured at the dawn of science to learn the truth about such matters. The animistic attitude of the 'primitives' is for Tylor thus literally 'childish,' since they commit the same error of ascribing life, intelligence, and feeling to inanimate things as children who weep for the pain suffered by an abandoned broomstick. No matter how he may have tried to disguise the antireligious intent of such odious comparisons, a good number of Tylor's critics recognized his theory of animism as an attempt to reduce religion to a 'childish' belief in spirits, or to dwell on its "puerilities [and] … terrible cruelties … the coarse rudiments of religion." This eventually caused some students of religion of the day to do what they called studying the "noncivilized … separately – from the religious point of view" (Réville 1883, p. 25).

It is important to note that when Tylor likened 'primitives' to children, he was not only describing them. He was also casting aspersions upon the mental capacities and nobility of all those peoples that he included under this label. Today, terms like 'primitive' and 'savage' stir the modern moral conscience of students of human societies.

But to Tylor and his generation, this sort of pejorative labeling was normal, and was carried on without a moment's hesitation about the possible moral offense such terms might give to those thus labeled. Indeed, for Tylor, morality was measured by conformity with the *forward* thrust of evolutionary development, much as the moral judgment of adults trumps that of children. The most highly evolved was by definition the measure of the good: parents know best. To be short of higher levels of development was to be deficient in ultimate goodness, to be 'childish' or 'immature.' Therefore, it was the duty of the highly evolved both to protect their level of development, and to teach lower stages of development the path to their higher fulfillment, again much as adults guide the education of children. For those at lower stages of development, resistance to 'growth' was analogous to children refusing to learn or grow up. In the eyes of Tylor and his ilk, immorality lay in resisting 'improvement' or 'education,' or in willfully refusing to recognize this, not in calling attention to the undeveloped condition of various peoples, beliefs, and practices.

The moral conscience of today's academic community firmly rejects the use of the language of the primitive and savage, because such terms are loaded with egregious belittling prejudices. Even though a modern-day thinker like Claude Lévi-Strauss employs the term in the title of his influential book, *La Penseé sauvage* (Lévi-Strauss 1966), it is clear that he does so strategically to undermine pejorative uses of the term. Thus he observes that "social evolutionism is, too often, no more than the falsely scientific covering up of an old philosophical problem, to which it is not at all certain that observation and induction may one day provide the key" (Lévi-Strauss 1976, p. 323). This applies with special force to the term 'savage,' although the paternalistic language of the primitive as children that we have just discussed is equally well subject to the same sort of repudiation. When one speaks of something 'savage,' one will have to think very hard of any case where the term is even used neutrally. 'Savage' means vicious, brutal, mean, and so on, as in the phrase a 'savage' attack. At best, it suggests a kind of pure, if fierce, energy, as in saying that two people were committed to each other with a 'savage' loyalty. Nonetheless, with the exception of this last example, few people would pretend to use this term in a morally neutral way. 'Savage' is an out and out term of violation, destruction, and abuse. So, let us move on to a fuller discussion of the more problematic language of the 'primitive.'

By contrast with 'savage,' 'primitive' is somewhat less morally problematic, although far from being wholly so, as we have seen with Tylor's patronizing comparison with children. There may be some cases where a neutral sense of the term 'primitive' applies, and the belittling moral sense is absent. Indeed, when we refer to 'primitivism' in modern painting, for example, we actually celebrate it. We mean that there is a bold simplicity or archaic look to it. Here, nothing much of moral note arises, unless we assume, as we often enough do, that this is the way our prehistoric ancestors or the tribal peoples painted. Taken positively in this way, primitivism may suggest a bold, pure energy, but it may also suggest the absence of a higher order of artistic skill. In its pejorative sense, the term primitive means something crude, childish, undeveloped, or wild, as we have seen. One might, for example, criticize a painting as primitive, because it was poorly made, as in the case just discussed where one claimed that creators of 'primitive' art lacked certain levels of skill. Thus, one might criticize a religious tradition as 'primitive,' because it was deemed to be 'superstitious' or plainly false. Further, even morally neutral uses of the term still carry at best dubious, and at least confusing, connotations. How do we know, for example, that Picasso's 'primitivist' paintings, with their strong lines and bold, sharp figures, such as his famous *Les Desmoiselles d'Avignon*, is 'primitive' in the sense of being 'archaic' or *old* looking, especially when we know that the cave art that can be dated to 30,000 years or so shows precisely the opposite features? But, less problematically, we might say that a stone-headed axe was an example of 'primitive' technology, compared to an axe with a steel head, because the steel head would stand up better under certain conditions, while the stone head might shatter.

Ironically neither positive nor pejorative uses really do justice to the great range of kinds of peoples usually included under the label 'primitive.' In the case where we celebrate the supposed pure energy that we lack, we project our own 'hang-ups' and longings as much as when we assume that they are deficient in some way. We make of other folk the objects of our rarified patterns of consumption – here not in terms of curios or 'art,' but in terms of the far more insidious belief that we can consume and exploit the ways of life of others. These other people are not there for our convenience, nor to be mirrors for us – no matter whether we think the mirroring flatters them or not. They are their own folk, and not to be subsumed, however we may imagine them, by our own uses.

Does Religious or Cultural Evolution Make Sense?

I have in effect been arguing against the embrace of an evolutionist approach to human culture from at least a moral point of view. To wit, it is immoral to belittle other folk by applying the term 'primitive' to them, by denigrating their cultural achievements, in effect, by likening them to children. But in order to be fair not only to Tylor but to the other cultural evolutionists whom we will meet in the immediately succeeding chapters – James George Frazer and William Robertson Smith – we need to try to understand how and why they thought they were right to think this way about aspects of human culture that do not seem to evolve at all, or at least not in ways that show sure signs of improvement. Further, it was not only naturalists and rationalists like Tylor and Frazer who were firmly convinced of this picture of broad human cultural evolution. As Tylor himself asserted before a meeting of the Royal Anthropological Society in 1888:

> the institutions of man are as distinctly stratified as the earth on which he lives. They succeed each other in series substantially uniform over the globe, independent of what seem the comparatively superficial differences of race and language, but shaped by similar human nature acting through successively changed conditions in savage, bar-baric, and civilised life. (Tylor 1888, p. 269)

Nor was the doctrine of social and cultural evolution restricted to scientists. Liberal Protestants, in particular, embraced radical progressive religious and social evolution as a "quasi-certitude," as one of their number asserted in the 1880s (Goblet d'Alviella 1885, p. 173). Have humans really evolved in terms of their kindness or trustworthiness, in their success at achieving happiness, in their native intelligence or honesty, in their range of emotional responses or abilities to sympathize with others, and so on? Similarly, is a stone axe really "better made," as Lévi-Strauss argued, than a steel axe just because the materials of which it is made are more durable (Lévi-Strauss 1968, p. 230)? Is not the design fundamentally the same in both cases, and thus are not these two kinds of axe equally "well made"? These questions are not at all easy to answer, and thankfully we do not have to solve these problems here. The point to be made is that it is not at all clear that it makes sense to speak about cultural institutions like religion, art, politics, and such as evolving at all, but Tylor and his generation had none of our scruples and doubts.

The thinkers of the late nineteenth century, however, thought they knew quite well what it meant to speak of 'progress' in religion. It meant the movement from polytheism to monotheism, from priesthood and sacrifice to prophecy and ethical purity of heart, from hieratic and hierarchic religious structures to a godly egalitarianism, from ritual to morality, from myths to beliefs, and from superstitions to rational beliefs, and so on. In short, in the nineteenth century and earlier, evolution and progress in religion meant the broad program of the Protestant Reformation. Liberal Protestants, in particular, embraced radical and progressive religious and social evolution as a "quasi-certitude" (Goblet d'Alviella 1885, p. 173). But can this viewpoint be much more than the projection of the reformation religiosity of the day? Is it really progress to diminish the role of myth, and thus imagination, from religion in order to replace it with doctrines? Is it really progress in religion to ignore the body, and thus ritual, and replace it with a series of ethical dos and don'ts? Is it really progress in religion to eliminate all sense of mystery and sublimity from religion and replace them with rational discourse? Is it really progress when monotheism enforces uniformity on religion, at the expense of the vitality and diversity of polytheism? Does not the insistence upon monotheism put monotheists into an arguably impossible position regarding the existence of evil? The one god is all good and all powerful, yet since evil exists, either the one god's power over things or his goodness (or both) are put into question. A polytheistic system would allow some gods to be good and others to be the causes of evil. What is the more highly evolved or progressive position? The answers to these queries depend on so many factors that it seems impossible to reply in the abstract. Whence then Tylor's confidence that progress could be tracked in the human mental and cultural realm?

The answer here lies not only in the optimism of the age, greatly encouraged by the great strides in technology made by the Victorians, nor even in Tylor's own Reformed-tradition religious principles and prejudices, although all these played their parts. The answer we would like to develop here gives Tylor and the other evolutionists the great benefit of the doubt and cuts loose for the moment from any of these 'external' influences bearing upon him. I believe that the very logic of evolutionary thinking itself explains much of why Tylor and others found evolutionism so compelling. Evolution was for them a "quasi-certitude," if not more, because of the power of its core insight. It made sense. Evolutionism holds that a given state of affairs – say, a piece of material technology like the DVD disk and player – required previous facilitating stages of material and social technology – say, the laser that reads the tracks on a DVD disk, electronics, a supply of electricity, the technologies of metallurgy, plastics, and so on – without which DVD technology would not have been possible. This is the wisdom captured by the Bizarro 'cave man' cartoon seen here (figure 4.2). Why is the situation absurd? Why do we laugh? We grasp the absurdity, nay impossibility, of the modern inventions mentioned in the cartoon – a blow dryer and record player – because all these examples of twentieth- and twenty-first century technology required *previous enabling steps* in order to make possible even the thought of the modern items in the cartoons. Technology does not leap from stone wheels or chunks of unworked wood to hair dryers at one go. This required a long series of steps, one laid upon the other, and mounting steadily to places others would take them. Such appliances required laying in place an entire series of such steadily facilitating steps, gradually assembled in place and in the proper order, to make it possible

Figure 4.2. Dan Piraro's 'Bizarro' strip cartoon makes sense of evolution
Source: Dan Piraro, 1995.

not only to *conceive* hair dryers, for example, but also to manufacture them. Modern sources of energy, along with electricity and metallurgy, a knowledge of basic physics, electronics, chemistry, and engineering, as well as modern monetary and financial systems and such, are among the hundreds of pieces of technology and science that had to be assembled before hair dryers and record players and all the rest could come to be. They laid the successive stages of development that culminated in the technological products that populate our world.

Now, Tylor in effect asked himself what enabling steps or stages had to be presumed in order for the mental and moral cultural things in our world to have come to be in the first place, and to have survived over the course of so many years. How did modern-day Protestant ethical and rational monotheism, for example, come to be when we know that people had been religious for ages in a riotously different series of ways? How did we get from Brixham cave's religion to the Church of England or to Tylor's own Quakerism – presuming that we do not get there by way of supernatural intervention into our world? That is the problem of religious evolution that Tylor sets for us. It is why he deserves to be taken seriously. He and other evolutionary anthropologists started with data we can all agree upon – the material data of the ancient technologies found in places like Brixham cave – and then proceed to ask us how we got from stone implements and bone tools to hair dryers, record players, and all the other products that are so characteristic of our world. In this study of how problems of religion generate theories of religion, Tylor in effect asks us how we got the religion we have today from the religion of our prehistoric ancestors, who, as we will see later, are analogous with the 'primitive' folk of our own time? Tylor seeks to put this question forward knowing full well that modern-day religious believers will not fare well. Either modern-day religious belief in one God – monotheism – will turn out to be only trivially evolved from the belief in many gods or spirits – the animism – of 'savages,' or modern-day religion will be seen as a fusty 'survival' of old, obsolete, and fundamentally ignorant ways of thinking about how to explain the world.

We Have Met the Primitives, and "They" Are "Us"

A second great jolt to European religious consciousness was now set to double the impact of the discovery of prehistoric Europe. We will recall how in the sixteenth century the first encounters between Europeans and so-called 'primitives' provoked problems of religion for pious Christians, in particular about the status of the religions of the peoples of the New World. We will also recall how those problems stimulated the early deists to imagine an ideal Natural Religion that formed a common human basis or capacity for religion. In this way, the deists were able to absorb the strange religions of the New World under the same 'umbrella' that included Christianity, Judaism, and other religions familiar to them. All the religions of the world were for them at the very least local manifestations or variants of Natural Religion. The task before the study of religion was then to mark how far or near a given historical religion was from the ideal of Natural Religion. However, Hume, Darwin, and the rise of natural history changed all this.

Just as Müller had sought, in effect, to answer Hume's challenge to provide *empirical and historical* examples of such a Natural Religion by producing a detailed picture of what was at that time regarded as the oldest of all religions – Vedic religion, Tylor gave the wheel of the dialectic another turn and, in effect, challenged Müller about the identity of the oldest and most fundamental religion. With the discoveries of human prehistory, geology, and evolutionary biology, a new developmental historical landscape, with new scientific investigative criteria, lay before anyone seeking to make claims about Natural Religion. And now with the new discoveries of ethnography, Tylor was ready to advance the case against Müller even further. From these new data and theories, Tylor felt that he had found in the belief in spirits – in animism – the very essence of religion. Here was the most ancient of religions, one that "survived" with only the most trivial of changes wrought by evolutionary development, and which had now lodged in place in modern times cloaked in the sophisticated jargon of theology. The trick, however, was to link the two sorts of inquiries so that Tylor could show that he was right about animism being the first and essential religion. This meant joining the discourse of the prehistory of the folk of Europe with the ethnographic research on contemporary 'primitives.' Tylor's way of making this all-important link lay in the proper application of developmentalist and evolutionist *theory*.

We owe this new vision of the equivalence of prehistoric folk to our 'primitive' contemporaries to the developmental thinker and geologist Charles Lyell. Although everyone in the human sciences at this time bore something of the mark of the influence of Darwin, Lyell arguably made more of a specific impact upon Tylor. Tylor's evolutionism was thus pre-Darwinian and more generic in style than anything that conformed to Darwinian orthodoxy. Tylor never applied a strict Darwinian principle such as 'survival of the fittest' to his analyses of culture, for example – even though Max Müller had done so in arguing that Indo-European languages showed how certain synonyms were "eliminated" by virtue of just such a Darwinian struggle (Leopold 1980, p. 31)! Indeed, the problem standing in the way of a Darwinian outlook for Tylor is that quite often the *unfit* survived! Tylor's 'survivals' were just this sort of useless fossil washed up on the shores of the present.

Anthropology was nonetheless for Tylor, as it was for Darwin, a branch of natural history, thus making Tylor a Darwinian in the relatively weak sense that he felt that human cultural evolution proceeded in a lawful and natural way:

> To many minds there seems something presumptuous and repulsive in the view that the history of mankind is part and parcel of the history of nature, that our thoughts, wills, and actions accord with laws as definite as those which govern the motion of waves, the combination of acids and bases, and the growth of plants and animals. (Tylor 1958, p. 2)

Adopting nature as a whole, instead of local cultures, as his strategic level of inquiry provided Tylor with a powerful comparative tool. It meant that he could aim at human species universals and pass over the endless oddities of individual cultures. Human nature was something fundamentally universal, constant, and invariant. All humans shared a common psychic unity much as they did a common physical anatomy (Stocking 1994, p. xx).

> For the present purpose it appears both possible and desirable to eliminate consider-ations of hereditary varieties or races of man, and to treat mankind as homogeneous in nature, though placed in different grades of civilization. The details of the enquiry will, I think, prove that stages of culture may be compared without taking into account how far tribes who use the same implement, follow the same custom, or believe the same myth, may differ in their bodily configuration and the colour of their skin and hair. (Tylor 1958, p. 7)

Nowhere did Tylor's commitment to the universal and constant species nature of humans have more impact than on his approach to religion. Religion for Tylor was to be studied just like any other feature of the natural world:

> To fall back once again on the analogy of natural history, the time may soon come when it will be thought as unreasonable for a scientific student of theology not to have competent acquaintance with the principles of the religions of the lower races, as for a physiologist to look with the contempt of past centuries on evidence derived from the lower forms of life, deeming the structure of mere invertebrate creatures matter un-worthy of his philosophic study. (Tylor 1958, p. 24)

Implied in this association of natural history and religion was the further association, owed to Lyell, of the study of European prehistory with the results of anthropological fieldwork among 'the primitive.' Notably, Tylor faithfully followed a program of identi-fying the prehistoric Europeans with the 'primitives' of today, anticipating the arguments of Darwin's *The Descent of Man* (1871).

> The main conclusion arrived at in this work, namely, that man is descended from some lowly organised form, will, I regret to think, be highly distasteful to many. But there can hardly be a doubt that we are descended from barbarians. The astonishment which I felt on first seeing a party of Fuegians on a wild and broken shore will never be forgotten by

me, for the reflection at once rushed into my mind – such were our ancestors. (Darwin 1970, p. 276)

And so it was that Tylor thought he was right to identify the religion of the folk of prehistoric Europe with the religion he met on the ethnographic field: both were examples of 'primitive' religion, in the loose Darwinian sense of the term, as the first and least developed of the human species (Stocking 1994, p. xvi). Without 'their' efforts in the dim past of prehistory, 'we' could not have mounted the heights of progress that Tylor felt the nineteenth century had achieved – even if in religious terms this progress would be relatively slight. 'They' provided the enabling first stages of animism upon which all later developmental steps of human religious progress were painfully constructed over many eons. By thus bringing religion into the sphere of disciplines such as natural history, Tylor hoped to revolutionize the religious world of his day.

From the point of view of providing a tool for explaining religion, Tylor's theoretical approach had manifest obvious and (for religious believers) ominous power. With the merger of the study of prehistoric societies with those encountered on the ethnographic field, both could be explained at one go, without the bothersome details of local histories. Both were for Tylor (and Darwin) "primitives" or "savages" in the identical sense of occupying a common place on the trajectory of human cultural evolution. Tylor believed that the prehistoric, proto-European folk whose remains we find in places like Brixham cave are at an equivalent level of species maturity as the modern-day primitive 'other' we meet on the ethnographic field, and close as well to the peasant folk of the Europe of Tylor's day. As Tylor colorfully put it, "the European may find among the Greenlanders or Maoris many a trait for reconstructing the picture of his own primitive ancestors" (Tylor 1958, p. 21). They can be compared, because they are comparable sorts of people in terms of their technologies, social patterns, and, most pointedly, their religion.

Thus, we would expect to find many parallel religious beliefs and practices between these far-flung folk and ourselves. We should be able to fill in details missing from one set of folk by matching them with the other. If we find a belief in many spirits in 'primitive' societies, we can expect to find (slightly) 'higher' forms of such beliefs – monotheism – in more 'advanced' societies. If we find human sacrifice in today's ethnographic contexts, we would do well to look for it in the historic domain: if today's Yanomami tribal folk do human sacrifice, we might expect those proto-Europeans inhabiting the caves at Lascaux tens of thousands of years ago to have done the same. The inferences flow in the opposite direction as well – from what the Paleolithic folk did, such as fashioning stone axes, to what we might expect among the Yanomami in terms of their technology of axe-making. Whether it be ultimately valid or not, such examples show how powerful Tylor's evolutionist style of comparison could be. In *Anahuac*, Tylor remarks on the similarities of stone axes:

> The family-likeness that exists among the stone tools and weapons found in so many parts of the world is very remarkable. The flint-arrows of North America, such as Mr. Long-fellow's arrow maker used to work at in the land of the Dacotahs, and which, in the wild northern states of Mexico, the Apaches and Comanches use to this day, might be easily mistaken for the weapons of our British ancestors, dug up on the banks of the Thames.

With diffusionists (like Müller, no doubt) in mind, Tylor is also quick to head off any explanation of the similarities between cultural traits that might be attributable to cultural borrowing or transfer:

> The wonderful similarity of character among the stone weapons found in different parts of the world has often been used by ethnologists as a means of supporting the theory that this and other arts were carried over the world by tribes migrating from one common centre of creation of the human species. The argument has not much weight, and a larger view of the subject quite supersedes it. (Tylor 1861, pp. 101, 102)

With this encompassing vision, Tylor moved ahead confidently to become the English-speaking world's leading proponent of "anthropology" – a universal science of humanity, a science that encompassed all of human history from its 'rudest' beginnings to the modern day.

Müller argued that the study of religion must be historical (chiefly philological), but unlike Tylor, Müller saw religion on the whole as being in a state of degeneration. Every religion of which we have any direct evidence signaled to Müller that it was somehow defective, showing a kind of degeneration from a better state, after a kind of 'Fall.' Thus, to study religion by comparison with Tylor's present-day or past 'savages' was to err, because one was trying to understand one degenerate form of religion by comparison with another. Such comparisons were likely to be unfruitful because they had little 'traction,' so to speak. That is to say, they did not supply us with any perspective, since they consisted of comparisons with essentially the same kinds of thing.

The problem for the student of religion was both to chart and explain why and how things had declined. This presumption of decline, rather than development, in turn called for comparison between later degenerate forms with earlier lofty forms of religion. Müller felt that historical comparison was best undertaken within the context of 'developed' (rather than 'savage' or 'primitive') societies. In many ways, he translated the spirit and some of the techniques of the new critical attitude to the Bible to his own studies of Vedic religion and the religions of ancient India. What Max Müller was doing was thus one thing: a "science of religion," to employ his own language; Tylor, on the other hand, in his ambitions to found a "Science of Man," was certainly doing 'anthropology of religion.' His not-so-secret desire "all theologians to expose," thus shaped his research program for religion in ways which would present even modern-day religion as a 'survival' of long-since outmoded ways of thinking, or at the very best, a trivial development of 'savage' animistic beliefs. In these respects, then, the two men could not have differed more in their approaches to the problems of religion that their age threw before them.

Notes

1. Some of the features of Müller's approach to the study of religion that have survived among present-day naturalistic Religious Studies are his focus on the rigorous study of languages, beliefs, and myth, his thoroughgoing comparativism, his typologizing of religions – in the form of present-day and classical 'phenomenology of religion,' his openness to theorizing religion and myth as a central feature of the non-empirical side the study of religion. With these, present-day Religious Studies has also incorporated much of the anthropological tradition of Tylor and his later generations in the study of customs, institutions, rituals, and material culture.
2. See in particular Tylor's dismissal of Müller's conception of Aryan as involved with his theological tendencies: "If we could admit Prof. Müller's starting-point of theology in a

state like that of the Aryans of the Veda, his consequence would no doubt follow" (Tylor 1880, pp. 456–7). As Stocking shows, this dismissal of Müller's theorizing as fundamentally "theological" was even more forcefully put forth by Herbert Spencer (Stocking 1987, p. 308).

References

Bataille, G. 1955. *Lascaux*. Lausanne: Skira.

Darwin, C. 1970. The Descent of Man. In *Darwin: A Norton Critical Reader*, ed. P. Appleman. New York City: W. W. Norton.

Durkheim, É. 1995. *The Elementary Forms of the Religious Life*, trans. K. E. Fields. New York: Free Press.

Frankenberry, N. K., ed. 2002. *Radical Interpretation in Religion*. Cambridge: Cambridge University Press.

Goblet d'Alviella, C. E. 1885. Maurice Vernes et la methode comparative. In *Revue de l'histoire des religions* 12.

Gruber, J. W. 1965. Brixham Cave and the Antiquity of Man. In *Context and Meaning in Cultural Anthropology*, ed. M. E. Spiro. New York City: Free Press.

Leopold, J. 1980. *Culture in Comparative and Evolutionary Perspective: E. B. Tylor and the Making of Primitive Culture*. Berlin: Dietrich Reimer Verlag.

Lévi-Strauss, C. 1966. *The Savage Mind*. London: Weidenfeld and Nicolson.

——— . 1968. The Structural Study of Myth. In *Structural Anthropology*, vol. I. London: Allen Lane.

——— . 1976. Race and History. In *Structural Anthropology*, vol. II. New York: Basic Books.

Lyell, C. 1863. *The Geological Evidence of the Antiquity of Man*. London: John Murray.

Marett, R. R. 1914. *The Threshold of Religion*. New York: Macmillan.

——— . 1936. *Tylor*. London: Chapman and Hall.

McCutcheon, R. T. 2001. *Critics Not Caretakers: Redescribing the Public Study of Religion*. Albany, NY: SUNY Press.

Müller, F. M. 1886. On Manners and Customs. In *Chips from a German Workshop*, vol. 2. London: Longmans, Green, and Co.

——— . 1891. *Physical Religion*. New York: Longmans, Green, and Co.

——— . 1892. *Natural Religion*. London: Longmans, Green, and Co.

Oldham, T. 1989. *The Complete Caves of Devon*. England: T. Oldham.

Réville, A. 1883. *Les religions des peuples non-civilisés*. Paris: Fischbacher.

Stocking, G. W. 1987. *Victorian Anthropology*. New York: Free Press.

——— . 1994. Introduction. In *The Collected Works of Edward Burnett Tylor: Anahuac: Or Mexico and the Mexicans, Ancient and Modern*, vol. 1, ed. G. W. Stocking. London: Routledge/Thoemmes Press.

——— . 2001a. Books Unwritten, Turning Points Unmarked: Notes for an Anti-History of Anthropology. In *Delimiting Anthropology*, ed. G. W. Stocking. Madison: University of Wisconsin Press.

——— . 2001b. Edward Burnett Tylor and the Mission of Primitive Man. In *Delimiting Anthropology*, ed. G. W. Stocking. Madison: University of Wisconsin Press.

Strenski, I. 1985. Comparative Study of Religions: A Theological Necessity. *Christian Century*, Feb. 6–13, pp. 126–9.

——— . 1996a. Misreading Max Müller. *Method and Theory in the Study of Religion* 8, pp. 291–6.

——— . 1996b. The Rise of Ritual and the Hegemony of Myth: Sylvain Lévi, the Durkheimians and Max Müller. In *Myth and Method*, eds. W. Doniger & L. Patton. Charlottesville, VA: University of Virginia Press.

Tylor, E. B. 1861. *Anahuac: Or Mexico and the Mexicans, Ancient and Modern*. London: Reader and Dyer.

—— . 1866a. On the Origin of Language. *Fortnightly Review* 4, pp. 544–59.

—— . 1866b. The Religion of Savages. *Fortnightly Review* 6, pp. 71–86.

—— . 1873. *Religion in Primitive Culture*. New York City: Harper.

—— . 1880. The President's Address. *Journal of the Anthropological Institute* 9, pp. 443–58.

—— . 1881. *Anthropology*. Ann Arbor: University of Michigan Press.

—— . 1888. On a Method of Investigating the Development of Institutions. *Journal of the Anthropological Institute* 18, pp. 245–72.

—— . 1958. *Primitive Culture*. 2 vols. New York: Harper and Row.

Evolution in the Religion of the Bible: William Robertson Smith

5

Dear, dear! So Moses did not write the books of Moses! (As if anybody ever believed he did.) If you republish, read (unless you have read) Spinoza, who proves the late date philologically.

–Letter of Sir Richard Burton to William Robertson Smith, 1880
(Black & Chrystal 1912b, pp. 406–7)

The Religion of the Bible and Its Problems

A consistent theme in this book has been that much of the progress in the study of religion has been due to questions about religion arising in connection with the study of the Bible. For this reason I have tried to throw relatively more light on thinkers like Spinoza, F. C. Baur, D. F. Strauss, Ernest Renan, Julius Wellhausen, and their present-day successors than is usually done in most attempts to comprehend the rise of religious studies. Of course, once we give it a moment's thought, the connection between biblical studies and religious studies makes perfect intuitive sense. After all, the Bible is the focus of so much passionate religiosity in the West that attitudes to it must make a difference to the way religion would be studied. Recently, we have begun to see a future for academic religious studies in the Muslim world, spurred on by critical study of the Koran, that promises to provoke at least as much religious problematizing turmoil as it has over the past two centuries in the West. A simple search on the internet for Muslim critics of the Koran, such as "Christoph Luxenberg" (pseudonym), turns up massive results. As *New York Times* columnist Nicholas D. Kristof recently wrote about Luxenberg and the entire movement of what we might call 'Higher Criticism' of the Koran: "But now the same tools that historians, linguists and archaeologists have applied to the Bible for about 150 years are beginning to be applied to the Koran. The results are explosive" (Kristof 2004, p. A23).

Despite the importance of the Bible for religion in the West itself, scholars in the different camps of biblical studies and 'religious studies,' respectively, have for too long behaved as strangers to one another. Part of the new vision this book has sought to promote is about reducing the mutual ignorance that biblical scholars and students of religion have had about each other. Indeed, I want to do my bit to end it by showing how fruitful the 'cross-pollination' between these two flowering fields within general religious studies has been. Thus, after having just seen how the example of scientific study of sacred texts practiced by the Higher Criticism formed the mind of a comparativist like Max Müller in chapter 3, and after having seen how the same period saw the beginnings of anthropology of religion with the work of Edward Burnett Tylor in chapter 4, I want to turn my attention to the critical study of the Bible as it was undertaken in light of the efforts of *both* Müller and Tylor taken together. The comparative and textual-critical work of Müller and the ethnographic and evolutionary thinking of Tylor merge in the remarkable and influential work of William Robertson Smith. He was "the first person in Britain to apply the comparative evolutionary anthropological approach to the study of an entire family of religions, the Semitic" (Ackerman 1987, p. 58).

Hailed (and cursed) in his own time for this disturbing approach to the study of biblical religion, Robertson Smith soon became a world-famous (or infamous) figure in the study of religion as a whole. Robertson Smith's own junior colleague at Cambridge, Sir James Frazer, nicely sums up Smith's contribution to the naturalistic study of religion that has become fundamental to modern religious studies.

> The idea of studying the religions of the world not dogmatically, but historically – in other words, not as systems of truth or falsehood to be demonstrated or refuted, but as phenomena of consciousness to be studied like any other aspect of human nature – is one which hardly seems to have suggested itself before the 19th century. (Frazer 1927, pp. 281 ff.)

In 1895, for example, within a year after its first publication, Smith's classic work, *Lectures on the Religion of the Semites*, was favorably reviewed in *The New World*, an important journal in general religious studies published out of Harvard University. The American reviewer reported that Smith's lectures "were received with marked consideration by all persons interested in Semitic and general religious study." Further, not only were Smith's theoretical innovations exciting, but the book itself was nothing short of "revolutionary in its teaching" (Toy 1895, p. 389).

Some of the problems concerning biblical religion tackled by Robertson Smith or inspired by his work would be the following. How, in its own terms, does the religion depicted in the Bible change? Granted some changes are putative results of divine decree. But does all of it follow this principle? Does the Bible explain why, for example, temple worship or an institutionalized priesthood arise? Does it change according to any regular principles that we might discover, such as evolution or degeneration? Does biblical religion change in terms of its own internal dynamic, or does it change in terms of its relation to other cultural systems or religions – say, by imitation or direct opposition? How do biblical religion's ideas and practice of sacrifice bear on the conception of the nature of a deity? Just why is sacrifice offered to the deity? Does sacrifice sustain the deity? If it sustains the deity, in what sense is the deity superior to its human devotees? Why does biblical religion exclude women from sacrifice? Does biblical religion, when it is featuring intense ritual life, tend to be more hierarchical, while it is more likely to be egalitarian when it eschews ritual?

The case of Robertson Smith shows in particular how attempts to deal with problems arising in the study of the Bible have made significant contributions to the overall study of the religion of the Bible. This happened in two steps. First, Robertson Smith's new contributions to biblical studies were in part made possible because they attempted to integrate the new ethnographic insights and fieldwork research practices urged by John F. McLennan and E. B. Tylor. McLennan in particular argued that the study of modern-day 'primitives' could illuminate ancient historical sources. Thus, as Smith noted in a review of McLennan's discussions of the worship of plants and animals, otherwise known as 'totemism,' "the prevalence of the totem system in modern savage races over a very large part of the globe, opens up a line of inquiry of the first importance, and suggests points of view for the study of ancient religions" (Robertson Smith 1912a, p. 456). Thus, while the previous centuries saw the rise of Higher Criticism of the Bible based largely in the sciences of history and philology, thanks to the influence of McLennan, Tylor, and other partisans of ethnographic sciences, Robertson Smith leveled new challenges at the status of the biblical narrative. For Robertson Smith, the Bible was no longer only to be seen as literature – although he was a master linguist and philologist – but as containing data about the religious *life* of biblical folk, and a 'life' that could be made more understandable by ethnographic fieldwork. Instead of just studying the Bible, we could say that Robertson Smith studied the *religion of the Bible*. An appendix listing Robertson Smith's citations of biblical sources shows that he was as much a master of the text as any student of the literature of the Bible. I count approximately 700 biblical entries for a book of about 400 total pages. Yet what makes him special is that he went well beyond the study of texts alone and engaged the religious life of biblical times – its rituals, customs, myths, social institutions, and such.

In Robertson Smith's hands, as well, the Bible and its religion became an episode in the *general history of religion*, and not just a document reflecting a particular people and the local peculiarities of their religion (Robertson Smith 1912c, pp. 229–33). Thanks to the same influences that inspired the comparative study of religions as practiced by Max Müller, Robertson Smith carried on his researches into biblical religion in a spirit formed by the realization that, as Müller said, "one who knows only one religion understands none." In order to understand any one religion, we need to see it in the comparative context of other religions – within the context of other members of its class of scientific objects. In this, Robertson Smith should rightly remind us of Müller, since both began as students of comparative linguistics – Robertson Smith working in the Semitic languages and Müller of course in Indo-European – then with both moving in their own ways to extend the lessons learned in the comparative study of language to the comparative study of religion.

In a way, Smith had the potential to be even more influential upon Western religious consciousness than Müller, because he started his general study of religion with the more familiar subject of the Bible (Bediako 1995). His classic, *Lectures on the Religion of the Semites*, goes beyond just the study of biblical texts, such as we have seen in our discussion of biblical criticism. Robertson Smith studies the Bible for the sake of studying the *religion of the Bible* or prebiblical times. He is only remotely interested, for example, in the internal or external discrepancies that troubled the first generation of biblical critics. His interest in miracles is slight, if not non-existent. Instead, Robertson Smith seeks to know what the religion of the Bible was at various stages of the development of religion among the Israelite community, all the while made intelligible by comparing it and its practices to other known religions. What was the original meaning of critical aspects of the lived religion of the Bible, such as priesthood, prophecy, sacrifice, ritual, purity, the sacred, totemism, and other religious institutions? Robertson Smith greatly enriched the study of religion at large by marrying critical study of the biblical text with the comparative study of the content of the religion we find there in the text.

What also shows the greatness of Robertson Smith is the continuing appeal of his style of inquiry even into our own times. Following in his spirit, modern anthropologists like

Mary Douglas have demonstrated how fruitful Robertson Smith's marriage of biblical studies, ethnography, and comparative study of religions has been. In her classic, *Purity and Danger*, Douglas shows how the sometimes opaque features of biblical *religion* – proscriptions against eating certain animals, for example, can inform our general understanding of religion – can be understood in terms of more general features of religious life. She also shows to biblical scholars how *problematizing* aspects of biblical religion can be made possible by comparative analysis with other religions (Douglas 1970). Her investigations into the intricacies of avoidance of various animals aim at bottom to show how these apparently trivial proscriptions reveal something of the religious vision of the Hebrew Bible, and by analogy with it to religious practices of the kinds of societies studied by anthropologists, such as taboos. Douglas has also applied herself to following up her work on purity and danger with an extensive study of the *Book of Numbers* (Douglas 1993). Robertson Smith therefore showed us how by starting from the study of biblical religion, we can go on to problematize religion in general, and thus how to devise and put questions that raise fundamental issues about the nature of religion. Who then was this man, what does he have to say about how we should study religion, and why did he think he was right in arguing as he did?

The Great Renown and Short Heretical Life of William Robertson Smith

Robertson Smith (1846–94) was born into a religiously conservative clerical family of the Scottish Free Church. A precocious young man, he began his university education at 15 in Aberdeen, where he studied classical languages and theology, but also did rigorous work in the natural sciences and mathematics. Early in his career, from 1869 to 1873, Robertson Smith even published a series of technical academic papers dealing with such rarified issues as theory of geometry, fluxional calculus, electricity, and the metaphysics of the sciences (Black & Chrystal 1912a, p. xi). As Robertson Smith matured, he shifted his academic venue to Edinburgh and focused increasingly on biblical studies and theology, the interests that would become dominant in his intellectual life.

Despite his strict Calvinist upbringing, Robertson Smith was attracted to the liberal theological scene then in vogue in Germany, and especially to the Higher Criticism of the Bible, then represented by Julius Wellhausen (1844–1918) and Paul Lagarde (1827–91). It is worth recalling that this liberal theological and Higher Critical world was, by the way, the same German intellectual ferment out of which Max Müller had emerged at roughly the same time. Although Müller and Robertson Smith differed in many ways, their connections with that liberal German religious world were for them a constant liability for careers in contexts as theologically different as Anglican Oxford and Calvinist Scotland. In both cases, the dominant biblical literalism of the leadership of these institutions presented a forbidding opposition to anyone bold enough to advance the cause of the Higher Criticism of the Bible.

After several shorter visits to Germany, in 1869 Robertson Smith decided to stay on in Germany to study Arabic, and later to embark on advanced biblical studies with Wellhausen and Lagarde. Wellhausen and Robertson Smith became lifelong friends, as did Robertson Smith and the chief liberal theologian of his day, the Lutheran Albrecht Ritschl. Despite the suspicions that these relationships and Robertson Smith's orientation to German theology created among the theological conservatives in Scotland, he overcame local suspicions – at least at first. In 1870, he took ordination in the Free Church and immediately won appointment as Professor of Hebrew and Old Testament at the Free Church College in Edinburgh.

Robertson Smith's troubles began when he was attacked for teaching the critical approach to the Bible that he learned from Wellhausen, what one of Smith's biographers, T. O. Beidelman, called a "freer, more historically accurate interpretation of the Bible" (Beidelman 1974, p. 7). In his heart, Robertson Smith never believed that this new freedom was inconsistent with his profound religious faith, and even less that he was the heretic he would be accused of being. Thus, in 1870, he wrote passionately in defense of Higher Criticism of the Bible from a *strictly religious point of view*, much as Max Müller had spoken for the scholarly study of the world's religion from a source deep in his own Christian heart:

> The higher criticism does not mean negative criticism. It means the fair and honest looking at the Bible as a historical record, and the effort everywhere to reach the real meaning and historical setting, Scripture records as a whole: and to do this we must apply the same principle that the Reformation applied to detailed criticism. We must let the Bible speak for itself. Our notions of the origin, the purpose, the character of the Scripture books must be drawn, not from vain traditions, but from a historical study of the books themselves. This process can be dangerous to faith only when it is begun without faith – when we forget that the Bible history is no profane history, but the story of God's saving self-manifestation. (Robertson Smith 1912c, p. 233)

Like Max Müller again, Robertson Smith pursued his scientific studies of the Bible and biblical religion motivated by a progressive religious faith. He never felt that this optimistic faith was fatally threatened by the tremendous growth in human knowledge that typified the age in which they both lived and flourished. So, accordingly, he went forth full-tilt following the call of his divinely inspired curiosity and quest for knowledge. The more he learned about the world, the closer he believed he came to God.

Nevertheless, despite Robertson Smith's sincere and courageous religious faith, a great theological battle ensued over Smith's teaching of Higher Criticism of the Bible. When he was branded as a heretic by his enemies, the charges tore at his pious heart. As a firm and constant believer in the ultimate divine inspiration of the Bible, Smith intended to pursue historical scholarship in order to get to the deeper spiritual, "inner" core of revelation that he felt was hidden beneath the "outer" layers of scribal composition, redaction, and editing added over the centuries (Robertson Smith 1912c, p. 224). The Reformation fathers knew how to read the Bible maturely, Smith claims. They sought "the *real meaning* of every heart-spoken word." A mature reader "pierces through the expression and sees in the words this and this alone." Mature readers grasp "the personality of God's word," because the Bible is "the direct personal message of God's love to me" (Robertson Smith 1912c, pp. 225–6). It is small wonder Robertson Smith found the charges of heresy both deeply galling and dispiriting.

Inspiring as his theological language was, it would not deter the conservative opponents of Robertson Smith from seeking to destroy him professionally. By 1876, the church fathers successfully brought Smith to trial for heresy. He was accused of denying the divine inspiration of the Hebrew Bible, in particular; for example, of denying that Moses had written the book of Deuteronomy, that the sacred authors were free from all error in terms of factual statements, or that no part of the Bible was fiction, such as the love poem, the Song of Solomon. Smith was cleared of all charges except his rejection of Mosaic authorship of the book of Deuteronomy. Convicted in 1881, he was dismissed from his professorship at the Free Church College in Edinburgh.

Robertson Smith of Arabia

While waiting for the verdict of the church assembly over the winter of 1879–80, Smith spent six months or so in Egypt, Libya, Palestine, Syria, and Arabia. In the Libyan desert, he reports traveling for 20 hours by camel and spending two nights with the local Bedouins (Black & Chrystal 1912b, p. 333). He also kept company with the famous explorer and 'orientalist,' Sir Richard Burton. In Arabia, he visited various local religious and political leaders. It was during this visit to Arabia that Robertson Smith moved about the peninsula on an expedition into what was, for his orientalist mind, a secret world of alluring exotica. While in Arabia, Smith assumed the name Abdullah Effendi, and traveled in the region near Mecca by permission of its emir. Donning local garb at the "serious" urgings of his Arab guides, but also in order "to avoid intrusive curiosity," Smith successfully disguised himself for the duration of his visit (Robertson Smith 1880, p. 497). (See figure 5.1.)

Robertson Smith's rather dry descriptive account of his travels in the Hejaz is recorded in his long essay, "A Journey in the Hejaz." The essay is a curious mixture of dull, matter-of-fact reporting sprinkled with gratuitous opinions about Islam and Arab culture. For us,

Figure 5.1. William Robertson Smith in disguise as Abdullah Effendi, 1880

Source: J. S. Black and G. Chrystal, *The Life of William Robertson Smith* (London: Adam and Charles Black, 1912), facing p. 336.

this essay has value – say, in the same way Max Müller's German romanticism did – in what it says about the religious and cultural prejudices that shaped Robertson Smith's views on religion. In the course of his report, Smith routinely reveals the evolutionist notions that cast him and his European culture as 'developed' while the Semites are not. Thus, Smith opines, for example, that Arabs *as well as Hebrews* are of the "sensuous Oriental nature." People like this, says Smith, are somewhat pitiful in that they cannot help but respond

> to...physical stimulus with a readiness foreign to our more sluggish temperament; to the Arab it is an excitement and a delight of the highest order merely to have flesh to eat. From the earliest times, therefore, the religious gladness of the Semites tended to assume an orgiastic character and become a sort of intoxication of the senses, in which anxiety and sorrow were drowned for the moment. (Robertson Smith 1923, p. 261)

In the same vein, Smith continues to betray the mind-set of late nineteenth-century European high culture when he argues, for instance, that Arabs are insensitive to the beauties of the natural landscapes. He, on the other hand, describes these landscapes in the most tedious detail, implying that such sensibilities were signs of cultural refinement – much as Max Müller's paean to the glories of the English Lake District were intended by that German Romantic to suggest (Robertson Smith 1880, p. 499). Confident, then, in his lofty position atop the ladder of human development, like Tylor in relation to Mexican Catholics, Robertson Smith often looked down with contempt on cultures and religions that he perceived as differing significantly from his own. Smith's remarks on Catholicism and rabbinic Judaism are other particularly noteworthy examples of this, as we will see.

Difficult as it may be to abide Robertson Smith's biases, we must not be summary in rejecting what he has to say about religion. He was very important in stimulating interest in tribal religion with his serious, first-hand ethnographic field observations of the religious and social lives of the tribal peoples of Arabia. His book, *Kinship and Marriage in Early Arabia*, as well as articles such as "Animal Worship and Animal Tribes among the Arabs and in the Old Testament" (1880), are cases in point (Robertson Smith 1885; 1912a). By contrast, the so-called father of 'anthropology,' Edward Burnett Tylor never equaled the serious fieldwork of the 'biblical scholar' (*sic*) Robertson Smith! In his ethnographic work, Robertson Smith relied heavily on the work of John F. McLennan (1827–81), a pioneer in the study of the development of systems of marriage, kinship, and religion, especially animal worship, or what became known as 'totemism.' Robertson Smith also owes a great deal to McLennan for his sense of what evolution itself might be like in terms of the development and growth of *cultural* realities. For Robertson Smith, the developmental stages by which marriage had grown were a certainty, since they were "now known, mainly through the researches of McLennan" (Robertson Smith 1880, p. 578).

With the practical ethnographic model of a McLennan, plus his evolutionary outlook in hand, and the good fortune of gaining access to the kingdom of Arabia, Robertson Smith was able to make real headway. Newly informed by McLennan's theoretical perspectives, he traveled about freely and widely, gathering data and impressions that would inform these and subsequent works on religion, such as his writings on sacrifice, animal worship, kinship, and totemism. While this six-month sojourn in the Middle

Eastern Muslim world does not seem like much by today's standards, it was as close to fieldwork as Smith would get. By the standards of Smith's own time, his 'fieldwork' experience was respectable, since it lasted half again as long as the 'anthropologist' Edward Burnett Tylor's four-month stay in Mexico. Moreover, what Smith wrote was far more intensely attentive to detail than most of Tylor's accounts of Mexican culture.

Robertson Smith's 'Arabian Revolution' in the Study of Religion

In terms of the study of religion, Smith's experiences among the nomadic tribes in Arabia convinced him of an idea that would revolutionize the study of the religion of the Bible, and take him far beyond even what ordinary historians of religion were likely to assume. He would use fieldwork and history in a unique way to amplify each other's results! In particular, he dared to use his fieldwork in contemporary Arabia as an interpretive 'key' for unlocking some of the mysteries of the Hebrew Bible.

Robertson Smith's revolution proceeded in two steps. First, like the good historian he was, he was committed to the view that to understand the present, we must understand the past. Thus, behind "positive religions" like Judaism, Christianity, and Islam,

> lies the old unconscious religious tradition, the body of religious usage and belief which...formed part of that inheritance from the past into which successive generations of the Semitic race grew up as it were instinctively, taking it as a matter of course that they should believe and act as their fathers had done before them.

This meant that far from being historically unique and unprecedented, the religion of the Bible owed much to its pagan forebears, even though the Bible never admits it. Historical events abhor a vacuum, and always rest on the stages in history that enabled them to come forth.

> The positive Semitic religions had to establish themselves on ground already occupied by these older beliefs and usages;...No positive religion that has moved men has been able to start with a *tabula rasa*, and express itself as if religion were beginning for the first time; in form, if not in substance, the new system must be in contact all along the line with the older ideas it finds in possession. A new scheme can find a hearing only by appealing to religious instincts and susceptibilities that already exist in its audience, and it cannot reach these without taking account of the traditional forms in which all religious feeling is embodied. (Robertson Smith 1923, pp. 1–2)

But this straightforward historical approach to biblical religions was only the first dramatic jolt Robertson Smith would give the religious conservatives of his day.

Robertson Smith also believed that his ethnographic observations in Arabia were another way to do *history*! In a way this is only explicable by his embracing of ideas of evolution that he shared to some degree with Tylor and other developmental thinkers such as McLennan. For him, long since disappeared historical beings could, as it were, be *directly observed* in the present, because they were living 'survivals' of things and institutions that evolutionists like him 'knew' them to be – not the fossils that Tylor's 'survivals' were (Bediako 1995, p. 121). "The religion of heathen Arabia...displays an extremely primitive type, corresponding to the primitive and unchanging character of nomadic life," Smith tells us (Robertson Smith 1923, p. 14).

Despite the brevity of Robertson Smith's stay in Muslim lands, his experience of Arabian nomadic folk convinced him that what he indeed saw there with his own eyes were living 'survivals' of the kind of religion practiced by the Hebrews in the days of their desert wanderings thousands of years earlier! The nomadic tribal Arab peoples and the ancient Hebrews, while differing in various respects, were actual kin!

> I start from Arabia, because the facts referring to that country belong to a more primitive state of society than existed in Israel at the time when the Old Testament was written, and because in Arabia before Islam we find a condition of pure polytheism. (Robertson Smith 1912a, p. 459)

A stunning realization this, since it reinforced Robertson Smith's belief that he could better understand ancient Jewish religion from the Higher Criticism of biblical *texts*, but in a real sense, now realized in his fieldwork, where he could actually *observe* something very close to ancient Hebrew religion being lived in 'surviving' form among the nomadic tribes of Arabia at the end of the nineteenth century. "The defects of historical tradition must therefore be supplied by observation" (Robertson Smith 1923, p. 6). Evolutionary theory and ethnographic observation had fitted Robertson Smith out with a kind of 'time machine' for traveling far back into remote, prehistoric times in order to encounter face-to-face the religious life of the people who wrote the Bible itself – the ancient Hebrews!

With this vision of how the quest for the roots of Jewish, and thus Christian, religion could successfully be realized, Robertson Smith plunged into the Arabian religious world. From 1880 onward, he published on kinship, marriage, sacrifice, totemism, and other subjects, using his Arabian experience as a major database. This experience and his subsequent writing about Arab society set the stage for his great work, *Lectures on the Religion of the Semites* (1889) (Sharpe 1986, p. 78; Robertson Smith 1880, 1885, 1923). Here, then, is where the marriage between Robertson Smith's training in Higher Criticism of biblical texts and Tylorian evolutionary anthropology would take place. And here, therefore, is where Robertson Smith's wholly new way of aiding interpretation of the Bible and religion at large would come into its own as well. Recognizing the radical nature of Smith's work, one of his representatives in France referred to Smith as "the author of a veritable revolution in the study of religion" (Reinach 1922, p. 104). The upshot of Robertson Smith's revolution, as reported in James Frazer's obituary of Smith, was nothing less than to "first to show ... [that mystical or sacramental sacrifices] are not confined to Christianity, but are common to the heathen and even savage religions ... The discovery was Robertson Smith's, and it is of capital importance for the history of religion" (Frazer 1927, p. 288).

Upon returning in 1881 from his Middle Eastern travels to find himself dispossessed of his teaching position, Robertson Smith was fortunate enough rapidly to regain employment when invited to serve first as co-editor and principal contributor to the ninth edition of the prestigious *Encyclopedia Britannica*, then subsequently as its editor-in-chief. In that influential position, Smith was able to maintain and expand his contacts in the academic world, and eventually move on to a professorship in Arabic at Cambridge a mere two years later in 1883. As the *Britannica*'s editor-in-chief, Smith enlisted distinguished Continental authors to write for the encyclopedia, but he also 'discovered' and thus patronized such future luminaries in the study of religion as James Frazer. In the next chapter, we will see how Frazer, then a classicist at Cambridge, continued many of the efforts that Robertson Smith had begun, especially the attempt to interpret Christianity and other modern religions in terms of their supposed 'primitive' roots. Smith assigned Frazer the key articles in the *Britannica* on totemism and taboo.

Robertson Smith and Higher Criticism: Wellhausen, Comparison, and Context

Much of what made Robertson Smith's revolution in the study of biblical religion heretical in the eyes of the religious conservatives of his day can be traced to at least two key ideas of Julius Wellhausen, Robertson Smith's German mentor in the Higher Criticism of the Bible. Wellhausen taught that religions should never be approached in splendid isolation – as unique and unparalleled in all respects, only to be studied in and for themselves. Instead, a religion should be studied as belonging in significant ways to its concrete, cultural, and social human contexts. The Germans called this religion's *Sitz im Leben*. Frazer recognized that this meant for Robertson Smith that religion was for him, as it was for Wellhausen, "largely modified and determined by physical surroundings, material culture, manner of life, social and political organization, and relations with neighboring peoples" (Frazer 1927, p. 286). In the opening pages of his classic work on ancient Hebrew religion, *Lectures on the Religion of the Semites*, Robertson Smith testifies to Wellhausen's vision of the larger, 'situated' Semitic nature of ancient Hebrew religion:

> You observe that in this argument I take it for granted that, when we go back to the most ancient religious conceptions and usages of the Hebrews, we shall find them to be the common property of kindred peoples, and not the exclusive possession of the tribes of Israel. The proof that this is so . . . will hardly be denied by anyone who has read the Bible with care. In the history of old Israel before the captivity, nothing comes out more clearly than that the mass of the people found the greatest difficulty in keeping their national religion distinct from that of the surrounding nations . . . The national basis of Israel's worship was very clearly akin to that of the neighbouring cults. (Robertson Smith 1923, pp. 3–4)

To understand the religion of ancient Israel, on this view of Wellhausen's, then, demanded that Smith consider the *situation* of Israel – at a particular period in its history (exilic, pre-, or post-exilic?), in terms of how it achieved its livelihood (pastoral, agricultural?), in terms of how it organized its overall political life (kingdom, republic, tribes?), and so on. Robertson Smith did just that. For Wellhausen, history and concrete environments all had to be considered if we were rightly to interpret the words of biblical times, and thus be true to what sacred scripture taught. Unless we let the Bible speak in its own idiom, we risk projecting the prejudices of our own time and place and reading scripture through our own eyes only, and thus not really attending to the word of God.

Implicitly Wellhausen's approach encouraged those, like Robertson Smith, who felt that religions should be studied *comparatively* – although for Wellhausen this meant the narrow comparative context of ancient Israel. While Wellhausen does not consider comparing the religion of Israel with the religions of the Muslims, ancient Romans, and Greeks, as well as small-scale societies in Polynesia and North America, as Robertson

Smith did, his approach opens the way for an expansion of the context of proper comparison later exploited by Robertson Smith. If this more focused approach to comparison reminds us of Wellhausen's fellow German religious liberal, Max Müller, it is because they both emerged from a common philosophical background that insisted that all aspects of culture, religion included, should be studied *comparatively* – at least within a common cultural area. Robertson Smith adopted the same position, but took it to higher levels of generality, making him one of the great students of the comparative study of religions. The Hebrews belonged "to the whole circle of nations of which they formed a part" (Robertson Smith 1923, p. 3). James Frazer noted this comparative quality in Smith's approach to religion, and celebrated it accordingly:

> Now, when . . . we examine side-by-side the religions of different races and ages, we find that, while they differ from each other in many particulars, the resemblances between them are numerous and fundamental, and that they mutually illustrate and explain each other, the distinctly stated faith and circumstantial ritual of one race often clearing up ambiguities in the faith and practice of other races.

Frazer also observes that Robertson Smith's comparative study of religion can be a mighty weapon against what Frazer and others consider the superstitious nature of modern religion. Evolutionary thinking shows that many supposedly lofty beliefs and practices are survivals of primitive ones. Comparison

> indirectly . . . proves that many religious doctrines and practices are based on primitive conceptions, which most civilized and educated men have long agreed in abandoning as mistakes. From this it is a natural and often a probable inference that doctrines so based are false, and that practices so based are foolish. (Frazer 1927, pp. 282 ff.)

Whether or not the church fathers considering Smith for trial as a heretic realized these implications, one does not know. But it would not be surprising if they had.

The second great way that Wellhausen seems to have left his mark on Robertson Smith was with his view of Jewish history, a conception of the history of biblical religion that will take us directly into the main arguments of Robertson Smith's *Lectures on the Religion of the Semites*. To Wellhausen, Jewish religious history was divided into periods of varying religious refinement. The ethical religion of reform of the prophetic age epitomized the loftiest levels of the religion of the 'Old Testament' (Anon 1960). Opposed to the prophetic strand of the religion of Israel was the corrupting priestly strand, with its lavish rituals, sacrifice chief among them. For Wellhausen, ritualism spelt trouble for real religion, because it exposed a tendency for Israel to lapse back into the idolatrous "crude nature religion" so hated by the prophets (Hubert 1901, p. 218).

While it was true that Wellhausen romanticized the ancient Hebrews for their primitive religious vitality, especially as revealed in their sacrificial rites, he was not unqualified in his admiration of them. As with the later ritualistic priestly religion, he was uneasy about sacrifice. The only way Wellhausen felt that this sacrificial ritualist religion of ancient Israel could be said to have value was essentially to impute to it a hidden spiritual essence. For him, then, the very earliest level of ancient Hebrew sacrifice was really highly spiritual. It was a pure act of communion between humanity and deity – not the external ritual thing it may have seemed to be. Wellhausen felt that the prophets had proven that the ritualistic part of sacrifice was exposed as something dispensable. For the ancient Hebrews, it only expressed a noble, but groping, attempt to approximate a spiritual and ethical ideal, later to be realized in full as humanity matured in its evolutionary growth to higher forms of ethical religion like those championed by his beloved prophets. Now, let us see how Robertson Smith adapted Wellhausen's teachings and combined them with the other strands of thinking we have already met.

Smith's *Lectures on the Religion of the Semites*

Perhaps the best way to understand the significance of Robertson Smith's classic is to see it as an answer to that great fundamental question posed by the earliest founders of the naturalistic study of religion like Jean Bodin – what was the first religion or earliest religion? What was its character? What was, for some at least, primal Natural Religion? I believe we can better understand Robertson Smith by seeing him as a person pursuing a solution to this early problem of religion by trying to delve into the depths of the history of Semitic religion.

For obvious reasons, Robertson Smith felt that the religion of the ancient Hebrews had a reasonable claim to being one of the older, if not the oldest, religion known to the human mind. And even if he did not think that he had hit rock bottom when he understood ancient Hebrew religion, he was satisfied that he had got quite far down to the most basic level of the history of human religion. As he said about the kindred religion of the Arabian nomads, it "displays an extremely primitive type, corresponding to the primitive and unchanging character of nomadic life" (Robertson Smith 1923, p. 14). Robertson Smith was then to some extent satisfied that he had indeed got quite close to the roots of religion in uncovering the nature of the religion of the Semites. What he concluded in his findings was to have far-reaching consequences for the study of religion.

Lectures on the Religion of the Semites is a great book because it not only deals with big issues, but also tries to deal with a number of them at the same time. The *Lectures* primarily deal with two important subjects in the study of religion. First, in terms of theoretical advances in the study of 'primitive' religion, the *Lectures* provide a novel theory about the original nature of sacrificial rites, and they introduce perhaps the most influential thesis on the meaning and function of totemism. But, second, in terms of their contribution to social theory and the general study of religion, the *Lectures* could equally well be said to offer an explanation of the origins of morality and the development and growth of religion.

The *Lectures* provide an ingenious theoretical solution to both kinds of problems at the same time. As an evolutionist with affinities to Tylor, Robertson Smith believed that our own institutions grew out of older ones. 'Primitive' institutions set the conditions and provided the necessary facilitating stages to ensure that future 'modern' institutions came into being. Human history did not leap from stone wheels or chunks of unworked wood to hair dryers or washing machines at one go. Unlike Tylor, who saw religion from the beginnings to the present day as animism, Robertson Smith, as a *religious* evolutionist, believed that religion evolved in substantial ways. Both sacrifice and totemism, for example, were 'primitive' rites that over the course of eons would, under the right circumstances – as they had in the Protestant West, in Robertson Smith's view – develop into higher 'modern' forms of spirituality and morality. Sacrifice, which had been at one time in the early stages of history a calculating offering to lay "the deity under a social obligation," or to buy the favor of the gods, would – given the right conditions – develop into the lofty ethical ideal of altruism, a pure uncalculating giving of the self for others (Robertson Smith 1923, p. 434).

That was what had actually happened in the Protestant West in Robertson Smith's view. What was at one time in the dim past a gross and 'material' kind of ritualism would gradually and thanks to divine interventions, become the high-minded and purified 'spiritual' morality that Robertson Smith thought his brand of Calvinism was. Original religion thus seemed devoid of elegant doctrines or ethical vision, properly speaking, that would characterize religion as Robertson Smith knew it in his own domain. Instead, "in ancient religions all the ordinary functions of worship are summed up in the sacrificial meal, and the ordinary intercourse between gods and men has no other form" (Robertson Smith 1923, p. 265). This requires nothing less than sacrifice: "sacrifice is the typical form of all complete acts of worship in the antique religions" (ibid., p. 214).

But true religion would in time, as it were, cast off the dullness of matter and take on the luminosity of spirit. Robertson Smith spoke from the perspective of someone who felt that he was living in the latter days of this magnificent religious evolutionary drama. Likewise, totemism, at one time a rite in which the animal or vegetable symbol of the divinity was killed and eaten for the sake of communion with the deity, would – under the right circumstances – evolve into the Christian Eucharist. There, the body and blood of the sacrificed God-man would be eaten by the faithful in communion. Under the right circumstances again, this concept of the Eucharist would itself evolve into more and more spiritual forms, such as seeing in it Jesus' altruistic giving up of himself to the Father, and all that implied as a model of divine community with humanity. Significantly, the conception of Jesus' death as an *expiation* is removed from the second edition of *Lectures on the Religion of the Semites*.

Robertson Smith's problem was how to establish his brilliant interpretation of the course of religious growth and development. Religious people differed – often significantly – about what sacrifice was. For Jews, at a certain later period in their history, sacrifice was a "gloomy" affair, "filled in times of distress with the cowardly lamentations of worshippers, who to save their own lives were ready to give up all they held dear, even to the sacrifice of a firstborn or only child" (Robertson Smith 1923, p. 415). How did it come to be that way – especially when biblical evidence pointed to an earlier joyous festival, replete with sacrificial banquet, among the Israelites (Robertson Smith 1923, p. 254)? And then there were the Roman Catholics of Smith's own day, repeating as it were all the theological errors of Israel in decline, not to mention those of "heathen" or "antique ritual" (Robertson Smith 1923, p. 439). Catholics asserted forcefully that the Eucharist was a sacramental reenactment of the passionate sacrificial death and immolation, done primarily to make up, atone for, or expiate the sins of humanity against God. For Catholics, in Robertson Smith's view, the sacrificial death of Jesus was a bloody repayment of a debt incurred by humanity to deity. It was their vain way of ensuring their own salvation by performance of a mechanical ritual. There was little of the sense of union with the divine or sublime joy of kinship in this that spoke to the religious heart of Robertson Smith. Indeed, sacrifice as expiation was a dreary affair, dominated by conniving priests, and dependent upon a mechanical ritual. To Robertson Smith, such a conception of sacrifice seemed deficient – he described it as "materialistic" – and he accordingly went to work to uncover what he believed would be a purer conception of sacrifice rooted in the biblical tradition itself (Robertson Smith 1923, pp. 439–40). How was it, further, that his own Protestant Reformation tradition taught this antimaterialist doctrine in contrast to the one pronounced by the Catholics? Was this just coincidental?

To do this, Robertson Smith felt that he had to justify his theory of sacrifice from history – bearing in mind how he believed that ethnography let him travel through time, unlike ordinary historical scholarship. He had, in effect, to go back even further in the history of Israel and show how expiatory, mechanical, priest-ridden conceptions of sacrifice were *later* than the kind of sacrifice he felt was primitive in the 'purest' levels of biblical religion. The main effort of *Lectures on the Religion of the Semites* was to delve into the biblical material and then to integrate it with the ethnographic data Robertson Smith had accumulated in Arabia to establish the sequence of development of sacrifice. When he had plumbed the past as far as he could, he discovered evidence for a primal conception of sacrifice as communion, rather than as the later occurring sacrifice of expiation. He argued that the oldest stratum of sacrifice consisted in the communal banquet of sharing in the sacrificial victim. This banquet knew nothing of cosmic bribery of the deity by humans. It was instead a precious time in which humanity and divinity 'sat at the same table,' so to speak, and enjoyed their kinship with each other.

> When men meet their god, they feast and are glad together, and whenever they feast and are glad they desire that the god should be of the party. This view is proper to religions in which the habitual temper of the worshippers is one of joyous confidence in their god, untroubled by any habitual sense of human guilt, and resting on the firm conviction that they and the deity they adore are good friends, who understand each other perfectly and are united by bonds not easily broken. (Robertson Smith 1923, p. 255)

As such, the important point to be made about sacrifice was its festive, high-spirited, and joyful marking of kinship of people with their deity – an occasion "full of mirth" (Robertson Smith 1923, p. 414).

But why was Robertson Smith so sure that sacrifice as communion was *earlier* than sacrifice as expiation or bribe/gift? For one thing, his reading of the Hebrew Bible led him to conclude, as we have just seen, that early in the history of Israel the main religious events were joyous public sacrificial festivals. Robertson Smith specifically cites the Book of Samuel (1923, p. 254, nn. 1–6) for details of the such a "merry sacrificial feast" (p. 257). Furthermore, these festivals constituted the "dominant type of Hebrew worship" for the Israelites of that early time (p. 254).

However, a second factor immediately intrudes into Robertson Smith's thinking – evolutionary doctrine about the developmental growth of the human race.

> The communities of ancient civilisation were formed by the survival of the fittest, and they had all the self-confidence and elasticity that are engendered by success in the struggle for life. These characters, therefore, are reflected in the religious system that grew up with the growth of the state, and the type of worship that corresponded to them was not felt to be inadequate till the political system was undermined from within or shattered by blows from without. (Robertson Smith 1923, p. 260)

Robertson Smith's mention of "struggle" in this citation is an apparent reference to Herbert Spencer, and not to Darwin, since Robertson Smith doubted whether "there is anything in Darwinism" (Robertson Smith 1880, p. 532). As a special case of general human evolution, then, the joyous stage of human religious evolution lays the foundation for its successor, just as the innocence of youth produces the conditions that call for its transcendence in the sobriety of adulthood. Thus, while the early stage of Hebrew religion seemed blissful indeed, it is immature. After all, Robertson Smith believed that the human race was itself immature at that time anyway. People at this early stage of human development exhibit a

> measure of *insouciance*, a power of casting off the past and 'living in the impression' of the moment, which belongs to the childhood of humanity, and can exist only along with a childish unconsciousness of the inexorable laws that connect the present and the future with the past. (Robertson Smith 1923, p. 257)

But, as time goes on, an inevitable change begins to occur as "the more developed nations" emerge from "national childhood," and they soon

> find the old religious forms inadequate...and are driven to look on the anger of the gods as much more frequent and permanent than their fathers had supposed, and to give to atoning rites a stated and important place in ritual, which went far to change the whole attitude characteristic of early worship, and substitute for the old joyous confidence a painful and scrupulous anxiety in all approach to the gods. (Robertson Smith 1923, pp. 258–9)

And thus the latter-day religions of guilt, gloom, and sin, with their expiatory and god-fearing sacrifices, were born as the inevitable results of the working out of the laws of human evolution.

But as well supported as Robertson Smith's view was, he also had his own personal religious reasons for wanting to emphasize this particular reading of the scriptures of the West. This is to say that we must take account of his own religious commitments and beliefs, because they directed his reading of the Hebrew Bible. That the Protestant Reformation marked real progress in the course of religious evolution was for Robertson Smith incontestable. And that his brand of Calvinism stood at the pinnacle of religious progress was also equally indubitable for Smith. Like Max Müller, Robertson Smith was an intensely, if unconventionally, pious Protestant. In his view, for the reformers, the central significance of the sacrifice of Jesus was the reestablishment of the unity enjoyed between divinity and humanity at beginning of time. Thus, strictly speaking in Robertson Smith's view, the coming of the prophets and Jesus was less an easy evolution than a radical restoration, albeit at a more mature level.

This view of Jesus as restorer conforms with the implications of Wellhausen's view of the Jewish prophets – of which Jesus was a prime instance. The prophets returned Israel to a lost level of communion with God. Strictly speaking, one can look on the prophets less as inaugurating a totally new religious regime than as returning humanity to its proper relationship with God. It is nonetheless true, for Robertson Smith, that the prophets represent revolutionary *evolution* beyond previous historical stages of Jewish religion, such as that exemplified by priestly ritualism. In that case, we can see what it means for Robertson Smith to be a "qualified" evolutionist about religion, since for Smith the religion of Israel evolves, but only after it has somewhat degenerated, and is then raised up again by divine revelation through the prophets. Israel has, as one knows, not always been faithful to its covenant with God. God himself had to lead Israel back to himself – by virtue of the supernatural agency embodied in prophecy. Otherwise, why were the prophets needed at all?

> It is a favourite speculation that the Hebrews or the Semites in general have a natural capacity for spiritual religion. They are either represented as constitutionally monotheistic, or at least we are told that their worship had in it from the first, and apart from revelation, a lofty character from which spiritual ideas were easily developed. That was not the opinion of the prophets, who always deal with their nation as one peculiarly inaccessible to spiritual truths and possessing no natural merit which could form the ground of its choice as the people of Jehovah. Our investigations appear to confirm this judgment, and to show that the superstitions with which the spiritual religion had to contend were not one whit less degrading than those of the most savage nations. . . . It does not appear that Israel was, by its own wisdom, more fit than any other nation to rise above the lowest level of heathenism. (Robertson Smith 1912a, pp. 482–3)

In absolute terms, nothing surpasses the state of unity humanity and divinity enjoyed at the creation. Both the prophets and Jesus, himself a prophet, try to restore what had been lost. Israel's religious evolution is simply not an absolute one, proceeding from zero.

One point ought to be made here in relation to Robertson Smith's religious motivations for his scientific work. While Robertson Smith was thus a great "critic" of the religion of his day, and indeed one of our greatest classic theorists, he was also someone who saw himself as a "caretaker" – someone who felt he was also advancing a religious agenda at the same time. Like Max Müller, Robertson Smith saw science (here the historical sciences) and religion as not only compatible, but mutually reinforcing. He would see himself as pursuing his caretaking work precisely by means of his critical, theoretical work (Bediako 1995, p. 118)! Thus, far from the dichotomy authors like Russell McCutcheon would draw everywhere between what he calls "critics" and "caretakers," we have seen how two of the most seminal classic theorists in the study of religion, Max Müller and Robertson Smith, for starters, are both "critics" and "caretakers" at the same time. (Tylor, on the other hand, had no interest in religious caretaking, and as he tells us, set out to delegitimize the pretensions of contemporary religion in the form of its theologians, as highly *evolved*. He is, as we may recall, an 'undertaker of religion.') Thus, the real history of the study of religion indicates that a combination of the two – 'critical caretaking' or 'caretaking criticism' – reflects the vital middle ground occupied by a certain set of religious theorists between the two extremes McCutcheon provides us (McCutcheon 2001).

What Robertson Smith Can Still Teach Us

Whether or not his views of the earliest religions were true, the study of religion has benefited a great deal from Robertson Smith's conception of the earliest religion as being primarily a matter of ritual, relationship, and action. It is going much too far to say that so-called 'primitive' religions lack doctrines, myths, and anything that might indicate an intellectual reflectiveness among their adherents, as Robertson Smith himself believed:

> But it is of the first importance to realise clearly from the outset that ritual and practical usage were, strictly speaking, the sum-total of ancient religions. Religion in primitive times was not a system of belief with practical applications; it was a body of fixed traditional practices, to which every member of society conformed as a matter of course. (Robertson Smith 1923, p. 20)

But it is useful to begin thinking about religion as rooted in other aspects of human life than just cognitive or intellectual activity, such as doctrines, creeds, beliefs, and even myths. Tylor's approach to religion was just this sort of theory, since he thought religion seeks to *explain* the world. While some religious beliefs do purport to explain the way the world is, in the long run Tylor implied that religion was basically just a second-rate – false – version of science. By affirming the possibility of religion as having to do with establishing relationships with both the divine and with other humans, as having to do less with thinking about things than about behaving properly, as ritual directs, Robertson Smith has greatly enhanced our appreciation of the multidimensional character of human religiosity. After all, there is more to human life than making theories or explaining the world. There is worship itself – a doing, an action, a performance directed at the divine, that is not in itself a piece of theoretical thinking.

Nor are we obliged to denigrate this aspect of human action as Robertson Smith felt he needed to do by labeling it 'primitive' and 'materialist' (Robertson Smith 1923, p. 440). He felt that the first religion was crude and imperfect. Frazer notes how Smith even finds primitive forms of Christianity, by which he means Roman Catholicism – doubtless because of the importance of ritual practice there – in a "low stage of society and in a very crude phase of thought" (Frazer 1927, pp. 288–9). Taking his hostility to Catholicism directly to its heart – the priesthood and sacramentalism – Robertson Smith levels a scathing attack on a fellow Christian community:

> The doctrine of the *opus operatum* in the sacraments unquestionably reduces certain features of the spiritual life to the level of a physical process, and this doctrine alone makes it possible for the Church of Rome to regard with complacency a degree of ignorance on the part of the laity, which is quite inconsistent with truly moral growth.
> But in Protestantism, at least, it should be otherwise. When the Reformers taught that the means of grace are effective only in so far as they bring the Word of God into contact with personal faith, they distinctly asserted that all true religious life is morally nourished. (Robertson Smith 1912b, p. 318)

"A ritual system," such as Smith believes is prevalent in Catholicism, "must always remain materialistic, even if its materialism is disguised under the cloak of mysticism." Leaving no role for ritual in the 'real' religiosity of his own faith, Smith proclaims that the "real living power . . . in Christianity is *moral*" and that "personal Christianity is not a play of subjectivities, but moral converse with God practically dominating the life." We should also not forget that Smith here followed his teacher Paul Lagarde's anti-Judaism and anti-Catholicism. Lagarde disapproved of the rabbinic Jewish and Roman Catholic ritualism of his own day because he felt that both exemplified the "dessication" of a religious life dominated by rituals.

Even in 1875, when Smith seemed to move toward a position granting substantive importance to liturgy, he could not muster the courage to cross the threshold. For while it is true that he thinks liturgy matters, it matters because of and is dependent upon the state of individual personal piety and moral rectitude. On the ritualist side, Smith says that "the church is not a fellowship of Christian love which requires no unity of organization – but a fellowship of worship," and that "church fellowship has a moulding and upbuilding power on those who take part in it." But then putting ritual into dependent status, he undercuts what he seems to mean by this. In Smith's view, this "common worship of many individuals" is only an "expression in intelligible form of their common relation of faith towards God." That is to say that ritual again comes second to the inner condition of the Christian soul. This likewise fits with his Reformation view earlier expressed in the same essay, that "the effectual factor in the sacraments is not the outward sign, but the word of promise signified. [Thus] all participation in the benefits purchased by Christ is to be gained in converse with God, in hearkening continually to His Word" (Robertson Smith 1912b, p. 319).

But we are not obliged to accept these anti-Catholic, anti-Jewish, and antiritualist prejudices, any more than we are obliged to raise up ethical behavior as the sum total of what it means to be 'spiritual.' For Robertson Smith, the glory and reality of religion lay in its future growth and evolution beyond the ritualistic stage, beyond its remote and 'primitive' past. Smith's religious evolutionism was a somewhat mild one. He always declared his pious loyalty to the Free Church of Scotland, and never doubted the divine inspiration of the Bible (Stocking 1995, p. 65). For Robertson Smith, the true nature of essential and 'pure' religion lay, however, in the forward-looking, reforming message of the Hebrew prophets and Protestant Reformers. The culmination of religious evolution lay in the ethical monotheism they and their Christian successors preached – and not in the ritualistic materialism of its origins (Robertson Smith 1923, p. 439).

Robertson Smith thus studied the evolution of Semitic religion into modern Christianity in the spirit of a triumphalist and supercessionist *Heilsgeschichte* – a qualified religious evolutionism in the service of casting his own Christianity as the religious cutting edge of progressive human spirituality (Reif 1995). His ambitions were to accomplish a "gathering up into one whole of all God's dealings with men from the fall to the Resurrection of Christ, the history of true religion, the adoption and education, from age to age, of the Church, in a continuous scheme of gradual advance" (Robertson Smith 1912c, p. 232). But the truth may be that religion is sublinguistic and prerational in its origins, and may just be the name of the ultimate shape people give to the way they live. But so what? As long as human beings are *embodied* beings, it would be odd indeed if our embodied nature should have nothing positive to do with being religious. We can at least thank Robertson Smith for recognizing that human religiosity can be firmly embodied, even if, as a good Victorian, he seemed to have been too embarrassed by the fact to exploit and celebrate it.

References

Ackerman, R. 1987. *J. G. Frazer: His Life and Work*. Cambridge: Cambridge University Press.
Anon. 1960. Wellhausen, Julius. In *The Jewish Encyclopedia*, vol. 12. New York: KTAV.
Bediako, G. M. 1995. "To Capture the Modern Universe of Thought": *Religion of the Semites* as an Attempt at a Christian Comparative Religion. In *William Robertson Smith: Essays in Reassessment*, ed. W. Johnstone. Journal for the Study of the Old Testament Supplement Series. Sheffield: Sheffield Academic Press.

Beidelman, T. O. 1974. *W. Robertson Smith and the Sociological Study of Religion*. Chicago: University of Chicago Press.

Black, J. S. & G. Chrystal, eds. 1912a. *Lectures and Essays of William Robertson Smith*. London: Adam and Charles Black.

——. 1912b. *The Life of William Robertson Smith*. London: Adam and Charles Black.

Douglas, M. 1970. *Purity and Danger*. London: Penguin.

——. 1993. *In the Wilderness: The Doctrine of Defilement in the Book of Numbers*. Journal for the Study of the Old Testament Supplement Series 158. Sheffield: JSOT Press.

Frazer, J. G. 1927. William Robertson Smith. In *Gorgon's Head and Other Literary Pieces*. London: Macmillan.

Hubert, H. 1901. Review of Wellhausen, *Prolegomena zur Geschichte Israels*. *L'Année sociologique* 4, p. 218.

Kristof, N. D. 2004. Martyrs, Virgins and Grapes. *New York Times*, Aug. 4.

McCutcheon, R. T. 2001. *Critics Not Caretakers: Redescribing the Public Study of Religion*. Albany: SUNY Press.

Reif, S. C. 1995. William Robertson Smith in Relation to Hebraists and Jews at Christ's College, Cambridge. In *William Robertson Smith: Essays in Reassessment*, ed. W. Johnstone. Journal for the Study of the Old Testament Supplement Series. Sheffield: Sheffield Academic Press.

Reinach, S. 1922. La théorie du sacrifice. In *Cultes, Mythes et Religions*, vol. 1. Paris: Leroux.

Robertson Smith, W. 1880. A Journey in the Hejaz. In *Lectures and Essays of William Robertson Smith*, eds. J.S. Black & G. Chrystal. London: Adam and Charles Black.

——. 1885. *Kinship and Marriage in Early Arabia*. Cambridge: Cambridge University Press.

——. 1912a. Animal Worship and Animal Tribes among the Arabs and in the Old Testament. In *Lectures and Essays of William Robertson Smith*, eds. J. S. Black & G. Chrystal. London: Adam and Charles Black.

——. 1912b. The Place of Theology in the Work and Growth of the Church. In *The Lectures and Essays of William Robertson Smith*, eds. J. S. Black & G. Chrystal. London: Adam and Charles Black.

——. 1912c. What History Teaches Us to Seek in the Bible. In *Lectures and Essays of William Robertson Smith*, eds. J. S. Black & G. Chrystal. London: Adam and Charles Black.

——. 1923. *Lectures on the Religion of the Semites*. London: Adam and Charles Black.

Sharpe, E. J. 1986. *Comparative Religion: A History*. La Salle, IL: Open Court.

Stocking, G. W. 1995. *After Tylor: British Social Anthropology, 1888–1951*. Madison: University of Wisconsin Press.

Toy, C. H. 1895. Review of William Robertson Smith, *Lectures on the Religion of the Semites*. First Series, 1894. *The New World* 4, pp. 386–90.

6

Setting the Eternal Templates of Salvation: James Frazer

"Le roi est mort, vive le roi! Ave Maria!"
The king is dead; long live the king! Hail Mary!

–James Frazer, *The Golden Bough*

The Long Life and Great Renown of Sir James Frazer

Although he was a classicist by training, and generally regarded as an "embarrassment" by today's practitioners in the profession of 'anthropology,' Sir James Frazer (1854–1941) was hugely influential in bringing the commonplaces of anthropology into Western intellectual, literary, religious, and neoreligious discourse (Ackerman 1987, p. 1). Frazer was raised in the same kind of pious Calvinist religious home as Robertson Smith, and was also a member of the same religious community, the Free Church of Scotland. When Frazer had come of age for university training, he stayed close to home and attended Glasgow University where he, like Robertson Smith, studied a wide range of subjects. These included the classics and philosophy, especially the empiricist and skeptical thinker David Hume. We will recall from our discussion of the critics of deists like Herbert of Cherbury, that Hume wrote the first critical and naturalistic history of religion – *The Natural History of Religion* (Hume 1963). Like Robertson Smith again, while at Glasgow, Frazer devoted serious study to the natural sciences, under such figures as Lord Kelvin, after whom the system of the absolute measurement of temperature was named. Upon taking his degree from Glasgow, Frazer planned for postgraduate work. His parents made sure that he would steer clear of Oxford, where the Catholicizing 'Oxford Movement' had inspired many to convert to the Church of Rome. So, it was off to the more hospitable religious environment of Cambridge that Frazer was sent, thanks in part to a scholarship. Frazer went on to win honors at Cambridge, and wrote a prize research dissertation on Plato that provided him a research fellowship that enabled him to stay on at Cambridge.

Although philosophy was in many ways dearest to his interests, Frazer always balanced the abstract and generalizing tendencies of this discipline with a profound love of literary, historical, and even archeological fact. He was fond of travel and the amateur exploration of ancient archeological sites on the Continent, especially its sunnier southern parts. Although he knew Spain and Greece, Frazer had a special love of Italy. It was on one of those trips to southern Europe that a Cambridge colleague encouraged him to read Edward Burnett Tylor's *Primitive Culture* (Fraser 2005). This put Frazer into the Tylorian camp from that moment on (Stocking 1995, pp. 131–2). So informed by Tylorian principles was Frazer's work that we can say that virtually all aspects of his evolutionist thinking about human cultures are "essentially Tylorian" (Stocking 1995, p. 145). Frazer accepted Tylor's theory of survivals, his method of comparison, his general evolutionist conception of the step-wise growth of cultures, his preference for independent origination over diffusionist transmission as the explanation for similarities among cultures, and his conception of anthropology as a "reforming science," aimed fundamentally at discrediting religion in modern society. On top of Tylor's methodological gifts to Frazer, the former's association of the primitives and ancients, combined with all that Frazer knew about the ancient classic civilizations (and their languages), would make 'primitive' cultures an integral part of the data that he would subject to the analytic rigor he had gained from philosophy.

It was perhaps that strength of analytic grip that made Frazer the most persuasive and powerful master of comparative cultural studies in modern times (Jarvie 1964, p. 32). In his tribute to Robertson Smith, Frazer outlines his theory of cross-cultural comparison in ways that Robertson Smith and Max Müller would surely recognize:

> Now when laying aside as irrelevant to the purpose in hand the question of the truth or falsehood of religious beliefs, and the question of the wisdom or folly of religious practices, we examine side by side the religions of different races and ages, we find that, while they differ from each other in many particulars, the resemblances between them are numerous and fundamental, and that they mutually illustrate and explain each other, the distinctly stated faith and circumstantial ritual of one race often clearing up ambiguities in the faith and practice of other races. (Frazer 1927b, p. 282)

Like Max Müller in particular, Frazer would try to fill in the 'unknowns' of one set of data by applying the parallels from an analogous set of data, as we have seen Müller do with related languages.

Unlike his close colleague and mentor at Cambridge, William Robertson Smith (1846–94), Frazer never quite ventured into the ethnographic 'field' the way later anthropologists, notably Malinowski, would. Frazer's interest in ethnographic materials seems to have begun with the reading of the classical author Pausanias. His detailed descriptions of the customs of the Greek world outside the major cities seems to have stimulated Frazer's imagination to know more. Accordingly, Frazer undertook extended journeys on horseback into the Greek hinterlands in 1890 and 1895 to observe what was left of the customs and practices of long ago. That, however, seemed to be the extent of Frazer's fieldwork. When invited in 1898 to join one of the earliest organized extensive fieldwork expeditions (to the Torres Straits), Frazer declined (Fraser 2005). Instead he remained the bookish scholar. Indeed, it was the influence of Tylor's *Primitive Culture* and his personal relationship with Robertson Smith at Cambridge that directed Frazer to evolutionist ideas and ethnographic materials (Ackerman 1987, pp. 58–9).

Still, the influence of Frazer is something with which to reckon. Mary Douglas tries to disarm some of the criticism aimed at Frazer simply for reflecting the prejudices of his own age.

> Anyone who criticizes Frazer now is criticizing not so much a writer, as a whole period that he represented, a period of about a hundred years ago. This is in itself a reason for reading *The Golden Bough*. It is not so certain that the pinnacle from which we look back to that time is so clearly elevated above it. We have our own self-esteem and arrogance which mark us as members of our own civilization. (Douglas 1978, p. 15)

The philosopher of science Ian Jarvie, some years ago created a stir by suggesting that Frazer's style of engaging in bold comparative investigation was still to be preferred over the more cautious approaches to anthropology current in our own day.

> Consider for a moment: whom can we take as an archetypal comparative sociologist? I am afraid the answer will be rather disconcerting to social anthropologists: the dead father: Sir James George Frazer is the comparative sociologist par excellence. Frazer is by no means perfect.... Nevertheless Frazer had the intellectual capacity, the historical and classical training, and the absorbent memory which well fitted him for the job of comparison....
>   I must say I find Frazer glorious and thrilling reading; there is an excitement to be found there which is sadly lacking in the work of the later generations and I am ashamed to have to report that he is not properly appreciated. My explanation for this would be that no one really knows how to appreciate him. (Jarvie 1964, pp. 32–3)

The Polish anthropologist Bronislaw Malinowski (1884–1942) was perhaps the last "anthropologist" to lavish praise on the significance of Frazer's work for the new discipline. In a 1925 public lecture, he declared that "anthropology, as presented by Sir James Frazer, is a great science, worthy of as much devotion as any of her elder and more exact sister studies, and I became bound to the service of Frazerian anthropology" (Malinowski 1992, p. 94). What Malinowski had specifically in mind was Frazer's 12-volume *The Golden Bough*. Among other things, it posed an all-encompassing cross-cultural theory of the evolution of religion that had particular import for the status of Christianity. Frazer had devoted major portions of *The Golden Bough* to demonstrating that images, accounts, and motifs regarded as unique to Christianity were in all likelihood of 'pagan' origin.

In all these matters of influence we of course need to maintain a mature distance, since oftentimes an author will either not recognize their mark on the work of another or totally disown it. For whatever it may be worth noticing, Frazer seems to have made a habit of doing this sort of thing. For example, Rickard A. Parker observes that although T. S. Eliot acknowledged an immense debt to *The Golden Bough*, Frazer claims that he found Eliot's poem impenetrable (Parker 1997–2002). Of course, we should not read Malinowski's remarks about Frazer naively, since he sought to trade upon the reputation of Frazer to enhance his own career. This caused Malinowski sometimes to interpret Frazer's work in ways that Frazer himself did not recognize as fitting. Malinowski had once prominently made a special point of attributing his own functionalist theory of myth to Frazer in his most important public lecture on the subject (Malinowski 1992, pp. 93–5). But in a letter acknowledging receipt of Malinowski's offprint of the lecture, Frazer flatly disowned Malinowski's theory! "I confess that I have been in the habit of regarding myths as explanations, and I am not sure that I follow your reasons for rejecting this view," was how the ungrateful Frazer delivered the bad news to his erstwhile successor, Malinowski! (cited in Strenski 1987, p. 5).

As for the study of religion in particular, unlike his progressive Christian friend, William Robertson Smith, Frazer quite early rejected Christianity. That rejection made a vast difference to the way he would study religion. It put him more in the camp of Hume and Tylor, as opposed to that of Max Müller, Herbert of Cherbury, Jean Bodin, and Robertson Smith. It ruled out his being a 'caretaker' of religion from the start. Instead, Frazer moved between this role of being a 'critic' to one I have called being an outright 'undertaker of religion.' It is explicit in Frazer's own words that he is deliberately disaffiliated from Christianity: "I am not a Christian, on the contrary I reject the Christian religion as utterly false" (Stocking 1995, p. 128, quoting Frazer 1935, p. 132). This early departure from the faith of his stern fathers no doubt prepared Frazer for his new allegiance to Tylor's idea of anthropology as "reforming science." In this way, Frazer's idea of the relation of religion to science was the opposite of Robertson Smith's and Max Müller's. For now science did not prepare the way for a deeper faith, it was the ultimate device in undoing the work of religion. Science was to provide Frazer with the 'shovels and picks' he required to 'bury' religion – for his career as an 'undertaker of religion.'

Contrary to common opinion, not all 'critics' or nonbelievers necessarily become or need to become 'undertakers of religion.' Such a move requires the *additional step* of commitment to the destruction of religion itself. Many critics, as we will see in the case of the phenomenologists, feel no need to embark on the program of burying religion. They, on the other hand, maintain neutrality about the ultimate value of religion, or whether it is worthy of continued existence. Such matters are left to the loving 'caretakers' of religion and to their mirror images – the equally zealous 'undertakers of religion.'

Now, while disaffiliation from a particular religion is not enough reason to become one of its 'undertakers' or an 'undertaker of religion' in general, in Frazer's case it was. His contemporary detractors and admirers alike have a great deal to say to confirm this picture (Lord 1912; 1916). George Bernard Shaw, one of Frazer's more prominent admirers and himself an 'undertaker of religion,' cites *The Golden Bough* in a sustained attack on some key Christian doctrines, especially the Christian – at least Catholic – doctrine of the Eucharist. But Shaw does not stop there in relating the lessons he has learned from Frazer. Shaw homes in on the Christian doctrine of the resurrection, exposed, he believed, by Frazer as resting upon the template of age-old pagan myths of vegetative regeneration and cults of fecundity.

> And from the song of John Barleycorn you may learn how the miracle of the seed, the growth, and the harvest . . . taught the primitive husbandman . . . that God is in the seed, and that God is immortal. And thus it became the test of Godhead that nothing that you could do to it could kill it, and that when you buried it, it would rise again in renewed life and beauty and give mankind eternal life on condition that it was eaten and drunk, and again slain and buried, to rise again forever and ever. You may, and indeed must, use John Barleycorn 'right barbarouslee,' cutting him 'off at knee' with your scythes, scourging him with your flails, burying him in the earth; and he will not resist nor reproach you, but will rise again in golden beauty amidst a great burst of sunshine and bird music, and save you and renew your life. (Shaw 1912)

So, in his own way Frazer shared the 'reforming' spirit of Tylor, Shaw, and others of their ilk eager to tear the mask off the mysteries of religion – especially of Christianity – and in doing so to reform society in the process.

There is one final point about caretakers, critics, and undertakers of religion worth reiterating in the case of James Frazer, as we have with Max Müller and Robertson Smith. In some sense, although it helps us *understand* the intellectual strategies and theories of the great thinkers about religion to know what their *motivations* concerning religion might be – caretaker, undertaker, etc.? – the mere fact of their being motivated to study religion for one of these purposes can and ought to be separated from how they actually propose we study religion. Just because Müller undertook comparative studies in which he sought to discover Natural Religion does not *invalidate* his method of comparative study of religions – a method that he borrowed from comparative historical phonology anyway! Similarly, although I shall endeavor to uncover the underlying motives and intellectual strategies behind Frazer's comparative study of religions, I do not feel this constitutes a critique of it as a method for studying religion. Indeed, along with Jarvie, I think it, together with Max Müller's comparative study of religions, present really powerful ways of studying religion which are insufficiently practiced today. Note that while Müller takes the role of 'caretaker of religion' as often as Frazer takes that of 'undertaker,' both theorists have a great deal to offer anyone who aspires to be a critic of religion. Now, let us see how Frazer works his way through these various approaches to religion. Once more, the idea of key problems of religion takes center stage. What sorts of problems afflicted Frazer?

How Did We Get from 'There' to 'Here'... Again?

In some ways, the same cluster of closely knit problems drove the thinking of James Frazer as that of Edward Burnett Tylor, and to a lesser extent William Robertson Smith. The 'shock of the old' jolted Frazer even more dramatically than it had the other evolutionist thinkers we have already met. George W. Stocking records how Frazer's belief in the power of a 'primitive' past caused him to speak in metaphors even more disturbing to the everyday certainties of modern life. A "volcano underfoot" was how Frazer described the threat of the lurking, potent, primitive forces threatening the 'civilized' society of Europe in 1908. In his lecture entitled *Psyche's Task: A Discourse Concerning the Influence of Superstition on the Growth of Institutions* (1909), Frazer warned that "the "smooth surface of cultured society" was "sapped and mined by superstition" (Stocking 1995, p. 146).

Even decades earlier, when Frazer was not gripped by these fears, with a zeal equal to his mentor in anthropology, Edward Burnett Tylor, Frazer delved into the deepest depths of what would later so trouble him as 'primitive' superstitions and the human past. His interest was to engage questions about human origins: 'How did we get from there to here?' 'Where did we come from and where are we going?' And, finally, amidst their perception of the impressive record of human progress in the late nineteenth century, 'What is the place of so retrograde an institution as religion in this story of unprecedented growth and development?'

It may be difficult for us to realize in our 'high-tech' times just how impressive was the perceived scientific and technological progress of the late nineteenth century. It is thus hard for us to really empathize with the kind of mental world someone like Frazer inhabited when he first started publishing *The Golden Bough* in 1890. The last two decades of the nineteenth century saw a tremendous burst of technological innovation, widely deployed as well in the lives of ordinary people. In 1879, the first hearing-aid came onto the market, and Thomas Edison first publicly demonstrated the incandescent light. In 1880, the world's first electric streetcar made its inaugural run near Berlin, and news of the Afghan war was received by telegram dispatch in London. In 1882, after having constructed the first electricity generating plant, Thomas Edison illuminated a square-mile area of New York City. In 1884, the first long-distance telephone call was made, between Boston and New York City, and the basis of information storage used by early computers – the hole-punch card system – was invented. By 1885, most people in the urban areas of the Western world could expect home delivery of their favorite newspaper. In 1886, Karl Benz patented the first successful gasoline-driven car, the process of manufacturing aluminum was developed, and the first typewriter ribbon was patented. In 1887, Sherlock Holmes debuted on the literary stage, employing all the dazzling methods of technical crime investigation – such as the earlier use of fingerprint identification (1885) – that has become the hallmark of the private detective ever since. The first Kodak 'box' camera (100 exposures) could be had for $25 in 1888. 1889 saw the first dishwashing machine for sale. Patents on both the screw cap and the coin-operated telephone were granted in the same year. In 1891, one year after Frazer published the first volume of *The Golden Bough*, the first telephone connection between Paris and London was established, followed in 1896 by the first use of the X-ray machine, and in 1897 by Marconi's first radio communication. It is no wonder, then, that Frazer was at once so impressed with what looked to him like evidence of human progress, especially in the area of human control over the environment and the general enhancement of human mastery of the world (Ratnikas 2005).

At the same time, the last two decades of the nineteenth century marked a great burst of colonization by the major European powers. Now not only were older colonial powers like France, the Netherlands, and Great Britain busy locking up vast areas of the globe, but newly formed nations, such as the United States, Italy, Max Müller's Germany, and Belgium also got into the colonialism business. This expansion of Western power was largely in the service of supplying the late nineteenth-century industrial economies with the raw materials needed to produce the very technologies of which Frazer and his ilk would be proud. Thus, the rise of late nineteenth-century industry came in considerable degree at the expense of technologically less well-developed peoples, their natural resources and markets – precisely those folk Frazer and others like him would call the 'primitives.' The juxtaposition of these two facts – the power of the industrialized nations over the newly colonized tribal peoples of the American West, Africa, Latin America, Melanesia, and the Pacific; the corresponding sophistication of the technology of the West over against the 'primitive' crafts of the newly colonized peoples – was puzzling to those who pondered these things. Why are 'we' *here* and 'they' *there*? To play once more upon Bizarro's caveman cartoon, why do 'we' have electric lighting (by 1882, thanks to Edison), while 'they' still light their dwellings with open flames?

This contrast between 'primitive' and modern was altogether more acute and powerful, since evolutionists like Frazer assumed, as we have seen with Tylor and Robertson Smith, that the 'primitives' were developmental "survivals" of people who were in most respects just like our own prehistoric ancestors (Stocking 1995, p. 131). Tylor taught that all peoples passed through the identical developmental stages. Frazer agreed completely (Stocking 1995, pp. 131–2). What 'they' are, 'we' once were. After all, had not the archeological finds of the mid-nineteenth century shown that 'our' prehistoric technology was identical to that of today's 'primitives,' and thus by extrapolation, that many of the other institutions of our own prehistoric past were as well? Tylor had argued as much in identifying both the essence of the polytheism of the 'primitives' and the high-god of Abraham, Isaac, and Jacob as animism. So once more the original question came back at European thinkers like Frazer in an especially salient and humbling form. How did 'we' get from *there* (and the way today's 'primitives' were) to *here* – to the level of sophisticated science and technology that made us who we are?

For Frazer, the answer to these big questions lay in understanding how humans took control of their environments, in how our modern applied science and technology – what Frazer lumps together under the label "science" – had originated. Frazer was fixated on the practical, "utilitarian" problem of how 'primitive' people survived by seeking, at least, to *control* their environments by understanding the real mechanisms by which nature operates (Stocking 1995, p. 131). 'Primitive' folk were not primarily interested in *explaining* how nature worked in and for itself, but in finding a "key" to the nature of the universe that would let them make material progress.

> Here at last, after groping about in the dark for countless ages, man has hit upon a clue to the labyrinth, a golden key that opens many locks in the treasury of nature. It is probably not too much to say that the hope of progress – moral and intellectual as well as material – in the future is bound up with the fortunes of science, and that every obstacle placed in the way of scientific discovery is a wrong to humanity. (Frazer 1958, p. 825)

Although the differences between science and technology are minimized by Frazer, as they tend to be in our own ordinary speech, it must be emphasized that what mattered to Frazer was practical mastery of the world, not its pure or theoretical comprehension. This is at any rate how one of Frazer's greatest confessed followers, the anthropologist Bronislaw Malinowski, read Frazer. Yet much of what Malinowski has to say about Frazer is more or less on the mark. Malinowski, for example, rightly uses Frazer to support his own pragmatic view of religion as a device for *controlling* features of the world, not for *explaining* them.

> *The Golden Bough*, in this regard, shows us primitive man as he really is, not an idle onlooker on the vast and varied spectacle of Nature, evolving by reflection a sort of speculative philosophy as to its meaning and using all the means in his power towards the attainment of his various needs and desires: supply of food, shelter, and covering; satisfaction of social ambitions and of sexual passions; satisfaction of some aesthetic impulses and of sportive and playful necessities. He is interested in all things which subserve these ends and are thus immediately useful. (Malinowski 1962, p. 272)

As we will see in chapter 10, Malinowski diverges from Frazer in asserting forcefully that the so-called 'primitives' have *both* religion *and* science at the same time!

From Magic to Religion to 'Science' . . . More or Less

How, then, could religion take its place in the evolutionary development that prepared the way for the stunning inventions of Frazer's time? What were those necessary steps that the human species was obliged to take in order for us to enjoy the benefits of telecommunications, medical miracles, or the computer? Attentive readers will note that in a subtle way Frazer's entire orientation differed on this point from Tylor's. Frazer felt that the most important human activity to chart through its evolutionary stages of development was not pure theoretical *science*, as Tylor had thought, but useful or applied science, what some may call 'technology.' It was not the pure speculative domain of the human adventure, the need to *explain* things, that was the critical area of human evolution. Therefore, the key questions were not about how the belief in spirits or souls inhabiting things functioned to make sense of the world for the 'primitives.' Something far more humble and basic must have been at play for our prehistoric ancestors, as it now was for the tribal peoples encountered in the colonial domain. It was the ability of human beings to *control* the environment in which we lived that mattered most – both then and now, both far away on the colonial frontier, and near to hand in the modern world.

Frazer's answer to this question was given in his argument for the evolution of what he called "science" ultimately from magic, by way of religion.

> If then we consider, on the one hand, the essential similarity of man's chief wants everywhere and at all times, and on the other hand, the wide difference between the means he has adopted to satisfy them in different ages, we shall perhaps be disposed to conclude that the movement of the higher thought, so far as we can trace it, has on the whole been from magic through religion to science. (Frazer 1958, p. 824)

In Frazer's view, the most primitive of human beings lived in fear of the vicissitudes of life. Danger threatened our prehistoric ancestors from every quarter. When ordinary means of protecting themselves failed, our ancestors resorted to a special sort of primitive 'technology' – what Frazer calls 'magic.' For him, magic is a mechanism for *controlling* events in the world by other than ordinary, everyday means. "In magic man depends on his own strength to meet the difficulties and dangers that beset him on every side. He believes in a certain established order of nature on which he can surely count, and which he can manipulate for his own ends" (Frazer 1958, p. 824). Instead of the employment of brute force or strength, our prehistoric ancestors thought that 'magic' effects changes in the world by means of spells, amulets, incantations, rituals, and such. Although Frazer believed that the power of magic operates in a different way from the physical use of force, magic is still somehow thought to be a power inherent in being human. Some people are believed to be able to tap this special human power; others are not. Those people who can access the hidden human resources to control nature are what we call 'magicians.'

However, Frazer says that sooner or later people conclude magic fails. They need a more powerful 'technology' for controlling nature, a mightier means of ensuring that nature will not overcome them. Realizing that nature cannot be managed by their own means, however special these may be, people call upon higher than human powers – upon gods and spirits.

> When he discovers his mistake, when he recognises sadly that both the order of nature which he had assumed and the control which he had believed himself to exercise over it were purely imaginary, he ceases to rely on his own intelligence and his own unaided efforts, and throws himself humbly on the mercy of certain great invisible beings behind

the veil of nature, to whom he now ascribes all those far-reaching powers which he once arrogated to himself. Thus in the acuter minds magic is gradually superseded by religion, which explains the succession of natural phenomena as regulated by the will, the passion, or the caprice of spiritual beings like man in kind, though vastly superior to him power. (Frazer 1958, p. 824)

In this way, religion is born – indeed religion of the sort that Tylor, for one, discussed. As in Tylor's animism, Frazer believes at this second stage of evolution that people implore the spirits, gods, or god to assist them in times of need. They offer sacrifice to placate the anger of the gods or to win their support for the causes that neither ordinary human physical power nor magic can affect. People learn to pray and worship. They become 'religious,' and divine intercession becomes a special kind of 'technology' whose sources of power come from distant places beyond the human realm entirely.

Finally, people mature to the point where they realize that the gods do not answer prayers, nor that sacrifices do not win divine approval or aid for human projects. People fall back again upon themselves – returning in a fashion to the self-reliance of magic – and labor to produce the kinds of modern technologies that can effect real changes in the world. We no longer dance for rain (magic), nor do we implore god to send rain (religion), we seed clouds with iodine crystals.

the keener minds, still pressing forward to a deeper solution of the mysteries of the universe, come to reject the religious theory of nature as inadequate, and to revert in a measure to the older standpoint of magic by postulating explicitly, what in magic had only been implicitly assumed, to wit, an inflexible regularity to the order of natural events, which, if carefully observed, enables us to foresee their course with certainty and to act accordingly. In short, religion, regarded as an explanation of nature, is displaced by science.

We thus resort to modern science and technology because they are the sources of power and productivity that Frazer and his generation were beginning to experience all round them. But, as firm a part of Frazer's mentality as his devotion to science and technology was, it would not be an untroubled one. This is one reason no doubt that George W. Stocking contrasts the sunny optimism of Tylor's evolutionary thinking with Frazer's "disenchanted later Victorian" outlook on life, and the life of religion, as we will now see (Stocking 1995, p. 146).

An Anxious Lust for Life

Oftentimes, however, answering one question only succeeds in triggering another. This is one of those times. While we now can understand how Frazer thought he was right to see the epic of human evolution in control over nature pass from magic through religion to science and technology, we still do not know why he thought he was right to fix on practical control over nature as the leading edge of human evolution. This means that we need to press on to a deeper, more basic level of Frazer's worldview and his intellectual motivation for his studies of religion. Why did Frazer think he was right to identify the forward thrust of evolution with the story of the development of *applied* science or technology, rather than, say, as Tylor did, on *pure* science? Or, why were other choices, reflecting other essential dimensions of human life, such as the evolution of art, music, social organization, or morality, not considered worthy of Frazer's devotion? Robertson Smith, for example, felt that the origins of the morality of altruism and generosity were our most vital questions about human evolution. And as we will see, Durkheim felt the key to understanding the more important aspects of human life depended upon understanding how our social life had changed over the ages. Why not Frazer? What was so critical for him about applied science and technology?

Interestingly enough, however, Frazer's basic motivations are even more complex. While he was strongly motivated to admire applied science and technology, he also registered great reservations about its fruits as well as about the strength of modernity to resist the return of more primitive forces in human life. In *Psyche's Task: A Discourse Concerning the Influence of Superstition on the Growth of Institutions* (1909), Frazer warned that

> "the ground beneath our feet" was "honeycombed by unseen forces"; we were "standing on a volcano which may at any moment break out in smoke and fire to spread ruin and devastation among the gardens and palaces of ancient culture wrought so laboriously by the hands of many generations." He could still believe in progress, but only as "the avowed creed of the enlightened minority"; in contrast, "the real, though unavowed creed of the mass of mankind appears to be almost stationary [because] in the majority of men, whether they are savages or outwardly civilized beings, intellectual progress is so slow as to be hardly perceptible." (Stocking 1995, p. 146)

On top of this latter-day hysteria about the solidity of modern society, one might argue that Frazer was already profoundly prepared to be skeptical about the sufficiency of modernity. He can also be seen as a passionate lover of the natural, rustic, old, and rural – in short a 'romantic' not unlike Max Müller! Of his reservations as to what science and technology had wrought, we catch a glimpse in his translation of the poem of the clergyman Charles Jean Marie Loyson (Père Hyacinthe), "Pour un chiffon de papier" – "For a Scrap of Paper." The poem memorializes the murderous tragedy of the First World War invasion of neutral Belgium by the Germans. The mention of the 'scrap of paper' refers to the Prussian Chancellor von Bethmann-Hollweg's cynical dismissal of protests against the invasion because of the formal international accord on Belgium's neutrality. Frazer's translation may well convey his own sense of growing disillusionment with scientific and technological 'progress' that eventuates in mass warfare:

> Why bursts the cloud in thunder, and to devastate the world
>   The levin bolt of battle from heaven, or hell, is hurled?
> Why march embattled millions, to death or victory sworn?
>   Why gape yon lanes of carnage by red artillery torn?
> For a scrap of paper, for a scrap of paper, nothing more!
>
> (Frazer 1927a, p. 425)

What seems to lie beneath these at first perplexing orientations is, I believe, Frazer's having been seized by a general sense of anxiety about life and fecundity. This sensibility was strong in the late nineteenth and early twentieth century, and even gave birth to a broad cultural and philosophical movement of the time known as vitalism. This sensibility looked on life in the modern world as lacking in vitality and spirit. To the vitalists, modern culture was sterile and needed a spark of life to revive it. Poets and playwrights of the time such as George Bernard Shaw and T. S. Eliot gave voice to vitalist ideas, and it is no accident that they were themselves influenced by Frazer.

Much of the spirit of Frazer's age, with its anxieties about fecundity and sterility, was reflected in his work, and left its mark on T. S. Eliot and his modern classic, *The Waste Land*. In a section of the poem called "What the Thunder Said," the poet laments the desiccation of both material and spiritual landscapes in the modern machine age. All round one hears rumbling promises of rain and thus of the replenishment of life. But instead the promise of life is unmet, for this is "dry sterile thunder" – " without rain." Only death prevails.

> Here is no water but only rock
> Rock and no water and the sandy road
> The road winding above among the mountains
> Which are mountains of rock without water
> If there were water we should stop and drink
> Amongst the rock one cannot stop or think
> Sweat is dry and feet are in the sand
> If there were only water amongst the rock

In his notes to *The Waste Land*, T. S. Eliot records his special debt to *The Golden Bough* and to the immense influence of Frazer's obsession with the themes of life, fecundity, and growth:

> To another work of anthropology I am indebted in general, one which has influenced our generation profoundly; I mean *The Golden Bough*; I have used especially the two volumes *Adonis, Attis, Osiris*. Anyone who is acquainted with these works will immediately recognise in the poem certain references to vegetation ceremonies. (Eliot 1922)

In the case of Shaw, *Man and Superman*, act III, a debate in hell between the reckless, life-affirming Don Juan and his captor, the Devil, is carried on with vitalism at the center. Don Juan tries to answer the Devil's charge that life – here known as "The Life Force" – is reckless and creates havoc and disorder, along with whatever good it may bring forth. Don Juan answers like a true devotee of vitalism that it is preferable to the alternatives, since it is for all that a creative force.

> DON JUAN. Well, the Life Force is stupid; but it is not so stupid as the forces of Death and Degeneration. Besides, these are in its pay all the time. And so Life wins, after a fashion. What mere copiousness of fecundity can supply and mere greed preserve, we possess. The survival of whatever form of civilization can produce the best rifle and the best fed riflemen is assured.

Shaw is incidentally not shy about his intellectual debts to Frazer, although I do not claim any more here than their being rooted in a common vitalist mentality. Thus Shaw is quite explicit in his admiration for *The Golden Bough*, largely, as we will see, for its special brand of criticism of Christianity that Frazer as an 'undertaker of religion' is eager to engage.

> There is yet another page in the history of religion which must be conned and digested before the career of Jesus can be fully understood. People who can read long books will find it in Frazer's ... From Frazer's magnum opus you will learn how the same primitive logic which makes the Englishman believe today that by eating a beefsteak he can acquire the strength and courage of the bull, and to hold that belief in the face of the most ignominious defeats by vegetarian wrestlers and racers and bicyclists, led the first men who conceived God as capable of incarnation to believe that they could acquire a spark of his divinity by eating his flesh and drinking his blood. (Shaw 1912, pp. 19–20)

What makes Christianity a work of – for Shaw, malignant – genius in eyes now illuminated by Frazer's *The Golden Bough*, is how Christianity has melded together and exploited age-old mythological vitalistic themes of fecundity, fertility, and regeneration, setting them firmly upon a foundational template for use throughout its 2,000-year history.

> And from the interweaving of these two traditions with the craving for the Redeemer, you at last get the conviction that when the Redeemer comes he will be immortal; he will give us his body to eat and his blood to drink; and he will prove his divinity by suffering a barbarous death without resistance or reproach, and rise from the dead and return to the earth in glory as the giver of life eternal. (Shaw 1912, pp. 19–20)

If Frazer thinks, as we will see, that the most fundamental of all religious cults seek to guarantee that people will conquer death and attain increased life in this world and everlasting life in the next, the anxious spirit of his age, as witnessed by Shaw and Eliot, gave him every reason to think that his intuitions were on target. Even more impressively, as we have just seen, Frazer reciprocates those sentiments amply and casts his influence widely among creative members of his own generation.

Frazer's exploitation of vitalist ideas is thus itself a great work of genius, whether it be correct or not as to the nature of religion. Let us now see how Frazer finds the elements of his vitalism in the religions of the ancient world and exotic societies. These discussions fill the many pages of his great classic of comparative study of religions, *The Golden Bough*. But what makes special *problems for religion*, at least for Christianity, are Frazer's attempts to undermine the uniqueness and supernatural origins of Christianity by showing how it fundamentally trades on 'primitive pagan' attempts to control the environment. After all, do not both 'pagans' and Christians want people to have "life, and have it more abundantly" (John 10:10)? Let us first see how Frazer works out his vitalist convictions in a general way in *The Golden Bough*, and how he then tries to undermine Christianity using the same analytic tools.

The Golden Bough: From Norseland to Nemi

If we are to believe Frazer's own words, the records of a strange ancient Roman rite set him on a quest that would culminate in the publication in various editions, stretching from 1890 to 1915, of his ultimately 12-volume classic study of religion, myth, and folklore, *The Golden Bough*. The 'bough' of the book's title refers to mistletoe. In winter, Frazer tells us, when the when the oak tree which hosts mistletoe has lost its leaves and seems drained of all life, the "golden" mistletoe bursts forth from the trunk and upper branches of the dormant oak. It promises the return of new life by embodying the very life of the oak itself. True both to his inclination toward the encyclopedic and to the comparative method, Frazer tracks down any number of instances in which mistletoe figures in ritual uses. Without following Frazer down every turning along this rather long corridor, we can trace two major comparisons that both illustrate his method and the major theme of *The Golden Bough*. These concern the puzzles he tries to solve involving the sacrificial death of the god and the promise of new life in the process, all with the help of a sprig of mistletoe!

First, consider the myth of Balder, the Norse hero and son of the father-god, Odin. Traditionally, Balder is symbolically associated with mistletoe. Balder's very life is embodied in the mistletoe – "his own existence is inseparably bound up" in it, and tragically "his own death is the result of it" (Frazer 1958, p. 812). The myth tells of the intention of the gods to make Balder invulnerable to attack by getting the gods of all materials that make up earthly existence – iron, stone, water, etc. – to agree not to harm him. They do so pledge. Thereupon, the other gods test Balder's resistance by submitting him to attacks from all the standard weapons of warfare – axes, swords, arrows, and such. Nothing even slightly fazes the hero. But one additional test, suggested by one of the divine assembly, named Loki, consists of attacking Balder with a blow from a mere twig of mistletoe. This is done. Then, horrible to behold, one of the gods hurls the mistletoe at Balder, and as soon as it strikes him, the 'golden bough' – that sprig of mistletoe – "pierced him through and through, and he fell down dead" (Frazer 1958, p. 704). After Balder's death, the gods cremated his body upon an immense funeral pyre, producing an appropriately large blaze.

Frazer feels that the point of the myth was profound and central to what he had come to see in myths across the globe – the tragic inner relationship between life and death, wherein each force mutually makes possible its opposite in a never-ending cycle of life and death. He says this because, thereafter, in the northern reaches of Europe, people celebrated the death and cremation of Balder by sacrificing human 'Balders' in fire festivals at critical times in the growing season. Summing up, Frazer says that "we may reasonably infer that in the Balder myth on the one hand, and the fire-festivals and custom of gathering mistletoe on the other hand, we have, as it were, the two broken and dissevered halves of an original whole." What seemed like unconnected rites, customs, or religious practices are actually held together by reference to a deeper human sensibility. The lust for life is symbolized in the blazing fires of sacrificial immolation and the bouquets of the mysterious new growth of the 'golden boughs' of mistletoe from otherwise barren-looking oak trees!

> In other words, we may assume with some degree of probability that the myth of Balder's death was not merely a myth, that is, a description of physical phenomena in imagery borrowed from human life, but that it was at the same time the story which people told to explain why they annually burned a human representative of the god and cut the mistletoe with solemn ceremony.

Unlike Robertson Smith, who saw the ritual instinct as primary, Frazer saw myths as vital and primitive in human civilization's formation. Moreover, the myths that mattered were those related to cults and religions working to enhance life by means of the performance of the sacrifice of the god.

> If I am right, the story of Balder's tragic end formed, so to say, the text of the sacred drama which was acted year by year as a magical rite to cause the sun to shine, crops to thrive, and to guard man and beast from the baleful arts of fairies and trolls, of witches and warlocks. (Frazer 1958, p. 770)

Now, thanks to Tylor's influence, Frazer was a devoted, if sometimes confusing, evolutionist and comparativist. As such, in general, he believed that all human societies pass through the same stages of human development, just as human individuals all grow according to a common order of development from childhood to adulthood. There may be occasional reversals or untidy mixtures of stages, but overall the evolutionary line is set out on a progressivist course. In this, religion is no exception. Indeed, the thrust of Frazer's undercutting of Christianity presumes this religious evolution, the greater implications of which we will see shortly. Now, since religion evolves, Frazer believes in the universality – or at least wide deployment among human societies – of certain religious patterns, much as Max Müller believed that there were cross-cultural linguistic and mythological patterns in Indo-European languages and mythologies. The problem with trying to understand cultures – especially ancient ones – at this late stage in history, however, is that our data are often fragmentary and incomplete. We do not have the complete mythologies of the Greeks, Hindus, or Romans, still less complete knowledge of them, and still less anything approaching complete knowledge of cultures of the ancient world. Much has been lost over the course of history; there are many gaps. The strategy of comparison speaks directly to this problem of gaps in our knowledge. If we find gaps, say, in one language or mythology, we should be able to fill these in with what we know from analogous related languages, mythologies, cultures, and so on, where those same gaps might not exist.

In true evolutionist style, Frazer 'knew' – among other things – that all cultures passed through identical stages of development and that the human mind was everywhere essentially the same. Thus, even though old Norse culture is a long way in time and space from, say, ancient Rome, Frazer was confident in the explanatory power of comparative method.

> recent researches into the early history of man have revealed the essential similarity with which, under many superficial differences, the human mind has elaborated its first crude philosophy of life. Accordingly, if we can show that a barbarous custom, like that of the priesthood of Nemi, has existed elsewhere; if we can detect the motives which led to its institution; if we can prove that these motives have operated widely, perhaps universally, in human society, producing in varied circumstances a variety of institutions specifically different but generically alike; if we can show, lastly, that these very motives, with some of their derivative institutions, were actually at work in classical antiquity; then we may fairly infer that at a remoter age the same motives gave birth to the priesthood of Nemi. (Frazer 1958, p. 2)

Thus, Frazer believed that he could move by various leaps and bounds to connect what he knew (or did not know) about Balder and mistletoe to what he did not know (or what he knew) about other accounts of a hero or god being killed, and in which mistletoe was connected. Frazer found precisely – at least by his standards – an analogous case in the rite of the murder of the priest at the shrine of Diana along the shores of the lake at Nemi – where mistletoe figured as well! By this kind of comparison, Frazer felt that he could get at something deeply human, given that historical borrowing seemed out of the question.

Because Frazer thought that he recognized similarities, despite this separation of one case from another, and despite the lack of evidence of historical influence in these matters, Frazer was, in effect, also arguing against Max Müller. The old Norse and the ancient Romans were unlikely to have adopted their practices from one another – by *diffusion* or historical borrowing – as say Max Müller felt the analogies of language, myth, and culture among Indo-European folk were to be explained. They *invented* them *independently* of any historical connection. These analogous rites merely expressed aspects of a common cultural evolution that these widely dispersed peoples shared. Let us then look at Frazer's famously dramatic account of the gloomy goings on at Nemi.

In his excellent study of the life and work of Frazer, Robert Ackerman has recorded a remarkable letter Frazer wrote on November 8, 1889, to the future publisher of *The Golden Bough*, George Macmillan. In it, Frazer essentially sums up the argument and intentions that will carry through from the first edition of the book in 1890 to its third and final full version of 12 volumes 25 years later:

> By an application of the comparative method I believe that I can make it probable that the priest represented in his person the god of the grove – Virbius – and that his slaughter was regarded as the death of the god. This raises the question of the meaning of a widespread custom of killing men and animals regarded as divine ... *The Golden Bough*, I believe I can show, was the mistletoe, and the whole legend can, I think, be brought into connexion, on the one hand, with the Druidical reverence for the mistletoe and the human sacrifices which accompanied their worship, and, on the other hand, with the Norse legend of the death of Balder. (cited in Ackerman 1987, p. 95)

We know the story of Balder to which Frazer refers in his letter. Now, in order to follow the links in Frazer's thinking, let us proceed to the story of "Virbius," the god-priest of the sacred grove at Nemi, and see what Frazer makes of it. Since the literary quality of Frazer's *The Golden Bough* is so much a part of the distinctiveness of his work, let me quote its opening passages as they set the initial dramatic scene of a kind of extended murder "mystery" thriller – a 'why-dunnit?' rather than a 'who-dunnit?'– played out over the balance of its remaining 11 volumes (Stocking 1995, p. 139). We are at act I, scene 1, so to speak, "The King of the Wood."

Frazer at once invites us into a nostalgia-infused scene at the shores of the lake at Nemi, warmed by the romance of a nature idyll:

> Who does not know Turner's picture of the Golden Bough? The scene, suffused with the golden glow of imagination in which the divine mind of Turner steeped and transfigured even the fairest natural landscape, is a dream-like vision of the little woodland lake of Nemi – "Diana's Mirror" ... One who has seen that calm water, lapped in a green hollow of the Alban hills, can ever forget it. The two characteristic Italian villages which slumber on its banks, and the equally Italian palace whose terraced gardens descend steeply to the lake, hardly break the stillness and even the solitariness of the

scene. Diana herself might still linger by this lonely shore, still haunt these woodlands wild.

Breaking the spell of this pastoral, a murder mystery now begins to unfold in a crime scene that is – of all places – also a sacred precinct of some apparent woodland nature rite.

In antiquity this sylvan landscape was the scene of a strange and recurring tragedy. In the northern shore of the lake, right under the precipitous cliffs on which the modern village of Nemi is perched, stood the sacred grove and sanctuary of Diana ... or Diana of the Wood ...

Enter the criminal:

In this sacred grove there grew a certain tree round which at any time of the day, and probably far into the night, a grim figure might be seen to prowl. In his hand he carried a drawn sword, and he kept peering warily about him as if at every instant he expected to be set upon by an enemy.

Learning more, we find out as well that the "grim figure," armed and ready for his deadly deed, is no common homicidal thug, but a holy man. "He was a priest and a murderer," charged with a brutal and paradoxical commission of that holy site.

and the man for whom he looked was sooner or later to murder him and hold the priesthood in his stead. Such was the rule of the sanctuary. A candidate for the priesthood could only succeed to office by slaying the priest, and having slain him, he retained office till he was himself slain by a stronger or a craftier. (Frazer 1958, p. 1)

Frazer tells us more about the holy stalker who himself can anticipate the same crime committed against him. This murderous priest is likewise a "king," but a king who would also become the target for the next killer-priest, his successor. The king is dead; long live the king.

The post which he held by this precarious tenure carried with it the title of king; but surely no crowned head ever lay uneasier, or was visited by more evil dreams, than his. For year in, year out, in summer or winter, in fair weather and in foul, he had to keep his lonely watch, and whenever he snatched a troubled slumber it was at the peril of his life. The least relaxation of his vigilance, the smallest abatement of his strength of limb or skill of fence, put him in jeopardy; grey hairs might seal his death-warrant. (Frazer 1958, pp. 1–2)

All this finally may make us want to ask, 'why dunnit?' There is no mystery in 'who dunnit,' since Frazer tells us so from the start – even though it will be a different priest-king each time as the role of hunter and hunted revolves. The mystery of the killing of the priest-king by his successor, the next priest-king to be, lies in the rationale for such an apparently irrational custom. 'Why dunnit?' Frazer is ready with a beginnings of an answer. "The strange rule of this priesthood has no parallel in classical antiquity, and cannot be explained from it. To find an explanation we must go farther afield" (Frazer

1958, p. 2). We must become the kind of comparativists that Frazer, Tylor, and others have been, and make significant links with such examples "farther afield" such as Balder. Without going into all the complexities of the detail that Frazer laboriously presents to us, let me provide some idea of how Frazer's comparative thinking operated here.

Both in the case of Balder and the priest-king of Nemi, a sacred personage is killed by other sacred persons – whether this be the gods in Balder's case or the priest-king to be in the case of Nemi. Also, associated with both is the change of seasons and the return of new life that corresponds to them. The midsummer fires lit in honor of Balder, and the ancient custom of annual human sacrifice in connection with these "Balder fires," parallel the high summer fire worship of Diana, the "huntress" and fertility goddess to nubile and expectant women, at Nemi, and the hunting down and killing – the death and resurrection, as it were – of the priest-king by his successor. "*Le roi est mort, vive le roi! Ave Maria!*" – The king is dead; long live the king! Hail Mary! (Frazer 1958, p. 827). Linked as well with Diana as goddess of the hunt is Virbius. He too is worshiped at Nemi, as a kind of male counterpart to the goddess, reminiscent of the way Attis, for example, is linked with Cybele. Like the near invincible Balder, Frazer suggests that Virbius too is characterized by a tremendous ability to resist death, and therefore is a powerful emblem of ever-renewed life (Frazer 1958, pp. 4–6). What would seem to clinch the analogy for Frazer are two additional details. First, Virbius is acknowledged as the "mythical prede-cessor or archetype of the line of priests who served Diana under the title of Kings of the Wood, and who came, like him, one after the other, to a violent end" (Frazer 1958, p. 9). He then shares the fecundating nature of Diana, now linked with the period hunting/killing and renewal of the life of the priest-king of the Wood. Second, the priest-king of Nemi, like Balder, is identified with mistletoe. He personifies the oak tree upon which the 'golden bough' of mistletoe grows. And, like Balder again, as embodying the spirit of the oak, he can only be killed when a sprig – of mistletoe, in this case – is broken from the sacred oak itself. When the Balder fires are lit at midsummer, this also signals the gathering of mistletoe in the northern woodlands (Frazer 1958, p. 769).

> As an oak spirit, his [Virbius'] life or death was in the mistletoe on the oak, and so long as the mistletoe remained intact, he, like Balder, could not die. To slay him, therefore, it was necessary to break the mistletoe, and probably, as in the case of Balder, to throw it at him. And to complete the parallel, it is only necessary to suppose that the King of the Wood was formerly burned, dead or alive, at the midsummer fire festival which, as we have seen, was annually celebrated in the Arician grove [Nemi]. (Frazer 1958, p. 815)

This then is the story that lies behind the title of Frazer's great book. The ceaseless rhythm of life, death, and rebirth, and the human desire to see life triumphant, lie at the heart of the strange rites of the sacrifice of the god. It may seem as if we have followed a long and tortuous route to reach this conclusion. But, unraveling Frazer's thinking, we are at least true to the character of the intricately detailed mystery stories that seem to have inspired Frazer in the first place. One great burden of Frazer's book is to show that this pattern and this human sensibility are universal and particularly compelling. This is surely a tall order, but Frazer's attempts to prove his case provide stimulating, if at times maddening, reading and, at the very least, wonderful stimuli for thinking about problems of religion.

In concluding these comparisons of Balder to the deities at Nemi, Frazer teases us by dangling before the eyes of his readers – but just out of reach – the target at which his work is ultimately aimed. "The resemblance of many of the savage customs and ideas" – such as those having to do with the death and 'resurrection' of gods like Balder or Virbius – "to the fundamental doctrines of Christianity is striking." But Frazer will not exploit the gains he thinks that he has made. Coyly, he stops at the threshold. "I make no reference to this parallelism, leaving my readers to draw their own conclusions, one way or the other." I, however, lack Frazer's reluctance to say what he really thinks, and shall now lay out the conclusions that Frazer seems only willing to insinuate.

Old Templates, New Meanings: 'Baptizing' Ancient Pagan Beliefs and Practices

We have now seen along the way that Frazer deliberately introduces religious ideas, motifs, myths, ritual, and so on that echo Christian ones. The death and return to life of both Balder and Virbius, their connection with the enhancement of life, and so on, all have reasonable Christian echoes. As Frazer himself is aware, some may think that such comparative likening of central Christian motifs to pagan ones proves how the coming of Jesus was 'prepared' by God over a long history of pre-Christian religious life, or on the other hand, perhaps, is evidence of Satan's attempt to lure Christians into accepting counterfeits of their own faith. Thus, in connection with the Mediterranean god Mithras, Frazer notes how problematic the interpretation of analogies with Christianity has been, even among early Christian scholars and theologians.

> In respect both of doctrines and of rites the cult of Mithra appears to have presented many points of resemblance not only to the religion of the Mother of the Gods but also to Christianity. The similarity struck the Christian doctors themselves and was explained by them as a work of the devil, who sought to seduce the souls of men from the true faith by a false and insidious imitation of it. (Frazer 1958, p. 415)

For other Christians, these ancient pagan religions were more akin to ancient Judaism in establishing what we can call certain religious *templates* in myths, rites, images, and so on. These more accommodating Christian thinkers would believe that the religions outside the Jewish world might have served the same divine plan of *preparing* the way for Christ. These pre-Christian religions got people ready for Christianity so that when the missionaries came with the Gospels, Christianity would not seem all that foreign to them. In our survey of theories of religion, we will recall that the devotees of Natural Religion felt somewhat the same way. Some of them believed that the religious aptitude or capacity that was built into human nature was part of a divine plan for laying the foundations of what would be 'revealed' to Jews and Christians in the 'fullness of time.' Christianity was still unique, but its outlines had been imprinted on the human religious mind millennia before the coming of Christ.

Now, Frazer did not feel this way, at least early on in his career. For him, especially as argued in the second edition of *The Golden Bough* in 1900, the many analogies to Christian motifs that he found in the religions of the ancient world and across the globe only showed how much Christianity *belonged* to the general history of religion, and therefore how lacking in uniqueness it was. These comparisons did not show how the pagan religions were really Christian underneath the surface, but rather how 'pagan,' 'primitive,' and 'savage' Christianity in truth actually was (Stocking 1995, p. 131). This method was Frazer's way of trying to undermine Christianity and to fulfill his career as and 'undertaker of religion.' To appreciate the power of his attack, let us consider some special examples of how he believed comparison could be the corrosive force against Christianity that he wished it to be.

Consider the supposedly unique Christian idea of Jesus as an incarnate god. Frazer attacks this belief in a series of ways. In Frazer's view, Christians have become comfortable in thinking that the idea of the god-man comes late in the history of religions – perhaps because one does not find this belief in the Jewish background out of which Christianity grew. But is this true according to what we can know from historical data, Frazer asks? Not so, since the

> notion of a man-god, or of a human being endowed with divine or supernatural powers, belongs essentially to that earlier period of religious history in which gods and men are still viewed as beings of much the same order, and before they are divided by the impassable gulf which, to later thought, opens out between them. Strange, therefore, as may seem to us the idea of a god incarnate in human form, it has nothing very startling for early man, who sees in a man-god or a god-man only a higher degree of the same supernatural powers which he arrogates in perfect good faith to himself.... Thus beginning as little more than a simple conjurer, the medicine-man or magician tends to blossom out into a full-blown god and king in one. (Frazer 1958, p. 106)

Are there other religions, Frazer asks, where we find the same thing? Yes indeed, answers Frazer again. Take India, and the god-man Krishna for example: "perhaps no country in the world has been so prolific of human gods as India; nowhere has the divine grace been poured out in a more liberal measure on all classes of society from kings down to milkmen," Frazer tells us (Frazer 1958, p. 115). So, to Frazer's way of seeing things, Christianity fails the first test of establishing its uniqueness – many religions can lay claim to worship incarnate deities, and thus the first piece of a pre-Christian template would seem to be in place.

What about other features essential to the basic structure of Christianity? Are the crucifixion, atoning, self-giving sacrificial death, and miraculous resurrection of Jesus not just too specific to Christian history to have their uniqueness diluted by comparison with other religions? Is not the poignant figure of Jesus' mother, at once – mostly for Catholics and the Eastern Orthodox – miraculously preserved from sin, and at the same time virgin and mother, too specifically Christian to fall prey to the corrosive effects of Frazer's comparison? Not so again, would be Frazer's reply. Specifically to undermine such standard Christian beliefs, Frazer develops extensive and detailed comparisons with non-Christian gods who do all the key things that Jesus is believed to have done – to die suspended from a wooden structure, if not a cross precisely, and whose death is seen as an atonement for human sin – the god giving themselves up for the salvation of their people, only to return in some form once more to life.

Frazer begins to show how the modeling of Christian symbols upon pagan ones occurred in a deliberate way. Early Christians, Frazer argues, deliberately tried to compete with pagans by, in a way, stealing their symbols outright. Consider the oddity of the present-day Christian celebration of Jesus' birth on December 25. Indeed, the gospels make no mention of the nativity's date, and most Christians previously had celebrated it on January 6. So why is it that ever since 375 CE, December 25 has been designated as the 'true' date of the birth of Jesus? Supported by the confirmation of Christians of the time, Frazer replies that it was rivalry with devotion to the Mediterranean sun-god Mithras that decided the issue of when to celebrate the birth of Jesus, then also known, analogously, as the "Sun of Righteousness" (Frazer 1958, p. 417). The religion of Mithras

> proved a formidable rival to Christianity, combining as it did a solemn ritual with aspirations after moral purity and a hope of immortality. Indeed the issue of the conflict between the two faiths appears for a time to have hung in the balance. An instructive relic of the long struggle is preserved in our festival of Christmas, which the Church seems to have borrowed directly from its heathen rival.

The main reason for seizing on December 25 was then to replace the main celebration of the birth of Mithras with the birth of Jesus. Picking up Frazer's belief that religion was really about fertility and increase of life, we can see why he was attracted to what he perceived in the early Christian attempt to supplant Mithraic religion with its own symbols. On December 25, new life was thought once more to begin, since that day was the sun-god Mithras's birthday and in

> the Julian calendar the twenty-fifth of December was reckoned the winter solstice, and it was regarded as the Nativity of the Sun, because the day begins to lengthen and the power of the sun to increase from that turning-point of the year.... The Egyptians even represented the new-born sun by the image of an infant which on his birthday, the winter solstice, they brought forth and exhibited to his worshippers. (Frazer 1958, p. 415)

But early Christians were not satisfied to let pagans have their way. Christians would fill the old 'pagan' template with new Christian meaning.

This is a pattern of behavior of the early church that might be termed a 'baptizing' of pagan customs, beliefs, and practices. The old pagan form – or 'template' – remains, such as the December 25 date or the winter solstice, but a new, Christian content – Jesus, "Sun of Righteousness" – is added to replace the pagan meanings having to do with Mithras. Indeed, the key to Christianity's success lies in its brilliant exploitation of pagan motifs. What Frazer tries to show is that this pattern of 'baptizing' pagan beliefs and practices was not exceptional, it was indeed the *rule* by which the church dealt with pagan rivalry in the early centuries of the Christian era, and succeeded in replacing the 'pagan' religions. It became the 'rule' for the Christian missionizing of pagan Europe, with broad and profound implications, as we will see.

> When we remember that the festival of St. George in April has replaced the ancient pagan festival of the Parilia; that the festival of St. John the Baptist in June has succeeded to a heathen midsummer festival of water: that the festival of the Assumption of the Virgin in August has ousted the festival of Diana.... we can hardly be thought rash or unreasonable in conjecturing that the other cardinal festival of the Christian church – the solemnisation of Easter – may have been in like manner, and from like motives of edification, adapted to a similar celebration of the Phrygian god Attis at the vernal equinox. (Frazer 1958, p. 418)

To conclude this chapter on Frazer, let us now turn to the telling case of Frazer's comparison of the Christ story to that of Attis and his mother, the goddess, Cybele. This brings out how Frazer, among other things, reprises Robertson Smith's themes of the sacrifice of the god and the theory of totemism and the totemic communion connected with it. In this comparison, Frazer is making several powerful points that need carefully to be separated out.

First, Frazer goes to the extreme of arguing that the comparisons are remarkably *precise*. The powerful Christian images of Jesus' life, death, and resurrection along with Mary, Jesus' mother, rest on rather detailed correspondences between the *templates* of ancient pagan dying gods and 'Great Mothers' and the Christ story.

The story of Cybele and Attis, as Frazer tells it, is at once tragic and odd. Frazer notes to begin that Attis, the Good Shepherd, "was said to have been a fair young shepherd or herdsman." He does not make any explicit comparisons with Jesus. Then, echoing the Christian belief in Jesus' virgin birth, reports that Attis's "birth, like that of many other heroes, is said to have been miraculous. His mother, Nana, was a virgin." There is some confusion in the several stories of Attis, since Cybele, "the Mother of the Gods, a great Asiatic goddess of fertility," who loves Attis dearly, is also said to be his mother, and not Nana (Frazer 1958, p. 403). Still, if the matter of Attis's precise maternity can be set aside for the moment, we can see behind Frazer's words another implication – namely that Cybele, 'mother of the gods' and goddess bringing life and fertility, corresponds to Mary,

Figure 6.1, Cybele, as the Great Mother, holding her infant son, Attis, in her arms (see also figure 9.1)

virgin mother of Jesus, known by many Christians as "Holy Mary, *Mother of God*," who is also "*full* of grace," and as such the medium conveying Christ, the giver of divine eternal life, unto the world. Then, while the precise details of the death of Attis vary from myth to myth, most agree that he died in some close relation to a tree and hung from a tree – the pagan precursor, one imagines Frazer thinking, to the cross upon which Jesus is crucified. Thus, in one version of his myth, Attis dies at the foot of a "pine tree" after having bled to death from a self-inflicted castration (Frazer 1958, p. 407). Save for this violent unmanning, perhaps this foreshadows Jesus' plaintive "Thy will be done" – his submitting entirely to the will of the Father on Calvary? In another version of the Attis story, he is tied up in a tree and there he is killed (Fraser 1994, p. 355). Without trying too hard to disguise his belief that the Christ story is ultimately the same as the Attis story, and that no doubt the Catholic Lenten Passion pageants repeated old pagan rites, Frazer then recounts the cult that was widely celebrated to remember Attis's bloody death and fixing upon a tree. On the appointed day at the Spring equinox:

> a pine-tree was cut in the woods and brought into the sanctuary of Cybele, where it was treated as a great divinity. The duty of carrying the sacred tree was entrusted to a guild of Tree-bearers. The trunk was swathed like a corpse with woollen bands and decked with wreaths of violets ... and the effigy of a young man, doubtless Attis himself, was tied to the middle of the stem. (Frazer 1958, p. 405)

Like Jesus as well after his death, the effigy of Attis is "laid in the sepulchre," and just as in the Christ story, his resurrection follows straight on:

> But when night had fallen, the sorrow of the worshippers was turned to joy. For suddenly a light shone in the darkness: the tomb was opened: the god had risen from the dead; and as the priest touched the lips of the weeping mourners with balm, he softly whispered in their ears the glad tidings of salvation. The resurrection of the god was hailed by his disciples as a promise that they too would issue triumphant from the corruption of the grave. On the morrow, the twenty-fifth day of March, which was reckoned the vernal equinox, the divine resurrection was celebrated with a wild outburst of glee. (Frazer 1958, p. 407)

Finally, in commemoration of the death and resurrection of Attis, a sacramental meal and communion that Frazer calls a "blessed sacrament" are celebrated, albeit, Frazer claims, in secret private settings.

> Our information as to the nature of these mysteries and the date of their celebration is unfortunately very scanty, but they seem to have included a sacramental meal and a baptism of blood. In the sacrament the novice became a partaker of the mysteries by eating out of a drum and drinking out of a cymbal, two instruments of music which figured prominently in the thrilling orchestra of Attis. (Frazer 1958, p. 408)

It is not clear whether this is a reference to Robertson Smith's concept of the totemic meal, but we might at least look at Frazer's account here of the death and ritualization of the dying god as such. Frazer does not call the communion sacrament of Attis specifically a "totemic" one, yet it is clear from the logic of Frazer's argument that it conforms in large part to totemic characteristics. The god is ritually celebrated by a group of devotees that display him and his death in a totem-like effigy, after which they partake of the essence of the dead totem in a sacramental meal.

As we have just seen, Frazer was struck not only by similarities in the narrative accounts of the Christ story and the Attis/Cybele story, but also with the fact that the cults built upon them seemed likewise to mirror each other. Ever attentive for evidence of vitalism, such as the rhythms of seasonal vegetative death and rebirth, Frazer argues that the first days of Spring seem to have been chosen by both cults for celebrating the deaths and resurrections of Attis and Jesus, respectively. Their mystical new lives cohered with the new life of nature's Spring season of rebirth.

> Now the death and resurrection of Attis were officially celebrated at Rome on the twenty-fourth and twenty-fifth of March, the latter being regarded as the spring equinox, and therefore as the most appropriate day for the revival of a god of vegetation who had been dead or sleeping throughout the winter. But according to an ancient and widespread tradition, Christ suffered on the twenty-fifth of March, and accordingly some Christians regularly celebrated the Crucifixion on that day without any regard to the state of the moon. (Frazer 1958, p. 417)

These analogies gave Frazer the additional opening he sought to indict Christianity – especially Roman Catholicism – as a survival of "savagery." After all, Frazer in effect will ask us, does not the logic of salvation according to Christianity adhere to the same atonement theology of human redemption as the old cult of Attis? Does it not preach the salvation of the faithful by means of the 'Passion,' with its scourgings, beatings, killing, and copious shedding of the blood of Jesus?

> The barbarous and cruel character of the worship, with its frantic excesses, was doubtless repugnant to the good taste and humanity of the Greeks, who seem to have preferred the kindred but gentler rites of Adonis. Yet the same features which shocked and repelled the Greeks may have positively attracted the less refined Romans and barbarians of the West. The ecstatic frenzies, which were mistaken for divine inspiration, the mangling of the body, the theory of a new birth and the remission of sins through the shedding of blood, have all their origin in savagery, and they naturally appealed to peoples in whom the savage instincts were still strong. (Frazer 1958, p. 414)

Frazer's implications seem clear enough, even down to his sly identification of the *Roman* Catholics of his day with those who adhered to the murderous cult of Attis – those "less refined Romans and barbarians of the West."

Second, in the case of the comparison of Attis/Cybele to the Christ story, the analogies between the pagan and the Christian show an *unconscious* and *unpremeditated* aspect. Frazer's remarks suggest, for instance, that there may be some kind of latent cultural 'memory' or imprinted unconscious 'template' that reasserts itself even though layers of historical change may have been applied over it.

> At least it is a remarkable coincidence, if it is nothing more, that the Christian and the heathen festivals of the divine death and resurrection should have been solemnised at the same season and in the same places. For the places which celebrated the death of

Christ at the spring equinox were Phrygia, Gaul, and apparently Rome, that is, the very regions in which the worship of Attis either originated or struck deepest root. It is difficult to regard the coincidence as purely accidental.

Going on immediately at the same place, Frazer also suggests that at the very least there is a common, universal response to the life-giving rhythms of nature that explain these comparisons:

> If the vernal equinox, the season at which in the temperate regions the whole face of nature testifies to a fresh outburst of vital energy, had been viewed from of old as the time when the world was annually created afresh in the resurrection of a god, nothing could be more natural than to place the resurrection of the new deity at the same cardinal point of the year. (Frazer 1958, p. 418)

Thus, unlike what Frazer reported about the cynical maneuverings of the Church Fathers to celebrate Christmas on Mithras' birthday, Frazer suggests as well that there was something deeply appropriate to these policies that bespoke some sort of common human religious orientation. This comparison then carries a more special weight of implications about the universal nature of religion than any deliberate attempts to trade on the structures or templates of other religions for the self-conscious benefit of one's own. Once again Frazer notes how we can learn about the nature of religion from studying how the cults and rites of a religion are celebrated – even down to the selection of the dates for such celebrations. Thus,

> the tradition which placed the death of Christ on the twenty-fifth of March was ancient and deeply rooted. It is all the more remarkable because astronomical consid-erations prove that it can have had no historical foundation. The inference appears to be inevitable that the passion of Christ must have been arbitrarily referred to that date in order to harmonise with an older festival of the spring equinox. (Frazer 1958, p. 417)

Frazer seems to be saying that people think in a certain religious way *naturally*, without coaxing or premeditation. There was no "historical foundation" for the church fathers *deliberately* selecting the March 25 to celebrate Easter. Its selection rested on some more "ancient and deeply rooted" factors. Discovering what that natural religious inclination might be has always been, I believe, part of the way Frazer thought about religion – as we know always for him, in vitalistic style, a matter of enhancing life and fertility.

Third, in the case of Attis and Cybele, Frazer not only observes the same *template* – unconscious or otherwise – as seen in Christianity, he suggests this template is more than just *structure*. It carries with it into Christianity itself a good deal of the *meaning and content* of the old pagan rites and ideas. To tie these three points together, Frazer believes this mostly because Frazer believes that the very ideas that lie at the foundation of the Attis/Cybele religion and Christianity, respectively, lie at the basis of all religions. All the religions of all people in the end want people to 'have life and have it more abundantly.' They want to be vitalists – like Frazer!

References

Ackerman, R. 1987. *J. G. Frazer: His Life and Work*. Cambridge: Cambridge University Press.

Douglas, M. 1978. "Introduction." In *The Illustrated Golden Bough*, by Sir James Frazer, ed. S. MacCormack. London: George Rainbird.

Eliot, T. S. 1922. *The Waste Land*.

Fraser, R. 2005. Frazer, Sir James (1854–1941). Article in *The Literary Encyclopedia*, www.litencyc.com, accessed June.

——, ed. 1994. *James George Frazer, The Golden Bough: A New Abridgement*. Oxford: Oxford University Press.

Frazer, J. G. 1926. Letter to Bronislaw Malinowski, Feb. 14, 1926, ed. B. Malinowski. Bronislaw Malinowski Papers, Manuscripts and Archives, Yale University Library.

——. 1927a. For a Scrap of Paper (From the French of Paul Hyacinthe Loyson). In *Gorgon's Head*. London: Macmillan.

——. 1927b. William Robertson Smith. In *Gorgon's Head*. London: Macmillan.

——. 1935. *Creation and Evolution in Primitive Cosmonogies and Other Pieces*. London: Macmillan.

——. 1958. *The Golden Bough*. New York: Macmillan.

Hume, D. 1963. The Natural History of Religion. In *Hume on Religion*, ed. R. Wollheim. London: Collins.

Jarvie, I. C. 1964. *The Revolution in Anthropology*. London: Routledge & Kegan Paul.

Lord, Daniel A., SJ. 1912. The Christianity of George Bernard Shaw. *America* 16.

——. 1916. *The Christianity of George Bernard Shaw*. New York: America.

Malinowski, B. 1962. On Sir James Frazer. In *Sex, Culture and Myth*. New York: Harcourt Brace.

——. 1992. Myth in Primitive Psychology (1925). In *Magic, Science, and Religion and Other Essays*, ed. R. Redfield. Prospect Heights, IL: Waveland Press.

Parker, R. A. 1997–2002. Exploring *The Waste Land*. http://world.std.com/~raparker/ exploring/thewasteland/explore.html, accessed June 2005.

Ratnikas, A. June 2005. Timelines of History, at http://timelines.ws/

Shaw, G. B. 1912. Preface to *Androcles and the Lion*: On the Prospects of Christianity. In *A Penn State Electronic Classics Series Publication*, ed. J. Manis. Philadelphia: University of Pennsylvania Press.

Stocking, G. W. 1995. *After Tylor: British Social Anthropology, 1888–1951*. Madison: University of Wisconsin Press.

Strenski, I. 1987. *Four Theories of Myth in Twentieth-Century History*. London/Iowa City: Macmillan/Iowa University Press.

Classic Twentieth-
Century Theorists of
the Study of Religion:
Defending the Inner
Sanctum of Religious
Experience or
Storming It

PART III

From Evolution to Religious Experience: Phenomenology of Religion

7

Problems of Evolutionism, Problems with Evolutionism

The classic nineteenth-century founders of the study of religion, such as Friedrich Max Müller, James Frazer, or Edward Burnett Tylor, proceeded under (at least) four major assumptions. First, they presumed that religion was a *simple* thing and therefore that religion only required *simple* explanations. Religion required minimal description, almost no account of its constitution, and virtually nothing about how its constituent parts might articulate. Second, since the nature of religion was presumed to be well understood, the nineteenth-century founders thought that the way was cleared for them to *explain* religion. Third, in terms of *explaining religion*, the nineteenth-century founders simply took for granted that the only questions worth asking about religion, and thus the only explanations worth having for religion, were historical ones. These were given either in the rather narrow sense of history as chronology – what institutions came first and gave rise to, or *caused*, succeeding ones – or in the more theoretically informed strategies of exploring developmental or degenerative processes – what historical stages laid the necessary facilitating conditions for the evolution or 'devolution' of what stages of religion were to follow.

In 1885, the Belgian student of religion, Comte Eugène Goblet d'Alviella, attested to how deeply entrenched in nineteenth-century thinking about religion was the notion of religious evolution. To him, the evolution of religion seemed not even to be a 'theory,' but rather a "quasi-certitude"(Goblet d'Alviella 1885, p. 173). Goblet d'Alviella's co-religionist in Paris, the liberal Protestant historian of religion Jean Réville, revealingly argued that if the objectivity of religious "progress" were shaken, it would have the intolerable result of placing Christianity at the same evolutionary level as other religions (Réville 1903, p. 432). Thus the fourth shared assumption: the conviction that the problems of historical evolution were foremost in importance, which led the nineteenth-century founders of religious studies to play down the role of *empirical ethnography* or *fieldwork study* and the method of *"participant observation"* of religion and religious institutions that became part and parcel of the so-called 'anthropological method' of studying religion. This is not to say that the founders had no place for fieldwork, only that their evolutionist priorities led them to rank it lower than their need to confirm already devised historical schemes of developmental growth.

For Max Müller, latter-day romantic devotee of Enlightenment Deism, religion was thus simply – and for him, self-evidently – essentially the contemplation of the Infinite. What required explanation was how and why so much of what passed as 'religion' failed to live up to the essence of 'religion.' His answer was given in terms of a narrative of decline, degeneration, or devolution of essential religion (the same virtually as the "natural religion" of the Enlightenment and earlier) into the many religions. For one reason or another, humanity had simply lost its way and strayed from an aboriginal blessedness where humanity and divinity were at one, and the lion lay down with the lamb. Significantly, Müller never set foot in India, nor did he immerse himself in the social life of emigrant Indian communities, such as they were, in Europe. For him, the texts were all he needed for his work (van den Bosch 2002, p. 137).

For his part, Frazer sized up religion as just an attempt by 'primitive' peoples (and Catholics!) to control their environment by supplicating the deity, or variously preserving or reviving the deity. On Frazer's evolutionary scale of progress, religion was a developmental prelude to technology, and itself successor to exotic human attempts to manage reality – 'magic,' so-called – and nothing more. 'We' had learned that magic did not work, so 'we' resorted to petitioning the deity. When humanity finally understood that religion failed as well, 'we' once more took matters into our own hands and developed technologies. But while Frazer was an avid holiday traveler, especially throughout the Mediterranean world so beloved of his classicist's heart, these journeys were unsystematic and casual. Thus, when William James asked Frazer whether he might want to sojourn a while to study at first hand the 'primitives' about whom he had written so much – if only for the sake of confirming these lavish theories – Frazer replied "God forbid!" (Young 2004, p. 229).

Tylor too felt that no great mysteries for understanding and explaining religion lay at the surface of things. Religion is plainly just the ultimately childish belief that active spirits directed events of the observable world. Whether this be one single spirit, such as the one God of the monotheism of the Abrahamic tradition, or the many souls that many sorts of traditional folk felt inhabited the objects and visible beings of their everyday experience, the answer was the same. Religion is the belief in the active existence of these 'spirits' in the world. Unlike Müller and Frazer, at least Tylor took himself off to the ethnographic 'field' about which he was to write – the Mexico of his first book, *Anahuac*. However, unlike the classic modern anthropology that would emerge at the end of his career, Tylor's approach was still that of the casual adventuring 'traveler' making less than perfectly systematic investigations and observations of his subjects. Tylor never stayed in the ethnographic field long enough carefully to observe or deeply to understand the goings on in the social and cultural fields about which he wrote. He had other scientific interests foremost in his mind – that of gathering just enough examples to support the evolutionary scheme to which he was already deeply and incorrigibly committed. Ironically, like the theist believer in miracles fitting any sort of unusual event into a scheme that would confirm a doctrine of divine providence, so also Tylor and others committed to an evolutionist ideology never let contrary 'facts' interfere with their presumption of the truth of general cultural evolution. Instead, these 'facts' were simply added to the 'evidence' confirming the developmental worldview.

How and Why Did 'Phenomenology of Religion' Really Come to Be?

We sometimes think that the great changes in the way people think happened magically in a flash of brilliant insight. We imagine that one day some great genius woke up with a totally new idea that neatly and cleanly broke with what everyone thought before then. From that moment on, the progress of the new idea just rolled in like a great tsunami crashing onto the land, sweeping everything before it. In the popular imagination, one tends to think that new ideas happen like Isaac Newton arriving at the theory of gravitation after getting bopped on the head by a falling apple. This way of understanding how new ideas come to be and take hold is not true. It is especially not true for the way people who thought about religion took the radical turn to what can loosely be called phenomenology of religion after so many generations of thinking about religion in developmental and evolutionary terms. They found it quite difficult to let go of evolutionary ideas, especially the idea that Christianity represented the highest, or most highly 'evolved,' form of religion. It is ironic, from our present viewpoint, where evolutionism and some forms of Christianity stand starkly opposed to one another, that Christians have been among the most active supporters of evolutionary worldviews, even Darwinian ones. The Christian attraction to evolutionary ideas of religious development was part of the reason that Christians were at first well disposed to Darwin's theory of evolution – even though the Christian idea of religious progress ought not, of course, to be confused with Darwin's theory.

This is also to recognize that especially in the late nineteenth and early twentieth centuries among Christians in the West, the belief that Christianity rode the rolling tide of religious progress was very deeply entrenched. Indeed, the belief in *religious* progress or evolution is still very much alive today, even as the very same Christians may combat Darwin's ideas! This is because many faithful Christians believe in the superiority of Christianity as the epitome of religious development, growth, and evolution, all the while disparaging the ideas of human origin put forth by Darwin. In this regard, I do not mean to single out Christianity, although it needs to be featured, since our religious theorists either were Christians themselves or at least operated within a thought-world dominated by Christianity. For this reason it is well to point out that many segments of Islam share ideas of progressive religious development with Christians, leading to a belief in the 'advanced' nature or religious superiority of Islam. For their part, Muslims, like Christians, do not deny the prophets of the Hebrew Bible. Instead, like Christians who claim that Jesus supersedes and fulfills the Jewish prophets, so also Muslims take the same attitude to both Judaism and Christianity, and even to Jesus: Muhammad is the "Seal of the Prophets" – the final, culminating message of God to humanity. Muhammad does not negate those who led up to him, even Jesus. He only fulfills the preaching and teaching of Jesus and all the prophets of Israel. So, religious evolution is a far more prevalent and 'normal' part of the way religious folk look on themselves and other religions than one might imagine, given the tendency these days to think of (Darwinian) evolution and religious faith in opposite camps.

How then did it happen that those we may first call 'phenomenologists of religion,' all of whom were not only Christians, but ordained ministers of one or another Christian church, began to break with evolutionary thinking about religion?

The first point to be made is that while there was indeed a general shift in focus in the way religion was being studied in the late nineteenth and early twentieth centuries, this reorientation was shared across the board by other humanistic and social-scientific disciplines. The problem immediately arises, however, that the term used to name this shift – 'phenomenology' – has been used vaguely and without much effort at consistent usage. There is, fortunately or unfortunately, not much to be done about this. I have resigned myself to the vagueness of this term, a position in keeping with those much more expert in the field than I. As Herbert Spiegelberg, author of the authoritative two-volume survey of the phenomenological movement, has said, "the underlying assumption of a unified philosophy subscribed to by all so-called phenomenologists is an illusion.... there are as many phenomenologies as there are phenomenologists".

Some of these new ways of looking at data tried, for example, to adhere strictly to an understanding of the term 'phenomenology,' often linking this with philosophical precedents, such as G. W. F. Hegel's great work *Phenomenology of Spirit*. Others, such as the famous Dutch phenomenologist of religion Gerardus van der Leeuw, attempted to attach his work to the philosophical phenomenology of Edmund Husserl. There, one posited objective structures of consciousness and sought to explore that world from a highly rigorous point of view. It is a mistake, in my view, to try to make more precise the idea of 'phenomenology of religion' *as it actually is practiced* than it can be. Some thinkers widely recognized as classic phenomenologists of religion, such as Gerardus van der Leeuw, have done just this by forcing their somewhat eclectic phenomenological approach to religion onto the Procrustean Bed of, say, Husserlian or Heideggerian *philosophical* phenomenology. In the pursuit of precision, one can sometimes offend accuracy – the main reason van der Leeuw's claims to be following Husserl's phenomenological method have generally not been taken seriously.

Accordingly, I shall adopt a general sense of the term 'phenomenology of religion' to apply to the main figures in this chapter. As we will see, for the most part they sought a general style of approaching religion with significant 'family resemblances' that makes sense of employing this usage. We can also look on other thinkers treated in this book – especially Max Weber, Émile Durkheim, Bronislaw Malinowski, and Mircea Eliade – as embodying one or another aspect of this general sense of the phenomenological approach to religion. This is to say that everyone of these thinkers, for example, either rejected the idea of the evolution of religion, at least implicitly, or did without it. Even when we can detect certain touches of evolutionist thinking in the famous twentieth-century greats of religious studies, such as Durkheim, Weber, or Freud, the developmental or progressive assumptions so prominent in the thinkers of the late nineteenth century remain in the background or are absent entirely. Every one of the thinkers with whom we will deal from this chapter on out, had, as well, to take seriously the idea that the study of human culture and society required certain methods especially tailored to the human subject – even if they finally opposed giving the human realm special status. I have in mind here the admission of subjectivity into the human sciences ushered in by the phenomenologists.

Another feature of what I take to be a phenomenological approach to religion is the conviction of this new generation of thinkers that in order to understand human beings, it was necessary to *empathize* with the viewpoint of the people one was studying. While this did not mean sympathizing or *agreeing with* the human subjects that one studied, it meant that human subjectivity had to at least be considered. One had to approach human subjects with the idea that one was acting as an *interpreter* of human action, not like a physicist, for example, objectively seeking to *explain* what people were doing in terms of *causes* determining their actions. Therefore, it is safe to say that something big happened to the way culture and society were studied, dating from the late nineteenth and early twentieth centuries, and that things were never quite the same again. Phenomenology of religion represents *one instance* of 'what happened' in the study of religion, but also one instance of what happened as well in anthropology, history, philosophy, psychology, sociology, and so on (Spielberg 1969a; 1969b).

Further, while phenomenology of religion emerged in the context of late nineteenth and early twentieth-century reformations of thinking in the humanities and social sciences as part of the various critiques of 'historicism' of the same period, its delivery was largely difficult, often delayed, or then again resulted in its still-birth. This is to say that we must not fall into unexamined assumptions of evolutionist thinking ourselves in viewing changes in the study of religion as automatically indicating *progress*, and a one-way, irreversible development. Some thinkers took up with the new phenomenological study of religion, and dispensed with evolutionist ideas entirely. Others never took to phenomenology at all, and continued along lines familiar to us from the work of Tylor, Frazer, and others. Still others, as we will see, like Cornelis P. Tiele, arguably the first phenomenologist of religion, tried to combine evolutionism with phenomenology at the same time. This is to say that the transition from developmental to phenomenological methods in the study of religion has been, and continues to be, a messy affair. When, for example, Comte Eugène Goblet d'Alviella, the Belgian religious scholar, excitedly reviewed an attempt by one of Tiele's French confederates, the French historian of religions Jean Réville, to counter the monopoly of historicist scholarship in religion, he was struck by the upsetting potential of phenomenological approaches. Goblet d'Alviella noted that "grouping things into more general syntheses" would be, in effect, to go beyond "analytic" history (Goblet d'Alviella 1910). Thus, the change in orientation away from evolution to phenomenology was neither unanimous, clean, sudden, nor complete, nor was it even necessarily long-lasting across the field. Still, it did become at least one of the available approaches that students of religion could add to their repertoire of ways to study religion.

Arguably this shift in orientation began with two Dutch scholars of the late nineteenth and early twentieth centuries, Cornelis P. Tiele and Pierre Chantepie de la Saussaye. But, as I have just noted, the sudden and complete changeover to phenomenology from evolutionism is in many ways an illusion – at least as far as their intentions were concerned. While both men talked about their work in 'structural' or 'morphological' terms as seeking to lay out certain elementary or basic 'forms' of religious life, they always subsumed this early phenomenological task to their primary interest in placing these 'forms' in an overarching evolutionary scheme. This is why we can say that they make good examples of *transitional* figures in the phenomenological movement. Let us turn to the example of Tiele in order to see how the transition from evolutionism to something entirely different took place.

Phenomenology of Religion's Liberal Christian Inspiration

Born in Leiden in 1830, Cornelis P. Tiele trained in theology at the university of Amsterdam and at a liberal Calvinist ("Remonstrant," as we will see later) seminary there. He was ordained into the ministry in 1853, and served as a pastor in the Remonstrant church until 1873. While a pastor, Tiele studied world religions and ancient languages to the point that he was able to become professor of the history of religions at the Rotterdam Remonstrant seminary in 1873, and later its director when it moved to Leiden. In Leiden, at the same time, he also held the post of professor of the history and philosophy of religions (1877), in which post he remained until his death in 1902.

What makes Tiele especially interesting is how his example shows yet again how *religious ideas and commitments* stood behind the emergence of *scientific projects*, such as the phenomenological study of religion! In this way, Tiele should remind us of that other progressive Christian, Friedrich Max Müller. The theological positions of the two men were, as well, quite close to one another. Both were sincere and believing Christians, with neither man seeing their respective commitments to Christianity as being in any way at odds with scientific commitments and academic work. Indeed, if anything, Tiele, like Müller, saw religion and science as solidly complementary to one another. For Tiele and those like him, scientific activity led to spiritual vision (Molendijk 2000b, p. 90). Since both religion and science sought truth, and since truth was one, both the paths of scientific exploration and religious questing should lead to the same divine resting place. That was at least one reason why both Müller and Tiele spoke with wholeheartedly pious enthusiasm of their style for studying religion as the "science of religion."

This optimistic belief in the ability of religion and science to be reconciled to one another was a mark of the fearless and progressive Christianity of their age – Müller was born in 1823, Tiele in 1830. Reminiscent of the Deist devotees of Natural Religion, Tiele believed that religion was thus a "natural fact and spontaneous tendency of human nature," not something "superadded" as the partisans of revelation held. He also taught that human beings contained within themselves "the germ of a spiritual development, the objective ideal of which is God Himself" (Réville 1864, p. 283). By contemplating the natural world, people could come to see and know God as he expressed himself in and through his creation.

These beliefs reflected the common membership of both Müller and Tiele in the more liberal branches of the Protestant traditions of northern Europe. Tiele was by theological persuasion a "Remonstrant," and thus a special kind of religious liberal. The Remonstrants broke with the dominant Dutch Reformed Calvinists in rejecting the belief in predestination. This belief dictated that all people were fated for either damnation or salvation in advance of the kinds of lives they lived. As such, it struck the Remonstrant theologians as both antihuman and at odds with the biblical Christian ideal of a God of Love. In theological terms, it led the Remonstrants, like the Deists we have met earlier, to conclude that a true God of Love must have some secret plan for the salvation of all people – even those who had never known or never could have known Jesus because they just happened to have been born before his time. Thus, it makes sense that Tiele and his community should be committed to a variant of the belief in Natural Religion, much as were the Deists and Max Müller, since this belief implied that all people had an innate capacity for religiousness which humanity inherited from the very beginnings of the race. Natural Religion was a religion given to all humanity in equal proportions as a pure and unsullied primordial, monotheistic revelation. In a way, therefore, the gospel had been preached to all people from the very beginnings of time. This belief inspired Tiele's desire to study religion in order to track the ways Natural Religion was evidenced in the religions of humankind.

Thinkers like Tiele are particularly interesting to us at this point in discussing the origins of phenomenology of religion because he put his own special spin on the idea of Natural Religion. As the basic, underlying religion of humanity, Natural Religion was what the philosophers of the time called a *noumenon* – the thing that lies beneath appearances ('phenomena'), but that controls how phenomena appear. The natural contrast to 'noumenal' – 'phenomenal' – arises in other areas of life. We could, for example, think of the fundamental human *artistic* or *moral* capacities and ideas as 'noumenal,' while the various different and varied cultural forms of art and morality of humanity throughout its long history would be considered 'phenomenal.' All humans seem endowed with a sense of 'justice,' for example, although what counts as 'just' in one society or another may differ. Ideas of justice may as well differ within a society or culture, such as that between the standard of 'an eye for an eye' over against a morality of forgiveness. Natural Religion for Tiele – as indeed for some of the Deists we have met earlier – was the basic underlying religion, indeed the nature of religion itself, while the many religions were only manifestations, appearances of this *noumenal* religion – the *phenomena* of religions. As Tiele put it so well, some troubled people fearing the loss of faith

> do not see that the form of religion in which they have been brought up, and to which they are with heart and soul attached, is but one of the forms of religion, and that religion itself is entirely independent of such forms; that forms may change and vary without sacrificing the eternal ideas and the immortal aspirations which constitute the essence of religion. (Tiele 1896, p. 222)

Ultimately, Tiele wanted to discover empirical evidence of the "religion itself" beneath the phenomena or "manifestations" of it.

In historical terms, some thinkers akin to Tiele have even posed the idea that the religion of Adam and Eve in Paradise was just this noumenal Natural Religion, then of course not hidden or divided, but just the simple religion of the beginnings. In Paradise, noumenon and phenomena coincided and were one, because humanity had full and direct knowledge of God. After the Fall, however, as the story goes, humanity lost this intimate acquaintance with God, and descended into 'history.' Humanity's access to this noumenal Natural Religion weakened and religious affairs degenerated along the broad lines of what we recognize today as the 'religions,' with all this entailed in terms of their violent warring and feuding among each other, their magical practices, such as found among the Catholics and primitive religions, and their crude and inhuman customs, such as polygamy, bloody (sometimes human) sacrifice, fetishism, and such.

All these aspects of religion represented corruptions of our original religiousness. Nevertheless, they were the empirical reality of religions as given to us in our present, 'fallen' state. More than that, however, the religions were traces of the original Natural Religion, and thus provided the clues for getting back to the religion of the beginnings. Along these lines, Tiele understood the mission of the study of religion as examining the relation of the 'phenomena' of the many ('fallen') historical religions to their source in the 'noumenon' – in the primordial and real nature of religion. If we studied the 'phenomena' sufficiently well, and if we did so across all human cultures, we could perhaps find their common denominator beneath them. In doing so, we could then identity the main features of Natural Religion and return humanity to its service. The motivating energy behind Tiele's approach to religions was then to proceed from phenomenal religions to noumenonal religion.

Tiele's "Morphology" and the Hesitant Beginnings of Phenomenology of Religion

Tiele did not, however, refer to his approach to religion as "*phenomenology* of religion" for several reasons, as we will see. He called what would later be known as *phenomenology* another name more familiar to the natural scientists of his day – "morphology," a word generally used in the study of organic life *forms*, such as plants and animals in the biological sciences of the time. One reason for Tiele's choice of words may well have been to reinforce his belief that religion and science were just two ways to the same goal of learning the truth about things. A French student of Tiele's sums up these sentiments eloquently.

> In virtue of his religious consciousness, man directly feels God, and even if he were to be the subject of a perpetual evolution, would never be able to avoid feeling Him. If we are able to admit the validity of this double method of finding God in nature and in the soul, I think that we may watch with perfect serenity all the progress, all the discoveries, all the transformations of science. If we open our eyes to the universe, God is there; and if we close them to look into out own nature, God is with us still. (Réville 1875, p. 242)

The term "morphology" was accordingly a term that Tiele used without difficulty in the study of religion. It made religion seem all the more 'natural' and the study of religion all the more scientific.

Because of the flavor of the nineteenth-century life sciences in Tiele's morphological enterprise, a certain odor of evolutionary thinking still lurked about it. In fact, Tiele had already written a widely used history of religion some 20 years before his book on religious "morphology." It was thoroughly informed by an explicit developmental outlook (Tiele 1877). There he introduces his study in language, suggesting a model of "natural" organic growth and development:

> the fundamental principle [of the history of religions] is that all changes and transform-ations in religions, whether they appear from a subjective point of view to indicate decay or progress, are the results of *natural* growth, and find in it their best explanation. (my emphasis; Tiele 1877, p. 2)

Significantly, Tiele then goes on to make clear that his book is "really history, and not a *morphologic* arrangement of religions, based on an arbitrary standard" (my emphasis; Tiele 1877, p. 2). But, after this somewhat offhand dismissal of 'morphological' approaches in 1877, Tiele turned toward "morphology" in his Gifford Lectures of 1896, *Elements of the Science of Religion: Part One: Morphological*. What had happened to his thinking about religion in the meanwhile? Just what did Tiele's embrace of 'morphology' imply?

As it turns out, including 'morphology' in his title gave a somewhat false impression of Tiele's real intentions. Even in 1896, Tiele sought to reinforce his abiding commitment to evolutionist thinking, all the while touting another kind of approach. Thus, when Tiele once said, "I would venture to say of myself, 'I am nothing if not historical,' " he really meant it for a much greater timespan than one may have had a right to expect (Tiele 1896, p. 17)! Accordingly, the titles of 9 of the 10 chapters of this book bear out how hard it was for him to let go of religious evolutionism – even if he had truly wanted so to do. These 9 chapters are all about *evolution* – religious 'development' or a variant of this idea (Tiele 1896).

Still, the beginnings of something at least resembling 'phenomenology' of religion did start to take shape in Tiele's 'morphological' approach. First, Tiele says: "Historical research must precede and pave the way for our science." But there is more, since historical research, strictly speaking, "does not belong to it." Spelling out this move beyond history, Tiele goes on: "Yet I believe that the science of religion requires a broader foundation than history in the ordinary sense of the word." For Tiele, this meant that ahistorical, structural, or synchronic kinds of studies must complement what history has to offer.

> Anthropology or the science of man, sociology or the science of our social relations, psychology or the science of man's inmost being, and perhaps other sciences besides, must yield their contributions in order to help us to learn the true nature and origin of religion, and thus to reach our goal. (Tiele 1896, p. 17)

Thus, by the nineteenth century's end, Tiele had in effect mounted an argument for, at minimum, the coexistence of *history* of religion with a *phenomenological* study of religion. As such, it foreshadows aspects of the later phenomenology of religion, especially its 'morphological' side, that go together to make up Tiele's composite "science of religion."

When Tiele writes of his "science of religion," he makes it clear that his model of *scientific* inquiry in the human realm draws directly from the "science of language," just as it did for Friedrich Max Müller in chapter 3. But Tiele's ideal of a "science" of language drew from the Yale philologist William Dwight Whitney, who, along with Tiele, was quite critical of Max Müller's conception of a "science of religion" (Tiele 1896, pp. 6, 12 ff.; van den Bosch 2002, p. 109 n. 434). An evolutionist like Tiele, Whitney was also a strong supporter of Darwin: "the religion of each race must be studied as a whole. Each is the result of long growth, a structure built upon by generation after generation, one working over, modifying, and adding to what was bequeathed it by another" (Whitney 1870, p. 243). Thus Whitney also felt that Max Müller's assumption of religious decline and his opposition to Darwin's theories fatally undermined the scientific status of what Müller had argued about religion (van den Bosch 2002, pp. 186–7). For another thing, both Whitney and Tiele felt that Müller's philosophically idealist conception of language made it too spiritual a thing. They instead felt that although the study of religion could be likened to the science of language, religion was more than words, but also rituals and moral norms (van den Bosch 2002, p. 529).

Whitney's approach thus adhered to an even deeper naturalism than Max Müller would entertain, and as such entailed a number of requirements ensuring the scientific status of his study of language. One was that a science of religion would be humanistic or naturalistic: "The object of our science is not the superhuman itself," says Tiele, "but religion based on the belief in the superhuman" (Tiele 1896, p. 4). Max Müller's belief that traces of a sublime Natural Religion could be found today in the religions of so-called 'primitive' folk, also drew Whitney's ire. It was simply "inadmissible" to assume a

> native and absolute intuition of the Infinite, or the Divine, or of a God – which Müller would make the basis of the science he is trying to construct. It is sheer folly to talk of a sense of dependence, a yearning after a Father, and the like, as felt by the generations who laid the foundations of race-religions. (Whitney 1870, p. 243)

Knowing what we know of Max Müller's Romanticist intellectual and cultural nurture, Whitney may have hit upon a key truth about the sources of Max Müller's fundamental assumptions about the nature of religion.

Thus, at least at first, Tiele believed as students of religion we should be 'critics' and not 'caretakers.' Phenomenology of religion as developed in modern times by Ninian

Figure 7.1.   Ninian Smart, Block Island, RI, May 1983
Source: author photo.

Smart, as we will see, would find this putting aside of theological agendas a defining mark of the academic study of religion. (See figure 7.1.)

A second aspect of this 'science,' now enhanced by his morphology, was what the later phenomenologists will call *epochê* – the practice of detached study, of what has also been called 'bracketing' one's beliefs, and what Tiele refers to as a "calm impartiality" (Tiele 1896, p. 8). One of the benefits of *epochê*, according to this model of Whitney's now so eagerly embraced by Tiele for religion, was its openness to the task of gaining knowledge, rather than seeking to launch an apologetics. In a science of religion, one will "investigate it [religion] in order to learn something about it" (Tiele 1896, p. 5). A true scientific study of religion will, therefore, study all religions without prejudice, just as a scientist of language will study all languages without prejudice. "Genuine science," says Tiele, "seeks nothing but the truth" about religion (Tiele 1896, p. 10) – to "investigate and explain [religion]; it desires to know what religion is, and why we are religious" (Tiele 1896, p. 12). Keen students of phenomenology of religion will note that Tiele does not shy away from *explanation*. He invites 'why?' questions; he invites inquiries into the *causes* of religious behavior. To Tiele's credit, this openness to explanation, cause, and so on shows him to be consistent with his evolutionism. After all, as we have seen with Frazer and Tylor, evolutionism is, among other things, a certifiable *explanatory* strategy, since it approaches religion by presenting us those facilitating stages of development that created the conditions for the emergence of religion. They showed how previous stages of development may be seen to have *caused* religion by laying in the necessary conditions for religion to exist at all. A good 'critic' should thus try to be fair to the religions that they study, and not try to be its 'caretaker' or even less its 'undertaker.'

Finally, these recommendations for the right method of studying religion should issue in the practice of requiring an early form of phenomenology of religion – Tiele's "morphology" of religion. In the science of language, this would involve formal tasks such as the construction of a lexicon, grammar, and the like. Recalling Max Müller, Tiele felt that his morphology should sort out the different 'kinds' of religions, as well as its different practices and so on. Any real 'science' as understood by Whitney and Tiele, should demonstrate the performance of the essential morphological task of showing "an inward connection of... facts which enables us to subject them to careful *classification*" (Tiele 1896, p. 6). Tiele continues to fret over the difficulties of "classification" as the study proceeds, whether schemes of classification might, for example, change or not (pp. 59–62). Thus Tiele discusses the differences between various kinds of "gods" (35 ff.), or between religions having founders versus those arising by " 'unconscious growth' " (42 ff.), or religions of " 'world-negation' " contrasted with those of world-affirmation (62 ff.), or "ethical" religions over against "nature" religions (63–8), or "Spiritism" versus "Animism" (72–83), and so on. In the same vein, Tiele's American friend, Morris Jastrow, Jr., called attention to Tiele's part in the debate about the *classification* of religions themselves. Published in his article "Religions" for Robertson Smith's ninth edition of the *Encyclopedia Britannica*, Tiele sets up a "successive scale" of the five major *classes* of religion (Jastrow 1981, p. 65).[1]

Nevertheless, however good a beginning in creating a real phenomenology of religion Tiele's 'morphology' may be, we should not forget that all these 'morphological' discussions, are conditioned by Tiele's submission of them to the question of how they fit in a scheme of religious *evolutionary* development. Tiele maintains an encompassing and overriding "teleological viewpoint," an explanatory strategy that was directed at seeking to establish the existence and character of the noumenal 'religion-as-such' that lurked behind the historical variations of the phenomenal religions, and provided the necessary *causal conditions* for their coming into existence at all (Molendijk 2000b, p. 92). "Morphology," then, as Tiele practiced it, can be seen as little more than the faintest forerunner of more familiar schemes of classification in fully-fledged phenomenology of religion.

The main difficulty with seeing Tiele as a "phenomenologist of religion" in the sense understood by the term in the light of the work of someone expressly identifiable by this title, such as Gerardus van der Leeuw, was that he probably would have rejected the description! Tiele gingerly approached a transformation that would carry his successor, William Brede Kristensen, over to the antihistoricist side, while Tiele let his weight rest comfortably on the historical side. One might then argue that Tiele did not fully appreciate the implications of the teleology of his own thought, since all his morphological or structural work still rested securely, in Tiele's view, upon a scaffold of evolutionary developmentalism. But we have no evidence for reading Tiele this way. He was what he was.

However half-hearted Tiele's phenomenology was, his successor in his chair at Leiden (1901), the Norwegian William Brede Kristensen (1867–1953), never looked back to the evolutionism that kept such a firm grip on Tiele. It was he who truly laid the foundations for what today has come to be known as the phenomenology of religion, even down to establishing the current usage of the term itself (Molendijk 2000a, p. 24). Kristensen was, in addition, the teacher of Gerardus van der Leeuw, the individual who, if anyone, can be credited with being the first truly undisputed phenomenologist of religion (Molendijk 2000a, p. 35). Let us now turn to the story of how the break with evolutionism occurred.

Problems with Evolutionism Prompt Phenomenology's New Problems of Religion

Even in a time dominated by rationalist and evolutionist approaches to religion, far more decisive movements of resistance and discontent than Tiele's would begin to stir in large part because of the increasing number and intensity of the problems thrown up by these nineteenth-century evolutionist treatments of religion. As we will see in our discussion of one of the first modern 'anthropologists,' Bronislaw Malinowski, the new social and cultural anthropology that he at the very least promoted, if not initiated, represented one such center of discontent and intellectual revolution. Both the phenomenologists and anthropologists like Malinowski eventually threw up their hands at the impossibility of trying to force all the diverse and confusing new facts that they had acquired from the comparative study of religions and direct observation onto a Procrustean bed of some evolutionary scheme or another. This final admission that the 'facts' would not fit the theoretical scheme devised by the evolutionists, seems precisely to have led Tiele toward a closer look at the religious data in question (with all that implies about sorting data in terms of their 'form'), to a 'morphology,' and later to the 'phenomena' of our phenomenologists of religion. That at any rate was the conclusion about Tiele's intellectual progress reached by an American review of his *History of the Egyptian Religion* (1882):

> The author, well known as an able student of the history of religions, had previously published a valuable little manual entitled *Outlines of the History of Religion to the Spread of the Universal Religions* (English translation, London, 1877), which many have called the first orderly presentation of modern views on this subject. But he saw that the attempt to construct a general history of religion was premature until the particular religions had been worked out in detail, and he has since devoted himself to more special studies. This is now the understanding among scholars every where, and solid foundations for the new science are being laid. (anon. 1882, p. 361)

In France, for instance, even Christian theologians were beginning to pick apart the pretensions of cultural evolutionism, and in doing so beginning to see how problematic its entire approach to religion had been. Paris's Maurice Vernes said that the idea of cultural evolution was bogus. Although touted as an historical approach to religion, cultural evolutionism was "not at all historical," but only "reflects the ideological preferences of the historian" (La Planche 1991, p. 93). Vernes argued, for example, that representatives of the various so-called 'stages' of religious evolution could be found at any given time in the life of a religion. Cultural traits considered 'primitive' could be found in supposedly higher stages of development. Is not the Roman Catholic cult of the saints a kind of ('primitive') polytheism, but comfortably existing alongside a strict ('higher') monotheism – and not as musty 'survivals' but as living, functioning parts of the religions in question? And, further, for polytheists, do they not enter the spiritual mindset of monotheists when they focus on a particular deity (d'Alviella 1885, p. 173)?

And, even when the historicity of the historical approaches of the evolutionists could be defended, were not the *problems* the evolutionists sought to address becoming increasingly outmoded or impossible to answer? Thus, since the Frazers, Tylors, and similar of the world shared an almost exclusive commitment to an *evolutionist* approach to religion, their '*problems* of religion' revolved around issues like identifying the chronological first religion, or discovering the origins of religion in time and place. Their curiosity was driven by a desire to know how religion 'grew' out of a particular historically comprehended stage of primitive human evolutionary development or 'fell' from the pristine archaic stage of spiritual perfection before the onset of human decline (Max Müller). But what was to guarantee that these questions would retain their pertinence? In a sense, the rise of phenomenology of religion amounted to a claim that indeed the *problems of religion* addressed by the evolutionists were irrelevant. After so many conflicting ideas about the identity of the original religion – assuming that there was *one* – even some evolutionist thinkers were beginning to give up on the historical quest for the *first* or *original* religion. They turned instead, as we will see, to the question of whether people had some kind of fundamental psychological predisposition to be religious, as basic, say, as the human sense of justice or aesthetic sense of beauty and ugliness. Even Tiele was beginning to think this way (Tiele 1877, p. 6).

In the Netherlands, the true home of the phenomenological movement of the study of religion, other arguments were brought to bear against evolutionist studies of religion. The Norwegian phenomenologist of religion William Brede Kristensen, for instance, charged that "historical" evolutionism, and any other form of religious evolutionism, was only a 'theory.' Later phenomenologists of religion would strengthen this stance, as we will see, by ruling out all explanations – especially *causal* ones – or theorizing from their approach to religions. Such attempts at *explanation* were really too speculative, ambitious, or premature, given our meager understanding of the conditions necessary for the emergence of religion and religious institutions. Kristensen challenged the prevailing view of the previous generation of students of religion that evolutionism was a certain virtual fact (Molendijk 2000a, p. 32). It was one, and only one, way of interpreting the data of religion. Thus, in his introduction to the work of one of the foremost phenomenologists of religion, William Brede Kristensen, the unlikely figure of the conservative, neo-orthodox theologian, Hendrik Kraemer – nonetheless a personal friend of Kristensen's – suggests that brave rebellion against the oversimplifications of religion by evolutionists and dogmatic theologians energized the rise of Kristensen's phenomenology of religion.

> The book I introduce contains many utterances of impatience with the genetic and evolutionist dogmatism of the day. His criticisms in this respect, made fifty years ago, are now more and more accepted, but for a long time they were lonely deviations from the dominant thinking which reveled in explaining and construing grand tableaux of religious evolution.

Worst of all, in Kristensen's view, the evolutionist preoccupation with these grand historical schemes rested on very shaky foundations. The evolutionists built these schemes

> without having ever asked the preliminary fundamental question of what religion really is. It was taken for granted that one knew this.... Kristensen showed himself a true phenomenologist, who does not measure and compare as to the stage of value, but whose sole aim is to understand. (Kraemer 1960, p. xxiii)

Pressing his attack even further, Kristensen judged evolutionism not only a theory, but ill-informed about the nature of religion and false on top of that. It had not really got *inside* religion, or indeed *inside* the minds of religious people to understand what religion really was.

Kristensen's condemnation of evolutionism was grounded in several ways, one of which was his commitment to the primacy, and apparent infallibility and incorrigibility, of the religious insider's point of view. "If the historian tries to understand the religion from a different viewpoint than that of the believers, he negates the religious reality," says Kristensen, adding: "For there is no religious reality other than the faith of the believers" (Kristensen 1960, p. 13). While readers today may puzzle at this somewhat extreme declaration of methodological faith, we need to understand it in light of its being intended to counteract a generation of confident efforts, like Tylor's or Frazer's, to *explain* religion, and indeed to 'explain it away': 'reductionism.' One reviewer of Tylor's *Anthropology* (1881) picked up on the reductionism in Tylor's work on religion, noting that "a religion is a body of connected beliefs and practices growing out of the views taken of the powers of nature in their relations to men. Thus, as compared with a philosophy, a religion is something posterior and derived" (anon. 1881, p. 181). On the other hand, the phenomenologists sought therefore to counter reductionist studies aimed at showing how religion was "derived" from or was sustained by nonreligious *causes*. Believers do not think that their religion is *caused* by their science-like desire to give an account of the way things happen in the world (Tylor), or their interests in controlling nature (Frazer). Therefore, Kristensen and those like him felt that we had actually to consult religious believers to see what they thought religion itself was about!

Despite the value derived from seeing how religion was *objectively* put together, Kristensen therefore felt that the vital perspective of the believer was missing. As a phenomenologist, he recognized that none of the *objective* comparative work one wanted to do would be possible if religious folk could not *recognize* themselves in the studies produced of them. Religious folk did not have to accept what the phenomenologists said about them, but they at least had to agree that their viewpoint was accurately stated. Kristensen felt, therefore, that something of the subjectivity of religious folk needed to be taken into account. Religious folk had no veto over the studies of their religion by scholars, but they at least had to be able to *recognize* their own religious beliefs, practices, situation, and so forth in the generalizations of scholars.

In general, phenomenologists of religion have sought to make this connection with the viewpoint of believers by adopting what they called an *empathetic* approach to the religious beliefs and practices of those they studied. At least in the beginning, an essential point of reference for phenomenologists would be the *believer's point of view*. The 'insider's' viewpoint might prove to be wrong, but one at least had to start by taking note of what it was. Scholars at least had to 'walk a mile in the moccasins' of religious people, before they *interpreted* or, certainly, tried to explain the causes of religious behavior. In that way, when it came to explaining religion, these future explanations would at least have been *about* the religions in question. This, as we will see, is a lesson that both Max Weber and Émile Durkheim took to heart and applied with great effect. Both of these great modern religious theorists never went about *explaining* religion as they did in their different ways without intense efforts to discover and convey the "native's point of view," as the interpretive anthropologist Clifford Geertz has put it (Geertz 1973; 1983).

Another way of expressing this subjective side of phenomenological method is by way of its adoption of *interpretive* ways of studying religion – its links with what is called *hermeneutics* and all that implies about the primacy of empathetic understanding of human action and the preference for *understanding* religion over *explaining* it. Unlike their predecessors, the evolutionists, the phenomenologists of religion did not really try to *theorize* about religion, and therefore did not try to *explain* what may have *caused* it. They tried instead to take religion as they saw it, as it was presented to them, and then to try to make sense of or interpret it – to achieve an *understanding* of religion rather than an *explanation* – rather than seeking possible *causes* of religion or religious institutions.

Surprising to some who see him mainly as the hyperscientistic 'undertaker' of religion whom we will meet in chapter 10, perhaps no one has summed up this approach better than, Bronislaw Malinowski:

> the final goal, of which an Ethnographer should never lose sight . . . is, briefly, to grasp the native's point of view, *his* relation to life, to realise *his* vision of *his* world. We have to study man, and we must study what concerns him most intimately, that is, the hold which life has on him . . . To study the institutions, customs, and codes or to study the behaviour and mentality without the subjective desire of feeling by what these people live, of realising the substance of their happiness – is, in my opinion, to miss the greatest reward which we can hope to obtain from the study of man. . . . (Malinowski 1961, p. 25)
>
> What interests me really in the study of the native is his outlook on things, his *Weltanschauung*, the breath of life and reality which he breathes and by which he lives. Every human culture gives its members a definite vision of the world, a definite zest of life. . . .
>
> The Science of Man, in its most refined and deepest version, should lead us to such knowledge and to tolerance and generosity, based on the understanding of other men's points of view. (Malinowski 1961, p. 517)

Perhaps no more impassioned and articulate profession of phenomenology's subjective point of view can be found than that which Malinowski gives us here.

Readers today might want to ask questions about this approach – especially as to whether Kristensen in particular assumes too much on behalf of religious believers. Do they really have 'perfect knowledge' of their own religions and religious commitments? Is the insider's point of view necessarily the right one? Can believers not make mistakes about their own religion? Is religious "faith" the sum total of religion? Does it exhaust the questions we might have about religion of other folks? Kristensen does not address these points, because, as I suspect, they are as fundamental to his own religious standpoint as the "quasi-certitude" about evolution of the developmentalist thinkers.

Nevertheless, despite this assertion of his own pieties, Kristensen's passionate denunciation of evolutionism merits some treatment for the lasting value of some of its polemic points. First, in showing how any evolutionary view of religion is just an *interpretation*, Kristensen in effect argues that they are what one might call 'impositions' upon the religions being studied. This is problematic in a scientific study since a minimum requirement of such a study of humans would at least be that the claims of the evolutionist investigator could be recognized by believers as even minimally describing their religion. This is not to say that such 'impositions' are either true or not, or whether the believers might be ignorant of their own religion in some way, or whether they may be in some state of 'denial,' not wanting to admit unpleasant truths to themselves. These are separate issues to be dealt with in due course. At his best, what Kristensen stands for is the view that interpretations of religions should at least produce an account of religion that would be *recognizable* to believers. To wit, Kristensen says that

> all evolutionary views and theories . . . mislead us from the start, if we let them set the pattern for our historical research. Believers have never conceived of their own religion as a link in a chain of development. Perhaps they have thought of it sometimes as the goal, but never as an intermediate link; yet in the evolutionary view, this is an indispensable concept. (Kristensen 1960, p. 13)

Second, Kristensen notes that to the extent that the investigator does not at least get the details of the insider's point of view correct, they invariably raise doubts about whether their explanations are even *about* the religion in question. In this case, the investigator never gets outside the closed quarters of their own minds to try to reach out to understand someone different than they: "No believer considers his own faith to be somewhat primitive, and the moment we begin so to think of it, we have actually lost touch with it. We are then dealing only with our own ideas of religion, and not the ideas of others." Do 'infidels' really think of themselves as 'unfaithful' (Kristensen 1960, p. 13)? And do they perhaps think of those so accusing them as 'infidels' as well? Do 'fetishists' really worship things? Do 'naturists' really worship rocks and trees? And how would we know if they did?

Third, Kristensen's remedy for this self-imposed solipsism is to allow the data from the religious believer to impinge on the thought processes of the investigator. Investigators must allow themselves to *learn* from their 'data' – an uncontroversial enough point, one would have thought, but apparently not one accepted by the evolutionists.

> The historian and the student of Phenomenology must therefore be able to forget themselves, be able to surrender themselves to others. Only after that will they discover that others surrender themselves to them. If they bring their own idea with them, others shut themselves off from them. No justice is then done to the values which are alien to us, because they are not allowed to speak in their own language. (Kristensen 1960, p. 13)

Kristensen therefore is arguing, in effect, that the proposals of scholars about religious people need to be governed by some kind of scheme of 'checks and balances,' some way of correcting or revising their ideas against the 'data' of religion. To do otherwise would really be bad scientific practice, since it could invite dogmatism. Even the ideas of scientists – indeed, especially *their* ideas – need to be open to correction or refutation, as philosophers of science like Karl Popper have argued (Popper 1963).

New Perspectives, New Problems

One welcome upshot of this more receptive approach to religion was the gradual replacement of the questions about religion guiding the evolutionists with an entirely new set of puzzles and problems about religion. These new problems were spawned primarily by Kristensen's desire to recognize the *interpretive* character of religious data and the need for *understanding* the viewpoint of religious believers. His desire to be faithful to the insider's point of view of a religion – perhaps *too* faithful – at least provided a means of getting one's *preliminary* bearings before we attempt to *explain* the religion or religious data in question.

I say "too" faithful to the insider's point of view, because Kristensen simply 'rubber stamps' the viewpoint of believers as true and complete. The student of religion has really nothing more to add to what the believer thus says – neither to correct nor extend the meaning of what religious folk believe and do. "For the historian only one evaluation is possible: 'the believers were completely right.' Only after we have grasped this can we understand these people and their religion" (Kristensen 1960, p. 14).

But Kristensen has made a great logical error in thus conflating empathy with understanding, when he should be showing how they differ. This difference is quite important to the way we will go about studying religion, and indeed, how Ninian Smart will advance the program of phenomenology of religion begun by the likes of Kristensen and others. One way they differ is that an *understanding* of religious action sometimes makes things clearer to a religious actor than they were before. Just relying on what believers say about themselves and their religious situation may therefore not be enough – indeed may be in need of supplementing information. For example, many pious Christians today pray on their knees, with hands folded together before them, although early Christians prayed with arms raised high. Why do praying Christians kneel and fold their hands in prayer today? If we tried to answer this question just by empathizing with today's Christians, or if we just assumed their 'insider's point of view,' we would learn something rather vague, such as this gesture being a sign of humility, reverence, or peace. Or, in the case where, while on bended knee, the hands are gripped tightly together with fingers wrapped around each other, they indicate that one is pleading, begging, and such. Why do many modern Christians pray in this way?

I am not arguing that any of this is wrong. But *understanding* why most modern Christians pray kneeling with hands folded, takes us further beyond empathy and the 'native's point of view.' We need to do better than Kristensen. Consider, for example, that the historian of feudal Europe, Marc Bloch, informs us that the style of praying we have just mentioned only came into being during Europe's feudal age (Bloch 1961, pp. 145–7). Praying on our knees with folded hands, argues Bloch, means acknowledging fealty to a divine lord, and the lord's reciprocal pledge to 'save' sinful humanity, much as medieval vassals pledged their service to a feudal lord, while their lord pledged to protect them by force of arms. Bloch bases this analogy on the fact that the gesture of kneeling with folded hands was employed by vassals pledging allegiance to their feudal 'lord.' The ceremony is known to us and moves through the following steps: to begin, the new vassal was first to kneel before the lord; then he folded his hands together with fingers pointed toward the lord; finally, the vassal placed his folded hands between the encompassing hands of the lord, who at that point secured the union between lord and vassal. Knowing this, we surely *understand* the particular religious behavior better than we would using mere empathy or by taking the believer's point of view – unless, of course, they knew the same history that Bloch relates.

Despite the obstacles Kristensen thus puts in the way of a 'scientific' or academic study of religion by slipping into the role of a 'caretaker of religion,' he nonetheless creates conceptual space for new and interesting problems of religion. Once we assume the 'native's point of view,' so to speak, new questions arise. How, for example, do the various religions hang together, knowing now what we do about their great variety and diversity? What are the key elements that go into making up what a religion is? What elements of religion are the most important for sustaining a religion – its myths, rituals, doctrines, or some other dimension of religion's constitution? How do we reconcile disparities between what believers say about their religions and what outside observers say? How is religion related to other aspects of culture? Is it utterly unique and independent of them, or does it fall into line along a spectrum of gradually differing cultural entities, such as morals, the arts, or politics? Once evolutionism had been thrown off, a host of such questions arose as if suppressed for a long time by hidden forces.

Because of the shift in perspective articulated by the likes of Kristensen, today's phenomenologists of religion are exercised by an entirely different set of problems of religion than had been seen before in its study. Although the phenomenologists too were on the whole, unlike the new anthropologists, content to remain in the comfortable confines of their studies, they shifted register from the 'diachronic' domain, the concern with historical problems such as evolution, to ones we can call 'synchronic,' problems and puzzles that had to do with religion taken as it stood. They thus wanted to know the answers to precisely the same *problems* that Kraemer said that Kristensen wanted to know – "what religion really is." The evolutionists had "taken for granted that one knew this" (Kraemer 1960, p. xxiii). But to the phenomenologists, such delving into the question of what religion "really is" meant a fresh start for the study of religion. It led, as we will see, to seeking an answer, at least, to the "preliminary fundamental question" of the *internal* constitution of religion, of the *structure* of the variety of things that went to make up one religion after another, and of how they interacted to make religions what they were. In short, said Kraemer, the phenomenologists' "sole aim is to understand" (Kraemer 1960, p. xxiii). This is, as we will see, what phenomenologists in the full sense – thinkers like Gerardus van der Leeuw and Ninian Smart – wanted to know.

Phenomenology of religion was thus another of these movements of dissatisfaction and reaction to the Frazers and Tylors of the day, as well as to the dogmatic theologians who so plagued Robertson Smith and Max Müller.

The Autonomy of Religion, Structure, and Empathy

It would, therefore, be unjust simply to see the phenomenologists of religion in a negative light as evolutionist 'undertakers' of religion! In reacting against evolutionism, the phenomenologists of religion promoted the "understanding" of which Kraemer speaks, with at least two great and continuing methodological innovations in the study of religion. These innovations are roughly to do with what I shall call structure and 'objectivity,' on the one hand, and, on the other, with empathy or 'subjectivity.' Structure and objectivity have to do with the constituting of religion as a phenomenon, and understanding its many shapes and forms, its typologies and main religious terminology, its attention to the 'anatomy,' morphology, or formal properties of religion. Again, somewhat in the style of an anatomy of religion, the phenomenologists, in effect, reasoned that if religion be likened to a human person, the nineteenth-century historians of religion might be said to have written 'biographies' of religion or traced the 'family trees' and 'genealogies' of the religions. The phenomenologists ought to be likened to 'anatomists,' 'biologists,' or 'kinesiologists' of religion, since they sought to understand how the human body 'hung together,' how its 'bones' and 'muscles' articulated and worked together to make a living, active whole.

On the other hand, empathy and subjectivity concern a technique by which one acquires the data for constituting religious phenomena from religious people themselves. While some phenomenologists of religion, such as Kirstensen, confuse empathy with understanding, the objective and subjective aspects of phenomenological method must finally also be linked with the claim made by them that religion was a *distinctive* – and irreducible in its essential nature – form of life, indeed for some an *autonomous* or *sui generis* form of life (McCutcheon 1997, pp. 57–61). As early phenomenologists like Cornelis P. Tiele stated, "Religion," understood in the sense of the Natural Religion reminiscent of the Deists or Max Müller, is "independent." This is to say that religion is not controlled by the other functions of the human mind or the other phases of human life, and is not hampered by limits detrimental to its growth, but appropriates from them, and assimilates, whatever conduces to its development. (Tiele 1896, p. 297)

However deficient Tiele's thought may be as a full expression of the phenomenology of religion, its basic principles began to emerge in his work, later to be realized by his student, William Brede Kristensen. There, structure, morphology, classification, empathy, the 'insider's' point of view, autonomy, religion as *sui generis*, interpretive understanding, *epochê*, and so on, rather than explanations, necessary preconditions, or causes, go to make up the fundamental stock of a vocabulary which has been used by phenomenologists of religion ever since.

This chapter will now turn to a discussion of three integrally related and influential representatives of the phenomenological approach – Gerardus van der Leeuw, Rudolf Otto, and Ninian Smart. We can assess the progress of phenomenology of religion by looking on van der Leeuw and Otto as respectively emphasizing two aspects of the movement. Van der Leeuw stands out for his extensive treatment of the 'objective' or structural side of phenomenology, while Otto excels at illuminating the 'subjective' or emotional, experiential, and empathetic 'inner' side of phenomenology of religion. Coming along a couple generations or so after these founding figures, Ninian Smart deliberately synthesizes both objective and subjective aspects of phenomenology, while adding what he calls a most important "dynamic" dimension to phenomenology of religion as a whole. Let us first consider Otto's stunning contribution to our understanding of the experiential and emotional dimension of religion.

Rudolf Otto and the Autonomy of Religious Experience

Rudolf Otto was a German Lutheran historian of religion and theologian who flourished during the years immediately on either side of the First World War. His great classic, *The Idea of the Holy* (1917), was written in large part to establish a strong case for the autonomy of religion. As a model piece of religious phenomenology, Otto elaborated the case for religion's autonomy by bringing out what he believed to be the single, central, constituent *category* of religion – the notion of holiness or the sacred. Otto left it for others to explore secondary features of the structural make-up of religion such as myth, ritual, sacrifice, prophets, priests, and so on. He went right to the heart of religious 'matter,' so to speak, and sought to understand what he felt made religion distinctive, indeed autonomous and thus irreducible in its being. In Otto's day, philosophers talked of morality as defined by the category of 'obligation,' by language of what we *ought* or *ought not* to do. Art was similarly delineated by the category of the beautiful or sublime. For Otto, religion should be delimited by the idea or category of holiness, the sacred, and so on. In this way, Otto can be seen to follow Kristensen's preliminary *structural* path of seeking to address the "preliminary fundamental question of what religion really is," since Otto tried to isolate and then extensively analyze 'holiness' or the 'sacred' as a fundamental *category* of the nature of religion.

What brings Otto to our attention here is that he undertook to identify and delineate the autonomous nature of religion by trying to isolate and grasp what he took to be the essential religious *experience*. For Otto, religion was not something in and for itself – *sui generis* – because it preached certain doctrines or was centered on certain rituals, for example. Religion was autonomous because it sprang from something unique in our emotional life, from some special vision, feeling, sensibility – some *experience* – that was unlike any other and that was distinctly and appropriately religious. By contrast with those who thought religion was *descriptively distinctive* such as reductionists like Freud, for instance, the phenomenologists claim a *distinctiveness* in the very nature and being of religion that no reductionist can abide.

In pursuing this quest for essential religious experience, Otto was painfully aware that he was up against some powerful opponents. Unnamed, nay-saying 'undertakers' of religion – arch-reductionists – were abroad not only dismissing the truth of religious doctrines, but denying that religion was something distinctive in being at all! And, no matter what degree of intensity of autonomy is claimed, it is always opposed to such attempts at *reduction* and the operation of what is called "reductionism." In fact, 'autonomy' and 'reduction' are exact opposites of each other. To affirm the *autonomy* of religion, say, is to claim that it cannot (or should not) be *reduced* to other forms of life. The assertion of autonomy and the resistance to reduction are really two sides of the same coin. Autonomy claims that religion has its own nature and identity; *radical reductionism* asserts that religion is really nothing particular, but is really better described and explained in nonreligious terms, because it is in its nature something else entirely.

In reaction to the 'reductionists,' the phenomenologists sought to articulate what they took to be the nature of religion as a 'phenomenon' – as something that could be looked on in terms of its characteristic *distinctiveness* or *autonomy* much as one would consider other distinctive domains or levels of human life such as society, art, music, politics, morality, and so on. Of music, Otto says pointedly: "Musical feeling is rather [like numinous feeling] something 'wholly other,' which, while it affords analogies and here and there will run parallel to the ordinary emotions of life, cannot be made to coincide with them by a detailed point-to-point correspondence" (Otto 1923, p. 49). Music and such were all things worth considering in themselves – as *phenomena* meriting serious attempts at understanding. So why not religion too? Reductionists, in Otto's way of speaking, were therefore those who "with a resolution and cunning which one can hardly help admiring...shut their eyes to that which is quite unique in the religious experience." Otto's contempt is hard to conceal as he entertains the notion that there are actually people who might admit all sorts of other kinds of distinctive experiences – one thinks of esthetic experience essential to our feeling for the arts, for example – yet are dumbfounded when it comes to recognizing an essentially 'religious' feeling. With withering irony, he continues, "But it is rather a matter for astonishment than for admiration! [that this should be so] For if there be any single domain of human experience that presents us with something unmistakably specific and unique, peculiar to itself, assuredly it is that of the religious life" (Otto 1923, p. 4).

Otto countered the reductionists by arguing that religion arose from a unique kind of subjective *psychological* datum – what he called a "numinous" experience. The term is derived from the Latin word *numen*, which is the term for a deity that presides over a particular place, such as Diana or Virbius did over the sacred grove at Nemi about which Frazer wrote in *The Golden Bough*. This numinous *experience* was what we feel when we encounter what is holy or sacred – an experience that for Otto was an experience of something that was "wholly other." The numinous experience was, thus, a feeling of being in the presence of a "*mysterium tremendum et fascinans*" – a tremendously powerful, yet magnetizing, fascinating mystery. Such feelings arose in people because in it they sensed their dependence upon that all-powerful mystery. Indeed, more than this, people sensed their *absolute* and utter dependence upon this power, a feeling totally appropriate for a creature to have regarding their creator (Otto 1923, chs. ii–v). To Otto, it was, therefore, an experience that transcended all others, as the terms applied to it imply. The kind of examples that Otto had in mind of the numinous experience should help us understand why he was so sure both that it was distinctive, unique, *sui generis*, but also why it made sense to see it as the underlying support for the autonomy or distinctiveness of religion.

Phenomenologists of religion like Otto believe that we can get at this subjective experience by examining our own religious feelings, and then by seeing if we can recognize the same emotional states in the great religious texts of the world. This is to say that Otto, like a true phenomenologist, felt that we needed to read religious texts with great sensitivity – indeed, what the phenomenologists of religion would call reading these documents *empathetically*. We needed to try to put ourselves into the mindset of the actors in the materials we were reading, as difficult as that may seem. Preserving one's neutrality in this process is critical, however. Thus, one should not confuse 'empathy' with 'sympathy,' the latter of which implies a favorable judgment about the phenomenon.

Consider the example of the conversion of Saul (soon to become the apostle Paul) on the road to Damascus, eager to continue his persecution of the early Christian community (Acts 9). As he rode forth nearing the city, the narrator of Acts says,

> As Saul was coming near the city of Damascus, suddenly a light from the sky flashed around him. He fell to the ground and heard a voice saying to him; "Saul, Saul! Why do you persecute me?" (Acts 9:3–4)

The phenomenologist of religion reads this text in the spirit of someone who tries to imagine what sort of force would throw a grown man from his mount. What sort of feeling would one then have when out of nowhere boomed a reproachful voice calling one to account for one's actions? It is not that hard to *empathize* with Saul/Paul as he is stunned by the power of the tremendous energy of divine wrath. Knocked from his horse, dazzled by a mysterious light in the heavens, all worked to send the blinded Saul into a perfect frenzy of fear before the holy, the sacred: "*mysterium tremendum et fascinans.*" We can well *understand* the feelings and emotions that must have surged through Saul/Paul's mind and body. It is as Otto says – a feeling of tremendous mysterious power, yet – adding to the mystery – a feeling that makes one want to draw near.

Or consider likewise, in the book of Isaiah, a similar type of powerful religious experience. In chapter 6 of the book of Isaiah, it says

> In the year that reign of King Uzziah, I saw the Lord. He was sitting on his throne, high and exalted, and his robe filled the whole temple. Around him flaming the creatures were standing each of which had six wings. Each creature covered its face, with two wings, and its body with two and used the other two for flying. They were calling out to each other: "Holy, holy, holy! The Lord Almighty is holy! His glory fills the world." The sound of their voices made the foundation of the temple shake and the temple itself became filled with smoke. I said, "There is no hope for me! I am doomed because every word passes my lips is sinful, and I live among the people whose every word is sinful. And yet, with my own eyes. I have seen the King, the Lord Almighty." (Isaiah 6: 1–5)

Again, this passage from Isaiah related an experience combining divine energy, over-powering force, and the densest mystery that results in the poor prophet being forced to the ground. There, he trembles in awe and quickly becomes aware of his abject creature-hood and utter dependence upon that transcendent 'wholly other' God. In light of what we read here, is it hard to see this as an experience of divinity of obvious religious dimensions? Understanding it as such, instead of as an attack of moral scruples or a spell of fey esthetic pleasure, surely seems the most obvious of ways to make sense of what we read in this extraordinary document of the religious consciousness. It is the creature, profane, powerless, and utterly dependent, brought low by the sacred.

Finally, no account of Otto's view would be complete without demonstrating the broad cross-cultural application of his grasp of *sui generis* religious experience as the experience of the numinous. A classic example comes to us from the Hindu scripture, the *Bhagavad Gītā*. Here again the essence of the divinity bursts forth into the cozy human world, blowing apart our neat attempts to domesticate the divine by means of an overpowering yet 'fascinating' experience. The scene is set on the field of battle central to the civil war dominating the great Hindu epic, the *Mahabharata*, of which the *Bhagavad Gītā* is a part. In a chariot on the front lines of the forces of one side are Prince Arjuna and his noble charioteer, the god Krishna disguised in human form. Arjuna is demoralized by doubts about the value of taking up arms against his own kin. He has lost the 'will to win' – the will to fight and kill – and confesses this to Krishna, who nevertheless urges him to do his duty and press on with the battle. First, Krishna shows Arjuna the real divine – numinous – form that lies hidden beneath his human bodily form:

> Having spoken thus, O king, Krishna, the great lord of the possessors of mystic power, then showed to the son of Pritha [Arjuna] his supreme divine form – having many mouths and eyes, having within it many wonderful sights, having many celestial ornaments, having many celestial weapons held erect, wearing celestial flowers and vestments, anointed with celestial perfumes, full of every wonder, the infinite deity with faces in all directions

And, when he had once done that, Krishna showed him the tremendous power of his divinity and inspires Arjuna to bow down in profound and humble worship:

> If in the heavens, the brightness of a thousand suns burst forth all at once, that would be like the brightness of that mighty one. There the son of Pandu [Arjuna] then observed in the body of the god of gods the whole universe all in one, and divided into numerous divisions. Then Arjuna was filled with amazement, and with hair standing on end, bowed his head before the god, and spoke with joined hands.

Tremendous fear seizes Arjuna as he comes face to face with the otherworldly reality of the numinous, as he realizes his utter and absolute dependence upon the lord of all the worlds:

> Seeing your mighty form, with many mouths and eyes, with many arms, thighs, and feet, with many stomachs, and fearful with many jaws, all people, and I likewise, are much alarmed, O you of mighty arms! Seeing you, O Vishnu, touching the skies, radiant, possessed of many hues, with a gaping mouth, and with large blazing eyes, I am much alarmed in my inmost self, and feel no courage, no tranquility. And seeing your mouths

terrible by the jaws, and resembling the fire of destruction, I cannot recognize the various directions, I feel no comfort. Be gracious, O lord of gods, who pervades the universe!

With data like this, it is natural that Otto should feel confident in the conceptions he had of both the autonomy of religion and its grounding in a peculiar kind of experience – even when these affronted conventional values. These dramatic eruptions of the holy, sacred, or numinous into the world of the everyday had no parallel in other modes of life, certainly not morality for instance. The God of Acts 6 is a violent being who inflicts fear (and temporary blindness) upon Saul. The "King, the Lord Almighty" of Isaiah 6 similarly has no scruples about plunging his loyal prophet into an abyss of despair. The God of the Hindus even demands that Arjuna kill his own kin; in the form of Krishna, he reveals himself as well as a violent slayer of the innocent, ruthlessly chewing human victims in his great grinding jaws. Compassion, mercy, fairness, justice, and other sweet moral values are conspicuously absent on the horizon of a landscape defined by the holy. It must be so, on Otto's view, since the numinous (as are all forms of experience of the numinous) is autonomous of all forms of human life and activity – just as is our experience of it, and religion too – the *sui generis* human response to such singular subjective states of consciousness.

This was another way for Otto of saying that religion as humanity's response to the sacred, to the holy, could not and should not be confused with its most likely object of comparison at the time – morality. We will recall Robertson Smith's Victorian sense that morality was indeed the very highest form of religious consciousness, echoing perhaps the English poet Matthew Arnold's definition of (at least nineteenth-century) religion as "morality tinged with feeling." Such were the prevailing views of the nature of religion in Otto's day. As a kind of revolutionary in religious thought, Otto was dead set against this moralizing of religion so typical of the nineteenth century. Such a reading of religion just did not reflect what was there in the religious traditions of humanity the world over. It domesticated religion by reducing it to human conceptions of right or wrong. To Otto, morality could not therefore be the essence of religion, since religion trafficked in the "wholly other," in the transcendent. Religion was not, therefore, to be *reduced* to morality – to human conceptions of obligation and duty. Religion was autonomous of morality, and every other thing as well. It was humanity's relation to the numinous. Or, at the very least, this is what we grasp when we seek empathetically to understand the religious experience of pious peoples, however unfathomable or illogical they may seem to us – as in the Maori ritual depicted in figure 7.2.

Perhaps, even more than refusing to allow religion to become 'reduced' to morality, Otto rebelled against the attempts by rationalists like Frazer and Tylor, respectively, to explain religion as either the result of a primitive scientific instinct (animism) or as arising from some wish of 'savages' for a technology to control nature (magic). For Otto, religion was not at all about reasoning about the world or controlling it. It was instead basically worship of the abject creature for the absolute creator – an all-consuming form of pious life, animated by powerful experiences of utter dependence upon the "Other," touching upon the most profound and disturbing mysteries that the human race had encountered. Most of all, religion was not mere cogitation, nor something ordinary. It was convictions such as these that led Otto to approach religion in a phenomenological way – from the inside, in and for itself, seeking only to map it out so that people could understand it. Given Otto's perspective, there was no 'explaining' religion at all, since

Figure 7.2.   The Maori religious 'specialist' or *Tohunga* is depicted here being fed with great care to guard against the dangerous power of the sacred

Source: J. C. Graham, *Maori Paintings: Pictures from the Partridge Collection of Paintings by Gottfried Lindauer* (Wellington: A. H. & A. W. Reed, 1965).

whatever *causes* there might be of this perplexing and amazing behavior lay well beyond human comprehension.

An Anatomist of Religion: Gerardus van der Leeuw

If Otto can be cast as making the most dramatic case for an elaborate exploration and exposition of *sui generis* religious *subjectivity* – experience – as exemplifying the way phenomenologists proceed, then Gerardus van der Leeuw shows us phenomenology of religion as an exercise in laying out the anatomy or structure of religion – its *objective* aspect.

Gerardus van der Leeuw (1890–1950) was professor of History of Religions and Theology at the University of Groningen from the tender age of 28 until his death in 1950. Like other phenomenologists of religion that we have met, van der Leeuw was a pious Christian, indeed an ordained minister and parish pastor in the Dutch Reformed Church, in which post he served from 1916 to 1918. Before the advent of his academic career, he had studied theology at Leiden and also for short periods in Göttingen and Berlin. Theologically, he was active in the reform of his church's liturgical life and also sought to influence its ethical teachings. As an historian of religion, he focused on ancient Egyptian religion. He later took up the study of small-scale societies especially as elaborated by Durkheim and his collaborators in Paris as well as by the work of a French philosopher and social thinker, close to the Durkheimian group, Lucien Lévy-Bruhl. In addition to his ecclesiastical and academic roles, he also participated in national public service as minister of education after the First World War, and again after the Second World War as his nation's secretary of cultural affairs. Van der Leeuw divided his writing between theological themes – liturgy, religious music, the sacraments, and history of Christianity – and phenomenological treatments of the arts in religion and the religion of small-scale societies (van der Leeuw 1918; 1948; 1949; 1952; 1963).

A persistent theme in van der Leeuw's intellectual journey is his attraction to philosophers or to theoretically minded historians like Edmund Husserl and Wilhelm Dilthey. It was probably during his period of early study in the German capital that van der Leeuw became acquainted with the work of the modern reviver of 'hermeneutics.' Van der Leeuw also claimed that his religious phenomenology was a precise adaptation of the *philosophical* phenomenology of the German philosopher, Edmund Husserl, but this claim was not made until the second edition of *Religion in Essence and Manifestation* (Spielberg 1969b, p. 606). It is perhaps for this reason that parallels between van der Leeuw's phenomenology and Husserl's lack precision. Nonetheless, Husserl did advance methodological notions later taken up by Dilthey – and through him, van der Leeuw – such as *epoché* and empathy (Spielberg 1969b, pp. 134, 158, 182, 207, 261 ff., 452). Dilthey and Husserl carried on a long and significant series of exchanges about phenomenological method. Although they did not always agree, Dilthey always acknowledged his intellectual debts to Husserl (Ermarth 1978, pp. 201–9). What is certain about the formation of van der Leeuw's thought is its embrace of Wilhelm Dilthey's advocacy of hermeneutic and interpretive methods of approaching human realities, which van der Leeuw puts forward as proper procedure in phenomenology of religion. His focal emphases on hermeneutics, interpretation, empathy, and understanding, for example, come directly from Dilthey (van der Leeuw 1964, pp. 671, 676). Taken together, in absorbing the influences of Husserl and Dilthey, van der Leeuw self-consciously located himself right in the midst of the phenomenological movement of thought, then at its peak in the late nineteenth and early twentieth centuries.

It has rightly been pointed out that van der Leeuw never really let go of his primary vocation as a Christian theologian, going even further to conceive of his academic work in phenomenology as a classic 'handmaiden' to Christian theology (Sharpe 1986, pp. 232–3). As such he never was interested in segregating his scientific and scholarly activities from his religious faith and heart-felt duty to his church. For him, phenomenology of religion was a discipline that should be placed at the disposal of Christian theology, the better to aid it in putting some degree of order into the data about the world's religions that had swamped the scholarly world in the late nineteenth century. We have seen how the same avalanche of data had overwhelmed the ability of cultural evolutionists to put them into a neat sequence of progressive development. Christian theologians like van der Leeuw felt that they too had to respond to all this new information. His phenomenology of religion was his way of trying to encompass all this new information under the dogmatic umbrella of a new theology. Having done the preliminary phenomenological job, van der Leeuw felt that as a Christian theologian his ultimate role was to pass judgment on the value of various religious facts in order to put them to use in the service of Christian doctrinal theology.

In this overriding commitment to Christian theology, van der Leeuw resembles no one more than Tiele's contemporary and modern co-founder of phenomenology of religion, Pierre Daniel Chantepie de la Saussaye. Chantepie de la Saussaye produced one of the earliest manuals of religious typology, his *Manual of the History of Religions*. This massive (700-page) volume surveyed all the great religions according to geographical region and specific religion, and brought to bear a host of comparative categories by which one might begin to match up the world's religions with one another. One religion, doubtless deemed to be 'incomparable' and which was therefore conspicuously absent from this survey, was Christianity!

Beginning with the structural or objective side of the methodology of the phenomenology of religion that van der Leeuw championed, four points should then be made. In the hands of perhaps the prototypical phenomenologist of religion, and in his classic of the phenomenology of religion, *Religion in Essence and Manifestation*, we see how this appreciation of the subjective dimension of religion gets worked into a deliberate and methodical approach, requiring a step-wise approach – none of the steps, one will note, culminating in an explanation, much less a reduction, of religion (van der Leeuw 1964).

First, for van der Leeuw everything about *understanding* religion begins with the same kind of *empathetic* approach we saw employed by Otto and spelt out by Kristensen. Van der Leeuw, incidentally, accepted Otto's account of the 'holy' and incorporated it into his theory of religion. But van der Leeuw adds to the subjective attitude of Otto and Kristensen something of a subjective attitude of his own – the mental act of *epoché*. *Epoché* means a 'bracketing' of what is experienced or derived from our empathetic understanding of the other so as to exclude judgments of truth or value regarding the phenomenon. The phenomenologist takes a 'step back,' so to speak, and withholds judgments until finished with the job of *understanding* what has been presented. Van der Leeuw wants us to 'bracket' religious data so that we regard it in a neutral and detached way, and do not therefore lapse into an all-too-easy partisan attitude to religious data. Phenomenologists of religion thus resist making leaps of faith or declaring unbelief in the religious data presented to them. They hold back on judging, theorizing, explaining, and seeking causes of the phenomenon in question. They simply take religious data as given without affiliating or disaffiliating themselves from the data. Hindus, for example, call Krishna "lord," and believe him to be sovereign in their lives today, as have Hindus in the past. The phenomenologist is only required to note or record that this is so *for Hindus*. Phenomenologists of religion are forbidden by the dictates of phenomenological method to go beyond *phenomena*, such as that believers say that 'Krishna is lord,' to a possible underlying reality of whether that religious claim is true. They 'bracket out' the *noumenal* of things, the level of the ultimate truth about the status of Krishna, and concentrate upon getting the phenomenological level of religion right. Once that is done, believers and skeptics may do what they want with what the phenomenologist has provided. Theirs is a preliminary scientific task.

Second, what sometimes seems to typify van der Leeuw for many readers is the next step he lays out for doing phenomenology of religion. The phenomenologist *classifies* phenomena – what is noted or recorded. Again without judgment or theorizing, the phenomenologist *names* the phenomena that appear. Thus, since the Hindus themselves speak of Krishna as "lord" (actually "*bhagavant*" (as in *Bhagavad Gita*) or as "*iśvara*," the phenomenologist might take the opportunity to explore the possibility that the category of lordship or indeed the Sanskrit *bhagavant* and "*iśvara*," as Ninian Smart urges, might be more broadly or differentially deployed in religion. 'Lord' as '*bhagavant*' or '*iśvara*' might actually turn out to be a useful cross-cultural *religious category* or *type* – indeed a religious *phenomenon* – that could be part of an entire long list of such basic or elemental religious phenomena! Actually, there is ample reason to think this would be so, while the Buddhists also refer frequently to the Buddha as 'lord' in the sense of "*bhagavant*," at least in the Theravada tradition, he is never "lord" as "*iśvara*." With allowances made for translation and nuances between different languages, Christianity, of course, entitles Jesus with the status of 'lord' – '*kyrios*' or '*dominum*.' How does a 'kyrios' differ or resemble a 'bhagavant,' and so on? What then is the range and either common or differential meaning of lordship as used in these three great world religions? Can one now see a bit better why a phenomenologist of religion like Kristensen was so irked by the sweeping generalities of the evolutionists, that he declared through his editor, Henrik Kraemer, that the reductionists and evolutionists proceeded "without having ever asked the preliminary fundamental question of what religion really is. It was taken for granted that one knew this" (Kraemer 1960, p. xxiii)? Kristensen and other phenomenologists understood well that religion was far more complex than the *simple* thing that the Tylors and Frazers of the world would lead one to believe. For the phenomenologists of religion, the job of *understanding* religion – much less *explaining* it – had hardly begun.

Devoted as they are to bringing out the detailed and complex nature of religion – at the very least to head off sweeping critical attacks on religion – the phenomenologists of religion would actually welcome the problems of religion provoked by teasing out how alike and different the meanings of 'lord' as '*bhagavant*,' '*iśvara*,' or many terms used to apply to Jesus as 'lord.' Such a question would be hard to imagine ever arising in evolutionist discourse about the status of sacred figures like Krishna or Jesus. But, because *empathy* and nonjudgmental *epochê* are at the heart of the phenomenological approach to religion in its quest to comprehend the believer's point of view, this conversation is encouraged. The pursuit of the ultimate truth (or falsity) of religion – the noumenon – is left either to 'caretakers of religion' or to the 'undertakers of religion,' respectively. Phenomenologist are pleased to leave such metaphysical matters to others, while they instead enrich our understanding of the religious data.

In pursuit, at the very least, of religion's descriptive distinctiveness, phenomenologists like van der Leeuw then assembled long lists of such basic categories or structural pieces that made up *religion* as they understood it. Just as politics was made up of a set of basic 'parts,' and thus had its own distinctive vocabulary of political terms – sovereignty, nation, king, and so on – so also did religion. Thus, terms like prophet, priest, sacrament, sacred, taboo, savior, and such clearly fell into the class of distinctively religious notions. The *phenomenon* of religion was made up of elements such as these – prophet, priest, sacrament, and many others. And thus the phenomenology of religion was devoted to the study of phenomena characterized by such elements. A glance through the table of contents of van der Leeuw's 1938 classic *Religion in Essence and Manifestation* lists four pages of chapters in which such categories are explored. This includes everything from Power, Taboo, Sacred, Savior, The Father, Medicine-Man, Priest, Sacramentals, The Sacrament, Divination, Myth, to The Founder, The Preacher, The Mediator, and more. Kristensen's *The Meaning of Religion* similarly lists three full pages of chapters devoted to such basic religious ideas as Death, Oath, Curse, Offering, Altar, Cosmos, Heavens, Moon, Sacred Earth, Tree Gods, Plant Gods, and so on. Moreover, when one unpacks these chapters in the list of topics in the index to *Religion in Essence and Manifestation*, one is struck by the myriad phenomena contained there – about 700 terms in all. Religion in the hands of the phenomenologists of religion looks less and less '*simple*.' In a more economical vein, Ninian Smart's attempt to update van der Leeuw's classic, *Dimensions of the Sacred: An Anatomy of the World's Beliefs*, lists only the core seven dimensions of Smart's phenomenology of religion – doctrine, myth, ritual, social organization, moral codes, experience, and material expressions (Smart 1996). Thus, whatever the style of their conception of the phenomenon or the elements included in it, the result is the same – religion is composed of a complex of innumerable and identifiable parts that go together to fill out what we mean by religion as it is in real life.

Although we cannot go into great detail here, it would be revealing just to sample how van der Leeuw treats a particular religious 'phenomenon,' such as 'lord.' In this case, the term van der Leeuw chooses is the related notion of 'king' (van der Leeuw 1964, ch. 13). In a survey of world cultures and religions rivaling Frazer, van der Leeuw touches on this notion in Masai and Maori cultures, in France, Egypt, Melanesia, Hawaii, China, Israel, Norway, England, and as well in Frazer's ancient Rome of the sacrifice of the king at Nemi.

The contrast with Frazer's approach and aims is instructive in showing us how the phenomenologists sought a different path from that of reductionist evolutionists like Frazer. Because van der Leeuw accepts that the phenomenologist of religion must begin with an empathetic understanding of the worldview of those one studies, he knows that – in their minds – the ancients, for example, sacrificed someone they regarded as their god because they believed the sacrifice of the god would restore fertility to the land (van der Leeuw 1964, p. 122). But, unlike Frazer, van der Leeuw is not trying to *explain* that the king must die, for example, because such a sacrificial death is *supposedly* proper to a certain evolutionary stage of human mental development where the 'primitives' believe in the causal efficacy of such sacrifices. Van der Leeuw is not trying to *explain* the institution of the sacrifice of the god-king as what one would *expect* from certain people at certain levels of human evolution. Instead, he connects this institution with other phenomenological categories and religious institutions, such as the belief in the existence of the "savior" (van der Leeuw 1964, p. 122). We cannot understand, he argues, why the killing of the god-king would bring fertility to the land, unless we first understood that the people in question already participated in a religious life in which they expected a "savior" to solve their cosmic problems for them. These peoples and their style of being religious would then stand at one extreme from other, more self-reliant, peoples who felt that matters of this gravity were in their own hands. Those who made the category of "savior" focal to their religious lives stood, as well, at the opposite extreme from other, more fatalistic peoples who, like orthodox Calvinists or many Muslims, felt that the course of human events was *predestined* or *predetermined* from the beginning.

Thus, in the case of the dying, sacrificed god, van der Leeuw was even less trying to do the job of an 'undertaker of religion' (like Frazer) by *explaining* how the Christian idea of the saving death of lord (king) Jesus was readied for acceptance by being foreshadowed and inscribed in the preexisting pagan rites of the sacrifice of the god-king. Van der Leeuw is really not trying to explain anything at all. He was, rather, trying to *understand* the many meanings of the phenomenon of 'king' itself in religious contexts, by linking it to other religious ideas and institutions, as we have seen in his connecting it with the "savior" idea. By comparing instances of its occurrence in the history of religions, he seeks to discover what they share. He is trying to fill out the phenomenological category 'king' by surveying and *understanding* what religious people have had *in mind* when they used kingly language about their gods. When he does so, van der Leeuw lays out a number of common factors, many of them obvious: the king is chief emblem and bearer of power;

he was a healer; and so on. But to these van der Leeuw adds some more interesting features of kingship: the power of the king is not personal, but belongs to a facilitating force of which the king is but a bearer. In this way, we can *understand*, van der Leeuw adds how and why kings are often thought to be able to control, or at least channel, cosmic forces such as luck, weather, fertility, peace, or health. The king may also be (or become) a god, and in this way embody the ultimate of cosmic powers. He is 'augustus' and so on (van der Leeuw 1964, ch. 13).

It is thus important to note for our own understanding of phenomenology of religion that van der Leeuw seeks to do a job that is *descriptive*, not *explanatory*. The job is to fill in the content of categories, to assemble all the elements that would go toward informing an *understanding* of the term 'king,' and together with other constituent unit ideas and an *understanding* of religion – all the while abiding by the rules of structured empathy by which this approach to religion operates. We will seek in vain for claims about what necessary preconditions or causes were required to produce religion. That is to say, that we will only meet with disappointment if we seek *explanations* from phenomenologists like van der Leeuw.

Ninian Smart's "Dialectical" Phenomenology

While a scheme like van der Leeuw's may be impressive for how it deepens our understanding of the 'vocabulary' of religion, of the bits and pieces of religion, his phenomenology did not really gain a wide following. Van der Leeuw's efforts may have won professional admiration, but there have not been any attempts at close imitation, except briefly the work of Hans Penner around 40 years ago. Significantly, after working to bring out the current English edition of *Religion in Essence and Manifestation*, even Penner was soon to reject the phenomenological method completely (Penner 1970).

Puzzled by the oddity of the failure of van der Leeuw's work to catch on, Ninian Smart suggested that one reason may have been that van der Leeuw's approach lacked dynamism. It was too *static* an approach to such a lively and contested reality as religion. At best, with van der Leeuw, we may come to better *understand* certain entries in the 'vocabulary' of religion, along with an accompanying 'glossary' of these key terms, so to speak. But, in doing so, we have not *understood* religion as 'alive' – as an organic, internally interactive whole. We have not even begun to understand a *single religion* as a kind of living, changing, historical reality by adopting van der Leeuw's method.

This is not to say, of course, that the evolutionists helped us much in this regard either, only that they at least presented students of religion with a stirring story in which religion played a significant role. As reductionists, the evolutionists thought the 'days' of religion were numbered: it was no better than an irrelevant "survival," useful at one time to get us to a certain point in human history, but now discarded like an obsolete piece of technology. The evolutionist thus waved religion off the 'stage' of history as the drama of human growth and development moved toward what they thought would be its secular culmination. Van der Leeuw put religion back onto the 'stage,' so to speak, but failed to supply the 'stage directions' to get it into action. His phenomenology is like a set of slides, with appropriate commentary to distinguish one from the other. Smart instead produces a kind of dynamic 'moving picture' of religion, where actors interact, scenes change, and real drama is played out. Like them or not, then, evolutionist accounts of the place of religion in human history were at least *dynamic*, even if faulty. Van der Leeuw's rather static phenomenology of religion, on the other hand, tells us no story at all. This is not to his credit.

Smart tries to set religion in motion first of all by providing a sense of the religious totality or whole. Beyond van der Leeuw's affirmation of Otto's conception of religion as an orientation to the numinous or holy, his phenomenology of religion fails to provide an *overall* understanding of the 'whole.' This failure of van der Leeuw's to grasp religion as a totality resulted precisely in producing an approach to religion that would be static. The two features of van der Leeuw's approach went together.

This insight of Smart's can be applied to understanding of the religion as such as a whole, and also to understanding particular religions. For Smart, religion should be seen as a structured 'whole' made up of seven mutually interdependent or "dialectically" related "dimensions": myths, rituals, doctrines, ethics, social forms and organizations, emotions and experiences, and material or esthetic elements. Now, although each of these dimensions may exist independently or in relation to other human formations, when they are clustered into an interactive complex, we have what is usefully called a "religion." A religion is defined by its social institutions, actual buildings and physical property, a clergy, a set of sharply defined beliefs, a program of prescribed rituals, a group of adherents, an experiential and emotional life involving a world beyond the material one. Smart is not only concerned with the 'parts' of religion, or even the 'sum of the parts,' but the 'whole' of religion, which – like all 'wholes' – is always greater than the 'sum of its parts.'

There is one more point that follows. Once Smart has decided to bring out the totality that religion is and that particular religions are, he becomes a very different kind of thinker than previous phenomenologists. Smart's style of "understanding" religion approaches, and in some cases becomes, an *explanation* of religion (Wright 1971). This is not to say that Smart lapses back into evolutionism, where we talk of *necessary preconditions* for the emergence of religion or religious institutions. Nor does Smart claim to know what ultimately *causes* religion, religious experience, and all the rest. But he does feel that we can make a great deal more sense of religion – we can address at least some of the 'why' questions – when we grasp that what happens in religion can often be accounted for in terms of its own inner dynamic. There are *religious conditions* of religious behavior, so to speak. As we will see, Smart wants to bring out how this inner conditioning dynamic works in religion. And why not? Every other form of life has its own inner dynamic. Why not religion? Religion for Smart, therefore, has systemic qualities, certain internally interconnected regularities, a particular way of fitting together and meshing into a unity. His phenomenology of religion is unique in exploiting this insight, and therefore in breaking down to a degree the hard and fast distinction between understanding and explanation so much a part of the thought of the founders of phenomenology of religion.

Thus, what Smart realizes – without abandoning the phenomenological ideal of seeking to *interpret* or *understand* religion, rather than explaining it *causally* – is that phenomenological interpretations have to go some way to slake the thirst of students of religion for the answer to 'why' questions. In order to 'catch on' in the way van der Leeuw's phenomenology of religion never did, Smart is effectively arguing that its 'interpretations' and 'understandings' of religion need to satisfy our natural curiosity in a way that at least approaches causal 'explanation.' There is just something perennially attractive about finding and citing *causes*, about *explanation* – or at least about not drawing a hard and fast line between explanation and interpretation. That is what I shall show in discussing the way Smart does his own version of phenomenology of religion.

Motivated both by dissatisfaction with the static character of van der Leeuw's phenomenology of religion and his failure really to boost our *understanding* (or explanatory grasp) of religion as such, or even of a particular religion, Smart proposed what he calls a "dialectical phenomenology" of religions (Smart 1996, p. 7). Here Smart not only focuses on bringing out the meanings of individual phenomena, such as 'lord,' for instance, but on how a single phenomenological element like 'lord' fits together with other distinctive bits and pieces of religion in the repertoire of the phenomenology of religion. Here is where Smart shows how his style of phenomenology of religion can address 'why' questions – how it can offer understandings and explanations of religion – accounts that rely on grasping the inner dynamic and interrelatedness of the things that go to make up a religion, but accounts that do not simply repeat what believers may say, or which do not rely on empathy as an infallible and incorrigible source of knowledge about religion.

To go all the way back to Tiele's adaptation to the study of religion of linguist William Dwight Whitney's analysis of language, what is the *grammar* of religion? Language is more than just its vocabulary or even a glossary or dictionary of key terms. It is a systematic scheme – something that has a grammar, syntax, and semantics – in short all those features that make for the unity and totality of religion. What parallels are there, then, with religion and the way it hangs together? How, for example, is being a "lord" related to the "ritual" acts of "devotion," "prayer," "sacrifice," "meditation," "worship," and so on? And would it depend upon what *kind* of "lord" – "incarnate" and human like Attis, Jesus, or Krishna, "heavenly" like the Amitābha Buddha or the Bodhisattva Avalokiteśvara, "transcendent" like Allah or Yahweh, and such? How does it inform a religion's "mythology" or the style of religious "experience" and "emotion"? Will it not perhaps cause one to expect one sort of experience rather than another? Is not, for example, Otto's analysis of the numinous more likely to apply to an experience of the radiant 'lord,' rather than, say, an experience of the transcendent vacancy of Buddhist Emptiness or the Taoist "tao"? Can we likewise expect that religions emphasizing the "lordly" qualities of their focus will express that in certain forms of 'materiality' – in the architecture of their sacred buildings, or as we have seen in the graphic arts brought into our discussion of Otto and the numinous, in graphic and musical dimensions of religious life? Likewise, and in Smart's "dialectical" style, would not certain styles of ritual, myth, material representation, and so on *induce* a sense of 'lordship,' even to the inducing of certain experiences of numinous lordliness? This same series of questions can be submitted to any particular religious context in which lordliness figures, whether that be ancient Israel, or *comparatively* – across contexts – such as ancient Israel compared to ancient India. Given that elemental religious categories might be quite numerous, the kinds of relationships open to questioning of this and other kinds is probably literally infinite.

Consider a 'why' question such as the reason for the institutionalization of religion. Today, it is commonplace for people to affirm their religiousness while at the same time complaining of alienation from so-called 'organized religion.' One even hears the idea mooted about that religious institutions are not necessary; only bodiless spirituality, purity of heart, and the right beliefs are required. This denatured view of religion should remind us of Robertson Smith's view that mature, highly evolved, "spiritual" religion would do away with the dense material of ritual life that typified religion in small-scale societies, such as he studied in the Arabian peninsula. Says Smith:

on the whole it is manifest that none of the ritual systems of antiquity was able by mere natural development to shake itself free from the congenital limitation inherent in every attempt to embody spiritual truth in material forms. A ritual system must always remain materialistic, even if its materialism is disguised under the cloak of mysticism. (Robertson Smith 1923, pp. 439–40)

With its reputation for simplicity and individual moral self-reliance, Theravāda Buddhism, for example, might, according to Robertson Smith, be seen as essentially the adherence to the Four Noble Truths or the Eightfold Path. But on closer inspection, by way of Smart's "dimensions" we would note that the "religion" of Theravāda Buddhism is not just a matter of ideas and ethics, as our nineteenth-century predecessors felt. True, it is those 'spiritual' dimensions, but also together with the institution of the Buddhist monastic order, the Sangha, the rich yogic experiential life of meditating monks, the cycle of calendrical rites, the veneration of relics and construction of stupas, as well as the cult of the *devatas* that, among other things, puts Buddhists in the right frame of meditative mind. A "religion" for Smart is all the seven dimensions taken together with other features in a condition of dynamic and "dialectical" interaction. The dimensions of Buddhism, like the "texts" of poststructuralism referring to other texts, "refer" to other dimensions of religion. One dimension takes its meaning and purposes from others within the Buddhist constellation. Rituals such as monastic begging reinforce *dogmas* of selflessness and detachment. Experiences of emptiness resonate with vows of poverty and material simplicity, with the refined austerity of the shaven head of the bhikkhu, with the purity of some of Theravādin architecture such as in the simple white stupas seen everywhere in these countries. Thus, by showing how interdependent the dimensions of religion are, phenomenologists of religion can address questions about the how and why of religion – without really going beyond religion itself.

The beauty of Smart's dimensional approach is that it can set up a perspective in which a whole series of 'why' questions can be addressed and answered. True to the ideal of autonomy or distinctiveness characteristic of the phenomenology of religion, these are questions and answers that do not pass outside the realm of religion itself. They are not efforts at 'explaining' religion in nonreligious – reductionist – terms. They are efforts to account for how and why things happen in religion in terms of religious factors, much as one would explain events within a sport in terms of the basic conditions and rules of the game. In a basketball game, for example, we might be asked by a novice spectator to 'explain' why shots made from beyond a certain line on the floor count for 3 points and others short of this line for 2 points. To do so, we would simply appeal to the overall structure of the game (to win by scoring the most points), and the conventional rules covering 3-point shots. We would not have to go beyond the rules of the game to dwell on the *psychological* causes or motives behind the behavior of the scorer, or bring out the causal relevance of their membership in a certain *sociological* class, or even proceed with a *kineseological* analysis of the muscular causes at work conditioning the action of the shooter's arm. We could, of course, go on to bring in all such matters lying *outside* the scope of the game of basketball – if we had reason so to do. Perhaps the shooter's highly competitive personality structure predisposed them to take long, risky shots? Perhaps, the shooter's low economic class origins caused them to overachieve by venturing shots from 3-point range? And so on. We could always ask these questions. But we need not necessarily do so in all cases. It depends on what we want to know, and upon what level of strategic inquiry we seek to pursue. We could, thus, perfectly well satisfy much of the curiosity about the way a basketball game unfolds by simply understanding – and in this noncausal way, *explaining* – the reasons for taking a 3-point shot. We could appeal to the conditions of the game at the time: time was running out and the shooter's team, behind by 2 points, needed 3 to win; the shooter *intended* to win the game, and therefore decided to attempt the 3-point shot needed for victory, and so on. How does the analogy to the game of basketball translate to religion?

We might ask what seems like a question with an obvious answer. To wit, why do certain religious folk engage in Smart's "ritual" dimension of human behavior? They pray, worship, or do sacrifice, for example. Why? One answer is that what it means to do these things – why these things are done – is bound up essentially in the "doctrinal" assumptions or "beliefs" made about the way the world is by the worshipers, sacrificers, et al. – to cite another of Smart's "dimensions." In a religion, however, in which lordship defines the nature of the religious focus, at least part of the reason for worship becomes clear: the lord is the source of all power and life; the appropriate attitude of the creature to their lord is to acknowledge that difference in status by bowing down – by 'worshiping' – or by giving of themselves to acknowledge their Otto-like status of absolute dependence – sacrifice. Such behaviors thus 'make sense' in light of the worldview dominated as it is by the conception of the lord, and following upon this, the proper intentions of the worshiper, sacrificer, and such, before that power.

Further questions may also be put in regard to these behaviors as well, questions that take us further into the complex reality of religions constructed about a 'lord.' What, for example, is the meaning of 'lord' in a particular religion's historic context – exactly the kind of question, as we have seen, to which Marc Bloch addressed himself in our discussion of the reasons why today's Christians pray on bended knee with folded hands. They behave as if they are directing themselves to someone lordly outside themselves, because their doctrinally defined worldview dictates that people are not alone, but in relation to higher, lordly, beings, understanding all the while how the idea of 'lord' has been built up historically.

These are nonetheless puzzling behaviors, since the transcendent focus of prayer, sacrifice, or worship is not given to common sense. Yet, people act *as if* the divine, lordly focus of their worship were present. Why? Some might answer that although empirical experience or common sense fail to give evidence of the truth of their "beliefs" and the meaningfulness of their "rituals," their religious "experience" – perhaps of the numinous kind elaborated by Otto – inspires them both to certain "beliefs" and "rituals." It is perhaps unnecessary to carry this exposition further, realizing that one might explain why these same worshipers adhere to particular "ethical" standards (they are given by the lord as law-giver), or assemble in certain distinctive kinds of organized "social" groupings (churches, a holy chosen people, an *umma* or particular political formation required by the lord) and so on. What we should see here is that Smart's "dialectical phenomenology" sets up a context in which the interrelatedness of religion to its parts can be explored. Smart has thus given us a phenomenology of religion, but one that is organic and that lives. This is his way of approaching how religions could be said to be *structured* – the same 'objective' side of phenomenology of religion that van der Leeuw so well exemplified. They believed that part of what it was to study religion was to study how its distinctive elements were related to one another.

Notes

1. Pierre Daniel Chantepie de la Saussaye also includes Tiele among those notable for their schemes of classification of religions. See Chantepie de la Saussaye, 1904.

References

anon. 1881. Tylor's Anthropology. *The Nation* 33, p. 181.

——. 1882. Tiele's Egyptian Religion. *The Nation* 35, pp. 361–2.

Bloch, M. 1961. *Feudal Society: The Growth of Ties of Dependence*, trans. L. A. Manyon. Chicago: University of Chicago Press.

Chantepie de la Saussaye, P. D. 1904. *Manuel d'histoire des religions*, trans. H. Hubert & I. Lévy. Paris: Armand Colin.

Ermarth, M. 1978. *Wilhelm Dilthey: The Critique of Historical Reason*. Chicago: University of Chicago Press.

Geertz, C. 1973. *The Interpretation of Cultures*. New York: Basic Books.

——. 1983. *Local Knowledge: Further Essays in Interpretive Anthropology*. New York: Harper and Row.

Goblet d'Alviella, C. E. 1885. Maurice Vernes et la méthode comparative. *Revue de l'histoire des religions* 12.

——. 1910. Review of Jean Réville's *Les phases successives de l'histoire des religions*. *Revue d'histoire des religions* 61, pp. 349–52.

Jastrow, Morris. 1981. *The Study of Religion*. Chico, CA: Scholars Press.

Kraemer, H. 1960. Introduction. In *W. Brede Kristensen, The Meaning of Religion*, ed. J. B. Carman. The Hague: Martinus Nijhoff.

Kristensen, W. B. 1960. *The Meaning of Religion: Lectures in the Phenomenology of Religion*, trans. J. B. Carman. The Hague: Martinus Nijhoff.

La Planche, F., ed. 1991. *La méthode historique et l'histoire des religions; les orientations de la Revue de l'histoire de religions* (La tradition française en sciences religieuses). Québec: Université de Laval.

Malinowski, B. 1961. *Argonauts of the Western Pacific*. New York: E. P. Dutton.

McCutcheon, R. T. 1997. *Manufacturing Religion: The Discourse on Sui Generis Religion and the Politics of Nostalgia*. New York: Oxford University Press.

Molendijk, A. L. 2000a. At the Cross-Roads: Early Dutch Science of Religion in International Perspective. In *Man, Meaning and Mystery*, ed. S. Hjelde. Leiden: E. J. Brill.

——. 2000b. The Heritage of Cornelis P. Tiele. *Nederlands Archief voor Kerkgeschiednis* 80, pp. 78–114.

Otto, R. 1923. *The Idea of the Holy*, trans. J. W. Harvey. New York: Oxford University Press.

Penner, H. H. 1970. Phenomenology, a Method for the Study of Religion? *Bucknell Review* 18, pp. 29–54.

Popper, K. R. 1963. Science: Conjectures and Refutations. In *Conjectures and Refutations*. London: Routledge.

Réville, A. 1864. Dutch Theology: Its Past and Present State. *Theological Review* 3, pp. 275–7.

——. 1875. Evolution in Religion, and Its Results. *Theological Review* 12, p. 243.

Réville, J. 1903. Leçon d'ouverture de M. Maurice Vernes. *Revue de l'histoire des religions* 47.

Sharpe, E. J. 1986. *Comparative Religion: A History*. La Salle, IL: Open Court.

Smart, N. 1996. *Dimensions of the Sacred: An Anatomy of the World's Religions*. London: Harper/Collins.

Smith, W. R. 1923. *Lectures on the Religion of the Semites*. London: A. & C. Black.

Spielberg, H. 1969a. *The Phenomenonological Movement: A Historical Introduction*, vol. 1. The Hague: Martinus Nijhoff.

——. 1969b. *The Phenomenonological Movement: A Historical Introduction*, vol. 2. The Hague: Martinus Nijhoff.

Tiele, C. P. 1877. *Outlines of the History of Religion to the Spread of the Universal Religions*, trans. J. E. Carpenter. Boston: James R. Osgood.

——. 1896. *Elements of the Science of Religion. Part I: Morphological*. Edinburgh and London: W. Blackwood and Sons.

van den Bosch, L. P. 2002. *Friedrich Max Müller: A Life Devoted to the Humanities*. Leiden: E. J. Brill.

van der Leeuw, G. 1918. *Plaats en taak van de godsdienstgeschiedenis in de theologische wetenschap*. The Hague: J. B. Wolters.

——. 1948. *Inleiding tot de theologie*. Amsterdam: H. J. Paris.

——. 1949. *Sacramentstheologie*. Nijkerk: G. F. Callenbach.

——. 1952. *De primitieve mensch en de religie. Anthropologische studie*. Groningen: J. B. Wolters.

——. 1963. *Sacred and Profane Beauty: The Holy in Art*, trans. D. E. Green. New York: Holt, Rinehart and Winston.

——. 1964. *Religion in Essence and Manifestation*, trans. J. E. Turner. London: George Allen and Unwin.

Whitney, W. D. 1870. Review of F. Max Müller, *Introduction to the Science of Religion*. *The Nation*, 242–4.

Wright, G. H. von. 1971. *Explanation and Understanding*. Ithaca: Cornell University Press.

Young, M. W. 2004. *Malinowski: Odyssey of an Anthropologist, 1884–1920*. New Haven: Yale University Press.

Religious Experience Creates the World of the Modern Economy: Max Weber

8

We ought not to prevent people from being diligent and frugal; we must exhort all Christians to gain all they can, and to save all they can; that is, in effect, to grow rich.

–John Wesley, as quoted by Weber in *The Protestant Ethic and the Spirit of Capitalism*

Weber and the Problems of Understanding and Explaining Capitalism

While it may seem unimaginative to begin a chapter on Max Weber with his life story, his biography can be read like an irresistible extended metaphor, capturing and reflecting essential tensions in his approach to religion. His tormented relations with his parents seem to pose some of the same dilemmas that he tried so successfully to bring out in his attempts to show how religion and modern economic life were related. Weber's deeply personal struggles with his own inner demons sometimes seem like other ways of dramatizing the great political battles of his day. His own ambivalence about the place of work and career in making for himself a whole human life seem to rehearse the tragic lessons of the discontents that characterize the modern world as a whole. So, although it may be conventional to begin discussing the ideas of an author by reciting the life story of that author, I believe the results of doing so in the case of Max Weber will be anything but conventional.

Born into a comfortable middle-class family living in the better days of Bismarck's German Empire, Max Weber (1864–1920) was well placed to make a good start in life. Unfortunately, the otherwise smooth exterior of late nineteenth-century bourgeois existence into which Weber was born concealed many of the tensions that troubled him and the entire age into which he was born. His dramatically conflicted personal life in many ways repeats at the level of biography the same irresolvable conflicts that emerge again in his intellectual struggles, including the study of religion. The family of his mother, Helene, had been French Huguenot refugee school teachers for generations; the family of his father, Max Sr., by contrast, had been long established in the trades and business. Max Sr. also served as a parliamentary deputy in the Reichstag, and was close to the inner circle of power around Bismarck in Berlin. Despite their more modest origins, some of Weber's mother's family had amassed considerable wealth and a certain level of social prestige, placing them in a social class higher than Weber's father and his family, with their petty bourgeois commercial manners and parsimonious style of life (Mitzman 1969, p. 44). These subtle differences in social class between Weber's parents only served to signal other, even deeper, differences between them that were to have lasting effects upon their son. As a result, it would also become a source of inner turmoil for Max Weber himself. A good deal of this turmoil would be fraught with emotion. While Weber was close to his mother in terms of his personal feelings, he dutifully followed the career example of his worldly, successful, rationalist father. His heart may have been with his mother, but Weber centered his life around his career.

Religion was one of these major areas of conflict within the Weber household. Weber's father was neither a practicing nor believing Christian of any stripe; Helene Weber was a pious religious Lutheran of a moderate sort. Weber's ways of resolving this parental conflict were creative. Thus, despite the power of the male role model provided by his father, Weber was always intellectually engaged by religion throughout his life. To a remarkable degree for a nonbeliever, he was, as well, quite literate in the theological controversies of the times, in part through his close relations with his Lutheran theologian cousin on his mother's side, Otto Baumgarten, but also because of his own intellectual and historical curiosity about the nature of early Christianity, especially its Christology. There he was fascinated by the claims made by Albert Schweitzer and others that Jesus needed to be seen within the historical context of later Jewish apocalyptic (Honigsheim 2003, pp. 229–30). At the intellectual level, Weber was also a great admirer of major figures in the Higher Criticism of the Bible, such as David Friedrich Strauss and Ferdinand Christian Bauer. So, although we can say that Weber conformed, at least externally, to the secular style of his father, these other dimensions of Weber's relation to religion raise doubts as to how deep his identification with his father's distaste for religion was.

Despite seeming to follow his father's secular ways, a small indication of a religious depth to Weber's character becomes evident in his engagement in the moral status of the individual. Thus Weber's intellectual concurrence with rationalists like Strauss may be less an indication of his religious sense than his passion about moral issues of a religious origin. Weber was, for example, vexed by the dilemmas of relations between the individual believer and collectivities such as church or state. In terms of the moral and political status of the individual, Weber shows himself to be a true inheritor of the Protestant prophetic spirit. He was, early in life, particularly impressed with the Prussian Hussar army officer, Christoph Moritz von Egidy (1847–98). A man revered by moral conscientious objectors to war in the years before the First World War, von Egidy's focus on the sacrosanct nature of the individual human conscience fed Weber's own sense, perhaps originally Lutheran, of the primacy of the prophetic spirit's independence of both the institutions of church and state. Von Egidy became a devoted purveyor of the ideas of nonviolent resistance of the Russian Count Leo Tolstoy. He also challenged the Lutheran orthodoxy of the day in Germany by bringing his pacificist ideas to the fore. However, he was forced to leave the army because of the publication of a tract arguing against "official dogmas of the established church" (von Suttner, April 18, 1906). Von Egidy in fact fearlessly taught that religious action was far more important than doctrines (Honigsheim 2003, p. 104). Weber's sympathies with von Egidy's ideas were soon to be revealed. Weber felt, for example, that the idea of a state church promoted by Kaiser Wilhelm II was distasteful in the extreme. Repellent as well was the state's religious ritualization of the Kaiser's vision of the fusion of the Prussian state and religion. For the young Weber, both the Kaiser's politicization of religion and the religious ritualization of politics violated Weber's classically Lutheran belief that the individual's response to God's calling was the only bedrock of real religion (Honigsheim 2003, pp. 103–5). Weber's subsequent attraction to Tolstoy, mediated as it was by von Egidy and a number of young Russian liberals then studying under him in Heidelberg, falls into place as part of a larger Protestant prophetic vision that informed Weber's view of the relation of the individual to society.

Another way that von Egidy seemed to have influenced Weber was precisely his prophetic Protestantism informing and inspiring what there was of Weber's Christianity. We might also recall that this was the same religious spirit beloved of Robertson Smith and his teacher, Julius Wellhausen. Standing for this strong, rebellious, and upright form of Christianity, von Egidy conceived the faith as a kind of concrete *ethic* directing the way one lived everyday life in the world. If these positions should again recall Robertson Smith's view of Christianity as essentially an *ethic*, it is no accident. Smith, as we know, had also sojourned in late nineteenth-century Germany and seems to have absorbed similar theological influences to Weber's. The example of von Egidy, therefore, justifies seeing Weber's conception of an ideal Christianity as a worldly force, as an ethic, in a new light as part of his own, perhaps never fully articulated, religious beliefs.

Von Egidy's ideas seem to have consequences both for what we will see in Weber's classic, *The Protestant Ethic and the Spirit of Capitalism*, and also for his life of social action. Weber joined a social movement, dear to his mother's heart, of sweet Lutheran ethical concern for social justice – the Evangelisch-Soziale Verein, the Lutheran Social Union – and even attended its meetings with her (Mitzman 1969, pp. 37–8). Gradually, however, Weber came round to his father's way of looking at political matters, since he came to feel that the Verein's program for Germany was soft and unrealistic. The Verein could not ultimately claim Weber's loyalty, since it lacked the fierce Nietzschean power of will that a 'real' politics required of its participants (Diggins 1996, pp. 87–8).

If these twists and turns in Weber's attitude to religion were not contorted enough, Weber's relation to religion gets even more complicated by the emotional interplay within the Weber nuclear family. The bitter relations between Weber's mother and father seem to have played an especially upsetting role in Weber's life, and in their own obscure way, influenced his professional attitudes to religion. The principal episodes in Weber's life that are most telling have to do with the way Max Sr.'s antireligious passion savaged the heart of Weber's own beloved mother, and in turn doubtless inflicted their own deep wounds upon the young Max Weber. In the presence of his son, Max Sr. would routinely and vehemently belittle his wife for her adherence to the softer Christian notions of compassion and charity toward the poor.

In this emotional distancing from an overbearing father, Weber will resemble Bronislaw Malinowski, as we will see in due course, and together with Malinowski, later in life would display something of the same psychological profile that was a source of so much torment and instability for the great Polish anthropologist. Although Weber does not seem as sexually driven as the libidinous Malinowski, his sexual life was nearly as vexed. He never consummated his marriage, but did engage in several extramarital affairs. As we will see, Malinowski was tormented by the ascetic impulse to harness his powerful and, for a while, polymorphous sexual appetites. At the other extreme, Weber was always fascinated by the subject of Protestant asceticism. Even though married, one might speculate that, his extramarital liaisons notwithstanding, he lived out this worldly monkish fascination by failing to consummate his union. Further, like Malinowski, Weber suffered from bad health all his life, some of which may have become complicated by psychological causes. At 12, he was stricken with a case of meningitis. This early trauma seems to have weakened his physical constitution and perhaps made him vulnerable to illness later in life. But like Malinowski, Weber was also prone to mental maladies such as manic-depressive episodes. In 1898, for example, he suffered a mysterious bout of paralysis that lasted until 1901, and which forced him into retirement from university teaching in 1902. He spent most of the remaining 18 years of his life working as an independent scholar.

If we turn from religion for a moment to Weber's educational career, by all accounts we find a young man who distinguished himself right from the beginning in Germany's excellent and rigorous primary and secondary school systems and in its lively universities, at that time the envy of the world. But again a certain conflict of interests seemed to lodge in the heart of the young man. Weber loved the Roman and Greek classics, and accordingly showed considerable aptitude for classical studies and history. Yet at university in Heidelberg he pursued a course in law, in the footsteps of his worldly and success-oriented father. Weber's career at the university also reflected the ways the young man was pulled one way and another. Like his pious and abstemious mother, Weber in part, at least, was the model of a disciplined and serious student at Heidelberg. But at the same time, like his worldly father, he also led the conventionally rowdy life of aggressive male bonding legendary at Germany's universities in the late nineteenth century. Dueling for sport and honor, boozing in the local beer halls, and carousing with his (male) contemporaries dominated Weber's leisure hours. Upon his return home after a season of university drinking and dueling, Weber's mother was horrified to see her most cherished son beer "bloated" and scarred about the face. She immediately greeted him with a resounding slap across the face (Mitzman 1969, pp. 23 ff.). No matter how Weber may have tried to mediate the tensions within his personality between ascetic discipline and spontaneous pleasure-seeking, this opposition will remain a central one, particularly, as we will see, in his tragic sense of the gains and losses of embracing the worldly asceticism that defined the central values of the new capitalist order.

Shortly after the completion of his law studies, Weber returned to his earlier love of ancient history, and at the precocious age of 25 did a doctoral dissertation on the history of medieval Italian and Spanish trading companies. He went on to write a further dissertation – the German *Habilitation* – that made one eligible for university teaching posts. This second doctorate confirmed Weber on his eventual intellectual course as an economic historian or historical sociologist. The subject of this second doctorate as well – Roman agrarian history – marked somewhat of a return to his old love of the ancient classical world, but now conditioned by his scientific approach to the study of other cultures. At the young age of 30, the first goals of Weber's professional academic ambitions were fulfilled when he became professor of political economy at the University of Freiburg.

Weber's indifference to conventional religious practice and his orientation to a secular professional life more in keeping with his father's ideals of success, did not, however, in any way affect his emotional affinities with his mother. Indeed, Weber's affection and emotional identification with her might only be said to have increased as he became more aware of the ill-treatment meted out to her by Weber's abusive father. Max Sr. would routinely ridicule his wife's piety and kind-hearted Christian attitudes towards the poor, seeking always to maintain tight "patriarchal" control over the members of his

Figure 8.1.   Max Weber, age 23, seated uncomfortably next to his hated father, Max Sr., but not close enough to his much-beloved mother, Helene. Berlin 1887.

Source. Marianne Weber, *Max Weber: A Biography* (New York: John Wiley and Sons, 1975), p. 345.

household. Incapable of fighting her husband, Helene "poured out her grief" to Weber, putting him thereby in the most profound opposition to the harsh master of the house (Mitzman 1969, p. 45). The decisive alienating act by Weber's father was the high-handed dismissal of a 'moral tutor,' hired by Helene to inculcate Christian values into her children. By all accounts, Weber never recovered from this act of his powerful but emotionally remote father. Max Sr. had tried quite brutally to squelch the religious passions of this beloved, ill-treated mother with whom the young man had such a close bond of feeling (Mitzman 1969, pp. 45 ff.). (See figure 8.1.)

A powerfully illustrative incident – and its aftermath – indicated the depth and emotional complexity of Weber's relations with his father. Many years after the expulsion of Weber's moral tutor, his parents arrived to visit their son and to glory in his success at winning a university professorship at Heidelberg. Weber chose that precise moment to exact revenge upon his father for Max Sr.'s demonstration of patriarchal control. Weber himself, now master in his own house – located significantly in his mother's home city – angrily refused his own father entry, literally driving the old man from his door. Weber's mother stayed on with her son for the duration of the planned visit, but Weber's father died only a few weeks later. It is speculated that the long depression and nervous breakdown which Weber suffered upon the death of his father was only symptomatic of the tortured emotional life that shaped his life, torn as he was by the impossibility of being a loyal and loving son to both parents in such a destructive emotional environment (Mitzman 1969, pp. 150 ff.). Even when Weber felt justified in avenging his mother by wounding Max Sr., who had so abused both his mother and himself, he could not control the surge of guilt that his own cruel act brought upon him. Thus, relations between Weber and his parents seem always to have been consequential. These relations were also, as I have argued and will continue to argue, illustrative of tensions within Weber's thought about religion. In a way, Weber could not live with religion, nor could he live without it. He might well have liked to avoid considering religion as active and important in the world, but his conscientious scholarship simply prevented him from denying what he came to learn.

Weber's biographers note that this last period of his life following on his father's death and his own mental breakdown, produced his most influential and profound work on religion. Although afflicted with bouts of debilitating depression, Weber also experienced periods of intense manic activity, resulting in the studies in religion and economic life for which he is now best known. *The Protestant Ethic and the Spirit of Capitalism* appeared in 1905, followed in 1915–20 by his studies of India (Buddhism and Hinduism), China (Confucianism and Taoism), and ancient Israel. By any standard, these books are models of the comparative study of religions in the way they both reflect encyclopedic knowledge of many different religious faiths and do so in a rich comparative context. Witness to the wealth and suggestiveness of Weber's insights into these different religions and their relation to economic values, these books are still read with admiration in our own time. Indeed, they have inspired many imitators as well, such as Robert Bellah's study of Japan's transition to capitalism by way of transformations of Japanese Buddhism, and Milton Singer's investigation of indigenous Hindu sources of a religiously based economic ethic (Bellah 1957; Singer 1972). So important indeed has Weber's way of posing (and solving) the problem of the possible relationship of religion to economic life been, that it is widely known as the "Weber thesis."

It is entirely possible that Weber began to develop this sensitivity to comparison and contrast from the social and geographical circumstances of the city of his birth, Erfurt, provincial capital of the German *Land* of Thüringia. Situated half way along the northeast axis between Frankfurt and Berlin in the heart of Germany, its population was roughly divided equally as well between Germany's major religious communities, the Catholics and the Protestants. Overall, the Catholics were well represented in Rhineland and the south and the Protestants were more numerous in the north and east. By contrast, Dessau, the birthplace of Friedrich Max Müller, lay midway again between Erfurt and Berlin, and therefore in mainly Protestant eastern Germany. Weber thus experienced at first hand the contrasting tempers of these religious communities, with their divergent economic orientations. Later in life, he experienced the same kinds of contrasts when he undertook research along the borders of Protestant Prussia and Catholic Poland (the latter still at that time part of the German Empire). This perception of difference seems to have left an indelible imprint on Weber that is evident in *The Protestant Ethic and the Spirit of Capitalism*. There, Weber took his point of departure from the comparative perspective of opposing Catholic and Protestant theologies and their related economic orientations. Weber's own family situation likewise reinforced this contrast. We might imagine Max the child pondering the differences between his father's practice of the traditional profession of law over against the impact made upon him by his father's entrepreneurial industrialist family, cited by Weber's biographers as the source of formative experiences in the nature of capitalism, especially its practice of modern rationalized management (Käsler 1988, ch. 1).

In terms of his own moral and political character, Weber presents the image of a principled conservative. He supported the Prussian-led German state under Bismarck, but felt at the same time that the sacrosanct rule of law and the rights of individual citizens were endangered by elements close to or inside the regime. He was especially dead set against the demagogic, jingoistic, and charismatic philosopher, Heinrich von Treitschke, who had begun to come into favor toward the end of the nineteenth century. In his opposition to the domineering styles of political life exemplified by Treitschke, Weber once more rehearsed and reaffirmed the oppositions between mother and father in very concrete ways. Weber became very close to his maternal uncle, the historian Hermann Baumgarten, a man of liberal politics with whom Weber had long, intellectually intense, and affectionate relations, especially during Weber's years at university. Instead of the domineering, high-handed – one is tempted to say Treitschkean – style in which Max Sr. lorded it over his entire family, Baumgarten and the young Weber enjoyed a lively intellectual meeting of minds, passionately contending with each other in a setting in which Weber was always treated as an equal by his good uncle. In this respect, Baumgarten became for Weber in part a source of emotional grounding for the filial feelings his own father never fulfilled. Baumgarten not only supplied the warm humanity that Weber enjoyed with his mother, but also the heady intellectual give and take that Max Sr. made possible through his extensive social connections with leading German luminaries of the day. Among the glittering array of guests in Max Sr.'s household were the likes of Dilthey, whom we have had occasion to consider in connection with the phenomenologists, and also the historian Theodor Mommsen, as well as Treitschke himself (Käsler 1988, p. 3; Mitzman 1969, p. 20).

In the matter of the evaluation of Treitschke and all he stood for, it is highly significant that Max Sr. lined up in bourgeois conformist style with the powers of his day behind Treitschke and the kind of antiliberal politics he represented (Mitzman 1969, p. 35). Weber was a firm and loyal German nationalist, but one who was repelled by his father's submission to Treitschke. Weber thought that Treitschke's insertion of charismatic authority into politics attempted to substitute instinct and other subrational forces for the respect for law and procedure needed to manage a modern nation-state. Weber did his tour of military duty faithfully while a young man in his twenties, but could never be classified as a mindless patriot. Treitschke also irritated Weber because as an academic he misused the position of trust that teachers of the young had a right to expect. In a passionate declaration of his moral commitment to fairness and objectivity, *Science as a Calling*, Weber insisted that teachers and intellectuals were solemnly pledged, as much as humanly possible, to maintain a *Wertfrei* – value-free – level of discourse in their classes in order to eliminate any intrusion of personal views into what should be a matter of scholarship and intellectual integrity. In the classroom, teachers should steer clear of using their privileged positions to benefit partisan politics. Teachers should never exploit the trust of their charges to sway the political views of their students.

Thus, in this somewhat hurried review of Weber's life, I think we can begin to anticipate some of the key issues that he will investigate and try to resolve. Some of them will draw us into concerns about how both individuals and societies should balance such perennial poles of human life as pleasure and restraint. Some of these will place us face to face with the consequences of opting for a particular style of economic life that, while producing many benefits, also seems to kill something of the human spirit. What makes Weber so important for the study of religion is that for him these great human dilemmas all point back to even more fundamental religious foundations. Let me then move on to a consideration of the way his work fits with and differs from the approaches to religion that we have lately been considering.

Description, Understanding, Explanation: Getting at Religion in Three Ways

A brief review of my exposition of the phenomenology of religion might be illuminating at this point. Roughly dating from the beginning of the twentieth century, the methods of approaching religion broke with assumptions dominating classic historic methods of the study of religion which had prevailed since the very beginnings of the field in the sixteenth century. In this transition, phenomenology of religion plays something of a pivotal or transitional role, marking features distinctive of the new style of approaching religion naturalistically. To do this, I shall again employ the analogy of likening the 'game' of religion to the game of basketball. At least three levels of access to these 'games' are possible, and at each level we can review distinctive features of the classic approaches to religion that we have already studied and anticipate characteristic traits of the new approaches that will engage us in the rest of this work. These 'levels' of ways of getting at religion are three: descriptive, hermeneutic, and explanatory.

First, the descriptive, involves a simple inventory or catalogue of the items making up the enterprise in question – if it were basketball, the description would include everything from the kind of ball, its degree of inflation, and such, to the size of the court, the nature and placement of the boundary lines on it, the nature and location of the 'baskets,' and so on. We would also want to include as much description of the players as relevant – their uniforms, kinds of athletic shoes, etc., as well as the kinds of 'shots' and 'passes' taken, and so on. By analogy, what the student of religion desires at this point are merely 'facts' or 'data' about religion. The tasks before the student of religion at this level of inquiry are to collect data, facts, and information by observation, reading, interrogation, and so on. At the end, what one achieves is a list, inventory, or encyclopedia, and at best, an arbitrarily arranged classification of facts, say, by alphabetical order or geographical origin of the data collected. In our experience of students of religion, James Frazer's *The Golden Bough* comes closest to this level of investigation of religion with its massive 12-volume collection of data, albeit arranged according to certain descriptive literary themes, such as "Priestly Kings," "Magic and Religion," "Worship of Trees," "Tabooed Acts," and so on. So, also, of course, does the phenomenologist of religion Gerardus van der Leeuw's *Religion in Essence and Manifestation* have that 'encyclopedic' classificatory catalogue look about it.

Second, once we decide to go beyond just registering facts, or once we become dissatisfied or suspicious about *arbitrary* classifications and arrangements of 'facts,' we will want reasonable and meaningful ways to connect data. The name one can assign to this level of inquiry is the *interpretive* or *hermeneutic* level – that level of strategic access that concerns matters of the 'meaning' of the facts so assembled and the *understanding* of what certain connections of facts involves. It is also at the level of interpretation that we have recourse to the critical operation of *empathy* – that operation by which we come to understand the meanings of things to the actors involved in what we study.

In the last chapter, I have shown how Ninian Smart, for example, puts empathy, interpretation, and hermeneutics to work by his demonstration of how the dimensions making up religion articulate and interact "dialectically" with one another over the issue of lordship. Such articulation or connection of disparate facts is what we might call 'interpretation,' since the relation of facts to one another is interpreted in a certain defensible – and nonarbitrary – way. The implication of such interpretations is that the facts fit together in some kind of logic. They hang together to form a whole, and the rules governing their coherence can be teased out as we study it.

Consider again the analogy between approaching religion and the game of basketball. Calling basketball a 'game' already implies that there is some kind of unity to the parts and bits of facts and data that we noted earlier. Indeed, to apply the word 'game' to the bits and pieces of data we named above, is already to *interpret* the data in a certain way. There are rules to be discovered that form a coherent unity; there are 'moves' to be made in the 'game; there is an aim or goal involved; and so on. During the normal course of a basketball game, we *understand* that when a player throws the ball intentionally into the opponent's basket, and it goes in, the *meaning* of such an action is a "goal scored." Within the context of the game, the interrelations then of certain facts – the ball, thrown by the player, at the opponent's basket, and so on – go to make up a *meaningful* action. Using the basketball analogy as we did in discussing Smart's approach, if the score had been tied, and the shot that had been taken did in fact go into the basket, we would know that this would *mean* that the score had changed. Knowing what we know about the nature of the game, we also would *understand* further that scoring this basket would *explain* why those supporting the scorer were now celebrating, and so on.

Understanding what those kinds of meanings are in religion is the aim of a student of religion at the hermeneutic level of access. At the *hermeneutic* level, then, the study of religion becomes a matter of *interpreting* the facts in certain – always contestable and corrigible – ways, and of *understanding* the way they relate to one another. There are not only lords, with people kneeling in prayer with folded hands, experiences of absolute dependence or of numinous awe, and so on, but dialectically related connections among them. We "kneel" before the "lord" with hands folded in "prayer" because this *means* in our culture an expression of fealty to God upon whom we depend and who in turn oversees our lives. One *understands* what the 'goal,' as it were, of the kneeling devotee is once one *understands* the *meaning* of the ritual gestures involved in their larger context of acknowledging divine lordship and responding appropriately to the emotions of absolute dependence that the devotee feels.

I have suggested that Smart advanced phenomenology of religion by bringing forth a new appreciation of religion as a dynamic and thus dialectically constructed reality. In this way, he has also stimulated the creation of an almost endless string of problems of religion by exploring the ways the internal dialectical dynamic of religion governs the shape of religion. Smart's instigation of many types of religious "why?" questions was thus a notable advance upon previous phenomenologists of religion. They had got us to begin looking closely at religion in and for itself, to begin paying attention to the believer's point of view, to learn the importance of empathizing with our human subject, and to take stock of what went into the making of a religion. But Smart started to show how we might interrogate religion in order better to *understand*, and to a degree *explain*, how the parts of religion that the phenomenologists identified worked together to account for *why* religion took shape as it did. In this way, Smart went beyond mere empathy, beyond as well merely assuming, as did Kristensen, that empathy was all there was to *understanding*. For Smart, understanding required 'structure' as well as empathy. It sought an account of religious action that brought in the "dialectical" interrelations he worked out among the dimensions of religion – accounts that could even make the religious actors in question even more aware of what they were doing than they had been before.

But, to the levels of description and hermeneutics, we can add a *third* level of strategic access to religion – the level of *explanation*. Smart built his dialectical phenomenology atop the earlier efforts of the founders of the phenomenology of religion. Their main contribution to the study of religion was the introduction of interpretive and hermeneutic approaches to religion, mostly derived in turn from thinkers like Wilhelm Dilthey among others. Much of the impetus in following Dilthey was the ammunition he gave the founders of phenomenology of religion for defending religion from the so-called 'reductionists.' Among other things, reductionists cast religion in a passive role of being something that needed explanation in terms of nonreligious causes, or was perhaps just an illusion that dissolved before our eyes as we perceived the real factors at work in human life. Karl Marx, for instance, can be said to have seen religion, at least at times, as an 'illusion' – as something that 'appeared' to be of a particular sort, but was actually something quite different. Religion was simply a cloak of deception hiding the real material economic forces that made the world what it was. Religion itself was not a *cause*, only at best an 'effect' of active features in culture. At the very least, the phenomenologists cast doubts on the merely passive nature of religion by arguing that it was something that could be studied in and for itself. Smart becomes important here because he also showed that far from being merely passive or a kind of illusion, religion had an organic or systematic nature that, in part at least, accounted for how religion took shape.

To take one final look at the analogy with basketball, the point I am trying to make in distinguishing this *third* level of access to religion should become clear. Let us say that all our questions about the meaning of what happens on the basketball court in terms of how the game is played, or why certain actions mean certain things and not others, are answered. We *understand* why players want to put the ball into the proper basket; we *understand* that the point of doing this is peculiar to a game, because the point of a game is to win – by scoring most points; we *understand* why only some spectators applaud when one team scores, while another part of the crowd celebrates when they do not. We *understand* what this game is about and how is all fits together.

But what would we say to someone who asked questions like these? *Why* do some people become 'players' at all? Why do some individuals involve themselves in such vigorous competitive activities, when many of us find no interest in them at all? Why do certain players seem to take particular delight in standing out among their teammates – either as team captains, or in scoring more (or less) than their teammates, no matter what the outcome of the game? Why is it that most players come from families of a certain socioeconomic classes? Why do most players hail from large cities, rather than small towns or the countryside? Why are so few players – if any at all – women?

These are questions concerning the game but that lie outside the interior aspects of the game. They are about factors influencing entry *into* the game in the first place, or factors determining how someone plays the game that are independent of the way the game is put together or *understood* by its players. There is no *understanding* why a player may be a selfish 'ball hog' by appealing to an *understanding* of the way the game is structured. There is no *understanding* why only males become members of major professional basketball teams simply by *understanding* how the rules of the game make a kind of coherent sense. Similarly, as long as it does not bear on the outcome of the game, we have no idea what selfless play in a game or the lack of women players may *mean* just by thinking harder about how the game is put together, or by asking players what their *understanding* of the nature and internal conditions of the game of basketball are. These are cases where we need to appeal to other – external – factors than those constituting the game itself. This is where we can most naturally talk of *explanation*. Let us turn back to religion again.

Let us assume by this time that we *understand* how a religion arrayed around the example of lordship hangs together – how the kneeling, praying, sense of dependence, and so on help us *understand* and, in the way Smart develops it, *explain* how a religion of lordship will work. Just as there may be additional questions one may want to ask of our basketball players, so also we might want to interrogate religion about such matters as why anyone would want to become a "devotee" – why anyone would want to be involved in a religion of "lordship"? Once one is a "devotee" already, other factors within the religion of lordship will reinforce that position. Having become a member of a community devoted to lordship, one will have formed human relationships that will encourage one to retain membership. Having enjoyed the emotional benefits of such membership, one will likewise become adapted to the affective support provided thereby. But how does such an affiliation begin in the first place? What are the effects of being a member of a certain socioeconomic class, racial group, gender, or sexual orientation? Why not an affiliation with another kind of religion – say where lordship is replaced by something like the self-reliance characteristic of major strands of Buddhism, or where the 'lord' is female rather than male, a mother goddess rather than a warrior king? Why does one 'play the game' of lordship religion, or certain *kinds* of lordship religion, so to speak, rather than some other or none at all?

In terms of these three ways of getting at religion, I submit that we might remind ourselves of the thrust of the work of classic theorists like Tylor, Frazer, Robertson Smith, and the Deists (Herbert of Cherbury, Bodin, *and* Max Müller). They all tried to *explain* the very existence of religion, or track down the first religion, whether that be the Deist idea of a divinely implanted Natural Religion or something as arising from secular interests – Tylor's idea of religion as proto-science or Frazer's understanding of the essence of religion as our need to control nature. But while twentieth-century theorists like Émile Durkheim, Sigmund Freud, Bronislaw Malinowski, and Mircea Eliade also tried to *explain* religion, they did so by trying to *explain* the nature and origins of religious *feelings* and *experience*. The quest for Natural Religion as an historical phenomenon was abandoned. The phenomenologists, on the other hand, avoided all talk and action about *explanation*, and at the very most sought to *describe* religion and *catalogue* its parts, after having admitted to themselves the need to consider seriously the view of the insider about their own religion. In this way, they sought to defend the autonomy of religion, say, in terms of a distinctive kind of numinous experience (Otto) or, moving onto other perspectives with Smart showing how religions were dynamically constituted and defined by the interaction of his seven dimensions.

What makes Weber, then, the perfect figure to treat after the classic theorists and before engaging the twentieth-century theorists is the mediating methodological position that he assumes. While he desires to *explain* things concerning religion, and is open as well to nonreligious influences upon religious behavior, he uses religion to explain secular realities, as well. Furthermore, like a phenomenologist, at the same time, he adheres to classic *phenomenological* methods in approaching religion in the first place by practicing its classic methods of empathy, understanding, classification, and a good deal of *epoché*.

Max Weber's Turning of the Tables: Religion Explains Things Too

Try as they might to elevate religion by seeing it as an autonomous phenomenon with its own concepts and rules of action, the phenomenologists never tried to 'turn the tables' on the reductionists and cast religion as some kind of *cause* acting in the world. Here, Weber stands apart from them.

> We must free ourselves from the idea that it is possible to deduce the Reformation, as a historically necessary result, from certain economic changes. Countless historical circumstances, which cannot be reduced to any economic law, and are not susceptible of economic explanation of any sort, especially purely political processes, had to concur in order that the newly created Churches should survive at all. (Weber 1976, pp. 90–1)

No phenomenologist ever 'turned the tables' on the various sorts of 'undertakers of religion,' such as Marxists, who attempted the 'reduction' of religion to economics. Although one must not overdo the differences between Weber and Marx, no phenomenologist of religion, for example, stood Marx on his head and declared economic life 'illusory' or derivative, and religion the primary underlying reality of economic life – at least not until our own day in quite singular phenomenology of religion of Mircea Eliade! Phenomenologists were allergic to speaking of 'causes' at all – even when religion might have been a cause! Positing 'causes' was by definition going beyond the level of phenomena and human experience to the level of unknowable noumena. It was an overambitious effort at *explanation*, while the phenomenologists only sought the more modest goal of *understanding*. All attempts at explanation, moreover, only produced hopeless conflicts because they attempted to operate at the level of the unknowable noumenon – a level only the subject of speculation and (endlessly inconclusive) theoretical argument. In this way, religion could never in principle become a *cause* as long as the phenomenologists had their way.

From the start, what makes Max Weber different from the phenomenologists is his embrace of both *explanation* in human affairs and *causal* explanation at that – even to the extent of assuming that religion could be used to *explain* things and that it acted as a kind of cause. In his own words, Weber declares, "we are merely attempting to clarify the part which religious forces have played in forming the developing web of our specifically worldly modern culture" (Weber 1976, p. 90). For Weber, human life is an arena in which causes are part of the reality of things as they are. We do things be*cause* of preexisting enabling reasons or conditions. And it is possible to discover what those reasons and causes are – even when they may be religious ones! While Weber never went as far as we will see Mircea Eliade go and declare secular things in effect unreal or illusory, he felt that religion was a robust reality, and that it took part in the 'rough and tumble' of human life, here exerting causal influence, there absorbing it from other sources. Weber's view of religion in society was thus a realistic, dynamic, and unsentimental one, and one that has set an independent course that has had many followers ever since.

But having said that Weber embraces causal explanation in human affairs, it is vital to understand that these causes are typically *immaterial* in the sense of having to do with the beliefs and values of people. Therefore, the kinds of causes in human affairs that Weber typically found most interesting and compelling were what we might call "*ideal*" causes, such as values, ideas, or beliefs. Although the ultimate source of Weber's belief that 'ideas matter' is still a subject of lively contest, Weber's wife, Marianne, claims in her great biography of her husband that Weber was convinced that "ideal" forces acted in the world as evidence of a lingering religiosity.

> Evidently he concerned himself at an early age with the question of the world-shaping significance of ideal forces. Perhaps this tendency of his quest for knowledge – a *permanent concern with religion* – was the form in which the genuine religiosity of his maternal family lived on in him. (Weber 1975, p. 335)

Deciding whether Marianne Weber's view here is true or not would take us well beyond the scope of this book. But it is worth keeping her assertion in mind, not least because the ambiguities of Weber's relation to religious belief and practice – about which we will see more shortly – raise such interesting lines of speculation.

An American philosopher, Sidney Hook, in his days as a 1930s Marxist, noted that Weber's use of religion to explain things amounted to assuming, for instance, that "some causal connection" exists "between the specific activities of man's life in this world and his conception of an after-life in the next" (Hook 1930, p. 477). The religious belief or "conception" here does the causal work of shaping human activities "in the world." Thus, for example, Weber *believed* that if one were committed to 'worldliness' – an engagement in the everyday world – as opposed, say, to 'other-worldliness' – escape from the world – as a *value* in living one's life, certain behaviors could be explained by reference to this. Beliefs are, at least at times, causally prior to actions. As a religious person, such beliefs might, for example, *explain* why one did not feel it necessary to run off and join a monastic order, but rather why one could become actively engaged in public affairs. The beliefs in question acted as conditions causing, enabling, or even inducing certain actions to follow. Thus, Sidney Hook characterized Weber fairly enough as holding that "ideas make history." Weber himself said of his great classic, "The following study may thus perhaps in a modest way form a contribution to the understanding of the manner in which ideas become effective forces in history" (Hook 1930, p. 478; Weber 1976, p. 90).

Billiard Balls and Excuses

Despite the understandable tendency of some critics to characterize Weber's 'idealist' thinking in the simple causal terms of pushes and pulls, it is rather more complex. On the billiard-ball view, for example, ideas would be seen as things that exert external force on human action. But there is more to Weber than that. Weber's understanding of how religion acts in the world is a rich one, as we will now see. As our Marxist critic, Sidney Hook, expressed it, "ideas make history." This means that instead of the crude push–pull billiard-ball view, we can also read Weber's 'idealism' as grasping the way in which beliefs, values, and such make certain actions 'legitimate,' 'justified,' 'sanctioned,' 'authorized,' and so on. Such beliefs or values give people 'excuses,' 'permission,' 'reasons,' etc., for doing what they do, and for defending those actions to others. In speaking in terms of *legitimacy*, we need not then think of Weberian explanations of human action only in terms of the 'billiard-ball' model of behavior in which a value functions like the forward thrust of a cue stick or cue ball to impel another ball to move across a billiard table. Instead, Weber looks upon the values agent in human behavior as rationales, bases, or legitimations that a person actually had in mind or tacitly presumed for doing things. Weber thus believes that a person committed to the world would appeal to certain values to give *legitimacy* to their course of action. Activity in the world is (religiously) legitimate *because*, for example, God ordered it, as we have seen in the case of Krishna's command to Arjuna in the *Bhagavad Gītā* to go to war against his kinsmen. As we will see, Weber believes as well that *religion* supplies perhaps the most powerful source of legitimacy that one could have for the actions one performs. What else could be more potent than a divine command, a declaration of divinely dictated *duty*?

In speaking in terms of *legitimacy*, we need as well to avoid naive approaches to the understanding and explanation of human action. Sometimes people will cite beliefs or values as the reasons or causes of certain behaviors, even though they may not have had these in mind when they acted in the first place. Our 'worldly' person may actually have committed themselves to a life in public affairs because they had been compelled so to do by their parents, or because of the dull force of habit, without any strong motivation at all. They may just have 'fallen into' a life in the world mindlessly. In the case, then, where our worldly actor in the public domain cites some kind of commitment to a value of the divine command of being worldly, they would be doing so *after the fact*. This might be an exercise in bad faith, simply to justify their position to others or to themselves. But it may also be a retrospective interpretation that discovers a deeply hidden reason for doing something that only later comes to the surface. Whatever the truth of such cases, their efforts to claim legitimacy for behavior signal at least a recognition or belief that values matter in one sense or another. As we will see, a further aspect of Weber's idealist approach to explaining human action will involve accepting the power of certain *feelings* and *experiences*, such as the dynamic influence of the power of the revelation of Krishna as the almighty lord in the *Bhagavad Gītā*. But whatever the range of Weber's understanding of idealist causality, it remains a feature of the way he approaches the ability of religion to function as a cause in the world.

Before leaving this preliminary discussion of Weber's idealist conception of causes of human action, we need to confront again the figure with whom much of his idealist approach is often 'shadow boxing' – Karl Marx. Weber, himself an economic historian by training, had great respect for Marx, especially for his historical analyses. Indeed, some scholars have argued that Weber had wanted to " 'round out' Marx's economic materialism," rather than starkly to oppose it (Gerth & Mills 1946, p. 47). Yet, I would prefer to think about Weber as an alternative to Marx rather than as a semi-Marxist himself. In understanding Weber, I therefore will stress the distance between his *idealist* approach to understanding and explaining human action as part of a deliberate counter to Marx's *materialism* and economic determinism (Ringer 2004, p. 113).

Marxists dwell on the compelling nature of the material conditions in which persons find themselves. What *economic* drives caused someone to prefer life in the world over life in the monastic cell, for example? These forces differ fundamentally from any array of Weberian ideal causes (or legitimations) of action such as beliefs, values, ideologies, theologies, moral positions, ideals, experiences, and such. Marxist 'causes' have to do with the compulsions of the brute conditions of material necessity and enabling contexts in which people find themselves, not with legitimations, ideologies, or religions. After all, being active in the world might help one secure one's economic advantage and thus improve one's material conditions and chances for survival. Being active in the world might as well only be a possible alternative in life because of the advent of social or technological change in a society – such as the creation of a money economy, the freeing of entry to trades and commercial opportunities, and so on. Our *material* interests in raw survival and power, or the simple availability of such material openings might do more to determine our behavior than lofty ideals or evanescent experiences. In 1930, Hook, the reviewer of the first English translation of Weber's *The Protestant Ethic and the Spirit of Capitalism*, thus concluded his discussion by saying that

> the chief objection to Weber's procedure is that he does not sufficiently weigh the possibility that both the spirit of capitalism and the ethics of Protestantism are effects of fundamental changes in the socio-economic environment induced by the discovery of new lands, the rise of a world market, the influx of gold and silver, and the improvements in mechanical technology.... Protestantism and the spirit of capitalism arose only there where the *objective* possibilities of a rational capitalistic economy were already given. (Hook 1930, p. 478; my emphasis)

The Marxist option should therefore not be ruled out. But in evaluating Weber's approach, we will have to think carefully about the plausibility of Weber's account of how religion supposedly shapes the economic system known as capitalism. We need to insist that both Marxist and Weberian approaches be tested in each case.

Weber's Phenomenological Side

At the risk of being paradoxical, we can also say from the start that what makes Weber interesting is his embrace of much of the approach of the phenomenologists, and his simultaneous desire to synthesize it with his commitment to causal explanation. The anthropologist of religion, Clifford Geertz, for example, claims that Weber was influenced strongly by Wilhelm Dilthey – like the arch-phenomenologist, Gerardus van der Leeuw (Geertz 1983, pp. 5, 7, 16, 21–2, 51, 69, 121). While there is evidence for this in the way Weber proceeds, he never accepted Dilthey's ideas totally. Moreover, students of Weber's life and works have argued persuasively that he in fact owed more to the German sociologists Georg Simmel and Ferdinand Tönnies and philosophers in the neo-Kantian movement of the times than he did to Dilthey. In particular, Weber was critical of tendencies in Dilthey's thinking that verged on an irrational conception of the nature of 'understanding' (Ringer 2004, p. 25). Weber was even more set against the more mystical interpretations of the method of empathy and understanding. Thus, for Weber, empathy was not some kind of mind-reading or "an identity of minds" (Ermarth 1978, p. 377 n. 11). It was just a normal attitude one took in pursuit of the understanding of other persons. As a contemporary put it, "Weber's ability to empathize with, and to interpret, the meaning of human action was, in a manner of speaking, unlimited" (Honigsheim 2003, p. 150). But it was not magical or extrasensory. Nor was the method of 'understanding' sufficient for the kind of social *science* that Weber sought to found as an alternative to the natural sciences (Ringer 2004, p. 18). "Understanding" (*Verstehen*) needed to be situated within an historical process that could be known objectively – without empathy. The objective course of history will condition who or what we try to *understand* (Honigsheim 2003, p. 247). Still, in all, despite Weber's careful qualifications of Dilthey's methods, his own method nonetheless represents an attempt to synthesize interpretive and hermeneutic approaches to understanding human religious behavior with explanatory causal ones (Käsler 1988, p. 178). How then does Weber show us his phenomenologist side?

Three features of the way Weber proceeds immediately stand out, and show us how he has been marked to some degree by the same revolution in the human sciences as the phenomenologists of religion. These are the employment of the method of *understanding*, the critical place that he assigns to religious *feelings* or *experiences*, and his attention to the need to *define* and *classify* what makes us the *phenomena* with which he deals.

First, Weber believes that in order to be in a position to use religion to *explain* the rise of capitalism, we must first employ – with the proper degree of care and commitment to rational inquiry – interpretive and hermeneutic methods to *understand* what the items in this chain of causality mean to the actors or believers. To begin with, that will require the famous phenomenological imperative of approaching human subjects with *empathy*. We need, first of all, to understand the way religious people "see things." As the philosopher Charles Taylor puts it, "Making sense of agents does require that we *understand* their self-descriptions." Neither for Taylor nor Weber does this mean falling back onto a naive acceptance of the 'believer's point of view,' typical of Kristensen. As Taylor wisely adds, we "may indeed, often must, take account of their confusion, malinformation, illusion." Still, we have to start with an empathetic grasp of the human subjects whom we propose to explain. Thus Taylor concludes, "we make sense of them if we grasp *both* how they see things *and* what is wrong, lacunary, contradictory in this. Interpretive social science cannot by-pass the agent's self-understanding" (Taylor 1985, p. 118).

The same approach applies to religion as to any social or cultural formation – such as capitalism. In precisely the same interpretive, hermeneutic way, making sense of capitalism, as we will see Weber attempt to do, will require understanding what capitalists say in speaking of their own behavior. Getting to these understandings will require *empathy*, as the phenomenologists said. But, it will also require both understanding the meanings the actors in question assign to things, as well as seeing where they are wrong in how they see things. Their key goal is to give an account of the rise of capitalism, in this case, in a way which "sets out the significance of action and situation" (Taylor 1985, p. 117).

Second, once we have understood what things mean to the actors in social contexts, we should follow solid scientific practice and construct a proper vocabulary of key terms – what the phenomenologists termed the process of naming and classifying phenomena. In Weberian language, these phenomenological classes are called "ideal types." Thus, for him, 'capitalism,' for instance, would conform to an 'ideal type' of economic formation. There might be variations in actual concrete cases one to another, but Weber would match these against the 'ideal type' of the phenomenon under study.

Third, besides doing the fundamental classificatory job of naming and classifying ideal type phenomena, Weber believes that we also need to *understand* the vital role of religious emotions, feelings, and experiences in causing an ideal type such as capitalism to arise. Like the phenomenologists of religion, such as Rudolf Otto, Weber places a great deal of importance upon psychological power in people of their religious feelings, especially their conviction of a personal sense of "calling." For him, religious feeling, emotion, or experience play powerful roles in effecting the changes that we might attribute to religion. In this sense, Weber falls neatly into the modern pattern. His main problems have nothing to do with questing after the original religion, with perhaps the pursuit of Natural Religion, but everything to do with grasping the place of religious *experience* in human affairs.

Fourth, Weber finally needs to persuade us that he understands the *meaning* of terms like 'capitalism' or 'religion.' Beyond empathy, this means that, like van der Leeuw or any of the other phenomenologists of religion, he needs to persuade us that he understands *objectively* what bits and pieces actually constitute capitalism or religion as 'phenomena.' He would, for example, have to show us that he knows what *kinds* of capitalism and religion there are, and which in particular have had to do with the goals he has set himself. He would, finally, also need to convince us that his *understanding* of these terms would, at least, in principle, be recognizable to those labeled by him as 'capitalists,' 'religious,' and so on. This means, in effect, that Weber will need to show how he adopts the insights of the *objective* side of the approach of phenomenology.

How the West Got Rich

With these considerations in hand, we can now focus down to the fine details of the way Weber proved himself to be one of the greatest of students of religion. Like all the thinkers we have considered thus far, Weber's work centers round a series of questions – a number of 'problems of religion.' These differ from other problems of religion we have met heretofore in that what troubled Weber was how religion was a 'cause' of secular institutions – specifically, what place religion had in the rise of the modern economy. Unlike others we have met, Weber had no interest at all in finding the 'first' or 'universal' religion, nor even, despite his German nationalist feelings, the original religion of the Germans, Aryans, and such that so fascinated another patriotic German scholar, Friedrich Max Müller. Nor did Weber really think *evolutionary* approaches to religion had much to teach us. He was not interested in how religion *grew*, but in how secular institutions like the economy grew *because* of religion. How, in particular, did the West get rich? What explained the manifest fact of the economic, scientific and technological superiority of the West in the late nineteenth and early twentieth centuries? How, especially, had Europe come to dominate the world *economically* – even to the point where the smallest nations, devoid of natural resources or other natural endowments of wealth – were major players on the world stage? In Weber's time, for example, some of the smallest nations of Europe, such as Belgium and the Netherlands, had extensive colonial possessions that made them economic giants. So, again the question kept at Weber: how did the West get rich and stay that way? Why were not India or China many times more prosperous than the West? Both countries had great natural wealth in terms of energy sources, raw materials, industrious populations, and millennia of sophisticated civilized life, artistic achievement, and so on. What *causal* factors could *explain* these discrepancies between the economic power of Europe over against that of other parts of the world?

Since Weber did not believe in some sort of *biological* superiority of the West over others, such as some of the evolutionary anthropologists we have met, he was compelled to look at the *history* and cultural composition of particular civilizations for his answer. The kind of prehistory that set Tylor speculating would, therefore, not make a parallel impact upon Weber. Although the discoveries at Brixham Cave, for example, might be interesting in themselves, they did not seem to hold any answers to the problems that puzzled Weber – not to mention the 'problems of religion' he entertained. At best, whatever we learned from prehistory only told us about the very distant past, and then sketchily at best. Prehistory was *prehistory* because it came *before* we knew anything very precise about the life and times of very ancient peoples, such as those who might have frequented Brixham Cave. Given this lack of real facts, was it not then more profitable to look to an *historical* past, to the foundations of our modern world, where documents and other rich sources of information could guide us, than to place so much emphasis on speculation about how our distant human ancestors lived, or to make the leap to assume that today's 'primitives' were good indicators of how our own prehistoric ancestors lived?

What elements of Darwinism are to be found in Weber's thinking are concentrated in his attitude to practical politics, rather than in his more general view of an overall story of human history. Some have classified Weber's politics as influenced by social Darwinist ideas of a will to power. He certainly felt that there was an iron law of 'survival of the fittest' inside economic systems like capitalism such as "in a wholly capitalistic order of society." There, "an individual capitalistic enterprise which did not take advantage of its opportunities for profit-making would be doomed to extinction," Weber tells us without a trace of sentiment (Weber 1976, p. 17). Yet, it is also true that Weber felt that social Darwinist ideas were "biases parading as objective science. He assumed that there could be no transcendent standard by which cultures can be judged superior and inferior" (Diggins 1996, p. 35). Nevertheless, Weber supported German imperialism and was in every way a true German nationalist. Further, in line with the political realism that we saw him begin to develop as he parted ways with the Evangelisch-Soziale Verein, Weber felt that power politics was a normal part of the competitive struggle for prosperity of one state over against others (Gerth & Mills 1946, p. 35).

How Weber went about answering the problem of how the West got rich is instructive for understanding how he went about making sense of society at large, and thus about how religion would fit into his logic of explanation (Weber 1976, pp. 17–31). The first approximation to an answer to the question of how the West got rich would be to consider its way of acquiring and producing wealth, its economic system – 'capitalism.' Here, thinking like a phenomenologist, Weber seeks to name and classify his key terms. But simply invoking the word hardly takes us any distance at all. We still need to *understand* what capitalism is – as an objective socioeconomic system – and who classic capitalists are – the real, historical individuals.

The Basic Values of the 'Spirit' of Capitalism

Weber approached this question with great historical and comparative erudition. The notion that Protestant values had something to do with the rise of capitalism was an idea widely accepted in the early twentieth century. Weber was the first, however, to try to show that this was the case with "an empirical proof of concrete historical connections" (Kippenberg 2002, p. 158). People the world over had shown propensities to often radically different styles of life, expressing different *value* orientations. Weber expressed these different value orientations as the result of systematic pairing of opposed values. Consider the hedonist/ascetic opposed values first. Some people, Weber believed – perhaps the common run of humanity – *valued* simple (or sometimes exotic) pleasure. Putting on his phenomenological 'hat,' Weber called them 'hedonists.' Opposed to the hedonists, others, such as Buddhist or Christian monks or Hindu sages, chose to control, limit, or restrain pleasure. Again, without judging the goodness or evil of this value choice, Weber 'bracketed' the value choices of these folk, like a phenomenologist again, and simply was content to label them 'ascetics.' Now, Weber then considers another pair of opposed values that he will then pair with the first pair – the hedonist/ascetic. Here, Weber opposed the value of 'worldliness' to 'other-worldliness.' By 'worldliness,' Weber means that one's behavior is directed at *this* world, such as, say, an architect or mechanic; by 'other-worldliness,' Weber means that behavior is focused on a realm *beyond* or *outside* of this world, such as, say, someone who seeks escape into trances or extrasensory states or sites. By matching these two paired sets of values against one another, Weber believed he could generate the key value clusters that defined the four basic 'ideal types' – worldly hedonist, worldly ascetic, other-worldly hedonist, and other-worldly ascetic.

On the face of it, one might think that it is obvious that some values merely repeat the other values, just doing so using other words. Are not, for example, all 'hedonists' by definition 'worldly,' since pleasure must necessarily be a thing of '*this* world'? And, are not all 'ascetics' necessarily 'other-worldly,' since self-denial would only make sense for the sake of meriting an eternal life *beyond* 'this world'? The brilliance of Weber's complex phenomenological work shows through, however, in his demonstration that what may seem 'obvious' is not so. For instance, while Weber believed that we can easily speak of *worldly hedonists*, by referring to the example of today's pleasure-seeking Westerners or, as we will see shortly, to the "traditionalist" style of life of precapitalist Europe, his scheme allows him to speak of 'other-worldly' hedonists as well. Example? Had he been alive in our time, Weber might have classified as 'other-worldly' hedonists various counterculture drug users, such as Dr. Tim O'Leary, seeking mystical experiences through LSD and other hallucinogenic drugs. Likewise, Weber will have much to say about 'other-worldly ascetics' because they would be represented by the great tradition of the Catholic ideal of monasticism – an institution of retreat from the world and mortification of the 'flesh' (ascetic), all the while focused on the spiritual world *beyond* this one in the here and now (other-worldly). But the most important ideal type of all for his *The Protestant Ethic and the Spirit of Capitalism* will be the apparently incongruous "*worldly asceticism*" – the value cluster that defines for Weber the ideal type embodied in capitalism. Here, Weber describes what may seem the unlikely combination of focus upon goals in this world, but inspired and guided by an ethic of self-denial, discipline, restraint, and so on.

Weber thus uses this set of value options to do the most precise phenomenological job that he can do regarding the definition of the "spirit of capitalism." It is for this reason that he can sharpen his definition of the "ideal type" of capitalism, and distinguish it from economic systems that only *appear* to be capitalist, but really are not. Thus, Weber notes that people, for example, have always *wanted* to be rich, and have always used various sorts of objective methods to become rich. But mere desire for riches is insufficient for providing the content of the phenomenological category "capitalism." 'Adventurers' – pirates, warring plunderers, brigands, thieves, treasure finders, gamblers, and such – have all sought to be rich, and often have attained great wealth, but we would not call them 'capitalists' (Weber 1976, p. 17). They might well be worldly since their activity was directed at *this world*. But most were hardly people one could describe as *ascetic*, since they either squandered their plunder in great gushes of expenditure, or at least were not rational in the way they behaved. They were, after all, 'adventurers.' By contrast, while some refer to nineteenth-century capitalist industrial magnates like Henry E. Huntington, Henry Ford, or Andrew Carnegie as 'robber barons,' the term is a metaphor. While these men may have come by their riches by manipulating the institutions of wealth creation, they were neither *literal* 'robbers,' such as those holding up the local bank, nor even less men of noble 'baronial' lineage. Instead, they were men whose distinction was establishing rationalized bureaucratic – capitalist – systems for producing wealth, that even survived their demise.

Similarly, rich folks – the mere *possessors* of wealth, such as the offspring of the Huntingtons, Fords, and so on – ought not necessarily to be called capitalists either, if Weber has his way in defining the term. Whether they were capitalists or not would depend on how they dealt with the wealth that they inherited, not simply upon their *being* wealthy. They may, for example, lack any interest in further production, or in *making* money at all, but are content to simply spend away what they have – much like the lucky folk who find the gold of the leprechauns at the end of the rainbow. People who are just lucky to be rich, or who are born rich, or who inherit great wealth, are not *ipso facto* capitalists. They are just rich. Real 'barons' and other sorts of rich people have always existed, even long before anything one might call 'capitalism' existed. So, therefore, we must look elsewhere to discover what the qualities of capitalism are that make it a distinctive category worthy of study and investigation. If Weber is right, we need to look to the source of the values of "*worldly asceticism*" and to the style of life it made legitimate.

Profit, More Profit, and the Rational Outlook

Weber believed that there was something both objective and subjective lacking among mere 'possessors' of wealth as it is lacking in 'adventurers' that excluded them from being identified as capitalists. In terms of their objective way of getting rich and/or their inner attitude about doing so, neither of these successful types of people – rich as they might be or want to be – necessarily conforms to the image of the classic capitalists like a Henry Ford. Paradoxically, someone who may not at the moment be rich might well be a capitalist despite their lack of wealth. Would not a small businessperson making a modest profit still be judged to be a capitalist even though they were not doing well at the time? Weber thinks so, because they practice an objectively distinct method of trying to get rich along with a distinctive attitude toward their effort so to do. Here, Weber believes someone known for their modesty, sobriety, industry, and self-discipline, like Benjamin Franklin, exemplifies the ideal type of the capitalist. Weber cites Franklin:

> "Remember, that *credit* is money. If a man lets his money lie in my hands after it is due, he gives me the interest, or so much as I can make of it during that time. This amounts to a considerable sum where a man has good and large credit, and makes good use of it."
>
> "Remember, that money is of the prolific, generating nature. Money can beget money, and its offspring can beget more, and so on ... "
>
> "He that loses five shillings, not only loses that sum, but all the advantage that might be made by turning it in dealing, which by the time that a young man becomes old, will amount to a considerable sum of money."
>
> "Remember, that time is money ... He that idly loses five shillings' worth of time, loses five shillings, and might as prudently throw five shillings into the sea." (Weber 1976, pp. 48–50)

This combination of outer techniques and inner attitudes puts Franklin at odds both with worldly hedonists such as the mere 'possessors' of wealth and irrationalist seekers after wealth such as the 'adventurers,' not to mention the monkish other-worldly ascetics and drug-culture other-worldly hedonists. But what precisely is the difference that "worldly asceticism" makes?

On the basis of historical investigation, first, into the *objective* changes in economic practice, Weber first determined that capitalist enterprises operated by what were then radically new and different procedures than those governing earlier forms of manufacture, service, retail, and other forms of business. Weber's words are very precise and to the point on the definition of capitalism: "*capitalism is identical with the pursuit of profit, and forever renewed profit, by means of conscious, rational, capitalistic enterprise*" (Weber 1976, p. 17; my emphasis).

Taking this definition apart to bring out the meanings of its individual terms, we first begin with (1) "the pursuit of profit." Capitalism is about *gain*, not about charity or giving. It is an economic system in which the capitalist seeks to be wealthier *after* the operation of their enterprise. 'Breaking even' is not good enough. Hand to mouth subsistence is not good enough. Steady state is not good enough. Thus, the capitalist is unlike the rich heir who has decided not to increase their wealth, but simply to enjoy it by spending it down so that it lasts throughout their life. By contrast, the capitalist is uneasy, and seeks to *increase* their wealth.

Second, for this reason, the capitalist can never really rest, and thus in order to ensure survival, Weber's 'capitalist' must seek (2) "forever *renewed* profit." The capitalist not only seeks profits for today, like a prospector hoping to make the one big strike that will set them up for life. The capitalist plans to seek profits for an endless string of tomorrows. The capitalist thus will defer gratification regarding the wealth they gain. They will do what we call "*invest*" part of the wealth, rather than consuming or enjoying it, so that part of the initial profits may be put aside to finance future "forever *renewed*" profit. One can never let down one's guard against the rise of potential competition, and so on. So, one must 'set aside resources' for future contingencies. The capitalist thus seeks to increase wealth in theory continuously and without limit.

Third, the manner in which profits are won and continuously won is by employing the methods of (3a) "conscious," (3b) "rational" capitalistic enterprise. In terms of being (3a) "conscious," the capitalist defines themselves as a deliberate and disciplined actor in pursuit of profits. Profits do not fall by accident into the laps of the capitalist like they would for the lucky heir. The capitalist is a deliberate actor in the world, making careful plans and reckonings for amassing ever-increasing wealth. Careful planning therefore means (3b) "rational" planning. Unlike the happy-go-lucky treasure hunter or the gambler, the capitalist calculates every significant move in their quest for profits. He rationally assesses his gains and losses, typically by keeping ledger books, measuring the output of his effort against the benefits of the effort expended. The capitalist figures whether or not his efforts have been 'profitable' – whether the gains won because of their labor exceed the losses incurred in paying laborers. And, in light of these calculations, the capitalist lays plans for the future – whether to continue or even expand their enterprise, or to give it up as a 'losing proposition.'

Moreover, the capitalist typically does not work alone, but instead establishes an 'institution,' such as a company, firm, or business. As such Weber believes we have to look past the capitalist hero, the 'entrepreneur,' to the lasting institutional changes made in society by the application of capitalist principles. Excessive attention to the heroic figure of the entrepreneur can reduce capitalism to the kind of precapitalist 'adventurist,' freebooting enterprises that Weber felt did not get to the heart of what made capitalism distinctive. The entrepreneur can indeed kick off a capitalist enterprise, but what distinguishes mature capitalism at least is its persistence over time by means of a rational organizational structure, such as a bureaucracy. Once more, for Weber *"capitalism is identical with the pursuit of profit, and forever renewed profit, by means of conscious, rational, capitalistic enterprise"* (Weber 1976, p. 17). Where workers are employed, the capitalist measures their output over against the productivity of their work, as well as the relative productivity of workers with respect to each other. Labor is measured out in precise packets of time of hours worked, measured by the ubiquitous time clock if necessary. Efficiency of labor is likewise measured by time/motion studies that determine how actual work matches with its results. All these go to making up the 'rational' character that defines capitalism in Weber's sense as a profit-driven, rational enterprise of gaining wealth.

But It Wasn't Always This Way

A moment's reflection upon this style of winning wealth is all that is needed to conclude that capitalism is a very demanding way to make a living. One could reasonably ask why, short of some dire necessity, would anyone voluntarily choose or desire this kind of life? Assuming that one could meet one's basic needs and have a little left over for discretionary purposes, why would anyone *choose* such a rigorous and disciplined style of life? Could the possibility of being wealthy be worth all the fussiness and self-denial of a Benjamin Franklin? Indeed, we know from anthropological studies of certain small-scale societies that some peoples deliberately choose *not* to pursue anything like the disciplined, rationalized profit-making economic activity that Weber sees as characteristic of capitalism. Few people would seem 'naturally' drawn to an 'ascetic' life, even if it be a 'worldly' one. They nevertheless achieve what the American anthropologist Marshall Sahlins called "an affluent society . . . one in which all the people's material wants are easily satisfied," not by "producing much, but by desiring little." They have little need therefore for the rigors of rationalized economic life of Weber's capitalist, since they do not feel the need to maximize their profits for ever and ever. Instead of the capitalist way of life, Sahlins refers to another approach to life that he calls the "Zen strategy," because of its focus on restraining human needs and desires. By limiting their desires, people enjoy a relatively comfortable – if not luxurious – standard of living more in balance with what they can produce with relative ease (Sahlins 1972, pp. 1–40). As Sahlins explains, the "Zen" strategy involves

> departing from premises somewhat different from our own: that human material wants are finite and few, and technical means unchanging but on the whole adequate. Adopting the Zen strategy, a people can enjoy an unparalleled material plenty – with a low standard of living. (Sahlins 1972, pp. 1–2)

I mention Sahlin's "Zen" strategy in particular because it describes an economic phenomenon that Weber thought was the prevalent style of economic life in Europe *before* the advent of capitalism. It was the style of economic life *against* which capitalism reacted and had continuously to struggle. To Weber, this most significant impediment to the rise of capitalism was known as "traditionalism." The two systems – capitalism and traditionalism – are inextricably linked as direct opposites of one another. As Weber notes, "one of the fundamental characteristics of an individualistic capitalistic economy [is] that it is rationalized on the basis of rigorous calculation, directed with foresight and caution toward economic success." This temperament is opposed to the fundamentally worldly hedonist value structure of traditionalism, and is thus "in sharp contrast to the hand-to-mouth existence of the peasant, and to the privileged traditionalism of the guild craftsman and of the adventurers' capitalism, oriented to the exploitation of political opportunities and irrational speculation" (Weber 1976, p. 76). We cannot understand one without understanding the other. Thus, if Weber is right in his analysis of the problem of the rise of capitalism, in order to understand how capitalism came about, we will need to understand how "traditionalism" was overcome. This is the same as our needing to understand how the worldly hedonist attitudes of traditionalism gave way to the worldly asceticism of capitalism.

This overcoming of "traditionalism" is of course an *historical* problem, having to do with real change, as well as a contest of ideas. It is a problem about what is happening in the human material world of time and space. As such, Weber seeks the historical *causes* that would *explain* the change from a traditionalist economy to a capitalist one. Weber's task is not just to classify and define terms any longer – to define certain "ideal types." He had already done that preliminary task. Nor was he endeavoring even to *understand* in phenomenological style *what it meant* that traditionalism faded and capitalism grew. The task of such a phenomenological *understanding* had already been pressed as far as it could go. Similarly, unlike the phenomenologists – except perhaps Ninian Smart – he does not seek only to *understand* how this change happened by empathizing with the actors in question, or simply referring – as Ninian Smart does – to the internal dynamic of how the traditionalism 'game' is played, hoping in this way to account for how an entirely new 'game' – capitalism – comes onto the field! Here, Weber moves to that *third* 'strategic level of access' to social processes with which I dealt in the opening pages of this chapter. Weber wants to operate at the *causal* level, because only in doing so does he believe that he can identify the *enabling conditions* that make the rise of capitalism happen – against the backdrop of the specific historical conditions of a society dominated by traditionalist economic values and practices.

Now, unlike a Karl Marx, as we know, the *causes* Weber seeks will not be primarily 'material' ones, although they will not therefore be *supernatural* causes. Weber is still operating within the rules of academic and scientific discourse the main principles of which were in effect laid down as long ago as David Hume's time. The causes Weber is intent upon uncovering in the transition from traditionalism to capitalism are the so-called *ideal* causes that we discussed at the outset of this chapter – beliefs, values, moral stances, theologies, ideologies, worldviews. Although these causes are not the same as more tangible causes, such as billiard balls or physical pushes and pulls, Weber and other idealists believe that they are *empirical* in the sense that they are all accessible by ordinary public human experience. They are in no way refractory to reason and public discourse. Weber was always alert to the importance of material causes and processes because of his respect for Marx, but the causes he sought would not be like those that his Marxist critic of 1930, Sidney Hook, cited – to wit, "the discovery of new lands, the rise of a world market, the influx of gold and silver, and the improvements in mechanical technology," and so on (Hook 1930, p. 478). Weber wanted to know what basic *values* had to come into play, or what *beliefs* had to gain acceptance, or what *theologies* or *ideologies* had to shape thinking in order *to take advantage of* Hook's new material factors – the new lands, influx of gold, and so on. What *values* had to be in place for capitalism to arise in a context where the worldly hedonism of traditionalism previously prevailed? Weber wanted to know how the transition from traditionalism to capitalism was made *legitimate* in the minds of actors involved in this tremendous social upheaval. What *defenses* were made in behalf of new capitalist ways of doing business or in negotiating wages that were not, or could not have been, made in the days when traditionalism prevailed?

This is why the second big problem that drove Weber's inquiry – beyond why the West got rich – and was so much of the history of the West *before* the rise of capitalism, was conditioned by a spirit analogous to Sahlin's worldly hedonist "Zen" strategy – "traditionalism." Thus, the rise of capitalism came hard up against the historical reality that the West had to *become* capitalist. It had *not* been capitalist for very long, and had been dominated by a spirit and an economic practice that, in fact, militated against capitalism and the rigors of rationalization and 'ascetic' discipline essential to it – that of pre-Reformation Catholic Europe. An old adage of the time neatly summed up some of these differences in values at least as traditionalism went:

> The Catholic is quieter, having less of the acquisitive impulse; he prefers a life of the greatest possible security, even with a smaller income, to a life of risk and excitement, even though it may bring the chance of gaining honor and riches. The proverb says jokingly, "either eat well or sleep well." In the present case the Protestant prefers to eat well, the Catholic to sleep undisturbed. (Weber 1976, pp. 40–1)

Traditionalism was reinforced by the Catholicism that had dominated Europe for centuries in a number of ways. Here was a religion that placed no restrictions against the easy-going traditionalism that we have noted, and which also valued ascetic practice with its extensive monastic establishments and spiritual practices of fasting and mortification. Here as well was a religion deeply embedded in the cultural ways of European life, with its elaborate system of mediating structures that negotiated between the faithful and the divine. Its cycles of holy days and ritual observances, its rich sacramental life, its system of indulgences, and its universe of holy persons (the saints) and holy places (shrines, cathedrals, springs, wells, mountains, and so on), all functioned as occasions of grace, as ways of channeling holiness to the faithful. Here was a religion that created an 'enchanted' world of religious meanings and occasions for sacramental encounters with the holy, and that sanctified ordinary life.

Weber had in mind the image of traditional Catholic European village life. There, people had attained a comfortable equilibrium between their needs and their means of fulfilling them, and a correspondingly well-integrated relationship to the holy. People were not rich, but their lives were unregulated and not particularly taxing. Most importantly, Catholic moral teaching helped prop up this "stone wall" of traditionalist work, while business was a scaffolding of sin-laden guilt. Enjoying wealth as good in itself risked two sins – "*turpitudo*" (feeling good about even justly won wealth) and avarice (the desire for gain). From his extensive research in the economic history of Europe, Weber learned that "the conception of money-making as an end in itself to which people were bound, as a calling, was contrary to the ethical feelings of whole epochs." And even when concessions were made by Catholic moralists in regard to the acquisition of wealth for its own sake, "the feeling was never quite overcome, that activity directed at acquisition for its own sake was at bottom a *pudendum* (figuratively, a cause of shame) which was to be tolerated only because of the unalterable necessities of life in this world" (Weber 1976, p. 73).

But despite these religious disincentives for acquisition, there was a certain leisure in the traditionalist world of Catholic Europe. There were no time-clocks to punch, no hourly calculations of wages, no precise piecework quotas of production to meet; the pace of life and work were slow and regular; and the rewards were proportionately moderate. Businesses avoided fierce competition with one another and preferred instead to find comfortable niches and guaranteed markets in the local economy with a regular circle of loyal clients and customers. As Weber describes the "traditionalist" business world, one detects a telling note of nostalgia for the loss of what he calls an "idyllic state" (Weber 1976, p. 68) betrayed in his words:

> The number of business hours was very moderate, perhaps five to six a day, sometimes considerably less; in the rush season, where there was one, more. Earnings were moderate; enough to lead a respectable life and in good times to put away a little. On the whole, relations among competitors were relatively good, with a large degree of agreement on the fundamentals of business. A long daily visit to the tavern, with often plenty to drink, and a congenial circle of friends, made life comfortable and leisurely. (Weber 1976, pp. 66–7)

A stunning example of why Weber felt that the values of worldly hedonist traditionalism were so deeply ingrained among European workers, for example, comes to us in his discussion of the paradoxes of piecework labor. At times like harvests, for example, it was in the interest of employers to speed up the rate of labor in order to gather in the harvest before changes in weather might cause crop loss. So, employers sometimes offered workers a higher piece rate amount in the expectation that this would provide an incentive for higher production. But this policy often had the surprising result that workers produced *less* than they did at the lower rate per piece produced. So embedded in the traditionalist style of life and patterns of thought were workers that simply worked less hard and thus produced *less* while still being able to earn the same wages as they had when the rate was lower. As Weber nicely sums up:

> The opportunity of earning more was less attractive than that of working less. He did not ask: how much can I earn in a day if I do as much work as possible? But: how much must I work in order to earn the wage . . . which I earned before and which takes care of my traditional needs? (Weber 1976, p. 60)

Matters did not improve either when wages were reduced. Laborers just worked less hard and produced correspondingly less, thus hurting the profits of the cheap labor business (Weber 1976, p. 61). Nothing seemed to be able to bring down traditionalism's "stone wall of habit" (Weber 1976, p. 62). Noticeably, these traditionalist workers showed no dedication to their work. For them, it was a disposable means for attaining a certain level of life, and no more. Labor to them was only a means to an end, never an end in itself worthy of perfection. In general, they felt no sense of responsibility to their work, and no need to 'advance.' Their lives revolved around other centers, such family and friends, membership in religious sodalities and social clubs, the cycle of liturgical religious rituals that marked births, baptisms, marriages, and deaths in the community or that sanctified other moments in the religious calendar, and so on.

Thus, with such massive moral disincentives and religious sanctions against people of the time for departing from the "traditionalist" style of economic life, it becomes even more challenging to try to explain the rise of capitalism. The emergence of capitalism was marked by tremendous struggles, as Weber tells us. Aiming a blow at the Marxists, Weber begins, "But the origin and history of such ideas is much more complex than the theorists of the superstructure suppose." Rather, Weber believed that these struggles occurred at the level of motivation and other psychological factors.

> The spirit of capitalism, in the sense in which we are using the term, had to fight its way to supremacy against a whole world of hostile forces. [Such a] ... state of mind ... would in ancient times and in the Middle Ages have been proscribed as the lowest sort of avarice and as an attitude entirely lacking in self respect. It is, in fact, still regularly thus looked upon by all those social groups which are least involved in or adapted to modern capitalistic conditions. (Weber 1976, p. 56)

How and why could capitalism have emerged at all, when so many factors were arrayed against this historical development?

How Traditionalism's "Stone Wall" Came Tumbling Down

With regard to the resistance of traditionalist workers to change to the worldly asceticism of a capitalist attitude toward their work and wages, Weber notices a peculiar anomaly in the data gathered about the paradoxes of piecework. Unlike the great majority of resistant traditionalists, a small class of workers actually did respond to the offer of higher rates for piecework! These workers differed from those in his traditionalism sample by their affiliation with a Protestant sect called Pietism. Unlike their traditionalist co-workers they displayed a sense of "obligation" to the job, a sense of the value of labor as an end in itself, a guiltless desire for gain along with the "self-discipline" and deferral of gratification needed for preserving and consolidating one's gains, and so on – in short all the traits that set traditionalism on its head. Weber later confirmed a possible link between religious affiliation and economic behavior by a series of statistical studies that pointed to something important. In the Germany of his time and place, where, as we have noticed, Protestant and Catholic populations mixed, there was nonetheless a strong tendency for the two populations to disaggregate in terms of economic status and occupation. Catholics, on the whole, gravitated to the traditional humanistic professions of law and medicine, while Protestants were disproportionately found among the managerial, commercial, technical, and business classes, and especially Protestants like the Pietists, who were drawn from Calvinist rather than Lutheran segments of the Reformation tradition (Weber 1976, p. 35).

This anomaly set Weber thinking along a series of steps – although not necessarily in chronological succession – toward his ultimate conclusion. First, are changes in objective conditions; second, are changes in values or ethos.

First, from place to place and for various reasons, the objective conditions of labor and business changed. Whether these were directly motivated by changes in values *in advance* or only *justified retrospectively* in terms of these values is immaterial. It is characteristic of Weber that while he thinks ideas and values matter, he does not think that objective changes do not matter. There is a subtle interaction between the two, as we will see. Thus, Weber describes a hypothetical case of how "at some time this leisureliness" of traditionalism "was suddenly destroyed," by attending to how the objective practices changed. His example is drawn from the textile business, and involves a model entrepreneur – "some young man" – who nevertheless hailed from one of the traditionalist textile producing families. Instead of maintaining the previous generations' long relation with his family's traditional suppliers, he seeks a better price for his raw materials from outside the local circle of his own region. This early capitalist thus ventured forth and went

> out into the country, carefully chose weavers for his employ, greatly increased the rigor of his supervision of their work, and thus turned them from peasants into laborers. On the other hand, he would begin to change his marketing methods by so far as possible going directly to the final consumer, would take the details into his own hands, would personally solicit customers, visiting them every year, and above all would adapt the quality of the product directly to their needs and wishes. At the same time he began to introduce the principle of low prices and large turnover. There was repeated what everywhere and always is the result of such a process of rationalization: those who would not follow suit had to go out of business.

For Weber, this shift to a entrepreneurial, profit-driven, competitive, rationalized economy spelled doom for traditionalism.

> The idyllic state collapsed under the pressure of a bitter competitive struggle, respectable fortunes were made, and not lent out at interest, but always reinvested in the business. The old leisurely and comfortable attitude toward life gave way to a hard frugality in which some participated and came to the top, because they did not wish to consume but to earn, while others who wished to keep on with the old ways were forced to curtail their consumption. (Weber 1976, pp. 67–8)

Objective conditions, after a while, do matter, Weber believes.

Second, quite possibly concurrent with these changes in the objective conditions of doing business, was the need for arguments defending them, for justifications or legitimations of these new arrangements. Weber believes that these new *legitimations* were as inescapable as the effects of fierce competition, introduced by our young capitalist entrepreneur. One can well imagine the opposition and social disruption caused by this sudden break with traditional ways of doing business. As Weber observes, a hard rule of competition takes hold, and "those who would not follow suit had to go out of business." The traditionalist suppliers, for example, either had to match or better the prices charged for their raw materials, or go under. Were they to go under, explanations would be required of the young man for causing such disruption. He would have to explain himself, justify or legitimize his decisions for suspending longstanding relations as well as disrupting the stability of the region that depended on these relations. How could he do this?

Weber believed that one way or another the young capitalist's actions would require legitimation in terms of the greater importance of the values behind his action. He might reply that his freedom to be ambitious and dynamic were *values* to be encouraged. He might also argue that the lower prices he could charge for his goods served the community better than the higher prices inevitably the result of the stagnant relations maintained with traditional producers. But whatever the *justifications*, they would need to speak to the ethics and morality of people.

> Along with clarity of vision and ability to act, it is only by virtue of very definite and highly developed ethical qualities that it has been possible to command the absolutely indispensable confidence of his customers and workmen. Nothing else could have given him the strength to overcome the innumerable obstacles, above all the infinitely more intensive work which is demanded of the modern entrepreneur. (Weber 1976, p. 69)

But it is not only others that would need to be persuaded of the rightness of the new ways of doing business. The new capitalist would have to justify things to themselves. Why was it good, as well, that he became wealthier in the process, especially while others went out of business entirely because of the competition he introduced into the local market? There would be a lot of *explaining* and *legitimating* to do – to the community, but also to his own conscience. Why are the new capitalist values of change *better* than the old traditionalist values of stability? But if the changes the young capitalist wrought were dire enough, he would need very powerful justifications indeed. Where would he obtain these?

Only Divine Duty – "Calling"– Can Crack Traditionalism's Wall

What Weber argues is that these changes in economic *values* were indeed momentous, and that therefore they required the most potent justification that could be had. In the period when the transition to capitalism began to take hold, Weber argues that such changes in values ultimately relied upon the powers of religion for their foundation. After all, the traditionalist way of life was undergirded by pre-Reformation Catholic religious beliefs and values, and thus it was so very deeply embedded in the traditionalist mentality, to dislodge traditionalists from their positions and convert them to such a radically different attitude toward life would require the power of religion as well. Weber, therefore, thought that only *religion* could bring about such changes, because religion was about ultimate sanctions. Only religion brought to the decision-making process the very power and prestige of the divine will. Nothing short of some kind of supernatural sanction could effect the profound transformations that throwing off easy-going, pleasurable traditionalism for the disciplined, rationalized, and hard life promised by capitalism would entail. There had to be some powerful overriding reason for people to adopt what in many ways was the prospect of an unpleasant life when they already enjoyed a life of comforts, however modest they might be.

Here Weber joins forces with phenomenologists like Ninian Smart and others who have argued for the importance of religious *experience*. For Weber, this experience amounted at times to an experience of power much like that described by Otto and other students of religion like R. R. Marett. It was far indeed from the rationalist instinct to *explain* the world that Edward Burnett Tylor advanced in his theory of animism (Kippenberg 2002, p. 165). The confidence of the new capitalist rested on nothing less potent than a sense that they were doing God's will, that their economic endeavors were the result of a special divine "calling," a feeling of an absolute *duty* toward God's will. As it happens, this notion of the faithful being led by a personally tailored "calling" to fulfill a divine duty was one of the strongest elements of the new preaching of the Protestant Reformation, first introduced by Martin Luther. The Lutheran appeal to a "calling" in effect asserted the primacy of the *duty* felt by the individual conscience over against the perceived Catholic doctrine of the governing role of the Church in deciding what one could and should do. It also reinforced the Lutheran ideal of a dramatic one-to-one relationship between a Christian and their God – a terribly fierce relationship in which the devotee stood alone and without excuses or supporting structures before God almighty. Only by placing absolute faith in God's saving power could one hope for salvation. One could not earn God's favor or negotiate the terms of one's ultimate fate. Only God decided. But once God issued a "calling," no other force in the world could stand against the dutiful obligation one had to fulfill it. Therefore, the confidence of the new capitalist could rely on an *experience* such as knowing that one was living in line with one's *duty* toward God, an obligation to heed this divine "calling." The ability of the capitalist to explain and justify their confident radical behavior took its strength from the same divine source as being called to a certain course in life. For Weber, God's "calling" broke the hold of traditionalism over the minds of pious Christians. Only a new *divine* duty could replace an older one.

There is, however, one significant additional point to be made about Luther's idea of "calling" that will enable him to link religion and economic behavior. Luther's view of "calling" does not quite suffice to account for the radical nature of the transition to capitalism from traditionalism, since it too was still too 'traditionalist.' Luther did link "calling" to our duties in the economic realm. Luther, for example, felt that retreating from the world into a monastery was a profoundly unchristian act, in part because of its selfishness (Weber 1976, p. 81). His sense of divine "calling" in the world – 'worldliness' as a positive value – concerned, however, one's obligation faithfully and dutifully to pursue a specific traditional profession or hold an appointed station in life. "The individual should remain once and for all in the station and calling in which God had placed him, and should restrain his worldly activity within the limits imposed by his established station in life" (Weber 1976, p. 85). Dutiful sons were thus obliged or 'called' to follow in the footsteps of their fathers. Sons of blacksmiths became blacksmiths as their fathers had been. Sons of weavers – Weber's name literally meant 'weaver' – took up the same economic niche as their forebears – in perhaps the same way Weber took up his father's life in law by enrolling in law at university himself.

Lutheranism had, thus, not broken sufficiently with traditionalism. "His calling is something which man has to accept as a divine ordinance to which he must adapt himself" (Weber 1976, p. 85). By contrast, the new capitalism knew no limits or restrictions placed in advance on what kind of business or profession one might be obliged to pursue. The world was a wide open arena of possibilities for gaining wealth, limited only by the current ability and imagination of the burgeoning capitalist scheme. 'The sky was the limit,' as the saying goes. The individual could aspire to any career they wished, even though breaking with tradition often caused pangs of conscience.

A perhaps little known passage from Daniel Defoe's *Robinson Crusoe* dramatizes this important turning point, and reflects the lingering power of traditionalism. We all know the main outlines of the Crusoe story, which by now, and for good reason, has become for us a kind of myth of the new capitalist world order. Crusoe goes forth on an enterprise and encounters hardship, but alone and by his single-minded endeavor succeeds in surviving and thriving in hostile conditions by dint of his diligence and hard work. What is seldom noted in the standard telling of the story are some intriguing details for anyone thinking about Max Weber. To wit, while Crusoe was born in the north of England (York) in 1632, his father was an immigrant from Bremen in Protestant northern Germany. The original family name was something like "Kreutznaer," Crusoe tells us. Establishing their Protestant *bona fides*, in the early seventeenth century, Crusoe's brothers fought as mercenaries in the Netherlands against the Spanish Catholic forces. Interestingly, these Catholic forces were the same as those against whom our old friend, Edward, Lord Herbert of Cherbury, had campaigned in the same time period (Defoe 1948, p. 3). On the economic front, we learn that Robinson's father was in what Weber would recognize as a typical Protestant occupation of the time – dealing "merchandise." But we also learn that Robinson had neither the desire to follow in his father's business, nor to obey this father's even more traditionalist wishes that his son become a lawyer. He wanted to venture forth on his own, and try something utterly new – the life of a commercial planter in the new world. Crusoe's father pressed his son with arguments about the great benefits of the traditionalist style of life that a position in law would afford him as against the risks that becoming a new capitalist would entail:

> He asked me what reasons more than a mere wandering inclination I had for leaving my father's house and my native country, where I might be well introduced, and had a prospect of raising my fortune by application and industry, with a life of ease and pleasure . . . [that] he had found by long experience was the best state in the world, the one most suited to human happiness. (Defoe 1948, p. 4)

Instead, Crusoe speaks in a voice that one could imagine issuing from our young, rebellious capitalist textile entrepreneur. He had no appetite for the life his father wished for him – a life in "easy circumstances sliding gently through the world, and sensibly tasting the sweets of living, without the bitter" – in short the life of the traditionalist (Defoe 1948, p. 5). Instead, being

> the third son of the family and not bred to any trade, my head began to be filled very early with rambling thoughts . . . but I would be satisfied with nothing but going to sea, and my inclination to this led me so strongly against the will, nay, the commands of my father and against all the entreaties and persuasions of my mother and other friends. (Defoe 1948, pp. 3–4)

Crusoe was determined to set his own course, offending all the normal moral constraints that might inhibit him, foremost among them the traditionalist norm of obedience to the will of his parents. Indeed, Crusoe's father even invoked the divine sanctions we know will become so important for breaking through the stone wall of traditionalism. In one last effort to dissuade Crusoe from his decision, his father calls down the warnings of a divine punishment. While Crusoe's father said he would continue to pray for his son, "yet he would venture to say to me that if I did take this foolish step, God would not bless me, and I would have leisure hereafter to reflect upon having neglected his counsel when there might be none to assist in my recovery" (Defoe 1948, p. 6).

We all know how the story turns out, and how indeed God seems to have punished Crusoe for his parting with the ways of traditionalism as his father prophesied. Nevertheless, it was the mark of this new breed of capitalist that Crusoe was so determined to become one against all obstacles and objections. How, Weber in effect asks, can such a decision be justified, legitimized, or defended? What *divine* justification could Crusoe throw up against the well-rehearsed *divine* disapproval of departing from traditional patterns of livelihood?

Calvinist "Calling" Can Overcome All Obstacles

In Weber's view, a far more radical degree of "calling" was required to effect the radical changes that capitalism in its fully-fledged, post-traditionalist form represented. It had to provide both the divine support for new economic decisions of Luther's concept of the divine calling, but also be free of traditionalist restrictions on the way that "calling" was expressed. To refer again to that great exemplary myth of capitalism, the story of Robinson Crusoe, he needed a "calling" that made his violent break with tradition, family, convention, and religious structures possible to justify, to legitimize and such. Weber also refers to that Calvinist paradigm of dutiful "calling," "Christian" of John Bunyan's allegory of the life of the new Calvinist, *Pilgrim's Progress* (1678). When Christian receives the "calling" to a higher life, "wife and children cling to him, but stopping his ears with his fingers and crying, 'life, eternal life,' he staggers forth across the fields...expressing the emotions of the faithful Puritan, thinking only of his own salvation" (Weber 1976, p. 107). The ability to make such a violent break with the deepest ties of human feeling is the essence of this freer, unrestricted concept of "calling," provided by the second great theological stream of the Protestant Reformation, the Calvinists. And, it is Jean Calvin's (1509–64) theology that Weber believed ultimately provided the theological justifications, or "ethical" basis, for the values that we have come to know as capitalist values – or the capitalist "spirit" from the title of Weber's classic. Indeed, it might have been more accurate for Weber to have entitled his masterpiece *The Calvinist Ethic and the Spirit of Capitalism*.

Calvin's conception of calling is rooted in a rigorous theological grasp of what and who God is. If God is who the Bible says he is, then God is like Otto described the numen – 'wholly other,' transcendent, and beyond all human conceptions. God is therefore all-good, all-knowing, and all-powerful, and so on. We depend absolutely upon God for everything, even our very existence, and cannot restrict God in any way, or reproach him for his deeds. Humans cannot hope to comprehend God's plans, simply because God's ways are not our ways, as the saying wisely puts it. From these theological considerations, several key Calvinist doctrines follow with a combination of "extreme inhumanity" and "magnificent consistency" (Weber 1976, p. 104).

The first of these, and the most unpalatable but most important for Weber's argument, is the so-called doctrine of predestination. By this, Calvin means that from all eternity, each human being is determined by God either for salvation or damnation. For Calvin, this makes eminent sense since an all-knowing God, such as he describes, not only must know the fate of each creature, but also must will that fate, since everything in the universe happens because of God's will. Moreover – and here this doctrine causes greatest controversy – humans can do nothing to alter God's decision. They cannot bargain with God, since that would imply equality between God and humanity. Nor can people appeal to moral rules of fairness to plead their case, since that would mean that God was subject to – and therefore inferior to – these rules. Nor can people earn the right to salvation if they have been predestined to damnation because, again, that would entail God's subordination to humans. This doctrine is laid out in the Westminster Confession (1647), chapter III, nos. 3, 5, and 7, regarding the general principle and the fate of the elect:

> By the decree of God, for the manifestation of His glory, some men and angels are predestinated unto everlasting life, and others foreordained to everlasting death.

As for those elected by God for salvation, the *Westminster Confession* says:

> Those of mankind that are predestinated unto life, God before the foundation of the world was laid, according to His eternal and immutable purpose, and the secret counsel and good pleasure of His will, hath chosen in Christ unto everlasting glory, out of His mere free grace and love ...

The text goes on to note that God's grace is granted irrespective of human *moral* behavior. God just wills that some will be saved, and others not.

> without any foresight of faith or good works, or perseverance in either of them, or any other thing in the creature as conditions, or causes moving Him thereunto, and all to the praise of His glorious grace.

In no. 7, we learn that the fate of the damned is also a consequence of God's supreme, unfathomable, arbitrary, and merciless will:

> The rest of mankind God was pleased, according to the unsearchable counsel of His own will, whereby He extendeth, or withholdeth mercy, as He pleaseth, for the glory of His sovereign power over His creatures, to pass by, and to ordain them to dishonour and wrath for their sin, to the praise of His glorious justice. (Weber 1976, p. 100)

There is never any possibility of dealings between God and humanity, because the gap between them is infinite. As Weber notes with perfect Calvinist theological consistency:

> For the damned to complain of their lot would be much the same as for animals to bemoan the fact they were not born as men. For everything of the flesh is separated from God by an unbridgeable gulf and deserves of Him only eternal death, in so far as He has not decreed otherwise for the glorification of His Majesty. (Weber 1976, p. 103)

As grim as this vision was for those not predestined for life eternal with God, it had its radiantly positive side for the elect. The second consequence of Calvin's theological vision then is that the elect *should* be able to enjoy enormous levels of self-confidence knowing that they are fated for heaven. But this condition is subject to an 'if' – and this is a *big if* – if they could be certain that they were predestined for salvation. If they *knew* that they had been "called" to salvation in the most complete and irrevocable way possible, what could be a greater source of self-assurance than that? But *knowing* whether one was among the elect was precisely the problem. Being predestined did not imply *knowing* that one was. People were still in doubt about the results of that divine judgment *for them*. As one can imagine, this became a huge source of anxiety – what critics have called their "salvation panic" – for Calvinists (Ringer 2004, p. 119).

Thirdly, making for even more anxiety was the recognition that whether predestined to be either saved or damned, the human individual was totally on their own and before God (Weber 1976, p. 104). One's only obligation or duty was to oneself, and to realize God's predestined plan for oneself. In this fierce one-to-one encounter of "extreme inhumanity" and "magnificent consistency" nothing could intervene between the individual and God to alter the fate that had been decreed from all eternity. "In what was for the man of the age of the Reformation the most important thing in life, his eternal salvation, he was forced to follow his path alone to meet a destiny which had been decreed for him from eternity. No one could help him" (Weber 1976, p. 104). This meant that all the old Catholic sacramental machinery of mediation became suddenly obsolete. It was totally useless for any priest or saint to intervene in behalf of the human supplicant. No rituals as well could serve the purposes of mitigating the judgment of God, and thus all previously holy places and spaces lost their magical ability to sanctify individuals. The world had been thoroughly and forever "disenchanted." Only God was 'enchanted,' as it were. All else was ungodly and thus corrupted by sin (Weber 1976, p. 105).

Such a rigorous scenario, however, created immense pressure to resolve anxiety among the faithful. In time, it led to a theological solution that both satisfied the religious needs of the faithful and, as it happened, played right into the hands of the new capitalist need for divine sanction for their new enterprises. The Calvinists theologians resolved this problem by preaching that a sure sign of 'election' was first of all a sense of confidence in one's being saved. It was a duty to dismiss all doubts that one was not among the blessed (Weber 1976, p. 111). A further remedy for temptations to doubt was worldly activity: one gained self-confidence in one's salvation by this "intense worldly activity" (Weber 1976, p. 112). Moreover, such a worldly life was not a mere casual life of "single good works, but a life of good works combined into a unified system" (Weber 1976, p. 117) aimed at the "glorification of God" – not, of course, any attempt to *earn* salvation (Weber 1976, p. 108).

Thus, those who were found among the successful in the world then could minimize their anxieties about the ultimate fate. The biblical parable of the servants in *Matthew* 25:15–31, who disposed of the 'talents' given them in different ways, held a lesson for Calvinists. The rejected servant was he who did not return the master's gift with profit! They thus knew definitely that salvation was assured to them because the predestination that had determined salvation for them was confirmed by visible signs in this world (Weber 1976, p. 268 n. 43). Those who were capitalists could feel assurance as well that their monetary successes were signs of being among the 'elect.' Indeed, on the Calvinist view, as Weber tells us, anyone who voluntarily wished to be poor, such as those in the Catholic monastic and mendicant orders, were wishing to be "unhealthy" (Weber 1976, p. 163). Further, of course, since success marked one as being among the elect, this put increasing pressure on the Calvinist capitalists to maintain a level of success. "If that God, whose hand the Puritan sees in all the occurrences of life, shows one of His elect a chance of profit, he must do it with a purpose. Hence the faithful Christian must follow the call by taking advantage of the opportunity" (Weber 1976, p. 162). We would not be far from the mark to see in this desire for continuous success the source of what Weber identified as one of the characteristics of capitalism – "*the pursuit of profit, and forever renewed profit*" (Weber 1976, p. 17). Appearances had to be maintained, because 'appearances' marked one as saved.

Thus, Weber arrives at an answer to his original questions: why was the West rich, and in particular, why was the Protestant West rich? His answer is simply that the economic system of capitalism made the West rich, and that the system required a certain 'work ethic' to motivate the efforts of those working within it. Finally, the origins of the capitalist 'work ethic' are to be sought in the justifications that people need to have for their participation in capitalist enterprise. Weber believed that these justifications or legitimations were ultimately to be found in Calvinist theology. Religion, therefore, in the form of theological legitimation can be said to cause or *explain* the rise and persistence of the great economic system of our own time. Describing this movement from precapitalist asceticism to the worldly asceticism of Calvinist engendered capitalism, Weber waxes poetic:

> Christian asceticism, at first fleeing from the world to solitude, had already ruled the world which it had renounced from the monastery and through the Church. But it had, on the whole, left the naturally spontaneous character of daily life in the world untouched. Now it strode into the market-place of life, slammed the door of the monastery behind it, and undertook to penetrate just that daily routine of life with its methodicalness, to fashion it into a life in the world, but neither of nor for this world. (Weber 1976, p. 154)

We have seen how this historical analysis not only reflected Weber's impressive grasp of historical realities, but also reflected some of the personal tensions afflicting him within his own life. We have not delved deeply into matters of his personal psychology, but only noted how they seem to have been a factor in the way Weber saw the world. In turning now to the monumental work of Sigmund Freud, we will be able to see how at least one great genius tried to solve the mysteries of the psychological life, some perhaps like Weber's themselves, and in doing so how the phenomenon of religion can itself be explained.

References

Bellah, R. N. 1957. *Tokugawa Religion*. Boston: Beacon Press.

Defoe, D. 1948. *Robinson Crusoe*. New York: Modern Library.

Diggins, J. P. 1996. *Max Weber: Politics and the Spirit of Tragedy*. New York: Basic Books.

Ermarth, M. 1978. *Wilhelm Dilthey: The Critique of Historical Reason*. Chicago: University of Chicago Press.

Geertz, C. 1983. *Local Knowledge: Further Essays in Interpretive Anthropology*. New York: Harper and Row.

Gerth, H. H. & C. W. Mills, eds. 1946. *From Max Weber: Essays in Sociology*. New York: Oxford University Press.

Honigsheim, P. 2003. *The Unknown Max Weber*. New Brunswick, NJ: Transaction Publishers.

Hook, S. 1930. Capitalism and Protestantism. *The Nation* 131, pp. 476–8.

Käsler, D. 1988. *Max Weber: An Introduction to His Life and Work*, trans. P. Hurd. Chicago: University of Chicago Press.

Kippenberg, H. G. 2002. *Discovering Religious History in the Modern Age*, trans. B. Harshav. Princeton: Princeton University Press.

Mitzman, A. 1969. *The Iron Cage*. New York: Grosset and Dunlap.

Ringer, F. 2004. *Max Weber: An Intellectual Biography*. Chicago: University of Chicago Press.

Sahlins, M. 1972. *Stone Age Economics*. Chicago: University of Chicago Press.

Singer, M. 1972. Industrial Leadership, the Hindu Ethic, and the Spirit of Socialism. In *When a Great Tradition Modernizes*. London: Pall Mall Press.

Taylor, C. 1985. Understanding and Ethnocentricity. In *Philosophical Papers: Philosophy and the Human Sciences*, vol. 2. Cambridge: Cambridge University Press.

Von Suttner, B. April 18, 1906. *The Evolution of the Peace Movement: The Nobel Lecture*. Stockholm.

Weber, Marianne. 1975. *Max Weber: A Biography*, trans. H. Zohn. New York: John Wiley.

Weber, Max. 1976. *The Protestant Ethic and the Spirit of Capitalism*, trans. T. Parsons. New York: Charles Scribner's Sons.

9

Tales from the Underground: Freud and the Psychoanalytic Origins of Religion

In the slow ample beauty of the world,
And the unutterable glad release
Within the temple of the holy night.
O Atthis, how I loved thee long ago
In that fair perished summer by the sea!

"I Loved Thee, Atthis" (Bliss Carman)

The Freudian Moment

In playing up the emotionally charged relations of Weber to his parents in the last chapter, I had two intentions in mind, only one of which I revealed at the time. As I argued then, one can see a mirroring of Weber's personal tensions in the dilemmas he observed and sought to understand in society's choice of economic systems. To oversimplify for the moment, this meant that the 'softer' side of his mother's charitable, but unrealistic, nature and nurture mirrored the gentler world of easy-going traditionalism; the 'harder' side of his father's disciplined and careerist bourgeois worldview neatly reflected the harsh, but realistic, Calvinist work ethic. I believe that Weber was caught between these extremes both in his personal life and in his analyses of the relations between religion and economic systems. By enlarging our conception of Weberian thought to include his personal torments, I also wanted readers to think about the horns of the perennial human dilemmas on which much of human life is poised. Here, gratification and its denial, most notably sexual gratification, presented Weber with some of his gravest anxieties. These may have been worked out to some degree in his pondering of the role of Protestant asceticism as a necessary ingredient in making the modern universe of rational capitalist enterprise.

But at the same time as I explored this set of tensions, I should also like to confess that I dwelt upon Weber's relations with his parents in part to ease the transition to our present chapter on Freudian psychological approaches to religion. The influence on Weber of childhood nurture and the agonies of sexual desire and their realization or frustration anticipate great Freudian themes such as "civilization and its discontents" – in part a meditation on the necessity of the same rational discipline and restraint on sexual gratification that so consumed Weber. Without anticipating the arguments I shall make about Sigmund Freud (1856–1939) and religion, is it not at least plausible that the deep and troubled relations of Weber to his parents played a role in the way he came to think and in the way he lived his professional scholarly life? We know, for instance, of Weber's failure to consummate his own marriage, yet of his record of extramarital affairs. As I have already noted, we know as well of Weber's fascination with Protestant asceticism when he, at other times, evinced a hearty desire for the life of a carefree 'worldly hedonist' and nostalgia for the lost world of traditionalism. We know too of his movements back and forth between the 'softer' interpretive modes of inquiry and 'harder' causal ones. What is one to make of these puzzles of personal life? How do they work together to form a coherent whole in the personality and professional life that Weber constructed?

The biographical materials of someone like Weber (and indeed Malinowski, as we will see in the next chapter) would be treated as an open invitation by Freud. He would, I believe, want to explore how the opposition between Weber's hard and emotionally remote father over against his compassionate and emotionally accessible mother holds a deeper story to tell than might appear obvious. In a way, the 'only' thing Freud seeks to do is tell us such 'stories,' designed to open up the deeper levels of our minds, and in doing so to reveal the causes of action we had not thought were at work before then. In this chapter, we will see how Freud believes that he can explain religion, and in particular of course *religious experience*, in terms of the psychodynamics of the human mind. Freud believes, as we will see, that the formative patterns of relationships established between the parental family unity and critical religious people explain the kind of religion those people have.

In this sense, Freud raises a whole series of *problems of religion* having to do with the extent to which one can say that religion – religious experience – is to be *explained* in terms of mental conditions that are themselves *not* religious. Touching base again with Weber, while, for example, we may accept that the *religious experience* of being "called" motivates or legitimizes capitalist economic endeavor, Freud asks what *explains* – at all – the existence of such a kind of religious *experience*, and in some people and not others? Short of an appeal to religious or supernaturalist claims that God really does "call" people to lead a certain kind of economic life, what *explains* 'why' some people have these experiences and others do not?

Besides the obvious contrast with supernaturalist explanations of religious experience – of whatever kind – it seems natural to compare Freud's approach with that of the phenomenologists of religion. It should be obvious for us that since Freud sets out what can be called a classic *reductionist* approach to religion, his approach stands starkly opposed to what the champions of the "autonomy" of religion advocated. He believed that all religious experiences are in reality only psychological ones. Freud thus reveals himself as a "critic" of religion, rather than any kind of "caretaker." While he may seem at times like an 'undertaker of religion' – a thinker who wishes to eliminate talk of religion from our language – he really has too much invested in keeping it around as a handy target for his polemics. To flesh out Freud's approach, we will look at how Freud handles the examples of great religious figures such as Moses, as well as religious movements such as early Christian devotion to Mary, and even religiously troubled individuals like Max Weber.

Mentalism and the Two Psychologies

While it is not possible within the compass of this book to review the entire range of kinds of psychologies, I want to make a few broad distinctions, and locate Freud and his work within them. The first and most obvious question is what the nature of any psychology is. Two broad answers can be given to this question – one a 'mentalist' answer, the other a 'behaviorist' one.

For 'mentalists,' such as Freud, psychology is about the 'mind' or 'mental states.' Taking the term 'psychology' literally, mentalist psychology is, as it were, the scientific study of the '*psyche*' – the Greek word for 'soul' or 'spirit,' and by extension, 'mental states,' or mind. Such an understanding of the meaning of 'psychology' is one reason Tylor's *animist* theory of religion – that religion is the belief in 'souls' or 'spirits' – is often called a 'psychological' theory. As we will see, Tylor's animistic theory is a far cry from the scientific psychology that Freud sought to establish. Tylor's theory is only psychological in an informal sense of having to do with mental matters, such as experience, as well as the experience of spirits. Freud's psychology belongs to another world altogether. It strives to be a *science* of the mind – one that explains all 'mental states' no matter what we call them.

What would such a science include? For Freud, psychology would be about mental states in the sense it is about the way people think and feel. It concerns the conscious and unconscious states of people – their intentions, motives, feelings, experiences, intuitions, inner states, drives, needs, desires, wishes, and so on. Because psychology would include such data as "numinous experiences" or "mystical experiences," some commentators have, for example, called Otto's approach to religion 'psychological.' But to compare Otto to Freud reveals a great rift. Otto never intended his work to be *scientific*, as Freud so very much did. Otto always thought the "numinous" mental states that he investigated really went beyond the natural realm and participated in the supernatural as well. Thus, when Otto states what the "psychological facts" of the numinous experience are, he waxes mystical, mysterious, and (frankly) obscure. The "creature-feeling" that he links with Schleiermacher's "feeling of absolute dependence" is, in his view, to be described as

> itself a first subjective concomitant and effect of another feeling-element, which casts it like a shadow, but which in itself indubitably has immediate and primary reference to an object outside the self.
>
> Now this object is just what we have already spoken of as 'the numinous.' For the 'creature-feeling' and the sense of dependence to arise in the mind the 'numen' must be experienced as present, a *numen praesens*, as is in the case of Abraham. There must be felt a something 'numinous,' something bearing the character of a 'numen,' to which the mind turns spontaneously. . . . The numinous is thus felt as objective and outside the self. (Otto 1958, pp. 10–11)

Translating this out of Otto's contorted philosophical parlance into more straightforward language, he is saying that a person has this "creature-feeling" or Schleiermachean "feeling of absolute dependence" because they really encounter the divine, the numen itself. In other words, it seems that Otto is saying that a numinous experience proves the existence of the object of that experience – the divine itself. As we will see, Freud will present a theory that claims that our numinous experiences are *not* caused by supernatural powers, but by our own unconscious or by encounters with other human beings. Freud even believed that some day scientists would show that all mental states would be reduced to physical states of the brain.

In a classic passage, Freud reacts against the suggestion of his mystically minded friend, the French philosopher and writer Romain Rolland, that there is such a fundamental, Otto-like religious experience. Rolland called this the "oceanic feeling," a descriptive term that suggests Otto's rendition of the numinous experience as wholly other, mysterious, tremendous and overpowering, irrational, yet fascinating feeling of dependence. Rolland further elaborated to Freud his own experience of this feeling as one of a sense of " 'eternity,' a feeling as of something limitless, unbounded...a purely subjective fact...[that is] the source of the religious energy" (Freud 1961, p. 11). Thus, like Otto, Rolland implied not only that such experiences came at one from outside and overpowered us, but therefore, like Otto, that such experiences were "the *fons et origo* of the whole need for religion" (Freud 1961, p. 12). They accounted for both the existence and persistence of religion, much as the phenomenologists of religion themselves all agreed.

However much he wanted to bring out the power of the irrational in life, Freud, as we will see, would have none of Rolland's theologizing of the forces of the irrational. For him, religion and religious experience will remain firmly earth-bound within the natural and human realms; they are expressions, as he will argue, of deep irrational and wholly human determinants of human thought and action. As a consistent "reductionist," Freud will claim that religious experience is nothing more than an outgrowth of the unconscious, irrational operations of the human mind. Religion, as believers *consciously* understand it, is nothing more than an illusion. Summarizing Freud's 'reductionist' and therefore antiphenomenological viewpoint, Freud "can reject the universality of the 'religious need' in human nature by dissolving that specific need into emotions characteristic of more than religion. There is no distinctively religious need – only psychological need" (Rieff 1979, p. 271). And, although these needs are beyond the powers of ordinary reason to control and, to some degree, to plumb, they are nonetheless part of that which is *irrational* in the make-up of human nature.

But whatever may divide Otto from Freud in terms of their feelings about the supernatural character or states of mind, the two of them agree on the same *method* of getting access to data 'in the mind.' These data are acquired through introspection and/or interpretation of first-person accounts of mental states. They are primary data, and become the things that the mentalist psychologist of religion tries to explain and understand. Thus, Otto relied on what people who have had religious experiences report having experienced. Or, he interprets what religious people say as evidence for the existence of certain religious mental states. The reports of believers about those inner states, visions, numinous feelings, and so on, or Otto's interpretation of them, become his data. For an Otto, there is no way around such 'evidence' provided by believers to get at what might *really* – reductively – be on people's minds. Like other phenomenologists, Otto tends to take the position that 'you get what you see' – that the data for a phenomenology of religion are the reports religious people offer by means of their own introspection or what is reflected in religious documents. As an antireductionist, Otto would in principal never challenge Arjuna, for example, as to whether in experiencing Krishna's divine form he may not have actually 'seen' what is reported in the *Bhagavad Gītā*. For Otto, it is enough that Arjuna is cast as speaking of Krishna's "having many mouths and eyes, having within it many wonderful sights, having many celestial ornaments," and so on. Freud too at least *starts* by basing his ideas about the nature of the mind upon the reports that people offer him. But unlike Otto and other antireductionists, he will not naively accept the 'believer's point of view' as decisive evidence, as the final word. In this sense, Freud stands diametrically opposed to the extreme view of Kristensen that the believer's account of his state of mind is final and incorrigible. To Freud, the reports of his clients (or religious believers) become the raw material of his *interpretations* of these states of mind. Freud is not at all committed to accepting their reports as final – and much less as true.

The Behaviorist Revolution

Now, whatever the differences among such different 'mentalist' approaches to religion, no difference is as great as that between 'mentalists' and 'behaviorists' – the second great kind of psychological approaches to religion. 'Behaviorists' might indeed describe Freudian psychology as a form of superstition, since Freudians, like all 'mentalists' believe in the existence of ghostly realities such as mental states, which in turn are thought to influence human action. Instead, as the name declares, 'behaviorists' study individual human *behavior*, and dispense entirely with all talk of intentions, motives, and other introspectively derived entities. If we could imagine a 'behaviorist' study of Arjuna which gave rise to his talk of "many mouths and eyes" and so on, it would focus on data such as Arjuna's intense excitedness, such as his hair standing on end, his trembling, sweating, cowering, and so on. But nothing would be said about anything one could call a mental state. Everything to which the 'behaviorist' referred would be public and observable.

Malinowski, as we will see, incorporates behaviorist insights into his approach to religion (Malinowski 1948, pp. 47–54). Although he also was a Freudian, this behaviorist aspect of his thinking comes out in a telling example of a mortuary rite in one of the small-scale societies that Malinowski studied. Referring solely to *observations of behavior*, Malinowski suggests a link between the stimuli created by the mortuary ritual *behavior* and the *behavioral* responses of the mourners. He implies that there may be some kind of as yet not well understood causal connection between a public rite and behavioral states of grief, depression, and such. All we know is what we *see* in the changes in behavior of people involved. Thus, Malinowski, first, notes his initial observed data – the sad, emotionally unstable, dejected condition of mourners at the beginning of the performance of the rite. These data could be read either or both as publicly observed behaviors, such as overt facial expressions, crying, and so on, or they might be read as unobserved inner mental states – 'grief,' 'despair,' 'upset,' feelings of being bereft and abandoned by the deceased, and so on (Skinner 1999).

By contrast, a phenomenologist who held to the magical, mind-reading view of empathy – that Weber, for example, explicitly rejected – at this juncture would say, as we would expect, that the observer could indeed directly know what the mourners were feeling by simply exercising their power of *empathy* to 'get inside the heads' of the mourners. Not only Weber – for his own reasons – but typically Malinowski and all 'behaviorists' on the other hand, would reject talk of the mental states of others. Even if they could be proven to exist, which behaviorists deny, a behaviorist would challenge the view that such putatively existing mental states can be known publicly, as if one were 'reading minds.' Nor, of course, is there any question of *observing* them, strictly speaking, since they do not take seriously the possibility of any evidence of their existence. Mental or emotional states are not *behavior*, but are instead illusory.

Second, like any good ethnographer, Malinowski observes the public and observable mortuary rites for the deceased, and dutifully records what he 'sees' in his notebooks. Third, Malinowski then draws some conclusions about what behaviors he has observed. He notes that *after* the performance of these ritual behaviors, the behavioral forms of grief seem to have given way to expressions of equilibrium, joy, gladness, relief, and so on – all behaviors fully observable to any onlooker simply by reading the body language and facial expressions of people. In perfect 'behaviorist' style, Malinowski concludes that somehow the mortuary ritual *behavior* acted as a *stimulus* to induce the *response* of emotional equilibrium among the people of the small-scale society. Although he may not understand the precise mechanisms governing this change in behavior, for Malinowski as 'behaviorist' it is enough to correlate the changes that he and others can observe.

As an example of this view of human nature, we are probably all familiar with the wide use of the therapy that behaviorist theory has informed – "behavior modification." Here, for example, one desires to correct an undesirable behavior: say, delaying the writing of essays for school courses. How to do this? One might, of course, exhort the student to correct this bad habit. One might, in effect, try to introduce a different mental state, intention, motive, and so on into the student's mind. But what if that failed, as it so often does? The 'behaviorist' would take a different tack. For every time the student turned in their essay late, the teacher would simply penalize the student in some conspicuous behavioral way, say by depriving them of certain privileges, or simply refusing to accept a late essay, eventuating in a severe grade penalty, and all that might mean in terms of parental ire, etc. Conversely, whenever the student produced an acceptable essay assignment on time, the student would be rewarded in some overt way. In doing so, the teacher would be following tried and true behaviorist principals by introducing certain *stimuli* into the life of the student and seeking in that way to generate favorable *responses* – positively stimulating desirable behaviors and discouraging undesirable ones. The behaviorist cares nothing for what 'went through the mind' of the student, only that the student behaved better. They care nothing for any possible mental state of the student, only for the performance of the objective task at hand – producing an acceptable essay in a timely manner. The behaviorist attends only to the cause–effect chain between selected stimuli and desired responses.

If we flip this example around slightly, we can also grasp more of the insights embodied in behaviorism, especially in its struggles with mentalism. This time we would ask the perennial procrastinator in our essay example what it meant when they repeated again and again that they *intended* to produce an acceptable essay, yet never did so? What status does the mental state of such an "intention" have, if we never see it realized? If mentalists think that mental states are 'causes' of our actions, then what would it mean to say that one 'had an intention in mind' if no effect of that appeared? Would we really not have to admit that it made no difference at all that such a fugitive mental state existed or not? If so, why talk of intentions, motives, and the like at all? Why not simply become a behaviorist, and drop all talk of internal mental states?

Part of the power of the behaviorist approach is then its comfortable place in our common sense. We have all had experiences such as that just mentioned, in which we said we had such and such an intention, yet never acted upon it. Ought we not to doubt that such shadowy things exist at all? In addition, we have all also had experiences in which our behavior, and perhaps our frame of mind, was altered by an external stimulus – the body, as it were, working on the 'mind.' As children, we may feel rebellious or experience antagonism to our parents. But, although it does not work in all cases, that *feeling* of rebellion or antagonistic *motivation* – mental states – can sometimes be 'broken' or changed by the application of the right sort of external stimulus. All I am saying is that in many cases, people do 'change their minds' (*sic*) by having their *behavior* altered or affected. In those cases, they do not 'change their minds' because their mental states have been addressed, but because their behavior has been.

Freudian Psychoanalysis: Pseudoscience and/or Therapy?

We should not let this talk of divisions in the *science* of psychology obscure two critical points about the thought of Sigmund Freud. First, even though Freud's first love was laboratory experimental science, Freudian psychology ought to be seen as about practical healing – *therapy*. And, even though he always felt that his task was to try to discover the physiological substrata of his talk of mental states, his theory – his model – of human mental life was 'mentalist,' and always conditioned by its subsidiary place to the practical task of dealing with problems of mental health. Thus, it might be borne in mind that a perhaps better general name for Freudian thought is "psychoanalysis" or "psychother-apy." Freud himself practiced medicine, although at first unwillingly, since he was unable to pursue a career in chemistry, zoology, or brain anatomy, as he had originally wanted (Rieff 1979, pp. 5–7). But once in the role of the physician, Freud devoted himself to relieving his patients of their pain and suffering. As someone with a caring humanist temperament, he departed from the standard practice of his peers in the medical profession: Freud actually *talked* with his patients! He sought to grasp the "intangibles" of the clinical situation, and thus focused on the patient, rather than exclusively on the disease, as his peers did. That Freud invited conversation with his patients did not mean that he was unaware of the dangers of emotional entanglement with them. He thus guarded against this with utmost rigor and maintained his own kind of "impersonal" style of practicing medicine (Rieff 1979, p. 10). Still, all in all, it was in large part because Freud began to *listen* to his patients that the classic techniques of psychoanalysis got off the ground at all. Whatever shows of emotional sympathy he held back in his clinical encounters with his patients, Freud more than compensated for by creating a body of theory that "focused on the personal factors in disease and cure" (Rieff 1979, p. 12). Given that Freudian theoretical (scientific) models of human thought and action therefore need to be seen as his imaginative creations, he aimed at *explaining* how and why certain strategies of healing worked, while other doctors did not. This is but one reason why among some of the most progressive of today's psychotherapists we find religious techniques of mental therapy, such as adapted Buddhist meditative practices, being taken into the clinic and synthesized with classic techniques of psychotherapy (Fulton 2005).[1]

Second, in this sense, we also should be alert to the many critiques of the *scientific* status both of Freudian psychological "theory" and the "psychotherapy" resting on this theoretical basis (Cioffi 1970). Strictly speaking, of course, psychotherapy is a practice or practical *technique* – a technology – not a "science." The same confusion arose, as we will recall, regarding how Frazer (and some of his commentators) also blurred the distinction between 'science' and 'technology' in referring to magic and religion as precursors to modern 'science' – rather than as forerunners of 'technology.' But the point to be made here is that, even after making allowances for imprecise usage, Freudian approaches have been criticized for their failure even to qualify for *broadly* "scientific" status.

The first kind of critique comes from the materialist or behaviorist charge that Freudian thought is unscientific because it has recourse to immaterial – 'mentalist' – entities acting as *causes*. Since materialists (and behaviorists, as well) see the world in material terms alone; they do not consider other sorts of causality, such as that 'ideas' or other mental states may influence behavior or bodily states. They do not even entertain the possibility of there being kinds of causality that conform to the 'billiard-ball' model, but where the balls are ideas rather than physical actions. They would dismiss immediately, for example, Weber's idea of religious values as *causes* of capitalism. For this reason, the materialists and behaviorists see science as a necessarily *empirical* venture, requiring that the causality involved be observable and thus physical, and that claims about causes be based on sense data. For them, Freudian psychoanalysis fails these tests.

In reply to such critiques, Freudians have adopted a number of strategies – one of which was Freud's puzzling claim that 'meanings' themselves were material! By far the most innovative reaction to these attacks has been to argue energetically for a radically antimaterialist counterattack, grounded in experimental practices. One of the central principles of psychoanalysis – that 'mind' acts on 'body,' to put it crudely – anticipates, for example, the whole phenomenon of psychosomatic illness. Here, 'mind' is seen to act on 'matter,' instead of the other way round, as the materialists would have it. The "body exists as a symptom of mental demands," one critic of Freudian thought charged (Rieff 1979, p. 8). If all so-called mental maladies are said to arise directly as mere 'expressions' of bodily states such as disorders of the body, do we find the attitudes, beliefs, wishes, desires, etc. of people – their mental states – giving rise to *physical* ailments? Why can depression increase our susceptibility to opportunistic infection, for example? Why, as contemporary anthropologists have shown, is *belief* in the care-giver often a vital factor in the efficacy of the care given (Lévi-Strauss 1968)? Freud himself asked why, if hysteria is supposed to be an expression of a malignant uterus, do we find 'hysterical' *men*? Why, moreover, can 'hysteria' be induced in patients by means of hypnotic suggestion, if 'hysteria' is just an expression of a state of the body (Rieff 1979, p. 8)?

The second kind of critique comes from those who feel that Freudian procedures fail the test of true science because their results are not repeatable. One Freudian analyst may see a situation in one way and prescribe one treatment, but another Freudian may see things in an entirely different way, and prescribe another treatment altogether. And this is to say nothing of the myriad 'schools' of psychotherapy aside from the Freudian! Worse yet, even when we restrict our test to Freudians, two therapists may achieve the same level of success or failure, even after producing different analyses and prescribing different remedies accordingly! In this, the critics are saying in effect that Freudian psychotherapy and psychology are more like an '*art*' than a 'science.' In the arts, virtuosity and variety of results are things to be celebrated. Perhaps Freudian thinking is more like this, and much less like the sciences in their ability to produce predictable and consistent results? Indeed Freud's earliest works were severely criticized as "unscientific" by his academic reviewers precisely for this lack of hard scientific quantification and experimental procedures. Freud's critics also likened his work to a kind of artistic endeavor. A Professor Leipmann (Berlin University), for example, excoriated Freud's efforts, saying that "the imaginative thoughts of an artist had triumphed over the scientific investigator" (Rieff 1979, p. 26).

We need not attempt to resolve all these matters here. But it is important to say that there is a positive way of resolving the issue of whether or not Freudian thought is a kind of 'art.' For the sake of argument, let us agree that the critics of Freudian psychotherapy are right, and that Freudian techniques are not the stuff of 'science.' If we accepted his insights, we would actually recapture a goodly part of the origins of Freudian medical practice in its creative employment of the art of interpretive decoding – of seeing things as *signs* of other things, of reading things as "*symptoms.*" Freud himself referred to his approach to the interpretation of dreams as a kind of hermeneutic that we should recall from discussions of biblical interpretation. He approached dreams "like a sacred text," was how Freud himself put it (Preus 1987, p. 185).[2] That act of seeing certain behaviors as 'effects' and so on is an artistic or interpretive task. According to the interpretive – hermeneutic – view of Freudian method, the psychoanalyst may also then be likened to a detective, car mechanic, or family doctor rather than to a chemist, physicist, or, even less, an engineer. If Freud did see himself as an artist, he sought to "grasp his subject," says Philip Rieff: "Freud had not to quantify and measure, but rather to intuit, to interpret, and . . . to evaluate" (Rieff 1979, p. 23). The point of the work of psychoanalysts is to read what they see as signs, indicators, effects, symptoms of certain underlying mental structures, and then to address those structures so that patients can be relieved of their suffering. As early as his first great publication, *The Interpretation of Dreams* (1900), Freud had been moving away from physicalist reductionism toward a wholly opposite approach. For Freud, dreams, for example, became "symbols" or expressions, even though he always maintained that they were "physiologically rooted" (Rieff 1979, p. 7).

But what then if Freudian psychotherapy *were* more an 'art' – more an exercise in *reading*, and therefore, in empathetic or phenomenological *understanding* of human behavior, as his early critics said (Ricoeur 1970)? Would this be such a tragedy, even if Freud himself, at certain points in his ever-evolving way of thinking about such profound matters, might have balked at the thought? I think not, and will accordingly proceed with this discussion of Freudian thought and religion on that basis. That is to say, that my evaluation of the Freudian impact on religion and the study of religion will not depend on whether Freudian psychotherapy or psychoanalysis merits a hard scientific status. What matters more to the impact of Freud upon the study of religion is the creativity and suggestiveness of his *interpretations* of religion. Freud creates '*problems of religion*' – he plants the 'worm of doubt' in the minds of religious folk, especially those who center their religion on a powerful god or other mighty sacred beings, such as Mary as 'mother of God.' To that degree, the problems of religion that Freud raises are some of the most intriguing and upsetting of all. They are, therefore, ones that I believe are most useful for getting us to think about religion, even if they may not qualify as scientifically sound.

What Lies Beneath: Freud and His Model of the Unconscious

While we have seen how 'mentalist' and 'behaviorist' psychologies differ in many ways, let me return to a point made in passing about behaviorists. For behaviorists, the putative internal mechanisms that some would say turn stimuli into responses simply lie outside their realm of scientific inquiry. We wait, to some degree, on the progress of the neurological sciences. Now, with that in hand, I want to note the fact that Freud, on the other hand, was all about shedding lots of light into what he took to be the internal mechanisms conditioning human thought and action. When presented with the same behavioral 'facts' as the behaviorists, Freud did not stop there. He speculated about what mechanisms may be inside the mind, so that its inner dynamic would be revealed. Like the good artist that both his critics and admirers claim him to be, he spun a theory about the content of the human mind. He turned behaviorist 'responses' into "symptoms." He turned brute facts into meaningful indications – *signs* – of the identity of what lies beneath. Freud was driven by the quest to understand what mechanisms existed within people that caused them to 'respond' in certain ways to certain 'stimuli.' What lies *beneath* the facts? What "latent" realities lie beneath the "manifest" appearances of psychological inquiry (Freud 1938, p. 238)? What behaviors are *symptomatic* of deeper realities than appear on the surface? Such attempts to get at what may be thus *latent* in publicly observable facts involves the *positing* of mechanisms or 'models' that are said to account for what is *manifest*. The Freudian unconscious is just such a 'model' of what lies beneath facts presented to public view.

The idea that there were unconscious mental processes did not originate with Freud. Still, in all, he conceived the unconscious in so radical and original a way that his ideas caused a major cultural revolution in Western society, while no other concept of the unconscious apparently has ever done. At least four critical features make up the salient architecture of the Freudian unconscious.

First, Freud's unconscious is an *absolute* unconscious. Freud *bifurcates* the human mind into the separate compartments of unconscious and conscious, such that the unconscious is opaque to introspection. The Freudian unconscious is thus 'absolute' in that it is unknown and unknowable to us under ordinary circumstances. In this way it differs from Freud's idea of the "preconscious" – those things that we happen from time to time not to remember, or of which we are not conscious: as Dan Pals amusingly notes, "things like the ages of our parents, what was served for dinner yesterday, or where we intend to go on the weekend" (Freud 1938, pp. 491, 518, 544–5; Pals 1996, p. 58). Another way that Freud conceives of this bifurcation of the mind is to say that contents of the unconscious mind are "latent," while those of the conscious mind are "manifest" (Freud 1938, p. 238). Individuals, acting on their own, cannot hope to penetrate into their own deeply hidden unconscious, but instead need to rely on the clinical therapeutic help of an expert investigator of the unconscious – the Freudian psychoanalyst! The one possible exception to this rule was Freud himself, who undertook his own self-analysis. But today, all Freudian analysts are routinely required to be in analytic relations themselves with another colleague.

Second, the reason the unconscious is absolutely separate from the conscious mind is that the unconscious has been deeply buried by actively suppressing certain memories (Preus 1987, pp. 179–80). The unconscious was originally formed, says Freud, by the "repression" of things in early childhood – wishes, desires, actual deeds – that we cannot really admit to ourselves because they are so threatening to our own personal integrity. Although Freud felt that classic "repression" thus occurred in early childhood, not in adulthood, we can get a sense of the power of his viewpoint by extrapolating to a perhaps more accessible example of the psychological mysteries of the celebrated case of an otherwise loving husband and father, the accused murderer, O. J. Simpson. To this day, Simpson denies having committed the murder. Let us assume, however, that he did the deed, as in fact his subsequent conviction in the civil trial held. But let us complicate matters psychologically, and assume that he is telling the truth in asserting his innocence because he may in fact have no memory of having done the murder. Consider the following scenario of how it might be possible then that Simpson both did the murder, yet would be telling the truth – as he knows it – in denying having done so. On this view, Simpson, emotionally overwrought in a blind rage, murdered his wife, Nicole, and her friend, Ron Goldman, just as the prosecutors tried to prove in the criminal trial. Further, in performing the deed, imagine as well the trauma and horror impressed upon O. J. by its ghastly results. Add to this the fact that while retaining consciousness of his act, O. J. could not escape the feelings of utter guilt of being the murderer of both his once treasured wife and the mother of his children. Freud would suggest that such a matter was so emotionally catastrophic that it could well have been like the classic "repressions" of early childhood in the sense that these 'repressed' feelings had become *constitutive* of O. J.'s sense of himself. That is to say that O. J. could not both *admit* his guilt to himself, and simultaneously maintain a desired image of himself, in the process retaining his sanity. He would have to "repress" the *consciousness* of his guilt, and confine it to an absolute unconscious. He would need to slip into a state of "denial," in which he would so deeply bury the conscious memory of the murder in his unconscious that he may truly no longer be able to remember it. He would have successfully repressed the memories of his murder in his unconscious – which in cases likes these in early child-hood, for Freud, is hermetically sealed off from access by our consciousness. Thus, Simpson's protestations of innocence, while attacked by many and, indeed, possibly false, may have been true *to him*, 'true' in *his own conscious mind*, and thus honest and sincere protestations of his own innocence. That, at any rate, is what would follow if Freud were right about the ability of people to "repress" formative early childhood memories and to seal them away in the deep locker of our unconscious.

Third, in Freud's view, not only are we absolutely not conscious of the Freudian unconscious, but we do not exert *control* over our unconscious either. Instead, the unconscious, in Freud's view, controls us. Freud overturns the classic humanist view of human nature, prevalent at least since the Renaissance, that human beings are self-aware and free, and substitutes instead a view that casts us as blind and subject to our deep inner nature. We are not, therefore, the 'masters of our own ship,' but have our behavior directed by our unconscious promptings. And even though we are unaware of its action upon us, the unconscious nevertheless works from great depths to cause us to think and behave in certain ways – and ways over which we have virtually no control of our own. The sometimes riotous and unscripted scenarios we experience in our dream-life were for Freud a rich source of knowledge about our unconscious – especially if they held clues to interpreting our walking thought and action. Why, as well, do some people 'obsess' about things? Shakespeare caught this mood when he cast murderous Lady Macbeth 'ritualis-tically' scrubbing her hands long after any signs of Duncan's blood had faded. "Out, damned spot! out, I say!," she complains in frustration, as she futilely seeks to see her hands 'clean' again (*Macbeth* V.i.38).

Fourth, for Freud, the unconscious is the most powerful *constitutive* force in shaping how we behave and think. This is why it is so vital to self-preservation that the matters we repressed in the unconscious remain buried. They have become part of who we are. To release repressed materials, and to disrupt this part of our identity, would shatter emotional stability. Thus, if indeed O. J. murdered his wife, the chief reason that he might persist in repressing his memories would be that *admitting* them would destroy his mental stability. The guilt felt in becoming *conscious* of the *unconscious repression* of his deed would be too much for a person to bear. His sense of who he is depends upon his keeping repressed and hermetically sealed off from consciousness the matters he may have buried in his unconscious. These memories may emerge when the mind 'relaxes,' as in dreams or – in the O. J. case – perhaps nightmares.

Reverting again to Shakespeare, whom Freud loved so well,[3] recall how Hamlet seeks to entrap his murderous uncle, Claudius, into exposing the guilt he has tried to repress. "The play's the thing wherein I'll catch the *conscience* of the King," says the young prince (*Hamlet* II.ii.633). Had Hamlet been a Freudian, he perhaps might have said the '*unconscious*' of the king instead of "conscience" (a matter for speculation and amusement, best left aside for the moment). The import of his words, nevertheless, remains clear. The 'relaxed' atmosphere of an evening's entertainment is arranged by Hamlet in the form of a playlet produced by the unforgettable traveling players, Rosenkrantz and Guildenstern. In their little court stage drama, upon Hamlet's explicit instructions, these two enact the famous murder of a faraway king – one who also has his widowed wife taken as bride by the murderer, his own brother. As all lovers of *Hamlet* know, upon witnessing the dramatic murder, and being stung by the parallels with his own dark deed, Claudius becomes enraged and bolts from the scene. Playing a bit of the Freudian *avant la lettre*, Hamlet has all the proof he needs. Hamlet's uncle has been exposed to him as the murderer of the old king by the unmistakable symptoms of his repressed guilt. Thus, although normally we keep a tight lid on the things that we feel need to be hidden because our identities would be threatened by their exposure, sometimes it is possible to trick out what we repress. While our modern 'courts' of law would not permit the spectacles Hamlet employed to entrap a suspect, one cannot help but wonder what would have happened had Judge Ito of the Simpson trial permitted a modern Hollywood Rosenkrantz and Guildenstern to work their stage magic in his courtroom.

The Structure of the Self: Ego, Superego, and Id

The originality of Freud's psychology is not limited to his theory of the unconscious. His way of looking at the workings of the human self are *dynamic* too. The human self, already a mixture of conscious and unconscious, now is revealed as a dramatic system of pressures and drives, made up of three components – ego, superego, and id.

At the most basic level – the "id" – people are still beasts, and as such are driven by the same biological needs, by the same bestial survival instincts. When we are hungry, we want to eat; when our lives are threatened, we fight to resist our attackers; when we are sexually stimulated, we want to achieve gratification, and so on. The id's deep origins in our animal natures are unconscious to us, although we have all felt and recognized the powerful compulsions associated with the id and its cravings for satisfaction.

In Freud's view, left to ourselves as *id*-driven beasts, we would never have evolved into a species that could be called 'human.' We would simply be raging appetites seeking satisfaction – we would act 'beastly,' so to speak. Luckily for the survival of a human species that rises above the level of beasts, the energy of the id is restrained. Freud calls that salutary engine of restraint upon the surging energies of the id the "superego." Freud identified the superego with morality, with the disciplining function of norms and values, such as those, for example, that Max Weber identified with the "worldly ascetic" *values* that guided capitalist enterprise. The mention of Weber here is deliberate because both he and Freud believed that however unpleasant the disciplining of our pleasure-seeking urges might be, that without them we could not have civilization. We would not have truly *human* life, organized on a large scale or not. We nevertheless pay a price for "civilization." These are what Freud referred to in the title of his classic on this great human dilemma – *Civilization and Its Discontents* (1930). If we think for a moment again of Max Weber returning from a season of debauchery and drunkenness to the stern rebuke of his Protestant mother, we can get some of the flavor of this aching choice for men of Weber and Freud's generation. On the one side, the sweetness of pleasure without substantial achievements; on the other, the impatient 'discontents' of moral restraint, but richly rewarded with constructive enterprises rising to the sky. A 'Hobson's Choice' indeed, and one for which there was no real solution, only a prudent, if erratic zig-zag between extremes. Pleasure and the restraint of pleasure: can't live with them, can't live without them!

Understood as values, moral norms, and such, the *superego* spans the whole range of human possibility from conscious through preconscious to unconscious. The level of consciousness of superego will depend upon its place in the lives of particular individuals. Some people may be conscious of their values, others, whose values malinger in a preconscious land of poor memory, may temporarily forget theirs; while still other people will have repressed certain values because they cannot face them in the lives they have constructed for themselves at the time. What do soldiers, for example, who are trained and conditioned to kill, do with their love of living things? What does a woman who feels it is wrong to abort a fetus do with that value because she has chosen to abort rather than carrying her baby to term? Repression is everywhere, and mighty.

As for the "*ego*," Freud is quick to dispatch it to the realm of relative unimportance. As he tells us in *Civilization and Its Discontents*: "Normally, there is nothing of which we are more certain than the feeling of our self, of our own ego. This ego appears to us as something autonomous and unitary, marked off distinctly from everything else" (Freud 1961, pp. 12–13). The ego is our normal self-consciousness, our waking, rational, and willing mind. Our awareness of the ego gives us a certain feeling of confidence that we are in control of our own selves. But, as we may gather from what has been said about the powers of the id and superego, Freud thinks that it the weakest of the three components of the self. It is thus "deceptive" to think of our conscious selves as most people do "normally." The human ego sits at the meeting points of the conflicting pressures flowing from the extremes of our make-up. Instead of the autonomous ego, 'normally' experienced by 'normal' people, "the ego is continued inwards, without any sharp delimitation, into an unconscious mental entity which we designate as the id and for which it serves as a kind of facade" (Freud 1961, p. 13). Instead of enjoying a false independence, this ego hangs onto the 'tail' of wild, biologically rooted, bestial id-drives until our 'lion tamer' superego brings the id to heel by applying the moral brakes and societal pressures that maintain a civilized life. But, in actuality, the most the ego can do is try to 'choose' the right balance between id-originated pleasure and the 'discontents' of pleasure's denials effected by the superego (Pals 1996, pp. 57–62). Given the imbalance of power between the unconscious and conscious, Freud is not optimistic that such choices will be free ones. Now the question becomes how this creative theoretical machinery can be wheeled in to *explain* and understand religion.

Totemism, Taboo, and Sacrifice: A Father's Burden to Bear

One way to appreciate the power and distinctiveness of Freud's explanations of religion is to focus narrowly on Freud and him alone. Another, and to me more preferable, way is to bring out Freud's distinctiveness by comparing Freud with some of the earlier figures we have met in the field of religious studies. Fortunately, Freud was a great reader of William Robertson Smith and James Frazer. He not only enjoyed what they wrote on religion, he also relied heavily upon them in two of his four main writings on religion, *Totem and Taboo* (1913) and *Moses and Monotheism* (1939). While the other two studies relying on religion, *The Future of an Illusion* (1927) and *Civilization and Its Discontents* (1930), do not dwell on Robertson Smith and Frazer as the first pair do, they nonetheless review the subjects of taboo and totemisms, thus bearing witness to the continued importance of these two great figures of the English school of anthropology for Freud.

But one point must be emphasized here in terms of Freud's relation to these anthropologists. To wit, however highly he may have esteemed the work of Robertson Smith and Frazer, Freud was not their slavish imitator. What Freud did with the materials with which those men provided him placed him into another class of students of religion altogether. No less an expert on Frazer than Robert Ackerman speaks ominously of Freud going "beyond Frazer in his investigations into the volcano" (Ackerman 1987, p. 213). I should like to complete this chapter by showing precisely how Freud established an entirely new approach to the study of religion by 'standing on the shoulders,' as it were, of his two great predecessors, Robertson Smith and Frazer.

The three great themes that Freud found irresistible in the work of Robertson Smith, and to some degree in Frazer, were totemism, taboo, and sacrifice. Freud took these themes and not only reinterpreted them, but placed them firmly in the context of his psychodynamic and psychoanalytic interpretation of the formation of the human self. With Freud, then, we get more than just an historical or social account of the institutions of totemism, taboo, and sacrifice, for example, but a psychological *explanation* of why these institutions took the social and historical form that they did. What, Freud asks, was the most fundamental – deep – reason for the sacrifice of the king at Nemi that puzzled Frazer, or for the joyous communal eating of the sacrificed totem that Robertson Smith reported among the Semites?

Let us look at Robertson Smith first. We will recall that Robertson Smith saw the ideas of totem, taboo, and sacrifice as intimately related to one another. Freud did as well. Indeed, he accepted all of Robertson Smith's general conclusions before adding his own special angle. We know from our discussion of Robertson Smith that his researches were meant to undermine the claims of Christianity to autonomy or uniqueness. He did this by showing that Christian rites and beliefs were foreshadowed by ancient 'pagan,' pre-Christian *and* pre-Jewish ones. Therefore, both Jewish and Christian religions owed great debts to the religious practices and insights of religious folk who came before them. Thus, along with Robertson Smith, Freud believed that totemism – worship of a 'totem' animal, at least provisionally – was the earliest form of religion. This worship took the form of a communal rite in which the totem was sacrificed, then shared and eaten by the entire community. Most important of all, it was by means of this common totemic, sacrificial banquet that the community achieved and enjoyed union with their deity. Robertson Smith drew this picture to suggest that these ancient totemic rites were actual historical precursors of the Christian, and primarily Catholic, Eucharist – which indeed Freud believed as well.

But Freud believed the rites described by Robertson Smith had considerably more significance. For starters, what Freud believed was something that he felt not only applied to the Semitic or even Western religious traditions, but to *all* religions everywhere and at all times. Therefore, Freud felt that he had discovered something with *universal* implications, and not just conclusions about the religions of the Semites or the West – as important as these nevertheless were for Christian self-understanding. For one thing, he believed that all animal sacrifices were only symbolic of an even earlier level of religious practice in which the main victim in the sacrificial killing was a human being! But, particularly in the first instance of these rites, the victim was not just any human. It was a certain specified person, fulfilling the role of father of the band. Let me explain. Following Darwin, Freud accepted that the earliest forms of human society were small bands. To Darwin's idea, Freud added that these primeval bands were mainly composed of brothers – males related by common blood to a common father – and dominated by that powerful father. Seeking selfishly to maintain a monopoly over sexual access to the females in the band, the father denied his sons the sexual pleasure and rights of generation that he enjoyed. As Freud saw it, this denial of sexual access made the brothers in the band deeply resentful and blindly angry. So infuriated were they with the father's tyranny and his monopolization of sexual partners that at one crucial point, the brothers rebelled *en masse*, killed their own father, and indulged the sexual appetites which had so long been frustrated. This murder of the father was of course a great crime, never mind the subsequent sexual chaos. The murder, however, developed a religious character and was seen as initiating sacrifice. This analysis reflects Freud's hostility to religion. Since the murder of the father founded religion as Freud saw it, the circumstances of that killing are significant. For Freud, this primal sacrifice is flavored with a hostility to religion, implicit in the vengeful motivations of the fraternal horde that is altogether lacking in the idea of sacrifice as a joyful communal meal shared between humans and their god as related by Robertson Smith.

An Oedipal Interlude

In Freudian parlance, this murder of the father by the son (or sons) and the subsequent sexual relations enjoyed by the brothers with his former wives gave rise to what is known as the famous "Oedipus complex" that later afflicted the brothers. The term is drawn from an ancient Greek myth that tells the tragic story of Oedipus. A boy child born of royal parents, Oedipus's birth is deemed inauspicious, in part because a soothsayer predicts that Oedipus will kill his father and marry his mother. To evade this fate, the king, Oedipus's father, has the infant abandoned in a wilderness so that he might be destroyed by wild beasts. As fate would have it, a shepherd rescues the child and raises it as his own son into adulthood. One day the king is abroad and meets the adult Oedipus at a pass on a highway. Neither the king nor Oedipus will yield right of way. A struggle ensues, and Oedipus slays the man that, unbeknownst to him, is his own father. Proceeding to the royal city some time later, Oedipus meets the widowed queen. Mutually attracted to one another, they marry and produce children of their own. Throughout, neither knows the identity of the other or Oedipus's role in the death of the former king. Once these secrets are revealed, however, the horror of the situation drives Oedipus and his wife–mother into emotional ruin. The queen commits suicide; Oedipus inflicts blindness upon himself in a vain attempt to alleviate his guilt.

For Freud, this drama holds many powerful lessons. The most germane for us is its indirect psychodynamic lesson: male children secretly desire to possess their mothers entirely and eliminate their fathers. What is repressed in our own unconscious seems to have been brought out into the open by the Greeks – as if some ancient Greek forerunner of Freud's incorporated the drama into a kind of therapy, to wake up the Greeks to their own repressed desires! This is but open speculation, but it is oddly enough like Prince Hamlet's playing of the king to make his unconscious repressions explode into the full and incriminating view of one and all: "The play's the thing wherein" drama will penetrate to the *unconscious* of the King and the Greeks attending the play of *Oedipus*, staged by our ancient Greek anticipation of Freud! Having noted the genesis of this Oedipal syndrome in Freud's mind, let us return to the dilemma faced by the murderous brothers.

Oedipal Consequences

Like all actions, the brothers' murder of their common father would have unforeseen consequences. In this case, because of the enormity of the act, the murder would be laden with ambiguities. On the one hand, while the brothers were overjoyed by having overthrown their tyrannical father, they realized that they had after all committed a terrible crime in murdering him. A father, even an unjust one, is still a father. The brothers responded to their complex feelings of joy and guilt by inaugurating a series of actions designed to embrace both aspects of their ambivalent feelings. These reactions to the primeval parricide are for Freud still alive and active in religion today the world over.

Responding, first, to their feelings of guilt – of sin – the brothers *repressed* the actual nature of what they did. In an *unconscious* attempt to distract themselves from coming to terms with their egregious act, and as well to make up for their misdeed, they began to revere and honor, and eventually to worship, their dead father – who, though now dead, is conceived to exist in a heavenly realm above this world. The brothers, in effect, invent *religion* by projecting the image of the dead father into the heavens, later to be regarded as a fit object of worship and devotion. The brutal father who sought to keep all the band's women for himself now becomes our father in heaven. The gods are born. In order to keep alive the sacred memory of the father, periodic animal sacrifice was thus inaugurated. Religious ritual practice begins to take place, the first of which was what Robertson Smith and Frazer would call totemism. The animal to be sacrificed in memory of the father was chosen as a fitting symbol of the band. And since the father had been the head of the band, the totem animal now was seen as the main symbol of the community. The totemic sacrifice served as a fitting commemoration, or ritual reenactment, of the slaying of the father, since it too, of course, was quintessentially a killing, and a killing of the being that symbolically represented tribe and father. Furthermore, because sacrifice demanded the giving up of something that was precious to the sacrificers, it functioned to propitiate their guilt and to mitigate their original sin of murder. The brothers and their successors tried to make up for their crime by thus depriving themselves of precious things, such as a prize animal from their herds. It was common as well for the successors of the murderous brothers likewise to inflict pain upon *themselves* in an effort to expiate their crime. This was, from Freud's point of view, how all religions really began, with a nexus of the feelings of guilt and sinfulness, the worship of heavenly father gods, bloody sacrifice to them in expiation for sin, and so on.

But since ambivalence reigned over the killing of the father, elements of joy would persist as well as sorrow and guilt. After all, the brothers were now liberated from the demeaning tyranny of the father and now free to become fathers and adults themselves. This is Freud's explanation for the joyous nature of the communal meal eaten by the community after the totem animal sacrifices, or for the totemic sacrificing community weeping over the animal that they had just killed sacrificially. The community felt that its self-assertion also earned it a degree of self-respect. This too was a cause – deep-running and silent, to be sure – for the joy felt at totemic rites. But joy arose partly because in the communal eating of the sacrificial victim, the entire community felt that it had regained union with the father, but on terms more in keeping with their own sense of self-respect and adulthood. While religious devotees surely feel the sense of dependence and submission to the will of the father characterizing religious attitudes, in Freud's view at least, they feel an abiding sense of joy in communion with the father along with a peace of mind that comes with the acknowledgment of unwavering divine authority.

Such a far-fetched tale would have little chance of acceptance today, one would hope. But, in Freud's day, we must recall that the possibility of literal readings of evolutionary accounts of early human social life was still taken seriously. Freud for one believed his story of the parricidal band of brothers more or less literally. He actually believed that there really had been primal hordes of early humans, and that there probably had been something like the original murder of the father that he described, and all the rest. Peoples living in the world many centuries removed from those foundational events, still bore memories of them. This idea of a kind of human collective memory will be picked up and exploited by one of Freud's most illustrious students, notably Carl Gustav Jung, and in turn by someone deeply influenced by Jung, Mircea Eliade, whom we will meet in the final chapter of this book.

Mighty Mothers and Their Dying and Rising Sons

Freud's transcending of Frazer's studies of religion gives us another opportunity to appreciate the way Freud approaches other domains of religion than those that emerge in his meditations on Robertson Smith and the origins of religious notions such as the father god, sin and guilt, sacrificial expiation, Eucharist and communion, and so on. Whatever else one may think of Freud's contributions to understanding these aspects of religion, the extravagant creativity and originality of Freud's interpretations are wonders of the human imagination. The second example that I shall use to demonstrate how Freudians can raise interesting questions about the nature of religion can be found in Freudian Michael Carroll's attempt to account for the psychoanalytic origins of the cult of the Virgin Mary. Without committing to the validity of Carroll's controversial arguments, his work makes an excellent example of a fresh use of Freudian attempts to explain religious phenomena that readers will find surprising and illuminating. Another reason for using Carroll's analyses is that they let us compare his Freudian approach to the way Frazer takes on the same materials. Both Carroll and Frazer are puzzled, as we will see, by the same religious mysteries of male asceticism intimately connected with the worship of the mother goddess in the ancient Mediterranean (Carroll 1992).

Moreover, Carroll's Freudian approach to the worship of Mary also helps us understand some of the puzzles we encountered in the life and works of Max Weber, and which I anticipated in the life and work of the (part-time) Freudian, Bronislaw Malinowski. Carroll attempts to show that the "asceticism" discussed by Max Weber originated in the same primal psychological dramas of putting aside the father, and the guilt felt for so doing, that we have just discussed in connection with Robertson Smith and totemic sacrifice. Although Carroll does not himself discuss Weber, his work suggests intriguing lines of inquiry. In an attempt to make good for guilt felt for their 'sins against the father,' people denied themselves pleasure or caused themselves pain. Without going deeply into Weber's case, this should at least make us think again both of Max Weber's personal travails and the obsessions evident in his scholarship. On the personal side, his inability to consummate his marriage, his pained agonizing over the enjoyment of simple pleasures, the deep shock over his mother's rebuke for his carousing student life – all point to deep disquiet, and dare I say it, Freudian "repression." Whatever really 'lies beneath,' there is surely something psychologically significant here. On the side of Weber's scholarship, we may add his lifelong fascination with Protestant asceticism, even though he was not conventionally religious. Taken together, the strong ascetic strands in Weber's life and scholarship only add to the mysteries lurking beneath the surface. I believe that what Carroll has to say about the cult of the Virgin Mary will shed light upon how a Freudian would *interpret* and *explain* these puzzles.

Let us review what Frazer attempted along these lines first. Like Robertson Smith, Frazer sought to undermine Christian uniqueness. As we know, so did Freud; so as well does Carroll. Frazer's way was to expose how early Christians 'baptized' pagan customs, beliefs, and practices, and converted them into Christian ones. Freud's way was to show that deeper psychological structures, common to all human beings, and involving universal dynamics among ego, superego, and id, would serve to provide a more profound account of Christianity's foibles. Agreeable as he was to Frazer's program of delegitimating Christianity, Freud wanted to do much, much more.

For Frazer, many of the Catholic saints of the Mediterranean world have uncanny resemblances to older pagan gods and goddesses. Now, Frazer argued that despite their being 'baptized,' the old pagan 'template' shone through. It remained despite attempts to Christianize it. Indeed, in this way pagan religion actually changed early Christianity. For example, the god-hero Attis, Frazer believed, was a prototype of Jesus. Carroll believes that Attis's life and death, as we will see, may have provided a template upon which the story of Jesus was written. His self-inflicted castration, as related by Frazer, further holds the secrets of such bizarre religious practices as the asceticism described by Weber (Frazer 1958, p. 407). Mary too was foreshadowed by the Mediterranean image of the Great Mother, a powerful goddess and often mother of the gods as well. Was not she preeminently recognized by early Christians as "Holy Mary, mother of God"?

This belief that the old Catholic practice of 'baptizing' pagan religious individuals, practices, and such effected a corruption of pure Christianity was one reason that the Protestant Reformers purged Christianity of the cults of the saints, holy places, and so on. This was what Max Weber described as the Protestant Reformation's "disenchantment" of the world. For the Reformers, Christianity could not incorporate non-Christian features, however well intended they might be, without corrupting its true nature. This purifying mania was one reason, for example, that the celebration of Christmas, with its 'survivals' of pre-Christian elements such as the Christmas tree, was forbidden by the English Reformers known to us as the Puritans.

The particular case Frazer delighted in parading before the public in *The Golden Bough* was the salacious story of that mother goddess, Cybele. and her son (or, in some versions, her lover), Attis. Frazer, as we will recall, felt that their story foreshadowed that of Mary and Jesus. Attis is, like Jesus, a Good Shepherd or herdsman. Like Jesus again, Attis was born to a virgin, or in some other miraculous way. For her part, Cybele is celebrated like Mary as 'mother of the gods' and depicted as the Great Mother, a kind of earth mother (see figure 9.1.). As a goddess, she brings life to the land. Mary is correspondingly "full of grace," and God's chosen vehicle for conveying Christ, the giver of divine life, to the world. Pressing the analogies further, Frazer relates that a reasonable consensus of accounts of Attis describes his death in terms of hanging from a tree, his burial as being laid in a sepulchre, and most stunning of all, his *resurrection* shortly thereafter on or about the date of Easter – the vernal equinox! Finally, harkening to Robertson Smith's and Freud's totemic communion notions, the devotees of Attis celebrate and commemorate his death and resurrection with a sacramental meal and communion that Frazer called, in full awareness of the implications of the term, a "blessed sacrament."

Figure 9.1. The Madonna of Sorbo with the infant Jesus, echoing motifs of the Great Mother with the infant, Attis (see also figure 6.1). From thirteenth-century wall painting in Santa Maria del Sorbo, Campagnano, Italy.

Source: J. Wilpert, *Die Römischen Mosaiken und Malereien der Kirchlichen Bauten vom iv. bis xiii. Jahrhundert: Unter den Auspizien und mit allerhöchster Förderung Seiner Majestät Kaiser Wilhelms II* (Freiburg im Breisgau: Herder, 1916).

These parallels gave Frazer lavish opportunities to indict Christianity, especially Roman Catholicism, as resting – unawares, *unconsciously* – on a template of 'primitive' religious practices and beliefs. Nevertheless, both Christian and pagan instincts, as embodied respectively in the Jesus and Attis stories, ought to be respected to some degree, as Frazer implies. Both, after all, seem to recognize the mysteries and value of life, even though they approach the enhancement of life by their benighted and primitive magico-religious means. His task was to expose modern Christianity as perpetuating these primitive ways of coping with human mortality. Once that was done, Frazer had pretty much finished what he had started to do. But here is where a Freudian like Michael Carroll picks things up, and applies the interpretive and explanatory approaches of Freud.

Some Questions about the Cult of the Virgin Mary, and Some Possible Replies

Carroll's book begins with the puzzle of the origins of the Marian cult. Why is there a cult of the Virgin Mary at all? Why is she worshiped and celebrated, especially among Catholic and Orthodox Christians? Why and how is it that she is conceived at the same time as both an ever-pure and perfectly chaste – 'ascetic' – virgin, and a bounteous, nubile, life-giving mother? How is it that she is believed to have conceived of her son, Jesus, without having had sexual intercourse with her husband or with any other being? Why is she believed to have given birth to Jesus "immaculately" – without taint of sin – and through the direct intervention of the third person of the Trinity, the Holy Spirit? Why is she believed to have never died, but instead to have been 'assumed' alive and bodily into heaven, or as the eastern Orthodox tradition sees her, to have 'fallen asleep' – in the state of suspended animation, the "dormition"? Why does she have the power to effect miracles in the world? And why, finally, in her heavenly abode, can Mary be the eternal object of devotion and prayer, and serve as a most powerful intermediary between God – either as Father or as Son – and human beings?

To some people – Roman Catholic believers, for instance – there are obvious religious or 'supernaturalist' answers to these questions. There are no problems with any of these queries because it is just *true* – by virtue of divine miraculous power, if necessary – that Mary was miraculously both virgin and mother, that she was divinely preserved from sin, and 'magically' assumed into heaven. There, in that supernatural realm of heaven, she serves as primary spiritual intercessor between Jesus and humans, also able to appear fantastically by virtue of divine power to her devotees on occasions where God determines that direct religious experience of her is necessary for his divine plan for humanity, and so on.

At least two problems prevent the Freudians from quietly acceding to the supernaturalist explanation that, in effect, such and such religious statements about Mary in my list of queries are just *true*. First, although this kind of answer may satisfy those who already *believe* in Mary's supernatural nature, it would not satisfy those many who do not, such as most Protestant Christians as well as non-Christians. As such, it could not serve as general public discourse about Mary, but would only be the way some segment of people in the world talked about her – her devotees. The supernaturalist way of talking about Mary would, as well, not be something that we could confirm by ordinary experience – one of the few common denominators among people for getting at even humble truths.

What about those of us who are not blessed with supernatural vision, or the 'eye of wisdom' that Krishna grants Arjuna to enable him to see the divine form of the Hindu god? Second, and in some ways even more puzzling, is why most of these beliefs came into being only 400 years or so *after* the time of Mary and Jesus, and then in only certain parts of the Christian world and not in others. Mary was not the object of a cult until almost 400 years after the time of Jesus, and then *not* necessarily for her virginity or only for being the mother of Jesus.

If, given the academic and public context of our inquiry in this book, we then put supernaturalist answers to my questions to one side, are we left with no alternative source of reply to my questions than the one a Freudian like Carroll will offer? There is at least one other approach, which by now we should know well – the phenomenological approach. Might not phenomenologists of religion be able to offer informative answers to the questions about the supernatural status of Mary and the Marian cult, and still remain within the realm of public academic discourse? Might they not offer *understanding*, if not a full *explanation*?

In adopting the phenomenological approach, for example, we would first seek the believer's point of view and empathize with it. But, unlike the believer, the phenomenologist does not commit either to the truth or falsity of these supernatural claims about Mary. Phenomenologists instead invoke the spirit of *epoché* and *bracket out* the question of the truth or falsity of these claims of Marian theology. Phenomenologists would say that by means of empathy and assuming the 'native's point of view,' we can at least begin to *understand* why the Marian cult exists among Roman Catholics. We can begin to *understand* what the Marian cult *means* to Roman Catholics, and how, therefore, it makes a kind of sense to them.

Indeed, the answers to our questions come easily if we adapt Ninian Smart's approach to this question and see how various beliefs are internally linked to practices, such as ritual practice, and give *meaning* to these practices. Devotees of the Marian cult *worship* Mary because of their belief in her sanctity. The rituals and beliefs likewise would help *make sense* of other "dimensions" of religion that Smart introduces into the approaches of phenomenology of religion, such as the formation of Marian sodalities, social organizations, or religious clubs, pledged, for instance, to emulating her purity and to committing to an ethic of chastity. Thus, as Smart might explain, according to Catholic *belief*, Mary was the mother of Jesus, and consequently deserves the honor of being the object of a *cult* or *rite*, and to no one's surprise also the subject of religious *experiences*, such as visions and apparitions of Mary to her faithful devotees. What else would one expect?

Once we thus had grasped these "dynamic" relations among dimensions of religion, Smart and other phenomenologists of religion would say that we had *understood* why there was a 'cult' of the Virgin Mary. Reverting once more to our example of trying to give an account of what occurs in a basketball game, the phenomenologist would have appealed to how certain moves in the course of the game produced certain results and not others. Even though players from one team handled the ball properly, had not taken steps without dribbling, and so on, they may, for example, have failed to bring the ball across half court in sufficient time, and been forced to surrender the ball to their opponents. We could *understand* and indeed in a way *explain* – simply and solely in terms of the rules internal to the game of basketball – that the first team had to surrender the ball, because they had failed to bring the ball across half court in sufficient time. For the 'phenomenologist of basketball,' that would be the end of the story. For the phenomenologist of religion, like Ninian Smart, citing the interconnections among belief, practice, experience – all dimensions internal to Marian religion – likewise would be the end of their story. They would have *understood* what was occurring in Marian religion.

But once we get some external purchase on the Marian cult, not even the phenomenologists of religion would seem to have answers to the questions one might ask. Once more, as I put it to the believers, why is it that no cult of Mary existed until 400 years or so *after* the time of Christ, and then only in certain parts of the Christian world and not in others? This would be analogous to our asking the 'phenomenologist of basketball' why certain players failed to remember that the ball had to be advanced beyond half court within a certain time. Since the question is really about matters *external* to the inner workings of the game, one would not expect there to be any answer forthcoming. Here, then is where Michael Carroll applies a Freudian approach to explain the coming into existence of the Marian cult – an explanation that will as well gather up some of the loose ends, left deliberately hanging, about Frazer's approach to Cybele and Attis, as well as the inner torments of Weber's life and the parallel tensions in his work.

A Freudian Explanation of the Marian Cult

Carroll first of all observes not only that the Marian cult comes relatively late to Christianity, but that its beginnings are particular to areas in the southern Mediterranean basin. And, since the Marian cult thus seems a very *particular* historical phenomenon, it calls out for *particular* causes. Delving further into its particularity, Carroll also claims that the first devotees of the Marian cult were recruited from populations of rootless young men, typically displaced from their home provinces of what is now north Africa, Spain, and other portions of southern Europe, to seek work in the metropolis, Rome. It was among these populations that rather exuberant and emotional Marian cults first arose as lower-class religious phenomena.

Although we generally think of early Christianity as a religion of the poor, in the Rome of the fourth century it was the property of a dignified aristocracy of Christian families. It was doubtless inevitable that the two styles of spirituality would clash, even as their economic interests and identities would. And they did. The newer Marian forms of religious practice, however, gradually gained acceptance into the mainstream of Christian life in Rome. This happened partly in response to the sheer numbers of the upstart Marian devotees, since the newcomers soon swamped the population of the somewhat staid older urban Roman Christians. After a period of agitation for recognition of the Marian cult, the church worked out a way to include the new spirituality. The official triumph of this new Marian spirituality can in fact be dated, Carroll argues, to two great church councils – Ephesus (431 CE) and Chalcedon (451 CE). Ephesus declared that Mary was what the Greeks called the "*theotokos*" – the God-bearer. In our parlance, this would be the "mother of God." For Carroll, Mary's elevation to this level, in effect, made her a kind of goddess. For its part, Chalcedon only accentuated this deification of Mary by promulgating the doctrine that she was eternally a virgin, even after having given birth to Jesus. Mary had thus been miraculously conditioned, and could no longer be regarded as just another person or even just another saint. She was very special. These conciliar declarations marked a kind of legitimation of the Marian cult by, in effect, imbuing her with divine qualities. They marked the triumph of a new spirituality that had swept in from the outer reaches of the Empire into the metropole.

At the same time as this legitimation of the Marian cult was under way, Carroll notes that the fourth century also marked the rise of what appear at first glance to be other distinct new religious movements and developments. Carroll claims, for example, that the origins of today's controversies over an exclusively male priesthood, in effect, can be dated to the fourth century in Rome, since it was then that such an exclusion of women from the priesthood became codified. Further, the drive to require male celibacy in the Roman priesthood culminated in the fourth century with its official approval and canonical enforcement. By contrast, the Eastern Orthodox and eastern rites of Christianity still retain a married clergy. In the fourth century as well, for the first time, the image of the suffering, dying, tortured, crucified Jesus gradually came into prominence. Likewise, bloody sacrificial language increasingly came to be used about the Eucharist. I mention these changes because Carroll believes they are not at all distinct from the dynamics that gave rise to the Marian cult. For Carroll, their rise and the rise of the Marian cult are one and the same. Before, however, I show how Carroll links these apparently disparate phenomena, let me turn to the data that Carroll assembles about the psychological and social conditions of the devotees of the Marian cult.

In addition to these historical facts, Carroll also claims we know significant things about the nurture and family situations of these young male devotees of Mary. He claims that because of economic and political instability in the southern Roman provinces, families were somewhat thrown into disarray. Fathers were often absent from the home for significant lengths of time, leaving the women of the household in charge. And, even when the fathers would return from time to time from their efforts abroad, they could not really reestablish male authority in households now accustomed to stronger female presences than had been the rule in more settled times. The young men of these households grew up in conditions of strong assertive mothers and weak or remote fathers. As a result, from their earliest years, they identified with their mothers, given that they were for the most part the only available adults to provide strong and constant role models of adulthood. Given the realities of the incessant power of the "id," they also wanted to possess their mothers sexually, and monopolize their love exclusively. The young men resented their inconstant and bothersome fathers, who although seldom on hand to take responsibility for the family, would return and presume ownership of their wives, the beloved mothers of these young men. They secretly wished to eliminate these interloper fathers altogether, perhaps by murdering them, as the band of brothers in Freud's account of the origins of religion did.

At some point, the pressures of superego forces acting upon these young men led them to recognize that they could not murder their fathers. The superego told them that it would be wrong, no matter how ill-disposed they felt towards their oppressive fathers. The youths were overcome with guilt, but because their notional act was so horrendous, they buried it deep in their unconscious by *repressing* it in the same ways they had earlier *repressed* their original desire to murder their father. Later, as well, these disturbances in their feelings became even greater, as these young boys became pubescent young men. In deep embarrassment, they realized that identification with their mothers challenged their identities as males. If recognized by themselves or other males, displays of identification with their mothers would become an immense source of embarrassment. No young man just coming into his manhood wants to be tagged as a 'momma's boy.' Indeed, they will do almost anything to fend off such charges of being effeminate. Acting tough and coarse in front of their peers, engaging in violent or dangerous sports, often provide a way for such mother-identified young men to hide the things they have repressed into their unconscious. Some such young men may even try to fend off their gender confusions by exaggerating their masculinity in displays of 'macho' behavior. It was as if these troubled young men, haunted by the female images of perfect adulthood that they had had unconsciously imprinted upon themselves as prepubescent youths, were trying to tell themselves that they were *real* men by behaving in exaggerated male ways.

In the cases Carroll investigated, these mother-identified young men from father-ineffective families typically sought out places where they could escape both their dysfunctional family scenes and the scarcity of economic opportunities in the provinces. Formed under these psychological conditions, many of these young men migrated in significant numbers to the city of Rome to seek employment and better lives. But though they might change their base of operations from countryside to town, so to speak, they could not escape their psychologies – the complex of deeply repressed feelings now lodged in the darkest recesses of their unconscious. Deprived as they had been from their early years of economic and familial stability of life, they carried with themselves to Rome the same confusion and psychological burdens of weak male role models and strong unconscious identification with their mothers. From this dynamic psychological ground, Carroll believed that the Marian cult sprang. But just how does Carroll pull these psychological factors together with what we know of the historical context and religious changes to make a plausible case for the "psychoanalytic" – Freudian – origins of the Marian cult?

On the face of it, Carroll will have his hands full. His case differs radically from the classic Freudian one involving father-killing and its associated feelings of guilt. Here, we have a case of goddess worship, and no expressions of guilt in connection with having 'killed' the mother, for example. Yet Carroll is not deterred. We have the standard Freudian Oedipal desire to kill the father and 'marry' the mother. We have, moreover, the makings of good psychoanalytic reasons for deifying the (strong) mother by worshiping her as a goddess, based upon unconscious repressions – a Freudian enough insight. In the case of these young men, we can readily admit it to be plausible that they should maintain their admiration for their mothers by projecting this out of the dangerous realm of human relations – potential incest with one's own real mother. Instead, then, of simply praising their actual mothers, or even less, seeking union with them, the young men now *project* their feelings for their earthly mothers onto a supernatural object – a mother goddess. They are free to seek and wish for total union with their heavenly mother in a way impossible with their earthly one: the devotees indeed 'fulfill' their wishes by reverting to religion. Such "wish fulfillment" is thus the core and origin of religion as much as the guilt of our murderous band of primeval brothers.

Carroll in fact suggests as much. These young men projected their conflicted feelings about their own mothers onto the convenient objects of the goddesses of religion, among them Mary. For these mother-identified, father-ineffectual men, Mary became at the one and the same time a goddess, worthy object of union, but safely preserved beyond access to their sexual advances, in heaven. At the feet of this perfect goddess, then, these males 'fulfill' their 'wishes' for union with the mother, and in that way could indulge their childhood feelings of identification with the feminine without risking incestuous relations with their own parent and without confusion with their own gender identities. But there were costs, as we will see.

What makes Carroll's analysis of these young Christian devotees of Mary especially powerful is that they were not alone. Nor were Mary and the Marian cult alone in the features found there. Something universal seems to be at work. Thus, in other parts of the empire a similar psychodynamic was working itself out with other similarly constituted male youths from other parts of the empire's Mediterranean territories – but now in relation to non-Christian mother goddesses, mostly notably in cults devoted to the Cybele that Frazer had found intriguing in *The Golden Bough*! Like Mary, non-Christian goddesses were explicitly available for worship, and indeed were conspicuously worshiped by young men with the same psychological profiles as the early devotees of Mary, as we will also see. Now a word about this so-called 'style.'

One thing that made this syndrome of goddess worship, both Christian and non-Christian, complex and troubling, but also very illuminating, was the costs to male identity that it entailed. The religious identification of the young men with Mary (or even other mother goddesses) entailed not only fierce, self-administered ascetic behavior, but also extreme forms of self-abuse and "masochism." Frazer, for example, described in detail, if somewhat prudishly, the spectacular features of this new religiosity of the goddess. Frazer first describes the fierce ascetic rites to which the devotees of the Great Mother submitted themselves. Here, we can recall his accounts of the spread to Rome from Asia Minor of the goddess worship of Cybele (and related to that, her son/lover, Attis). Frazer's reference to "emasculated priests" and "unsexed beings" in the citation portends something of the grotesque character of the rites of this religion that drew the interest of Carroll, and paints for us a vivid, if gruesome, picture of ways that Freudians think that religion can embody the dark secrets of the unconscious.

> We may conjecture, though we are not told, that the Mother of the Gods brought with her the worship of her youthful lover or son to her new home in the West. Certainly the Romans were familiar with the Galli, the emasculated priests of Attis, before the close of the Republic. These unsexed beings, in their Oriental costume, with little images suspended on their breasts, appear to have been a familiar sight in the streets of Rome, which they traversed in procession. (Frazer 1958, pp. 404–5)

Frazer also relates that the priests of this rite, the Galli or their superiors the Archigalli, officiated at a most ascetic rite. As Frazer is wont to do, he deliberately suggests, of course, that these 'pagan' rites will survive somehow in Christianity because both Christians and 'pagans' celebrate similar festivals on approximately the same dates. The rite here described was a fertility ritual and occurs on the date of the Christian version of a kind of Christian fertility festival – Easter, the celebration of the coming of the new life inaugurated by Jesus after his having suffered an awful violent death.

> The third day, the twenty-fourth of March, was known as the Day of Blood: the Archigallus or high priest drew blood from his arms and presented it as an offering. Nor was he alone in making this bloody sacrifice.... the inferior clergy... gashed their bodies with potsherds or slashed them with knives in order to bespatter the altar and the sacred tree with their flowing blood. (Frazer 1958, p. 405)

Then, as if not extreme enough in their ascetic practice, Frazer reports that these devotees to the Great Mother – all men – voluntarily mutilated themselves to the point of self-castration. Frazer reports that "it was on the same Day of Blood and for the same purpose that the novices sacrificed their virility...they dashed the severed portions of themselves against the image of the cruel goddess" (Frazer 1958, p. 405). Spelling out the gory details, Frazer tells us that these ascetic rites honoring the Great Mother, Cybele, took on a male-negating form that would be bound to draw the attention of a Freudian like Carroll: "man after man...flung his garments from him, leaped forth with a shout, and seizing one of the swords which stood ready for the purpose, castrated himself on the spot..." After having done the unmanning deed, the devotee put on "a suit of female attire and female ornaments, which he wore for the rest of his life" (Frazer 1958, pp. 406). These young men had, in effect, become 'women,' and as such constituted orders of "eunuch priests" that were well known across the southern portions of the Mediterranean basin and further to the east:

> Goddesses thus ministered to by eunuch priests were the great Artemis of Ephesus and the great Syrian Astarte of Hierapolis, whose sanctuary, frequented by swarms of pilgrims and enriched by the offerings of Assyria and Babylonia, of Arabia and Phoenicia, was perhaps in the days of its glory the most popular in the East. Now the unsexed priests of this Syrian goddess resembled those of Cybele so closely that some people took them to be the same. And the mode in which they dedicated themselves to the religious life was similar. (Frazer 1958, pp. 406)

Carroll notes that among these devotees of Mary and other 'goddesses,' such as Cybele, one should delve into a correlation that, at first glance, will surprise us. These young men, so eager now to negate their own male sexuality in religious rituals, were the same young males who had displayed their characteristic southern European machismo. One exaggerated form of male assertion – machismo – had now literally 'flipped' into its opposite – the ascetic and male negation of the devotees of the goddess. For Carroll, this is an invitation to wheel out the Freudian interpretive machinery, which he does with stunning imagination. To wit, in their particular psychological condition, the young men have repressed their feelings to be one with their mothers. First, this is expressed by exaggerated, and doubtless defensive, male behavior of 'machismo.' But, repressed though their deep feelings to be like their mothers are, given the right conditions they will emerge. And emerge they do in the gory rites of the Mother goddess. Instead of uniting sexually or otherwise with their real mothers, they project that image onto the heavens by worshiping a goddess, like Cybele, or of course Mary. In order to perfect this ritual identification with the Mother, some devotees even go so far as to alter their physical bodies to be like women – as Frazer notes, they remove the marker of male gender; they dress in women's clothing; and so on.

One last point remains. Although the new Christians may have devoted themselves to and identified themselves with Mary, they certainly do not seem to have engaged in the same self-mutilating or even gender-denying behavior. Carroll agrees. But this does not mean that Christianity avoids *ascetic* practice. Indeed, as we know from Max Weber, it is ascetic in many different forms. The other-worldly asceticism of the Catholic monastic tradition, notable for its suppression of sexual activity, as well as the worldly asceticism of Weber's "Protestant ethic," with its strong puritan militancy against sex, are but two cases in point. In both cases, male sexuality is put under wraps and restrained. For Carroll and his kind of Freudian, this would be for primarily psychodynamic reasons and not because of a religious experience of being "called" either to the contemplative life or to the life of worldly asceticism outside the monastery in capitalist enterprise. As we will now see with Malinowski, the ascetic ideal, often only identified with religion, can likewise show itself to be one of the psychodynamic effects of a particular kind of child-rearing. Malinowski's interpretation of religion is in part, at least, a reflection of essentially Freudian insights. Thus, although we will leave Freud as we move on to Malinowski, we should not forget all the possible ways of thinking about the causes of religious experience with which he has tantalized us.

Notes

1. See, for example, such workshops and conferences as "Mindfulness Meditation and its Clinical Applications" (2005), offered by the Institute for Meditation and Psychotherapy in collaboration with the Barre (Massachusetts) Center for Buddhist Studies: www.meditationandpsychotherapy.org/Current_Programs/Mar_05_Intensive.htm
2. Preus here cites Freud, *The Interpretation of Dreams*. New York: Modern Library, 1950.
3. However, Freud used Hamlet in quite a different way than I have – to dwell upon the themes of father-killing, mother-incest, and such. See Peter Gay, *Freud, Jews and Other Germans*. New York: Oxford University Press, 1978.

References

Ackerman, R. 1987. *J. G. Frazer: His Life and Work*. Cambridge: Cambridge University Press.

Carroll, M. P. 1992. *The Cult of the Virgin Mary: Psychological Origins*. Princeton: Princeton University Press.

Cioffi, F. 1970. Freud and the Idea of a Pseudo-Science. In *Explanation in the Social Sciences: Confrontations*, eds. R. Borger & F. Cioffi. Cambridge: Cambridge University Press.

Frazer, J. G. 1958. *The Golden Bough*. New York: Macmillan.

Freud, S. 1938. The Interpretation of Dreams. In *The Basic Writings of Sigmund Freud*, ed. A. A. Brill. New York City: Modern Library.

———. 1961. *Civilization and Its Discontents*, trans. J. Strachey. New York: W. W. Norton.

Fulton, P., ed. 2005. *Mindfulness and Psychotherapy*. New York: Guilford Press.

Lévi-Strauss, C. 1968. The Sorcerer and His Magic. In *Structural Anthropology*. London: Allen Lane.

Malinowski, B. 1948. Magic, Science and Religion. In *Magic, Science, and Religion*. New York City: Doubleday.

Otto, R. 1958. *The Idea of the Holy*, trans. J. W. Harvey. New York: Oxford University Press.

Pals, D. L. 1996. *Seven Theories of Religion*. New York: Oxford University Press.

Preus, J. S. 1987. *Explaining Religion*. New Haven: Yale University Press.

Ricoeur, P. 1970. *Freud and Philosophy: An Essay in Interpretation*. New Haven: Yale University Press.

Rieff, P. 1979. *Freud: The Mind of the Moralist*. Chicago: University of Chicago Press.

Skinner, B. F. 1999. From *About Behaviorism*. In *Problems in Mind: Readings in Contemporary Philosophy of Mind*, eds. I. Jack & S. Crumley. New York City: McGraw Hill.

10　Bronislaw Malinowski, Bipolarity, and the "Sublime Folly" of Religion

O death, where is thy sting? O grave, where is thy victory?

–1 Corinthians 15:52–5

His work will no doubt suffer periods of criticism and oblivion. Yet for those who will rediscover it after those intervals of shadow, from which no living thought escapes, it will without question hold the same vibrant freshness.

–Lévi-Strauss 1942, p. 45

Anthropology's Pragmatist

The gnawing effects of the 'worm of doubt' that Freud dropped into the midst of religious life are hard to overestimate, since it threatens to eat away at what seems the last solid place of security for religious consciousness – the autonomy of religious experience. If we begin to doubt the integrity of our own inner religious feelings and thoughts, just what safe harbor remains for the pious soul? If even our innermost religious experiences can no longer be trusted, many believers will have come up hard against a very substantial *problem of religion* indeed. And here I do not single out Christians. For those religious traditions centered on mental cultivation and meditation, such as many forms of Buddhism and Hinduism, the 'problem of religion' provoked by Freudian undermining of confidence in our own introspective powers is perhaps gravest of all. Part of the Buddha's claim to authority, for example, is to have given us a reliable 'map' of the pathways of mind, along with an accurate 'escape strategy' out of suffering and life's dead-ends (Strenski 1992). But, when the 'map' can no longer be trusted, nor the 'escape strategy' assured, what then?

As I hope we have learned throughout this volume, the story of the impact of 'problems of religion,' such as those thrown up by Freudian ideas and clinical practice, is not, of course, the *end* of the story. There never quite is an end to religious dispute. Problems are encountered only to be countered by solutions, and those solutions draw counterattacks of their own in their turn. In principle, there is no end to religious dispute – unless perhaps someone decides to withdraw from the field or surrender. In the case, for example, of problems of the status of religious experience, especially as they may affect

Buddhism, we find both vigorous 'solutions' to the 'problems' Freud provokes, but clever adaptations of Freud to bolster Buddhist conceptions of how the mind really works, and how Buddhist 'religious experience' fits in with even Freudian analyses (De Silva 1973; 1974). As we will see in our coming discussion of Durkheim, there may be different sources of religious experience of absolute dependence than childhood experiences of parental power. The religious experience of dependence and power may arise from our experience of collective life. Or, in the case of Mircea Eliade, Freud's 'worm of doubt' may also 'turn' on itself, so to speak. If Freud can show that religious experiences are *really* just disguised experiences of a powerful father or mother, perhaps an equally imaginative thinker, such as Eliade makes himself out to be, can show that these experiences of parental power are themselves only disguises of the sacred? Just as religious disputes can go on as long as the dialectic can be kept alive, so also can theoretical debates run on without any necessary reason to conclude. In the last analysis, theoretical imagination will have the last word.

In this chapter about the social anthropologist Bronislaw Malinowski (1884–1942), we will in part see some of the continuing legacy of Freud's critiques of religion. In the early part of the twentieth century, Malinowski was one of the earlier enthusiasts for the psychoanalytic movement of Freud within the social science community. He felt so strongly about the genius of Freud that he is reported to have sought nomination of the father of psychoanalysis for the 1938 Nobel Prize (Ellis 1936). This did not, however, imply Malinowski's being a sycophantic devotee of Freudian psychoanalysis. For some reason, Malinowski never really followed through with his attempts to adapt Freudian thought consistently to anthropology. And Malinowski's greatest claim to fame as a Freudian may be – ironically – his *criticism* of the universality of the Oedipus Complex (Stocking 1986, p. 42)! Nonetheless, in a good portion of Malinowski's work, especially that on religion, he believed that the theory of mental operations offered by Freud created real and insurmountable *problems of religion* that he, as a 'critic of religion,' welcomed.

Malinowski also figures in the overall story of the present volume for several other reasons. First, I would remind readers that he is very much a living part of the debates about the nature of religion and religious experience that we have tracked in the present volume. Recall, for instance, Malinowski's articulation of the phenomenological method of 'empathy.' But note especially how Malinowski links us directly to the first generation of anthropologists, such as Frazer, whom he knew personally, but also to the ethnographic traditions of empirical studies of small-scale societies popularized by Tylor and Robertson Smith. Malinowski was also deeply influenced by the sociologist Durkheim and his school. In turn, his *Argonauts of the Western Pacific* (1922) left a clear mark on the Durkheimian, Marcel Mauss, and his classic study of gift exchange, *The Gift* (1925). He, likewise, took careful aim on the theories of myth of Max Müller in his own considerable work on the nature of myth.

Second, Malinowski figures in this volume because, in addition to being part of the living conversation about earlier classic problems of religion, he also adds problems of his own – ones conditioned by his "pragmatism." While these can be looked on as further articulations of problems of religion analogous to those Freud raised, they nonetheless carry Malinowski into original territory as a 'critic of religion.' Malinowski finds that his studies of animal *biology* and *behaviorist* psychology throw up what he thinks are devastating problems of religion. Taken together with Freudian ideas, Malinowski produces what can be called a "pragmatist" or "pragmatic" critique of the sufficiency or autonomy of religious experience. While it is true that Malinowski's pragmatism was confirmed by his association with the famous American "pragmatist" philosopher and psychologist, William James – the very person who coined the term itself – Malinowski apparently had come to pragmatist conclusions about interpreting religion on his own (Young 2004, p. 82).

In Malinowski's hands, pragmatism becomes a powerful weapon forcing religion to square claims about its ultimate consequences and purposes with the *observable and measurable* results of being religious. Religious people may *say* one thing about why they are religious or the transcendent goals of being religious, but what about what we can see, feel, and hear with our own senses about the apparent *effects*, *functions*, and *consequences* – intended or unintended – of religion? Are these to be discounted? And, if not, how do they figure as possibly being the underlying reality of religious life? What if we *see*, for example, as Weber argued, that people who practiced certain forms of Protestantism were conspicuously more prosperous than their Roman Catholic neighbors who were in all other respects the same? Even if they discounted any connection between their religious affiliation and their economic performance, would we not tend to think, quite reasonably, that there might well be such a connection? Perhaps the 'cash value' of religious beliefs – their practical consequences or results – as it were, differs from what believers themselves imagine it to be, and that 'cash value' lies in the concrete practical effects of holding those beliefs?

No matter what religious people may *say*, for example, about the other-worldly realities revealed in religious myths and scriptures, Malinowski sees something else entirely. Malinowski, for example, calls myth a practical tool functioning to enhance real flesh and blood human survival, not a 'map' of the transcendent world or 'escape strategy' for eluding eternal death. Myth, in his words, is "indispensable" and "vital" – something a society needs; the proverbial 'crutch' without which people cannot materially persist (Malinowski 1992b, p. 82). Myth is thus not *really about the other world*, but is instead a "hard-worked active force," covering the "whole pragmatic reaction of man towards disease and death" and expressing "his emotions, his forebodings." As such, for Malinowski, myth is practically linked with our basic biological needs (Malinowski 1992b, p. 105). In using myth, the so-called 'primitive' is

> an eager actor, playing his part for his own benefit, trying to use all the means in his power towards the attainment of his various needs and desires. He is interested in all things which subserve these ends and...are thus immediately useful. (Malinowski 1962, p. 272)

In these later writings, Malinowski pressed his materialist utilitarianism to the extreme.

> The theory of myth, then, here propounded.... shows that the whole complex of cultural practices, beliefs, and myths expresses man's pragmatic reaction towards life and its vicissitudes. (Malinowski 1936, p. 310)

As he concedes to his audience in the 1931 Riddell Lectures, a "rationalist and agnostic" such as himself, "must admit that even if he himself cannot accept these truths [of religion], he must at least admit them as indispensable pragmatic figments without which civilization cannot exist" (Malinowski 1936, p. 62). He *must* admit them as such because he believes he has *seen* how religions *functions pragmatically* to hold society together.

For religion, as for myth, Malinowski, of course, does not believe it to be literally true. He thinks that accounts of 'another world' – of an Otto-like realm of the numinous, or of Max Müller's "Infinite" and so on – are false. But these religious images and concepts are much needed for most people to maintain order and a sense of meaning in their lives. Religion thus provides indispensable 'crutches.' And since religion *functions* to maintain social coherence, we need to keep religion on hand – if only for the pragmatic purposes it serves in keeping society from disintegrating. As a species, we humans simply cannot do without the fantasies of life after death, personal immortality, divine justice, or eternal blessedness that religion creates for us. As a *practical man*, despite his own private contempt for human weakness as revealed in religion, Malinowski is determined to conspire in maintaining religion in place. For the sake of social order and stability, after all, it is the only *practical* (*sic*) thing to do!

Bipolarity in Life and Letters

Knowing where Malinowski's thought comes to rest is, however, not enough for those of us who want to see inside the man and understand the 'madness in his methods,' to turn a phrase. In this chapter, I want to see that final resting place in relation to other orientations Malinowski pursued with equal vigor. Seeing how Malinowski shifted his theoretical ground can, I believe, give us an even greater insight into the heart of his thinking about religion, and perhaps explain what he does. In effect, doing this will mean turning a little bit of Freud back on Malinowski himself – a project about which Malinowski could hardly complain with any degree of consistency! Such a close, somewhat Freudian, look into Malinowski's life and work reveals evidence of what seems an almost clinical 'bipolarity' in thought and biography that gives rise to what I hope readers will find an interesting way to explore Malinowski's thinking about religion.

What I mean by Malinowski's bipolarities are, for example, oppositions in his life and work such as these. Beginning in orthodox Freudian fashion with Malinowski's parental situation, one notes that although Malinowski was virtually raised in the absence of his father by his mother and her family, and although she was to him the closest companion of his first 20 years, he always kept her at a distance from his most intimate thoughts. Could these be features of Malinowski's psychology common to those we saw (in the last chapter) afflicting the tormented young devotees of Mary in Michael Carroll's psychoanalytic explanation of the rise of the Marian cult in ancient Rome? First, in his younger years, partly because of his own father's emotional remoteness (parallels to Weber here), Malinowski identifies with his mother, but then as he comes into manhood, he needs to suppress this identification by such devices as emotional withdrawal from her as well as identification with aspects of the father, however remote. Thus, in his first vocational calling, Malinowski sought what some might cast as the 'feminine' career of an artist, especially when contrasted to his final decision to seek rigorous training in the more disciplined "masculine" (*sic*) fields of philosophy of science, mathematics, and physics at the Jagiellonian University in Cracow. Is this opposition between rebellion and conformism repeated at yet another level as well, in Malinowski's being for the most part the "sober scientist," yet nonetheless drawn to the excitement created by the Young Poland avant-garde movement of the *fin-de-siècle*? This esthetic and political avant-garde called Malinowski to the satisfaction of his own heightened erotic appetites, which, however, he opposed by resisting the total embrace of their debaucheries, and instead fixed his path on the strict discipline of a self-imposed regime of ascetic chastisement and purification. In religion, too, Malinowski engaged an atheistic humanism from an early age, but ironically one that nevertheless taught the identical puritan morality of the Catholic upbringing Malinowski sought to escape! Finally, although as urbane and cosmopolitan as any other member of his well-established, rather genteel social class, he sought out a career of relative deprivation in a remote anthropological field; while always attached to the ideal of Polish nationality, he wanted above all to be like his acquaintance and compatriot, Joseph Conrad, a 'British' Pole; although a devotee of positivist thinkers such as Max Planck, Richard Avenarius, and especially Ernst Mach, Malinowski devoured the writings of their opposite numbers, the antipositivists, Wilhelm Dilthey, Henri Bergson, and Friedrich Nietzsche (Young 2004, chs. 5–6).

We can round out our biographical considerations about Malinowski by noting their instructive polarities as well. On the one side, Malinowski was the consummate *professional* academic – a teacher of legendary repute at the London School of Economics from 1910 to 1939, author of a dozen or so books and about 50 or so articles and book reviews, Malinowski held forth on subjects as varied as economics, gift exchange, the family, myth, ritual, religion, language, totemism, sexual life and marriage, crime, and magic, all the while making one of the earliest efforts to engage the problems thrown up by the implications of Freudian thought for social science. Much of Malinowski's fame derived from promoting his own reputation as founder of the intense and systematic methods of fieldwork that he practiced in his six years of on-and-off study of the native people of the Massim peninsula of eastern Papua, and in some of the island groups off the east coast of Papua New Guinea – Mailu Island, the Amphletts, and the Trobriands. On the opposite side from Malinowski the 'professional' academic and scientist, there was also the active public intellectual of his London years. Beyond writing and teaching in ethnology, he wrote for the wider general reading public on folklore, literary criticism, linguistics, philosophy, psychology, psychoanalysis, religion, and, as I have noted, sexuality. Malinowski was an exciting and provocative thinker – one who tried to combine scientific styles of thinking with the big issues of life and death, and our so-called existential human problems. Such an interesting set of inner contradictions literally calls out for deeper explanation than I for one feel prepared to offer. At least, with these in mind, the readers of this book might be enticed to think harder about the deeper meanings of Malinowski's work than they might otherwise have been.

Bringing his professional academic and social activist sides together was Malinowski the teacher and mentor. After his studies at LSE, Malinowski put in six years or so of fieldwork, and there were wartime restrictions upon his travel in New Guinea and Australia. He would return to London in 1920 to begin what would be a two-decade long association with the LSE. In 1939, while visiting the United States, Malinowski had already been entertaining plans to emigrate to America. The advent of the Second World War forced his hand. During the early 1940s Malinowski lived in New York City, often making trips up to New Haven to give seminars at Yale, while teaching at the New School. He had also begun to do field studies of traditional economies in Mexico. In the year of his death, 1942, Malinowski accepted Yale's offer of an appointment to a permanent professorship there. He was, however, never to assume this post, since he died suddenly of a heart attack in May of that year.

It was in those two decades at the London School of Economics, I shall argue, that Malinowski made trend-breaking contributions to the advancement of women's professional training and advancement at the LSE. So marked is this effort at advancing women in the scientific field of anthropology, and so marked, as we have seen, are the other gender-charged 'psychodramas' of Malinowski's life, that one cannot but wonder what a good psychoanalyst would make of Malinowski's professional relation with so many of his women students. Malinowski's youngest daughter, Helena Wayne, noted that his efforts in behalf of the dignity of women in the profession of anthropology grew out of a genuine *sympathy* with his fellow 'outsiders' on the opposite side of the gender divide. Malinowski's women students, notes Mrs. Wayne,

> had great affection for him not just because he was attractive as a man, as his detractors have said, but because, in England at least, women were not really accepted in academic life, it was still cranky to go to university, and the middle-class woman was expected to be cultured but not really efficient at anything. As Audrey [Richards] put it, there was a horror of the clever woman, but [Malinowski]...didn't have it at all, and women blossomed in this atmosphere of being taken completely seriously. (Wayne 1985, p. 537)

But perhaps Mrs. Wayne just demonstrates the natural tendencies of a loving daughter to enhance the reputation of her father? Did Malinowski's behavior to women perhaps rather underline other paternalistic qualities of his character, so much easier to deploy over a more dependent audience? Or does it represent, perhaps, the avant-garde nurture of his youth, with its egalitarian ethos that became so apparent in his comfort in the company of clever and accomplished women – especially when this would have been so unusual in the 'patriarchal' British academic world of those days? One wonders as well what the same analyst would make of Malinowski's attractiveness for those very same women. Again, is paternalism at the root of this, or is it genuine regard and admiration for a true champion of women's rights and dignity?

I note these matters not just for their obvious salience but, as I shall argue below in concluding this chapter, also because they fit into the larger pattern of the overall shape of Malinowski's thinking about religion. To venture to interpret or explain them in themselves would take us too far afield. At any rate, what jumps out at one is that Malinowski was, without doubt, the leading scholar-teacher of his time to take a direct and forceful hand in promoting the careers of the entire first generation of women anthropologists in Britain. And that is certainly something so unusual that it must be noted. The list of women anthropologists trained and formed by Malinowski include the likes of Hilda Beemer Kuper, Phyllis Kaberry, Rosemary Firth, Lucy Mair, Monica Wilson, Elsie Clews Parsons, Camilla Wedgwood, Hortense Powdermaker, Margaret Read, Audrey Richards, and so on. Malinowski helped the women students in his charge overcome one of the chief internal obstacles working against them in their time – the particularly debilitating self-limiting feeling of which the feminist historian of science, Evelyn Fox Keller has written so eloquently – the hard time women in professions had *"taking themselves seriously*, being professional" (Keller 1997, p. 25). Perhaps because he, like Max Müller, never forgot the wounds inflicted on an outsider like himself in Britain, Malinowski well understood the pain of his women students, and thus did a great deal to lift its burden. Perhaps sympathy for the plight of the outsider explains the marked character of Malinowski's relations with his women students, although given all the other unusual features of Malinowski's relation to gendered relationships, one would still like to know what a Freudian and feminist psychoanalysis would turn up.

Frazer and Malinowski

But while I believe the make-up of Malinowski's thought (and the life nourishing it) reveals interesting possibilities for analyses in the terms of bipolarity already noted, there is one glaring biographical oddity that needs to be cleared up. Why does Malinowski makes himself out to be a single-minded devotee of the less complicated thought of Sir James Frazer – when in his heart Malinowski is really an anti-evolutionist, antirationalist, and thoroughgoing pragmatist? How then, for example, does Malinowski's pragmatist desire to maintain the place of religion fit with what we have seen of Frazer's desire to undermine religion completely, first by discrediting Christianity? How, as well, if Malinowski be a kind of Frazerian developmental thinker, does his pragmatic acceptance of the value of religion for modern societies square with Frazer's desire to see religion replaced by 'science' (technology), its natural evolutionary replacement?

The short answer to these questions is that Malinowski is not much of a Frazerian at all, although he very much wants his readers and lecture audiences to think that he is. And here the modest psychoanalyzing I have done at Malinowski's expense sheds more light on what makes Malinowski 'tick' regarding religion. Malinowski's promotion of Frazer as a kind of 'second father' confirms the depth of his own difficulties with his natural father, and thus the other oppositions I have noted in Malinowski's life and work. I think we will find that he seems deliberately to have sought to promote Frazer as his intellectual 'father,' and moreover to foster this self-serving 'myth' for no more nobler reason than to advance his own career by riding the reputation of the illustrious Sir James.

One of the main sources of this myth is Malinowski's classic dedication to Frazer of his major essay, *Myth in Primitive Psychology* (1926). Originally read at the University of Liverpool in 1925 as an address honoring Frazer, this dedication fills in the mythologized autobiographical information Malinowski promoted about his own intellectual formation. It shows how he attempts to wrap himself in the mantle of his popular idol, and thus to enhance his own reputation in the process.

Always one ready to dramatize his life and efforts, Malinowski begins by conjuring a romantic image of himself when a 'poor' student, absorbed in the mysteries of *The Golden Bough*. All these romantic inner struggles are set amid the haunting gothic arches and towering steeples of his home town and *alma mater*, the Jagiellonian University in old Cracow:

> If I had the power of evoking the past, I should like to lead you back some twenty years to an old Slavonic university town – I mean the town of Cracow, the ancient capital of Poland and the seat of the oldest university in eastern Europe – I could then show you a student leaving the medieval college buildings, obviously in some distress of mind, hugging, however, under his arm, as the only solace of his troubles, three green volumes with the well-known golden imprint, a beautiful conventionalized design of mistletoe – the symbol of *The Golden Bough*.

To this historic 'romance' Malinowski adds a personal note, evoking a sympathetic image of himself as a troubled, sickly lad, nevertheless now raised up to the position of lecturing at the very university (Liverpool) where a chair had just been established expressly for Frazer.

I had just then been ordered to abandon for a time my physical and chemical research because of ill-health, but I was allowed to follow up a favorite side line of study, and I decided to make my first attempt to read an English masterpiece in the original. Perhaps my mental distress would have been lessened, had I been allowed to look into the future and to foresee the present occasion, on which I have the great privilege of delivering an address in honor of Sir James Frazer to a distinguished audience, in the language of *The Golden Bough* itself.

Malinowski tells how his reading of Frazer had lowered him a virtual a life-line – the vision of his eventual vocation as an anthropologist.

For no sooner had I begun to read this great work, than I became immersed in it and enslaved by it. I realized then that anthropology, as presented by Sir James Frazer, is a great science, worthy of as much devotion as any of her elder and more exact sister studies, and I became bound to the service of Frazerian anthropology.

Giving himself over entirely to his sense of occasion, Malinowski inaugurates the 'festivities' honoring Frazer, and 'pulls out all the stops.'

We are gathered here to celebrate the annual totemic festival of *The Golden Bough*; to revive and strengthen the bonds of anthropological union; to commune with the source and symbol of our anthropological interest and affection. I am but your humble spokesman, in expressing our joint admiration to the great writer and his classical works; *The Golden Bough, Totemism and Exogamy, Folklore in the Old Testament, Psyche's Task*, and *The Belief in Immortality*. As a true officiating magician in a savage tribe would have to do, I have to recite the whole list, so that the spirit of the works (their '*mana*') may dwell among us.

And, finally, he pledges himself and his career to the great man and his legacy.

In all this, my task is pleasant and in a way easy, for implicit in whatever I may say is a tribute to him, whom I have always regarded as the 'Master.' (Malinowski 1992b, pp. 93–4)

Now it would be fair to say that *some* of this picture corresponds to the truth. Some of the key themes we saw so deeply embedded in *The Golden Bough* are Malinowski's themes as well. Consider the theme of the value of life, which we will see as we explore Malinowski's thought further. We already have seen how gripped Frazer was by the fear of the loss of fertility, fecundity, and growth, and how, therefore, he saw in the movement of human technological progress the promise of control over the forces of death and disintegration. Death and sterility are also some of Malinowski's deepest dreads. In a letter from Frazer (August 13, 1936), the "Master" praises Malinowski for bringing out the "important part which magic appears to play in the economic activities of the natives" (Frazer 1936).

But, as seductive a story as Malinowski may have spun for us and his rapt audience in Liverpool, the truth is rather different. While one should not discount thematic continuities and preoccupations running from Frazer to Malinowski, the record behind the rhetoric needs to be set straight. In terms of Malinowski's interest in mythology itself, we know that his real father, Lucjan, was already a well-known professor of folklore at the Jagiellonian, and something of a professional ethnographer himself (Young 2004, p. 12). The young Malinowski could, therefore, have acquired the taste for ethnography from his own flesh and blood. Perhaps it was he, the father, as well who made a gift of those costly green volumes to his son? Despite an estrangement from the emotionally remote Lucjan, like the young Max Weber, Malinowski incongruously followed his father's career path more than he cared to admit to the world.

While this is only speculation, the possibility at least puts in doubt Malinowski's implicit claim to have converted to Frazerian anthropology on Cracow's chilly cobble-stoned streets, since he apparently did not make such a career change to the social sciences until some years after he had left Cracow – and then apparently under the influence of his latest lover at the time, Annie Brunton (Young 2004, p. 130). Mal-inowski, therefore, did not, as one might be forgiven for assuming, go straight into anthropology from his studies in mathematics and physics, but rather sojourned for a year or so in Leipzig – where his father, incidentally, had taken his advanced degree – studying with the experimental psychologist and budding social psychologist, Wilhelm Wundt (1832–1920). There, before his departure for the London School of Economics in 1910, Malinowski may well have absorbed a humanistic vision of the social and historical sciences that may be credited to Wilhelm Dilthey's interpretive methodological thought (viz. 'empathy') (Young 2004, pp. 128–50). This was a long way from what Frazer represented.

Finally, when Malinowski arrived in England to pursue these new studies at the LSE in 1910, he immediately and without hesitation sought out teachers like the ethnographer Charles Seligman and the philosopher-historian Edvard Westermarck at the London School of Economics, rather than Frazer in Cambridge. For his part, Frazer seemed rather distant from Malinowski and his newly emerging functionalism and pragmatism – no matter how much Malinowski wanted to attribute these theoretical orientations to Sir James. Indeed, Frazer seems to have flatly repudiated Malinowski's claim to be following him as his "Master," particularly in the important area of myth studies. In a letter to Malinowski dated February 14, 1926, Frazer thanked Malinowski for "two lectures on myth" that had been sent to him shortly before. The "Master," apparently somewhat frustrated at having been misunderstood by Malinowski on myth, writes: "I confess that I have been in the habit of regarding myths as explanations, and am not sure that I follow your reasons for rejecting this view." These "two lectures" were apparently drafts of the lecture Malinowski gave at Liverpool in November 1925, later published under the title "Myth in Primitive Psychology" (Frazer 1926).

While Malinowski could not have wanted publicly known what Frazer's ungrateful little note said directly, he was very far from Frazer on essential issues like his "Master's" evolutionary perspective. The very title of one of Malinowski's most important books of religion, *Magic, Science and Religion*, seems to mock Frazer's evolutionist perspective of the gradual development of magic into the succeeding stages of religion and science. More than this, the very revolution in thinking about this trio of vital subjects that Malinowski initiated relied on the fundamental opposition to Frazer's evolutionist ra-tionalist assertion that 'the natives' (*sic*) knew only 'magic,' leaving 'religion' and 'science' for the second and third respective great stages of evolutionary growth. As Malinowski loudly and clearly proclaims in the opening sentence of his *Magic, Science and Religion*:

There are no peoples however primitive without religion and magic. Nor are there, it must be added at once, any savage races lacking either in the scientific attitude or in science, though this lack has been frequently attributed to them. In every primitive community, studied by trustworthy and competent observers, there have been found two clearly distinguishable domains, the Sacred and the Profane; in other words, the domain of Magic and Religion and that of Science. (Malinowski 1992a, p. 17).

If this is not a sharp and decisive slap delivered to the entire Frazerian evolutionary and rationalist perspective on culture, it is hard to know what would be.

A Biology of Religion: Survival Fits

With the myth of the Frazerian legacy and Malinowski's tireless self-promotion out of the way, we can home in on understanding Malinowski's real theoretical arguments concerning religion – what we have already referred to as his "pragmatism."

Following much of Durkheim's lead in terms of *functionalist* analyses of religion, Malinowski tried to adapt the French sociologist's functionalism to both Freudian and behaviorist psychologies respectively. The end result would be something of a psychology of denial, bound to a pragmatic perspective on human nature. Malinowski reveals at least part of this grand synthesis in his 1935 *Coral Gardens and Their Magic*, where he tells us that he seeks to study culture by "reducing Durkheimian theory to the terms of Behavioristic psychology" (Malinowski 1935, pp. 236, 258). With regard to religion, therefore, Malinowski makes a clear and explicit declaration of its *practical function* in society

The function of religion and its value we have learned to understand in the survey of savage creeds and cults given above. We have shown there that religious faith establishes, fixes, and enhances all valuable mental attitudes, such as reverence for tradition, harmony with environment, courage and confidence in the struggle with difficulties and at the prospect of death. This belief, embodied and maintained by cult and ceremonial, has an immense biological value, and so reveals to primitive man truth in the wider, pragmatic sense of the word. (Malinowski 1992a, p. 89)

The stages in Malinowski's thinking about this pragmatic functional approach to religion follow a tight step-by-step logic.

First, Malinowski argued not only that societies were systematic wholes, held together by mutually functioning subsystems, such as magic, myth, politics, religion, economy, and such, but that social wholes were at such risk to dissolution that every subsystem was *necessary* to the existence of a particular society (Malinowski 1948, pp. 39–41, 46). His functionalism thus takes a "pragmatic" or "utilitarian" view of culture. Everything in culture serves a "pragmatic," 'work-a-day,' or practical *function* – which is the same thing as saying that everything in a culture serves a "useful" or "utilitarian" purpose. Malinowski thus saw social wholes as organisms in crisis, fragile unities that one disturbed only at great risk to those societies. If one by chance were to disrupt their functioning, one would have in effect risked destroying this culture by having disrupted one of the practical or utilitarian functions that maintained a culture in existence.

Second, Malinowski felt that cultural functions were rooted in and finally *determined* by biological needs. He thought that no matter what else we think we may be, we humans are still living, organic beings, and as such beings, our organic needs trump all others. Cultural things, such as religion, were 'practical,' 'useful,' or worked – functioned – because they directly corresponded to biological needs. They fulfilled certain organic needs of the human biological unity. As such, so-called religious experiences were to be looked on as mere expressions of the biological conditions of human beings in crisis, impelled, as it were, by our biological drive to survive (Malinowski 1948, pp. 51–3). Along with all other life-forms, we organisms seek to enhance life and to ensure our own survival. Our biological natures impel us do those things that will function for our survival. If even plants exhibit phototropism – a tendency to grow in the direction of life-giving light to enable their photosynthetic processes – humans too exhibit their own 'vivotropism,' a drive for survival, so to speak – an affinity for enhancing life. We are drawn toward life as surely as chlorophyll-based plants are drawn toward light. Suicides, as we will see in what follows in our next chapter on Durkheim, are 'deviants' in some drastic way, and deserve to be regarded as mentally ill. Those who may seem as if they are suicidal, but who really are not – the altruistic suicides, such as soldiers, who give their lives to preserve the lives of others – fall into another class altogether, since they would live, if they could, but volunteer to die in order that others may live. They are thus as much driven by the desire to live as others, but divert that desire to the greater good of the survival of their group, which in turn will enhance the chances of life of other members of the group. This realization likewise entails that, at the biological level, people are equals, subject to the same basic needs and drives for survival.

Further, Malinowski wishes to point out that we are incredibly canny and intelligent biological systems. As Freud implied, and as Malinowski agreed, we understand at some deep level what we want and need to survive, and thus we take appropriate action to protect ourselves from harm. We may try to prevent such harm to ourselves in many ways, beginning, of course by taking simple everyday precautions against danger and risk. By we have other, more subtle – psychological – ways of minimizing the wounds that have been inflicted upon us. We may practice what I referred to in the previous chapter as "denial," for example, in order not to increase the impact upon ourselves of the harm that may have been done. We may try to lessen our sense of depression over being harmed, for instance, and thus try to maintain a sense of confident control. Freud also wrote of so-called "wish-fulfillment" in the same way. Things may not turn out as we wish, but we cling to hope that our wishes may be 'fulfilled' – or even in some remarkable way *that they are* fulfilled – in order to overcome the depression of our wishes not having turned out as we might have wanted. Getting back to the theme of 'life' once more, wish-fulfillment might take the form, for instance, of a mechanism by which we imagine that life goes on after death – that, say, the human soul is immortal – and thus that our 'wishes' for life are 'fulfilled' in the face of the counterevidence of death.

This would be yet another way that we maximize pleasure and minimize pain for ourselves – unless we are deranged in some way, or called to some higher conception of survival. We maximize those behaviors and states of mind that *function* for our survival, and minimize those that do not – even to the extent we seek to fulfill these functions *unconsciously*, as Freud would well understand. We therefore also reject or avoid those things that do not function. In Malinowski's view, therefore, instinctively we reject those things that do not function for our betterment.

Malinowski thus rejects Tylor's theory of "survivals" because Malinowski believes that these institutions, traits, and so on would not 'survive' their own impracticality, their own irrelevance. The things that Tylor wished to label 'survivals' must actually serve some kind of function – even though they seem only to be holdovers from a previous stage of evolutionary development. Presented with a Tylorian 'survival,' Malinowski would set about discovering just what actual useful function it actually served. As far as a society or an entire culture may be concerned, everything in them functions for the sake of the overall maintenance of the whole culture or society. Everything works together, then, to keep a culture alive and coherent.

Addressing Our Inability to Accept Death

A choice example of the way Malinowski believes that he can expose the way that religion works in this pragmatic functionalist context can be found in his analysis of a funeral rite in a small-scale traditional society (Malinowski 1948, pp. 47–53). Indeed, Malinowski cites the authority of his old teacher at Leipzig, Wilhelm Wundt, that the forebodings around death and immortality formed the "very nucleus of all religious belief and practice" (Malinowski 1992a, p. 48). If we can understand the death–immortality nexus, we can, Malinowski suggests, understand religion itself. So, what can be learned about the nature of religion from what we meet in actual on-the-ground encounters that people have with death, such as in the funeral rites Malinowski witnessed in the South Seas?

Part of Malinowski's anthropological method of intense fieldwork entailed the assumption that careful observation can tell us many things – indeed perhaps all we need to know – about what is really happening in a society. This is equally true of what we can learn about the essence of religion from observing religious rites such as those societies use to deal with the death of a member. Faced with such a death, the survivors realize, to a degree unconsciously, that each and every death threatens the survival of the entire group. Individual members of the group accordingly suffer real psychological as well as physiological stress in the face of such loss. Thus, death is a serious matter in such contexts, and needs to be managed in order to maintain a psychological – and ultimately physiological – equilibrium in the group. Malinowski believes that in response to the death of one of its members, societies resort to *rituals*. In a way, as we will see, rituals seem effective in addressing this threat to the society.

Here is what Malinowski 'sees.' First, he establishes that the death of one individual is, in fact not a solitary event, but a communal or *social* one:

As death approaches, the nearest relatives in any case, sometimes the whole community, forgather by the dying man, and dying, the most private act which a man can perform, is transformed into a tribal event. (Malinowski 1992a, p. 48)

Second, once the man finally dies, Malinowski calls attention to the highly *emotional* features of the preparations surrounding the corpse.

As soon as death has occurred, the body is washed, anointed and adorned...Then it is exposed to the view of all, and the most important phase, the immediate mourning, begins... There is always a more or less conventionalized outburst of grief and wailing in sorrow, which often passes among savages into bodily lacerations and the tearing of hair. This always done in a public display and is associated with visible signs of mourning...

The immediate mourning goes on round the corpse... The body is sometimes kept on the knees of seated persons, stroked and embraced... (Malinowski 1992a, pp. 48–9)

But, third, the group must in the end part with the corpse. Somehow they must dispose of the dead body. But this need to separate the corpse from the group runs counter to all the *emotions* of tenderness and attachment that have gone before, as Malinowski says –

the two-fold contradictory tendency, on the one hand to preserve the body, to keep its form intact, or to retain parts of it; on the other hand the desire to be done with it, to put it out of its way; to annihilate it completely...

In all such rites, there is a desire to maintain the tie and the parallel tendency to break the bond. (Malinowski 1992a, pp. 49–50)

Fourth, this contradiction results in a most remarkable outcome – the beginnings of a belief in the survival of the deceased in spiritual form. In effect, Malinowski believes he has discovered the origins of the native belief in the "soul" or spirit that Tylor's theory of animism attributed to the 'savage' desire and need for *explanation*. Instead of an *intellectual* origin of such a belief in the existence of souls or spirits, Malinowski is claiming that something in the *emotional* character of mortuary rites bears responsibility for this elemental religious belief. Despite the repugnant features of dealing with the dead,

the mortuary ritual *compels* man to overcome the repugnance, to conquer his fears, to make piety and attachment triumphant, and with it the belief in a future life, in the survival of the spirit.

Malinowski explains this recourse to the idea of compulsion by recalling the role that emotions have in the mortuary rite.

In the foregoing analysis I have laid stress on the *direct emotional forces* created by contact with death and with the corpse, for they primarily and most powerfully *determine the behavior* of the survivors. But connected with these emotions and *born out of them*, there is the idea of the spirit, the belief in the new life into which the departed has entered. (Malinowski 1992a, p. 50; my emphases)

In a classic neo-Freudian analysis in terms of wish fulfillment, Malinowski argues that it is our emotions – our *desires* for the dead to be thought yet alive – that produce our belief that they are indeed alive in some heavenly realm. A *belief* in immortality thus emerges out of deep unconscious wishes for that end to be fulfilled in reality.

Fifth, and finally, when Malinowski asks why this should be so, by what psychological mechanism an emotional condition is transformed into a 'belief,' his answer is again pure Freud – wish fulfillment – albeit riding a surging wave of the biological undercurrents that make up our physical organisms.

The savage is intensely afraid of death, probably as the result of some deep-seated instincts common to man and animals. He does not want to realize it as an end, he cannot face the idea of complete cessation, of annihilation. The idea of spirit and of spiritual existence is near at hand, furnished by such experiences as are discovered and described by Tylor. Grasping at it, man reaches the comforting belief in spiritual continuity and in the life after death.

Summing up, Malinowski declares his position on the function of religion, and we are back once more with Freud seeing in religion only the pathetic expression of an immature desire of people to have their richest fantasies fulfilled.

> And here into this play of emotional forces, into this supreme dilemma of life and final death, religion steps in, selecting the positive creed, the comforting view, the culturally valuable belief in immortality...the continuance of life after death...
>
> Thus the belief in immortality is the result of a deep emotional revelation, standardized by religion, rather than a primitive philosophic doctrine...The real nucleus of animism lies in the deepest emotional fact of human nature, the desire for life. (Malinowski 1992a, p. 51)

Malinowski thus believed religious behavior could be *explained* by the inability of humans – simply as biological systems – to adapt easily to the idea of death. The biological aspect of our humanity simply resists permitting us to dwell upon the certainty of our end. We prefer denial of the reality of death to its acceptance. We prefer imagining some Otto-like *eternal numinous* realm beyond time and space into which we can escape. Denial therefore generates – as a biological reflex alone – both the *belief* in immortality and the concomitant religious *experiences* that confirm this belief (Malinowski 1948, p. 51). Humans simply cannot face death, and the body deludes them into persisting in this fantasy of immortality, using religious doctrines and *experiences* to mask the inevitability of this grim reality. Referring here explicitly to magic, Malinowski says, "Hence do we find magic an invariable adjunct of all important activities. I think we must see in it the embodiment of the *sublime folly* of hope, which has yet been the best school of man's character!" (Malinowski 1948, p. 90, my emphasis). Religious *experience* is for Malinowski one of the products of this noble – "sublime" – foolishness of people who refuse to acquiesce in the ineluctability of their own annihilation.

Malinowski Thinks He Knows All This because of Freud

Now that we know what Malinowski thinks about religion and religious experience, the critical question we want now to ask is again: why does Malinowski *think he is right* to believe that religion reflects "wish fulfillment" for endless life, and their concomitant inability to accept the finality of death and to therefore imagine that they actually survive death?

In the spirit of Malinowski's bipolarity, we can say that there are two answers to this question. First, Malinowski was personally convinced of the general validity of Freud's psychological analysis of human nature, especially Freud's partial emphasis on the power of the *id* – our drive to satisfy our appetites for life and thus to survive danger. To be sure

Freud also felt that these appetites for life reflected explicit conscious beliefs about the goodness of life, and thus fundamentally had roots in the *ego* as well – a position Malinowski tended to play down. Here, we should also recognize some of the same themes that drew Malinowski to the thought of Frazer, especially *The Golden Bough*'s obsession with fecundity, fertility rites, and the enhancement of life. As a champion of Freudian psychoanalytic ideas, Malinowski believed that human beings operated specifically on the basis of *unconscious drives* – forces that welled up from deep within our unconscious minds and sought to enhance our own lives. But Malinowski knew well that in fact such dreams of immortality were just that – 'fantasies' or 'illusions' – in more or less the Freudian sense, since Freud believes ultimately that religious 'illusions' will wither away. But ordinary people had not the strength to face the finality of death, and thus cheerfully cooperated in their own self-deception. They wanted life eternal, even if that meant lying to themselves that it was attainable. Common folk thus created a 'fulfillment' of these fondest of 'wishes' in their religious beliefs and practices. To repeat what Malinowski told the audience at his 1931 Riddell Lectures, the beliefs of religion, such as of immortality, are "indispensable pragmatic figments without which civilization cannot exist" (Malinowski 1936, p. 62).

If we press further and ask why Malinowski *thought that Freud was right* in teaching such a view of human nature, we enter a deep and murky area where one can only offer hypothetical suggestions. Since we have already considered Freud in an earlier chapter, here are some recognizable, Freudian-inspired possibilities. First, Malinowski was, from what we can tell, clinically involved as a patient of Freudian psychotherapy. Thus, he was convinced by his own personal experience of Freudian therapy that its theoretical underpinnings had some validity (Young 2004, p. 124). We know, as well, that Malinowski kept personal and intellectual company with other leaders of avant-garde movements sympathetic to Freudian ideas of the importance of sex in the make-up of human nature, such as Henry Havelock Ellis. Ellis repaid Malinowski's friendship by writing the Preface to Malinowski's *The Sexual Life of Savages*.

Malinowski's own engagement with Freudian theory came most conspicuously in his appropriately named *Sex and Repression in Savage Society* (1927), but was forecast in a published letter written to the editor of *Nature* in 1923 (Malinowski 1927; Malinowski 1992c). Briefly, while Malinowski honored Freud's great contributions to understanding the human mind, he felt that Freud's ideas had to be adapted to differences in cultures. In particular, Malinowski denied the universality of the Oedipus Complex – at least in the form Freud articulated it. Where Freud went wrong was in his *Totem and Taboo*, where he "assumes the existence, at the outset of human development, of a patriarchal family with a tyrannical and ferocious father who repressed all the claims of the younger men" (Malinowski 1992c, p. 56). It was there, we will recall, in the slaying of the father by the younger men over the possession of sexual partners that religion began, in Freud's view. But Malinowski's field studies in Melanesia reveal that families take different forms from that of the patriarchal model prevalent in nineteenth-century Europe. With these different forms of families, different psychological roles are thus attached to family members. In Eastern New Guinea, for example, Malinowski testifies from his first-hand experience:

> the mother and her brother possess . . . all the legal *potestas*. The mother's brother is the "ferocious matriarch," the father is the affectionate friend and helper of his children. He has to win for himself the friendship of his sons and daughters, and is frequently their

amicable ally against the principle of authority represented by the maternal uncle. In fact, none of the domestic conditions required for the sociological fulfilment of the Oedipus complex, with its repressions, exist in the Melanesian family of Eastern New Guinea. (Malinowski 1992c, p. 56)

The undertones of this letter may hint at the troubled nature of Malinowski's relation with his own father, and thus make sense of his receptivity to Freud and special sensitivity to the Oedipus Complex. As a recent biography of Malinowski put it, "Malinowski was inclined to see his own father...[as] pompous, wooden, tactless" (Young 2004, p. 19). Add to this that Malinowski's relation with his mother was unusually close, and it does not take much imagination to see why he found Freud intriguing. Malinowski spent most of his free time as a boy with his mother and her comfortably established family – most of whom were by this time women: Malinowski's aunts, female cousins, and such. But even beyond childhood, he remained intensely close to his mother, to the extent of vacationing for long periods of time with her as his sole companion – such as the nearly two years (1906–8) they spent together in the Canary Islands. There, Malinowski prepared for the *Habilitation* degree that would certify him competent to teach at the university level in the German-speaking academic world, to which his region of Poland then belonged. By contrast, as a youth, Malinowski had little to do with his father, and even less to do with him emotionally.

The possible Oedipal circumstances of Malinowski's youth are not the only factors that help us understand his attraction to Freudian theory. To this, one must add Freud's daring and wide-open explorations of the dynamics and dilemmas of sexual life – writings that can be favorably compared with those of Malinowski's friend Havelock Ellis for their frankness about what was then still a sensational, if not taboo, subject. Here again, as with Malinowski's position between different parents, his bipolarity rears its head. Malinowski was always tormented, but nonetheless thrilled, by his adventures with the unruly power of the libido. At once riding its wild energies, at other times trying to wrestle it into submission, Malinowski's infection with libido and his attempts to repress it are perennial themes in his personal diaries. It is no wonder then that he was magnetized by Freudian ideas – and not here for their scientific value. In Freud, Malinowski found mature meditations on the nature and causes of the oscillations of libidinal desire and the asceticism that so tormented him. Although Malinowski had cut himself loose from his puritanical Roman Catholic moral moorings at an early age, he understood the wisdom of its ascetic imperatives, which Freud as well admired for their contributions to 'civilization,' or which Max Weber conceded were necessary for the creation and maintenance of capitalist economic structures. Malinowski, Ellis, and Freud all shared the belief that human beings were closed hydraulic systems of scarce personal energies. Malinowski believed, along with his mentors in the science of sex, that if he were to divert those forces to the satisfaction of his insatiable id, and indulge his sexual desires, his scientific work would suffer for lack of sufficient inner energy. Of course, the careerist Malinowski scorned being a spent force – an indulgent wastrel – of no particular intellectual achievements. His ambitions were to be an ego of significance in the world. He thus needed to go to the hard school of ascetic denial. His ego needed to learn the lessons of self-restraint and to redirect his sexual energies toward his work. Aided and abetted in Malinowski's personal psychodrama was his ever-ready Catholic superego, patiently waiting to censure deviations from its rule with its ample reserves of guilt. Michael Young's psychoanalytically informed biography of Malinowski casts his intimidation by the superego's commandments in appropriately religious terms, saying that "Based on its ascetic imperative, Freudianism became a secular religion to which Malinowski was set to be converted" (Young 2004, p. 124). In the suppression of his wilder eros-driven nature, Malinowski was able to create – at least for stretches of time – a successful professional *scientific* identity and a conventional married family life, complete with house and children.

Malinowski Thinks He Knows All This because He Can "See" It

The mere mention of 'science' in Malinowski's milieu, was, however, to enter into contested territory. After all, Max Müller and Cornelis P. Tiele both believed they were doing a '*science* of religion.' They thought that scientific practice could lead one to the 'throne of God,' so to speak. Reason and religion were at peace with one another. But by the standards of a good half of the intellectual world that Malinowski inhabited – thinkers we can call 'empiricists,' or in their more extreme forms, 'positivists' – such a reconciliation was impossible. For the positivists, or at the very least, empiricists, all claims about human thinking need to be founded on talk about 'observables.' The religious entities or realities of which a Max Müller or Cornelis P. Tiele spoke were well beyond the scope of ordinary, empirical experience. Freud too thought that his psychology would be justified one day in terms of observables. The positivists, however, felt that Freudian psychology was a pseudoscience and thus not so different from religious thought. It too incorporated claims about nonobservable entities – *hidden* entities such as the egos, ids, or superegos that made up the Freudian 'unconscious.' No wonder Malinowski made use of Freudianism as a kind of religion, as Michael Young asserted – it was in part a kind of surrogate for religion, a systematic scheme for giving meaning to life!

But, although I have written about Malinowski's attraction to Freud and Freudianism, there were other influences shaping Malinowski's conception of 'science' that reach back into his early university education in Cracow. Although I have not mentioned it up to this point, for the most part the scientific nurture of Malinowski's student career in Cracow was shaped by positivism. Freudian ideas made their impact on Malinowski about the same time in the first decade of the twentieth century, and were apparently never fully reconciled with his positivism. From the viewpoint of this positivism, real 'science' needed to be based upon 'observables.' What we understand as Malinowski's "behaviorism" is nothing but a species of this positivism, since behaviorism lays down the strict rule that only observable behaviors may be counted as evidence for explanations of human action. But Freudian psychoanalytic analyses appealed to the inner dramas of hidden 'drives' of the deep unconscious – *nonobservable* entities – despite what Freud might have believed, or hoped one day to show. The wish for fulfillment of desires for the life of the deceased, for example, cannot literally be 'seen.' They float away into the realm of the occult. Unlike the overt *behavior* that forms the basis of behaviorism's database, key elements of Malinowski's Freudian explanation of the origin of religious beliefs in immortality are hidden from view.

One must therefore imagine Malinowski at some level in a state of theoretical confusion trying to be both positivist and Freudian at the same time. This seemed to push him into a strategy of trying to assure the scientific status of his theory, no matter the immediate risk of confusion, by grounding Freudian ideas in something empirical, observable, and (ideally) measurable. This is why we find in Malinowski's analysis of mortuary rites *both* his crude attempts to lay out a causal chain of classic observable behaviorist 'stimuli and responses' *lashed to* Freudian wish-fulfillment language. Speaking of the 'primitive man' of his fieldwork experience, Malinowski notes how a moment of crisis tells him all he needs to know about how religion can be said to work *from a scientific point of view*.

> Forsaken by his knowledge, baffled by his past experience and by his technical skill, he realizes his impotence. Yet his desire *grips* him only the more strongly; his anxiety, his fears and hopes, *induce a tension in his organism which drives him to some sort of activity* ... *His nervous system and his whole organism drive him to some substitute activity.* Obsessed by the idea of the desired end, he sees it and feels it. His *organism reproduces the acts suggested* by the anticipations of hope, dictated by the emotion of passion so strongly felt. (Malinowski 1992a, p. 79; my emphases)

What this means in the practice of Malinowski's fieldwork reports is that, from the behaviorist side, Malinowski *thinks he is right* about the way religion functions because of his *observation of the overt behavior* of people – even as he uses Freudian language to talk about it as well. He believes that he just needs to look, and that the inner goings on of people will be made manifest.

Maybe this explains his devotion to the *direct observation* fieldwork upon which his reputation as an anthropologist rests – rather than, say, on the more humanistic and romantic image that he promotes of *empathetic understanding*. So, there was always an inner tension – another bipolarity – in Malinowski's thought between the opposed forces of Freudianism and positivism – a tension that Malinowski finally resolved in favor of behaviorism. In his *A Scientific Theory of Culture*, published posthumously in 1944, Malinowski makes an emphatic statement of his behaviorist view and the concomitant rejection of reliance on hidden forces within human beings:

> the fundamental principle of the field-worker, as well as of the behaviorist, is that ideas, emotions and conations never continue to lead a cryptic, hidden existence within the unexplorable depths of the mind, conscious or unconscious. All sound, that is, *experimental psychology can deal only with observations of overt behavior* ... (Malinowski 1944, p. 23; my emphasis)

The 'Phenomenological' Malinowski?

What I have herewith outlined are the main elements of Malinowski's better-known, or what we might call his 'mature,' theory of religion, since it dominates most of the publications of his professional career. But, keeping to the theme of bipolarity once more, it must be pointed out that his behaviorism (and even his Freudianism) mark changes from an earlier, more humanistic theoretical position, closer to our phenomenologists of religion. Recall that when I wished to cite a classic statement of the empathetic method, I in fact chose to do so with a quote from Malinowski, not from one of the leading phenomenologists under discussion there. Here, Malinowski's bipolarity about styles of approach to religion is, in some respects, like that noted in the thinking of Max

Weber between a broadly phenomenological approach and one more readily identified with causal analysis. Both men not only have manifested similar 'bipolarities' in their troubled relations with their badly matched parents, but also polarities embracing the same opposition of phenomenological to causal approaches to religion. The two men differ, however, in that Weber seems to have succeeded in *synthesizing* these in the two-step program he used in his *The Protestant Ethic and the Spirit of Capitalism*. Malinowski, on the other hand, does not seem able to bring the extremes together.

Articulating the interpretive method – and also, against the implications of his later behaviorism, the priority of theory over experience – Malinowski says in what we could even call a romantic and vitalist way that what he seeks in facts is *the insider's point of view, the 'native' meaning and understanding* of their situation, not causal explanations delivered from on high:

> details and technicalities acquire their meaning in so far only as they express some central attitude of mind of the natives...
>
> What interests me really in the study of the native is his outlook on things, his *Weltanschauung*, the breath of life and reality which he breathes and by which he lives...a definite vision of the world, a definite zest of life. (Malinowski 1961)

In this, Malinowski seeks nothing less than access to the subjectivity of the natives. He seeks

> to grasp the native's point of view, *his* relation to life, to realize his vision of his world...We must study what concerns *him* most, ultimately, that is, the hold which life has on him. (Malinowski 1961, p. 25)

Statements such as these seem to echo the work of late nineteenth- and early twentieth-century antipositivist philosopher Wilhelm Dilthey, whom we have discussed for his role as founder of aspects of the way phenomenology of religion did its work – empathy, understanding, and such. And indeed this 'echo' seems to be a true one, since Malinowski is reported to have read and absorbed the works of Dilthey both directly from his writings and indirectly from his time of study with the Leipzig experimental psychologist and budding social psychologist, Wilhelm Wundt. In the 'Continental' – viz. 'German' – intellectual world in which the young Malinowski moved until his departure for LSE in 1910, Dilthey's interpretive methodological thought was a major force for anyone – such as Malinowski – who might have been considering a career in the human and cultural sciences. It was the likes of Dilthey who seems to have fed Malinowski sophisticated articulations of some of the leading notions in his first great book, the 1922 *Argonauts of the Western Pacific* (Strenski 1982). In lauding the empathetic method, Malinowski shows – at least the desire to promote – a certain willingness to hear the native folk out, to listen receptively to them in order to appreciate and understand the way they see the world both they and Malinowski inhabit together. In the beginning, Malinowski, then, was not one of our evolutionists of the previous generation, such as Malinowski's second father, Frazer. He did not merely gather enough data – and not necessarily first-hand – to confirm a scheme of developmental evolution that had been drawn up *a priori*. Malinowski felt that he needed to see for himself how small-scale societies 'worked' or functioned by using all the tools at his disposal so to do – even empathy. This was not to last, as we may imagine from Malinowski's embracing of behaviorism. In his last book, Malinowski consigns empathy to the methodological trash heap as "dangerous guesswork," in what must be one of the wildest swings of the intellectual pendulum even for so 'bipolar' a personality as we have seen Malinowski to have been (Malinowski 1944, p. 23).

Upon assuming a position in a British intellectual world at the LSE that was generally inhospitable to talk of 'empathy' and other such Continental concoctions, Malinowski seems to have adapted the justification of his advocacy of intense fieldwork to British empiricist tradition thinking, there since Tylor's appropriation of Hume's empiricism. As it happens, these traditions are not as foreign to one another as may seem to be the case, given that Dilthey believed himself to be something of an empiricist as well. So, in a way, for Malinowski the transition to British empiricism, aided as well by his Polish scientific education, was not a radical one.

On top of the "empiricist" and later behaviorist foundations of intensive fieldwork that we have seen Malinowski articulate, he did also continue along rather more critically non-empiricist lines. Over against empiricist canons of inductive styles of inquiry, where the mind of the observer is passive with respect to the impressions the outside world makes upon it, Malinowski felt that the mind had to be an active agent in knowing the world. He thus insisted that his students *select* their field data in terms of the *a prioris* of "universal functionalist categories" and – one may even speculate – in terms perhaps of his unempirical Freudian ideas. Rather than rely upon classic empiricist – and behaviorist – faith that the data of observed stimuli and responses dictated what the anthropologist should think, Malinowski believed that the anthropologist should enter the field with interesting theories, investigative strategies, and such – very much the approach preferred on the Continent (Stocking 1995, p. 409). A fieldworker had to prepare themselves with a problem or set of problems to be framed *before* they entered the field, and not leave such organizing activities to the vicissitudes of good fortune after the fact. So Malinowski shows us yet another set of polarities – he would be hopelessly committed both to a rigorous empiricism and behaviorism, on the one hand, but also to an ideal of study learned early in his life of letting theory take the lead over experience (Young 2004, pp. 87 ff.). By this time, however, we should not be surprised to have found yet another dichotomy in Malinowski's complex thinking. Bipolarity is his norm.

Malinowski Gendered?

But, in conclusion, is there a way to better understand Malinowski by probing more deeply into other possible factors that might illuminate such bipolar ways of thinking – especially in light of how salient the issues of gender were in his life? Some historians and philosophers of science have argued that an interpretive method such as Malinowski expounded in his phenomenological moments may reflect something of a more 'feminine' approach to science. On this view, by contrast, a causal or behaviorist approach, boasting of its 'objectivity,' would be considered 'masculine.' Given how powerful women were in Malinowski's life, but given as well his need to assert his identity as a 'man,' might we not see Malinowski's 'gendered' upbringing reflected in his opposed, and possibly gendered, methods of studying religion and society?

A distinguished historian of the biological sciences, such as Evelyn Fox Keller, suggests there may be something in this effort to link 'gendered' methodologies with a 'gendered' upbringing. But we will have to take as much care as Keller does herself in avoiding crude simplifications of what may only be suggestive analogies. Keller wisely suggests that an interpretive approach *may – under certain carefully spelled out conditions –* indicate a 'feminine' explanatory style, and a behaviorist one the opposite! In Keller's hands, this does *not* amount to the facile – and stereotyping – view that women are creatures of feeling and intuition, and thus 'naturally' favor empathetic or interpretive modes of human inquiry, while men are objectifying and 'scientific,' and thus 'naturally' favor 'hard,' 'masculine' modes of inquiry such as behaviorism or 'linear' cause/effect explanations of human thought and action. Rather, given a time and place where such oppositions were assumed by a consensus of scientific opinion, it would be significant if a male were to champion those methods of inquiry marked as 'feminine,' such as the kind of empathetic interpretive method of understanding dominant among the phenomenologists of religion we have studied. It would be significant if a male were to run counter to the stereotype of the way a *male should do science* – such as Malinowski's promotion of empathy in his first book, *Argonauts of the Western Pacific*! It would be additionally significant if that same male also ran counter to the stereotypes of his time, and not only *accepted* women as students in training for a scientific profession, but also distinguished himself by *promoting the scientific careers* of those same women – both of which Malinowski did.

Interestingly, like Keller, Malinowski advocates such an expansion of research attitudes in anthropology to include empathy and reflexivity precisely in the interests of producing *better* science. For him, as for Wilhelm Dilthey, who first articulated an extensive ideal of inquiry in the human sciences by means of empathy, the goal of understanding the other in their own terms was always to advance science in a way appropriate to the nature of humanity under study. Drawing out what she calls the "moral of the story," Keller sketches a similarly broadening vision:

> the moral of the story, is not a moral about the vision or perception of male scientists versus that of female scientists. Rather this is a story about how gender ideology shapes the ways in which all of us see the world, men and women alike. In fact, to read this story as a story of male scientists versus female scientists is simply to project on to science that same archetypal image, so basic to traditional gender ideology, of a war of the sexes, of a contest between sperm and egg, that shaped so much of our thinking in the first place. I want to emphasize: *this is not about women doing science differently to men. It is about everybody doing science differently when the gender ideology shifts.* (Keller 1996a)

What seems to have happened to Malinowski is a "shift" in approach to the study of religion – or at least a shift in what he *wants us to believe* – that corresponds to the, at the time, differently gendered approaches of empathy and understanding versus causality and explanation.

Although it was lacking gender focus at the time, one might today well want to characterize Malinowski's earlier empathetic methodology in terms of gender, as Evelyn Fox Keller has done with the great American biologist Barbara McClintock (Keller 1983). The culture of the life sciences that the men over McClintock dominated held to other models of scientific objectivity than the one McClintock practiced. Her *situation* as a woman advancing a distinctly unorthodox method of empathetic inquiry into life forms disadvantaged her with respect to her male colleagues, who operated in terms of positivist – and to Keller "masculinist" – conceptions of objectivity.

Malinowski's bipolar theoretical thinking seems, then, subject to analogous interpretation. Thus, although the early Malinowski's empathetic methods may yield fruitful and accurate results about human societies, those in a narrowly empiricist, positivist, or behaviorist camp might discount these results because they do not rest on overtly observable facts. Keller is right to be skeptical of those who would say that their approach is 'scientific' and 'objective' because, in this case – as the later Malinowski did – it treats people *without* considering their 'subjectivity' and the meaning their own acts have for them. She (and ironically, the early Malinowski) would be tempted to retort by asking how an investigation of meaning-making 'subjects,' such as human beings, could purport to be *objective* or 'scientific' with respect to human beings, *unless* their *subjectivity* were considered?! These people, and the later Malinowski, suffer from what Keller calls "the *objectivist illusion*" (Keller 1996b, p. 30). The earlier Malinowski and the work of Keller attempt to "question the very assumptions of objectivity and rationality that underlie the scientific enterprise" (Keller 1996b, p. 30), and to "legitimate those elements of scientific culture that have been denied precisely because they are defined as female." This program would entail precisely what Malinowski had done with respect to his early celebration of empathy and phenomenological understanding, since he, like Keller long after him, sought "a process of critical self-reflection" and affirmed an "interaction between subject and other" (Keller 1996b, pp. 32, 35).

Malinowski's theories might, therefore, be said to be *gendered* in a way analogous to that we saw in the case of Max Weber. This suggests that people are more unified across different domains of their lives than we often think. Thus, Malinowski might 'think' about society the way he 'thinks' about the differences between what his mother and father meant to him. Along with Evelyn Fox Keller, then, I am placing 'gender' squarely within the cultural and social domains – and thus within the ambit of the familial socialization of both men. Gender, Keller says, is "a cultural rather than biological category – existing in social space, and exerting force on the world through its power to shape the development of individuals and institutions" (Keller 1989, p. 721). These would include not only Malinowski's relations with his parents and his unusual (but apparently above-board) relations with his women students, but also his maneuverings to install himself in the foreign world of British academe, where he played the game of trading on the reputation of his 'second father,' Sir James Frazer. Given the severity of these primarily intellectual oppositions that I have called Malinowski's 'bipolarities,' he seems to have made us an open invitation to treat him to some of the same psychoanalyzing that he freely applied to his native subjects. This, in part, is the way I have taken up his approach to the study of religion.

References

De Silva, P. 1973. *Buddhist and Freudian Psychology*. Colombo: Lake House Investments.
——. 1974. *Tangle and Webs: Comparative Studies in Existentialism, Psychoanalysis and Buddhism*. Kandy, Sri Lanka: T. B. S. Godemunne and Sons.
Ellis, H. 1936. Letter to Malinowski, 1936. Bronislaw Malinowski Papers, Manuscripts and Archives, Yale University Library.
Frazer, J. G. 1926. Letter to Bronislaw Malinowski, February 14, 1926. Bronislaw Malinowski Papers, Manuscripts and Archives, Yale University Library.

Frazer, J. G. 1936. Letter to Bronislaw Malinowski, August 13, 1936. Bronislaw Malinowski Papers, Manuscripts and Archives, Yale University Library.

Keller, E. F. 1983. *A Feeling for the Organism: The Life and Work of Barbara McClintock*. San Francisco: W. H. Freeman.

——. 1989. Just What Is So Difficult about the Concept of Gender as a Social Category? (Response to Richards and Schuster). *Social Studies of Science* 19, pp. 721–4.

——. 1996a. Excerpts from Two Lectures on Human Biology. Sydney, Australia.

——. 1996b. Feminism and Science. In *Feminism and Science*, eds. E. F. Keller & H. E. Longino. New York: Oxford University Press.

——. 1997. Developmental Biology as a Feminist Cause? Osiris, 2nd series 12, pp. 16–28.

Lévi-Strauss, C. 1942. Souvenir of Malinowsky. VVV 1, p. 45.

Malinowski, B. 1927. *Sex and Repression in Savage Society*. London: Routledge.

——. 1935. *Coral Gardens and Their Magic*, vol. 2. London: Allen and Unwin.

——. 1936. The Foundation of Faith and Morals. In *Sex, Culture and Myth*. New York: Harcourt, Brace and World.

——. 1944. *A Scientific Theory of Culture and Other Essays*. Oxford: Oxford University Press.

——. 1948. Magic, Science and Religion. In *Magic, Science and Religion*, ed. R. Redfield. New York: Doubleday.

——. 1961. *Argonauts of the Western Pacific*. New York: E. P. Dutton.

——. 1962. On Sir James Frazer. In *Sex, Culture and Myth*. New York: Harcourt Brace.

——. 1992a. Magic, Science and Religion (1925). In *Magic, Science and Religion and Other Essays*, ed. R. Redfield. Prospect Heights, IL: Waveland Press.

——. 1992b. Myth in Primitive Psychology (1925). In *Magic, Science and Religion and Other Essays*, ed. R. Redfield. Prospect Heights, IL: Waveland Press.

——. 1992c. Psychoanalysis and Anthropology (1923). In *Malinowski and the Work of Myth*, ed. I. Strenski. Princeton: Princeton University Press.

Stocking, G. W. 1986. Anthropology and the Science of the Irrational: Malinowski's Encounter with Freudian Psychoanalysis. In *Malinowski, Rivers, Benedict and Others: Essays on Culture and Personality*. Madison: University of Wisconsin Press.

——. 1995. *After Tylor: British Social Anthropology, 1888–1951*. Madison: University of Wisconsin Press.

Strenski, I. 1982. Malinowski: Second Positivism, Second Romanticism. *Man* 17, pp. 766–71.

——. 1992. Gradual Enlightenment, Sudden Enlightenment and Empiricism. In *Religion in Relation: Method, Application, and Moral Location*, ed. I. Strenski. London/Columbia: Macmillan/University of South Carolina Press.

Wayne, H. 1985. Bronislaw Malinowski: The Influence of Various Women on His Life and Works. *American Ethnologist* 12, pp. 529–40.

Young, M. W. 2004. *Malinowski: Odyssey of an Anthropologist, 1884–1920*. New Haven: Yale University Press.

Seeing the Sacred with the Social Eye: Émile Durkheim's "Religious Sociology"

11

Think Group!

Whether we follow Freud, the Freudian Malinowski, or the behaviorist Malinowski of chapters 9 and 10, respectively, we have seen classic samples of attempts to explain religious experience, and hence religion, solely in terms of the individual. To that extent, it does not matter that the focus of Freud and the Freudian Malinowski rests on internal unconscious psychological dynamics, or that the gaze of the behaviorist Malinowski falls upon the logic of stimulus and response fundamental to the mechanics of all living biological organisms. Their explanations of religious experience rest upon the 'hard' reality of the individual human person.

From this hard ground of the concrete individual, Freud and Malinowski feel that they can build up explanations of *groups* of such individuals. To explain religious *institutions*, such as sacrifice, guruship, temple prostitution, sacred times and spaces, initiations, prophecy, sacraments, rituals, sin and expiation, and so on, we need only understand the individuals *inside* or *participating in* them, fully to comprehend what they are about and mean. Or, to explain religious *collectivities*, such as churches, movements, *ummas*, Chosen People, totemic clans, brotherhoods, sororities, *sanghas*, covens, cults, sects, priesthoods, sodalities, religious orders, *varnas*, and such, we need only understand their basic constituent parts or 'building blocks' – the individual human being. The workings of the individual just need to be multiplied or added together in sufficient number to tell us all we need to know about religious experience and religion. Thus Carroll can make sense of the entire movement of devotion to Mary in the Catholic church simply by reference to the psychological dynamics entailed by father-ineffective child-rearing among the fourth-century Roman devotees of Mary. And similarly, Malinowski thinks that he knows all he needs to know about funerary rites or beliefs about immortality anywhere in the world and at any time by knowing that the individual's awareness of the prospect of death produces powerful biological survival reactions in the human organism that compel people to act and think in certain ways.

Émile Durkheim (1858–1917) differs fundamentally from any thinker espousing such individualist ways of looking at religion, even as he follows a method of approach as academic, naturalistic, and 'scientific' as those pursued by Freud, Malinowski and others. He seeks to *explain religion* as much as any other thinker we have met.

> To explain religion, to make it rationally intelligible . . . we must find in the world which we can apprehend by observation, by our human faculties, a source of energy

superior to that which is at the disposal of the individual and which, nevertheless, can be communicated to him. (Durkheim 1975a, p. 183)

At any rate, Durkheim is, if not the first, then one of the most powerful, proponents of a 'holist,' 'social,' 'sociological,' or 'collective' way of looking at the human world. Even Max Weber, who might be considered to have placed the individual conscience of the pious Calvinist entrepreneur at the center of his study of the religious roots of modern capitalism, understood that a *collective Calvinist value system* was to be held responsible for taking charge of the individual mind of those receptive to its calling. Similarly with Durkheim, nothing is more important than his way of looking at the *religious* 'world' with a social 'eye.' In this chapter, I shall want to explore what this social way of seeing religion means, and how it contributes to the overall study of religion. Thus, as we have seen, Freudians try to explain religious experience in terms of the consequences of formative childhood experiences that condition the nature of the *individual* unconscious. Likewise, behaviorists think that religious experience can be explained equally easily in terms of being a clinical 'response' to certain 'stimuli' in the *individual* human organism. But Durkheim inverts the direction of causality by arguing that the *social location* of individuals shapes their individual consciousnesses and, in turn, conditions the religious experience of pious believers.

One somewhat crude, but still representative, version of this Durkheimian kind of social causality of religious experience would be the way the immersion of a believer in a religious group – say at a revival meeting – can have an effect of its own upon the consciousness of the believer. Pious believers *experience* a religious exaltation at revival meetings, as Durkheimians would say, because of the effects of being part of a crowd in a high state of excitement, or what the Durkheimians called "effervescence." Referring to his aim to find the "source of energy superior" to individual everyday life, Durkheim muses:

I ask myself if this source can be found anywhere other than in the very special life which emanates from an assembly of men. We indeed know from experience that when men are all gathered together, when they live a communal life, the very fact of their coming together, causes exceptionally intense forces to arise which dominate them, exalt them, give them a quality of life to a degree unknown to them as individuals. Under the influence of collective enthusiasm they are sometimes seized by a positive delirium which compels them to actions in which even they do not recognize themselves. (Durkheim 1975a, p. 183)

In this sense, 'society' – this powerful social force – can be said to be prior to individual 'psychology' – to forces that stem solely from within the lone person. Durkheim reverses the causal priorities of the Freudians and Malinowski. What we may 'experience' or feel going on 'in our heads,' so to speak, is the result of our participation in groups – even, and for Durkheim, especially, for *religious* experience and feelings.

It is because of his assignment of priority to social life over individual psychology that (like Max Weber, his contemporary) Durkheim can rightly claim the title of a founder of modern sociology. But while this is true and vital to our understanding of Durkheim, it is critical for us to see him in a far more rounded way than is customary. Durkheim was an immensely sophisticated and wide-ranging thinker, and for this reason also one of the most important figures in the development and growth of the academic study of religion. Even in his time, Durkheim's conception of what it was to be a sociologist encompassed being something of an historian and philosopher as well – two disciplines that Durkheim sought to reconcile to one another in his sociology. Moreover, Durkheim was also a major pedagogical thinker and moralist, and like Tylor, Frazer and Robertson Smith, an attentive student of small-scale societies. Outside the university, Durkheim also led an active political and public life, writing patriotic tracts during the First World War and championing charitable relief efforts for Jews fleeing the Russian pogroms of the early twentieth century. As a leading defender of Captain Alfred Dreyfus, the French Jewish artillery officer falsely accused of treason, Durkheim was a central figure in the Dreyfus Affair, that emblematic human rights struggle with so many far-reaching consequences in so many areas of life in the late nineteenth and early twentieth centuries.

In a way analogous to that in which Weber sought to bring religious considerations to our understanding of the formation of economic life, Durkheim sought to bring a *sociological* viewpoint to areas of human life previously thought to be exclusively the province of biological or psychological factors. One of Durkheim's earliest books, *Suicide* (1897), argues that frequency of suicides – Durkheim distinguishes several classes thereof – is to be correlated with membership in certain social groups, such as armies, religions, nations, villages, and such. To show this, Durkheim first eliminates the usual candidate explanations. First, are suicides *externally* caused by changes in the conditions of life afflicting its victims? Perhaps? But, as Durkheim observes,

> the circumstances are almost infinite in number which are supposed to cause suicide because they rather frequently accompany it. One man kills himself in the midst of affluence, another in the lap of poverty; one was unhappy in his home, and another had just ended by divorce a marriage which was making him unhappy. In one case a soldier ends his life after having been punished for an offense he did not commit; in another, a criminal whose crime has remained unpunished kills himself. The most varied and even the most contradictory events of life may equally serve as pretexts for suicide. This suggests that none of them is the specific cause. (Durkheim 1951, pp. 297–8)

If external circumstances are not to blame, then what of something biological or psychological, as Malinowski might opine – "in the intrinsic nature of the person, that is, his biological constitution and the physical concomitants on which it depends"? In the present state of knowledge in Durkheim's time, he could not find support for such causes either. Suicides were apparently not caused by something typically considered locked in the deepest private recesses of the human mind and independent of the place of the individual in a social group. This left Durkheim only one possibility:

> Wholly different are the results we obtained when we forgot the individual and sought the causes of the suicidal aptitude of each society in the nature of the societies themselves. The relations of suicide to certain states of social environment are as direct and constant as its relations to facts of a biological and physical character were seen to be uncertain and ambiguous. Here at last we are face to face with real laws, allowing us to attempt a methodical classification of types of suicide. The sociological causes thus determined by us have even explained these various concurrences often attributed to the influence of material causes, and in which a proof of this influence has been sought. (Durkheim 1951, p. 299)

The likelihood, therefore, of someone's taking their own life, Durkheim argued, was due not alone, or primarily, to independent psychological causes, such as sheer *feelings* of personal loneliness, or *experiences* welling up in the individual in terms of internal turmoil or metaphysical anxiety. Even if these personal experiences were individual, in the sense that all experiences are such, the individual cannot escape their membership in certain populations or groups.

> When considered in its [suicide's] outer manifestations, it seems as though these were just a series of disconnected events; for it occurs at separated places without visible interrelations. Yet the sum of all these individual cases has its own unity and its own individuality, since the social suicide-rate is a distinctive trait of each collective personality. That is, though these particular environments where suicide occurs most frequently are separate from one other, dispersed in thousands of ways over the entire territory, they are nevertheless closely related; for they are parts of a single whole, organs of a single organism, as it were.... Altruism is more or less a force in the army depending on its role among the civilian population, intellectual individualism is more developed and richer in suicides in Protestant environments the more pronounced it is in the rest of the nation, etc. Everything is tied together. (Durkheim 1951, p. 322)

Thus, it is because of the *collective* conditions of being a member in a certain *social group* – for instance, in a religious social group – that the causes of suicide are to be found. Thus, for Durkheim, the location of individuals in a given religious social group caused certain psychological factors to come into play – not the other way round.

But the question of what these sociological causes look like, and how they are themselves caused, is left essentially unanswered. True, Durkheim does invoke the metaphoric language of "energy" and "force" in the concluding section of *Suicide* to name these causes. But that is as much as Durkheim is willing or able to say in 1897.

> The conclusion from all these facts is that the social suicide-rate can be explained only sociologically. At any given moment the moral constitution of society establishes the contingent of voluntary deaths. There is, therefore, for each people a collective force of a definite amount of energy, impelling men to self-destruction. The victim's acts which at first seem to express only his personal temperament are really the supplement and prolongation of a social condition which they express externally. (Durkheim 1951, p. 299)

We will have to wait, at least, for the next decade and a half for Durkheim's last great work, *The Elementary Forms of Religious Life*, to see how he fills in the gaps – how he accounts for the creation of the social solidarity that is the source of the energy that sustains individuals against self-destruction.

'Society,' in this sense, then, for Durkheim was causally prior to 'psyche.' Being a member of a particular social formation, such as a religion, was a better predictor of the likelihood of taking one's own life than personal psychological factors, such as Freud or Malinowski might cite. Thus, there were emotional costs inherent in the heroic individualism and loneliness of the Protestant entrepreneur struggling to overturn "traditionalism," so well brought out by Weber in his discussion of the *Calvinist* ethic of early capitalists. On its other side, the loneliness of the entrepreneur opposing social conventions to start a new kind of business also meant that they would lack social support. And, as such, these lone individuals might well find themselves vulnerable to the psychological preconditions of suicide. Based on rigorous statistical surveys that made allowances for other variants, Durkheim discovered that the more collectively minded Catholics and Jews of his own day suffered much lower rates of suicide than their Protestant peers. Durkheim thus reasoned that the collective character of Catholic and Jewish life was the key variable in accounting for these differences in suicide rate with Protestants.

Life and Times

Born David Émile at Épinal in Lorraine in 1858, the future founder of sociology descended from a long line of rabbis. Yet the teenage Durkheim abandoned Jewish religious practice shortly after completing primary school. Under the influence of his secular education and the rising patriotism of the period just following the 1871 loss in the war against Prussia, Durkheim became, if anything, more a devoted, indeed 'religious,' French nationalist than an adherent to any traditional religion, including his own Judaism. His reverence for the ideals of the French revolution and its Declaration of the Rights of Man and Citizen counted as everything for him in his maturity, while a sense of distinct Jewish identity faded. In terms of Jewish beliefs, Durkheim felt that Judaism was straightforwardly "false," embodying "a confused and distorted form of morality . . . expressed in theological and mythological, rather than positive or scientific idiom" (Jones & Vogt 1984, p. 48). In social terms, Durkheim was also repelled by the notion of the Jews as "a people apart" (Lukes 1972, p. 627), and sought to avoid being recognized as Jewish or being singled out as an example of a Jewish success story.

These feelings of Durkheim did not, however, turn him into someone who actively hated his Jewish roots, nor into someone who shunned the companionship of other Jews. Indeed, Durkheim, as mentioned earlier, worked to seek civil rights for Jews suffering persecution under the Czar, and to care for those who had fled Russia for asylum in France. While he, like other dissenting Jews of his day, may have distanced himself from Jewish practice and belief, Durkheim nonetheless maintained solid relations with the many prominent Jewish academics in France. One might especially single out Durkheim's admiration for the chief Talmudic scholar of his age, Rabbi Israel Lévi, and the movement called "Science du Judaisme" (Scientific Study of Judaism) that Lévi embodied in the late nineteenth and early twentieth centuries. Perhaps the best way for readers to understand what "Science du Judaisme" meant to French Jews is to understand that it arose at the same time and in the same spirit as the Higher Criticism of the Bible – a movement that we know has had great influence in the rise of the academic study of religion, traceable – in spirit, at any rate – all the way back to our old friend, Spinoza. In terms of their scientific and critical attitudes to religion, the scholars who rallied round "Science du Judaisme" shared many of the same ideals of scientific scholarship evident among Durkheim and his 'team' of sociological co-workers (Strenski 1997, ch. 4).

In these respects, Durkheim was in addition like a significant number of similarly minded, liberal French Jewish intellectuals of his day. Thus, he may have found the transition to the French Enlightenment's universal values of social justice easier to accomplish than the adherents of other religious faiths. After all, in the minds of liberal Jews of Durkheim's time, the prophets of the Hebrew bible also preached values oftentimes indistinct from those of the Enlightenment. Thus, an editorial in the most important learned journal of Jewish studies in France in fact defined French Judaism as showing a native "Jewish universalism" that thus bore the "imprint of the French spirit" (Editors 1880, p. vii). Further, James Darmesteter, the principal proponent of the liberal universalist Judaism of Durkheim's era, felt that Judaism contained the seeds of a true universal religion embodying values common to the Enlightenment. Reminiscent of Robertson Smith, for example, Darmesteter distinguished ancient Hebrew religion from the later religion of the prophets – the so-called "prophetic faith." Darmesteter celebrated the Jewish prophets as idealist ethical reformers and iconoclasts, opposed to the "materialistic" ritualistic religion of the ancient Semites. To a liberal Jew, such as Darmesteter, this "prophetic faith" matched up so well with the spirit of the Enlightenment that he argued that his liberal modern Judaism could lay a valid claim to being the religion of a modern France (Réville 1892, p. 256)!

Still, while identified with the scholarly life of science-minded Jews (and Gentiles) in Paris and no stranger to the liberal Judaism of a Darmesteter, Durkheim does not seem to have been able to join up with his liberal co-religionists in any committed way. He not only found the old ways of the Judaism of his childhood inconsistent with the new, more cosmopolitan world he had inhabited ever since leaving Lorraine, but also could not join the ranks of liberal Jewry with a Darmesteter. While attending the religious commemoration of the death of his mother in his home town in Lorraine, Durkheim objected to being singled out for his academic successes by the presiding rabbi (Filloux 1970, p. 301). Further evidence of his estrangement from Judaism, Durkheim failed either to rear his children in a Jewish home, or to see that they married within the fold. One of Durkheim's children – his daughter – ceased being Jewish, and all three of his grandchildren married Gentiles, with two of them converting to Roman Catholicism (Mestrovic 1988, p. 6). Durkheim thus broke the generations-old lineage of professional calling prepared for him as the eldest son in a family with a long and illustrious history of service to the rabbinate. Like many a talented provincial youth, Durkheim left home for further studies and a new life in Paris. There, he attended the Lycée Louis-le-Grand in the capital, one of the most prestigious schools in the nation, renowned for preparing young men for entrance into yet another level of elite institutions of higher learning in the Third Republic – its "Grandes Écoles." In Durkheim's case, this would be the illustrious École Normale Supérieure. This elite institution trained France's instructors (instituteurs), staffing its nationwide system of rigorously secular lycées. Durkheim's main subjects there were philosophy and history.

Durkheim's years at the École Normale Supérieure (1879–82) gave the new life he had fashioned for himself a definite intellectual and personal formation. He gained entrance there in 1879, and found himself among the cream of French intellectual youth. Among his classmates were future luminaries such as the philosopher Henri Bergson and the great statesman and socialist, Jean Jaurès. Among instructors, Durkheim was greatly influenced by the 'scientific' history of Gabriel Monod and even more perhaps by the historian of Roman religion and domestic rituals, Numa Denis Fustel de Coulanges. Among philosophers, the neo-Kantian Émile Boutroux exerted direct influence upon Durkheim with his notions about the independence of different levels of being, such as the social over the psychological. Linked with Boutroux in terms of Durkheim's emerging social realism was Alfred Espinas. A major figure in the 'eclectic' tradition of philosophy and social thought in France, Espinas was dean of the Faculty of Letters at the University of Bordeaux when Durkheim was appointed there. Durkheim credited Espinas with being the source of his sense of autonomous reality of the social realm over against the realms of biology and personal psychology. For the future founder of sociology, this conception of the *autonomy* of the social level of reality gave Durkheim the intellectual warrant to treat society as a thing with its own properties – what can be called his 'social realism.' In this sense, Durkheim shares with the phenomenologists of religion, discussed in chapter 7, the same notion of the existence of independent realms of human reality that cannot and ought not to be subject to *reductionism*. In Durkheim's case, 'society' could not be explained in terms of either biology or psychology, much less economics, for instance. It was *autonomous* of them. On the other hand, he thought that much of psychology could be reduced to society, as we have seen from his ideas in *Suicide*.

Although not among his instructors at the École Normale Supérieure, another vital philosophical influence upon Durkheim was the neo-Kantian Charles Renouvier. The political liberalism of this influential thinker was realized in its affirmation of the sacredness of the individual human person, a value that Durkheim championed his entire life. Durkheim's defense of Captain Alfred Dreyfus was indeed articulated in terms of the sacred value of the individual. This meant that for Durkheim the individual was a sacred being, and as such could not be sacrificed for any purpose whatsoever – even to 'save face' for the state, as in the case for convicting Dreyfus, even though his innocence was widely acknowledged. Thus, despite the fact that Durkheim should be connected with bringing a social perspective into human affairs, he was not about to deny the value of the human individual. The point was to find a middle ground between the prevailing extremes of his day. These extremes were between a materialism and utilitarian individualism that we have seen in Malinowski's thought, on the one side, and a collectivism that denied dignity to the individual, on the other. We might also include here the sense we may get of the immersion of the individual in the divine from a religious mysticism, such as suggested in Rudolf Otto's idea of the overpowering energy of the numinous. Neither of these extremes appealed to Durkheim, since he wanted a world in which human dignity was respected, but one in which individuals acknowledged their fellowship with others in the community.

Following the normal practice for graduates of the École Normale Supérieure, Durkheim taught philosophy for several years at several provincial *lycées*, interrupted by a short state-sponsored study tour of German universities (1885–6). In 1887, his reputation had gained him sufficient acclaim to enable him to join the faculty of the University of Bordeaux in a position created for him in social science and pedagogy. He stayed on quite contentedly in Bordeaux until 1902; the peaceful environment enabled him to produce his first trademark books – *The Division of Labor in Society*, *Suicide*, and *The Rules of Sociological Method*, as well as many germinal shorter publications. In Bordeaux he also began to develop an interest in ethnological topics, such as totemism, and also religion.

Durkheim lived the final decade and a half of his life in Paris, where he succeeded Ferdinand Buisson in the chair of "Science of Education" at the Sorbonne. In Paris, Durkheim focused attention on organizing a 'team' of like-minded young thinkers, drawn mostly from the ranks of graduates of the various programs in philosophy. This team would become the social basis for the Durkheimian 'revolution' in sociology. Its members would act to support one another in various academic disputes. They would also work collaboratively with Durkheim to produce the famous annual review, *L'Année sociologique*. Its success was facilitated in very large part by his nephew, Marcel Mauss, and Mauss's close collaborator, Henri Hubert. These two Durkheimians also recruited members for what arguably was Durkheim's most important 'work' – the Durkheimian team of co-workers, also best known by its French name, the *Équipe*. This remarkable community not only absorbed and deployed Durkheimian ideas for generations but would also shape a good deal of what and how Durkheim himself would think and write. As historians of religion themselves, Hubert and Mauss, for example, made significant contributions to Durkheim's articulation of the central notion of sacrifice in *The Elementary Forms*. Others associated with the *Équipe* were Maurice Halbwachs, Robert Hertz, Célestin Bouglé, Antoine Meillet, Marcel Granet, Louis Gernet, Marc Bloch, Lucien Febvre, and Lucien Lévy-Bruhl, among others. His location in Paris also placed Durkheim in the thick of the struggles over the future of republic with its Catholic adversaries, and with that, all the attendant academic and national political struggles that shaped the times and Durkheim's work as well. In the capital, he also produced the work for which he is justly most famous, *The Elementary Forms of Religious Life* (1912). Durkheim died on the eve of the end of the First World War, considerably wounded in spirit by the death of his son, André, on the field of battle, but writing what he considered would be his masterpiece, a book to have been entitled *La Morale*.

Durkheim's Theory Begins with Problems

While we will see in some detail how Durkheim's theory of religion works in a subsequent section of this chapter, knowing what we know about his life, I want to reflect briefly on *why* the life he led should have compelled him to concoct a theory of religion, especially the kind of sociological one that he eventually produced. More than any other factor, I shall argue that Durkheim's passionate, indeed religious, devotion to and love of the French nation and its special values accounts for much of why he felt compelled to address the religious question as he did. Because the 'values' of the French nation were both contested and complex, we will need to consider them in some detail.

For most of Durkheim's formative years, France was in the throes of a national depression. The Prussians had soundly routed the armies of Napoleon III in 1871, and had taken as their prize the cherished eastern *départements* of Alsace and Lorraine. A mood of national humiliation and desire for revenge lay heavily on the nation, and especially on the young Durkheim, who himself grew up on France's eastern borders with Imperial Germany and who, as an early teen, witnessed the triumphal march of the Kaiser's forces through his own home town. These events alone seemed to have turned Durkheim from traditional religious loyalties to a truly religious devotee of France. Furthermore, this sense of national humiliation at the hands of an authoritarian Imperial Germany – so well exemplified by the harsh dictatorial manners of Max Weber's father, a staunch supporter of the Kaiser's regime, as we know – made devotion to the liberal French national community a natural outlet for an idealist young man like Durkheim.

As evidenced by his first book, *Suicide*, and by the attacks of other social critics of the time, Durkheim was also deeply troubled throughout his life by the social problem of how to establish a secure and viable social order in modern France. How, especially in the present grave national security threat of more war with Germany, could modern societies such as France hope to maintain sufficient cohesion to continue surviving, yet without surrendering human rights and becoming a kind of garrison state? How, in particular, could the energy of fissiparous individualism bred by modern urban life (political anarchism of the day also troubled Durkheim), be channeled into preserving the kind of liberal society that made such individual freedom and liberty possible? Were French society to fly apart because individuals could not find ways to coordinate individual freedom with the national interest, it would be a disaster not only for the French nation but also for its liberty-loving citizens.

Thus, although Durkheim's concern for the well-being of his country may not explain all of his orientation to the value of sociability, when we add to it the *religious* component that so well characterized the attitude of Durkheim's whole generation to the cause of the French nation's dignity, we can begin to see how Durkheim was pushed in the direction of trying to find an acceptable way to value society – but without destroying the individual liberty that French society had stood for ever since the Enlightenment.

But if the patriotic crises of Durkheim's youth help us somewhat understand his friendliness to community values, for what *particular* French community values would he be willing to make sacrifices? What 'France' would Durkheim worship? This was not such an easy question to answer, since the nation itself was divided about the definition of the essential values that it should embody. At the time at least two forces fought to control the core values of France – the right-wing Catholics and the Republican liberals.

One side held up a powerful image before its citizens of a radical right-wing 'Catholic France.' As the 'eldest daughter of the church,' with its authoritarian, monarchist, and antirepublican conception of the nation, this image was attractive to many seeking strong and uncomplicated visions of the future. After all, such a history connected ordinary citizens with the regal France of Charlemagne, Joan of Arc, Louis XIV, Napoléon, and such. The debacles of the recent past certainly urged the embrace of a glorious and even stern model of national identity. Was not the crushing defeat of France evidence enough of definite divine judgment upon the nation for its secular, revolutionary, and republican ways? France's citizens were accordingly called to repent and to *sacrifice* the willful individualism that they argued had brought the nation so much division and grief. Freedom of speech and intellectual dissent needed to be sacrificed to the need for maintenance of national order and to sustain national pride. This, however, would not be Durkheim's way, although he was impressed by Catholic devotion to collective duty and sense of seriousness about the need to overcome selfishness in the face of national need.

On the other side, the Republican liberals defined France as embodying the ideals of the Enlightenment and the French Revolution. They proposed an ideal of a very special kind of French patriot – freedom loving, individualistic, and thus in politics republican, democratic, and devoted to the Declaration of the Rights of Man and Citizen. In economics, the liberals were also pledged to capitalist or market economics, because they gave freest reign to the initiative of the individual entrepreneur. We will recall that Weber had tracked the origins of capitalism to its Calvinist religious sources. But when he did so, he also revealed how it tended to create a certain personality type – the lone individual, who easily cut the ties of tradition and community because he saw his singular, predestined, individual calling as dictated by an all-knowing, all-transcendent God. Despite its tendency toward individualist economics, we should note that the Republican tradition was also intensely *nationalistic*, and thus deeply devoted to *political society*, albeit the national French political society just as much as were the radical Catholics.

While Durkheim favored much of what the liberals wanted, he was put off, however, by the tendency of liberals to give unlimited freedom to the individual in all domains of life. Although he never became a socialist, he was somewhat tempted by socialism's promise of reining in individualism's more destructive effects on economic life. He certainly felt that the market was itself a social creation, and as such had no right to the absolute autonomy 'free marketeers' imagined it to have. Instead of socialism, however, Durkheim felt a better way of governing the market was through social movements that cooperated with economic powers for the overall good of society. Thus, he and his team supported labor unions and other workers' associations. Durkheim himself sought to create an ethic of social responsibility among the leading professional classes that wielded most power in a modern economy (Durkheim 1957; 1962). His economic thought also favored the kinds of argument advanced in Marcel Mauss's great work on gift economies, *The Gift*, itself informed in part by Malinowski's work on the *kula* in the South Pacific. Such works illustrate Durkheimian suspicions about the sufficiency of market values alone in guiding human life (Mauss 1967).

In politics, Durkheim also took a parallel middle route through the fierce conflicts typical of his time. Although he was always committed to the sanctity of basic individual human rights, he could not see how an unbridled individualism could be compatible with the needs of the national – or any – community. Nor was he ever tempted by communism, or by the other extreme collectivist movements at the right-wing end of the political spectrum – all of which were active in his day. Instead of pressing toward either of the extremes, Durkheim believed that France needed some sort of reconciliation between the values of community and the individual. He worked out his middle way between the extremes in a remarkable intervention into the Dreyfus Affair, his essay, "Individualism and the Intellectuals" (Durkheim 1898). It shows us a Durkheim who makes serious proposals about the desirability of a religion of the individual as the common religion of French society, especially as that conception of France rests on Enlightenment and French Revolutionary values.

In this essay, Durkheim defended 'intellectuals' such as himself for their support of the human rights of Dreyfus against the attacks made upon them by the radical right-wing Roman Catholic polemicist, Ferdinand Brunetière. In light of what I pointed out earlier about Durkheim's alienation from the Judaism of the provinces and his closer affiliation with a liberal, universalist Judaism such as that embodied in the thinking of Darmesteter, it is significant that Durkheim does not – rightly or wrongly – defend Dreyfus on the basis of his being a Jew, but rather as a human being with the full dignity that should accrue to a citizen of France. At the time Durkheim wrote, it was becoming increasingly clear that Dreyfus was quite plausibly innocent and thus that he had been unjustly condemned and punished, with promises of more to come. Due to spectacular new evidence in the case, the tide of a popular opinion began to shift to reopen the case and to exonerate Dreyfus. Brunetière, however, argued against any revision of the initial guilty verdict by the military tribunal that had sent Dreyfus to bitter imprisonment on faraway Devil's Island. He argued, in effect, that the admission of error on the part of the state, at what Brunetière and others deemed a period of particular vulnerability, would cause great damage to key national institutions charged with protecting the nation, such as the army. Brunetière therefore argued to suppress Dreyfus's individual rights to protect the collectivity – the reputations of the army and state. By 'sacrificing' Dreyfus on the altar of 'reasons of state,' and by silencing the dissent of the 'intellectuals,' he felt that France could 'ride out the storm' with its national dignity and reputation for infallibility intact. A government that apologized or admitted error, would, Brunetière reasoned, discredit itself. In a time of national danger, matters of mere individual innocence must be subordinated to saving the face of the national government. Better, like Jesus, that one man – even though innocent – suffer for the sake of the people of France, than that the nation's key institutions be humiliated and perhaps delegitimized by admitting their errors. The trouble in the France of his day, argued Brunetière, was those noisy protesting partisans of individualism – the Republican liberal 'intellectuals,' who were the chief advocates of Dreyfus's innocence. These so-called 'intellectuals' were no use to a nation endangered, since they were not only full of egoism but also languished in a "lazy melancholy," and were unable to mobilize for the *Patrie* (Weber 1959, p. 57).

For his part, a liberal like Durkheim argued in the name of transcendent values of justice and the integrity of the individual that Dreyfus should be rehabilitated, no matter what embarrassment this would cause to the army or the nation as a whole. Moreover, Durkheim pointed out that the defenders of Dreyfus were just the kind of "individualists" who actually would strengthen national solidarity, since their individualism was entirely French, given its foundation in the Enlightenment and French Revolution. Indeed, Durkheim argued, a core value of individualism – respecting the integrity of individual differences – was perhaps the only national collective value capable of reassuring the antagonistic parties of so divided a nation as France proved itself to be over an incident such as the Dreyfus Affair.

The case he made for the individual dignity of Dreyfus is remarkable. It shows, incidentally, how crass some of our assumptions about Durkheim can be. Against Brunetière, Durkheim argued that the proposed 'sacrifice' of Dreyfus violated the dignity of the human individual as a sacred being. Let the legal process take its course; if Dreyfus were proven guilty, let him suffer the consequences. But if, as it now appeared, Dreyfus were innocent, then let him enjoy the freedom due to any individual of a republic like France. As sacred, an individual like Dreyfus, was due justice absolutely. His rights as a sacred being were transcendent and could not be subordinated to the national interest, as Brunetière wished.

What makes this reply to Brunetière rhetorically brilliant, and such a perfect reconciliation of societal and individual values, was Durkheim's assertion that the *individual* was sacred *because* this was a *social* value – at least ever since the Enlightenment and French Revolution.

> We are now in a better position to understand the reason why certain people believe that they must offer an unyielding resistance to all that seems to them to threaten the individualist faith. If every attack on the rights of an individual revolts them, this is not solely because of sympathy for the victim. Nor is it because they fear that they themselves will suffer similar acts of injustice. Rather it is that such outrages cannot rest unpunished without putting national existence in jeopardy . . . The religion of the individual . . . is the sole link which binds us one to another, such a weakening cannot take place without the onset of social dissolution. Thus the individualist, who defends the rights of the individual, defends at the same time the vital interests of society.

More even than a general social value, individualism is a *French national* social value as well. Thus celebrating it could be seen as part of the effort at national renewal after the defeat by the Prussians in 1871:

> And, there is one country among all others in which the individualist cause is truly national, it is our own; for there is no other whose fate has been so closely bound up with the fate of these ideas. We gave the most recent expression to it, and it is from us

that other people have received it. That is why we have hitherto been held to be its most authoritative exponents. We cannot therefore renounce it today, without renouncing ourselves, without diminishing ourselves in the eyes of the world, without committing real moral suicide. (Durkheim 1975b, p. 69)

Durkheim's rhetorical defense of individualism as a religion at the height of the Dreyfus case not only affirms the generally positive place that religion has in his worldview, but also shows how cleverly he tried to balance social and individual sides of life. The conflict over Dreyfus showed that Durkheim aimed at a societism that responded to the national crisis of his time in his nation with something of a religious answer. It also was an original way of conceiving the relation of society to the individual. But what of the larger question-mark that usually hangs over the Durkheim's thought – the relation of society to god (or religion)? We might well see Durkheim's point of view that French *social* values invest the belief in the integrity and sacredness of the individual with authority. But we then might naturally want to ask whether he felt that all religions were likewise indebted fundamentally to society? The standard story is that Durkheim is a simple sociological reductionist, and believes that all references to 'god' or other sacred beings are only mistaken references to 'society.' But is this true? Has Durkheim perhaps been misjudged with regard to his sociological reductionism of religion, as badly as he was about his supposedly collectivist suppression of the individual?

God Is Really Society and Society Is Really Godly

While Durkheim introduces a social perspective to religion, he has also been – in part at least – rightly read as reducing the very reality of the sacred (in particular, God) to society. True as this is, I shall also argue that this reductionist reading of Durkheim is only one way of viewing him. For the study of religion, it is also possible to read him in a second, much different way, that seems to me far more fruitful for what it suggests about the relation of religion and society (Bossy 1982). Like many a thinker, Durkheim was a somewhat slippery fellow; that is to say, a creative mind who advanced systematically ambiguous ideas. Yet, among his contemporaries, none other than Malinowski found this ambiguity displeasing, even to the point of what he took to be a fatal inconsistency in Durkheim's view of the relation of god/religion to society:

> Prof. Durkheim's views present fundamental inconsistencies. Society is the source of religion, the origin of the divine; but is it "origin" in the sense that "the collective subject...thinks and creates the religious ideas"? This would be a metaphysical conception deprived of any empirical meaning; or is society itself the "god," as is implied in the statement that the "totemic principle is the clan," thought under the aspect of a totem? That reminds one somewhat of Hegel's Absolute, "thinking itself" under one aspect or another. Or, finally, is society, in its crowd aspect, nothing more than the atmosphere in which individuals create religious ideas? The last is the only scientifically admissible interpretation of the obscure manner in which M. Durkheim expounds the essence of his theories. (Malinowski 1962, p. 287)

While such ambiguity can simply be confusing, it can also generate creative insights. I think Durkheim's ambiguity about the relation of religion to society generates just the sort of creative insights that have been useful in the study of religion.

Let us turn first, then to the *reductionist* reading of Durkheim. In his classic in the study of religion, *Elementary Forms of Religious Life*, Durkheim says quite explicitly that "society has all that is necessary to arouse the sensation of the divine in minds" (Durkheim 1915, p. 236). Anticipating Otto, Durkheim claims that "society also gives us the sensation of a perpetual dependence" (ibid., p. 237). Society indeed has a special "aptitude...for setting itself up as a god or for creating gods" (ibid., p. 244). More to the point even than these words, in 1914 Durkheim used the occasion of a joint meeting of French thinkers on opposite sides of the religious divide to engage the relation between religion and society. This was the joint meeting of the agnostic or atheist Union of Free Thinkers and a corresponding liberal, mostly Protestant, body of traditionally religious folk, the Union of Free Believers. To the members of the Union of Free Believers, who had come to hear him discuss the threatening implications of his socio-logical reductionism for religious faith, Durkheim seemed at first to offer cold comfort in asserting what seemed an uncompromising sociological atheism. To these believers, he says that

> above and beyond all the dogmas and all the denominations, there exists a source of religious life as old as humanity and which can never run dry; it is the one which results from the fusion of consciences, of their communion in a common set of ideas, of their co-operation in one work, of the morally invigorating and stimulating influence that every community of men imposes on its members.

This "source" to which Durkheim refers is, obviously, society – the "fusion of con-sciences." Anticipating the objections of his audience of pious believers, Durkheim remarks immediately: "You may think, no doubt, that this religious life is not enough, that there is another one, which is higher, which springs from an altogether different origin." But no, says Durkheim, society is a sufficient object of our religious inclinations – and one that we can experience in the here and now:

> Is it not something to be able to recognize that there exists in us, outside us, religious forces which depend on us for their release, need us to call them into being: forces that we cannot but engender by the mere fact of coming together, thinking together, feeling together, acting together? (Durkheim 1975a, pp. 185–6)

Thus, it seems rather clear that Durkheim reduces the object of religion to society, and as a consequence, he thinks that religious experiences – such as those which formed the bases of the ideas of phenomenologists like Smart or Otto – are really misperceived experiences of social forces. There is no experience of God, or at least anything that we could prove so to be. But there is shared and direct experience of society – and its power feels like an experience of God.

Thus, if we look at this relation as one of *identity*, then we could express it in the following way: "God ≡ Society." I will call this "D1" for "Durkheim no. 1," because it stands for the *first* reading or interpretation of Durkheim's view of the relation between religion and society. Thus, by this reading, "God ≡ Society" implies that Durkheim believed that the underlying reality of religious experience, and thus of the nature of

God, is society. Religious experience is thus caused by those very social forces that can be detected and investigated in the public way we have just discussed.

But, as is so true of much of Durkheim's thought, ambiguities abound. What, therefore, of the *nonreductionist* reading of the god–society identity? Here, we pick up the interestingly ambiguous way Durkheim and his peers spoke of his 'sociology of religion' as a "sociologie religieuse" – a *religious* sociology! As an identity, this relation would then be read as "Society ≡ God." Let's call this one "D2" for "Durkheim no. 2." This second identity expressed nothing less than the idea that society had a religious, or at the very least, *spiritual*, nature! In the same address to the combined meeting of the Union of Free Thinkers and Union of Free Believers, Durkheim challenged the atheists of the former as vigorously as he had confronted the members of the latter. First, he dispelled charges that religion is a mere "illusion," such as we might associate with Freud (*The Future of an Illusion*) or Marx.

> Indeed, religion is not only a system of ideas, it is above all a *system of forces*. The man who lives according to religion is not only one who visualizes the world in a certain way, who knows what others do not know, he is above all a man who feels within himself a *power* of which he is not normally conscious, a *power* which is absent when he is not in the religious state. The religious life implies the *existence* of very special forces...
>
> This sentiment has been too widespread throughout humanity and is too established to be illusory. An illusion does not last in this way for centuries. So it is essential that this *force* which man feels to be there should *really exist*...
>
> ...these forces must be *real*, they must *really be there* inside me. (Durkheim 1975a, pp. 182–3; my emphases)

Durkheim's defense of the reality of religious forces at work in personal religious experiential life was naturally greeted with enthusiasm by his pious religious audience. They were still more stirred by his recognition of the importance of these self-same forces at the heart of social processes.

In contrast to Malinowski, for instance, Durkheim thus asserts that society is no mere sociobiological massing of individual organisms, responding automatically to behavioral stimuli, but a collectivity constituted and directed by 'spiritual' forces – by beliefs, values, and ideals, by ideas of the sacred and profane, pure and impure, and so on. Durkheim claims nothing less than that such spiritual or religious traits are necessary for the existence and maintenance of *any* society and the psychological health and integrity of *individuals* in that society. Reading the society–religion identity as D2 then takes seriously the idea that Durkheim was no materialist, but someone with something of a profoundly spiritual – although not necessarily traditionally religious – outlook. After all, as I have noted, Durkheim abandoned his native Judaism and showed no signs at all of converting to any other traditional religion. Stressing the antimaterialism at the core of his thought, Durkheim says:

> Nothing is wider of the mark than the mistaken accusation of materialism which has been leveled against us. Quite the contrary: from the point of view of our position, if one is to call the distinctive property of the individual representational life spirituality, then one should say that social life is defined by its hyperspirituality. By this we mean that all the constituent attributes of mental life are found in it, but elevated to a very

much higher power and in such a manner as to constitute something entirely new.
(Durkheim 1974, p. 34)

Malinowski, as one would imagine, took a dim view of such "spiritualist" tendencies in Durkheim's thought. At least as it emerged in *The Elementary Forms*, Malinowski indicted Durkheim's idea of society as "a metaphysical conception deprived of any empirical meaning" (Malinowski 1962, p. 287).

For Durkheim, this spiritualist outlook was so strong and persistent a part of his thought that he also felt – unlike Malinowski or Freud – that the human 'soul,' for example, could not be reduced to matter, or to innate psychological endowments. This is so because the human 'soul' was simply the presence of society in us, on Durkheim's view. When we think of aspects of 'soul,' such as conscience, is this not just ultimately our embodiment of social norms? Or, when we think of thinking or consciousness itself, are we also not finally being aware in terms of an 'inner voice,' addressing us in our own language? The notion that we had souls was not a brute or primary psychological fact of life for Durkheim, as it was for Tylor's animism. For Durkheim, people felt that they had souls as part of their being human. And being human always meant living together with other humans – as a social animal. Similarly, there was no such thing as language without there being human society. Language both *made* human society possible – because it made communication possible – and was made possible by our being social, because without others with whom to communicate, why would a lone animal even need a language or try to have one?

Thus, Durkheim believed, like Max Weber with regard to the religious origins of capitalism, that what moved the human world were our common consensus values, our socially formed consciences, our basic concepts and assumptions about what is to be done and what we should do. Further, given his belief in the *autonomy* of society that he took from his philosophical mentors of his formative years, Boutroux and Espinas, this social 'soul' of which Durkheim speaks was equally well something *irreducible* to matter. It existed on *its own level*, and needed to be grasped in terms of the laws governing it at its own level. Social laws did not really negate biological or physical laws – although Durkheim was so much the spiritualist that he was actually tempted by this prospect! Early in his career in 1884, while still a young *lycée instituteur* in Sens, Durkheim flirted with the idea that both 'soul' and 'body' might involve one another in paradoxical ways. "Our spiritualism admits," muses Durkheim, "that the soul is not a reality of a separate nature, arising suddenly in the scale of beings." Rather, "the mind finds itself in all degrees, only more or less rudimentary: everything lives, everything is animated, everything thinks"' – of course, as we have noted, for radically different reasons than the theory of animism of E. B. Tylor (Jones & Gross 2004, p. 279).

Émile Durkheim, Phenomenologist of Religion?

Before leaving Durkheim's address to the joint meeting of the Union of Free Believers and Union of Free Thinkers, I should like to call attention to one particularly notable consequence of his ambiguous and original attitudes to the study of religion. Most students of Durkheim will find these words at least as surprising as they may already have found what I have pointed out about Durkheim's spiritualism and its affirmation of the spiritual or religious heart of society. I write here of the scientist, often characterized as a crude positivist, Durkheim's declaration of allegiance to phenomenological method, especially the practice of *empathy*!

> In brief, what I ask of the free thinker is that he should confront religion in the same mental state as the believer. It is only by doing this that he can hope to understand it. Let him feel it as the believer feels it; what it is to the believer is what it really is. Consequently, he who does not bring to the study of religion a sort of religious sentiment cannot speak about it! He is like a blind man trying to talk about colour. (Durkheim 1975a, p. 184)

Indeed, perhaps going even further than other phenomenologists, Durkheim insists that students of religion assume a "religious" attitude to their data.

> we are no longer in danger of perpetrating the error and injustice into which certain believers have fallen who have called my way of interpreting religion basically irreligious.
>
> There cannot be a rational interpretation of religion which is fundamentally irreligious; an irreligious interpretation of religion would be an interpretation which denied the phenomenon it was trying to explain. (Applause). Nothing could be more contrary to scientific method. We may understand this phenomenon differently, we may even succeed in not understanding it, but we cannot deny it. (Durkheim 1975a, p. 185)

Nothing would be odd, of course, in our having found declarations like this in its classic locus among the works of Tiele, Kristensen, Otto, or Smart. Even reading such ideas in the works of unexpected authors, such as Malinowski and Weber, respectively, might raise some eyebrows. But it seems astonishing to find such methodological advice coming from Durkheim, a thinker who typically has the very different reputation of being a hardcore social scientist. Yet there the phenomenological side of Durkheim unmistakably is. Operating like a genuine phenomenologist, Durkheim directs his appeal to empathy in particular as a first step in *understanding* religion – even though, as we know, he will want, like Weber, to move further to an *explanation* of religion. What makes Durkheim's phenomenological attitudes a little less stunning is the work of his closest colleagues and co-workers, whom he inspired and directed along the same paths.

Both Henri Hubert and Marcel Mauss trained as 'historians of religion' at the École Pratique, Fifth Section, in a French version of '*science religieuse*' inspired by Max Müller. Hubert had trained in the study of Judaism and near Eastern religions under the leading scholar of Rabbinic Judaism of France, Israel Lévi, while Jewish-born Marcel Mauss worked on the religions of India under Sylvain Lévi. But even beyond their concern with the *histories* of particular religions, Hubert and Mauss also had *phenomenological* interests. They, for example, had also been attracted to Tiele's morphology of religion. Tiele, as we know, was William Brede Kristensen's teacher, and Kristensen trained van der Leeuw as a phenomenologist of religion. Durkheim had gone so far as to send Mauss on a mission to study with Tiele in Leiden as part of a year's tour of leading foreign university efforts in studying religion – a study tour including residence under Tylor at Oxford and Frazer at Cambridge. The common desire of the Durkheimians (especially Mauss) and Tiele was to produce a history of religion that was "philosophical" rather than merely documentary. What this meant was that both Durkheimians and the early phenomenologists sought to go beyond the mere facts by seeking the structures or morphological entities underlying them. Initially, Mauss lavished praise on Tiele's efforts at morphology – especially Tiele's creative classification and grouping of religion into different forms. For Mauss, category formation, such as he and Hubert undertook in their *Sacrifice: Its Nature and Functions*, was the part of Tiele's phenomenological work closest to the ambitions of the Durkheimian team.

In a similar spirit, Henri Hubert's French edition and translation of Pierre Daniel Chantepie de la Saussaye's massive handbook of the world's religions showed how much like the phenomenologists of religion Durkheimians wanted to revolutionize the study of religion. As we know from our discussion of the phenomenologists of religion, Saussaye was Tiele's colleague in Amsterdam and himself something of an early phenomenologist of religion. The Durkheimians were interested in any new way of studying religion that could advance it beyond the older approaches of the historians and theologians. So, in 1904, Henri Hubert and Isidore Lévy assembled a team of translators for a French edition of Saussaye's massive work, under the title *Manuel d'histoire des religions* (Chantepie de la Saussaye 1904). The French edition was, however, not done in the spirit of 'pure' scholarship, partly because they found much of Saussaye's approach to religion unscientific and secretly prejudiced in favor of Christianity. In his introduction to the new translation, Hubert exposed Saussaye's unscientific exclusion of both Judaism and Christianity from the *Manuel* on the grounds that they were incomparable to pagan religions! Since Chantepie de la Saussaye saw them as 'true' revelations of the divine plan for humanity, and not mere 'religions,' he felt that they could never be the subject of scientific study. In Hubert's scientific Durkheimian eyes, these theological prejudices could not stand if the study of religion was to move in an open religious environment. Once Saussaye's theologizing of the study of religion had been put aside, Hubert proceeded to use his introduction to sketch out the new sociological approach to religion that his master, Durkheim, was then in the process of conceiving: what we will come to know as his *sociologie religieuse* (Strenski 2003, pp. 160–5).

Durkheim's "Sociologie Religieuse" Explains Religion in General

The scope and detail of Durkheim's thought on religion – his *sociologie religieuse* – is so vast that one despairs of conveying its salience in the kind of introductory work that the present volume intends to be. Nevertheless, I shall propose to interpret how Durkheim's theory of religion hangs together. Whether or not Durkheim is correct in thinking about how religion works, the question we need to consider is *why he thought his theory of religion was right?* This reflects as well the ambiguities I have already described in Durkheim's complex view of the relation of 'god' and 'society' in the section above. How was it, then, that Durkheim imagined that he could say with equal conviction that 'god is really society' and that 'society is really godly'?

The first thing to appreciate about Durkheim's project is that he intended it to help make sense of religion in the present day *by means of* studying the kinds of small-scale societies usually treated by anthropologists. This may surprise some of us, since his great masterpiece, *The Elementary Forms of Religious Life*, is ostensibly devoted to the totemic religious life of aboriginal Australian folk. Does not the opening sentence of *The Elementary Forms* make this focus clear? "In this book," says Durkheim, "we propose to study the most primitive and simple religion which is actually known, to make an analysis of it, and to attempt an explanation of it" (Durkheim 1915, p. 13). Yet, at the same time, at the bottom of the same page of *Elementary Forms*, Durkheim distances himself from sole dedication to small-scale societies. In this guise, he appears more like the old self of his book on suicide, concerned with contemporary sociological problems: "The man of to-day ... There is nothing which we are more interested in knowing." Durkheim quickly reassures his readers that he has strayed off into the world of exotic primitivism. Thus, Durkheim says, "we are not going to study a very archaic religion simply for the pleasure of telling its peculiarities and its singularities." Rather, he promises to keep faith with his interests in the big sociological issues:

> If we have taken it [totemism] as the subject of our research, it is because it has seemed to us better adapted than any other to lead to an understanding of the religious nature of man, that is to say, to show us an essential and permanent aspect of humanity. (Durkheim 1915, p. 13)

So, in this respect, Durkheim is like his contemporaries, Tylor, Robertson Smith, Frazer, and Malinowski. All these students of exotic societies felt that they were venturing far afield into the world of small-scale societies, to better understand *modern* society, especially its religion! Thus, all the conclusions Durkheim reaches about aboriginal Australian religion are meant to refer – by analogy – to contemporary Western society, and thus to the universal nature of human religious life – to "an understanding of the religious nature of man, that is to say, to show us an essential and permanent aspect of humanity" (Durkheim 1915, p. 13). This grand universal aim of his scholarship demonstrates, in turn, Durkheim's practice of what I believe is proper to call his 'method of elementary forms.' Understanding this conception of the study of religion is essential to understanding what Durkheim has to say about the nature of religion, and why he feels he is right to say it.

Evolution and the 'Method of Elementary Forms'

Like all the evolutionist thinkers we have met, Durkheim was convinced that cultural and social things 'grew' or developed out of previous stages of growth and development. Recall Tylor, Robertson Smith, and Frazer again – not to mention the Bizarro cartoons – and their assumption that every cultural or social phenomenon relied for its existence upon an enabling level of cultural and social development. Durkheim felt that we owed debts to the past, because the past is causally agent in the present. Past events persisted into the present so that we could think of human history as a long chain of transmission, stretching back to the dim past. Durkheim even feels the people of the past are objectively alive in us. In one of his more beautiful moments of reflection on human life, Durkheim asks rhetorically:

> Indeed what do we even mean when we talk of contemporary man, the man of our times? It is simply the agglomeration of those characteristic traits whereby today's Frenchman can be identified and distinguished from the Frenchman of former times. But this cannot really give us a picture of the whole of modern man; for in each one of

us, in differing degrees, is contained the person we were yesterday, and indeed in the
nature of things it is even true that our past personae predominate, since the present is
necessarily insignificant when compared with the long period of the past because of
which we have emerged in the form we have today. It is just that we don't directly feel
the influence of these past selves precisely because they are so deeply rooted within us.
(Durkheim 1977, p. 11)

Emphasizing the importance of the objective – and thus causal – nature of the past upon
the present, Durkheim suggests that this fact would have certain consequences for how
we should study society and, of course, religion. "How can we fail to realise," Durkheim
asks in a somewhat mystical moment, reminiscent of Freud on the 'primal horde' of
brothers who first slew the father, "that we contain within us hidden depths where
unknown powers slumber but which from time to time may be aroused according to the
demands of circumstances?" What is critical, as it is for Freud, is that such an intimation
has *methodological* consequences. To wit, we need to do more than the kind of social
research that takes in only the data of the present: "This extended and expanded view of
humanity makes us realise more clearly how impoverished, flimsy and deceptive is the
one yielded by direct observation of ourselves." Beyond the study of the present in terms
of the present, we need to adopt an *historical* point of view, such as Durkheim's evolutionist peers had done. Going on to draw these conclusions, Durkheim says,

> for we must candidly admit that there exists in us something of all these styles of
> humanity which have historically succeeded one another, even if we are not currently
> sensible of the fact. These men of former ages were men like ourselves and it is
> consequently impossible that their nature should be foreign to us. Similarly, there live
> in us, as it were, other men than those with whom we are familiar. This proposition is
> confirmed by the findings of modern psychology, which reveal the existence of an
> unconscious psychic life beyond that of consciousness: a life which science alone is
> gradually managing to uncover, thanks to its special methods of investigation. (Dur-
> kheim 1977, p. 330)

In other words, the proper study of the *present-day* 'us' requires the study of the *historical*
'them' – whether 'they' be our actual historical ancestors or those historically *analogous* to
'ours' by virtue of their being at the same evolutionary level of development as our
cultural ancestors. These *analogous* ancestors were, for Durkheim and his evolutionist
contemporaries, the so-called 'primitives.'

Now, with these assumptions in hand, Durkheim suggested, for example, that the
modern-day 'primitives' – members of the small-scale societies studied by ethnographers
– were the equivalent of our ancient ancestors, such as the folk who had frequented
Brixham Cave. Thus, in studying the small-scale societies of aboriginal Australia in his
Elementary Forms, he believed that he was gaining insight into the religious and other
conditions of our own societal ancestors, and thus into ourselves, their heirs. Both in the
conditions of our ancient ancestors and in modern-day 'primitives' we could discern
cultural traits of religion, for instance, of an *elemental* or *simpler* sort. What Durkheim
therefore learned from Australia, could, he reasoned, be *analogically* applied to our own
cultural ancestors, as well as even further to ourselves! We were only more complex,
more developed or built-up versions of the *elemental* 'them' – whether 'they' be the folk
from old Brixham Cave or the Australian Outback. This meant that Durkheim could

understand and explain the more complicated 'us' – as he and his contemporaries assumed 'we' were – better by looking at the simpler (*sic*) 'them.' We could understand our presumably *complex* 'forms of religious life' by grasping 'their' supposedly *elementary* 'forms of religious life,' because 'ours' were only complicated forms of 'theirs.' In reports of aboriginal religion in the Australian Outback, Durkheim, therefore, thought he had data about the conditions of all humankind, since he believed in Australia he had found the most 'primitive' of all religions.

'Their' Secret Is Sacrifice

How is Durkheim's method of 'elementary forms' brought to bear on his conception of religion, especially as that is connected with Durkheim's outlook on his world and the possible place religion should have in it? We will recall how social and political problems afflicting the France of his day weighed upon Durkheim. The threats to national integrity presented by Germany, the twin but opposed dangers posed by right-wing Catholic attacks upon individualism and the parallel dangers of reckless individualism in the form of anarchism and social unrest, not to mention the social malignancy of suicide – all these surfaced in the midst of the prime of Durkheim's life. A good deal of Durkheim's thinking about religion can be seen in terms of a reaction to the complex social and political problems of a highly developed society like that of modern France. The method of 'elementary forms' gave Durkheim a unique way of dealing with these problems. He reasoned that if one could discover the way simpler societies managed problems *analogous* to those of modern complex societies, then 'we' might adapt and use some of the solutions of these simpler societies. Thus, if as was the case, France suffered from social dissolution, we might learn from societies which had solved such problems what their 'secret' was. It would then only be a matter of applying these solutions to France – all the while making allowances for local and historical differences.

In Durkheim's view, one place where the so-called 'primitive' or small-scale societies excelled was in their high degree of social cohesion. If one could isolate and identify the 'elementary' institutions, practices, and mechanisms that small-scale societies used to secure their own coherence, then perhaps modern folk could either create or retrieve analogous kinds of social technologies of order and coherence for their own use? *The Elementary Forms* is a book that attempts to answer this question by proposing aboriginal Australian society as something of a model for the France of its day. If *Suicide* taught us that anomie and lack of social cohesion could cause suicide, then what could Australian aboriginal religion teach us – analogically, at least – about how to remedy these causes of the voluntary taking of one's own life? What became obvious to Durkheim was that the social cohesion of aboriginal society had something to do with the elaborate *sacrificial* ritual religious life of these people. But why should this be so?

In a way, it was always clear to Durkheim that religion was a unifying force within society. It embodied the common values to which all members of society subscribed. But how did sacrifice fit into this picture?

While there are many reasons why Durkheim would have thought that sacrifice – of all things – was in effect the most important or typical sign of religious life, we should also recall that he read and admired thinkers like Tylor, Frazer, and, in particular, Robertson Smith. As we know, they dealt extensively with this ritual. Perhaps there was something special in their consensus concentration on this rite that made it essentially religious? Durkheim had, for example, studied Smith's *Lectures on the Religion of the Semites* carefully. Robertson Smith's book seems to have lent Durkheim an especially helpful 'hand' in conceiving the nature of so-called 'primitive' religion in such a way that some of Durkheim's questions were beginning to get answered. Robertson Smith, for instance, impressed upon Durkheim the idea of the religions of small-scale societies as consisting in ritual practices, rather than systems of beliefs or moral norms. Perhaps social cohesion was more a matter of achieving a kind of consensus of practice or morality, rather than risking the dangers of hoping to find uniformity in beliefs. This was one reason Durkheim was dubious about the long-term value of being too literal-minded about religious *beliefs* or *scriptures*: in the modern world, it was unlikely that we could ever achieve necessary consensus about such beliefs if we took them literally, rather than *symbolically*, say.

Durkheim's promotion of *symbolism* over literalism in religion indeed goes all the way back to his second publication – his 1887 review of Guyau's *The Irreligion of the Future*. There already Durkheim's religious symbolist sympathies are evident.

> To be sure, it has been said that dogma is untenable if taken literally, but why should we be confined to its literal expression? Words have no meaning in themselves; the mind has to seek the idea, and even the most sacred texts need interpretation. Unfortunately, once Luther had given the believer the authority to be an interpreter, he was instantly persuaded to put his own ideas in place of divine thought; and soon there were everywhere nothing but symbols, even in the most essential dogmas, including that of revelation. (Durkheim 1975c, pp. 27–8)

Even as late as Durkheim's address to the combined meetings of the Union of Free Thinkers and Free Believers in 1914, Durkheim reaffirmed the same principles first enunciated in 1887. Here, he clearly states his preference for the symbolic reading of religious doctrines, and thus finds little common ground with 'fundamentalists.'

> if he [the believer] values a denominational formula in an exclusive and uncompromising way, if he believes that he holds the truth of religion in its definitive form, then agreement is impossible and my presence here has no meaning.

Yet, for those willing to interpret dogmas more symbolically, there is hope of conversation across the gulf separating believer and skeptic.

> If, however, he considers that formulae are only provisional expressions which last and can only last a certain time, if he thinks that they are all imperfect, that the essential thing is not the letter of these formulae but rather the reality they hide and which they all express inexactly to a greater or lesser degree, if he thinks that it is necessary as a consequence to look beneath the surface to grasp the underlying principle of things, I believe that up to a certain point there is an enterprise we can embark upon by common consent. (Durkheim 1975a, pp. 184–5)

So, at the very least, Durkheim's de-emphasizing of religious beliefs made him open to a deep appreciation of noncognitive means of attaining the social solidarity he sought for his own country. This move to grasp the power of noncognitive – here, as we will see, ritual – means of making social solidarity can be seen to answer the questions left hanging from Durkheim's early book, *Suicide*.

This in turn made him receptive to Robertson Smith's view of small-scale societies and their religions as constituted by *ritual actions* – such as totemic worship and sacrifice. In Robertson Smith's mind – and thus in Durkheim's – they constituted the bulk, if not totality, of religion at this 'primitive' stage of its evolution, governed as well by elaborate systems of taboo and the sacred, and marked by concerns about physical matters, such as purity and pollution. Robert Alun Jones has even suggested that Durkheim's idea of religion as a locus of forces is owing to the influence of Robertson Smith (Jones & Vogt 1984, pp. 47 ff., 55). But this just pushes the inquiry along another step. Why should *sacrificial* ritual actions be so potent in achieving social solidarity in small-scale societies such as those Durkheim was discovering in his reading of the ethnographies of aboriginal Australia? Much of Durkheim's gravitation to sacrifice and an appreciation of its social power had to do with Robertson Smith too.

For Smith, sacrifice among the earliest level of Semitic religion was a celebration of community and kinship with the gods. As we will recall, Robertson Smith argued that the oldest Semitic sacrifice was far from any sort of attempt either to bribe the deity or to palliate the gods out of fear. Instead, it marked a special, preeminently social time of gods and people enjoying kinship with each other.

> When men meet their god, they feast and are glad together, and whenever they feast and are glad they desire that the god should be of the party. This view is proper to religions in which the habitual temper of the worshippers is one of joyous confidence in their god, untroubled by any habitual sense of human guilt, and resting on the firm conviction that they and the deity they adore are good friends, who understand each other perfectly and are united by bonds not easily broken. (Smith 1923, p. 255)

As such, what Robertson Smith saw when he thought about essential sacrifice was its joyful acknowledgment of kinship between human and divine – an occasion "full of mirth" (Robertson Smith 1923, p. 414). Because this presented such an attractive prospect, Durkheim doubtless felt that modern society might happily adapt festivals *analogous* to those described by Robertson Smith to promote social solidarity. Durkheim says as much when he reflects upon the wondrous unity of spirit that prevailed, say, in the French Revolution:

> This aptitude of society for setting itself up as a god or for creating gods was never more apparent than during the first years of the French Revolution. At this time, in fact, under the influence of the general enthusiasm, things purely laical by nature were transformed by public opinion into sacred beings: these were the Fatherland, Liberty, Reason. A religion tended to become established which had its dogmas, symbols, altars, and feasts. It was to these spontaneous aspirations that the cult of Reason and the Supreme Being attempted to give a sort of official satisfaction. (Durkheim 1915, pp. 244–5)

How, then, was modern France to recapture the social unity that manifested itself like this – but for only a time – in the French Revolution? Following Robertson Smith again, the answer lay in sacrifice. But what would be the appropriate modern-day *analogy* to some ritual sacrifice like the *Intichiuma*?

But there is more. Sacrifice was as well a joyous alimentary communion sacrament linked with totemism, and an instance of what Durkheim called the "positive cult," similar in ways to the "merry sacrificial feast" (Robertson Smith 1923, p. 257) of Robertson Smith's Semites. In *Elementary Forms*, Durkheim used, among others, the *Intichiuma* rite, from the Australian ethnographic materials, to demonstrate this "positive" cultic pattern of sacrificing the totem-god, then sharing it with all the members of the totemic clan in a 'primitive' communion meal. Through the *Intichiuma*, certain small-scale societies of aboriginal Australians renewed themselves, and revived their cherished values. This revival of society was not achieved by preaching sermons full of words or pledging allegiance to creeds but, as Durkheim believed appropriate to 'primitive' societies, by means of the ritual act of sacrificing the totem animal, and in the ritual eating thereof in a communion feast. Harkening back to Robertson Smith's conception of the earliest stages of Semitic religion as the enjoyment of kinship with the gods or God, Durkheim too saw in the Australian Outback the same kind of ritual practice. The "negative cult" was, by contrast, one that focused on interdictions or taboos, upon asceticism and a kind of dreary self-denial. It was not aimed specifically at facilitating kinship or communion – society – between gods and humans, but at keeping sacred and profane separate from each other, and in this way, protecting the sacred from dangerous pollution. Thus Durkheim declares his view of the positive priorities of the religious life:

> Whatever the importance of the negative cult may be, and though it may indirectly have positive effects, it does not contain its reason for existence in itself; it introduces one to the religious life, but it supposes this more than it constitutes it. If it orders the worshipper to flee from the profane world, it is to bring him nearer to the sacred world. Men have never thought that their duties towards religious forces might be reduced to a simple abstinence from all commerce; they have always believed that they upheld positive and bilateral relations with them, whose regulation and organization is the function of a group of ritual practices. To this special system of rites we give the name of *positive* cult. (Durkheim 1915, p. 366)

Beside being a 'positive' rite, in Durkheim's view the *Intichiuma* was a sacrifice as well, but one which was mainly a communion rite that was offered to sacred beings or forces that existed independently of human actions, like ritual. Along with Robertson Smith, then, Durkheim first saw sacrifice as *communion*; it was his *first* theoretical attempt to comprehend sacrifice. Accordingly Durkheim says that in sacrificing – killing and eating – the totemic animal, the devotees communicate with a preexisting "sacred principle residing in it" (Durkheim 1915, p. 378), or that the purpose of the "communion" is seeking "periodically to revivify the totemic principle which is in them" – the spirit of the totemic animal (Durkheim 1915, p. 379). For Durkheim at this *first* phase of his conception of sacrifice, the sacrificial victim to be offered is already sacred *before* any sacrificial ritual has commenced, even though from time to time, typically in the *Intichiuma*, at Spring, it needs to be revived.

Durkheim's opinion was, however, to change radically over the years, even though, oddly enough, he persisted in reciting his first theory – that the *Intichiuma* was such a "totemic sacrament" – long after this idea was discredited, even by his own 'team's' leading members, Henri Hubert and Marcel Mauss (Jones 1981, pp. 191–6). Therefore, as if just to confuse matters, in *The Elementary Forms of Religious Life* Durkheim also offered a *second* theory of sacrifice, borrowed from Hubert and Mauss, that in effect trumped the first, and indeed became Durkheim's mature view of the rite. This is the theory of sacrifice that we need to comprehend, because it is where we can see Durkheim's thought about religion and society at its most mature.

This shift in position turns up as well in the second chapter of book III of *The Elementary Forms of Religious Life*. There, Durkheim turns Robertson Smith's view that sacrifice is offered to a preexisting god or gods on its head, with an even more Smith-like assertion of the importance of ritual. Here, as a radical ritualist, Durkheim presses the thesis that ritual activity, such as *sacrifice*, creates and sustains the gods! First, sacrifice does not entail the presumed existence of a personal divinity, but is instead "independent of the varying forms in which religious forces are conceived" (Durkheim 1915, p. 385). Second, the gods depend on humans, such as by being fed by them with offerings of food in sacrifice. In calling attention to this dependence of the gods upon people, Durkheim levels an explicit critique at Robertson Smith: the gods would die without their cult, Durkheim tells us; the gods cannot do without worshipers any more than society cannot do without individuals (Durkheim 1915, pp. 388–9).

Further, if sacrifice literally makes the gods, it in effect produces the sacred. Accordingly, the sacred is therefore not a natural and preexistent condition of certain things which sacrifice only stirs up or revives (Durkheim 1915, pp. 378–81). Here, Durkheim turns his back again on Robertson Smith and on traditional religion. In his conclusion of the very same paragraph in which he had declared the preexistence of the sacred, Durkheim tellingly adds with respect to the *Intichiuma*: "The only difference we find here is that the animal is naturally sacred while it *ordinarily acquires this character artificially in the course of sacrifice*" (Durkheim 1915, p. 378; my emphasis). Not even the gods are sacred on their own, but only because people believe in them (Durkheim 1915, p. 386).

Thus, when we read closely the crucial second chapter of book III of *The Elementary Forms*, we see that it must be read as a treatise on the sacred which, for Durkheim, will be a treatise on society at the same time. *The Elementary Forms* is both about the social aspect of religion as well as the religious aspects of society. For Durkheim, here, there is no religiousness – no sacredness, no sense of obligation, no respect, no authority, no energizing force moving human beings to concerted action – outside the force-field generated by society. So also there is no society without a sense of sacredness: there are no boundaries, moral forces, proscriptions, inspiring ideals, respect, and so on outside the domain of sacredness. This interest in the social and sacred is why, I submit, Durkheim devoted the bulk of his discussion to what he called the "positive cult."

What Australians Can Teach Us

As Durkheim's *The Elementary Forms of Religious Life* shows us how ritual sacrifice functioned among the aborigines to weld the people into a coherent whole, so also he believed its analogue – civic sacrifice of duty and devotion to the various groups of which we are members – would ensure France's integrity against their foe. In virtually his last work, then, Durkheim completed the answer to the question he had raised early in his career in *Suicide*. How can our modern, complex, and largely secular societies attain analogous levels of social solidarity to that enjoyed by small-scale Australian aboriginal societies, sufficient to prevent the self-destructive malaises the causes of which he sought to understand and explain? The answer that comes to Durkheim from the Australian Outback is *sacrifice*. For not only is sacrifice a giving of the self, and by virtue of that a counteragent to the modern egoism that lies at the root causes of suicide, but it is also a powerful rite that creates, at the same time, the 'sacred' which, in its turn, puts the spiritual back at the center of social life as well. The meaning of the word 'sacrifice,' we will recall, is rooted in its Latin form, *sacra-ficium* – a 'making holy.' If we want to restore a measure of wholeness to our society, we need then, says Durkheim, to restore some sense of rising above our own individualities to embrace common values that we hold 'sacred' – that form the consensus that binds us together, that we seek to protect against *desecration* – our *sacred*. We need, in effect, a 'religious' core at the center of our lives, because for Durkheim that religious core was the sacred, and the sacred, by its very nature, functions to attract adherents to itself because it is the incarnation of what we value most.

References

Bossy, J. 1982. Some Elementary Forms of Durkheim. *Past and Present* 95, pp. 3–18.

Chantepie de la Saussaye, P. D. 1904. *Manuel d'histoire des religions*, trans. H. Hubert & I. Lévy. Paris: Armand Colin.

Durkheim, E. 1951. *Suicide*, trans. J. A. Spaulding & G. Simpson. New York: Free Press.

Durkheim, É. 1898. Individuals and the Intellectuals. In *Durkheim on Religion*, ed. W. S. F. Pickering. London: Routledge.

——. 1915. *The Elementary Forms of Religious Life*, trans. J. W. Swain. New York: Free Press.

——. 1957. *Professional Ethics and Civic Morals*, trans. C. Brookfield. Westport, CT: Greenwood Press.

——. 1962. *Socialism*, trans. C. Sattler. New York: Collier Books.

——. 1974. Individual and Collective Representations. In *Sociology and Philosophy*. New York: Free Press.

——. 1975a. Contribution to Discussion: Religious Sentiment at the Present Time. In *Durkheim on Religion*, ed. W. S. F. Pickering. London: Routledge.

——. 1975b. Individualism and Intellectuals. In *Durkheim on Religion*, ed. W. S. F. Pickering. London: Routledge.

——. 1975c. Review of *Guyau, l'irreligion de l'avenir* [1887]. In *Durkheim on Religion*, ed. W. S. F. Pickering. London: Routledge.

——. 1977. *The Evolution of Educational Thought: Lectures on the Formation and Secondary Education in France*, trans. P. Collins. London: Routledge.

Editors, T. 1880. A Nos lecteurs. *Revue des études juives* 1, p. vii.

Filloux, J.-C., ed. 1970. *Émile Durkheim, La Science sociale et l'action*. Paris: Presses Universitaires de France.

Jones, R. A. 1981. Robertson Smith, Durkheim and Sacrifice: An Historical Context for *The Elementary Forms. Journal of the History of the Behavioral Sciences* 17, pp. 184–205.

Jones, R. A. & N. Gross, eds. 2004. *Durkheim's Philosophy Lectures: Notes from the Lycée de Sens Course, 1883–1884*. Cambridge: Cambridge University Press.

Jones, R. A. & P. W. Vogt. 1984. Durkheim's Defence of *Les formes élementaires de la vie religieuse*. In *Knowledge and Society: Studies in the Sociology of Culture. Past and Present* 5, ed. H. Kuklick. Greenwich, CT: JAI Press.

Lukes, S. 1972. *Emile Durkheim*. New York: Harper and Row.

Malinowski, B. 1962. Elementary Forms of Religious Life (A Review of). In *Sex, Culture and Myth*. New York City: Harcourt Brace.

Mauss, M. 1967. *The Gift: The Form and Functions of Exchange in Archaic Societies*, trans. I. Cunnison. New York: W. W. Norton.

Mestrovic, S. G. 1988. *Emile Durkheim and the Reformation of Sociology*. Totowa, NJ: Rowman and Littlefield.

Réville, J. 1892. Review of Darmesteter's *Les prophètes d'Israel*. *Revue d'histoire des religions* 25, pp. 253–6.

Robertson Smith, W. 1923. *Lectures on the Religion of the Semites*. London: A. & C. Black.

Strenski, I. 1997. *Durkheim and the Jews of France*. Chicago: University of Chicago Press.

——. 2003. *Theology and the First Theory of Sacrifice*. Leiden: Brill.

Weber, E. 1959. *The Nationalist Revival in France, 1905–1914*. Berkeley: University of California Publications in History.

Mircea Eliade: Turning the 'Worm of Doubt'

12

That moment – unique, infinite – revealed to him the total beatitude he had yearned for for so many years. It was there in the glance she bestowed on him, bathed in tears. He had known from the beginning this was the way it would be. He had known that, feeling him very near her, she would turn her head and look at him. He had known that this last moment without end, would suffice.

–Eliade 1978, p. 596

A Real Religious Radical

Mircea Eliade (1907–86) was, without doubt, one of the most influential comparativists and interpreters of religion of the twentieth century. Almost single-handedly, he established the international reputation of the study of religions in North America, as perhaps no one else could. And, if anyone in this book can be called a sincerely and radically religious person, it would be Eliade. If anyone, moreover, could be said to have been a genuine mystic, it would be Eliade again. True, Max Müller may have had German Romantic nature-mystic inclinations, as evidenced by his reveling in the transcendence of natural beauty and his talk of "the Infinite" and "the Unknown." In our own modern-day appreciation of nature, says Müller, "do we not feel the overwhelming pressure of the Infinite ... from which no one can escape who has eyes to see and ears to hear?" (Voigt 1967, p. 32). Indeed, with such talk of "the Infinite," Müller even gives us every reason to imagine him hoping for, and perhaps even trying to participate in, an Idealist Absolutist dissolution of the self in the Great Self of the universe. This should come as no surprise, since Müller's scholarship on the religions of India participated, as we know, in the spirit of "Indomania," fed by such Romantic Monist philosophers as the Schlegel brothers and Schelling (Trautmann 1997, p. 138). Whether this neo-Hindu monistic spirituality expressed itself in any more than Müller's own pious thinking, we do not know. Eliade's thought bears the same marks, and more – he really did something about these ideas in his life.

Thus, among the great students of religion that we have studied, only Eliade can claim to have received official training in *yoga* and *tantra*, venturing to India to sit with gurus in the foothills of the Himalayas. I do not think the mature Eliade ever really abandoned

Figure 12.1. Mircea Eliade, aged 23 years, in the Calcutta home of philosopher S. N. Dasgupta, 1930

Source: Mircea Eliade, *Autobiography. Volume I: 1907–1937. Journey East, Journey West* (New York: Harper and Row, 1981), frontispiece.

the vision implicit in these youthful metaphysical commitments, especially as they took the form of a Hindu spirituality, known as Advaita Vedānta. A Sanskrit term literally translated as 'not-dual,' *advaita* is an interpretation of the Indian scriptures, dating from one of classic India's greatest religious thinkers, śankarācharya (788–820 CE). In our own time, it was propagated by Eliade's professor of philosophy at Calcutta from 1928 to 1931, the great Surendranath Dasgupta, among others. This philosophy holds to a metaphysics of the essential oneness of all reality. All difference is in the end only illusion. The only real reality is the one underlying *brahman*, which in turn consists of *sāt*, *cit*, and *ā nanda* – being, thought, and bliss. Eliade remained then a very unique kind of religious nondualist throughout his life. As a consequence, I believe, therefore, that Eliade's approach to religion remained more or less strongly marked by affinities with Advaita Vedānta thought and forms of Western thought congruent with it. And that is why we need to see Eliade's religious orientation as a key to understanding the whole man and his work.

In observing the character and depth of Eliade's religiosity, I am making less a biographical point than one about the fundamental character of Eliade's approach to the study of religion. Thus in calling attention to the seriousness of Eliade's religiosity, I do not mean to play down the sincerity of the more traditional Western religiosity of Bodin, Herbert of Cherbury, Robertson Smith, Max Müller, and all of the Deists and phenomenologists of religion put together. I claim in this chapter, however, that unlike the thinkers we have met in this volume, Eliade radically and systematically rejected the very epistemological and ontological foundations of the 'modern' secular world that we discussed in our introduction.

For Eliade, ordinary means of knowledge and experience are not only flawed, but really spread a veil of māyā over our knowledge of reality. Eliade's life-long commitment to a radical form of "new religious consciousness" is, I shall argue, a key to unlocking the otherwise refractory nature of his proposals for the study of religion. Two noted American scholars of religion, Robert Bellah and Walter Capps, recognized these religious implications in Eliade's thinking decades ago when they concurred in seeing a "revised methodology" for religious studies, inspired by Eliade, as a playing a role in "stimulating new religion." Bellah writes explicitly of " Religious Studies as 'New Religion' " (Bellah 1978, p. 111; Capps 1978, p. 103). Eliade is perhaps then the most radical student of religion we have met, not because he is either a 'critic' or less even an 'undertaker' of religion, but because he is a full-blown 'caretaker' of religion and, moreover, a 'caretaker' or – as Bellah and Capps correctly see Eliade –a 'maker' of religion who proceeds on the assumption that the epistemology of modern knowledge ought to be turned on its head.

For this reason, as the title of this chapter indicates, I allude to the image of the 'worm of doubt' – that metaphor signaling the slow gnawing away of religious vision and faith brought on by modern trends of secularization. Accordingly, I suggest that one way to look on Eliade's approach to the study of religion is as a deliberately (and contrary) religious assault on secularity – a 'turning' of doubts about religion into doubts about secularity at its very roots. As we will see, Eliade has a thoroughly religious purpose for studying religion – it is utterly to undermine the modern consensus about the character of human knowledge in order to smooth the way for a higher gnosis, as it were. Eliade thus not only tries to sustain a radical critique of modern irreligiousness, but he also seeks to shake the foundations upon which it, and everything else connected with it, could be said to stand. Eliade seeks to 'make' – to create – a new religious consciousness by the way he proposes that religion ought to be studied. In the spirit of Advaitin idealism, Eliade sees the sacred and timeless as real, as rich in *being*, and the profane and historical as not: as representing, as it were, the illusory realm of māyā. By contrast, as much as our phenomenologists of religion wished to show how autonomous religion was of, say, economic determinants, they would not have declared economic life languishing in a diminished state of being, and the sacred as the primary underlying reality – of economic and every other form of secular life. Nor did they go as far as we will see Eliade go in declaring the phenomenon of religion an absolutely autonomous domain! Eliade thus in effect rejected the naturalism that all the thinkers of this book have in one way or another kept as their lodestar, no matter how errant they may have become from time to time. His study of religion can thus be described as an attempt at a 'super-naturalist' study of religion.

This chapter then devotes itself to addressing the question of how Eliade approaches religion from a radically – for him – religious perspective, and why he *thinks that he is right* in doing so. The story of Eliade's revolution in the study of religion begins with his assault on the historical study of religion.

An 'Antihistorian of Religion'

During the course of this book, we have seen what a powerful contribution to the study of religion the discipline of history has made. Everything from the rise of historical criticism of the Bible, to Max Müller's tracing of the migration of the Indo-European language, myth, and religion, through to what we might call Max Weber's 'religious history' of modern capitalism, speaks loudly for the benefits of the historical sciences in the study of religion. Eliade seems to embrace this tradition by frequent affirmations of his regard and concern for history, even referring to his approach to religion as "History of Religion." Thus, Eliade says that "the historian of religions *sensu stricto* can never ignore that which is historically concrete," and that "religious documents are at the same time historical documents" (Eliade 1959, p. 88).

The problem is unfortunately that what Eliade gives with one hand, he takes away with the other. Indeed, he qualifies his approach to history so much that, at least to this reader, he seems to be talking out of both sides of his mouth:

> I am not denying the importance of history... for the estimate of the true value of this or that symbol, *as it was understood and lived in a specific culture* .... But it is not by 'placing' a symbol in its own history that we can resolve the essential problem – namely, to know what is revealed to us, not by any particular version of a symbol, but by the *whole* of a symbolism. (Eliade 1961, p. 63)

Just what it would mean to speak of the "whole of a symbolism" – especially in *contrast* to speaking of symbols in their cultural and *historical* contexts? While it is true that this is something Eliade will make clear when he reveals his theory of transcendent religious archetypes, it still puzzles historians as a criticism of their work. Similarly, when Eliade presents us with the apparently dichotomous claim that the history of religions "is attracted to both the *meaning* of a religious phenomenon and its history," any historian would see this distinction as false (Eliade 1959, p. 88). Historians try to do much more than "merely to piece together an event or a series of events," Eliade says (Eliade 1958, p. 5). They are just as concerned with the "meaning" of events as Eliade. No historian these days – nor in Eliade's time either – would accept such a loaded description of their discipline as Eliade offers. History proper only begins when chronicle has been superseded by the interpretive art of making an intelligible whole from the raw facts of the chronicle. Second, as we know from interpretive history as inspired by Dilthey, historical accounts thrive on informing their narratives with attempts to capture the intentions of actors. Historians as a rule do not ignore meaning and subjectivity – especially when attention to the intentions of actors in historical narrative is standard historical practice for any but the dullest positivists (Skinner 1969).

So, we are left to conclude that deeper purposes are being worked out in Eliade's writing about history and historical inquiry, as indeed proves to be the case. I conclude that Eliade is flat out opposed to the historical study of religion, and tries to hide his own reasons for being so under the cover of the weak arguments diminishing the status of historical inquiry we have seen. Rather than being a 'historian of religions' in any ordinary sense, Eliade's true loyalties are to what we will see is a kind of *psychological* study of religion – "creative hermeneutics." By 'trashing' the way historians really work, Eliade is free to celebrate his "History of Religions" as interested instead in "higher," "deeper," "primary," or "original" meanings (Eliade 1959, p. 94; 1964b, p. xiii; 1965, p. 210).

A 'History' of the Nonhistorical Is Not Possible

But before we explore the essence of Eliade's "creative hermeneutics," we need to try see in part why Eliade *thinks he is right* to denigrate the historical study of religion. As in other places where he seems to play on the ambiguity of language, we find something similar in the way Eliade talks about 'history.' For one thing, he talks about 'history' in both the sense of an approach or method for the study of religion, but also as a kind of ontological category. Thus, he tells us that he mistrusts "historical" *methods* of treating religion because he believes religion itself transcends the ontological category of "historical" *being*. Since, for Eliade, the object of the study of religion (for instance, God) is *beyond* historical reality, the student of religion must reflect that transcendence by adopting a method that also transcends history – an *ahistorical* method: "What distinguishes the historian of religion from the historian . . . is that he is dealing with facts which, although historical, reveal a behaviour that goes beyond the historical involvement of the human being" (Eliade 1961, pp. 32 ff.). Thus, Eliade says, "the history of religions is concerned not only with the *historical becoming* of a religious form, but also with its *structure*." But why does he go on immediately to insinuate that religious 'structures' are not part of historical change:

> For religious forms are non-temporal; they are not necessarily bound to time. We have no proof that religious structures are created by certain types of civilisation or by certain historic moments. When we consider religious structures historically, it is their statistical frequency which matters. But religious reality is more complex: it transcends the plane of history. (Eliade 1968, pp. 179–80)

So, there it is – a remarkable claim indeed – that because Eliade judges the "forms" or "structures" of religion to be beyond history, and thus to be impervious to historical change, the study of religion should not be an "historical" discipline. Eliade's "History of Religions" is then a distinctly odd, not to say confusing, kind of *history* of religions!

To give Eliade his due, there are the occasional places in his *oeuvre* where he admits to his true attitude to the historical sciences. This, of course, not only came *en passant*, but well after the web of confusion woven by Eliade had ensnared countless scholars and students in the belief that Eliade was an 'historian of religion' in any honest sense of that term. In this rare admission of mischief, Eliade says: "In short, we have neglected this essential fact: that in the title of the 'history of religions' the accent ought not to be on the word *history* but upon the word *religions*" (Eliade 1961, p. 29). Guilford Dudley captured Eliade's misleading use of the term 'history' in "History of Religion" decades ago, accurately labeling Eliade an "anti-historian of religions" (Dudley 1977, p. 148). Sad to say, Dudley's keen grasp of Eliade's deceptions counted for little against the fame Eliade enjoyed from his prestigious position in the academic world.

Eliade as Psychologist of Religion

Another reason that Eliade thought that he was right to sully the reputation of history is that he thought he had a far better method of getting at the fundamentals of religion – his own special variant of depth-psychological interpretation or hermeneutics.

> The history of religions is not merely a historical discipline, as, for example, are archeology or numismatics. It is equally a total hermeneutics, being called to decipher and explicate every kind of encounter of man with the sacred, from prehistory to our day. (Eliade 1969b, p. 58)

Eliade believes that a depth-psychology, much like Freud's, can get to the 'rock bottom' of religion. Eliade knew and sponsored Freudian ideas to some degree in the Romania of the early 1930s (Eliade 1982, p. 75). And, in doing so, he seems to have repeated the confusion (or attempted fusion?) of science and hermeneutics of which Freud himself is arguably guilty, as we have seen. On the one hand, Eliade says he is interpreting religion – doing a hermeneutics; but on the other hand, he thinks we can get to the nature of religion by a kind of magical employment of empathy – rejected by Weber, for instance – or by means of a mysterious sort of intuition or introspection. For what it is worth, some years ago, Professor Philip Hammond, now emeritus professor of religious studies at the University of California, Santa Barbara, informed me that he had heard that when Eliade was asked how he did his "scientific" writing, he replied "by intuition, the same as when I write my novels." Eliade's difficult style is thus no mere accident, but rather a deliberate choice. Therefore, he may inadvertently be correct when he says that the historian of religions proceeds "no differently" from the depth-psychologist, since Freud too, as we have seen, wobbled back and forth over whether he was just interpreting data or providing a scientific explanation of it. Nonetheless, Eliade wants there to be a very close analogy between his approach to decoding religious meanings and the 'uncovering' of the meanings of things the clients of psychoanalysis have to say (Eliade 1959, p. 95).

Let us consider Eliade's 'history of religions' as a *common* hermeneutic method. We will see shortly that he also proposes what he calls his own special kind of hermeneutics, "creative hermeneutics." In Eliade's view of this everyday hermeneutics, the depth-psychologist approaches human personality much as we saw Freud do. Freud's student, Jung, an inspiration of Eliade's in this area, worked in the same way. We will recall that for Freud psychoanalysis arose from medical practice. He adapted a 'hermeneutic' practice for interpreting physical data to applications having to do with the mind. This style of interpretation sought to decode the meaning of bodily states and verbal reports as signs of other hidden causes. These observable data became "symptoms" of what 'lay beneath.' Freud, like Eliade, referred to his approach as a kind of "hermeneutic." Like the interpreters of biblical materials who first employed the term, Freud approached mental data such as dreams, for example, "like a sacred text" (Preus 1987, p. 185). On this everyday hermeneutic view of psychoanalytic method, Freud (and Eliade) work like detectives, reading what they see as indicators of certain underlying mental structures. The task of psychoanalysis is to address those underlying meanings so that patients can be healed by reference to the hidden condition behind the particular set of symptoms.

As Eliade sees it, the historian of religions takes on the data of historical religious situations as the depth-psychologist takes on individual human situations. Both then apply theoretical models to these data in an attempt to make sense of them. The depth-psychologist is armed with a theory of the way the psyche works, as we saw with Freud's theory of ego, id, and superego, while Eliade's brand of historian of religion applies a theory of religious formation governed by the way he thinks religion works. For Eliade, religion works because, like Jung with the individual, certain archetypes shape religious data. As depth-psychology attributes certain experiences of an individual's history to the working-out of the psychic archetypes, so similarly does the history of religions interpret religious data from what Eliade calls a "more spiritual standpoint" – from the perspective of being an historical expression of a transcendental archetype (Eliade 1961, p. 31).

In an odd way, even though Eliade disdains the scientism of Freud and others, his conception of depth-psychology is remarkably scientistic, despite his embrace of hermeneutics. For Eliade, depth-psychology actually discovers new *facts* about religion; it does not just provide a creative or insightful *interpretation* of things. Eliade calls these facts "the archaic modes of psychic life." Like Jung, Eliade believes that the archetypes he discerns in his interpretation of religious data are also real structural elements that play a causal role in shaping and informing religious experience. These elements are what Jung referred to as real effects of human experiences accumulated through the long history of humanity (Dry 1961, p. 92). Significantly, Jung's view wins wide approval from Eliade: "Every historical man carries on, within himself, a great deal of prehistoric humanity" (Eliade 1961, p. 12). And again, Eliade claims that "archaic modes of psychic life are 'living fossils' buried in the darkness of the unconscious, which now become accessible to study through the techniques developed by depth-psychologists" (Eliade 1960, p. xix). So, although he embraces the freedom of hermeneutics, and even trumpets his loyalty to the openness of the interpretive art, at the same time he seems to want to claim that the models he uses to interpret experience are really 'set in the concrete' of the mind itself!

Whatever else may be true, this suggests that Eliade has a great deal of confidence in his abilities to plumb the truth of things. Indeed, he lays claim to powerful intuitive abilities that, in effect, guarantee the truth of what he says about the human mind and human religion – at least to his satisfaction. Thus, although the archaic psychic history of humankind is not accessible to empirical investigation, such as through history, it is, Eliade believes, accessible to depth-psychological introspection. Proceeding by what he calls "immediate intuition" (Eliade 1959, p. 95), the historian of religions can confidently go about his researches without being taxed with the laborious requirements of empirical study. Historians of religion only need to activate their intuitive powers. Thus, Eliade rejects ordinary empirical methods of learning about the "the mental universe of archaic man," such as, for example, inquiring into their "explicit beliefs." Rather, this set of mental structures can be grasped because they are "preserved to us in myths, symbols, and customs which still, in spite of every corruption, show clearly what they meant when they began" (Eliade 1958, p. 10). And, since Eliade is not saying here that this 'discovery' is only one possible interpretation among many, he is saying that the structures so preserved are objective facts. So confident is Eliade of his knowledge of the 'real' meaning of symbols that he thinks he knows these meanings better than the symbol users themselves. Should the 'natives' reject Eliade's intuitions, there is no evidence that he would back down from his assertion of the meanings he feels are 'there.' From his lofty perspective of superior knowledge, Eliade feels, therefore, that he can say that

> we do not have the right to conclude that the message of the symbols is confined to the meanings of which a certain number of individuals are fully conscious, even when we learn from a rigorous investigation of these individuals what they think of such and such a symbol belonging to their own tradition. Depth-psychology has taught us that the symbol delivers its message and fulfils its function even when its meaning escapes awareness. (Eliade 1959, p. 106)

So, together with Freud and others like him, Eliade thinks that 'doctor knows best.'

In this light, it is hard to know what would get Eliade to change his mind. Introspection is for him self-authenticating. That is at least one reason I think it might be useful to think of Eliade as a 'guru of religious studies,' adapting the radical spiritualist and intuitionist epistemology of his Yogic teachers in the Himalayas from far back in his youth to his new situation as interpreter of religious data. Eliade has made the self-authentication of his intuitions the epistemological grounds of his discipline – something that not even those who celebrated 'empathy' were willing to do – in particular, Max Weber, as we may recall. For Eliade, 'empathy' has taken on magical mind-reading proportions. Eliade has put himself into the position of saying that his judgments about the minds of others are infallible. His kind of historian of religions becomes potentially the one who knows other minds better than the owners of those minds themselves – an arrogant claim indeed for a man of such gentle reputation. Intuition may be the way we *discover* certain truths – if, say, the term stands for some special mode of knowing. But it cannot certify this discovery: intuitions are not self-authenticating, even if Descartes and others mistakenly thought so. Cannot our 'intuitions' ever be mistaken? Of course they can, just as easily as our hunches on winning horses or football teams can fall short of the truth. Why is Eliade an exception? We will want eventually to seek the reasons behind his *thinking he is right* about his ability to know what other people think better than they themselves, even beyond his experiences as a yogin and a devotee of depth-psychology. This will take us back into his intellectual and social nurture in Romania, where the same kind of intuitionist thinking prevailed. But looking at the conditions of Eliade's life that made it easy for him to think that yogic epistemology and depth-psychology ought to be the measure of interpreting religious materials, we need to flesh out Eliade's unique adaptations of these two influences on his interpretive craft – "creative hermeneutics."

The 'Worm of Doubt' Turns: Eliade's "Creative Hermeneutics"

Another way that we can appreciate Eliade's engagement in an interpretive style of the depth-psychologists is by focusing on Eliade's own novel method of interpretation proposed for the study of religion. This is his so-called "creative hermeneutics" – the "royal road of the history of religions" (Eliade 1969b, p. 62). In choosing to name his method as "creative hermeneutics," Eliade delights in a certain delicious ambiguity of the term. The journalist Claude-Henri Rocquet even drew such an admission from Eliade in an interview – of the "almost devilish gift," says Rocquet, "for throwing your listeners off the scent, for twisting and turning your plots so that one becomes unable to tell true from false, left from right." Without a blush, Eliade replied "That's true. I even think it is a specific character of at least some of my prose writings" (Eliade 1982, p. 48). Ambiguity and a kind of slipperiness characterizes Eliade's writing. Its frequent occurrence is, naturally enough, both 'good news' and 'bad news' for our attempts to understand what he is saying.

First, "hermeneutics" is an approach to cultural or human matters that we should understand from our treatment of the phenomenologists of religion and biblical critics. But even here there may be more to Eliade's invocation of hermeneutics than meets the eye. We should recall that Eliade himself studied Italian Renaissance "hermeticists" during his sojourn in Italy in 1928, and would have been well aware of the historical and religious pedigree of the term itself. In this sense, hermeneutics carries magical overtones, lent by its association with the god Hermes (the Latin, Mercury) or Hermes Trismegistus. Thus, 'hermeneutics' is the divine art of Hermes (Mercury), whom the dictionary names as the messenger and herald for the gods, but also the patron of travelers and rogues. Likewise, he is defined as the god of commerce and invention, but also the deity embodying cunning and theft. Do we have, as it seems, more of Eliade's suggestive and subversive ambiguities? Plausibly so, since, as we will see by Eliade's conception of the interpretive act, there is surely a 'mercurial' religious mind at work here, perhaps seeking to 'revive' the archaic wisdom of the god, Hermes, for the purposes of an interpretative method. And, insofar as Eliade acknowledges devotion to the divine Hermes, his 'hermen-eutics' is an act of piety.

Second, beyond the intriguing possibilities hidden away in the term "hermeneutics," what could Eliade mean in calling his exercise of interpretation "creative" – understood in the everyday sense of 'fresh,' 'original,' or 'inventive'? I mean, would any phenomen-ologist of religion willingly say that their interpretations were *not* creative – 'fresh,' 'original,' or 'inventive'? No, of course not, and neither would Eliade. So, we might fix upon another sense of the ambiguous word "creative," and enter more deeply into Eliade's own theory of religion. Here we need to bear in mind the central role in religion that Eliade gives to the act of creation – both by the divine creator and human creators as well. His "creative hermeneutics" is for him a way of actualizing the primary model, or "archetype," of religious activity itself – divine creation itself. Doing "creative hermen-eutics" – being an "Historian of Religion" in Eliade's special sense of the term – is to engage in a profoundly religious action, because one is recalling and being guided by the archetypal religious act itself – the divine creation of all things. Thus, Eliade seeks to rally historians of religion to a bolder, revolutionary approach to their subject. Many of them, he believes, have 'sinned' "through an excessive timidity and leave to others the task of interpreting . . . spiritual universes." Eliade urges them instead to embrace his radical "creative hermeneutics" (Eliade 1969b, p. 71). He challenges historians of religion to regain their 'nerve' and stem the "progressive loss of creativity and an accompanying loss of interpretive cultural syntheses" in the study of religion (Eliade 1969b, p. 58).

I take Eliade to be intending both these senses of "creative hermeneutics," and in doing so to be launching a truly radical approach to the study of religion, because it is at the same time a *making of religion*. To be "creative" Eliade means that his interpretive forays into religious data are active. They are meant to produce revolutionary effects in today's secular society. The mere act of his interpretations will, Eliade believes, make it impossible for secular people to see the world in quite the same way as before. They will be unable to resist seeing the world in a religious way, Eliade believes – or at least leaving open the door for a the possibility of a religious view of the world. The whole purpose of his intellectual career and all his many publications is directed at this active 'creative' goal: "the history of religions envisages, in the end, cultural *creation* and the *modification* of man" (Eliade 1969b, p. 67).

If this reminds us of the revolutionary features of Freudian thought, it is for good reason – a fact that Eliade well recognizes and approves (Eliade 1969b, p. 59)! Freud, albeit operating from "scientistic" principles, sought, like Eliade, to disrupt the everyday conventional consciousness of his contemporaries, few of whom would have granted his theories of the deep unconscious any plausibility (Todorov 1989). True or false, making a place for the mere plausibility of the existence of the deep unconscious posited by Freud has made it impossible for many modern folk to look at human affairs without, at least, *wondering* about unconscious forces at work. As we have seen for traditional religious belief of his day, Freud intended and in large part succeeded in planting the 'worm of doubt' into theism. This is a little like lovers having their confidence shaken by an act of infidelity. While the lovers may become reconciled and reunited after such infidelity, the 'worm of doubt' will have done its pernicious work. A kind of innocence will have been lost no matter how warm the reconciliation repairing the infidelity has been. The same can be said to be true of the corrosive effect of Freudian and other psychoanalytic ideas about religion, no matter whether they are ultimately discredited or not. The 'worm of doubt' that Freud insinuated into the midst of modern religious consciousness by linking it to the powerful influences of our childhood memories cannot cavalierly be dismissed. It will always be there for us no matter how far in the shadows it may lurk. There is no going back, even as we may want to revise or correct aspects of Freudian ideas. For this reason, Eliade consciously takes up an analogy between his "creative hermeneutics" and the impact of modern movements in the arts, such as surrealism. He praises the surrealists generously for their "attacks on bourgeois society and morality," and the way they "elaborated a revolutionary aesthetic" and "also formulated a technique by which they hoped to *change* the human condition" (Eliade 1969b, p. 65), even to the extent that it contributed to the "destruction of the official cultural world" (Eliade 1969b, p. 4). It is the secular world that Eliade's "creative hermeneutics" seeks to destroy (*sic*)!

Eliade in effect asks, if the Freudian "scientistic" breakthroughs *against* religion have destroyed the 'official religious world,' so to speak, why should not he engineer a religious 'destruction' of the confidence of *secular* consciousness? One might then look at Eliade's project as part of an insurgency against entrenched ideas by the secular scientific (and 'scientistic') 'establishment,' just as Freud's was the opposite kind of assault on the confident presumptions of the religious establishment dominant in his own time. In this vein, Eliade says that his "creative hermeneutics changes man" – meaning here irreligious "man," of course. Thus, for Eliade, creative hermeneutics "is more than instruction, it is also a spiritual technique susceptible of modifying the quality of existence itself" – again meaning an "existence" which is not religious. Thus, what Eliade writes – a "good history of religions book," for example – should make a difference to irreligious humanity. It "ought to produce in the reader an...awakening" (Eliade 1969b, p. 62). Eliade's "creative hermeneutics" thus aims to enlighten the benighted consciousness of the modern secularist with irresistibly religious meanings, and thus merit the 'creative' tag.

What then makes Eliade's hermeneutics – his "creative hermeneutics" – unique, and utterly revolutionary, is his belief that he can, in effect, turn the consciousness of the secular world upside-down. His 'history of religions' by way of the technique of "creative hermeneutics" can convert today's nonbelieving secular people into profoundly religious people. More precisely, Eliade believes that he can convince modern secular people to *realize* that they are *already* religious. Secularity then is a kind of *māyā*, an illusion that he seeks to dispel by instructing secular people to see the sacred lurking under their noses, disguised as profanity. This conviction that the therapeutic process is one of *realizing* who or what one already is, rests on Eliade's view of the nature of the human psyche, and conforms, as students of the religions of India will recognize, to models of ultimate release taught by the mystics of *Advaita Vedānta*. Thus, Eliade believes – like Freud – that buried in the unconscious of modern people are powerful meanings that only wait to be released into the consciousness, that only wait to be uncovered. For Eliade, it is our deep religiosity that waits to be 'awakened,' not, say, our troubled infantile sexual desires.

> in the case of those moderns who proclaim that they are nonreligious, religion and mythology are "eclipsed" in the darkness of their unconscious – which means too that in such men the possibility of reintegrating a religious vision of life lies at a great depth. Or from the Christian point of view, it could also be said that nonreligion is equivalent

to a new "fall" of man – in other words, that nonreligious man has lost the capacity to live religion consciously, and hence to understand and assume it; but that in his deepest being he still retains a memory of it as, after the first "fall," his ancestor, the primordial man, retained intelligence enough to enable him to rediscover the traces of God that are visible in the world. (Eliade 1957, p. 213)

Eliade believes that he can snap modern secular people out of their dogmatically antireligious 'slumbers' by his method of "creative hermeneutics."

Eliade freely offers examples of how "creative hermeneutics" works to achieve this revolutionary goal. Again, without for the moment judging the truth or falsity of his approach, let me try to say *why he thought he was right* in claiming that his "creative hermeneutics" could achieve the goals of religious transformation that I have just described.

Eliade's "Religion" in Time and Space

First, in order to understand how Eliade thinks his "creative hermeneutics" can effect the cultural transformations that he seeks, we need to grasp what he understands as religion. For him, 'religion' is a rather complex notion, and thus one that will require a bit of 'unpacking' and explication. To begin, for Eliade, religion has a specific content or nature. At its most preliminary level, Eliade posits (notably along with Otto, many of the phenomenologists, and Durkheim) that religion is the orientation of people to the "sacred." Indeed, one of Eliade's most influential books, *The Sacred and Profane: The Nature of Religion*, elaborates this point of view directly as the title and subtitle indicate (Eliade 1957). The salience of Eliade's theory of religion is, then, to be found in his theory of the sacred. There, explicitly echoing Otto, Eliade declares that for him too the sacred is above all "something wholly different from the profane" (Eliade 1957, p. 11). Or, as Eliade says, the "first possible definition of the sacred is that it is the opposite of the profane" (Eliade 1957, p. 10).

But such definitions are merely formal. What we want to know is what the *content* of Eliade's idea of the sacred is. We want to know this because we will want to bring this discussion eventually back to the way "creative hermeneutics" works to 'redeem' "the man who lives, or wishes to live, in a desacralized world," as Eliade puts it (Eliade 1957, p. 13). We will also want to know this since it will reveal Eliade's idea of a new method in the study of religion that Bellah and Capps applaud for its contribution to a new religious consciousness by way of their (pseudo-)academic study of religion. How does that happen, given Eliade's understanding of religion and the sacred?

In terms of content, Eliade tells us that he resists Otto's definition of the content of the sacred in terms of the "irrational." As if addressing potential dissatisfactions with a merely formal definition of religion and the sacred, Eliade expresses his understanding of the sacred in more concrete and positive terms: "We propose to present the phenomenon of the sacred in all its complexity, and not only in so far as it is irrational. What will concern us is not the relation between the rational and nonrational elements of religion but the sacred in its entirety" (Eliade 1957, p. 10).

The Sacred Space of the Creative Center

By "entirety," Eliade means to flesh out how the sacred is realized across the whole range of human religious experience. Beginning with the two most basic conditions of experience itself – time and space – Eliade articulates what he believes it means for something to be felt to be sacred – what it means to experience the sacred – in these two fundamental modalities of human experience. *Homo religiosus*, as Eliade calls the religious person, sees space in a totally different way than does the "the man who lives, or wishes to live, in a desacralized world." For *homo religiosus*, space is structured hierarchically and formed according to a definite set of values; it is not the space of "homogeneity and relativity of profane space" that a person living in a desacralized world experiences (Eliade 1957, pp. 20–2). Therefore, "for religious man, every existential decision to situate himself in space in fact constitutes a religious decision" (Eliade 1957, p. 65). To make this decision to value some spaces and places more than others, is to participate in the radical distinction of sacred from profane – and on the side of the sacred.

Some actual physical places will, therefore, be more important than other places for *homo religiosus*. A hierarchy of space exists that encodes the values of religious man. Eliade notes tellingly in an example that for

> a believer, the church shares a different space from the street in which it stands. . . . The threshold that separates the two spaces . . . indicates the distance between two modes of being, the profane and the religious. The threshold is the limit, the boundary, the frontier that distinguishes and opposes two worlds – and at the same time the paradoxical place where those worlds communicate, where passage from the profane to the sacred world becomes possible. (Eliade 1957, p. 25)

Homo religiosus thus divides the world into actual special – religious – sacred spaces and places, and others which are mundane, commonplace, profane. But on what basis is such a bifurcation of the world of experience made? How does some place or space *become* sacred?

Eliade can conceive of nothing more *sacred* nor more essentially holy than the divine creation of the world. But the route to our experience of the divine creation needs to pass through modalities of space and time, and for this Eliade needs to link creation to a configuration of space – or our experience thereof.

> It must be said at once that the religious experience of the nonhomogeneity of space is a primordial experience, homologizable to a founding of the world. It is not a matter of theoretical speculation, but of a primary religious experience that precedes all reflection on the world. For it is the break effected in space that allows the world to be constituted, because it reveals the fixed point, the central axis for all future orientation. When the sacred manifests itself in any hierophany, there is not only a break in the homogeneity of space; there is also revelation of an absolute reality, opposed to the nonreality of the vast surrounding expanse. The manifestation the sacred ontologically founds the world. (Eliade 1957, pp. 20–1)

For Eliade, then, among other things, a configuration of space that perfectly expresses the sacredness inherent in creation is the symbol of the center. *Homo religiosus* sees the world as created by the divine by seeing it as oriented about a focus, as an arena of value, as imbued with meaning. In creating the world, the divine orients life around a core set of values. Creation is not blind, according to Eliade, since it stands for an assertion of being in a domain otherwise characterized as nonbeing. The divine creation is itself the preeminent and most positively affirmative of acts. For *homo religiosus*, those things affirming this divine act of creation are unapologetically better than others, because in creating, the divine has laid down some principles, has declared some things 'central' and others 'peripheral.' This structured view of the world stands in stark contrast, then, to the secular view of things, where values are relative and existence meaningless because they are not anchored in a creative divine being. Here, in the religious world, nothing is meaningless, because everything is experienced as existing in subordination to a center from which creation emanates.

In more actual terms, Eliade points out that this 'centered' way of experiencing the spatial dimension of existence accounts for the remarkable number of instances in which religious sites are organized about concrete centers (Eliade 1957, pp. 36–47). Whether this be the Ka'aba at Mecca as the focal point of all Muslim devotion, the conception of Jerusalem, the holy city, as the 'navel' or center of the world, the location of the capital of the Chinese king at the center of the world, or Mount Meru of South Asian Hindu and Buddhist religious mythology likewise being thought to be the focal point of earthly space, the same idea seems apparent. *Homo religiosus* sees the highest value – the sacred – as the ultimate principle of existential orientation, and thus embodies the ideal of creation in the way actual sacred spaces and places are organized, or at least felt to be organized.

In Eliade's view, things become sacred by being associated with essentially sacred acts. Consider a favorite example of Eliade's – the Cosmic Tree, which for Eliade is supposed to reflect and embody an essentially universal sacred act – "the perpetual regeneration of the world." While this general meaning differs superficially from the local meanings of various sacred trees, such as we saw attached to particular cults such as those of Attis hung upon a tree to die, or Jesus' death upon the cross, these and other tree cults have embodied ideas of fertility, vegetal regeneration, and the new life of the Spring season.

> It is because the Cosmic Tree symbolizes the mystery of the world in perpetual regeneration that it can symbolize, at the same time or successively, the pillar of the world and the cradle of the human race.... Each one of these *new* valorizations is possible because from the beginning the symbol of the Cosmic Tree reveals itself as a 'cipher' of the world grasped as a living reality, sacred and inexhaustible. (Eliade 1959, p. 194)

So, the particular and local tree cults take their holiness from a model, universal one – Eliade's archetype of the Cosmic Tree of the original creation.

As a necessary byproduct of the arrangement of physical space, loaded with these powerful universal meanings, this external world, so alive with significance, becomes a way of engineering mental attitudes toward the sacred. Thus the *mandalas* of Buddhist and Hindu meditational practice or the mazes and labyrinths of medieval Christianity not only reflect the idea of the prestige of the center, they also help us experience the spiritual orientation implied in them. By drawing the viewer ever more inward to their sacred centers, these devices for centering consciousness function to condition human consciousness for the contemplation of the centering value of the sacred in life. As physical space is arranged, so also the mind follows.

Although this array of sacred centers is impressive, and although we also might see how the religious value of centers can induce experiences of existential orientation, given specific religious cultural contexts and ideals, Eliade believes something far more profound, radical, and controversial. He believes that the entire centering phenomenon is itself a primary and essential universal of religion. "To us, it seems an inescapable conclusion that the religious man sought to live as near as possible to the Center of the World" (Eliade 1957, p. 43). This is because for Eliade, the ideal (or in his words, "archetype") of the center refers ultimately, although unconsciously, to the ultimate act of centering, orientation, and such – the divine creation of the cosmos. These individual centers are informed by a fundamental and universal religious attitude of desiring to be close to the center of the world:

> We have seen that the symbolism of the center is the formative principle not only of countries, cities, temples, and palaces but also of the humblest human dwelling, be it the tent of a nomad hunter, the shepherd's yurt, or the house of the sedentary man, he places himself at the Center of the World and by the same token at the very source of absolute reality.

The religious reason for such a desire is, in Eliade's eyes, that in desiring to be at the Center of the World people are expressing their desire to be close to the ultimate creative act of the divine creation of the world – a desire expressing itself in a powerful nostalgia for absolute beginnings.

> Religious man's profound nostalgia is to inhabit a "divine world," is his desire that his house shall be like the house of the gods, as it was later represented in temples and sanctuaries. In short, this religious nostalgia expresses the desire to live in a pure and holy cosmos, as it was in the beginning, when it came fresh from the Creator's hands. (Eliade 1957, p. 65)

Thus, Eliade thinks that in terms of the modality of space, a "creative hermeneutics" supplies a *religious* interpretation of things, a sacred reading of things because it brings out their centering, orienting, focusing aspects. And these acts of centering are sacred for Eliade, because they model divine creation – which is itself quintessentially sacred. Thus, if he can persuade modern secular people to see in any of their centering, orienting, or organizing activities the expression of such religious nostalgias for the freshness and purity of the absolute divine beginnings of things, he would have succeeded in transforming secular consciousness. Like the post-Freudian who cannot any longer innocently see the proverbial cigar as a cigar, Eliade hopes his hermeneutic can make it impossible for post-Eliadeans to see everyday centers, foci, and other similar configurations of space as the mere mundane features of life that they seem to be on the surface. Eliade believes that he can plant the 'worm of doubt' among the doubters, so to speak. By unsettling the arrogant and self-confident world of antireligious modern folk, Eliade believes he can 'reenchant' their world, by pointing them in the direction of their unconscious nostalgias for divine creation and its establishment of an absolute center of the world. And how could it be any other way, Eliade pleads? "The creation of the World being *the* preeminent instance of creation" thus "becomes the exemplary model for 'creation' of every kind" (Eliade 1964a, p. 21).

Myth Tells Us of the Eternal Time of Origins

What, however, of time? How is time as sacred rendered to profane temporal consciousness? As centered space is sacred space, what kind of time would sacred time be? As centered space recalls the ordering, constructive quality of an archetypal divine creation over against chaos, what qualities of time recall the same archetypal creative moment when all things came to be 'by the grace of God'?

Put this way, and knowing what we already know about Eliade's point of view, some answers seem readily to present themselves. If the divine creation remains the commanding archetypal religious event, so to speak, then the time of *origins* must be a prime candidate for Eliade's definition of sacred time. And indeed it is. The data for Eliade's conception of sacred time come from "myth." As Eliade shows how sacred space is realized by reference to various mappings of the world, such as those putting Jerusalem at the Center, he turns to stories – 'myths' – to provide examples of how sacred time is made real. A few words of warning are necessary, though, in speaking about Eliade's theory of myth and how it bears on sacred time.

I have put quotes around the word 'myth' because Eliade's idea of myth will have to be scrutinized before we do much with it. This is because he is guilty of a little logical slipperiness in speaking of myth. He first appeals to an apparently neutral notion of myth as 'story' as evidence to support his view that in myths we find many references to divine creation of the world. Eliade is right if all that he is saying is that there are many creation stories in the world treasure-house of narratives. But Eliade does not tell us about one very important decision that shapes his dealings with stories before they have begun. He selects as 'myths' only those stories that are *creation stories*. He has in effect *defined* 'myths' as creation stories from the very start.

This makes matters quite easy for him as his arguments develop, since he can talk universally about 'myth' as if indeed all the stories one might call 'myths' were in fact creation stories. This is only true if, as Eliade has done, we count creation stories as myths! Thus, Eliade says without qualification that "a myth is always related to a 'creation,' it tells us how something came into existence, or how a pattern of behaviour, an institution, a manner of working were established" (Eliade 1964a, p. 18). In the context of recommending his "creative hermeneutics," Eliade declares that "In general, one can say that any myth tells how something came into being, the world, or man, or an animal species, or a social institution" (Eliade 1969a, p. 75). Or, Eliade claims that "all myths participate in some sort in the cosmological type of myth – for every account of what came to pass in the holy era of the Beginning...is but another variant of the archetypal history: how the world came to be" (Eliade 1968, p. 15). This means that if a story is not about creation – in the rich and analogical way Eliade speaks of creation, as we have seen – it is not, by definition, something we should or could call a 'myth.' If a story is not, therefore, about 'centering' people in the creative and existential way that he has shown meditation upon sacred space does, then it cannot be a 'myth' – in his sense: "This is why," as Eliade tells us, "myths constitute the paradigms for all significant human acts," and why myth has always taught humankind "the primordial 'stories' that have constituted [us] existentially" (Eliade 1964a, p. 12).

Now, Eliade may be right to legislate the way we use the word 'myth' in this way – as creation stories, as stories of existential centering. But it is not obvious that we *ought* to do so. The definition of 'myth' is, as I have argued elsewhere, notoriously contested, and many other proposals for our use of the term 'myth' are currently being debated, with no end in sight to the debate (Strenski 1987).

With these issues duly noted, let me return to the problem of the moment. How and why did Eliade *think he was right* to stipulate that myths as creation stories are essentially sacred? Why and how does he believe that myths are the key to understanding the way sacred time is realized in human experience? How would the conclusions that he reaches, moreover, work to achieve that transformation of secular consciousness into religious consciousness that we have just seen in his efforts at exploring the symbolism of the center? If he is getting secular people to open their minds to the possibility that their orientations to centers and creativity reflect a deep nostalgia for "the Center" and thus the Creation, how does Eliade's idea of 'myth' introduce the 'worm of doubt' into secular consciousness about the materiality and finality of mundane time? How does Eliade think 'myth' stimulates a sense of sacred time for people who know only the mundane time of the everyday?

The answers to these questions are several, and all intriguing. First, if we agree that 'eternity' is a good benchmark instance of sacred time, we can see how and why Eliade finds the Creation such a suitable point of reference. Is not the moment just before creation a time without temporal duration, a 'time' when the 'time of God' was all there was? And is not that what 'eternity' is? From the Creation onward mundane time begins, and the essentially sacred 'time' of eternity is left behind. Thus, the question becomes how myths awaken people to an experience of eternity and the sacred blissful nature of the 'time' before time began. How do myths work to shake the confidence of secular people in the sufficiency of the mundane world, and in doing so, begin the work of reenchanting the consciousness of secular folk?

For Eliade and for most who have tried to formulate a description of it, eternity can be considered a "timeless time." It is a 'time' that is not the 'time' of duration. Then, Eliade asks, what do we experience when we immerse ourselves fully in myths, or indeed, in stories of any kind? Eliade believes that in engaging a myth, we are conveyed to the timeless time which is narrated in the myth. Since all myths are creation stories, in hearing them, we enter another state of consciousness. Believers, therefore,

> emerge from their historical time – that is, from the time constituted by the sum total of profane personal and intrapersonal events – and recover primordial time...which belongs to eternity...it does not participate in temporal duration because it is composed of an eternal present. (Eliade 1957, p. 88)

To Eliade, this ability to attain a kind of spiritual 'transport' is even available to secular folk pursuing their otherwise nonreligious activities, such as going to the cinema or reading a good book. The pity of it is, for Eliade, that they do not realize the deeper meaning of their yearnings to 'escape from time' to the sacred "timeless time" of eternity. Bringing them to this awareness is the task Eliade has set for the "creative hermeneutics" of his 'history of religions.'

> A whole volume could well be written on the myths of modern man, on the mythologies camouflaged in the plays that he enjoys, in the books that he reads. The cinema, that "dream factory," takes over and employs countless mythical motifs – the fight between hero and monster, initiatory combats and ordeals, paradigmatic figures and images...Even reading includes a mythological function, not only because it replaces

the citation of myths in archaic societies and the oral literature that still lives in the rural communities of Europe, but particularly because, through reading, the modern man succeeds in obtaining an "escape from time" comparable to the "emergence from time" effected by myths. (Eliade 1957, p. 205)

As far as Eliade is concerned, the point is to bring secular folk to the realization that what they *really* seek is their 'escapist' moments watching films, immersed in novels, or sunning on a beach at some paradisal resort is the *ultimate escape* into the Paradise of eternity – into a timeless time, into God's time of never-ending bliss – sacred time.

By Way of Preliminary Critique

Critics of the scientific status of Eliade's views have been troubled by his so-called intuitive approach to things, by his stipulations about the meaning of symbols and myths. Indeed, critics of the scientific status of Freudian or Jungian psychology have raised the same kinds of objections. How do we know, for example, that the meaning of symbols and such offered by an Eliade, Freud, or Jung are what those symbols mean (and to whom?) – even assuming it makes any sense to talk about "the" meaning of a symbol, myth, and so on? The critics of psychoanalysis – whether of the secular or sacred variety – have apparently hit upon something fundamental in the way Eliade and others think about interpretation. Eliade seems fairly frank about his preference for 'creating' a compelling meaning or telling a good story, over against, say, something like historical or empirical truth. Celebrating, however obscurely, the anti-empirical hermeneutic style of a Romanian philosopher whom Eliade much admired – Lucien Blaga – Eliade claims that the approach to interpretation of Blaga and his followers ought to be celebrated and "considered . . . legitimate in that it enabled them to find those deeper meanings . . . that can be apprehended only from the viewpoint afforded by a certain level of speculation" (Eliade 1972, p. 236). It is hard to read this appeal to some "level of speculation" other than as a justification for coming to conclusions about cultural meanings without the interference of any sort of bothersome empirical falsifications of these claims. "Specula-tion" is its own justification! Not surprisingly, in his journals, *No Souvenirs*, Eliade urges what one can only call a triumphant will to meaning. In the face of difficulties in ascertaining possible meanings in religious data, Eliade says that the practitioner of "creative hermeneutics" ought to seek meanings "*even if they aren't there*" (Eliade 1977, p. 85; emphasis in original). So, Eliade is far from the ideal of naturalistic or scientific study of religion that we have seen develop since Herbert of Cherbury. He is a kind of throwback to the era when theologians ruled discourse about religion, even if the actual nature of the 'god' about whom he testifies seems far from anything that orthodox Christianity, for example, preaches.

Eliade, Autonomy, and Phenomenology of Religion

If we can put aside our critical faculties for a while, and suspend falsificationist or empiricist critiques of Eliade's style of interpreting religious data, there are one or two things yet to be reviewed in Eliade's work that instructively link him, and separate him, from those we have considered in this book. In particular, how does Eliade's "creative hermeneutics" look when put into the context of his often perceived role as a *phenomenologist of religion*?

While Eliade might in part be described as in some sense a "phenomenologist," it is in a very eccentric sense. First, Eliade does keep faith with phenomenology's assertion of the *autonomy* of religion, but he does so in the most extreme way by declaring his methods of studying religion absolutely autonomous. This means in practice that no other discipline has anything really pertinent to say about religion than Eliade's "creative hermeneutics" – his brand of History of Religion. Thus chiding his colleagues for not doing enough to distinguish the field by practicing "creative hermeneutics," he observes the following about the 'relevance' of the work of other disciplines:

> Instead of a creative hermeneutics in the perspective of the history of religions, we shall continue to submit to the audacious and irrelevant interpretations of religious realities made by psychologists, sociologists, or devotees of various reductionist ideologies. (Eliade 1969b, p. 70)

Taken at his word, Eliade is declaring that, in effect, no other discipline than the History of Religion has anything worthwhile or germane to offer about religion. That is because no other discipline can deliver real understanding of religion. Only the History of Religion is capable of doing that.

> Certainly, the unity of the human species is accepted de facto in other disciplines, for example, linguistics, anthropology, sociology. But the historian of religions has the privilege of grasping this unity at the highest levels – or the deepest – and such experience is susceptible of enriching and changing him. (Eliade 1969b, p. 69)

It is declarations such as these that are the real meaning of Eliade's claims that a discipline is absolutely 'autonomous.' Only 'we' – the Historians of Religion – are equipped to study the X of religion; 'your' studies of X – anything outside History of Religion – are irrelevant to what the X of religion really is.

Second, Eliade also pays lip-service to Dilthey's method of *Verstehen* and empathetic understanding. Eliade is forever writing about how the native's point of view must be represented and respected. For instance, he laments the loss of knowledge of "the spiritual universes that Africa, Oceania, Southeast Asia open to us." But, immediately upon saying this, Eliade just *assumes* that they are religious in the sense *he* understands by that term.

> All these spiritual universes have a religious origin and structure. If one does not approach them in the perspective of the history of religions, they will disappear as spiritual universes; they will be reduced to facts about social organizations, economic regimes, epochs of pre-colonial and colonial history, etc. In other words, they will not be grasped as spiritual creations; they will not enrich Western and world culture. (Eliade 1969b, p. 70)

Thus, Eliade's "creative hermeneutics," as we have seen, aims for much more than 'understanding.' Rooted as it is in psychoanalytic theory and practice, it is really about

explaining religion, as well as doing its part to *invent* or *create* a certain religious consciousness.

It should thus be clear from the analogies between Eliade and Freud, and my appreciation of Eliade's approach to religion as radical, that I think it an error to place him
alongside phenomenologists of religion like Cornelis P. Tiele, van der Leeuw, William
Brede Kristensen, and Ninian Smart. Eliade's approach is so unique, indeed, that he
merits the chapter of his own that I have given him. This is to say that while Eliade
makes himself out to be a phenomenologist of religion, I think it more accurate to look
upon his work as an attempt to *explain* and *make* religion, and as well to explain religion
in a way he considers 'religious' (in his own way) itself! Thus, Eliade is above all no
"critic of religion" and not even a "caretaker" of any traditional religion that one might
name. Instead, as he has forewarned us in his explanation of his "creative hermeneutics,"
he is a bold 'maker' of a new religious consciousness.

Another Life: Eliade's 'Ficciones'

Now, given such a radical and unprecedented approach to the study of religion, we might
well want to ask Eliade the recurring question running through this entire book. Why
would Eliade think such things? Why would Eliade believe *that he was right* to propose the
kind of antihistorical, antiscientific, "creative hermeneutic" study of religion that he
does? Is there perhaps something special about his life story that helps us to *understand* –
not necessarily 'explain' – why his study of religion turns out as it does? As I have
suggested in linking Eliade, depth-psychology, and yoga, I think that locating Eliade's
ideas in relation to his life can provide interesting lines of interpretation and inquiry.

The first dimension of Eliade's 'life' that I should like to bring to bear on a deeper
reading of his theories of religion and proposals for the study of religion is his 'other life'
as a writer of significant works of a very special sort of fiction. I refer here to what literary
critics call "objective fantasy" or "magical realism." I am arguing that although it is
conventional wisdom to separate a person's scholarly or scientific work from their artistic
life, we should rather bring these together in order better to understand Eliade. Putting it
somewhat starkly, I believe Eliade's History of Religion and his literary efforts are part of
a single whole. They are driven by many of the same motives, reveal many of the same
thematic interests, and express much the same worldview. Eliade's mind did not work
according to the rules of contemporary intellectual compartmentalization. He was a
much larger person than most of our conventional professional categories could contain.

In literary circles, Eliade is perhaps best known for his most impressive novel – the
massive work most beloved by Eliade himself – *The Forbidden Forest*. Its appearance in an
English translation in 1978 (first published in France as early as 1955) triggered a new
appreciation of a person already well known for scholarly works. But here, instead of the
short stories and tales that, for the most part, were all that announced Eliade's literary
ambitions, was a tome of epic sweep. Aside from wondering at how he found time and
energy to pursue both the career of a scholar and literary artist, one must admire the
esthetic qualities of what Eliade produced over a long lifetime. In *The Forbidden Forest*,
for example, dreamy narratives waft along, sustained for nearly 600 pages, broken by the
staccato machine-gun-like reports of civil anarchy in wartime Romania. People are shot
without pity to bleed their singular lives away on some anonymous pavement; political

foes assassinate one another in rapid, efficient, but unending succession. Despite their violent will to assert themselves into our consciousness, Eliade makes them fade like the tireless reportage of a 24-hour news cycle blabbing away in the background. It is *historical* events that fade into the insignificance of the 'white noise' of mindless, and thus *meaningless*, chatter. In the face of such banal evil, standing in the way of this pointless cascade of violent events, only retreat into another world, free of history, is possible. A world of eternal, blissful, nonhistorical reality, such as in a dream, beckons to both the novel's main characters and the reader, now grasping the 'terror of history' dominating the daily profane events of Romania in wartime. For Eliade, the heart of that blessed dream world of retreat from the terror of Romania's violent history is love itself. So, in the midst of the horrors of death and chaos that surround the daily histories of the many characters of the novel, Eliade carves out a place of refuge constituted by the precious love affairs he recounts there, and that he counterposes to the terrors of their historical moments. Loves are won, but lost again, as historical events trample them under. But significantly, some lost loves are restored, often in magical ways as the dead seem to rise again – we are never quite sure what is 'real' and what is 'imagined' – to embrace the living left behind. *The Forbidden Forest* thus concludes with its leading character, Stefan (Eliade himself?), reuniting with a love lost to death itself, his Ileana. But Eliade never lets the profane mind rest in its confident certainties, in the assurance of the clear and distinct cleavage between life and death. Is this reunion of Stefan and Ileana a 'real' one in 'historical time,' is it a waking dream or hallucination of a broken mind, or does Eliade offer a mystic vision of a magical reunion in death itself of these two? We do not know, and Eliade is surely not about to tell us.

> That moment – unique, infinite – revealed to him the total beatitude he had yearned for for so many years. It was there in the glance she bestowed on him, bathed in tears. He had known from the beginning this was the way it would be. He had known that, feeling him very near her, she would turn her head and look at him. He had known that this last moment without end, would suffice. (Eliade 1978, p. 596)

Whatever the 'truth' of Ileana's existence, Eliade shows us a deeply moved person for whom 'history,' in the sense of an ontological state of being, had become catastrophic. In *The Forbidden Forest* Eliade voices what seems the immediate cause of his distaste for historical reality and thus, as we will see shortly, for the 'science' of history that dwells upon it.

> "Today the master of all of us is the war," Stefan began again. "It has confiscated the whole of contemporary history, the time in which we are fated to live. All Europe's behaving like a monstrous robot set in motion by the news being released every minute from hundreds of radio stations...Even when we're alone we think about the war all the time. That is, we're slaves of History. The terror of events is not only humiliating to each of us as human beings, but in the long run it's sterile...what does this struggle reveal to us? Only terror...Against the terror of History there are only two possibilities of defense: action or contemplation...Our only solution is to contemplate, that is to escape from historic Time, to find again another Time." (Eliade 1978, p. 250)

Eliade had already introduced this line of criticism in an untranslated novel from 1935 about the political thuggery of the 1930s in Romania. *The Forbidden Forest*, written two decades later, renders the same judgment but seen in distant hindsight. The Romanian literary critic Matei Calinescu implies that for Eliade this novel, called *Huliganii* (*Hooligans*; 1935), became a judgment upon the "'collective self' of his generation of 'angry young men'" (Calinescu 1982, p. 142). Despite their passion and idealism the political radicals of Eliade's Romania – the 'hooligans' – were no more than apocalyptic anarchists, "furious *negateurs*" as Virgil Ierunca says – those who "seek a paradise reconquered by the paradoxical weapons of violence and eroticism (Ierunca 1969, p. 344). Does this perhaps also mark a point in Eliade's consciousness where 'creation' and 'creativity' attain a new depth of significance for him in the face of this experience of the anarchistic nihilism that eventually swallowed up his life and that of so many of his friends and associates?

Such a judgment upon ordinary historical existence, and even more so upon the extreme of political historicism characteristic of devotees of political apocalypses, may then account for Eliade's preoccupation with such themes as the possibility of erasing hard and fast boundaries between dream and waking states, fantasy and reality, with māyā over against *sat* (Being). Indeed, such literary themes mark a good portion of his literary output. I am suggesting therefore that the 'same mind' is at work in Eliade's fiction writing as in his History of Religion. It is a 'mind' that sees the everyday world – the world of historical events – as ultimately unreal when compared to the world of the sacred and transcendent. The possession of that common mind, then, might be cited as one reason why Eliade *thinks he is right* in making the methodological choices about sacred space and time, etc., that we have already glimpsed.

This orientation seems indeed to have been deep and broad. Some literary critics date the 'fantastic' or magical realist trend in Eliade's fiction to the 1930s, to the same formative period in which his thinking about religion was taking shape (Calinescu 1978). In his *Mademoiselle Christina* (1936), Eliade accepts the reality of ghosts, as Stefan seems to do of the dead Ileana. In *The Serpent* (1937), Eliade introduces a strong theme that would dominate his literary thinking – "the unrecognizability of miracle" (Ierunca 1969, p. 352). His fascination with this theme of the "camouflage of the fantastic (and the absurd)" in the "daily event" frames his whole epistemology of the sacred: for him the point is to *see* how the sacred is symbolized in the world (Perry 1975, p. 49). For Eliade, what matters is not to be fooled by the many disguises assumed by the sacred as it sojourns in 'history.' The point is to realize eternal, timeless Being, and to dispel the māyā of illusion that is history.

Accordingly, literary critics tend to place Eliade alongside such better-known masters of "fantastic" fiction as Gabriel García Marquez and Jorge Luis Borges. In the sense of Borges, Eliade too may be seen as a writer of *"ficciones"* – what the Argentine master calls his "notes on *imaginary* books," his "tales of fantasy" delighting in the "unreality" of purportedly actual historical events, persons, and places (Borges 1998). In their manic fact-mongering, Borges's 'fictions' mock the show of self-confidence historical writing seeks by parading detailed description. What better way to subvert historical consciousness than by turning it against itself? This ironic attitude to history may finally make further sense of Eliade's cosmopolitan associations with the "magic realist" Ernst Jünger, who with Eliade founded the literary journal *Antaios*. So too do his links with the Romanian émigré existentialist writer and fascist intellectual, Emil Cioran, reinforce Eliade's radical connections (Strenski 1987, pp. 78–9, 93). In his essay "Thinking against Oneself," Cioran voices an analogous, but ultimately nihilistic, version of Eliade's quest for the primordial and timeless time of God:

Perhaps...we shall regain our supremacy over time; unless, the other way round, struggling to escape the calamity of consciousness, we rejoin animals, plants, things, return to that primordial stupidity of which, through the fault of history, we have lost even the memory. (Cioran 1956, p. 47)

Having mentioned Cioran and thereby alluded to Eliade's associations with Romania's fascist past, let me turn to another level of Eliade's formation in order to draw out yet another facet of his life that may help us see how and why he *thought he was right* to have written both his fiction and his History of Religion in the 'fantastic,' history-negating style that he did. Why in taking the fantastic route, does Eliade so strongly affirm creativity and creation? This takes us straight to the political and historical calamities of his Romania, especially his ideological and political location in that period of anarchy and upheaval.

In and Out of Romania's 'Hooliganized' History

As a result of the in First World War, Romania experienced a kind of national renaissance. The nation had regained a number of provinces which were historically Romanian, and greatly enlarged her territory and population. She also found herself with a movement of hopeful "young generation" intellectuals who were ready to articulate the meaning of the revival of her national fortunes. Now was the time to consider the future. Eliade was a significant player in this Romanian national drama. Born in 1907 in Bucharest, Romania, he was always, as we have seen, far more than a scholar. He was even more than the author of the numerous enchanting works of fiction, novels, and shorts stories, written in a literary genre known as "objective fantasy," that we have briefly discussed. He was a man born into a peculiarly explosive time for the politics of his native Romania from the end of the First World War to the beginnings of the Cold War. After being a student of philosophy and religions at the University of Bucharest, then some months in Rome to study Renaissance hermeticism, followed by three years in India (1928–31), Eliade returned to his native Romania richly and broadly educated. Shortly after his return from foreign travels, Eliade took up a post in the philosophy department at Bucharest, then headed by Nae Ionescu. The year was 1932. It was the beginning of a period of intense turmoil both in Romania and across Europe, as the fascist right and communist left battled each other for the control of the continent. Emil Cioran proudly recalls Eliade's role in those days as a leading intellectual combatant against the traditional conservatives and liberals of the 'old generation':

> In those days, the 'new generation' idolized him. We scorned the 'old duffers' and 'doters'– anyone over thirty, that is. Our mentor [Eliade] was waging war against them; he would take aim and fell them one by one. Rarely did he fire wild.... The struggle between generations seemed to us the key to all conflicts, the explanatory formula of every event. Being young was, in our eyes, a certificate of genius. (Cioran 1969, p. 407)

Here, Cioran apparently refers to the kind of regular opinion pieces Eliade was then writing for Nae Ionescu's newspaper *Cuvantul*. In one of his first published diaries, Eliade recalled one of these with some embarrassment at his youthful zeal. This fiery article,

"Apologia pro causa sua," was, as Eliade tells us, lobbed "right into the middle of the polemics about the young generation . . . And I shut up the 'old fellows' once and for all" (Eliade 1977, p. 19).

For those "old duffers" in the secular or Europeanist camp, Romania's new fortunes called for closer ties with the liberal West, especially the France of the French Revolution and Enlightenment. It marked for them another chance to revive the Romanian Enlightenment of the nineteenth century, and thus to reassert an ideal of a cosmopolitan Western nation.

In the other camp were Eliade and his friends, who populated the membership of groups heavily influenced by "traditionalist" thought. To them the entire program of Western liberalism was poisonous to the development of a specifically Romanian national spirit (Hitchins 1978, pp. 142–4). Eliade's cherished mentor and life-long friend, the philosopher Nae Ionescu, also figured prominently in the "traditionalist" movement, and especially on its "irrationalist" side. Along with Cioran, Eliade was then one of a group of young Romanian intellectuals to whom Ionescu provided a mix of religious and political nourishment and encouragement for the "traditionalist" campaign to control Romania's future. To them, Western liberal democracy seemed a failure. It was somewhat the preserve of the *deraciné*, secular, urban, francophile middle classes. The Romanian Orthodox peasant masses seemed to be left out of the picture. Lacking any aptitude for the mythological and symbolic dimensions of nationalism, these rationalist liberal democrats failed to give compelling expression to the increasingly frustrated national spirit of Orthodox Romanians. Rooted in the intellectualism of the French Enlightenment, liberal democracy was unable to tap the 'irrational' mythico-religious forces of Romanian identity, the power of which only political romantics and European fascists seemed to grasp well (Gentile 1996). Although the liberals had succeeded among the Romanian intellectuals in the nineteenth century, they not only could not capture the imaginations of the masses, but also failed miserably to inspire Cioran, Eliade, Ionescu, and the "new generation" of intellectuals in the 1920s and 1930s. The "new generation," like the Orthodox peasantry, insisted on a politics dominated by Romanian tradition, mythico-religious values, and populism.

Interestingly, the political stances and strategies of Eliade's "new generation" corresponded with attitudes to reason, science, and thus critical historical thinking. The "new generation" embraced the relativism and mystical transcendentalism of Ionescu that had "rediscovered security, authority and discipline in God and religion" (Weber 1965, p. 535). Ionescu and others contrasted the naive sincerity and supposed depth and simple wisdom of the Romanian peasant with the superficiality and shallowness of worldly empirical or historical "knowledge." For Ionescu the quest for positive human knowledge was a proud assertion of human power against the divine. Salvation was possible for this sinful humanity only if we surrendered our desire for knowledge, and immolated our intellects upon an altar of religious faith. Indeed, Ionescu embraced (and taught!) the trademark slogan of religious irrationalism and anti-intellectualism: "I believe because it is absurd" (Hitchins 1978, pp. 145 ff.). It is not difficult to see in Eliade's History of Religion the same disdain for the historical sciences and the concomitant glorification of intuition as a method for doing History of Religion.

Many "traditionalists" went further than intellectual engagement, and rallied round the banner of a messianic politico-religious organization called the Legion of the Archangel Michael. A better-known and somewhat more militant wing was called the *Garda Fer* or Iron Guard. Both elements were led by their charismatic founder, Corneliu

Codreanu (1899–1938). Accounts of Codreanu's campaigns feature his uncanny ability to rally the Romanian peasantry to his cause by exploiting native symbolism and traditional religious affiliation with the Romanian Orthodox church, many of whose clergy were vigorous supporters of the Legion. Mounted dramatically on his splendid white charger and done up in lavish peasant costume, Codreanu celebrated a kind of mythic identification between his modern political movement and the nativist 'soul' of an imagined indigenous Romanian people. Merging religion with his political program, he led his green-shirted Legionaries in rowdy, often violent, demonstrations of 'bully-boy' political power, yet all the while bearing lighted candles and holy icons as they marched.

While this movement had all the trappings, and many of the doctrines of the 'fascisms' of the 1920s and 1930s, it would be well to try to resist the all-too-easy lumping of these 'fascisms' into one. Yes, the Legion, like Nazism, was essentially and from the beginning anti-Semitic; but the fascisms of Salazar, Franco, or Mussolini were not. Commenting on this difference, a modern-day scholar of this movement warns us accordingly:

> The Legionaries were always aware of their great differences with the Nazis and Fascists...One of their leading intellectuals...explained: "Fascism worships the state, Nazism the race and the nation. Our movement strives not merely to fulfill the destiny of the Rumanian people – we want to fulfill it along the road of salvation." Another Legionary intellectual...called the Legion, "the only political movement with a religious structure," even to the point of seeing the "ultimate goal of the nation [as] Resurrection in Christ." The Legionaries perceived the whole history of mankind, and particularly that of Rumania, as an uninterrupted Passion, a mystical Easter, in which every step, every motivation, consequently every goal, was a struggle between light and darkness. The road of the Legion must be the road of suffering, sacrifice, crucifixion, and resurrection. (Nagy-Talavera 1970, p. 266)

Extravagant, adventurist, and other-worldly – fatally so, as we will see: the politically unrealistic Legion has even been cast as akin to Cargo Cults. Instead of bringing to Romania an apocalypse of prosperity – material consumer goods of the Western world – the Legion sought to call down from heaven the politico-religious 'goods' of a spiritually unified and deeply rooted national culture (Wiles 1969, p. 176). This is not to deny for an instant the many violent and murderous political acts they led against Jews and their other perceived enemies in their quest for a paradise on earth.

Although there is no evidence that Eliade ever took active part in such Legionary atrocities, he was a prominent sympathizer and a well-known ideological apologist and *porte-parole* for them and Codreanu. He never distanced himself from them or disavowed his association with the Legion (Eliade 1981, pp. 280–1; Wasserstrom 1999, pp. 131–2). As one of their senior advisors, Nae Ionescu was even more closely associated with forming the thought and policies of the Legion than Eliade, and in ways that linked his plans for Romania directly with Hitler's revolution in Germany. In his *Autobiography*, volume I, Eliade seems to make clear that he was aware of the tendencies of Ionescu's political thought, noting that in 1933 Ionescu spoke of being "very impressed" with the "revolution" taking place in Nazi Germany. "A similar revolution would have to take place some day in Romania," said Ionescu (Eliade 1981, p. 263). Eliade's sympathies for the political analysis of the "European right" – "what we young people were thinking... between 1925 and 1933," is, therefore, in large part clearly identifiable (Eliade 1977, p. 197). It may be called by many names; the late Susan Sontag – who also translated some of Cioran's short pieces into English – argued that Cioran and Eliade display a rightist "Catholic sensibility" (Sontag 1966, p. 88).

But as the tensions provoked by Eliade's ideological fellow-travelers inside Romania intensified in the early 1930s, civil conflict erupted. Given the Legion's undomesticated and explosive nature, the government sought to suppress it. The anarchy described in Eliade's *Hooligans* seems to refer to these bouts of suppression. But with each attempt at government suppression, the Legion only grew in strength and motivation to retaliate against the authorities. The elite Iron Guard organized themselves into death squads. The government retaliated with summary executions of Guardists, often leaving their corpses to rot unburied in the open air. Nor did the ramifications of Romania's internal anarchy stop at her borders.

Even though this conflict was, technically speaking, an internal civil war, the conflict had such international ramifications that *both* Western and Nazi governments urged Romanian governmental forces to end the civil war by totally liquidating the Legion. We might recall that Hitler's Nazi Party had dealt similarly with the adventurist 'Brown Shirts' of its own movement, and installed itself as the 'party of order' in Germany. After exhausting its own 'spiritual' inspirations, Hitler apparently felt he could do without those even more undisciplined and extreme members of his own movement. After all, as in Romania, there was governing to do, and order to be reestablished. Yet, despite suppression after suppression, in the 1937 elections, the Legion emerged third in the tally of votes – apparently giving evidence that it could not be so easily eradicated.

At this point, the king, Carol II, staged a royal coup, dissolved parliament, and manufactured his own version of the Legion. Moving swiftly, Carol had Codreanu imprisoned and secretly executed in 1938. The adventurist and idealistic wing of the Legion thus became victim of its own success at stirring up the masses. It could not control the forces it unleashed; nor could it make the transition from charisma to a bureaucracy. While it could campaign and inspire, it could neither govern nor ensure order. As a result, from within its general ranks, the king found a willing coterie of Legionaries eager to assume the role of the 'party of order,' and eager as well to enforce discipline upon the revolutionary fervor of Codreanu in the form of violent suppression of their own fellow Legionaires. The king's counter-revolution did not succeed, and whatever anarchy there had been before his royal coup, what followed completely overshadowed it. After Codreanu's murder, what remained of his Legion lost all sense of restraint. The hooligans ruled. It was at this time in 1940, with Codreanu's 'spiritual' revolutionaries losing the battle, that Eliade fled his country, never to return again. Speaking perhaps of himself and the catastrophe that rained down upon him and the political enthusiasms of his youth, in *The Forbidden Forest* Biris describes Stefan (Eliade?) in words that might well indicate Eliade's own desperate and defeated internal condition at the time:

> He suffered a nervous shock, that's all . . . History has taken revenge on him. He has a phobia against History. He has a horror of events. He'd like things to stand still the way they seemed in the paradise of his childhood. So History takes revenge and buries him as often as it can. It throws him into the detention camp by mistake. It kills men in his place, always by mistake. (Eliade 1978, p. 214)

Luckily for Eliade, the intervention of influential individuals permitted him to escape his own premature death, not to mention the further disintegration of his country as well as the advance of the Red Army. Eliade waited out the war as Romanian cultural attaché in Portugal (1940–5), continuing to write while there, among other things, a book on the rightist counter-revolution of the Portugese dictator, Antonio Oliviera Salazar, *Salazar y la contrarrevolución en Portugal* (Eliade 1942; 2000, p. 30). Eliade was quite convinced that there were lessons for Romania to be learned from Salazar's rightist counter-revolution in Portugal, and vice versa (Eliade 2000, p. 30). In an interview that Eliade was able to obtain with the dictator in 1942, Salazar expressed interest in the existence of a "common front" – "*espíritu de frente*" – in Romania as a force for making modern-day social revolutions. Salazar clearly had Eliade's Legion in mind, or at least recognized in Eliade – and rightly so – someone who would know such things (Eliade 2000, p. 39). One does not know what became of these explorations, in part because Eliade did not stay on long in Portugal. From Lisbon, he began the migrations that marked the next decade or so of his life. By various routes and turns of good fortune, he taught for a brief time in Paris at the École Pratique des Hautes Études (1950–5), and went from there to the post at the Divinity School in the University of Chicago that he held from 1956 until his death in 1986.

Eliade had thus experienced the 'terror' of the failure of 'historical' events to turn out as he and his generation had wished them to do. It seems a modest and reasonable interpretation of his orientations regarding 'history' in the study of religion to suggest that Romania's historical catastrophes might well have been influential in either reinforcing or initially shaping his later thought about religion. What I think emerges is that a person who lived through political and historical disasters as Eliade did would be motivated to look on political and historical ambitions with a peculiar tragic sense, even to the extent of scorn for the often cruel vicissitudes of history and politics. History in Romania had been for Eliade literally a murderous disaster, not only for him, but for every political and social value to which he had adhered since returning from India to assume a leadership position in the ambitions of the Romanian "new generation." It is for reasons such as these that I have tried to suggest that Eliade was motivated to *think he was right* to declare history the source of terror, rather than an arena of salvation and happiness, and therefore to *think he was right* to turn his mind to places beyond those that history could reach – to blissful realms of transcendence – where no historian had any business to meddle. Salvation, or at least personal mental survival, could be found by an escape into a world stabilized by transcendent, unmovable centers and heavenly archetypes that exist in the unchanging, but creative and life-affirming, 'timeless time' of eternity, of mythical time.

From this new set of priorities, it may also be easier to see that Eliade might want to have recourse to the methods of superior knowledge that likewise condition his approach to the study of religion. Eliade the yogin, the would-be guru, lived on in his intuitive approach to understanding religion. With history a wreckage, would not someone like Eliade, who had imbibed both yogic methods of attaining higher knowledge as well as Nae Ionescu's irrationalist contempt for ordinary means of attaining knowledge, feel that he could access higher (or deeper) ways of understanding religious data? Did not Eliade *think he was right* precisely because he felt that he *knew* he was right at the deepest core of his being?

References

Bellah, R. N. 1978. Religious Studies as "New Religion." In *Understanding the New Religions*, eds. G. Baker & J. Needleman. New York: Seabury Press.

Borges, J. L. 1998. Fictions: The Garden of Forking Paths. In *Jorge Luis Borges: Collected Fictions*, ed. A. Hurley. New York: Penguin.

Calinescu, M. 1978. The Disguises of Miracle: Notes on Mircea Eliade's Fiction. *World Literature Today*, pp. 558–64.

——. 1982. The Function of the Unreal: Reflections on Mircea Eliade's Short Fiction. In *Imagination and Meaning: The Scholarly and Literary Worlds of Mircea Eliade*, eds. N. J. Girardot & M. L. Ricketts. New York: Seabury Press.

Capps, W. H., ed. 1978. *The Interpenetration of New Religion and Religious Studies: Understanding the New Religions*. New York: Seabury Press.

Cioran, E. 1956. Thinking against Oneself. In *E. M. Cioran, The Temptation to Exist*, ed. S. Sontag. New York: Quadrangle.

——. 1969. Beginnings of a Friendship. In *Myths and Symbols: Studies in Honor of Mircea Eliade*, eds. J. M. Kitagawa & C. H. Long. Chicago: University of Chicago Press.

Dry, A. 1961. *The Psychology of Jung*. London: Allen and Unwin.

Dudley, G. 1977. *Religion on Trial: Mircea Eliade and His Critics*. Philadelphia: Temple University Press.

Eliade, M. 1942. *Salazar si Revolutia in Portugalia*. Bucharest: Gorjan.

——. 1957. *The Sacred and the Profane*. New York: Harcourt, Brace and World.

——. 1958. *Patterns in Comparative Religion*, trans. R. Sheed. London: Sheed and Ward.

——. 1959. Methodological Remarks on Religious Symbolism. In *The History of Religions: Essays in Methodology*, eds. M. Eliade & J. Kitagawa. Chicago: University of Chicago Press.

——. 1960. Encounters at Ascona. In *Papers from the Eranos Yearbooks* 4, ed. J. Campbell. London: Bollingen.

——. 1961. *Images and Symbols*. London: Harvill.

——. 1964a. *Myth and Reality*. London: Allen and Unwin.

——. 1964b. *Shamanism*. New York: Bollingen.

——. 1965. *The Two and the One*. London: Harvill.

——. 1968. *Myths, Dreams and Mysteries*. London: Harvill.

——. 1969a. Cosmogonic Myth and "Sacred History." In *The Quest*. Chicago: University of Chicago Press.

——. 1969b. Crisis and Renewal. In *The Quest*. Chicago: University of Chicago Press.

——. 1972. The Clairvoyant Lamb. In *Zalmoxis: The Vanishing God*. Chicago: University of Chicago Press.

——. 1977. *No Souvenirs*. New York: Harper and Row.

——. 1978. *The Forbidden Forest*. South Bend, IN: Notre Dame University Press.

——. 1981. *Autobiography. Volume I: 1907–1937. Journey East, Journey West*, trans. M. L. Ricketts. New York: Harper and Row.

——. 1982. *Ordeal by Labyrinth: Conversations with Claude-Henri Rocquet*. Chicago: University of Chicago Press.

——. 2000. *Diario Portugués*, trans. J. Gariggós. Barcelona: Kairós.

Gentile, E. 1996. *The Sacralization of Politics in Fascist Italy*, trans. K. Botsford. Cambridge, MA: Harvard University Press.

Hitchins, K. 1978. Gindirea: Nationalism in Spiritual Guise. In *Social Change in Romania, 1860-1940*, ed. K. Jowitt. Berkeley: Institute of International Studies, Research Series vol. 36.

Ierunca, V. 1969. The Literary Work of Mircea Eliade. In *Myths and Symbols: Studies in Honor of Mircea Eliade*, eds. J. M. Kitagawa & C. H. Long. Chicago: University of Chicago Press.

Nagy-Talavera, N. M. 1970. *The Green Shirts and Others*. Stanford: Hoover Institution.

Perry, T. 1975. The American and Romanian Literature. *Cahiers roumains d'études littéraires* 3, pp. 40–50.

Preus, J.S. 1987. *Explaining Religion*. New Haven: Yale University Press.

Skinner, Q. 1969. Meaning and Understanding in the History of Ideas. *History and Theory* 8, pp. 3–53.

Sontag, S. 1966. *Styles of Radical Will*. New York: Noonday.

Strenski, I. 1987. *Four Theories of Myth in Twentieth-Century History*. London/Iowa City: Macmillan/Iowa University Press.

Todorov, T. 1989. *The Deflection of the Enlightenment*. Stanford: Stanford Humanities Center.

Trautmann, T. R. 1997. *Aryans and British India*. Berkeley: University of California Press.

Voigt, J. 1967. *Max-Müller: The Man and His Ideas*. Calcutta: Firma K. L. Mukhopadhyay.

Wasserstrom, S. M. 1999. *Religion after Religion: Gershom Scholem, Mircea Eliade, and Henry Corbin at Eranos*. Princeton: Princeton University Press.

Weber, E. 1965. Romania. In *The European Right: A Historical Profile*, eds. H. Rogger & E. Weber. Berkeley: University of California Press.

Wiles, P. 1969. A Syndrome, Not a Doctrine. In *Populism*, eds. G. Ionescu & E. Gellner. London: Macmillan.

Conclusion: Science of Religion, the Bible, and Prince Charming

13

We have traveled far over the course of this book. Having done so, it would be fair enough to ask the inevitable "So what?" question. What value is there in the journey taken? Where have we arrived?

More than anything else, I believe we have gained immensely in our understanding of theories by submitting ourselves to the discipline of trying to understand the reasons and purposes that gave rise to these theories. While this means that although there may be no 'Prince Charming' of theories ready to carry us off to the palace of truth about the way religion should be studied, it also means that there remains much value still in the various approaches represented by the theories examined here. This book has not then been written as an antiquarian effort, even though the thinkers considered here are not living today. While they may not be alive today in the flesh, they nonetheless can claim immortality inasmuch as many thinkers of our own times lay claim to their heritage. The study of religion is notoriously peopled by Weberians, Durkheimians, Freudians, Chicago School (Eliade) products, biblical critics working in the spirit of Spinoza or Robertson Smith, functionalists thinking about religion much as Malinowski did, anthropologists of religion tracing their lineage to Tylor and beyond, cross-cultural comparativists of many sorts, such as those working in the light cast by Max Müller or even Frazer, and finally the many species of phenomenologists – both of the classic variety or of the more recent vintage exemplified by Ninian Smart or Mircea Eliade. How true, then, the words of novelist William Faulkner that "The past is not dead. It's not even past" (Haizlip 1999). Part of what I have sought to do in *Thinking about Religion* is to recognize the value that the creators of theories found in them – to understand 'why theorists thought they were right' – all the while also understanding their persistent value for us as well as their weaknesses. I have sought to do this by pursuing the novel approach of beginning this process by delving as far as I was able into the mindset and sociocultural conditions that gave these theories their salience and life.

The point of thus recognizing the originally perceived and persistent value of these theories of religion is to encourage even more theorizing. The last thing I wanted to produce was a book that culminated in a glittering show of clever dialectic demonstrating why all theories are wrong! It is at the level of creative theory-making where ideas burn at their brightest, where intellectual enthusiasms become most passionate, where the creative human mind engages its world most fundamentally. My purpose has been to help students access some of that passion, and to stimulate them to make it their own. The stories I have told about great theorists have been intended to engage readers in the delights of restless curiosity about religion and creativity in how to make sense of it.

I know no better way of stimulating more theorizing than to take readers into the heroic minds of theorists and let them revel in the excitement of their quests. This book has been written to celebrate the lust for knowledge so conspicuously part of the theorizing mind. I want to stimulate that same curiosity in students, not to thwart or censor it. Do we not discourage the study of theorizing if we make of the study of theories the incessantly negative activity of fault-finding it has too often become?

Put in other, now familiar words, my aim has been to understand 'why theorists thought that they were right,' not primarily or exclusively to show why they were wrong. In most cases, it is either obvious or soon discovered why a theory was wrong. It is a far harder task to divine why a theorist would think that they were right in the first place. Without then overlooking the role of the critic of theories, I have selected another kind of emphasis. Theorizing is an often passionate, engaged activity driven by an intense desire to find meaning in what passes before us in the world. I believe that students are owed an opportunity to venture into the inquiring minds of theorists, and to make that journey their own by discovering why theorists thought as they did.

As such, I see theorizing as a fundamental human orientation to the world – not something strange, or foreign to broader human purposes. For this reason, understanding theories in a full sense calls us to see how theoretical thinking coheres with the life choices thinkers make in other than academic domains as much as with related academic work. While theorizing may excel in dedicated settings, such as the laboratory, think-tank, or academic environments, it is not something exclusive to these places. Of course, there is a difference between the rigorous exercise of dedicated theorizing by intellectual workers and everyday 'folk' theorizing informally every time they hazard an account of a state of affairs. But these two kinds of theorizing are kin, not alien to each other. Part, then, of the purpose of my writing this book is to bring out the ramified sense of the reach of the concerns of life into theorizing. Ought we to wonder why the general public attitudes toward science fall so easily into belittling caricature of the scientist and the sciences when so much of the world we have created rarifies the vocation of science, the pursuit of knowledge? I want to put theorizing back into life by shedding light on how the exigencies of life in the world – those oft-mentioned 'problems of religion' – spurred theorizing about religion.

Unusual? Religious Motives Sometimes Made Religious Studies

On another subject, as a proponent of what one might call a naturalistic (or nontheological) approach to the study of religion, in *Thinking about Religion* I have doubtless taken a somewhat *unusual* line in accounting for the rise of the study of religion. To wit, I have argued that the historical record shows that *religion itself* has been a powerful factor in the origins and growth of the study of religion. True, the Humes, Tylors, Frazers, Freuds, Malinowskis, and others in the skeptical tradition were driven to study religion by the desire to uproot and discredit it. But in case after case, I have shown how religious *motivations* have driven the very creation of some classic theories in the academic study of religion. The scientific study of religion came about because of devoted *religious* concerns to uncover ultimate truth about the world – not in spite of them. Whether this be the quest for Natural Religion by 'deists' like Bodin, Herbert, or even Max Müller, or whether this be the pursuit for religion-as-such by the likes of proto-phenomenologist of religion

Cornelis P. Tiele, the same lesson of the dynamic influence of religious motives in the pursuit of 'scientific' knowledge is there to be learned. Such motivation does not, of course, justify or give added value to the theories thus created. But recognizing that religious motives may inspire critical scientific *thinking about religion* as easily as might the desire to discredit religious viewpoints, should go some way toward closing the gap that yawns so widely today between religious believers and scientific skeptics.

I believe that it is in the interests of skeptics of religion to deter dichotomizing of religion from science, and thus in the process to deter the eventual demonizing of the scientist by the believer. What I have shown is that such sentiments are not mere good wishes, but are grounded firmly in the history of the very rise of the scientific study of religion itself. The study of religion was, as Sam Preus late in life argued so well, as much a product of religious piety as it was of skepticism. From the very beginnings of the study of religion, we find creative minds like Herbert of Cherbury, Jean Bodin, Baruch Spinoza, and the 'deists' carried forward by their curiosity about the nature of religion as much as by the attendant belief that this curiosity was itself a divine endowment. No less heroic in facing the often fierce conservative religious opposition of later generations, even when that opposition took the form of formal trials for heresy or public calumnies, were their successors, Max Müller, Robertson Smith, Cornelis P. Tiele, and others. For them, as for the Cherburys, Bodins, and the others, the human quest for knowledge was creative, and as creative would, in the end, only lead them closer to the ultimate truth of things.

I call this result of my study '*unusual*' since, aside from excellent work of Peter Byrne, Sam Preus, and Donald Wiebe, no other comparable account of methods and theories in the study of religion pays the religious roots of theories of religion much – if any – attention at all (Byrne 1989; Preus 1998; Wiebe 1999a; 1999b; 1999c). This omission arises in part from simple ignorance about the objective historical conditions of the origin and persistence of many theories of religion – the 'why did they think they were right?' perspective. Part of the benefit then of knowing the objective history of the rise of the study of religion is precisely to learn that many of the founders of the study of religion thought of their scientific and religious activities as mutually complementary.

Religious Studies without (the Usual) Metaphysics

In paying heed and giving due credit to religious motivation in the rise of the study of religion I have deliberately sought to expose the historically unfounded and needlessly dichotomizing pronouncements of scholars like Russell McCutcheon. While, like McCutcheon, I personally find no need to justify naturalistic approaches to the study of religion in terms of a religious worldview, there is nothing stopping believers from seeing reason as God-given or the pursuit of scientific knowledge as divinely inspired and even conducive to deepened religious commitment. Indeed, history teaches precisely the opposite lesson. Most founders of the study of religion felt that it was only by virtue of the God-given nature of reason that their researches into religion were possible!

In terms of what the historical record plainly implies, McCutcheon's assertions that religion "can be conceptualized and then explained as a thoroughly human activity, with no mysterious distillate left over," or that the study of religion is "the study of an ordinary aspect of social historical existence," are therefore not so much true *or* false as they are fatuous (McCutcheon 2001, pp. xi, xii). Ironically and in effect, such assertions of a naturalistic foundation to the study of religion as McCutcheon sees it, in effect, reintroduces metaphysics into the field. Ironically, on top of this, McCutcheon then represents a reversion to the *theological* discourse of many of the founders, albeit as their mirror image. Such an assertion is nothing less than to play the theologian's game, and to engage in a deviant 'theology' of its own. Where the founders felt compelled to link their pursuit of knowledge about religion – their 'scientific' inquiry about religion – with their belief in the divine nature and purposes of human curiosity, McCutcheon feels he needs to link his naturalist approach to religion with commitment to a naturalistic metaphysical ground – that he feels he must "presume . . . claims [about religion] as historical, meaning they arise from and are in support of social, economic, political, and so on, situations" (McCutcheon 2001, p. 148).

But one must immediately raise the challenge as to why McCutcheon believes he is required to 'stand up and declare for' a naturalist metaphysics? Who needs it? Certainly not the study of religion, any more than it needs a theistic foundation. Granted, I have sought to *recognize* the place of religious motivations in the genesis and persistence of many theories of religion. But, I do not *advocate* that one do so – mostly because no such metaphysical foundation, supernaturalist *or* naturalist, is required for doing the study of religion. In a review article of a recent book of McCutcheon's, Don Wiebe, himself one of McCutcheon's mentors at the University of Toronto, devastatingly characterizes McCutcheon's style of discourse in precisely the same quasi-theological way that I have just done. Says Wiebe, McCutcheon's

> wish to replace the religio-theological studies of religion and their ideological agendas with the engaged, public intellectual is, so far as I can see, simply to pit a new ideological agenda over against the old. Calling this 'redescriptive scholarship' simply does not differentiate it . . . from the currently dominant religio-theological scholars in the field since neither group of scholars is primarily concerned with gaining objective knowledge about the (religious) world. (Wiebe 2004, p. 12)

Not only is it ironic that McCutcheon should require a naturalist metaphysics before he launches into a naturalist study of religion, but he fails to realize that study of religion has no need of any such ideological or metaphysical foundations at all. As implied in his locutions describing the ontology of religion as "thoroughly human" or "ordinary," McCutcheon would have us commit first to a particular naturalist ontology, or what I have called as well a metaphysics. But our understandings and/or explanations of religion are not one whit better for making these self-styled brave pronouncements. We are still left with no other choice than to study religion as we find it. We are still left to study religion by all the means available for intellectual inquiry in the 'sciences' as we have come to accept them. We are still left to study religion, at most, *as if* it were accessible to human reason, whether or not it finally and in fact is! We don't need to decide whether or not religion really has a supernatural origin or not in order to go ahead and study it. Whether or not religion has a supernatural origin, our human abilities to *know* are limited to the same restrictions in either case.

Furthermore, such descriptors as "ordinary" have no power to stop a potential future theistically founded study of religion from making the same assertions about confining their attention to "ordinary" states of affairs. After all, from a theistic point of view, what could be more "ordinary" than what the creator has created? Theists are always in a position to encompass scientific facts within larger religious schemes of interpretation.

Indeed, this is how many of the founders of the study of religion spoke about science, reason, nature, and such. For them, not only was reason itself God-given, but so also was it always possible to encompass any scientific fact within a larger religious perspective! Although many Evangelicals, for example, find science and religion at odds with one another, and rail, for example, at godless Darwinian evolution, today's Roman Catholics find no problems with their co-existence. The Vatican finds no difficulty establishing accord between a doctrine of divine creation of humanity *and* Darwin! For Roman Catholics, Darwin accounts for the "ordinary" facts of how God may have decided to work out the origins of living beings. And, like all genius, Darwin's genius is God-given, while his God-given theory of evolution says nothing of the ultimate beginnings of this world. Like today's Roman Catholics, a number of critical early theorists never thought of their *science* of religion as being at odds with their own religious impulses. Indeed, as I have reiterated as often as it has been appropriate, many founding thinkers believed that by pursuing *knowledge* about religion, they were at the same time pursuing a *religious* quest. Albert Réville gives voice to this point in a full-throated manner typical of the sort of thinker who refused to separate science and religion.

> I think that we may watch with perfect serenity all the progress, all the discoveries, all the transformations of science. If we open our eyes to the universe, God is there; and if we close them to look into our own nature, God is with us still. (Réville 1875, p. 242)

One is accordingly tempted to ponder why such an irenic attitude to the relation of science to religion is not good enough for believers today?

Thus, in order to do studies of religion, we can begin either as believers or as skeptics. We do not need to decide beforehand whether supernaturalist views of the world are true *or* not. We neither need, nor want, McCutcheon's atheistic metaphysics nor, for example, its mirror image, Eliade's mystical theistic one, as a foundation for the study of religion. We do, of course, need rules of evidence – just as we need them in courts of law, as Jean Bodin in effect argued centuries ago – but these are practical, not metaphysical (Wiebe 2004). Our rules of evidence in the study of religion, no more than in jurisprudence, do not require us to prove or disprove the existence of a supernatural world. Such questions, as indeed the existence of such a world at all, are strictly speaking *irrelevant* to the pursuit of a study of religion that passes all the tests of being 'naturalistic.' The believing scholar of religion, like so many of the founders, simply rejects McCutcheon's self-serving dichotomy between natural and religious. For them, as for many a believing scholar of religion today, the 'natural' is suffused with the divine purpose, and the study of the 'natural' is seen as leading to a deeper appreciation of that divine plan. This may not be my way, since I am proposing we proceed without foundations. But I can understand, and indeed admire, those who go about the study of religion this way, so long as we all play by the same rules – as we would in a court of law.

Bringing the Bible back in

Further, in the vein of reconciling often needlessly separated forces, I have given full credit to the way critical studies of the Bible have contributed essentially to the rise of the scientific study of religion from as early as the seventeenth century. The time has come to bridge the present-day gap between biblical studies and religious studies so called, because the two derive in large part from a common parentage. *Thinking about Religion* tries to do its part in legitimizing the affinities, lineages, and intellectual 'blood lines' between these frequently opposed traditions of the study of religion by providing the historical arguments that establish these relationships as genuine. Therefore, *Thinking about Religion* is unique among treatments of theories of religion because it devotes an entire chapter to this page in the development of critical approaches to religion. But not only that, *Thinking about Religion* extends that discussion well beyond biblical studies proper into the powerful influence that the scientific ideals and practices of biblical studies have had on major nineteenth-century founders of religious studies, such as Robertson Smith, Max Müller, and even Durkheim. These men were consciously, willingly, and profoundly influenced by both the seventeenth-century pioneers of the critical study of the Bible, and moreover by those representing the flowering of this scholarship going under the name, Higher Criticism of the Bible. Robertson Smith took what he learned from his teachers of Higher Criticism of the Bible into the study of religion on the ground – a commitment that arguably led a sociologist like Émile Durkheim to focus intently on the study of small-scale societies that is now so much a part of our field. For his part, Max Müller thought that the methods learned from critical study of the Bible were so powerful that he generalized their methods to the 'Bibles' of other religions, such as the scriptures of the ancient religions of India. A major theme of the early portions of *Thinking about Religion* has been the historical links between those recognized as various sorts of scholars of religion – comparativists, Indologists, sociologists, folklorists, and such, and the great traditions of Higher Criticism of the Bible. As one could not consider oneself an educated scholar of religion in those times unless one grasped the importance and the intellectual thrust of the great movements of Higher Criticism of the Bible, so I believe the same should apply to scholars of religion today. If it was good enough for one of the greatest nineteenth-century novelists and intellectuals, George Eliot, to know her way around the Higher Criticism of the Bible, how could it not be good enough for us today, especially in a time when the Bible is at the center of so many controversies, both in public and in academe, that bear on the future of religious studies and public policy as well?!

'Theories' of Religion, or Theoretical 'Ideas'?

In looking closely at the classic 'theories' of religion in *Thinking about Religion*, I have finally tried to reveal what so-called 'theories' of religion really are. In truth, I think we would conclude that they are not 'theories' at all, but at best theoretical *ideas*. (Still less of course, as any quantitative sociologist can attest, do we have *methodologies* for the study of religion!) Our so-called 'theories' are little more than suggestive, albeit uniformly interesting, starting points for thinking about religion. Nowhere can the study of religion claim to own anything remotely approaching a Darwinian *theory* of evolution or a Newtonian *theory* of the physical universe. That is just a fact, and one to which we should not blind ourselves just to maintain usage of the often pretentious language of 'theory.' Again, rather than theories, we have a good number of interesting and fruitful theore*tical* ideas, approaches, 'takes,' or 'angles' with which to approach religion. Our 'theories' are thus not much better than 'bright ideas' that might one day – if we chose – contribute to the creation of rigorous theories of religion in the proper sense of the term as it applies in the exact sciences. We may someday actually have in hand what might be justly called a 'theory of religion,' but not yet. It is at best premature to talk as if we did.

For this reason, I have assumed that we need to accept the *de facto* situation of a pluralism of theoretical *ideas* that fall in and out of fashion or that may be found fruitful for 'getting a handle on' religion; or in other cases, that are jettisoned as unproductive, misdirected, or otherwise unsatisfactory. For example, in case to case, Durkheim's view that religious experience is a result of our relation to social groupings may be defensible. What harm is there in exploring the extent that this is so? In principle, why could it not be the case that a given instance of religious experience had something to do with the location of the believer in a social group? Or, to take another example, we might want to see religious behavior as Malinowski did – namely something that can be directly connected to the biological conditions of our organisms. As yet, I know of no evidence for making this link in a rigorous way. But is such a possibility *ipso facto* absurd? Or, to take the opposite view, what would compel one to see religious behavior as biologically conditioned, even if one could? Why would one bother? Even in the case of early forms of explanatory modes now empirically discredited and out of fashion as well, such as the unilinear cultural evolutionism of a Tylor, Frazer, or Robertson Smith, is it absurd to entertain the, admittedly *minimal*, version of the *theoretical* idea that religious institutions can be said to develop because of the prior conditions established by their predecessors? To be sure, the nineteenth-century models of unilinear stage-wise 'growth' advanced by religious evolutionists like Frazer and such – *maximal* versions of this powerful theoretical idea – may not stand up to empirical challenges. But that does not mean that it is always absurd or false to think about cultures and religions to some degree from the point of view of a "growth story" (Gellner 1964, ch. 3). Students of religion ought to note that in our sister discipline of anthropology, cultural evolutionism is still very much alive, whether in Marxist and non-Marxist or unilinear or nonunilinear forms (Harris 1979; Rappaport 1968; Sahlins 1972; Service 1975; White 1959). Further, even though Max Weber is not the kind of evolutionist that the cruder unilinear progressivist Tylors and Frazers were, his view that the *growth* of social (mostly economic) institutions is made possible by prior religious conditions is still widely held in the social sciences. Similarly, is Durkheim's idea that the modern Western view of the sacredness of the individual can be meaning-fully seen as an out*growth* of Christian valuations of the human person to be dismissed because it too presumes a kind of developmental model with evolutionist overtones? After all, no less a major contemporary social thinker than Louis Dumont argues much the same brief (Dumont 1982).

All this is to say that many of the classic theoretical ideas that we studied still seem to be fruitful for spurring present-day research into religion, despite their failings. Why should the creativity of past thinkers be pushed aside and our curiosities stifled because the theoretical proposals of the past cannot be swallowed whole and entire? In striving to appreciate and understand why the theorists in this book 'thought that they were right' about their approaches to religion, I am in effect accepting the imperfect, partial, and corrigible nature of the theoretical ideas advanced over the years for guiding the study of religion. This book accepts that the study of religion is done without a God's-eye view of the reality of religion. We no longer need to wait expectantly for Prince Charming. The study of religion is done with tools that we might one day cast aside, refashion, or replace. We do not need Prince Charming to sweep us away. Instead, this book stands for the will to press on with positive studies of religion – with studies of religion employing what may be imperfect theoretical ideas. I believe we should want to carry on despite imperfections because the alternative is not to try to understand and/or explain religion at all. This book celebrates attempts to tackle religion in ways we may later find limited because the alternatives do not commend themselves to people who seek positive knowledge. I think it a colossal waste of time and talent to opt for the first alternative – to sit around waiting for that hoped-for handsome Prince of theories. Similarly, the second alternative to pressing ahead with positive studies of religion reduces them to conceptual criticism. In effect, it amounts to spending our time and talent obsessing about the shortcomings of our theoretical ideas. In the pursuit of purity, those choosing the second alternative retain that pristine condition at the risk of guaranteeing their own intellectual sterility.

Regrets?

Finally, if anything is to be regretted in the effort represented by *Thinking about Religion*, it is having to limit my selection of authors to those I felt were both most influential in the study of religion and most distinctive in their style of inquiry. A fuller, but much longer and perhaps redundant work, would have included such honored names in religious studies as Joachim Wach, Karl Marx, Ludwig Feuerbach, Friedrich Heiler, William James, Carl Jung, and Raffaele Pettazoni, not to mention the many scholars writing today in our diverse and prospering field. Such a 'book' might, of course, have grown into one very large book, or even into several volumes. But, in doing so, it would surely have undermined the practical purpose of being accessible to students in a compact and affordable form. One is forced at times to choose, even if the outcomes are not perfectly satisfactory. Even with the best of intentions, and virtually limitless resources, something meritorious will always get left out. I have resigned myself to accepting that there is not much to do about this. Still, I think readers will find that while I may not have given extensive treatment to some favorite figures of their choice, I have at least given the main classic approaches and thinkers in our field a good and honorable hearing.

References

Byrne, P. 1989. *Natural Religion and the Nature of Religion*. London: Routledge.

Dumont, L. 1982. A Modified View of Our Origins: The Christian Beginnings of Modern Individualism. *Religion* 12, pp. 1–27.

Gellner, E. 1964. *Thought and Change*. London: Weidenfeld and Nicolson.

Haizlip, S. T. 1999. Living in Black History Today (Sigh). In *Los Angeles Times*, Feb. 21, 1999, p. M8.

Harris, M. 1979. *Cultural Materialism*. New York: Random House.

McCutcheon, R. T. 2001. *Critics Not Caretakers: Redescribing the Public Study of Religion*. Albany: SUNY.

Preus, J. S. 1998. The Bible and Religion in a Century of Genius: Part I: Religion on the Margins: *Conversos* and Collegiants. *Religion* 28, pp. 3–14.

Rappaport, R. 1968. *Pigs for the Ancestors*. New Haven: Yale University Press.

Sahlins, M. 1972. *Stone Age Economics*. Chicago: University of Chicago Press.

Service, E. 1975. *Origins of the State and Civilization*. New York: W. W. Norton.

White, L. A. 1959. *The Evolution of Culture*. New York: McGraw Hill.

Wiebe, D. 1999a. *The Politics of Religious Studies*. New York: St. Martin's Press.

——. 1999b. Religion and the Scientific Impulse in the Nineteenth Century: Friedrich Max Müller and the Birth of the Science of Religion. In *The Politics of Religious Studies*. New York: St. Martin's Press.

——. 1999c. Toward the Founding of a Science of Religion: The Contribution of C. P. Tiele. In *The Politics of Religious Studies*. New York: St. Martin's Press.

——. 2004. The Reinvention or Degradation of Religious Studies? Tales from the Tuscaloosa Woods. *Reviews in Religion and Theology* 11, pp. 3–14.

Index